Learning
Disabilities

Learning Disabilities

The Interaction of Learner, Task, and Setting

Corinne Roth Smith

Syracuse University

 Little, Brown and Company
Boston   Toronto

Library of Congress Cataloging in Publication Data

Smith, Corinne Roth.
    Learning disabilities.

    Bibliography: p.
    Includes indexes.
    1. Learning disabilities.   I. Title.
LC4704.S618 1983   371.9   82-20835
ISBN 0-316-80165-8

Library of Congress Catalog Card No. 82-20835

ISBN 0-316-80165-8

9 8 7 6 5 4 3 2 1

MV

Published simultaneously in Canada
by Little, Brown & Company (Canada) Limited

Printed in the United States of America

Text Credits

Chapter 1, p. 15: From A. A. Strauss and L. E. Lehtinen, *Psychopathology and Education of the Brain-Injured Child,* p. 2. Copyright 1974 by Grune & Stratton. Reprinted by permission; *p. 21:* From Helmer R. Myklebust, *Auditory Disorders in Children,* pp. 331–333. Copyright 1954 by Grune & Stratton. Reprinted by permission.

Chapter 3, p. 103: From M. A. Wyke, ed., *Developmental Dysphasia.* Copyright 1978 by Academic Press Inc. (London) Ltd. Reprinted by permission; *p. 109:* From S. D. Clements, J. S. Davis, R. Edgington, C. M. Goolsby, and J. E. Peters "Two Cases of Learning Disabilities," in Lester Tarnapol, ed., *Learning Disorders in Children: Diagnosis, Medication, Education,* pp. 26–27. Copyright © 1971 by Little, Brown and Company (Inc.). Reprinted by permission.

Chapter 4, p. 138: From Macdonald Critchley, *The Dyslexic Child.* Copyright 1970 by Charles C.

Thomas, Springfield, Ill. Reprinted by permission of William Heinemann Medical Books Ltd.

Chapter 8, p. 276: From Ellen Lamar Thomas and H. Alan Robinson. *Improving Reading in Every Class: A Sourcebook for Teachers,* 2nd ed. Copyright 1972 by Allyn and Bacon. Reprinted by permission.

Chapter 9, p. 294: From Macdonald Critchley, *The Dyslexic Child.* Copyright 1970 by Charles C. Thomas, Springfield, Ill. Reprinted by permission of William Heinemann Medical Books Ltd.

Illustration Credits

Chapter 6, p. 192: Peter Vandermark/Photographer.

Chapter 13, p. 459: Copyright © 1971 by United Feature Syndicate, Inc.

Part opener photos: p. 2, Robin M. Smith; *p. 80,* Meri Houtchens-Kitchens/The Picture Cube; *p. 178,* Robin M. Smith; *p. 310,* J. Holland/Stock Boston; *p. 480,* David S. Strickler/The Picture Cube.

To my husband Lynn:
> whose confidence and encouragement motivated me to
> pursue this project.

To my children Julie and Rachael:
> whose love, faith, and pride strengthened my persistence
> throughout this project.

To my parents Drs. Elizabeth and Zolton Roth:
> whose model of dedication to inquiry and human service
> is reflected in this project.

Preface

This book was written primarily for students in the introductory learning disabilities course. Given the many characteristics that all children share in common, whether typical or disabled, this text would also be of interest to students concerned with educational interventions that are based on need rather than disability label. This text's broad overview of the field of learning disabilities also meets the informational needs of many who work with these children: parents, administrators, psychologists, counselors, special and regular education teachers, and communicative disorders specialists.

How we define learning disabilities is determined not only by educational practices and research findings, but also by the times in which we live. It is society's priorities that determine whether or not a particular child will be considered handicapped. Because of the emphasis placed on reading proficiency in recent years, many individuals tend to think of learning disabilities in the most narrow sense—as reading disabilities. Given the growing influence of the computer, however, it may be that mathematical skills will become as important a determiner of being labeled learning disabled, as physical prowess may have been in Greek and Roman times, musical talent in the Elizabethan era, or social reparté in Edwardian days.

It is our demands and attitudes that heavily determine if children's learning difficulties are to be ameliorated or if they are to be permitted to become debilitating, life-long handicaps. Therefore, in trying to meet handicapped children's educational, personal, and social needs, our looking glasses must be turned inward to ourselves as well as outward to society. By successfully matching the nature of our learning tasks, teaching strategies, and interpersonal interactions to children's strengths and weaknesses we can do much to enhance their learning and life adjustment.

This book is based on an empirical orientation which maintains that learning and behavior patterns are best studied and understood against the framework of normal child development. By bringing together the most relevant information from child development, psychology, the medical sciences as well as from special and general education, a broad view of learning disabilities is achieved. A preference is evidenced throughout the text for dealing with observable behaviors that relate directly to teaching objectives and important life goals.

We have attempted to present fairly the various perspectives on learner, task, and setting factors which pertain to the condition we call learning disabilities. Such an eclectic approach not only offers a comprehensive survey of the field, but it also reflects the fact that we do not as yet have enough data to enable us to follow one theory with full confidence to the exclusion of others.

Much can be learned from different theoretical perspectives. Each offers a valuable vantage point from which to evaluate the role of learner, task, and setting factors in learning disabilities. Consequently, the text presents the controversies and lack of consensus in learning disabilities, while also acknowledging the healthy nature of our differences in opinion. These differences already have had several valuable outcomes: a proliferation of research on learning difficulties, a greater appreciation of individual differences within the classroom, a nurturance of intensive teaching geared toward the needs of the individual, and a reexamination of our curricular and vocational expectations.

The content of this book is divided into five units. The first unit introduces the students to the historical, definitional, identification, and prevalence issues in learning disabilities. Unit II reviews the many learner-, task-, and setting-based factors that may contribute to learning disabilities, and the way in which learning becomes affected. Unit III uses a normal child development framework to understand the strengths and weaknesses of the learning disabled preschooler, elementary school student, and adolescent. Since learning problems often do not disappear with age, the vocational, independent living, and social-emotional needs of the learning disabled adult are also discussed. Unit IV focuses upon the academic tasks that we expect children to accomplish. It examines multi-dimensional assessment approaches and programming strategies. Since learning problems can be accentuated by mismatches between child and task characteristics, we also look at the facilitative effects of matching task content and teaching methods to the learner's abilities and style. Unit V is devoted to the notion that children's learning and behavior need to be understood within the context of their social networks. Emphasis is placed upon the role of the parent as model, advocate, and teacher. Attributes of the school environment that may impact upon the learner, such as organizational structure, class placement, and teacher characteristics also are highlighted. Since each learning disabled individual is unique, only by understanding how the child's characteristics interact with the tasks and individuals within his/her social settings can we comprehend the learning strengths and weaknesses and how best to intervene.

Writing a major textbook involves the assistance of many people. I am especially indebted to reviewers who spent hours critiquing various drafts of the manuscript and offering many useful suggestions. They are: Anna Gajar, The Pennsylvania State University; Paul Gerber, University of New Orleans; Karen Greenough, Eastern Kentucky University; Jean Harber, formerly of University of Maryland; Harold Hiebert, The University of Wisconsin, La Crosse; Jeffrey Hummel, The State University of New York at Buffalo; Donald Maietta, Boston University; Barry McNamara, Hofstra University; Maurice Miller, Indiana State University; Linda Patriarca, Michigan State University; Thomas Swem, Appalachian State University; Barbara Tymitz-Wolf, Indiana University; and Stanley Vasa, The University of Nebraska, Lincoln.

It is also with deep gratitude that I recognize the outstanding editorial assistance of Mylan Jaixen, Senior Editor College Division. In his professorial style he masterfully helped guide and organize the evolution of this text. He, along with the Little, Brown Book Editors Dana Norton and Virginia Shine, deserve applause for their ability to keep my production speed, motivation, and morale high.

I would also like to gratefully acknowledge Suzanne Gilmour's significant contribution in researching and writing the first draft of Chapter 13. Suzanne's talents as an experienced special education teacher and teacher trainer were particularly helpful in selecting those instructional strategies most likely to be useful to future teachers. Maria Joyale, a skilled word-processor operator, deserves heartfelt thanks for the cooperation, speed, professionalism and good humor with which she persevered through nearly 4000 pages of typing. I also wish to express my sincere gratitude to my graduate assistants, Lori Getman and Sue Woytkewicz, who so masterfully fulfilled far more than their fair share of clinical and administrative responsibilities while I buried myself in the library's stacks. Finally, my graduate students in Learning Disabilities, School Psychology, and Mental Retardation deserve acknowledgement. Their valued feedback and insights over the past eleven years have taught me far more than any books. In more ways than they'll ever know, they've influenced this text's philosophical approach and the selection and organization of its content.

Dr. Burton Blatt deserves special mention. He nurtured me in my student days and has pushed me in my professional life. I am indebted to his teachings, model, and support for having enriched and guided my professional development. Finally, the expertise of the authors of the four contributed chapters helped this text present a comprehensive, scholarly overview of learner, task, and setting factors in learning disabilities. Dr. Eleanor Williams, a clinical professor at New York State's Upstate Medical Center and a pediatrician in private practice, lent her expertise in family assessment to Chapter 14 and coauthored the chapter on the preschooler with me. Bringing her daily experiences with learning disabled adolescents and drug and alcohol abuse to Chapter 8, Dr. Debrah Shulman, a practicing school psychologist masterfully highlighted the issues facing LD adolescents and their teachers. Dr. Harold Keller, chairperson of Syracuse University's school psychology training program, reflected his talents in multidimensional assessment procedures in Chapter 10. His colleague on the school psychology faculty, Dr. Robert Hiltonsmith, brought his interests in ecological research to Chapter 15's discussion of school factors impacting learning disabled youngsters. To all of these individuals, I am deeply grateful.

Brief Contents

Contents

Learning
Disabilities

Part One

The Concept of
Learning Disabilities

Chapter One
The Birth
of a Field

Learning disabilities is by far the fastest growing, most controversial, and often the most confusing area within special education. The card catalogues and journal indices of libraries overflow with listings on learning disabilities. Journals ranging from the scholarly (*Journal of Learning Disabilities*) to the popular (*Parents Magazine*) carry articles on the subject. This literature is directed not only to teachers and parents of learning disabled children, but also to a vast array of professionals such as the physicians, nutritionists, and juvenile court judges, who feel that knowledge about learning disabilities is relevant to their work.

This broad-based interest stems from the multidimensional efforts required to prevent, study, and deal with learning disabilities. Figure 1-1 will help you to understand this point. It suggests the wide range of factors that contribute to learning disabilities, from physical causes within the learner to characteristics of the curriculum, school, and home environment. These learner-, task-, and setting-based factors can adversely affect the development or efficiency of an individual's information-processing abilities. The person may experience difficulty in taking in, organizing, storing, recalling, or reproducing information through visual, motor, language, and attention processes. Any combination of these contributors and information-processing weaknesses are found in mild, moderate, and severe degrees of learning disabilities. Since these factors impact on so many aspects of a person's life, many different professionals need to be involved in prevention, research, and intervention efforts. The behaviors addressed by these professionals are delineated in our current very general federal definition of learning disabilities:

> "Specific learning disability" means a disorder in one or more of the basic psychological processes involved in understanding or in using language, spoken or written, which may manifest itself in an imperfect ability to listen, think, speak, read, write, spell, or to do mathematical calculations. The term includes such conditions as perceptual handicaps, brain injury, minimal brain dysfunction, dyslexia, and developmental aphasia. The term does not include children who have learning problems which are primarily the result of visual, hearing, or motor handicaps, of mental retardation, of emotional disturbance, or of environmental, cultural, or economic disadvantage (Federal Register, Dec. 29, 1977, p. 65083).

Concern about learning disabilities is relevant to disciplines that study (normal child development, medicine), teach (general, special, and vocational education), or are affected by (the law, social welfare institutions) significant variation from typical learning and behavior. The scope of learning disabilities is further broadened by its relevance to all ages, races, and socioeconomic levels.

A broad-based approach to learning disabilities is important since no one theoretical perspective comprehensively integrates our present state of knowledge regarding causes, characteristics, and teaching methodology. Each posi-

Figure 1-1   Factors that contribute to learning disabilities

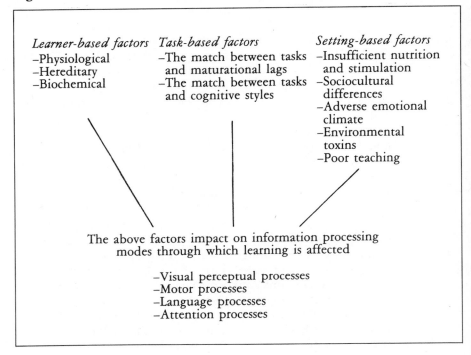

Learner-based factors   *Task-based factors*   *Setting-based factors*
–Physiological   –The match between tasks   –Insufficient nutrition
–Hereditary   and maturational lags   and stimulation
–Biochemical   –The match between tasks   –Sociocultural
                            and cognitive styles   differences
                                                         –Adverse emotional
                                                           climate
                                                         –Environmental
                                                           toxins
                                                         –Poor teaching

The above factors impact on information processing
modes through which learning is affected

–Visual perceptual processes
–Motor processes
–Language processes
–Attention processes

tion offers unique strengths which, when taken together, help us to better understand the learning disabled individual's needs as an interaction of learner, task, and setting factors.

We begin by tracing the evolution of educational philosophy and advocacy work that led to the birth of learning disabilities ("LD") as a new field in special education. We shall see how the LD field emerged from a long line of theory, research, and program development dating back to the 1800s. In the late 1950s and early 1960s this work combined with a heightened public awareness of the special educational needs of children who fit no existing category of disability, yet could not achieve in one or more academic areas. Along with greater public awareness, advocacy work, and changes in educational philosophy, the numbers of such children continued to grow. Some felt that this growth was due, in part, to advances in neonatal care over the past twenty-five years. That is, many children survived who in previous generations would have died. The pre- and postnatal trauma frequently linked to learning disorders suggest that some of our learning disabled may be coming from these ranks. By the late 1960s the learning disabilities concept had a large following, although its definition remained vague. Finally, in 1975 special services for learning disabled students were mandated and funded by federal law.

Educational Philosophy

The birth of the field of learning disabilities was influenced by parents and professionals who sought ways to view children's learning and behavior patterns from a large variety of vantage points. They desired a concept that would deal with each child's unique learning strength and weakness patterns, focusing not only on what children can't do, but also on what they can do and how they learn best. They were aware that characteristics of the tasks we have children do and the settings in which they do them must be altered to further their learning. That is, whether a child's particular strengths become assets, or weaknesses become liabilities, depends on how the child, task, and setting characteristics combine (Smith, 1980). This multidimensional, individualized perspective contrasted with special education classification and grouping practices, as well as the popular instructional philosophy of the time. This perspective also complemented research indicating that, for some children, appropriate instruction reduces learning weaknesses and raises intelligence test performance. The learning disabilities concept also had particular appeal to those who sought to avoid the mental retardation stigma.

Special Education
Classification and Grouping Practices

The development of learning disabilities into a new special education category was precipitated by a growing awareness that existing means of classifying children for special educational services often ignored their individual characteristics and instructional needs. Children carrying one handicapping label were assumed to have similar educational needs when, in fact, they each had unique needs. It also was generally assumed that a child carrying one label had little in common with a child carrying a different label, and that their instructional needs would differ. But the learning and behavior in different groups of mild to moderately handicapped children proved over and over again that some children in one group had abilities and educational needs similar to those in another group. For example, some moderately retarded children could learn certain types of information just as well as their brighter peers (Jensen, 1963; Klausmeier, Feldhusen, & Check, 1959 in Spicker & Bartel, 1968) and their social skills were not the lowest in a typical classroom (Lapp, 1957). Given the needs differentiating children carrying the same label, and the similarities across different exceptional categories, planning special class programs based on labels rather than individual instructional needs made little sense. The existing categories tended to ignore unique patterns of development in each person.

The learning disabilities concept had appeal because it expected each child's learning characteristics to differ from others'. It advocated grouping children for instruction based on similar educational needs. The learning disabilities concept promised that the nature of children's strengths and weaknesses would be highlighted, that instruction would be planned for each child individually, and that youngsters who did not clearly fit into existing categories would be served.

Special Class Philosophy of Education

The learning disabilities concept arose in part as a challenge to the notion that all children learn automatically, "when they're ripe and ready." Handicapped children had been placed in segregated classes so that special instruction in smaller groups and with specially trained teachers would help them progress at comfortable rates. Yet progress was not overwhelming and what made the methods special was unclear (Dunn, 1968; MacMillan, 1971; Morse, Cutler, & Fink, 1964). Johnson (1962) proposed that children profited no more from special than from regular classes because the special class therapeutic environment was geared toward children's inadequacies, lowering teacher pressure and children's motivation.

Parents and researchers became less willing to excuse children from intense teaching attempts because they were too retarded or disturbed to learn. Adherents to the learning disabilities concept wondered whether unique learning problems caused some children to be mistaken as retarded or disturbed. They questioned whether learning failure was perpetuated by a lack of individualized teaching that matched tasks to what children did and did not know, and how they learned best. They urged schools to stop emphasizing weaknesses by trying to eliminate disabilities, and instead concentrate on strengths by teaching new behaviors. Teachers were encouraged to develop more positive expectations (Trippe, 1963). Researchers were pressed to provide a solid scientific foundation for intensive teaching practices, tailored toward individual learning needs.

The Educability of Intelligence

Programming advances led to the discovery that some children had been misclassified as mentally retarded. For example, Samuel Kirk found that some of the mentally retarded children at the Wayne County Training School had greater intellectual and learning potentials once their language disorders were corrected. After intensive remedial reading instruction, these youngsters' reading and IQ scores rose significantly. The children were deinstitutionalized and eventually became self-supporting citizens (Kirk, 1976).

Similarly, Kirk (1958) found that intelligence quotients of institutionalized mentally retarded children enrolled in a preschool program increased, while those of children not enrolled decreased. Kirk (1976) reported that six of the fifteen enrolled children later left the institution, and one became a college graduate. None of the nonenrolled children ever left the institution. Kirk felt that many of these children had been falsely diagnosed as retarded. Rather, they had specific learning disabilities in some areas, but were normal in other respects. Programming successes with the socioeconomically disadvantaged also highlighted this educability of intelligence (Hess & Shipman, 1968; Klaus & Gray, 1968; Kohlberg, 1968). The learning disabilities concept was attractive because it advocated sorting out and remediating specific disabilities that could mistakenly masquerade as retardation.

Mental Retardation Stigma

The label *learning disabled* also appealed to parents whose children might at some point be labeled mentally retarded. It avoided the devaluation, segregation, and compromise of potential often faced by the retarded. Parents whose children tested at intellectually higher levels, yet in some areas appeared to be retarded learners, hoped to avoid the stigma. A more acceptable alternative, "LD" meant that their children's difficulties were a learning phenomenon, and the responsibility for correction rested with the schools.

The mental retardation field itself inadvertently spurred on the LD movement when, in 1973, the American Association on Mental Deficiency (AAMD) dropped 13 percent of those classified as mentally retarded by eliminating the borderline category (IQ 69–84). Only children with IQ's two standard deviations below the mean on intelligence tests (IQ's below 69) and who were equally impaired in adaptive behavior (everyday living skills) were considered retarded. The now unlabeled children still needed intensive, individualized teaching. In those states that followed the AAMD's recommendation, parents turned to learning disabilities to secure appropriate educational programs (Kirk, 1976).

Advocacy

Certain advocacy groups helped make the times right for learning disabilities to emerge as a new handicapping classification. These included federal bodies that took a role in special education, and also professional and parent organizations.

Growing Federal Role in Special Education

The growth of the learning disabilities field was encouraged by federal court decisions that gave all children equal educational opportunities. In 1975, Congress responded by enacting Public Law 94-142, which mandated special services for all handicapped children and was the first law to include the learning disabeled among those labeled handicapped.

Court Guarantee of Equal Educational Opportunities. The Soviet launching of Sputnik I in October, 1957, shocked America into upgrading its educational system. A decade later, when man walked on the moon, the American Commissioner of Education launched the "right to read" program for all citizens (Allen, 1969). Yet, federal funding for special educational programs was slow in coming. Of the seven million handicapped children existing in 1971, one million received no educational services due to exclusion, suspension, and denial or postponement of entry by school officials (Weintraub & Abeson, 1974).

Equal educational opportunities for the handicapped eventually were won on two arguments: that certain educational practices violated the equal protection clause of the 14th Amendment to the United States Constitution; and that the Civil Rights Act of 1964 guaranteed an equal educational opportunity to every citizen.

Access to a free public education for the retarded was first recognized by the federal judicial system in *Pennsylvania ARC* v. *Pennsylvania,* 1971. A year later, the same rights were extended to all children regardless of exceptionality (*Mills* v. *Board of Education,* 1972). But learning disabilities still were not handicapping conditions for which special educational services could be federally reimbursed. The only reimbursable categories were mental retardation, hard-of-hearing, deaf, speech-impaired, visually handicapped, seriously emotionally disturbed, and crippled. In order to receive federal aid for learning disabled children, school systems had to apply under one of these categories or "other health impaired."

Legislative Recognition of Learning Disabilities. Formal federal recognition of learning disabilities began when the Elementary and Secondary Education Amendments of 1966 (P.L. 89-750) added a new Title VI, Education of Handicapped Children, to the 1965 act (P.L. 89-10). This authorized formation of a National Advisory Committee on Handicapped Children, which in turn urged Congress to deal with learning disabilities. In 1969, the Second Task Force of the Minimal Brain Damage National Project on Learning Disabilities recommended that LD be legislated as an exceptional category.

Pressure from these committees and from parent organizations resulted in the Children with Specific Learning Disabilities Act of 1969 (Title VI of the Elementary and Secondary Education Act of April 13, 1970; P.L. 91-230). This act authorized the spending of one million dollars for teacher training, research, and demonstration projects in learning disabilities, but appropriated no money for educational services (United States Office of Education, 1970a). In subsequent years, the U.S. Office of Education disbursed funds to forty-four states to establish LD Child Service Demonstration Centers (Kirk & Elkins, 1975a).

By 1975, forty-five states had created LD categories for state funding of special educational services. The remaining five states included the learning disabled among other handicapping categories (Gillespie, Miller, & Fielder, 1975). It was not until November 29, 1975, with the passage of the Education for All Handicapped Children Act (P.L. 94-142), that special educational services to learning disabled students were federally mandated and reimbursable.

Those states accepting federal reimbursements for education are mandated by P.L. 94-142 to provide a free, appropriate education to all handicapped children. Public Law 94-142 has had a dramatic impact on special services, financial aid, assessment practices, educational planning, due process rights, and teacher-training needs.

In the act, Congress stated that the number of handicapped children for whom reimbursements for special services would be provided was not to exceed 12 percent of the school population aged 5–17. This 12 percent figure was based on estimates of the number of handicapped, collected between 1948 and 1966 (Mackie, 1969; Mackie & Dunn, 1954).

Before funding was granted, state plans that outlined the procedures by which states would comply with the federal statute needed to be approved. Federal regulations permitted states to develop their own reimbursement formulae to local districts, to limit the number of children labeled LD, to recommend specific ways of determining significant discrepancies between potential and achievement, and to set the number of children that an LD resource teacher served per week.

By 1979, approximately 8 percent of the expected 12 percent of school aged children were identified as handicapped (*The Condition of Education,* 1980). States' LD percentages varied from approximately one-half of 1 percent (Indiana, Mississippi) to over 4 percent (Alaska, Utah) of the school-aged population. During the 1981–82 school year, 8.8 percent of school-aged students (4.2 million) were identified as handicapped (Special Education Programs, 1982). Of these, 38 percent were being educated under the LD label. The learning disabled had become the largest group of handicapped students being served. The number of teachers specializing in learning disabilities was second only to the number specializing in mental retardation (*The Condition of Education,* 1980).

Because federal law does not mandate programs at the preschool and young adult levels, services for the handicapped at these ages have been slow to develop. As of 1977, only .7 percent of the 18–21-year-old group (*Progress Toward a Free Appropriate Education,* 1979) and 2 percent of preschoolers (215,000; U.S. Dept. of HEW, 1979) were being served as handicapped. To increase preschool services, federal incentive grants and child identification projects were increased (U.S. Dept. of HEW, 1979). Yet, as of the 1981–82 school year only 228,000 handicapped preschoolers and 160,000 handicapped 18–21 year olds were receiving educational services.

Public Law 94-142 provides that handicapped students be educated in as close to normal a setting as possible, the "least restrictive environment." In addition, they should participate for as much of the school day as possible with their nonhandicapped peers in academic or nonacademic periods (homeroom, lunch, art, gym, or music).

Public Law 94-142 mandates that two assessment procedures as well as observation within the regular classroom be used when identifying children as handicapped. The testing materials cannot be racially or culturally discriminatory, and test administration must be in the child's native tongue. The curriculum is detailed yearly in an individualized education plan (IEP), which is prepared and signed by appropriate school personnel and the parents or guardian. P.L. 94-142's regulations also give parents detailed rights to involvement in the educational planning process.

Growth of
Professional and Parent Organizations

Parent and professional advocacy groups had a powerful role in bringing about this litigation and legislation. William Cruickshank (1967) noted that the growth of parent power reflected society's increasing understanding and tolerance for the handicapped. This parent advocacy, in turn, fostered professional interest in special children.

Parents demanded a concept that appreciated the individual, recognized the child's successes and failures and allowed these to dictate instructional plans. Parents were tired of hearing their children described as "dumb," "mixed up," and "lazy." They knew that their children were smart in some ways, not crazy, often tried very hard, and that "they would learn if only they could." Cruickshank (1972) aptly described the situation: "Parents of tens of thousands of children in the United States knew that [their children] had [learning disabilities], even if professional educators and psychologists and pediatricians did not" (p. 381). Therefore, parents demanded a category distinct from all other recognized handicapping conditions.

Advocacy groups for children with subtle learning problems began at the local level (Evanston, Illinois' Fund for Perceptually Handicapped Children; New York City's New York Association for Brain-Injured Children). On April 6, 1963, local parent organizations banned together at a national conference in Chicago. The term *learning disabilities* was used in an invited address by Samuel Kirk. He never intended this term to become another label for children, and cautioned parents against establishing another exceptional category (Kirk, 1976). Nevertheless, the title Association for Children with Learning Disabilities (ACLD) was adopted and this parent advocacy group was formalized in 1964.

Educators followed suit in 1968 by forming the Division for Children with Learning Disabilities (now the Council for Learning Disabilities, CLD) associated with the Council for Exceptional Children (CEC). Both groups felt that, without a name to call children who did not fit existing handicapping categories, funding for special services would not be easily secured.

The conference and newsletters sponsored by ACLD and CLD have been valuable means of information dissemination and catalysts for research, program development, and advocacy through the judicial system. Each organization formed a strong national lobbying group to promote legislative recognition of learning disabilities. Input from over 2,200 parents, professionals, and advocacy groups was involved in setting P.L. 94-142's LD identification criteria, diagnostic procedures, and monitoring processes. The presence of a strong national group strengthened state and local affiliates, thereby influencing legislation and practice at the state and local levels.

Research and Program Development

Three major areas of study — visual-perceptual development, language development, and program development — constitute the history of learning disabilities. In each area pioneers challenged existing assumptions and practices and forged new areas for research. Their insights laid the foundation for today's research, which continues to address issues of individual differences and teaching techniques. Although the pioneers' emphasis may appear to have been learner-based, their modifications of teaching materials, strategies, and environments clarified the role of tasks and settings in learning disabilities.

Visual Perceptual Research

The appreciation of individual differences in behavior began with Kurt Goldstein's study of the brain-injured adult. It was continued in Heinz Werner and Alfred Strauss' research with retarded children, some of whom had histories and characteristics suggestive of brain injury. The study of more intellectually normal children who had learning disorders but who were not clearly brain-injured began with William Cruickshank, Newell Kephart, and Marianne Frostig.

These pioneers believed that behavioral style and learning underachievement could be caused by visual-motor difficulties, and that visual and motor learning precedes higher-level cognitive skills. This led some to develop visual-perceptual and motor assessment measures (Kephart, Frostig) and remediation programs (Cruickshank, Kephart, Frostig). Although these measures and practices were later challenged, they led to important research into the relationship between visual-motor processes and learning. These pioneers' work formed important building blocks for current LD practices: neuropsychological and educational research (Werner, Strauss); behavioral assessment (Werner, Strauss); structured and individualized teaching approaches (Strauss, Kephart, Frostig); class grouping by educationally relevant characteristics (Cruickshank); and development of social skills (Frostig).

A description of the kind of brain-injured child from whom these theories and practices evolved is found on p. 15. This child's inability to attend to visual stimuli for sufficient periods of time led to learning and behavior difficulties. Carefully planned interventions successfully overcame many of these problems. Fifty years ago this child may have been called emotionally disturbed or brain injured. Today the same child would be classified learning disabled.

Kurt Goldstein. Goldstein contributed to the development of the learning disabilities field by showing that brain abnormalities could alter a person's behavior. He attributed certain unusual behavior patterns to the defective processing of visual information, and to the subsequent reaction to these misperceptions.

Goldstein studied the aftermaths of head injuries in World War I soldiers (Goldstein, 1936, 1939, 1942). He identified six behavioral characteristics that were present, in one degree or another, in his wounded soldiers:

1. Forced responsiveness to stimuli — they were easily distracted by objects and people around them; any fleeting movement, noise, or thought might compel attention.

2. Figure-ground confusion — because they reacted indiscriminately to everything, the soldiers were unable to sort out the essential (a speaker) from the trivial (dining room noise).

3. Perseveration — because their attention was caught and recaught by the same stimuli, the soldiers kept repeating behaviors they had just engaged in.

4. Hyperactivity — the constant attention shifts created extreme, purposeless motor activity.

5. Catastrophic reaction — the soldiers suffered emotional breakdowns when they were unable to alleviate the bizarre perceptions and chaotic behavior. Goal-oriented, energetic, or creative activities were difficult to initiate.

6. Meticulousness — as a defense against excessive stimulus input, which produced a confusing world of misperceptions, soldiers became overly rigid in arranging their personal time schedules and possessions.

These characteristics provide a framework for studying children with learning difficulties even today.

Heinz Werner. Werner, a German psychologist, immigrated to the United States and became one of the leading theorists of developmental psychology. Werner worked with many other pioneers in learning disabilities at the Wayne County Training School for retarded children near Detroit, Michigan.

For teaching a concept such as counting to 2, Werner recommended following a sequence from earlier to later developing skills: begin with materials that can be manipulated (matching blocks, counting blocks), then use more visually taxing but less manipulative methods (counting drawings of 2 lines or cars), until the concept is finally mastered abstractly (learning the numerals 1 and 2). He felt that remedial programming was aided more by observing how

CASE STUDY: J

J. . . . Father a prominent attorney, mother educated according to the standards of the upper social class. Parents 31 and 17 years old respectively at the time of marriage. An only child. Pregnancy and delivery were both normal but the child was blue [oxygen deprived] at birth . . . He walked and talked somewhat later than usual and had no serious childhood diseases. He was an extremely disobedient and "obstinate" child with destructive tendencies, very easily excited. He seemed to be fearless. Not accepted by other children because of his constant teasing and tormenting . . . When six years old, he was entered in a private school but could not be admitted to a class with other children. Two teachers were employed for him alone since one teacher refused to stand it without relief for the entire day.

At eight years and six months of age he was admitted to our clinic. He had a second grade school achievement; psychometric testing was impossible because of extreme restlessness and distractibility. He was always "on the move," exploring everything in the house, particularly technical equipment, electric switches, door bells, elevators, etc. Asked questions incessantly, like a machine gun. Very affectionate with all the persons in the house. When taken to bed, he did not sleep until midnight but asked another question every five minutes. On the days following his admission he was still very restless and disinhibited [wouldn't stop moving] but meticulous and pedantic in the arrangement of his belongings and everything handled by him at the table or in the classroom. Play in the garden consisted in trying to destroy flowers or bushes but without ill-humor or anger. Always smiling and good-humored. At dinner time he ate enormous quantities of food and drank a glass of water or milk in one gulp. In church he was very distractible, wishing to give money to all the collection boxes. After two weeks in the clinic, he was more adjusted but still very distractible. He was discharged after one and one half years with an intelligence quotient within the normal range and admitted to a private school. Then attended class with children of his age and in an examination proved to be ninth in placement among forty children (Strauss & Lehtinen, 1947, p. 2).

children performed tasks, than noting scores earned on tests (Werner & Strauss, 1939). For example, children often answered correctly, but with no understanding of how the problems had been solved, or incorrectly although their thought processes were appropriate (Werner, 1937, 1944). Some children were well organized while others were disorganized; some had *global* mental processing styles, for example, attending to outlines of shapes. Others had *analytic* styles, attending to parts. These patterns called for different programming strategies.

Werner noted similarities between the behaviors of some of his school's children and Goldstein's brain-injured adults. He and Alfred Strauss assumed that these children's unique behaviors also could be explained by brain injury (Strauss & Werner, 1942; Werner & Strauss, 1940, 1941). Werner and Strauss called these children *exogenously* retarded because brain injury was presumed to have been inflicted by outside sources before, during, or after birth. The remaining children they called *endogenously* retarded because something was presumed to have occurred within the child's inherited brain structure (for

RESEARCH BOX 1-1
Performance Differences Between Werner and Strauss' Exogenous and Endogenous Children

Werner and Strauss' investigations compared the performance of exogenous children, who had presumably suffered brain injury, with endogenous children who had not. They found that exogenous children behaved very similarly to Goldstein's adult brain-injured: forced responsiveness to stimuli (impulsive and distractible), repetitiveness (inappropriate fixation on a task or thought), visual-motor disorganization (hyperactivity), figure-ground confusion, use of nonessential elements when categorizing, and inability to integrate parts into a whole.

One example of differences between the two groups occurred when they looked through a tachistoscope at common objects (a hat, a bird). Endogenous children reported seeing the object, but exogenous children instead were attracted to the nonessential background (Werner & Strauss, 1941). On a visual-motor task requiring copying a marble design on a marble-board and then drawing the pattern, the exogenous children had no sense of form or organizational pattern. Their approach was erratic and incoherent. The endogenous children produced continuous, symmetrical patterns in a planned manner, as did nonretarded children of a similar mental age (Werner & Bowers, 1941). Similarly, exogenous, but not endogenous, children performed very poorly on an auditory-motor task in which children were to vocally reproduce simple melodic patterns played on a piano. The endogenous children improved with age, resembling the performance of the normal children. The exogenous children did not. The errors of the latter children were "of a kind not known in normal development" (p. 98).

Because of the exogenous children's difficulties in all senses, Werner concluded that the responsible factors are general and not specific to any one sense. The difference found between children in strategies for problem-solving (organizational style, global *vs.* analytic style) is currently a major area of research for cognitive psychologists.

example, inherited mental retardation). The two groups differed greatly in behavior and problem-solving strategies (see Research Box 1-1).

Though the tendency of Werner and Strauss to infer neurological problems from behavior rather than from medical information was severely criticized, Werner and his colleagues highlighted the fact that children can be heterogeneous even when they all bear one label. Their focus on individuality, on how children solve problems, and on ordering the teaching process so as to parallel typical development, represents key concepts within learning disabilities today. Werner's work also encouraged others to research the causes of brain injury, its effect on learning and behavior, and the nature and effects of different information-processing styles.

Alfred Strauss. Strauss, a German neuropsychiatrist, is credited with introducing the term "brain-injured" into this country (Sarason, 1949). The way in which Strauss and his colleagues tested children, and matched the academic materials and classroom environment to their learning styles, has become an important guideline for practice within learning disabilities (Strauss & Kephart, 1955; Strauss & Lehtinen, 1947).

Strauss and his associates developed several psychological measures (Strauss & Werner, 1942) and a behavior-rating scale (Strauss & Kephart, 1940) to evaluate performance differences between the exogenous and endogenous child. As part of his evaluation program, Strauss took continuous measures of the intelligence of Wayne County Training School residents. The exogenously retarded tended to decrease in IQ (−2.5 points) over a four- or five-year period, whereas the endogenous children increased (+4 points) (Kephart & Strauss, 1940). Strauss concluded that the exogenous children's decrease in IQ was due to a mismatch between their tendency to overreact to stimuli and the overstimulating educational program. Therefore, irrelevant environmental stimuli were reduced and the saliency of materials essential to learning was increased, so as to engage attention before irrelevant stimuli could do so (Strauss, 1943; Werner & Strauss, 1940).

Strauss believed that attention would increase as both the controlled environment and the child's voluntary control diminished his or her hyperactivity and distractibility. In turn, perceptual, conceptual, mental organizational, and behavioral skills would be enhanced (Strauss & Lehtinen, 1947). One environmental means of engaging attention incorporated movement into learning tasks. For example, by placing pegs into a pegboard while counting, the child would slow touching and counting so that one object was counted at a time, instead of several objects being counted as one or omitted. Similarly, reading materials contained no pictures and exposed only a few words at a time to decrease distractions. Additional environmental modifications to reduce distractions included small group instruction, seating children at a distance from one another, teachers wearing plain clothing with no accessories, minimal room decorations and bulletin boards, screening the lower quarter of windows, screening study areas, and facing desks toward the wall.

Though Strauss and his colleagues stressed the development of visual-perceptual foundation skills, academic instruction was not withheld until the perceptual problems were resolved. Instead, special teaching methods helped compensate for the problems: for example, heavy black crayon outlined a figure to be colored, so confusion with the background was avoided; letters that could be confused (b,d) were color-coded; only one problem was presented on a page at a time. Active teacher guidance was essential to accommodate the child's learning style. For example, a teacher might work with a child at such a rapid pace that several steps were completed before the child became distracted.

Strauss (1943) reported remarkable academic gains in short time periods using his individually tailored methods. Through intensive teaching that matched children's learning styles, many children eventually moved on to normal school programs (Strauss & Lehtinen, 1947).

William Cruickshank. Cruickshank linked knowledge about brain-injured, retarded children to normal intelligence children displaying similar behaviors. He grouped children into classes based on behavioral characteristics and instructional needs, rather than diagnostic category. This practice was a forerunner of present noncategorical placement procedures.

Taking direction from his student work with Werner and Strauss, Cruickshank found that the perceptual attributes of brain-injured (cerebral-palsied) children of near-average (above 75 IQ) to above-average intelligence were similar to those of exogenously retarded children (Cruickshank, Bice, & Wallen, 1957). Therefore, Cruickshank and his colleagues (1957, 1965) concluded that perceptual disabilities were due to brain dysfunction, and not mental retardation. Like his predecessors, he felt that perceptual disorders implied underlying neurological dysfunction (Cruickshank, 1976).

Cruickshank then expanded his work to nonbrain-injured, extremely hyperactive, behaviorally disordered children with perceptual difficulties (Cruickshank, Bentzen, Ratzeburg & Tannhauser, 1961). These children were taught perceptual and academic skills in a manner similar to that used to teach the exogenous retarded. They were placed in classes based on common educational needs, regardless of their diagnostic labels. These children's success suggested that Werner and Strauss' way of understanding and meeting individual needs was applicable to children regardless of intelligence level.

Cruickshank (1976) laments that, when he bridged the gap between similarly behaving retarded and normal intelligence children, he inadvertently created an intellectual "line of demarcation between mental retardation and learning disabilities" (p. 106). This led many professionals to erroneously believe that a child could not be learning disabled and mentally retarded at the same time.

Newell Kephart. Kephart strongly influenced the 1960s *process training* movement in learning disabilities by advocating perceptual-motor training for poor learners. He, too, expanded the study of perceptual disorders to brain-injured children of normal intelligence, describing their characteristics and instructional needs, and the reliability and validity of measures distinguishing the brain-injured from nonbrain-injured (Strauss & Kephart, 1955).

Kephart's work (1960) reflected Werner and Strauss' assumption that perceptual and motor development form the basis for behavior, language, and conceptual learning. For example, Kephart believed that if a child was unable to tell left from right body parts, the child would be confused when trying to differentiate left from right in letters (b–d; p–q). Kephart also believed that motor development preceded perceptual development. Therefore, he felt that all school information that was seen or heard had to be linked with a spoken or movement response (*perceptual-motor match*) so as to lay the motor foundation for cognitive development.

Kephart devised a survey "to identify those children who do not possess perceptual–motor abilities necessary for acquiring academic skills by the usual instructional methods" (Roach & Kephart, 1966, p. iii). His corresponding perceptual–motor, remediation program goals were: balance and coordination, eye-movement control, eye–hand coordination, and visual perception (Kephart, 1960). Kephart called these children *slow learners* because their complex, puzzling needs defied a single label. He was one of the first to engage in intensive remedial work with normal-intelligence poor learners.

Kephart's perceptual–motor training assumptions have come under a great deal of criticism in recent years. However, had he not made them our research into the relationship between motor, perceptual, and learning skills would not have advanced as far as it has.

Marianne Frostig. Frostig greatly influenced educational practice with the learning disabled. Frostig, like Kephart, Werner, Strauss, and Cruickshank, hypothesized that perceptual development precedes the conceptual, and that poor development in the former creates learning problems. She felt that most learning is acquired visually and that neurological dysfunction might be a reason for many learning difficulties (Frostig & Horne, 1964).

Frostig and her colleagues developed a visual–perceptual assessment measure, the *Developmental Test of Visual Perception* (DTVP) (Frostig, Lefever, & Whittlesey, 1961, 1964), which remained popular through the early 1970s. Frostig's test data indicated that many neurologically impaired children have deficits in particular areas of visual perception. In 1964 Frostig and Horne developed a gross–motor and workbook program for perceptual dysfunctions identified by the DTVP. They reported that their remedial programs produced measurable visual perceptual gains in the weaker areas.

Frostig's program remained popular through the early 1970s until studies surfaced challenging the validity of the DTVP and showing unimpressive reading gains after perceptual training (Larsen & Hammill, 1975). Although some criticism of the remedial program was justified, the fault was not Frostig's. Practitioners had hoped that her test and workbooks alone would resolve their students' reading problems. They did not heed Frostig's early cautions that the exercises would only facilitate efficient use of visual skills during reading and other activities; reading improvements could occur only if reading instruction accompanied the visual perceptual training (Frostig et al., 1961).

Like Kephart, Frostig cautioned that test scores alone cannot appraise a child's characteristics and teaching needs. Tests are flawed, and scores may be misinterpreted or earned for the wrong reasons (guess-work, anxiety, misperceived directions). She felt that programs cannot be planned until the effects of such factors as past education, social environment, interests, attitudes, temperament, abilities, and disabilities are understood (Frostig, 1967). This philosophy is important to today's investigation of task- and setting-based factors in learning disabilities.

In 1947, Frostig founded the Marianne Frostig Center of Educational Therapy in Los Angeles (Frostig, 1976). Her unique emphasis on the development of moral, socially appropriate, and cooperative behaviors in her students has become an important focus in current LD research and practice.

Language Development Research

Reading and written expression translate language abilities into a new symbol system. A child who can hear well, but is unable to understand what is said, is likely to have difficulty understanding, organizing, and remembering what he or she reads. A child who can speak, but cannot organize or communicate thoughts orally, is likely to have trouble with written expression. The development of language competency is an important prerequisite to adequate academic progress.

Theoretical assumptions about how the brain processes language have been important to the development of teaching and remedial methods in learning disabilities. These investigations began with phrenology (a system of identifying character through the structure of the skull) in the early 1800s (Gall, Bouillaud). Shortly afterward speech was thought to be located in one brain site (Broca) and comprehension in another (Wernicke). Knowledge about adults who had become language-impaired due to brain injury (Wernicke) eventually was generalized to children who developed language skills slowly. Similar auditory processing disorders seemed to account for both the adults' loss of language and the children's language delays (Eisenson). But Osgood, Wepman, Myklebust, & Kirk pointed out that these children's language processes were still developing and that they generally were not suffering a loss of function. Therefore, they created models of normal language development against which disordered language could be compared. Both the disordered and normal development models contributed to remedial methods of teaching language skills to children.

Language disorders were solidly linked to learning disabilities when Helmer R. Myklebust conceptualized reading and written expression as the highest levels of language attainment. Language disabilities were found to impact academic skills as well as general intelligence (Jackson, Kirk) and abstract conceptual thought (Head). The pioneers' understanding of language strengths and weaknesses significantly influenced individualized instruction methods in the classroom. Language became appreciated for its significant role in higher level learning processes. Remediation of language disabilities as early as the preschool years became one means of trying to prevent learning disabilities.

Bobby's case is presented on page 21 to illustrate one type of language-disordered child with whom the pioneers worked. Today Bobby, along with

CASE STUDY:
Bobby

Bobby was first seen by an otolaryngologist when he was two years of age. The parents were concerned about his lack of speech. The otolaryngologist found infected tonsils and an adenoid mass causing a postnasal obstruction. He concluded further that the child could hear noises but not conversation. The diagnosis given was deafness due to recurrent respiratory infections. A tonsillectomy and adenoidectomy was performed two months later. Approximately six months after this the otolaryngologist requested further evaluation because speech development continued to be seriously retarded.

Summary of History Data

Bobby was seen at the center for auditory disorders in children when he was two years and ten months of age. His parents were professional people with deep concern about him but without handicapping anxiety. Bobby was the fourth pregnancy; the siblings were without defects. The parents stated frankly that although Bobby had no speech, they were confident that he had a great deal of hearing and doubted that his lack of speech could be attributed to peripheral deafness. The pregnancy was uneventful and of nine months' duration. Labor was precipitous, being of only two hours' duration. There was no evidence of injury at the time of birth. Birth weight was six pounds and there was no difficulty in swallowing or feeding immediately after birth. The illness history was negative. Bobby sat alone at eight months and walked at fourteen months. He was retarded in feeding and in acquiring toilet habits as compared to his siblings. He had a preference for the right hand and the parents had not observed unusual awkwardness or incoordination motorically. They reported that he had always been re-

sponsive to people, was playful and in general was a happy contented boy. The history of auditory behavior revealed responses to many environmental sounds including speech. He did not babble and only rarely produced meaningful sounds in play, such as "choo-choo" while engaging with a toy train. Moreover, he used a very few gestures and these had occurred only recently. . . . Interestingly, in view of the previous diagnosis of peripheral deafness, he comprehended speech rather readily. He made no attempts to imitate speech but used "mom" to refer to many objects and wants. . . . He was expressive in laughing, crying and smiling and these expressions manifested good emotional tone.

Behavioral Symptomatology

Bobby was a friendly boy who presented no unusual behavior symptoms with the exception of his lack of verbal ability. He was normally shy, inhibited, playful and manifested good relationship to his environment. He responded to simple verbal commands and engaged himself integratively and imaginatively with toys, crayons and other objects. His behavior was unlike that of children with peripheral or psychic deafness and was not typical of receptive aphasics [difficulty processing language input] or the mentally deficient. The clinical impression was distinctly one of predominantly expressive aphasia [difficulty expressing in speech what has been understood].

Test Responses

. . . Recommendations were made for immediate training and such training has been in progress for six months. The eventual outcome in terms of verbal language is not known but adjustment and progress are good. Receptive language is judged to be normal (Myklebust, 1954, pp. 331–333).

other children who have more subtle speaking or comprehension disorders, would be called learning disabled.

Franz Joseph Gall. The investigation of spoken language disorders can be traced to Gall, a Viennese physician (Wiederholt, 1974). In the early 1800s Gall hypothesized that loss of speech and memory for words resulted from injury to the brain's frontal lobes (Head, 1920a). After Gall's death, John Baptiste Bouillaud, a French physician and ardent follower of Gall, continued to try to locate speech in these lobes by offering "a sum of money to anyone who would produce the brain of an individual who had lost his speech in which the anterior lobes presented no lesion" (Head, 1920a, p. 393).

Gall and his colleagues pursued their theories through the art of phrenology, an analysis of skull size, shape, and bumps. Although phrenologists were unsuccessful and subject to much derision (Head, 1920a), they established the importance of exploring brain–behavior relationships.

Pierre Paul Broca. In the 1860s Broca, a French physician, continued Gall's and Bouillaud's study of brain–behavior relationships. Broca was among the first to hypothesize that the function of the left hemisphere of the brain was different from that of the right hemisphere, and that language may be located in the left hemisphere. Hemispheric specialization continues to grow as an important research area in learning disabilities today.

Broca worked at a time when other investigators discovered that vision and movement were controlled by specific portions of the brain (Eggert, 1977). Broca autopsied the brains of two men who had lost their ability to talk and found a portion of each brain's left frontal lobe to be atrophied (Osgood & Miron, 1963). Thus, he anatomically demonstrated a relationship between the left hemisphere and the ability to speak. This area of the brain was later labeled *Broca's area,* and the loss of ability to speak is referred to as *expressive aphasia* (Geschwind, 1968). Broca's work offered an important basis to subsequent theorists who tried to understand how auditory information was received, understood, memorized, and then repeated.

Carl Wernicke. Wernicke, a German physician, continued Broca's work in the 1870s. He expanded Broca's focus on speech production by studying the inability to understand the speech of others (Wernicke, 1874, in Eggert, 1977).

While working with adult stroke victims, Wernicke noted instances in which they lost their ability to comprehend language. These patients were unable to think of appropriate words when speaking, but the overall meaning of their garbled, incorrectly produced sentences was always reasonable. Even though they could not name simple objects such as a hat or pencil, the patients did know how to use them correctly. Along with their inability to understand, think of, or use words appropriately, they lost their ability to remember words when reading and writing. As the patients recovered their ability to understand words, speech and reading also improved. However, the more difficult ability to quickly call a word to mind or to express oneself in writing remained very poor (Wernicke, 1906, in Eggert, 1977).

Prior to Wernicke's work, such severe comprehension problems were attributed to low intelligence, hearing deficits, craziness, or brain deterioration in old age. In contrast, Wernicke suggested that this loss was the result of damage to certain portions of the temporal lobe, which had neural connections to the frontal areas described by Broca. Wernicke (1906) hypothesized that when these connections were damaged, speech that had been understood (Wernicke's area) could not be translated into spoken language (Broca's area). This explained why some stroke victims could understand what others said, but could respond only with unrelated emotional, automatic, and jargon-like expressions.

After Wernicke's death, his theories were anatomically proven (Geschwind, 1968). The comprehension difficulty is referred to as a *receptive* or *sensory aphasia*. The disorder existing in the neural connections between Wernicke's and Broca's areas is known as a *conduction aphasia*. Difficulty searching one's memory in order to come up with the right word is called a *word-finding problem;* this is a key characteristic associated with learning disorders. Assessment and remediation methods in use in schools today commonly analyze behavior along Wernicke's receptive, expressive, and connectionist (associative) dimensions. His work laid the foundation for understanding the important relationship between language processing, reading, and writing.

Hughlings Jackson. Jackson was a contemporary and follower of Broca. He agreed with his predecessors that the left hemisphere was used for speaking, and that damage to it usually caused aphasia (Head, 1915). However, he was among the first to suggest that, in some people (for example, left handers), language could be located in the right hemisphere. Although some of his patients had suffered left hemisphere damage, they still had command of all or certain types of speech. Jackson hypothesized that the right hemisphere processes certain types of messages, such as emotional and habitual responses, thereby controlling language expressing that content ("Oh my God," "Come on," "yes," "no," "very well").

Jackson defined aphasia as a disturbance of symbolic thinking and expression that was not due to a voice defect, paralysis of the tongue and other articulatory muscles, or deficient hearing (Head, 1915). Since behavioral disturbances often accompanied speech disorders, he argued that speech was controlled by complex interconnections within the whole brain (Jackson, 1931). Consequently, damage to any single portion of the brain reduces a person's overall abilities. This reasoning led Jackson to propose that language is thought, and therefore is linked to intelligence. Aphasia, according to Jackson, diminishes intelligence by interfering with ability to understand or to express thoughts.

Jackson's ideas stimulated a great deal of continuing research in hemispheric specialization and the link between language and intelligence. The right hemisphere's role in language has been confirmed and has helped us to understand ability differences among individuals. Although Jackson's suggestion that any brain damage reduces overall abilities has not been confirmed, a diminution in one ability may impact several other specific skills. Jackson's equating language proficiency with intelligence is now considered a valid concept because what our society defines as intelligent achievement and problem-solving depends a great deal on verbal skills.

Sir Henry Head. Sir Henry Head was the editor of the British journal *Brain* from 1905 to 1922. He monopolized its pages, lauding the works of Jackson and cruelly chastising localization theorists, especially Broca and Wernicke, who assigned certain behaviors to specific brain regions. He severely criticized Broca's and Wernicke's oversimplification of the neural connections between different portions of the brain (Head, 1926). Because he saw the brain as a complex neural network, Head (1920a) did not feel that a brain injury would produce a purely receptive or expressive disorder. Rather, it also would affect functions not associated with language, while leaving some speech functions intact. Due to the brain's complex connections, he urged researchers to focus on patients' behaviors rather than on pinpointing sites of brain lesions. He also stressed the meaninglessness of labels like "aphasia" because they do not describe the behaviors affected by the lesions.

True to his own preachings, Head developed an observational technique and tests to study the language characteristics of aphasics (Head, 1920b). Studying World War I victims of gunshot wounds to the head, he enumerated "the various activities which are found to be affected" (Head, 1920b, p. 157).

Head expanded on Jackson's concern with language and intelligence. He pointed out that abstract conceptual ability is the most serious process affected by aphasia (Head, 1920b). In so far as conceptual processes depend on the perfect exercise of all mental aptitudes, language disabilities dull a person's reasoning skills (Head, 1923). These individuals' intellectual capacities may function well in some ways (speaking), but be dull in other ways (reading). Head noted that once a person appears less competent to others he or she unfortunately becomes isolated from communication and information that might sharpen intelligence.

Many of Head's ideas are reflected in key premises within current learning disability theories: children may have intellectual potential that shows up only through specific sensory modalities and on certain types of tasks; describing behaviors is more important than labelling and diagnosing sites of brain lesions; if language and intelligence become synonymous in our society, then early intervention is critical.

Jon Eisenson. Eisenson (1954) expanded findings with adults who had *acquired aphasias* to children. He was responsible for a new era of investigation into the reason for and implications of language disabilities in children.

Eisenson (1954) hypothesized that children experienced *developmental aphasias* (poor language development) due to brain damage before, during, or after birth; or to a lag in the normal rate of cerebral maturation. These children's irregular brain waves often indicated problems in the left cerebral hemisphere (Eisenson, 1968), just as did those of adult aphasics. However, the children differed from the adults in that, instead of losing the ability to speak, they were slow to develop speech or did not develop it at all.

Like his predecessors' work with adults, Eisenson's tests found that language deficits such as small vocabulary, poor grammar, short sentence length, and poor comprehension were not the only difficulties experienced by these children. They frequently did not realize that people were speaking to them, had inconsistent responses to sound, experienced disorders in one or more sensory modalities, had intellectual, attention and memory inefficiencies, perseverated, showed emotional lability, or responded inconsistently from day to day (Eisenson, 1968). He felt that the majority of these children could not speak correctly because they lacked the capacity to meaningfully process the speech they heard (Eisenson, 1954). He speculated that these children's storage system for speech signals was defective, that they had difficulty receiving and processing auditory signals at a normal rate, and that their ability to tell sounds apart or sequence auditory stimuli and other events was impaired (Eisenson, 1968).

Eisenson's theories and treatment approaches stimulated research into the information-processing elements, especially processing of auditory elements, that may underlie children's learning difficulties. Eisenson's distinction between the adult brain and the child's developing brain is an important concept, which was not heeded sufficiently until the recent birth of child neuropsychology as a specialty.

Charles E. Osgood. While Eisenson dealt with language disorders in children, Osgood used *normal* language development as a key to understanding learning disorders. Osgood (1957a) proposed a communication model based on stimulus-response theory. He suggested that there were two stages to all behaviors: *decoding*, interpreting the significance of signals received from the environment; and *encoding*, expressing intentions through overt acts. Each stage has three levels of organization: a projection level, where sensing and motor action signals are wired to appropriate brain areas; an integration level, where incoming and outgoing neural events are organized; and a representation level, where meaning and thinking takes place. The integration and representation of information was thought to be dependent on the number and strength of stimulus-response pairings at the projection level. Osgood incorporated reinforcement theory into his model to account for motivational variables (Osgood, 1957b).

Osgood's assumptions proved valuable to individuals seeking to assess and treat information processing disorders in children. His model was incorporated into tests and became a means for conceptualizing remedial programs for children with learning problems. Osgood's use of behavioral theory to explain brain activities helped people understand that just because we can't see what's going on in the brain does not preclude us from theorizing about brain processes.

Joseph Wepman. Wepman, a contemporary of Osgood's, developed a similar framework for examining spoken language disorders (Wepman & colleagues, 1960). Wepman believed that clinicians oversimplified information processing theory, viewing input as leading directly to output, and ignoring the integrative process. Wepman's conception of the central nervous system's role in receiving, integrating, and expressing information is presented in Figure 1-2. He hypothesized that the central nervous system processed information in two ways: through the *transmission* of language by receiving or expressing it, and through the *integration* of previously learned transmissions so as to gain meaning.

Wepman and his colleagues' model was able to integrate all previous models. They limited aphasia to a disruption of integration, and gave new labels to receptive (*agnosia*) and expressive (*apraxia*) deficits. The model could account for all clinical types of language disorders: failure of language to arouse a meaningful state (*pragmatic aphasia*), difficulty selecting the appropriate words (*semantic aphasia*), and faulty or absent grammar and sentence structure (*syntactic aphasia*).

Wepman's model stimulated the development of assessment measures that would test its validity (Wepman & Jones, 1961). It also contributed greatly to therapy approaches aimed at remediating the transmission or integration process believed to be responsible for language disorders.

Helmer R. Myklebust. Myklebust also concentrated on a model of normal language development as a means of understanding language disturbances. His theories grew out of his work with deaf and aphasic children in the 1950s. By expanding normal language development theory to include reading and writing as the highest levels of language accomplishment, Myklebust linked language disorders to learning disabilities.

Myklebust (1954) described aphasia as a disorder in the use of language symbols. Aphasia is present at birth, but only becomes apparent later when the child cannot understand spoken language (*receptive aphasia*), or cannot verbally express what he or she understands (*expressive aphasia*). Myklebust (1952) found that these two aphasias often coexist (*mixed receptive-expressive aphasia*). He also suggested a category of *central aphasia,* in which thinking and reasoning

Figure 1-2 Wepman and his colleagues' conception of the central nervous system's role in information processing and its disorders. They proposed that language transmission (reception, expression) and integration (meaning) processes could operate at either a reflex level, perceptual level (imitation without meaning), or conceptual level (thought and language). The perceptual and conceptual levels had connections with memory. Once a child said or did anything, "external feedback" could modify subsequent thought and behavior.

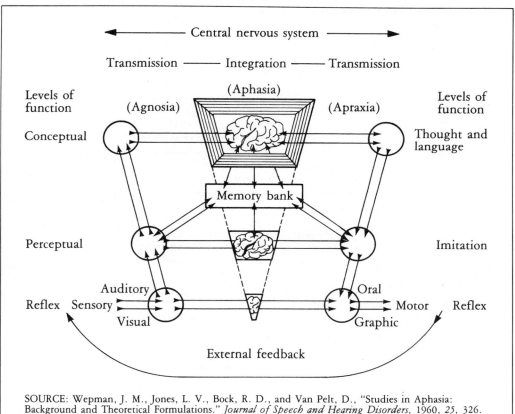

SOURCE: Wepman, J. M., Jones, L. V., Bock, R. D., and Van Pelt, D., "Studies in Aphasia: Background and Theoretical Formulations." *Journal of Speech and Hearing Disorders*, 1960, *25*, 326.

through inner speech (verbal or nonverbal silent reasoning) was disturbed. *Amnesic aphasia* occurred when language functioning was well-established but patients could not remember words, even though they knew what they intended to say and could recognize the correct words when spoken or written (Myklebust, 1954). Today we refer to amnesic aphasia as *word-finding difficulties*.

Out of these clinical observations grew Myklebust's theory of normal language development. This schema is depicted in Figure 1-3. Myklebust

Figure 1-3   Myklebust's hierarchy of normal development of language systems

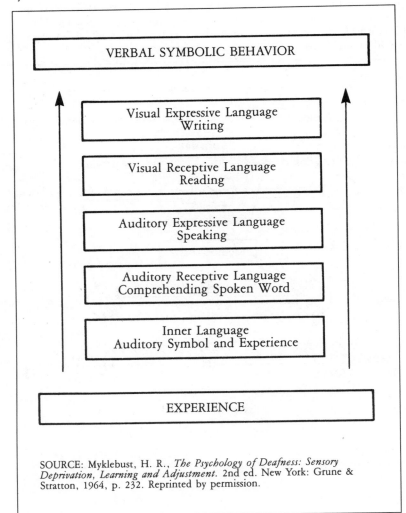

SOURCE: Myklebust, H. R., *The Psychology of Deafness: Sensory Deprivation, Learning and Adjustment.* 2nd ed. New York: Grune & Stratton, 1964, p. 232. Reprinted by permission.

(1964) viewed reading as the superimposing of the read word onto a known auditory word. Writing is superimposed on all earlier acquired language functions, and is the highest level of language attainment (Myklebust, 1965). Myklebust suggested that, in normal development, a child cannot express him- or herself in writing until he or she can comprehend the written word through reading, and formulate vocabulary and grammar. Written language disorders could be due to difficulty with motor movements required in writing (*dysgraphia*) and difficulty remembering (*revisualizing*) what letters or words look like. An impairment at any lower level of development impairs all higher levels. Subsequent reading and writing theory has been based on this important connection between language, reading, and composition skills.

Samuel Kirk. It was not until Kirk's work in the early 1960s that language development theory was widely translated into classroom practice. After successfully increasing some retarded children's intellectual functioning through language training, Kirk devised a test that isolated children's abilities and disabilities, and then led to remedial suggestions. The Illinois Test of Psycholinguistic Abilities (ITPA) (Kirk, McCarthy, & Kirk, 1961, 1968) was based upon Osgood's (1957ab) model of communication, and measured strengths and weaknesses in the way children processed information. Kirk and his colleagues conceptualized information processing in three dimensions: the channel of communication (hearing-speaking, seeing-doing), the psycholinguistic process (receiving, organizing, or expressing information), and the level of organization (automatic or requiring thought).

The ITPA's model became popular for designing educational programs aimed at using children's strengths to overcome their weaknesses. Although its theoretical validity and use in remediating weaknesses that underlie learning disorders has been criticized (Hammill & Larsen, 1974), Kirk's work made visible the critical relationship between language and learning disorders in children. Prior to Kirk's work, education-related tests and programs had a primarily visual-motor orientation. Kirk's work also focused attention on the importance of individually tailored, intensive remediation efforts. Due in part to Kirk's contributions, the American educational system stresses preschool education as a means of preventing learning disorders.

Program Development

The theoretical work discussed above and a proliferation of new educational materials, methods, and equipment in the 1960s made individualized instruction more sophisticated and manageable. A large volume of published teaching materials was directed toward bolstering visual-perceptual, language, and motor weaknesses that affect higher level learning. Other materials taught academic objectives. Individualized remedial programming approaches were based on which information processing channels were stronger or weaker. Children's strengths were analyzed and used to overcome or work around their weaknesses. Multisensory methods often were used and the school curriculum was adapted to what the individual was ready to learn. Assessment devices aimed at guiding teaching instead of only establishing a label. Programming concern shifted beyond reading to written expression, arithmetic, social communication, comprehension, and even nonverbal learning. Students also benefitted from greater numbers of ancillary personnel and new educational hardware such as tape recorders, educational television, Moore's talking typewriter, and automated instruction.

These advances in program development were stimulated by the work of several pioneers in learning disabilities. These pioneers viewed learning difficulties primarily from a visual-perceptual (Hinshelwood) or a language (Orton) perspective. Their hypotheses that areas of brain defect (Hinshelwood) or immature brain development (Orton) accounted for learning difficulties led to sophisticated neuropsychological research and creative remedial programming. By assessing children's information processing strategies, Fernald, Myklebust and Johnson developed remedial approaches that increased programming options and encouraged individualization of instruction in all school subjects. These pioneers worked with individuals having mild to severe problems in one or more areas of development (motor movements, language) and learning (behavior, reading).

A case study of a young man who appeared normal in all other respects, yet who had great difficulty learning to read is presented on page 31. This is one of the earliest reported observations on reading disorders; it communicates how these puzzling children could excite the pioneers' clinical interests. The contributions of these pioneers are so important to the evolution of the learning disabilities field that we shall discuss each briefly.

James Hinshelwood. Hinshelwood, a nineteenth-century Glasgow ophthalmologist, published observations on the effects of brain damage on adult reading skills. When he noted similar difficulties in children, he also attributed them to brain injury.

Hinshelwood's case studies, summarized in Research Box 1-2, led him to hypothesize that the brain had separate contiguous centers for the storage of visual memories of everyday objects and places, letters, numerals, and words. He supported his thesis by noting that each of these functions returned separately, not simultaneously, in brain-injured adults (Hinshelwood, 1899). Hinshelwood felt that a proficient reader no longer analyzed words letter by letter, but remembered them merely by recalling a visual picture.

Hinshelwood applied the term *congenital word blindness* to children of normal vision and intelligence whose reading disabilities were similar to those acquired by his adult patients. He hypothesized that they had a defect in the portions of the left hemisphere, where visual word and letter memories were stored (Hinshelwood, 1917). He attributed this brain defect to birth injury, faulty development, or disease. Hinshelwood suggested a three-stage process for overcoming word-blindness: 1) teach individual letters to be stored in the visual-memory center of the brain; 2) teach recognition of words by spelling the printed words out loud so as to use the person's good memory for letter sounds; and 3) use oral and written practice to aid storage of the reading words. By analyzing each word into its individual sounds, the child would finally learn to recognize it as a complete picture.

CASE STUDY:
Percy F.

Percy F. — a well-grown lad, aged 14 — is the eldest son of intelligent parents, the second child of a family of seven. He has always been a bright and intelligent boy, quick at games, and in no way inferior to others of his age.

His great difficulty has been — and is now — his inability to learn to read. This inability is so remarkable, and so pronounced, that I have no doubt it is due to some congenital defect.

He has been at school or under tutors since he was 7 years old, and the greatest efforts have been made to teach him to read, but, in spite of this laborious and persistent training, he can only with difficulty spell out words of one syllable.

The following is the result of an examination I made a short time since. He knows all his letters and can write them and read them. In writing from dictation he comes to grief over any but the simplest words. For instance, I dictated the following sentence: "Now, you watch me while I spin it." He wrote: "Now you word me wale I spin it"; and, again, "Carefully winding the string round the peg" was written: "calfuly winder the sturng rond the pag."

In writing his own name he made a mistake, putting "Precy" for "Percy," and he did not notice the mistake until his attention was called to it more than once. I asked him to write the following words:

Song	he wrote	scone
Subject	"	Scojock
Without	"	wichout
English	"	Englis
Shilling	"	sening
Seashore	"	seasoiv

He was quite unable to spell the name of his father's house though he must have seen it and spelt it scores of times. In asking him to read the sentences he had just written a short time previously, he could not do so, but made mistakes over every word except the very simplest. Words such as "and" and "the" he always recognizes.

I then asked him to read me a sentence out of an easy child's book without spelling the words. The result was curious. He did not read a single word correctly, with the exception of "and," "the," "of," "that," etc.; the other words seemed to be quite unknown to him, and he could not even make an attempt to pronounce them.

I next tried his ability to read figures, and found he could do so easily. He read off quickly the following: 785,852017, 20,969, and worked out correctly: $(a + x) (a - x) = a - x$. He could not do the simple calculation $4 \times \frac{1}{2}$, but he multiplied 749 by 867 quickly and correctly. He says he is fond of arithmetic, and finds no difficulty with it, but that printed or written words "have no meaning to him," and my examination of him quite convinces me that he is correct in that opinion. Words written or printed seem to convey no impression to his mind, and it is only after laboriously spelling them that he is able, by the sounds of the letters, to discover their import. His memory for written or printed words is so defective that he can only recognize such simple ones as "and," "the," "of," etc. Other words he never seems to remember no matter how frequently he may have met them. . . .

I may add that the boy is bright and of average intelligence in conversation . . . his eyesight is good. The schoolmaster who has taught him for some years says that he would be the smartest lad in the school if the instruction were entirely oral. It will be interesting to see what effect further training will have on his condition (Morgan, 1896, p. 1378).

RESEARCH BOX 1-2
Hinshelwood's
Case Studies

Hinshelwood's clients suffered from such brain insults as strokes and chronic alcoholism, and had acquired strange forms of "word blindness" or "dyslexia" (inability to read). One individual had lost the ability to read print, or write more than the first few words of a line, after which the words lost meaning for him. He was a tailor and could not remember how to fit pieces together, where he had just placed objects, and where his home was located (Hinshelwood, 1896). Another client could not read words, but could read letters and numbers, write from dictation, and copy words. If allowed to spell each word aloud, letter by letter, he could read the words laboriously (Hinshelwood, 1898).

Hinshelwood found that word-blindness was often accompanied by "letter-blindness." One patient could not recognize letters but, if allowed to trace them with his finger, could eventually name them (Hinshelwood, 1898). Another client, Tom, exhibited "'letter' without 'word' blindness." He could neither read, write, nor point to individual letters (with the exception of *T*, which he called "Tom"). However, Tom could read familiar and unfamiliar words rapidly, and also wrote well (Hinshelwood, 1899). It was not long before Hinshelwood and others generalized the theoretical notions about the injured brain processes in these adults to children who also experienced significant difficulties acquiring reading and writing skills.

Hinshelwood's visual interpretation of reading deficits had a strong impact on later visual-perceptual theories. His work helped subsequent investigators understand that the purpose of diagnostic assumptions about brain-behavior relationships is to create remedial programs that use children's strengths to overcome their weaknesses.

Samuel T. Orton. Orton (1937), a neuropathologist, proposed a language basis for severe reading disabilities. Like Hinshelwood, Orton saw similarities between children's reading, writing, spelling, and speaking delays, and the disorders of brain-injured adults. His theory that the failure of one cerebral hemisphere to establish dominance over the other leads to reading disorders is summarized in Research Box 1-3.

To remediate reading disorders, Orton (1937) suggested using one-sided motor training to establish cerebral dominance in children whose reading difficulties were accompanied by writing, speech, and coordination problems and in whom handedness had not yet developed. Once one hemisphere became superior, progress in language, reading and reasoning was expected to follow. Orton recommended training right-handedness in children with no hand preference because it is the most commonly used in our society.

RESEARCH BOX 1-3
Orton's Theory of Reading Disability

Orton (1925) attributed reading disorders to the failure of one cerebral hemisphere to establish dominance over the other. His clients were children who had language acquisition difficulties, but no known brain-injury. Many were mixed dominant; that is, neither the left nor right hand, eye or foot was consistently preferred. In the adult, the dominant hemisphere controls motor movements of the opposite body side and often language as well. Therefore, Orton concluded that his children's failure to establish motor dominance was related to their language disabilities. In support of this proposition, Orton noted that forcing a child to use the nondominant hemisphere by shifting handedness (due to accident or teaching) at critical ages for language development (ages 2–3 or 6–8) markedly interfered with language function.

Orton felt that the balance between each hemisphere's areas of strength determined which hemisphere ultimately gained superiority for language and motor acts. Pure left-handers were presumed to be no different than pure right-handers in reading, writing, and speech. It was only when a weak left- or right-sided tendency was present that its controlling hemisphere was not sufficiently strong, and academic troubles were expected. Since family histories of mixed-dominant, reading-delayed children often included left-handedness and language disorders, Orton concluded that brain specialization was hereditary. He felt that reading disabilities varied from mild to severe, depending on the amount of cerebral dominance a child had developed.

How did reading failure actually happen? Orton proposed that the nondominant hemisphere stored mirror-images ("engrams") of words that were correctly stored in the dominant hemisphere (Orton 1925, 1928). If superiority of one hemisphere over another was not established, the dominant hemisphere could not suppress these reversed images. This resulted in "strephosymbolia" (twisted symbols), so that reversals occurred with letters (p–q, b–d), words (was–saw, from–form), syllables within words, words within sentences, arithmetic (12–21), and directionality in math carrying or borrowing. Speech (motor movements, reversals, stuttering), comprehension (remembering order of what was said), foreign language learning, and motor movement difficulties often accompanied reading disorders.

Orton's (1937) work represented a major theoretical break with the brain-injury theorists. Contrary to those who thought that reading difficulties were "brain deficits," Orton viewed them as developmental patterns. Since the brain was intact, it could respond to training if initiated early enough. Orton felt that these developmental disorders could occur at all intelligence levels.

Orton's dominant hemisphere theory has not been confirmed the way he had conceptualized it. Nevertheless, it stimulated neuropsychological research that found different areas of each hemisphere to be dominant for different functions. At times, one of these areas can interfere with the efficiency of the same region in the opposite hemisphere. In addition, his conceptions about reversals in visual memory led to some important experimental work in visual sequencing and memory processes.

Since most children had already developed handedness, they did not meet Orton's qualifications for dominance training. For these children, he urged reading remediation methods that built associations between auditory, visual, and kinesthetic (feedback from body movements) information. For example, he suggested "having the child trace [the letter] over a pattern drawn by the teacher, at the same time giving its sound or phonetic equivalent" (Orton, 1937, p. 159). Maintaining consistent left to right tracing was essential to aid recall of "word pictures" and to overcome confusion caused by reversed letter and word images, which Orton assumed were stored in the nondominant hemisphere. He recommended repetitive oral and written drills on letter-sound associations (Orton, 1925). Since spelling presented even greater difficulties than reading, Orton (1937) stressed spelling training through analysis of sound sequences (*phonetic analysis*). Orton (1928) felt that the "look-say" approach in America's schools was responsible for a great deal of reading failure because the nondominant hemisphere's reversed letter and word images confused recall.

Orton influenced educators to use phonetic analysis and kinesthetic activities. The value of phonetic over sight approaches to reading has since been confirmed. Practices in learning disabilities today reflect several of Orton's influences: materials are geared to the individual's ability and interest level; no one remediation package is considered adequate for all children; instruction is individualized by analyzing the content and processes involved in learning (Johnson, 1967); negative personality characteristics (apathy, emotional blocking, inferiority, antagonism or paranoia) that can arise from academic struggle and failure are recognized. Most importantly, Orton's emphasis on the relationship between language and reading created a theoretical move away from the visual–perceptual perspective of learning problems. By the 1970s, the language, rather than perceptual, viewpoint had become primary.

Grace Fernald. Orton's methods were developed further by individuals interested in reading remediation: Marion Monroe, Anna Gillingham, Bessie Stillman, Romalda Spalding, and Grace Fernald. Of these, Fernald has had the most widespread influence. Fernald (1943) blamed much of reading disability on schools' visual teaching methods being incongruent with the needs of children who had difficulty remembering (*revisualizing*) what they had seen. Instead, she used a multisensory approach to reading and spelling that combined kinesthetic methods like tracing, with phonic associations like saying word sounds, while looking at the whole word. Kinesthetic instructional methods had never before been advocated with as much energy and focus. Fernald's methods first became popular in the instruction of severely retarded children, but are used today in most special classrooms.

Fernald's *Remedial Techniques in Basic School Subjects* (1943) was a landmark work. Besides reading remediation methods, it described how to remediate arithmetic difficulties and to apply her ideas to all school subjects, within the normal classroom. Today teachers in both regular and special classrooms use many of Fernald's methods to adapt curricula to individual needs and to teach reading through all subject matter.

Doris Johnson and Helmer R. Myklebust. Johnson joined with Myklebust to further develop his theories on auditory language, reading, arithmetic, non-verbal learning, and written language disorders (Johnson & Myklebust, 1967). They assumed that the brain was made up of discrete information-processing systems involving input-output systems, sensory modalities (visual, motor, auditory, vocal), and the integration of these systems and modalities. They proposed that information could be received, processed, and expressed via one sensory system and be relatively independent from another. This involved the *intraneurosensory* integration of visual inputs with motor outputs, or auditory inputs with vocal outputs. Many other tasks required the interneurosensory integration of two systems transferring information from one to another (visual-vocal or auditory-motor). Reading is an example of interneurosensory integration: a visual stimulus (letter) must be looked at, matched to its auditory correlate (sound), and then vocally expressed (read). Copying represents the intraneurosensory integration of looking and drawing.

Johnson and Myklebust categorized reading failure (*dyslexia*) as: *auditory dyslexia* (inability to process sounds), *visual dyslexia* (difficulty processing information seen), comprehension disorders, and written production problems. They felt that difficulty learning arithmetic (*dyscalculia*) could be due to language or reading problems, disturbance in quantitative thinking, difficulty revisualizing or writing numbers, and problems remembering instructions. They also described the spatial, conceptual, memory, and social difficulties of children with learning difficulties, and presented detailed instructional ideas.

Myklebust and Johnson's educational practices brought together the perspectives of many fields: medicine, psychology, neurology, psychiatry, education, and language pathology. Their theory of learning disorders and emphasis on *clinical teaching* (ongoing assessment while teaching) greatly influenced subsequent research, and the development of assessment, teaching materials, and teaching methods.

Later Work in Learning Disabilities

The pioneers were all wise people with tremendous observational powers and ability to integrate diverse information. Although discussed here within discrete areas of interest, none of the pioneers harbored fanatically narrow views of learning difficulties. The visual-motor theorists acknowledged the importance of language. The language theorists spoke about visual and motor difficulties. All were concerned with learning and most developed sensible teaching approaches. They understood that an eclectic, holistic approach was important because most developing functions play a role in an individual's overall performance.

The pioneers' followers, however, often stuck to a single theoretical position in spite of the limited state of research at the time or the pioneers' intentions. Others held narrow interpretations of the pioneers' work which led to severe, unwarranted attacks on their positions. For example, Orton's followers jumped onto a cerebral dominance training bandwagon. In his entire book (1937), Orton devoted less than one page to this type of training. Similarly, Marianne Frostig developed a visual–perceptual test and program, but never intended, as her followers assumed, that remediation of these underlying abilities would automatically increase a child's reading skills. Wernicke was terribly maligned by Head for drawing diagrams of specific brain areas' functions. Wernicke's theories were, in fact, very much in agreement with Head's; his diagrams were merely intended as visual aids, not truths. Kephart developed a survey on a small number of children in order to guide observations; his followers misused it as a standardized instrument. The unjustified approaches and attacks by those who followed the pioneers unfortunately led to many camps within learning disabilities.

The pioneers' provocative works stimulated scientific inquiry that resulted in many of the current theories, research, and practices in learning disabilities. Their early influences live on throughout our present theories and practices. If we look closely enough, we'll recognize them: when we teach a child "through all his senses," that's Fernald; when we build a study carrel to help a child attend better, that's Strauss; when we caution not to teach too much, too fast, too soon, that's Werner. Even theories that have fallen into disrepute stimulated research and enriched our knowledge in the field.

During the early 1960s, educators began actively translating pioneering research into classroom methodology. Instruction was geared to individual needs, with special emphasis on visual and motor skill development. Early identification and prevention of potentially handicapping conditions had priority during this period. In the late 1960s, educators found that children with reading difficulties often had been language-delayed as preschoolers and continued to display more subtle communicative disorders at older ages. These students frequently had more complex educational difficulties than did children with visual–motor weaknesses.

By the 1970s, the visual–motor emphasis had diminished. Both language-processing and attention deficits became major focal points for understanding learning disabilities. By this time behavior modification techniques had become sophisticated and were successfully applied to classroom programming (Whalen, 1966). Behavior modification uses well-researched relationships between behavior and environmental events to facilitate learning. These techniques offered systematic ways of observing and shaping the learning and behavior of children with school problems. Behavioral technology had been inadvertently fostered by Werner, Strauss, and Cruickshank. Their students (Bijou, and McCandless among others) translated their mentor's behavioral assessment and environmental structuring techniques into systematic means of dealing with learning and behavior disorders in the classroom. These behavioral psychologists and educators focused only on observable behaviors, rather than the underlying causes of learning difficulties. They developed ways of analyzing classroom tasks that determined exactly what and how to teach, and made individualized instruction all the more possible (Bijou, 1970; Mann, 1971).

Secondary educational and vocational training needs also came into focus in the 1970s. Interest in the emotional-social effects of learning difficulties grew. Sophisticated neuropsychological studies began on information processing patterns, their relationship to academic learning, and their modifiability with drugs, diet, and teaching strategies. Behavioral observation and task analysis systems were further refined, and the unique adolescent and adult needs of the learning disabled were recognized. It became clear that physiological differences did not cause all learning failures. Adverse life circumstances like poor parent models, lack of appropriate learning experiences (as in missing school due to frequent illnesses), and inappropriate school tasks also could lead to poor achievement (Quay, 1973).

The ever-broadening focus of learning disabilities has been accompanied by confusion and conflict. By the 1970s, a schism had developed between the behaviorists and individuals who understood learning disabilities as an information processing disorder of the visual, motor, language, or attention channels (Smead, 1977; Ysseldyke & Salvia, 1974). Equivocal academic gains after attempts to train underlying weaknesses led the behaviorists to severely criticize such remediation (Hammill & Larsen, 1974a, 1978a). Behaviorists were unconcerned about the cause of the learning difficulty, concentrating instead on teaching specific academic objectives.

Though the behaviorist position is the most prominent today, information processing research has increasingly flourished in the late 1970s and early 1980s. Its findings remind us that it may be unwise to concentrate only on what the child is supposed to be learning, and neglect brain-behavior research that helps us better understand how the child learns. For the most part, educators who remain biased toward the underlying process approach use this information only to better understand the nature of the child's difficulties and needs. Like behaviorists, their actual instruction is geared toward pertinent academic and life skills. As we become increasingly able to measure and understand the relationship between neuro-chemical brain processes and learning, we will be able to develop more refined individualized instruction methods. To do this we must integrate knowledge about the child's underlying processes with the already sophisticated behavioral technology. Research continues on many of the constructs that originated with the pioneers. These individuals laid the foundation for conceptualizing the important learner-, task-, and setting-based components of learning disabilities.

Summary

In the mid–1960s several forces came together to catalyze the birth of a new field in special education: learning disabilities. Parents whose children displayed uneven patterns of development were concerned with the appropriateness of existing educational classification and placement practices. They sought a way to focus greater attention on their children's strengths and weaknesses, what they needed to learn, and how they could best be taught. Parents and professionals advocated a systematic, intense, direct approach to instruction within a broader range of service delivery options.

Parents and educators recognized that teaching methods and settings needed to be analyzed so as to best accommodate to each child's learning abilities and style. The possibility for such individualized instruction was enhanced by research relating visual-perceptual and language difficulties to learning disorders, development of individualized programming materials and methods, and classroom application of behavior modification techniques. Reports of intellectual growth following intense individualized instruction heightened incentives to narrow the gap between a child's actual and potential achievement. The concept that specific disabilities were responsible for learning difficulties also had particular appeal to parents because it avoided the mental retardation or emotional disturbance stigma and encouraged intensive teaching efforts. With increasing numbers of high-risk births, greater government role in education, and strong parent-professional advocacy groups, learning disabilities became a recognized, funded handicapping condition. Currently, approximately 38 percent of all handicapped children are educated under the LD label.

The learning disabilities concept has attracted a broad range of professional expertise. Educational theories, assessment tools, and teaching practices are being keenly reexamined and put to an empirical test. This text will examine research and programming progress in learning disabilities from this eclectic vantage point. Our eclectic conceptual models give meaning to our observations, guide and catalyze research and programming efforts, and systematize our knowledge. They form a framework against which we test the validity of our philosophies and methods. Each theoretical perspective offers unique research evidence that, when taken together, helps us to narrow the gap between research and practice.

Suggestions for Further Study

1. If you are interested in learning more about similarities between the learning disabled, emotionally disturbed, and educable mentally retarded, consult Hallahan & Kauffman's (1977) article. They discuss the overlaps between these exceptional groups, and clarify which types of behavioral characteristics are more prevalent in one or another category. Their article underscores the incongruity in segregating children by their disability labels, when their educational needs overlap greatly. The learning disabilities concept also emphasizes instruction based on individual rather than group needs.

2. The concept that intelligence can be educated was originally introduced by Alfred Binet. His intelligence test (Stanford–Binet) was intended to identify educational needs rather than to label children. Kirk & Lord (1974) provide an interesting discussion on how Binet's concept was rediscovered nearly seventy-five years later. This educability premise underscores many instructional objectives with the learning disabled.

3. Educational rights were not easily won in the United States. Should you be a history or law buff, you would enjoy reading Cruickshank's (1967) and Church & Sedlak's (1976) accounts of the political and attitudinal forces that shaped special education in America. Other articles present excellent reviews of how the right to education movement began when Nebraska tried to outlaw teaching German in schools (*Meyers v. Nebraska,* 1923) and, over a fifty-year period, finally won full educational rights for all handicapped children: Ross, deYoung, & Cohen, 1971; Weintraub, 1972; Weintraub & Abeson, 1974.

4. The reference librarian in your university's Government Documents collection can help you find originals of laws mentioning LD; important articles and regulations regarding laws printed in the Federal Register, the government's daily communication source with the public; reports of national advisory councils that are not reprinted elsewhere; government-funded research reports that have not yet been summarized in professional journals, etc. This brief search will give you an appreciation of the large role that government plays in LD policy setting, direct service, teacher-training, and research.

5. Read a psychological report or IEP recently written for a learning disabled student. Now glance through Strauss & Lehtinen's (1947), Strauss & Kephart's (1955), Cruickshank, Bentzen, Ratzeburg, & Tannhauser's (1961), Fernald's (1943) or Frostig & Horn's (1964) books. How different are the programming strategies? Although materials have been expanded, and strategies refined over the past thirty years, their origins in the works of these pioneers are still evident. Fernald's book presents interesting self-descriptions by famous individuals who could learn only through kinesthetic methods (Rodin, William James). Her book is an invaluable aid to understanding how learning occurs through many senses, how one sense can compete with and confuse another, and how the senses can be used or selectively not used in instruction.

6. We explored how political and parent pressure influences professional practices. The professional philosophies held within any training institution also strongly influence the direction that their graduates take. For example, the emphasis on underlying process disorders and classroom remediation techniques in part can be traced to the research department of the Wayne County Training School in Northville, Michigan. Its director, Dr. Robert Haskell, attracted outstanding scholars and postgraduate students to the school (Strauss & Lehtinen, 1947). These individuals' later professional contributions strongly reflected the philosophical directions gained in their earlier years. Examine their works closely and see if you can detect their common origins: Alfred Strauss, Heinz Werner, Samuel Kirk, Newell Kephart, William Cruickshank, Sidney Bijou, Boyd McCandless, Thorleif Hegge, Laura Lehtinen, Bluma Weiner, Winifred Kirk.

7. The cases that the pioneers in language development reported were classic opportunities for clinical study. Many of these can be found in a medical school library. The pioneers' observations on adults gave subsequent researchers who worked with LD children a mind set from which to observe and interpret their behaviors. Reading these cases will help you conceptualize similar but more subtle signs in learning disabled youngsters. Give some thought to whether it is valid to suppose that the brain organization of the brain-injured adult and LD child who have similar disabilities is the same.

Chapter Two
Definition, Identification, and Prevalence

Now that we have described the historical roots of learning disabilities, let us explore how our terminology and definitions developed and the issues we face with LD identification practices and prevalence estimates. The LD child is characterized by major discrepancies between his or her potential for achievement and actual achievement levels. There is no single, best way to measure these discrepancies because each LD child differs from the others in personal characteristics and reasons for underachievement. Measurement error is also a concern. Whether or not a child is ultimately identified as LD depends on a clinical judgment that incorporates multiple dimensions. Although 38 percent of handicapped school children currently are labelled LD, research indicates that far greater numbers may be eligible for LD services.

The Search for a Definition

Before the term "learning disabilities" was accepted, many labels were used synonymously to describe children whose learning and behavior patterns did not fit existing handicapping conditions. Each professional's theoretical orientation dictated which term he or she preferred. These labels had little meaning; one term could refer to several different behaviors, or several terms might describe similar behaviors.

In 1964, Clements' (1966) national task force on minimal brain dysfunction tried to come to grips with the terminology issue. It found that thirty-eight terms applied to the same children (see Table 2-1). Some terms referred to the brain as a cause of the learning problem, while others described specific behaviors associated with the disorder. Common terms not on Clements' list were *slow learner, neurological handicap, brain injury,* and *educational handicap*. Strauss (1943) had even tried out the term *cripple-brained*.

Among these, the first term to gain general acceptance was *brain injury*. But the brain injury often could not be validated, and the term proved irrelevant to programming and offensive to many. Therefore, these children were redefined as having *minimal brain dysfunction* (MBD). Similar arguments were then levelled at this term. In contrast to the term "brain injury," MBD referred only to children of at least near-average intelligence.

A shift toward a more educational focus brought the term "learning disability" into vogue. Its definitions stressed individual strengths and weaknesses, and did not necessitate proof of central nervous system impairment. The current federal definition presumes that a child's severe discrepancy between expected and actual achievement is not caused by emotional, intellectual, visual, hearing, motor, or environmental deficiencies. A learning disability can, however, coexist with these conditions.

Brain Injury

In the 1930–1950s, Werner, Strauss, Lehtinen, & Kephart worked with many mentally retarded children whose learning problems were traced to biological

Table 2-1 Task Force I's listing of terms that different professionals used to describe the child with minimal brain dysfunction

GROUP I: ORGANIC ASPECTS	GROUP II: SEGMENT OR CONSEQUENCE
Association deficit pathology (Anderson & Plymate, 1962)	Hyperkinetic behavior syndrome (Denhoff, Laufer, & Holden, 1959)
Organic brain disease (Bender, 1949; Silver, 1951)	Character impulse disorder (Frosch & Wortis, 1954)
Organic brain damage (Bradley, 1957)	Hyperkinetic impulse disorder (Laufer & Denhoff, 1957)
Organic brain dysfunction (Burks, 1957)	Aggressive behavior disorder (Morris, Escoll, & Wexler, 1956)
Minimal brain damage (Clemmens, 1961)	Psychoneurological learning disorders (Myklebust & Boshes, 1960)
Diffuse brain damage (Daryn, 1961)	
Neurophrenia (Doll, 1960)	Hyperkinetic syndrome (Ounsted, 1955)
Organic drivenness (Kahn & Cohen, 1934)	Dyslexia (Park, 1953)
Cerebral dysfunction (Laufer, 1962)	Hyperexcitability syndrome (Prechtl & Stemmer, 1962)
Organic behavior disorder (Milman, 1956)	Perceptual cripple (Silver, 1958)
Choreiform syndrome (Prechtl & Stemmer, 1962)	Primary reading retardation (Rabinovitch, Drew, DeJong, Ingram & Withey, 1954)
Minor brain damage (Strauss & Lehtinen, 1947)	Specific reading disability (Hermann, 1959)
Minimal brain injury (Strauss & Lehtinen, 1947; Eisenberg, 1957)	Clumsy child syndrome (Walton, Ellis, & Court, 1962)
Minimal cerebral injury (Gesell & Amatruda, 1941)	Hypokinetic syndrome (Clements, Lehtinen, & Lukens, 1964)
Minimal chronic brain syndromes (Paine, 1962)	Perceptually handicapped
Minimal cerebral damage (Knoblock & Pasamanick, 1959)	Aphasoid syndrome
Minimal cerebral palsy (Wigglesworth, 1961)	Learning disabilities
Cerebral dys-synchronization syndrome	Conceptually handicapped
	Attention disorders
	Interjacent child

SOURCE: Clements, S. D., *Minimal Brain Dysfunction in Children: Terminology and Identification. Phase One of a Three-Phase Project* (NINDS Monograph No. 3, U.S. Public Health Service Publication No. 1415). Washington, D.C.: U.S. Government Printing Office, 1966, pp. 9, 16–17.

events or accidents that had injured their brains. Strauss & Lehtinen (1947) defined the brain-injured child as

> a child who before, during, or after birth has received an injury to, or suffered an infection of, the brain. As a result of such organic [brain] impairment, defects of the neuromotor [motor movements] system may be present or absent; however such a child may show disturbances in perception [receiving information], thinking, and emotional behavior, either separately or in combination. These disturbances can be demonstrated by specific tests. These disturbances prevent or impede a normal learning process (p. 4).

In the 1960s, Cruickshank expanded the study of brain-injured children to include those who had more normal intellectual potential. He described brain injury as a perceptual dysfunction — trouble attending to, organizing, storing, retrieving, or expressing information. It could occur at any age or level of intellectual capacity (Cruickshank, 1976).

Some experts were adamant that brain injury must be considered when evaluating learning problems, so as not to overlook life-threatening conditions (Hallahan & Cruickshank, 1973). However, others argued that it was not essential to consider brain injury, which they found a noxious term for several reasons:

1. It implied that the child's situation was hopeless; injured brain cells cannot be repaired.

2. It was too global to be meaningful. There are many types of brain-injured people, and they differ greatly. The term neither described a child's characteristics nor suggested teaching methods (Stevens & Birch, 1957; Wortis, 1956).

3. The nature and extent of brain injury cannot aid remediation because it is not directly related to the nature and extent of functional problems. For example, Cohn's (1964) autopsy studies showed that massive neurological destruction could result in very few learning and behavioral abnormalities. Conversely, numerous learning and behavioral deficiencies could result from very limited neurological damage.

4. The term "brain-injured" most often was reserved for children for whom the label could not be validated (Gallagher, 1966). When brain injury could be proved, the label was more specific: for example, cerebral palsy, hydrocephaly. Such presumptions could not be justified given the practical uselessness of the term.

5. Even if children had verified brain injury, it was their observable ability patterns that needed to be described rather than the cause of these learning problems (Gallagher, 1966). Ability patterns could guide programming, but the "brain injury" label could not.

Stevens and Birch (1957) suggested using the term "Strauss syndrome" as an alternative, to describe children whose thinking, behavioral, and especially perceptual disturbances were similar to those of Strauss' brain-injured children. However, their term was criticized because it limited brain-related learning disorders to the severe behaviors observed by Strauss (Johnson & Myklebust, 1967), because children can have perceptual problems even when not brain-injured, and because not all brain-injured children have perceptual disorders (Gallagher, 1966).

As an alternative to "brain injury," Gallagher suggested the term "developmental imbalances" to reflect the developmental ups and downs in these children's learning processes:

> Children with Developmental Imbalances are those who reveal a developmental disparity in psychological processes related to education of such a degree (often four years or more) as to require the instructional programming

of developmental tasks appropriate to the nature and level of the deviant developmental process (p. 28). . . . They have, in common, that they are all different — not only different from average children but different from one another (p. 32).

Gallagher felt that any child, whether brain-injured, mentally retarded or emotionally disturbed, could have developmental imbalances. Although Gallagher's term did not take hold, his concept of disparities in functioning is reflected in our current definition of learning disabilities.

Minimal Brain Dysfunction (MBD)

During the 1960s professionals took greater note of the many children of near-average or higher intelligence who had difficulty learning and displayed behaviors similar to the brain-injured. These children had sustained no known brain damage, and were neither mentally retarded nor emotionally disturbed. They had been commonly viewed as underachievers. Their underachievement was often blamed on parental pressure, birth order, sibling rivalry, inadequate home environment for studying, anxiety, and poor motivation.

It was becoming evident that many youngsters tried very hard but still could not achieve. Others achieved adequately, but had to put forth extraordinary efforts just to keep up. Their behavioral characteristics were similar to, though less striking than, those of brain-injured children. For example, instead of having a dysfunctional limb due to a stroke, a child might have awkward copying or motor-coordination skills; although able to speak, a youngster might have difficulty recalling words or sequencing sounds when reading.

A natural connection was made between these students' subtle deficits and the more severe disabilities of the brain-injured. Professionals, reluctant to call these children brain-injured, began to use the term "minimal brain damage" in the early 1960s. Strauss and Lehtinen had used the terms "minor brain damage" and "minimal brain injury" as early as 1947 (p. 108, 128). Gesell and Amatruda had used the term "minimal cerebral injury" with reference to infants and young children in their 1941 book (p. 240). These writers implied that some minimal injury to the brain had caused the learning difficulties. Since the damage could not be proved, the term "minimal brain damage" eventually was modified to "minimal brain dysfunction" (MBD). The term "dysfunction" was favored because it emphasized the consequences of the damage on learning and behavior.

Clements' (1966) Task Force I of the Minimal Brain Dysfunction National Project on Learning Disabilities used minimal brain dysfunction to refer to

children of near average, average, or above average general intelligence with certain learning or behavioral disabilities ranging from mild to severe, which are associated with deviation of function of the central nervous system. These deviations may manifest themselves by various combinations of impairment in perception, conceptualization, language, memory, and control of attention, impulse, or motor function (Clements, 1966, pp. 9–10).

Three important elements in the task force's definition of MBD contrast sharply with the earlier conception of brain-injured children:

1. *Cause:* MBD can be due to factors other than injury that affect the brain's functioning (for example, structural variations, biochemical irregularities, inherited maturational lags).

2. *Who can have MBD:* MBD is the sole province of youngsters with at least near average intelligence. The neurological deviation was believed to subtly affect learning and behavior, without lowering general intellectual capacity. In contrast, the earlier pioneers in brain injury had not limited this term to children of normal intelligence.

3. *Characteristics:* MBD included language disorders, whereas the brain injury school recognized but did not highlight the role of language in learning.

Clements' group compiled ninety-nine symptoms of MBD (see Table 2-2). The ten most frequently agreed upon characteristics, in descending order of frequency, included: hyperactivity, perceptual-motor impairments, emotional lability, general coordination deficits, disorders of attention, impulsivity, disorders of memory and thinking, specific learning disabilities (reading, arithmetic, writing, spelling), disorders of speech and hearing, and equivocal neurological signs and electroencephalographic irregularities. Table 2-2's list of symptoms highlights the great variations in behavior exhibited by children with learning disorders. Even if two children share a cluster of symptoms, they are unlikely to have identical instructional needs. Each child requires unique curriculum modifications to match what they already know, what they need to learn, and how they learn best.

By the late 1960s, the MBD label had come under fire for several reasons:

1. Its medical orientation was unfounded; the neurological abnormalities could not be proved. Only one medical indicator was among the ten most frequent characteristics of what was defined as a brain dysfunction.

2. A cerebral abnormality is a major event; there is nothing minimal about it (Benton, 1973).

3. Several screening kits had been marketed in the late 1960s so that doctors could diagnose MBD. These primarily measured developmental milestones in motor, language, social, visual-perceptual, and academic areas. Since these skill areas were to be remediated, not the brain, it made no sense to infer a medical dysfunction from these behaviors. It was said that, "MBD is a sophisticated version of 'The Emperor's New Clothes,' with onlookers pretending to 'see' something that is invisible" (Silberman, 1976, p. 78).

4. A minimal brain dysfunction could not be directly cured.

5. The term was irrelevant to programming and conjured up unnecessary, negative expectations.

Besides these objections, the term MBD became a useless, catch-all label for all underachievers (McIntosh & Dunn, 1973). Though the term MBD can

Table 2-2 Symptoms attributed to children with minimal brain dysfunction, as compiled by Task Force I

A. *Test Performance Indicators*
  1. Spotty or patchy intellectual deficits. Achievement low in some areas; high in others.
  2. Below mental age level on drawing tests (man, house, etc.)
  3. Geometric figure drawings poor for age and measured intelligence.
  4. Poor performance on block design and marble board tests.
  5. Poor showing on group tests (intelligence and achievement) and daily classroom examinations which require reading.
  6. Characteristic subtest patterns on the Wechsler Intelligence Scale for Children, including "scatter" within both Verbal and Performance Scales; high Verbal-low Performance; low Verbal-high Performance.

B. *Impairments of Perception and Concept-Formation*
  1. Impaired discrimination of size.
  2. Impaired discrimination of right-left and up-down.
  3. Impaired tactile discrimination.
  4. Poor spatial orientation.
  5. Impaired orientation in time.
  6. Distorted concept of body image.
  7. Impaired judgment of distance.
  8. Impaired discrimination of figure-ground.
  9. Impaired discrimination of part-whole.
  10. Frequent perceptual reversals in reading and in writing letters and numbers.
  11. Poor perceptual integration. Child cannot fuse sensory impressions into meaningful entities.

C. *Specific Neurologic Indicators*
  1. Few, if any, apparent gross abnormalities.
  2. Many "soft," equivocal, or borderline findings.
  3. Reflex assymetry frequent.
  4. Frequency of mild visual or hearing impairments.
  5. Strabismus.
  6. Nystagmus.
  7. High incidence of left, and mixed laterality and confused perception of laterality.
  8. Hyperkinesis.
  9. Hypokinesis.
  10. General awkwardness.
  11. Poor fine visual-motor coordination.

D. *Disorders of Speech and Communication*
  1. Impaired discrimination of auditory stimuli.
  2. Various categories of aphasia.
  3. Slow language development.
  4. Frequent mild hearing loss.
  5. Frequent mild speech irregularities.

E. *Disorders of Motor Function*
  1. Frequent athetoid, choreiform, tremulous, or rigid movements of hands.
  2. Frequent delayed motor milestones.
  3. General clumsiness or awkwardness.
  4. Frequent tics and grimaces.
  5. Poor fine or gross visual-motor coordination.
  6. Hyperactivity.
  7. Hypoactivity.

(*Table continued on following page.*)

Table 2.2   continued

F. *Academic Achievement and Adjustment (Chief complaints about the child by his parents and teachers)*
  1. Reading disabilities.
  2. Arithmetic disabilities.
  3. Spelling disabilities.
  4. Poor printing, writing, or drawing ability.
  5. Variability in performance from day to day or even hour to hour.
  6. Poor ability to organize work.
  7. Slowness in finishing work.
  8. Frequent confusion about instructions, yet success with verbal tasks.

G. *Disorders of Thinking Process*
  1. Poor ability for abstract reasoning.
  2. Thinking generally concrete.
  3. Difficulties in concept-formation.
  4. Thinking frequently disorganized.
  5. Poor short-term and long-term memory.
  6. Thinking sometimes autistic.
  7. Frequent thought perseveration.

H. *Physical Characteristics*
  1. Excessive drooling in the young child.
  2. Thumb-sucking, nail-biting, head-banging, and teeth-grinding in the young child.
  3. Food habits often peculiar.
  4. Slow to toilet train.
  5. Easy fatigability.
  6. High frequency of enuresis.
  7. Encopresis.

I. *Emotional Characteristics*
  1. Impulsive.
  2. Explosive.
  3. Poor emotional and impulse control.
  4. Low tolerance for frustration.
  5. Reckless and uninhibited, impulsive then remorseful.

J. *Sleep Characteristics*
  1. Body or head rocking before falling into sleep.
  2. Irregular sleep patterns in the young child.
  3. Excessive movement during sleep.
  4. Sleep abnormally light or deep.
  5. Resistance to naps and early bedtime, e.g., seems to require less sleep than average child.

K. *Relationship Capacities*
  1. Peer group relations generally poor.
  2. Overexcitable in normal play with other children.
  3. Better adjustment when playmates are limited to one or two.
  4. Frequently poor judgment in social and interpersonal situations.
  5. Socially bold and aggressive.
  6. Inappropriate, unselective and often excessive displays of affection.
  7. Easy acceptance of others alternating with withdrawal and shyness.
  8. Excessive need to touch, cling, and hold on to others.

L. *Variations of Physical Development*
  1. Frequent lags in developmental milestones, e.g., motor, language, etc.
  2. Generalized maturational lag during early school years.
  3. Physically immature; or
  4. Physical development normal or advanced for age.

Table 2.2   continued

M. *Characteristics of Social Behavior*
    1. Social competence frequently low average for age and measured intelligence.
    2. Behavior often inappropriate for situation, and consequences apparently not foreseen.
    3. Possibly negative and aggressive to authority.
    4. Possibly antisocial behavior.

N. *Variations of Personality*
    1. Overly gullible and easily led by peers and older youngsters.
    2. Frequent rage reactions and tantrums when crossed.
    3. Very sensitive to others.
    4. Excessive variation in mood and responsiveness from day to day and even hour to hour.
    5. Poor adjustment to environmental changes.
    6. Sweet and even tempered, cooperative and friendly (most commonly the so-called hypokinetic child).

O. *Disorders of Attention and Concentration*
    1. Short attention span for age.
    2. Overly distractible for age.
    3. Impaired concentration ability.
    4. Motor or verbal perseveration.
    5. Impaired ability to make decisions, particularly from many choices.

SOURCE: Clements, S. D. *Minimal Brain Dysfunction in Children: Terminology and Identification. Phase One of a Three-Phase Project* (NINDS Monograph No. 3, U.S. Public Health Service Publication No. 1415). Washington, D.C.: U.S. Government Printing Office, 1966, pp. 11–13.

still be heard in some medical circles, most individuals have sought a more acceptable alternative. For example, Johnson & Myklebust (1967) borrowed the term "psychoneurological learning disability" from Benton (1959) and Luria (1961). *Psycho* referred to behavior and learning processes that were altered by a *neurological* (brain) disability. Because this disturbance was not believed to create a generalized incapacity to learn, it applied only to children of average to high intelligence.

Learning Disability (LD)

Specific learning disabilities was one of the ten most frequent characteristics of MBD listed by Clements' (1966) task force. Over ten years earlier, Lehtinen (1955) had suggested that brain-injured children be referred to as children with *learning disabilities,* the term "least likely to thrust additional obstacles into the child's way" (p. 223).

Samuel Kirk, in his 1962 book on exceptional children, provided the major impetus for the term "learning disability." He defined it as follows:

> A learning disability refers to a retardation, disorder, or delayed development in one or more of the processes of speech, language, reading, spelling, writing or arithmetic resulting from a possible cerebral dysfunction and/or emotional or behavioral disturbance and not from mental retardation, sensory deprivation, or cultural or instructional factors (p. 253).

Interestingly, Kirk included emotional, as well as neurological factors, as causes of learning disabilities. His major criterion for identifying a learning disability was the existence of a major discrepancy between the disability area and other abilities.

In 1963, Kirk popularized the term by using it in his keynote address to "The Conference on Exploration into Problems of the Perceptually Handicapped Child." The term "learning disabilities" was generally agreed on by leaders in the field (Cruickshank, 1976) because its definition shifted away from medical causation toward educational relevance.

Barbara Bateman (1965) solidified this shift. Bateman borrowed the following definition of children with learning disorders from the unpublished proceedings of a United States Office of Education sponsored conference at the University of Kansas Medical Center, November 23–25, 1964:

> . . . children who have learning disorders are those who manifest an educationally significant discrepancy between their estimated intellectual potential and actual level of performance related to basic disorders in the learning processes, which may or may not be accompanied by demonstrable central nervous system dysfunction, and which are not secondary to generalized mental retardation, educational or cultural deprivation, severe emotional disturbance, or sensory loss (p. 220).

Bateman listed three broad types of learning disorders: reading problems, visual-motor disturbances, and verbal communication disorders. Three important elements characterize Bateman's definition:

1. *Discrepancy clause.* Learning-disordered children are defined by educational achievement significantly below their intellectual potential for achievement.

2. *Irrelevance of central nervous system dysfunction.* Evidence of brain injury is not important in determining educational disorders.

3. *Exclusion clauses.* The learning difficulty cannot be caused by mental retardation, educational or cultural deprivation, emotional disturbance, or vision or hearing impairment. Bateman implies that a learning disorder could be responsible for disturbed behavior and scores within retarded ranges on intelligence tests. Therefore, learning disabilities are not necessarily limited to near-normal intelligence, well-behaved children.

Bateman's ideas were reflected in Samuel Kirk's National Advisory Committee on Handicapped Children's definition, September 1967:

> Children with special learning disabilities exhibit a disorder in one or more of the basic psychological processes involved in understanding or in using spoken or written language. These may be manifested in disorders of listening, thinking, talking, reading, writing, spelling, or arithmetic. They include conditions which have been referred to as perceptual handicaps, brain injury, minimal brain dysfunction, dyslexia, developmental aphasia, etc. They do *not*

include learning problems which are due primarily to visual, hearing, or motor handicaps, to mental retardation, emotional disturbance, or to environmental disadvantage (USOE, 1968, p. 34, emphasis added).

The definition of learning disabilities that we currently follow, put forth by Public Law 94–142, is similar. Not all professionals were pleased with P.L. 94–142's broad definition, based on exclusion clauses. An alternative, inclusionary definition that stated what LD was, rather than what it wasn't, was proposed by Joseph Wepman's committee, within Nicholas Hobbs' National Project on the Classification of Exceptional Children (Wepman, Cruickshank, Deutsch, Morency, & Strother, 1975). They defined "specific learning disability" as referring

> to those children of any age who demonstrate a substantial deficiency in a particular aspect of academic achievement because of perceptual or perceptual-motor handicaps regardless of etiology or other contributing factors. The term perceptual as used here relates to those mental (neurological) processes through which the child acquires his basic alphabets of sounds and forms (p. 306).

This definition emphasized neurologically based visual- and auditory-perceptual, and motor handicaps. It accepted, rather than excluded, a wide range of causal factors. Wepman's suggestion subsequently was attacked for prematurely pinning learning disorders to perceptual causes, without adequate research support for this assumption (Hallahan & Kauffman, 1976).

More recently, the National Joint Committee for Learning Disabilities proposed a new LD definition:

> Learning disabilities is a generic term that refers to a heterogeneous group of disorders manifested by significant difficulties in the acquisition and use of listening, speaking, reading, writing, reasoning, or mathematical abilities. These disorders are intrinsic to the individual and presumed to be due to central nervous system dysfunction. Even though a learning disability may occur concomitantly with other handicapping conditions (e.g., sensory impairment, mental retardation, social and emotional disturbance) or environmental influences (e.g., cultural differences, insufficient/inappropriate instruction, psychogenic factors), it is not the direct result of those conditions or influences. (Hammill, Leigh, McNutt, & Larsen, 1981, p. 336).

This definition intended to show that LD applies to adults as well as children. It attempts to clear up the ambiguity surrounding the phrase "basic psychological processes" by clarifying that the underachievement is due to a neurological dysfunction within the child. Here spelling is subsumed under written expression. The authors did not confuse the definition by including such terms as "dyslexia" and "developmental aphasia," and tried to clarify that LD is not caused by, but may coexist with, other handicapping conditions and adverse environmental circumstances. The definition has not become an official document of the committee because it has not met with approval from all six of its member organizations.

The Current Federal Definition of Learning Disabilities

Federal law (P.L. 94-142), states:

> "Specific learning disability" means a disorder in one or more of the basic psychological processes involved in understanding or in using language, spoken or written, which may manifest itself in an imperfect ability to listen, think, speak, read, write, spell, or to do mathematical calculations. The term includes such conditions as perceptual handicaps, brain injury, minimal brain dysfunction, dyslexia, and developmental aphasia. The term does not include children who have learning problems which are primarily the result of visual, hearing, or motor handicaps, of mental retardation, of emotional disturbance, or of environmental, cultural, or economic disadvantage (Federal Register, Dec. 29, 1977, p. 65083).

After P.L. 94-142 recognized LD as a fundable handicapping condition, the law's regulations set the following identification criteria:

(a) A team may determine that a child has a specific learning disability if:
  (1) The child does not achieve commensurate with his or her age and ability levels in one or more of the areas listed in paragraph (a) (2) of this section, when provided with learning experiences appropriate for the child's age and ability levels; and
  (2) The team finds that a child has a severe discrepancy between achievement and intellectual ability in one or more of the following areas:
      (i) Oral expression;
      (ii) Listening comprehension;
      (iii) Written expression;
      (iv) Basic reading skill;
      (v) Reading comprehension;
      (vi) Mathematics calculation; or
      (vii) Mathematics reasoning.
(b) The team may not identify a child as having a specific learning disability if the severe discrepancy between ability and achievement is primarily the result of:
  (1) A visual, hearing, or motor handicap;
  (2) Mental retardation;
  (3) Emotional disturbance; or
  (4) Environmental, cultural or economic disadvantage. (Federal Register, Dec. 29, 1977, p. 65083)

Before a child can be labeled LD, it must be documented that learning outcome has been poor in spite of good educational opportunities; and the LD child must require special educational strategies beyond those generally used at his age or ability level (Federal Register, December 29, 1977).

Public Law 94-142 did not legislate a narrow definition for learning disabilities "because there is still much research required to further delineate the components of specific learning disabilities" (Federal Register, Nov. 29, 1976, p. 52404). The broad definition best reflected the multiple characteristics of learning disorders and the many etiological perspectives that still needed to be sorted out. Intervention approaches too were broad-based because they grew out of research in such different disciplines as medicine, psychology, education and sociology (Keogh, 1977a). The experts and legislators found it easier to say more about what cannot than what can cause learning disabilities.

A goal of future research is to provide precise operational definitions for the causes and characteristics of learning disabilities in homogeneous subgroups of children. These multiple definitions could connect the many camps that now exist within the field. Until then, it is important that we understand the key implications of and concerns about our current LD definition and regulations.

Severe Discrepancy Between Achievement and Potential. The learning-disabled child is defined as achieving below what would be expected from his or her intellectual ability. This underachievement can occur in oral language, listening comprehension, reading comprehension, reading, writing, spelling, arithmetic reasoning, or calculation. The child has areas of intellectual strength, but development is uneven. For example, a child may be especially talented in solving puzzles and math problems, but be weak in understanding word meanings, in verbal communication, and in learning of letter sounds. Each state regulates how large the discrepancy between ability and achievement must be before it is considered severe. When the discrepancy is set high, only the most severely learning disabled are identified and served.

Educational Orientation. Federal regulations deal less with medical causes of LD than with educational relevance. Underachievement, rather than central nervous system dysfunction, determines LD identification.

Basic Psychological Processes. The educational orientation of LD regulations does not mean that the brain is considered irrelevant to learning. On the contrary, P.L. 94-142's LD definition states that a learning disability is a disorder in one's "basic psychological processes" that results in learning underachievement. The federal definition does include such brain-related examples as perceptual handicaps, brain injury, minimal brain dysfunction, dyslexia, and developmental aphasia. Other examples of these processes include receiving information by listening, looking, or touching; processing this information through attention, discrimination, memory, integration, concept formation and problem-solving, and responding through speech or body movements (Chalfant & King, 1976).

The law emphasizes an educational orientation because we cannot yet clearly define the psychological processes underlying learning disabilities, and we are not sure whether these brain processes can be directly remediated. If they can be remediated, we don't know whether educational progress would be any more rapid than if only educational interventions were used. We are also unclear about whether knowing which brain area is damaged may help us decide whether one educational program is better than another.

Basic research in neuropsychology is just beginning to offer insights into the brain functions of typical learners and those with learning difficulties. Some investigators have begun to experiment with training one or another collection of brain sites. These neuropsychological advances eventually may lead to a shift back to brain-related descriptions of learning disabled children. For the time being, however, observable developmental delays in preschoolers and educational underachievement in school-aged populations remain the criteria for LD identification.

Exclusion Clauses. The federal exclusion clauses have come under particular criticism and have been subject to misinterpretation.

The LD definition excludes mental retardation, emotional disturbance, visual (blind), hearing (deaf), and motor (polio, muscular dystrophy) handicaps from being the primary causes of learning disabilities. However, learning disabilities can co-exist with these conditions. Retarded, disturbed, and physically handicapped children can have uneven developmental patterns that are not attributable to intellectual, emotional, or physical handicaps (Padula, 1979). These uneven patterns, rather than the other handicaps, can cause achievement to be less than the child's potential. For example, a blind teenager who loses the ability to speak, understand language, and read Braille after removal of a brain tumor has acquired a learning disability. This disability bears no relationship to the other handicap, blindness.

The word *primary* in the LD definition has often been ignored in practice. The law has been misinterpreted to mean "if you're mentally retarded, emotionally disturbed, or physically handicapped you can't also be learning disabled." Cruickshank (1976) addressed this issue with respect to the mentally retarded:

> Learning disabilities are characteristic of children and youth of any chronological age and of *any and all intellectual levels.* The artifact of differentiation between the two clinical groups is just that, a recent manmade artifact. It is illogical . . . the exclusion of the perceptually handicapped mentally retarded child from the specialized teaching and learning situations which are germane to his peculiar learning needs is an unnecessary tragedy, and the situation must be rectified quickly (p. 106).

Kirk (1976), too, notes that many of the exclusion clause children are very much like the learning disabled, are not being understood or served well within their categories, and could profit from services provided to LD children.

It is often difficult to determine whether a learning disability coexists with, yet is independent of, another disability, whether this other disability has caused the underachievement, or whether a learning disability might have caused emotional disturbance or mental retardation in particular. For example, a child may be emotionally disturbed due to poor family relationships, as well as learning disabled due to a brain insult suffered during a car accident. It is also possible that the car accident had no significant effect on learning, and that the emotional disturbance led to the academic underachievement. On the other hand, the academic and social frustrations of the learning disability could have promoted emotionally disturbed behavior and poor family relationships.

Similarly, a retarded teenager's written expression skills may lag so far behind reading and arithmetic abilities that a learning disability seems to exist independent of the retardation. On the other hand, the mental retardation may have put an upper limit on how far written expression skills can be developed. Or this teenager's language lags may have decreased performance on intelligence items that measure verbal reasoning, resulting in an underestimated potential; lower IQ scores make it harder to demonstrate a significant discrepancy between achievement in written expression and potential. Whether it was the retardation or learning disability that caused poor performance on the IQ test or poor progress in written expression is hard to tell.

Environmental, cultural or economic disadvantage are also listed as primary conditions that exclude a child from identification as learning disabled. Clearly, poor teaching or cultural differences are environmental circumstances that can cause underachievement, but they are *not* justifications for labeling a child learning disabled. However, this exclusion clause raises particular concerns about the low-income poor learner who fits no other category of exceptionality and has not profited sufficiently from past teaching attempts. Because the environment may not provide optimum health and social conditions for learning and development, this child has a higher probability of academic failure than a more advantaged age-mate (Kavale, 1980a). Research Box 2-1 shows that lower socioeconomic status individuals have a higher incidence of brain-related disorders that can cause learning disabilities than do higher economic groups. Many have neurodevelopmental disabilities to an extent similar to that of learning disabled middle-income children (Gottesman, Croen, & Rotkin, 1982). It is often impossible to tell whether a child had a learning disability to begin with or whether the disadvantaged circumstances altered the child's learning processes. Middle-income children with similarly uneven learning patterns are not excluded from the LD definition because their environments are not considered at fault.

Because environmentally disadvantaged children often need the intensive instruction offered in LD programs, ACLD's National Advisory Board has

RESEARCH BOX 2-1
The Environment, Brain Dysfunction, and Learning

It has long been known that lower-income children are more susceptible to traumas that affect development and learning than are middle-income children. This is attributed to inadequate prenatal care and nutrition (Pasamanick, Knobloch & Lilienfeld, 1956), more childhood diseases and injuries, and greater numbers of maternal diseases during pregnancy (Hurley, 1969). Organic brain damage is more likely among lower- than middle-income groups (Birch & Gussow, 1970; Pasamanick & Knobloch 1958, 1961) and may contribute to a range of intellectual, learning, and behavioral difficulties. Coleman and Sandhu's (1967) study demonstrated the relationship between health-related factors and intelligence. Of their lower intelligence subjects, 30 percent had experienced birth difficulties and 26 percent had suffered serious injuries. Of the average intelligence children, 23 percent had experienced birth difficulties. For above-average intelligence subjects, the figures were even lower, 17 percent for birth difficulties and 11 percent for serious injuries. This indicates that intelligence decreases as health related complications increase.

There is abundant data showing that lower-income children have a higher incidence of behaviors attributed to the learning disabled than do middle class children (impulsivity, Schwebel, 1966; Zucker & Stricker, 1968; immature language development, Kappelman, Kaplan & Ganter, 1969). Blacks seem to fare less well than whites on variables related to achievement (Bronfenbrenner, 1967): such as copying (Amante, Margules, Hartman, Storey & Weber, 1970); language, attention span, and reading (Deutsch, 1960); delay of gratification (Deutsch, 1960; Mischel, 1961); and social factors such as family disorganization due to paternal absence (Pettigrew, 1964) and home environment fostering education (Deutsch, 1960). Other social factors related to achievement are quality of housing, population density, rate of social assistance, and number of juvenile court cases (Miller, Margolin, & Yolles, 1957). Miller et al. found that 3rd and 5th graders with the highest reading levels came from school districts where the above factors ranked at least one quartile better than did the poorer readers. Similarly, Coleman & Sandhu (1967) found that intellectual potential of children was higher with higher father educational and occupational levels.

Of course health-related and social factors' relationship to achievement are intertwined, and a single cause of learning difficulties is hard to isolate. Whether children's poor learning is due to brain trauma or to lack of opportunity to learn appropriate behaviors at home or school, it is clear that environmental factors significantly impact subsequent learning.

recommended that they, and all other handicapped children, no longer be excluded from the LD definition (Kirk, 1976).

Further Concerns. The broad LD definition has encouraged overlabeling. Regulations state that only those children who need very intensive, special, out-of-the-ordinary teaching are to be labeled LD. Yet, many of the children labeled LD perform poorly because of insufficient motivation, poor teaching, little home support for school achievement, general immaturity, or general low ability (Ames, 1977; Cruickshank, 1976; Kirk & Elkins, 1975a). In their zeal to serve children and receive some reimbursement for their expenses, school personnel identify a large number of underachievers as learning disabled, regardless of the factors responsible for the lack of academic progress (Lovitt, 1978; Sartain, 1976). They argue that the LD label provides services to children having no alternative funding sources, is less stigmatizing and restrictive than other labels, is the most flexible label given the overlapping characteristics and instructional needs of mildly handicapped children, and forces an individualized approach to instruction. However well-intentioned, this overlabeling provides a body of research data that is difficult to interpret. It hampers the narrowing of etiological, assessment, and intervention concepts in learning disabilities. Liberal labeling has resulted in poorly conceptualized programs (Wallace, 1976) and dilution of remedial services (Larsen, 1976). Children with the most severe learning disabilities are often cheated of the intensive help that legislators intended to offer them (Kirk, 1976; Poplin, 1981).

A number of additional concerns about the vagueness of the LD definition and regulations highlight the need to establish more specific definitions and identification and service guidelines in the future.

1. The learning-disabled population is heterogeneous. Attaching one common label to all these children implies that they have the same causes of learning disorders, characteristics, and that they profit from the same teaching methodology.

2. The LD definition implies that the disability rests only within the child and that we need to cure it. It ignores the possibility that the tasks that we expect children to learn and their learning environment may also aggravate the disability (Smith, 1980). When the child is blamed for every nonconforming behavior, schools and society are relieved from blame and from finding real solutions (Bateman, 1974; Cohen, 1971; Divoky, 1974).

3. Learning disabilities are limited to academic areas. The LD definition ignores other manifestations of disorders underlying written and spoken language, such as social skills, abstract reasoning, organization of thoughts, study skills, planning ability, and emotional adjustment.

4. The LD definition does not specifically recognize the young adult whose persisting learning disabilities require unique vocational, emotional-social, daily living, and academic intervention.

5. Some extent of uneven development is normal. Yet, due to the LD regulations' appreciation of strengths and weaknesses, every variation from the norm can be misinterpreted as a disability. This limits the boundaries of normalcy, and leads to labeling normal children handicapped (Blatt, 1979; Divoky, 1974; Silberman, 1976).

6. The LD definition simplifies complicated services by not addressing teaching methods (Senf, 1978). Its broadness reflects the gap between laboratory research and classroom practice, and impedes our understanding of learning disabilities (Keogh, 1977a).

7. The LD definition reflects society's competitive, academic achievement values. It does not address how school curricula can maximize postschool vocational and social adjustment so that the learning disabled can still be viewed as worthwhile, productive citizens.

Identification Practices

In this section we discuss practices and issues surrounding LD identification of the preschooler, young elementary school child, and the older student who has had sufficient opportunity to profit from academic instruction. Part IV is devoted to a fuller description of screening and referral procedures, specific assessment measures and strategies, and placement and programming decisions.

The Preschooler

Developmental weaknesses in preschoolers should be identified as early as possible and growth in these areas facilitated in case these weaknesses delay later learning. Preschool LD identification presents a special problem because the child is not yet underachieving on the school achievement criteria by which federal regulations measure learning disabilities. On the other hand, the child's delays on other factors in the LD definition such as listening, thinking, speaking, and the motor movements involved on paper-pencil tasks, as well as those not in the definition (for example, the ability to attend well, to organize learning strategies, or to analyze visual information), are measurable. Discrepancies between these areas of development, rather than underachievement, must be evaluated since preschoolers are not expected to have achieved much academically.

The child's stronger developmental skills are considered an indication of potential, because what we call intelligence in young children is the same as their progress in these normal developmental areas. Intelligence scores are not very useful in calculating severe discrepancies at the preschool level because IQ scores below the ages of three or four are highly unreliable estimates of potential (McCall, Hogarty, & Hurlburt, 1972). The scores can vary greatly in the span of several months because they reflect the rapid developmental gains taking place in the preschool years.

No one preschool test battery has yet been developed that can definitely predict whether a preschooler is a high learning disabilities risk. Nevertheless, existing screening measures can identify preschoolers who show uneven developmental patterns that warrant early intervention.

Confidence in these measures' predictions of LD and pinpointing of instructional priorities increases as:

1. a child's delays become more severe in language, attention, and visual perceptual abilities (Kinsbourne, 1977a).

2. the child nears kindergarten entrance age and the test items are more similar to what children are expected to learn in school (Bower, 1978; Keogh & Becker, 1973; Magliocca, Rinaldi, & Crew, 1977). For example, observing a five- rather than four-year-old child's learning style, relationships with others, and performance on school-type tasks (impulsivity, attending, sharing, knowledge of alphabet, patience, independent work habits) offers a more accurate prediction of whether the child is likely to encounter difficulty in school (Keogh & Becker, 1973; Kinsbourne & Caplan, 1979).

3. specific environmental circumstances that can cause or aggravate developmental delays, or that may help to overcome these delays are considered (Bradley, Caldwell, & Elardo, 1977; Majoribanks, 1972).

Although many scales for evaluating setting variables have been developed, they are still of uncertain reliability and validity for predicting learning problems in children of different ages and sociocultural backgrounds (Bradley & Caldwell, 1978; Walberg & Majoribanks, 1976).

LD prediction remains a calculated guess until a child is old enough to be tested for underachievement on the school's academic criteria. Some professionals, therefore, urge us not to stigmatize and lower expectations for preschoolers by labeling them LD (Keogh & Becker, 1973; Warren, 1977). They recommend programs for preschoolers who show any kind of delays that might impinge on future learning. However, intervening without forecasting is easier said than done. Federal funding of special education early intervention programs requires that we label children handicapped. When states apply for federal P.L. 94-142 reimbursements for serving learning disabled 3 to 5 year olds, they must label.

The Young Elementary School Student

Identification among five and six year olds is an easier matter. The child now is spending six hours a day in the school setting. Identification depends on whether or not the child can handle class requirements as well as might be expected from his or her age, intelligence, and past learning opportunities. Evaluation should also consider whether the child has mastered those preacademic skills that make for success in kindergarten or first grade. Early identification is critical so that developmental gaps do not widen and appropriate modifications can be made in curriculum, grade placement, and special services.

In the early elementary school years, three common techniques are used to identify lags: tests administered to children, teacher checklists, and parent checklists. Poor performance at the beginning of kindergarten on visual, language, motor, and attentional aspects of easy academic tasks relates to later learning disabilities. Among these, the best predictors are

- reciting the order of the alphabet (Satz, Taylor, Friel, & Fletcher, 1978)
- naming letters of the alphabet (Jansky & de Hirsch, 1972; Lowell, 1971)
- naming pictures (Jansky & de Hirsch, 1972)
- vocabulary comprehension (Satz et al., 1978)
- copying designs (Satz et al., 1978)
- determining which finger was touched when eyes are closed (Satz et al., 1978)
- reading readiness tests that sample such areas as vocabulary, number knowledge, comprehension of sentences, copying, visual discrimination, following directions, identifying or substituting initial and final sounds in words, auditory discrimination, identifying alphabet letters (Colligan, 1977ab; Ferinden & Jacobson, 1970; Glazzard, 1977; Hawthorne & Larsen, 1977; Lessler & Bridges, 1973)
- auditory discrimination of sounds in words (Lowell, 1971)
- teacher observation of learning rate and strategies (Kirk, 1966).

Teacher ratings of a child's readiness skills and learning strategies often are more proficient than screening tests (Feshback, Adelman, & Fuller, 1974; Glazzard, 1981; Haring & Ridgway, 1967; Keogh & Smith, 1970; Stevenson, Parker, & Wilkenson, 1976). Teacher observations are valuable because teachers actually assess the interaction of child characteristics with the classroom tasks and setting. Screening tests alone may not measure the most relevant criteria for achievement in a particular school setting. Teachers assess areas that are difficult for tests to tap such as speed of learning, ability to focus and sustain attention, ability to avoid distractions, creativity, social relationships, ability to work independently and in groups, motivation to learn, and verbal participation (Durkin, 1978; Forness & Esveldt, 1975; Magliocci & colleagues, 1977).

Parental observations offer another valuable means of identification (Colligan, 1981; Colligan & O'Connell, 1974; Smith & Solanto, 1971). In addition, environmental factors such as the amount of schooling the family desires for the child and learning activities encouraged by the parents are predictors of learning success (Keeves, 1972; Whiteman, Brown, & Deutsch, 1967).

When parent–teacher observations and screening test data are collected at the end of kindergarten, identification of delays and prediction of future learning disabilities becomes even more accurate (Cowgill, Friedland, & Shapiro, 1973; Novack, Bonadventura, & Merenda, 1973). This is because the content observed and measured has become more similar to the academic criteria to which we are predicting (Keogh & Becker, 1973). For example, it now matters not only whether the child can name letters, but also whether the child can integrate this knowledge into reading words.

The Older Elementary
and Secondary School Student

Professionals agree that children who have had sufficient opportunities to profit from instruction should be identified as learning disabled if they show severe discrepancies between expected and actual achievement. Numerous formulas have been used to detect these discrepancies and determine eligibility for LD services (Hoffman, 1980). To make wise use of these formulas, we must understand what constitutes a severe discrepancy, common means of calculating discrepancies, and strengths and weaknesses of discrepancy formulas. Discrepancy formulas consider such major factors as intelligence, achievement, past educational experiences, and age. In addition, alternative approaches to measuring discrepancies address a broader range of variables impacting on learning. There is no one best way to determine whether a learning disability exists. That is a clinical judgment, made after careful evaluation of multiple child, curricular, family, and teacher variables.

Severe Discrepancy. How large must the discrepancy between expected and actual achievement be in order to be considered severe? Since federal and most state LD regulations do not dictate this decision, individual school districts usually can decide for themselves whether they will serve the mild to moderate, as well as severe, underachiever. Cutoffs generally are determined in two ways: by setting a percent of discrepancy between potential and actual achievement, and by setting achievement grade-level cutoffs above which LD services are not offered.

Setting a Percent or Standard Discrepancy Score. Some school systems set a percentage or standard degree of deviation. A child's achievement must lag behind expectations to this degree in order for the child to be identified as learning disabled. For example, New York State's regulations suggest an ability-achievement discrepancy of 50 percent; in order to be labeled LD a child roughly can achieve no better than half as well as would normally be expected. Achievement discrepancies evaluate progress from the beginning of kindergarten through the child's current grade.

The problem with high fixed discrepancies, such as 50 percent, is that the average child cannot be half behind *academically* until at least third grade. These high fixed percentages disqualify many children from services, thereby increasing their chances for school failure.

In addition, the meaning of any fixed discrepancy is more serious at lower than higher grade levels (Sulzbacher & Kenowitz, 1977). Since year to year academic gains slow up with age (Simmons & Shapiro, 1968), more grade levels behind at older ages is as serious as a few levels behind at younger ages. For example, an otherwise average third grader who is over one and one half years behind because he or she still hasn't mastered the sounds of the alphabet is far more delayed than the otherwise average fifth grader who can read at the mid-second grade level. The fifth grader already has mastered the sounds, although at a slower rate than expected. In order for the fifth grader to be equivalently delayed in learning skills, the discrepancy would have to be greater than 50 percent. The only way to equalize the significance of discrepancies across grades is to gradually increase the percentage difference between ability and achievement with age (Hammill, 1976).

Setting Grade Level Cutoffs. Educators commonly equate severe discrepancies with measures of how far below grade level a student is achieving (Kline, Ashbrenner, Barrington & Reimer; in Goodman & Mann, 1976; Salvia & Clark, 1973). Frequently a criterion of one year behind is set for grades one through three, and two years behind for grades four and up. Some educators suggest that secondary level students should qualify for LD services only if they are achieving below the third grade level (Wiederholt, 1975), mid–fourth grade level (Hammill, 1976), or sixth grade level (Goodman & Mann, 1976). Anyone with skills above these cutoffs is assumed to have sufficient learned skills for life adjustment.

Measuring only the grade level a student is behind ignores the student's *potential for achievement,* as required by P.L. 94–142. It doesn't deal with whether a particular student is expected to have learned more or less. For example, under P.L. 94–142 a very bright sixth grader who is one grade level behind in reading could be identified as learning disabled. A much slower classmate who is achieving two grade levels behind in reading, but is working to capacity, would not be identified LD. The grade level method might produce the opposite results.

A further problem with grade level cutoffs is that a grade equivalent is not a valid entity. Tests for grade level sample only a few items at each difficulty level, and error can be high. The test merely indicates whether a student got as many test questions correct as the average student in a particular grade. The skills that are measured actually overlap greatly with the performance of children in many other grades.

Finally, the same degree of underachievement may have different implications, depending on the subject area. For example, at age 15 a four-year lag in mathematics may not be considered as ominous as a four-year lag in reading. Therefore, judgments about the value of remediation in different subject areas influence whether or not parents and educators decide to label a child LD.

Calculating Discrepancies. Reading clinicians were the first to use formulas to assess the reading level that students could be expected to attain. Educators adapted these formulas to learning disabilities by plugging into them achievement scores from additional subject areas.

Most formulas first estimate a student's *expectancy* for performance from intelligence test scores. The *intelligence quotient* (IQ) reflects mental ability relative to one's age group, with a score of 100 as average. The achievement test scores are then compared with the *expectancy*. At times achievement in other school subjects and past educational experiences are added to the calculations. When achievement is below expectation, school personnel must determine whether the underachievement is severe enough to warrant LD identification.

Formulas Using Achievement, Intelligence, and Age. Harris' (1962) method is the most well-known and simplest means of calculating expected achievement levels:

$$RE = MA - 5$$

or

$$RE = (CA \times IQ/100) - 5$$

RE = reading expectancy *grade* level
MA = mental age (mental age = chronological age × IQ/100)
5 = 5 years old at school entry

Using this formula, Harris charted expected reading grade levels for children of different IQs and ages. For example, Nancy, who is eight years old and has a 100 IQ would be expected to be spelling at the third grade level.

$$RE = (8 \times 100/100) - 5$$
$$= 3$$

If her actual achievement is below the third grade level, she is performing below her potential.

Harris recently modified his formula, reasoning that mental ability is twice as powerful as age in predicting school achievement (Harris & Sipay, 1979):

$$MGE = \frac{(2\,MA + CA)}{3} - 5.2$$

MGE = mental grade expectancy
5.2 = a more accurate age for school entry

The expectancy grade table derived from this formula (Table 2-3) shows reading expectancy for Nancy still at a third grade level. However, if she had a 120 IQ, her reading expectancy would be higher than if calculated by the previous formula.

$$MGE = \frac{2(8 \times 120/100) + 8}{3} - 5.2$$
$$= \frac{2(9.6) + 8}{3} - 5.2$$
$$= 27/3 - 5.2$$
$$= 3.8$$

Table 2-3 Reading expectancy grades for selected combinations of chronological age and intelligence quotient

	CHRONOLOGICAL AGE											
IQ	7.2	7.7	8.2	8.7	9.2	9.7	10.2	10.7	11.2	11.7	12.2	12.7	13.2
140	3.9	4.4	5.1	5.7	6.4	6.9	7.7	8.2	8.9	9.5	10.2	10.7	11.5
135	3.6	4.2	4.9	5.4	6.1	6.6	7.3	7.9	8.6	9.1	9.8	10.3	11.0
130	3.4	3.9	4.6	5.1	5.8	6.3	7.0	7.5	8.2	8.7	9.4	9.9	10.6
125	3.2	3.6	4.3	4.8	5.5	6.0	6.7	7.1	7.8	8.3	9.0	9.5	10.2
120	2.9	3.4	4.1	4.5	5.2	5.7	6.3	6.8	7.5	7.9	8.6	9.1	9.7
115	2.7	3.1	3.8	4.2	4.9	5.3	6.0	6.5	7.1	7.5	8.2	8.6	9.3
110	2.4	2.9	3.5	4.0	4.6	5.0	5.7	6.1	6.7	7.2	7.8	8.2	8.8
105	2.2	2.7	3.2	3.7	4.3	4.7	5.3	5.8	6.3	6.8	7.4	7.8	8.4
100	2.0	2.5	3.0	3.5	4.0	4.5	5.0	5.5	6.0	6.5	7.0	7.5	8.0
95	1.7	2.2	2.7	3.2	3.7	4.1	4.5	5.2	5.6	6.1	6.6	7.0	7.5
90	1.5	1.9	2.4	2.8	3.4	3.7	4.3	4.7	5.2	5.6	6.2	6.5	7.1
85	1.2	1.6	2.2	2.5	3.0	3.4	3.9	4.3	4.8	5.2	5.7	6.1	6.6
80	1.0	1.4	1.9	2.2	2.7	3.1	3.6	4.0	4.5	4.8	5.3	5.7	6.2
75	1.0	1.1	1.6	2.0	2.4	2.8	3.3	3.6	4.1	4.5	4.9	5.3	5.8
70	1.0	1.0	1.3	1.7	2.1	2.5	2.9	3.3	3.7	4.1	4.5	4.9	5.3
65	1.0	1.0	1.1	1.4	1.8	2.1	2.6	2.9	3.4	3.7	4.1	4.4	4.9
60	1.0	1.0	1.0	1.1	1.5	1.8	2.3	2.6	3.0	3.3	3.7	4.0	4.6

Suggested Significant Differences
Grades 1–3: 9 months below expectancy
Grades 4–5: 1 year below expectancy
Grades 6+: 1½ years below expectancy

SOURCE: Harris, A. J. and Sipay, E. R. *How to Teach Reading: A Competency-Based Program.* New York: Longman, 1979, p. 213. Copyright © 1979 by Longman Inc. Reprinted by permission of Longman Inc., New York.

Had she been less bright, Nancy's expectancy would be lower than estimated from the 1962 formula. Harris' formula is the most frequently used method of quantifying a severe discrepancy (Cone & Wilson, 1981).

Alice Horn's (1941) formula is similar to Harris' (1979). Horn's formula was based on actual data indicating that, as one gets older, intelligence becomes more related than age to achievement. She weighted MA and CA differently with age: equally up to age 8½, 3 MA and 2 CA from 8½ to 10; 2 MA and 1 CA from 10 to 12; 3 MA and 1 CA above age 12 (in Bruininks, Glaman, & Clark, 1973). With this formula, Nancy with 120 IQ would be expected to learn at a faster rate with age, while a far duller Nancy would slow down in learning gains from year to year.

Adding Achievement in Other Subjects as a Predictor. Academic predictions become more reliable when the child's achievements in areas that require similar skills are considered. Marion Monroe (1932) suggested averaging arithmetic computation age, mental age, and chronological age to estimate a child's expected performance level in reading:

$$RE = \frac{MA + CA + ACA}{3}$$

RE = reading expectancy age
ACA = arithmetic computation age

She felt that a reading disability existed if the child achieved less than 80 percent of what was expected from this formula.

Adding Past Educational Experience. Several formulas calculate expectancy by considering the child's past educational experience.

Bond and Tinker (1967) reasoned that a child who spends several years in school or in a given grade can be expected to have gained more knowledge than the child who received instruction for fewer years. They suggested the following formula:

$$RE = (YIS \times IQ/100) + 1$$

RE = reading expectancy grade
YIS = years in school, beginning with grade one.
1 = beginning of grade one.

If Nancy is 9 years old and completing her second year in third grade, she is expected to achieve above her grade level:

$$RE = (4 \times 100/100) + 1$$
$$= 5$$

Myklebust (1968) proposed a well-known *expectancy age* (EA) formula that averaged the child's intellectual development (mental age), physiological maturity (chronological age), and school experience (grade age = present grade level + 5.2 years):

$$EA = \frac{Mental\ Age + Life\ Age + Grade\ Age}{3}$$

EA = expectancy age

If Nancy were completing her second year in third grade, this formula would more realistically expect her to read at the mid–third grade level, at which most 8.7 year olds read:

$$EA = \frac{9 + 9 + 8}{3} \text{ (most 3rd graders are 8 years old)}$$
$$= 8.7$$

Myklebust's Mental Age was the higher of the verbal (language tasks) or performance (blocks, puzzles) portions of an intelligence test, because the higher score was believed to best represent potential for growth.

Myklebust converted the child's achievement grade level test scores into an *achievement age* (AA) by adding 5.2 (average age of school entry). A *learning quotient* (LQ) was then determined by dividing achievement age by expectancy age and multiplying by 100 percent:

$$LQ = \frac{AA}{EA} \times 100$$

Myklebust felt that an LQ of less than 90 indicated the presence of a learning disability. His formula became popular for a time in large-scale LD screening projects.

Strengths of Discrepancy Formulas. Discrepancy formulas have several advantages:

1. They encourage objective (though still inaccurate) measurement devices to be used, together with subjective judgments, for LD identification.

2. They provide a uniform means of choosing research samples that share the same percent of discrepancy, so that findings can be better compared and interpreted.

3. They place no limits on intelligence level so that the degree of underachievement of mentally retarded as well as gifted children can be evaluated.

Weaknesses of Discrepancy Formulas. Clearly, a student's expectancies depend on the particular discrepancy formula used. While one formula might indicate that Nancy is a severe underachiever and in need of LD services, another formula might indicate that she is achieving normally. Figure 2-1 illustrates these differences in formulas. Bruininks, Glaman & Clark (1973) found that, depending on the formula used, 16 to 54.6 percent of third graders could be identified as functioning one or more grades below expectation. The formulas were least reliable for those students who need a sound identification method most, the lower and higher IQ children. In addition, no one formula can be used with equal confidence across different grade levels, genders, ethnic groups, and tests (Macy, Baker, & Kosinski, 1979).

More recently developed mathematical techniques convert children's test scores to standard scores. This way the IQ/achievement interrelationship is treated similarly at different age levels, the errors of measurement due to test unreliability are taken into account, and the increased range and variability of achievement scores at the upper grade levels when compared with IQ measures are dealt with. In addition, *regression analysis* methods control for scores that revert toward the mean on repeated measurements (Cone & Wilson, 1981). All

Figure 2-1   Reading expectancies for grades 8 and 12 according to Bond–Tinker, Harris, and Los Angeles formulas. (The Los Angeles formula is another name for Horn's formula.)

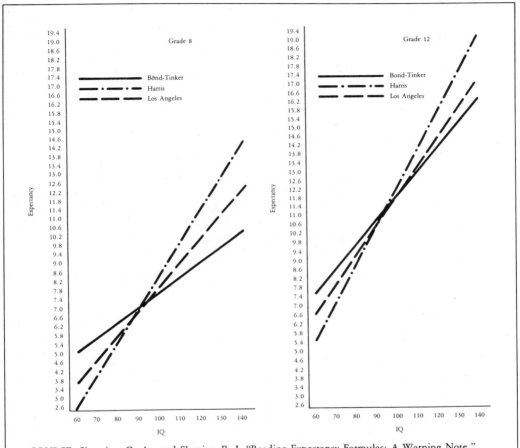

SOURCE: Simmins, G. A., and Shapiro, B. J. "Reading Expectancy Formulas: A Warning Note." *Journal of Reading,* 1968, *11,* p. 627. Reprinted with permission of the authors and the International Reading Association.

formulas require additional clinical judgments to interpret the meaning of discrepancies between expected and actual achievement.

Key Considerations in Identification. Discrepancy formulas are a way to begin determining whether a child is learning disabled. But they do not address many learner, task and setting factors that also play a role in learning failure (Hammill, 1976; Hoffman, 1980). These factors include the child's motivation, learning progress with different teachers and materials, progress in different settings, teacher expectations, home support for study, the need for special teaching or a slower pace, indicators of visual, motor, language or attentional deterrents to progress, vocational and daily living skills, and social–emotional needs.

There is no substitute for good clinical judgment and experience in LD identification (Bateman, 1965; McLeod, 1979). The same degree of discrepancy in two children of equal age, intelligence, and grade levels may have two entirely different meanings. One child may be underachieving due to an impulsive learning style and a language handicap. The other may have relocated so many times that the child has received little consistent instruction and has lost the motivation to try. The former student is learning disabled, while the latter is not. If both students put forth equal effort, the former student would not profit as much from the typical curriculum as would the second.

Learning disabilities identification judgments must be based on a multidimensional assessment framework. Educated consideration of intellectual abilities, achievement levels, past educational experiences, and age is imperative. An awareness of alternative identification approaches that help broaden the scope of learning-related variables also is important.

Intellectual Abilities. In general, intelligence tests are the best predictors of school achievement. McClelland (1973) humorously explains that: "The games people are required to play on aptitude tests are similar to the games teachers require in the classroom" (p. 1). IQ scores and school programs share several features: acquired knowledge from school or environment, cognitive processes (abstract reasoning, speed of information processing), and motivational and personality factors related to learning (Zigler & Trickett, 1978). Due to these commonalities, IQ tests do help predict children's academic successes. But alternate measures must be substituted when discrepancies are being determined for particular school subjects and cultural groups, and when the IQ test taps a student's weakest abilities. It is always important to consider IQ as a range of functioning rather than a fixed value.

1. There is no evidence that IQ tests are equally good predictors of potential for all school subjects (Lloyd, et al., 1977). For example, IQ is probably not as important a contributor to handwriting as to listening comprehension skills. *Years of instruction in writing* might be a more relevant index against which to compare handwriting achievements.

2. IQ tests do not predict academic ability for minorities and low-income groups as well as they do for other Americans. For example, the correlation between IQ and achievement for first grade blacks is far less than that for whites (Sewell & Severson, 1975). In fact, in one study the IQ-achievement correlation in 6- to 11-year-old blacks and Mexican-Americans was almost zero (Goldman & Hartig, 1975).

Intelligence tests underestimate the intellectual potential of lower income and culturally different Americans, because IQ scores are highly correlated with social class, parental educational level, and parental achievement expectations (Bayley, 1970; McClelland, 1973; Reese & Lipsitt, 1970). Because they have often learned different things than those required by IQ test questions, these children score lower on intelligence tests (see Research Box 2-2). Intelligence tests especially discriminate against minorities who do not share the white middle-class language abilities, reading skills, problem solving approaches, concepts, and knowledge that IQ test content incorporates (Bernal, 1975; Jackson, 1975).

When minority and low-income youngsters earn low IQ's, the likelihood of LD identification is reduced because a major discrepancy with achievement is less apparent. This results in inequities. For example, Franks' (1971) survey of grades one through eight in eleven Missouri school districts found that special classes for the educable retarded contained 67.8 percent whites and 34.2 percent blacks. In contrast, the LD special classes contained primarily white middle and upper social status children (96.8 percent) and only 3.2 percent blacks.

Alternate approaches must be explored when IQ tests do not fairly assess the minority and lower socioeconomic status child. Adaptive behavior measures which evaluate how a child gets along in everyday life are one alternative to IQ measures. Research Box 2-2 reviews the issue of intelligence test bias and further discusses testing modifications.

3. When intelligence tests tap children's weaker skills, their IQ's are underestimated, thereby reducing their opportunities for LD identification. Since standard intelligence tests are highly related to capacity to learn verbal content, children with severe language difficulties may be unable to demonstrate their knowledge and earn high potentials for achievement. Similarly, the student with severe reading disabilities cannot succeed on portions of IQ tests that demand reading or general knowledge gained from reading (Lloyd et al., 1977). Group IQ tests also underestimate IQ when children have severe reading, visual perceptual, coordination, attentional, and organizational difficulties.

In these instances alternative IQ tests that bypass weak areas need to be used to estimate expected achievement. Some alternatives are nonverbal tests, individual rather than group test administration, and tests that demand only a pointing response. Since each IQ test measures different types of abilities, it is often possible to select one that samples a child's strengths.

4. Although IQ becomes more stable above age six (Bayley, 1949), the score still may vary as much as fifteen points from one test to another (Honzik, Macfarlane & Allen, 1948). Therefore, it is wiser to consider a range within which intelligence is likely to fluctuate than a single intelligence number.

RESEARCH BOX 2-2
Overcoming Intelligence Tests' Cultural Bias by Use of Adaptive Behavior Measures

Intelligence tests' bias against those of different cultural backgrounds has resulted in a disproportionate number of children from low income and nonwhite families placed in classes for the educable mentally retarded (Dunn, 1968; Tobias, 1969; Wakefield, 1965). These placements are then associated with lower academic achievement than had the children remained in regular classes (Rubin, Krus & Balow, 1973).

Jane Mercer's work on intelligence test bias is well known. When she tallied the races of Riverside, California special class students (IQ 79 or below), she found three times more Mexican-Americans and two and one-half times more blacks than would be expected from their percentage in the general population (Mercer, 1970).

She then tested out the American Association on Mental Deficiency's definition of retardation on these students: *intellectual and adaptive* (daily living) skills must both be retarded in order for the child to be classified as mentally retarded (Grossman, 1977). A majority of the blacks and Mexican-Americans had to be declassified because their adaptive skills were normal, and their IQ's were within normal limits when evaluated relative to their own culture's norms on the test (Mercer & Lewis, 1978).

Mercer's famous 1973 study confirmed that the disproportionate numbers of black and Mexican-American retarded were due to the IQ test bias and the socioeconomic bias of the decision makers. Before testing, the percentage of special service referrals for these groups was equal to their representation in the general population. Similarly, when neighbors, parents, and friends were asked to identify their retarded, the ethnic proportions were the same as that in the general population. These findings were repeated in another study in which 66.7 percent of educable retarded youngsters were declassified after adaptive behavior measurement proved that, in the nonschool world, these students functioned normally (Coulter, Morrow, & Tucker, 1978).

In October of 1979, California's Judge Robert Peckham ruled that IQ tests for placing minority children in EMR programs are discriminatory and banned their use (a moratorium had been in effect since 1974). This precaution is equally valid in learning disabilities. By underestimating potential for achievement we might deny youngsters educational opportunities from which they could benefit. Adaptive behavior measures need to be refined, but may promise an alternative to IQ as an estimate of expected achievement in LD identification. Another alternative, Mercer's (1979) *Estimated Learning Potential* score adjusts IQ upward in relationship to the socio-cultural factors that could underestimate standard IQ scores: urban acculturation, socio-economic status, family structure, and size.

Achievement Levels. In choosing the achievement test to use in the LD identification process, we must consider how well it matches classroom content and methods, and whether or not it has overestimated achievement.

Achievement tests' content must match classroom content as closely as possible. We are trying to determine how much of what the child should have learned was actually learned. If the contents don't overlap, then we're not assessing achievement fairly. For example, reading tests ask the child to read words that commonly appear in standard reading programs. If the child had been taught by a language experience approach (materials made up from the child's speaking vocabulary), then the overlap may be poor. The child's low score may represent nothing more than a difference in content. Such an erroneous discrepancy could lead to an LD label.

The most valid measures of achievement for LD identification purposes reflect the nature of the classroom methods as well as content. For example, spelling achievement can be tested by having a child point to the one of four words that is correctly spelled, or write the word from dictation. Only the writing method is similar to how a child is supposed to function everyday in school. On the former test, the student may score too high and not be accepted for special instruction. Back in the classroom, however, the child may continue to fail spelling tests and written compositions. Therefore, achievement tests must evaluate achievement in the same way as the child demonstrates this knowledge in the classroom.

Since grade equivalent scores are not always valid indicators of actual achievement, they serve best when taken as indicative of ranges of achievement rather than absolute values. Often these tests overestimate achievement by one year because successes are added up across all levels, and motivation and attention are heightened in an individualized testing situation. This overestimation of achievement results in lower discrepancy figures and denial of special LD services to children who could profit from them.

Educational Experience. The number of years a child has spent in school, the quality of the instruction, and what learning experiences as a preschooler prepared the child for school entry are all important to consider. A child who continues to have severe, persistent learning difficulties despite adequate educational opportunities and ability has a learning disability. When opportunities have been poor, the amount of learning progress expected may be overestimated.

Age. Age at school entry may vary considerably, and too much may be expected from a student who is merely young for the grade. Age is an important factor to consider in such skill areas as reading comprehension, but declines as a factor in areas such as grammar and handwriting.

Alternative Approaches. Several alternatives or adjuncts to the use of discrepancy formulas help broaden the scope of learning-related variables considered in LD identification.

Behaviorists have suggested that *learning rate with various teaching approaches* be the focal point for educational decisions (Cohen & Martin, 1971; Lovitt, 1978). This process might involve systematic classroom observation on several occasions, use of tests that determine what a child knows and doesn't know in given subjects (Lloyd & colleagues, 1977), and observation of the teacher's behaviors (Hoffman, 1980). Lloyd and his colleagues (1977) also suggested evaluating the quality of instruction, or *teaching quotient* (p. 70). The model for learning and behavior laid down by the parents is also important to consider.

Harris (1979), as had some of his predecessors (Strang, 1964; Durrell & Sullivan, 1945), suggested that *listening comprehension* be used to estimate a child's potential. A student was said to have a reading disability if he or she could recall information that had been read aloud at a level over a year higher than the student's oral reading skills. The reasoning behind this discrepancy notion is that, if a student can understand and interpret information well (a skill highly related to intelligence), then reading abilities should be raised so that higher level material can be learned.

Since learning disabilities are characterized by uneven maturation in basic psychological processes, these too could be measured (Kirk, McCarthy, & Kirk, 1968). This method contrasts with others that focus on the educational manifestations of these basic processes such as arithmetic calculation scores. A processing test's average is presumed to reflect potential. Any major subtest deviation below this average would be considered a significant discrepancy. This method presumes that all children should develop in all information-processing subskills at the same rate. But not all children do, or should. Since strengths and weaknesses are common, these tests may inaccurately label typical learners as disabled (Kaufman, 1976; Larsen, Rogers, & Sowell, 1976). A further problem posed by process-oriented tests is that the relationship of the skills they measure to academic learning is still uncertain (Colarusso, Martin, & Hartung, 1975; Hammill & Larsen, 1974b; Larsen & Hammill, 1975).

Discrepancies also can be calculated from achievement differences among academic areas. This method presumes that the highest academic achievement score represents potential. Relatively poor performance in one area would indicate a specific learning disorder (Kirk & Elkins, 1975b). At times, however, the higher score does not represent hope for higher functioning in weaker areas. The high score may merely be a special talent, and not indicative of what would ordinarily be expected of a child.

Prevalence of Learning Disabilities

How many learning disabled children are there? Estimates from various studies and "off the top of the head" guesses have ranged from 1 percent to over 40 percent of our school population (Meier, 1971). The larger estimates reflect the LD definition's broadness and schools' liberal interpretations of federal identification guidelines. The smaller estimates come from schools serving only the severely learning disabled. These estimates also reflect the fact that some school districts find the bureaucratic process too cumbersome and professional salaries too expensive to warrant full identification of the learning disabled (Luick & Senf, 1979).

Accurate prevalence estimates are essential to preparing adequate numbers of teachers, programs, and financial allocations to meet the service needs of the learning disabled. Though the learning disabled currently account for 38 percent of handicapped school children, empirical studies suggest that approximately twice this number could qualify for services. Definitive estimates will not be possible until uniform assessment measures and degrees of discrepancy are used across states and studies.

Prevalence studies eventually will have to parcel out which types of children continue to experience severe, persistent learning difficulties on specific types of tasks and in specific teaching settings. The relative role of learner, task, and setting factors in learning disabilities may then be sorted out. Three types of prevalence figures are currently available: national policy estimates, state counts of labeled children, and findings from experimental studies.

National Policy Estimates

Over the years, national bodies have set guidelines that assumed 1 to 5 percent of school children were learning disabled (see Table 2-4). Currently, the Bureau for the Education of the Handicapped uses a 3 percent prevalence estimate as its working figure (*Progress Toward a Free Appropriate Public Education*, 1979).

State Counts

The first survey counting numbers of LD children was done in 1970. Approximately 2000 public elementary and secondary school principals were surveyed by the National Center for Educational Statistics of the United States Office of Education (Farnham-Diggory, 1978). The percentage of students considered LD by their schools averaged 2.6, but only 1.3 percent were receiving special services (Grant & Lind, 1978). The lower the socioeconomic status of the school district, the greater was the incidence of learning disabilities. By the 1978–79 school year, approximately 2.3 percent of the nation's 15–17-year-old students were being served within the LD category (*The Condition of Education*, 1980). By 1981–82 LD students represented 38 percent of the school-aged handicapped, or 3.4 percent of school-aged children (Special Education Programs, 1982).

Although we know how many children are being labelled learning disabled, we still do not know the nature and extent of these children's strengths and weaknesses, or how many who could qualify for LD services go unlabeled. This is due to variability across school districts and states in the degree of discrepancy between potential and achievement required for identification, measures used for identification, and maximum numbers allowed to be identified.

Experimental Studies

Empirical studies would seem to be the way to determine how many children actually deserve the LD label. Studies that have used the same test battery and discrepancy formula for all subjects report a 4 to 5 percent incidence of learn-

Table 2-4 National-level LD prevalence estimates

SOURCE	LD PREVALENCE ESTIMATE	STATED RATIONALE
U.S. Department of Health, Education and Welfare (1977) (information booklet on minimal brain dysfunction)	5%	None
Kass & Myklebust (1969) (meeting of 15 experts in 1967)	3–5%	Liberal enough to include children needing special LD services, yet conservative because some LD children would be receiving services in other special education programs and categories
National Advisory Committee on Handicapped Children (1970) and the U.S. Office of Education (1970ab)	1–3%	A low ceiling justified until research establishes objective criteria by which to define LD children
U.S. Office of Education (1976) Federal Register Proposed rule-making	2%	Based on a national survey, a 2% cap (limit) recommended on numbers of children who could be identified LD
U.S. Office of Education (1971) (estimated numbers of learning disabled in the U.S.)	1%	None

ing disabilities in school children when two criteria for significant under-achievement are required, and a 7.5 percent incidence when only one criterion is required (see Table 2-5). Interestingly, the 4 to 5 percent figure coincides with reports from states that actually identify the maximum 12 percent of handicapped school children permitted by federal law (*Progress Toward a Free Appropriate Public Education,* 1979). The far lower number of children served by most states under the LD label may be related to:

1. politics, appropriations, and tax issues

2. LD adolescent high school drop-out rates which decrease the number of students available for evaluation

3. the development by some students of compensatory techniques which mask the existence of underlying problems and delays identification and remedial services

Table 2-5   Empirically derived LD prevalence estimates

STUDY	SUBJECTS	MEASURES	PERCENT MEETING LD CRITERION
Meier (1971)	Over 2000 children in 80 second grade classrooms in 8 Rocky Mt. States representative of the U.S. urban-rural population density, and public-private school distributions No culturally disadvantaged children included	Teacher checklists identified 15% of children to be tested in the following areas: intelligence, achievement, perception, eye-hand coordination, articulation, and hearing The Myklebust Learning Quotient was calculated for each test	4–5% of children's learning quotient averages were less than 90, or two or more quotients were less than 85
Myklebust & Boshes (1969) 1965–66 pilot project on minimal brain damage	160 third and fourth graders	Intelligence; achievement in reading, arithmetic, written language; auditory receptive and expressive language; nonverbal tasks The Myklebust Learning Quotient was calculated for each test	7.4% of children scored one or more quotients below 85 A cutoff of 90 on one or more measures would have identified 24.3% of children as LD
1966–69 study	2704 third and fourth grade children from four suburban school districts	Intelligence, reading, spelling, arithmetic, nonverbal measures	7.5% of children earned one or more quotients of less than 85 A cutoff of 90 on any one quotient identified 15% of children as LD

4. enrollment in high school program options such as work study and vocational courses, which by the very nature of their less rigorous academic requirements camouflage the existence of certain learning problems

Although studies find males and females to be equally intelligent (Hier, 1979), learning difficulties are far more prevalent among males than females. Several large-scale screening studies report approximately a 2:1 ratio of LD males to females (Bentzen, 1963; Miller, Margolin, & Yolles, 1957; Rubin & Balow, 1971). Others find that males outnumber females by 4:1 (Owen & colleagues, 1971) and 6:1 (Coleman & Sandhu, 1967). Researchers are just beginning to uncover clues that relate various medical, maturational, sociolog-

Table 2-6 Hypotheses regarding greater male than female incidence of learning disabilities

HYPOTHESES	INVESTIGATOR
Medical factors	
The male may be more biologically vulnerable to brain damage prenatally and postnatally than the female. Although more males than females are conceived, more males die in utero or in infancy, females outlive males, and males face a higher risk of diseases that may lead to learning disorders (e.g., meningitis)	Bentzen, 1963; Critchley, 1970
Boys tend to have greater birth weights, larger heads and are more often firstborns; these conditions are associated with increased risks of brain injury and learning disorders	Silver, 1971a; Strauss & Lehtinen, 1947
Maturational factors	
Males lag behind females from the start; at birth males are one month less mature than females; they complete maturation at age 18, 2 years later than girls, growth rate is 80% that of the female through adolescence; slow physical maturation often is correlated with slow behavioral maturation	Bayley, 1943; Bayley & Jones, 1955; Farnham-Diggory, 1978
The male brain's protective sheath has been found to grow slower than the female's; therefore, the male has more prenatal and postnatal opportunities for damage to later developing cortical functions	Goldman & colleagues, 1974
The neural maturation of boys' cortical regions is known to differ from that of females; these differences may increase the probability of learning failure; males have been found to lag behind females in development of brain regions responsible for attention and such reading-related left hemisphere skills as verbal expression, stuttering, articulation and perception of the order of sounds in words	Goldman & colleagues, 1974; Hier, 1979; Bakker, 1970, 1972; Denckla & Reidel, in Denckla, 1979; Denckla & Heilman, 1979; Kinsbourne & Caplan, 1979; Kinsbourne & Warrington, 1963; Townes & colleagues, 1980
Males' greater variability in development may make them more susceptible to learning and behavior disorders	Kinsbourne & Caplan, 1979

ical, and brain organizational factors to sex differences in learning disabilities. These hypotheses are summarized in Table 2-6. Regardless of the reason for these sex differences, the fact is that boys are in greater jeopardy of school failure than girls.

Summary

The term *learning disabilities* evolved from the labels *brain injury* and *minimal brain dysfunction*. By the current definition, LD is due to a disorder in a basic psychological process that causes achievement severely below one's potential.

Table 2-6 continued

HYPOTHESES	INVESTIGATOR
Sociological factors	
Because males mature at a slower rate, research indicates that they often are unready for school entrance or the work of their grade	Ames, 1968
It has been suggested that our society expects more achievement from boys than girls and therefore is more apt to be aware of their learning difficulties or put pressures on them that they are too immature to meet; their more aggressive general behavior and reaction to failure seems to increase chances for LD referral because there are no sex differences in learning problems of unreferred children	Bentzen, 1963; Caplan, 1977; Vernon, 1957, in Critchley, 1970 Caplan & Kinsbourne, 1974; Lambert & Sandoval, 1980
Failing boys have in the past been more open to secondary behavioral difficulties upon school failure; their alternatives for success, being leaders and athletes, were harder to accomplish than girls' alternatives of being nice and quiet	Caplan & Kinsbourne, 1974
Brain organizational factors	
Impulsivity and certain types of information processing disorders have been found to be male-linked genetically	Kinsbourne & Caplan, 1979
The male's cerebral hemispheres are known to be more strongly specialized than the female's; therefore, in the event of left hemisphere damage, their right hemispheres are less flexible for assuming language functions important to academic achievement. Conversely, data indicates that boys whose left hemispheres become overloaded with inappropriate right hemisphere strategies (global, holistic) compromise their left hemisphere analytical, sequential reasoning skills so important to reading	Hier & colleagues, 1978; Heir, 1979; Farnham-Diggory, 1978; Davidoff & colleagues, 1978 Witelson, 1976, 1977

This definition's educational orientation requires measures of achievement and potential, but does not emphasize measurement of neurological factors. By federal law, the retarded, emotionally disturbed, physically handicapped, and economically disadvantaged can also have learning disabilities if these conditions are not directly responsible for the learning problem.

Our LD definition and regulations are broad because many questions regarding etiology, characteristics, and intervention remain unresolved. These questions are causing us to examine the roles that our task and setting requirements play in learning disabilities and whether the economically disadvantaged should be included in the LD definition.

Experts agree that the LD child is characterized by major discrepancies between expected and actual achievement. But there is no single way of measuring this discrepancy that is right for all children. Judging whether a learning disability exists is difficult, involving consideration of intelligence, achievement in different areas, past educational experiences, age, rate of learning with various instructional approaches, quality of present teaching, and several other factors.

Using various discrepancy measures for identification, approximately 3.4 percent of school-aged children, over one-third of all handicapped children, are now labeled LD. Experimental studies, however, indicate that 4 to 5 percent of children may be underachieving in two or more areas, and as many as 7 percent of children underachieve in one area. The fact that boys far outnumber girls in incidence of learning disorders has been linked to possible medical, maturational, sociological and brain organizational factors.

Suggestions for Further Study

1. Try checking off those characteristics in Table 2-2 that describe your own behaviors. Are you minimally brain injured? Clearly, not all maladaptive traits result in learning difficulties. LD focuses on particular clusters of traits which increase the likelihood of learning difficulties. Due to the wide gamut of possible symptoms, it's been said that "virtually any child with any problem falls within the domain of the learning disability specialist" (Bryan & Bryan, 1978, p. 26). Visit a local LD classroom. Do any two children share similar symptoms? If they do, does this make them alike in what and how they need to learn?

2. Many individuals, in addition to those mentioned here, commented on and influenced the direction of terminology in learning disabilities. To research these viewpoints, begin with the following: Freidus and Reitan's definitions (in Hallahan & Cruickshank, 1973); the educational definition developed by Myklebust's conference of experts in 1967 (Kass, 1969a); and the ACLD definition (in Kass, 1969b). Cruickshank's (1966) conference of nineteen experts deadlocked without reaching a definition (in Cruickshank, 1976). More recently, Hobbs (1975a) commented on why the federal LD definition was too loose and how Wepman's perceptual definition could add precision to the term. Cruickshank (1976) also argues for a definition based on perceptual disorders stemming from neurological dysfunction. At the other extreme, Ray Barsch describes "an individual as being learning disabled whenever he or she is *unable to consistently profit from the curriculum to which he has been assigned*" (Barsch, 1976; p. 73). For Barsch, as for many, LD is more valuable as a concept than as a category.

3. Several other definitions of learning disabilities were not discussed in the text. These are referenced here so that you can consult them for a more complete picture of variations in definition. The second National Advisory Committee on Handicapped Children (1970) put forth an LD definition that slightly changed the wording of the first advisory committee's definition. In 1969, Clements continued his role with the Minimal Brain Dysfunction National Project on Learning Disabilities in Children, by directing the second of its three Task Forces. The second Task Force adopted Bateman's

ideas, thereby shifting its terminology from MBD to LD, eliminating reliance on central nervous system dysfunction, and emphasizing educationally relevant functions. Finally, even prior to P.L. 94-142, most states had come up with their own definitions of what constitutes a learning disability. Mercer, Forgnone, & Wolking (1976) and Mercer (1979) present this data.

   4. If you are interested in researching discrepancy formulas not discussed in the text, consult: Martin (1963), Erikson (1975), McLeod (1979), and Reeve's (1979) methods. In addition, the Federal Register (Nov. 29, 1976) printed the government's proposed formula for determining a 50 percent discrepancy between achievement and ability. This formula created such protest that it was deleted one year later from the federal regulations. You will find Danielson and Bauer's (1978) article particularly worthwhile reading because of what it says about elements that the 1976 formula shared in common with others presented in this chapter. Statistical concerns about these formulas are reviewed by Cronbach & Furby (1970), Thorndike (1963), and Cone & Wilson (1981).

   5. Mercer (1973) stated that our intelligence test bias seems to breed the "situationally retarded" within a system of "institutionalized Anglocentrism." Could schools' fears of litigation if children are mistakenly labeled retarded lead to LD becoming a popular label for minorities? Read Tucker's (1980) survey of fifty Southwestern school districts. What happens to retarded minority youngsters when they are declassified? Could LD become another subtle form of discrimination?

   6. One of the consequences of a broad LD definition is overlabeling due to the many identification criteria different people apply. Divoky's (1974) article describes abuses of the LD label. She concluded that "the truth is that the learning disabled are whomever the diagnosticians want them to be" (p. 21). Similarly, Sylvia Farnham-Diggory (1978) summarizes the state of the art in learning disabilities in the following manner: "Whatever learning disability is, then it is 2 percent of something" (p. 6). She reviews LD's history and shows how we are becoming clearer as to what the "something" might be.

   Another consequence of our broad LD definition is variability in subject identification criteria from study to study. Consequently, research results are difficult to replicate and their findings are hard to generalize. Kavale & Nye (1981) present an excellent analysis of the variability in subject identification practices between 1968 and 1980, and Olson & Mealor (1981) do the same for 1975–1980.

   7. Witelson's theory of why boys underachieve more than girls is a hot item in neuropsychological circles. The studies that led to her assumptions are remarkably simple and easy to understand; perhaps their titles will induce you to read them: "Sex and the Single Hemisphere" (1976) and "Developmental Dyslexia: Two Right Hemispheres and None Left" (1977).

Part Two

Causes of
Learning Disabilities

Chapter Three
Physiological Difference Theories

Theorists do not agree on the exact cause of learning disabilities. Some feel that learning disabilities are caused primarily by physiological factors. Others feel that the tasks we ask children to do contribute to learning problems by making demands on their maturity levels or learning styles that they are not prepared to meet. Still others blame such factors as nutrition and stimulation in the children's living and learning settings. Appreciation of the relative roles of these learner, task, and setting factors helps professionals more accurately assess, observe, program for, and explain the factors contributing to particular children's learning disabilities.

The *physiological difference* theory maintains that a brain dysfunction alters specific brain processes, which in turn affect particular aspects of the child's learning and behavior. This chapter will consider three learner-based factors that may lead to learning disabilities: brain injury, heredity, and biochemical irregularities.

Brain Injury

Injury to brain tissue can cause a wide gamut of delays in early childhood development and difficulties in later school learning. Yet brain injury and learning disabilities are not the same thing. Brain injury does not always deter learning, and learning disabilities can be caused by many other factors. The child whose learning disorders are due to brain injury is referred to as *organically, centrally* (central nervous system), or *neurologically* impaired. Strauss and Lehtinen's classic case study of J.S., page 84, illustrates the types of learning difficulties that may follow an insult to the brain.

J.S.'s accident is only one possible cause of brain injury. While brain injury is often associated with learning difficulties, such a diagnosis has questionable relevance to instructional programming. Instead, clarifying the unique brain patterns that distinguish poor learners has better potential for guiding our daily teaching.

Causes of Brain Injury

Those areas of the brain that are newest in evolution and the latest to mature are responsible for high-level cognitive and academic reasoning abilities (Calanchini & Trout, 1971). They are susceptible to damage by carbon monoxide (sometimes caused by oxygen deprivation during suffocation or unconscious states), nutrient and oxygen deprivation (such as inadequate blood flow due to blood vessel constriction or blockage), free-flowing blood (as when a hemorrhage after a stroke or concussion blocks nutrients from cells), and pressure (as from tumor or pus infection). These events may occur in prenatal, perinatal, or postnatal life and are more common among children with learning and behavior difficulties than among average learners.

83

CASE STUDY: J.S.

J.S., youngest son of American parents of average intelligence and economic level. Two older children were progressing normally in school. Birth normal, psychophysical development uneventful until eighth year of age, when he fell 35 feet from a viaduct, landing on the fender of a passing car. He was unconscious for 24 hours, with bleeding from the nose and left ear and a severe black eye. Hospital diagnosed a fractured skull. In personality he had always been attractive and alert; this had not changed but his mother observed that he was more stubborn and impulsive at home following the accident. On returning to school, he no longer recognized the letters of the alphabet which he knew before, had "forgotten" how to read everything but a few words. Teachers soon saw that the earlier skills showed no evidence of returning. He could not read or write without scribbling, could not memorize or remember things from one day to the next. When admitted to the institution at 10 years of age his intelligence quotient was 82, performance quotient . . . 106. Still showed slight neurological signs of brain-injury. After 18 months of special training, he reached the end of the third or beginning of the fourth grade in reading and arithmetic. He returned to his family to enter school with a slow group of normal children (Strauss & Lehtinen, 1947, p. 3).

Prenatal Factors. Prior to birth, brain injury is associated with RH factor incompatibility, maternal diabetes and hypothyroidism, x-rays, too young or old maternal age, greater number of previous births, measles, cigarette smoking and medication causing oxygen deprivation, placental insufficiency, and maternal kidney malfunction and bleeding (Pasamanick & Knobloch, 1973). A higher incidence of prematurity (birth weight under 5½ lbs.) also exists among children with academic failures than normal learners (Meier, 1971).

Minor physical anomalies that occur prior to birth often are associated with later learning difficulties. These include facial asymmetry, atypical placement of ears or tear ducts, skin at the inside corner of eye covering tear ducts, unusually long index finger and short or curved fifth finger, tongue furrows, malformations of teeth, high arch in mouth, large gaps between toes or unusual length of toes (Steg & Rapoport, 1975; von Hilsheimer & Kurko, 1979). These physical anomalies do not disappear with age, are inversely related to intelligence, and are predictive of first grade school failure (Rosenberg & Weller, 1973; Waldrop & Halverson, 1971).

Perinatal Factors. At the time of labor and delivery, brain injury may occur due to shortage of oxygen, prolonged or precipitous labor, premature separation of placenta, and difficult delivery. Studies have found that 9–12 percent of all surviving newborns have evidence of intracranial hemorrhages at birth (Colletti, 1979). Colletti reports that the births of underachieving children differ from national birth statistics in greater numbers of mild and severe problems at birth, short first and longer second stage of labor, lower general health at birth, birth more often induced by the physician, greater length of hospitalization, more labor complications, more forceps deliveries.

Postnatal Factors. After birth, events that may cause brain injury include serious head injuries, accidents, strokes, high fevers, dehydration, brain tumors, and diseases such as encephalitis and meningitis.

Colletti's (1979) literature review and data suggest that by age six as many as 20 percent of all children may have suffered a significant insult to the brain. Given the many ways besides brain injury that children can become handicapped, why then is the national estimate of handicapped children only .12 percent? Clearly, the relationship between extent of brain damage and subsequent learning and adjustment difficulties is not perfect. The next section describes why this is so.

Effects of Brain Injury

Does knowing that a child is brain-injured help a teacher understand which learning functions are impaired and to what degree? No. Individuals who have cerebral palsy or epilepsy are all brain-injured. So are many individuals who are learning disabled, blind, or deaf. Yet all have different abilities, behaviors, and instructional needs. Some have severe learning difficulties while others have very few. Why is there such variability?

The effect of brain injury on learning and behavior varies because it depends upon several factors: the reason for the damage, its location, the extent of the damage, the individual's developmental maturity at the time of damage, how much time the damage has been progressing, the time passed since the insult, the individual's state of development at the time of testing, and the nature and extent of retraining attempts (Reitan, 1974). All these considerations relate to the fact that our brains are *plastic*. That is, although a brain cell won't regenerate or repair itself once destroyed, new neural connections are often formed between nondamaged cells so that learning and performance continue. Therefore, brain areas that just malfunction and are not totally destroyed can be exercised and can recover function when presented with stimuli that they are meant to respond to.

The brain's plasticity declines with age. Although brain insults in infancy usually create greater damage and immediate functional losses than in adulthood, infants are more likely than older individuals to recover function (Lenneberg, 1967; Ross, 1968). Because the brain is modifiable, theorists are hesitant to set upper age limits after which certain skills, such as speaking and reading, are unlikely to emerge. Research Box 3-1 further explores research on the brain's modifiability.

Due to the brain's plasticity, a history of brain damage does not necessarily predict the extent of later learning difficulties. Nevertheless, until recently it

RESEARCH BOX 3-1
Brain Plasticity

Damage to a specific brain site reduces the ability of the individual to perform a certain function. However, this functional loss may not be permanent. The human brain has approximately 12 billion neurons which, whether in adjacent or distant areas, often are capable of taking over functions of damaged regions. This can occur if a *primary*, densely enervated, receptive (visual, auditory) and expressive (motor, speech) area is not altogether destroyed; and the dysfunction is in the more sparsely enervated areas where neurons spread out and come together from several primary sites (Aljouanine & Lhermitte, 1965; Lenneberg, 1967). For example, a child's right hemisphere will take over many of the left hemisphere's language functions when the latter is damaged. The trade-off is that the visual-spatial functions slated for the right hemisphere and some higher order language functions may still be compromised (Annett, 1973; Searleman, 1977).

Animal research indicates that recovery after brain-injury occurs in several ways (Frostig & Maslow, 1979):

1. Inactive, intact axons (nerves that send messages) take over for cut axons' inability to repair themselves (Goodman & Horel, 1966; Scott & Liu, 1964).
2. New connections sprout from the axons of undamaged neurons, repairing damaged circuits (Diamond, Cooper, Turner, & Macintyre, 1976; Garey, Fisken, & Powell, 1973).
3. Synapses (areas where nerve endings meet) that had been vacated by other axon terminals are a growth stimulus for new neuronal sprouting; the sprouting pattern is not similar to the original normal connections (Raisman & Field, 1973).
4. Groups of dendrite branchings (nerves that receive messages) may form new circuits if stimulated appropriately (Scheibel & Scheibel, 1976).

5. Glial (connecting) cells regenerate and make contact with neurons so that transmission can occur (Hyden, 1973).
6. Enriched environments may result in positive changes in brain structure (for example, glial/neuronal ratio, enzyme activity, nucleic acid concentration, cortical weight) (Rosenzweig & Bennett, 1976).
7. Conductance changes in the outer surface of neural membranes may aid learning (Adey, Kado, McIlwain, & Walter, 1966).
8. Better conduction may occur due to changes in synapse density after stimulation (Garey & Pettigrew, 1974) or increased numbers of synapses (Cragg, 1972).

These findings are promising for people, but for obvious reasons cannot be tested out. We do know that the human central nervous system recovery ability varies with age, reason for, location of, and extent of damage (Reitan, 1974), as well as with intensity and type of retraining efforts. Because of variability in these factors, stroke victims may experience only temporary or reduced loss of function. No data on brain plasticity is more astounding than the remarkable relearning after an entire cerebral hemisphere or lobe has been surgically removed due to epilepsy, tumor, or trauma (Griffith & Davidson, 1966; Searleman, 1977).

There is less recovery of function after brain injury for the adult than child because neuron regeneration is less efficient (Lenneberg, 1967; Ross, 1968). In addition, there is less room for one area to take over the activities of another because the former has already specialized for a specific function (Geschwind, 1968).

Once damage and recovery have occurred, the reserve power of the brain is limited in the event of further damage (Lehrer, 1974). Nevertheless, the reserve is usually large enough to develop some compensatory skills. This is gratifying to educators, who train skills related to specific brain functions.

had been a common practice to try to explain or predict learning outcome by testing for whether or not a child might be brain-injured.

Testing for Brain Injury

Gross medical indicators of brain injury, electroencephalograms, and hard and soft neurological signs have been used to connect learning problems with the presumed cause, brain injury. Although these brain injury indicators are more prevalent among poor learners, they also are so frequent among children with no learning problems that they cannot be used as proof that the brain abnormality has caused a child's learning problem. This is due to the brain's ability to overcome some adverse effects of injury on learning, and also to the fact that our neurological indicators do not measure patterns of brain functioning involved in high-level academic reasoning.

Gross Medical Indicators. Although prenatal, perinatal, and postnatal factors associated with brain injury are more prevalent among learning impaired than nonimpaired children, they also are very prevalent among the latter group. Coleman and Sandhu's (1967) study of 364 middle class, 7–15-year-old children is representative of studies illustrating this point. They determined percentages of brain injury indicators for four groups differing in reading achievement:

	2 OR MORE YEARS BEHIND	1–2 YEARS BEHIND	LESS THAN 1 YEAR BEHIND	OVER 1 YEAR AHEAD
Birth difficulties	30%	23%	17%	19%
Serious injuries	26%	23%	11%	15%

Even though events related to brain injury were most prevalent among the poorer learners, they nevertheless were present in large percentages among better learners as well. Therefore, gross medical factors cannot be used to predict learning disorders in any one individual, or to state whether an existing learning disorder is definitely due to the brain insult.

Electroencephalograms. Electroencephalograms (EEGs) use electrodes to measure electrical activity at many points near the outer surface of the brain. The electrical signals are amplified and graphed on continuously moving paper. Because EEGs don't tap high-level cognitive functions, they correlate with neither IQ nor achievement (Hartlage & Green, 1971, 1972). Nevertheless, many investigators assumed that since the EEG could detect tumors, convulsive disorders, sleep states, and coma, it also might shed light on the brain functioning of the learning disabled. These hopes were not fulfilled.

The following percentages indicate no differences in numbers of typical and handicapped learners who have abnormal EEGs:

TYPICAL LEARNERS	POOR LEARNERS	
10%	10%	Meier (1971)
30%	41%	Myklebust & Boshes (1969)
22%	14%	Owen, Adams, Forrest, Stolz, & Fisher (1971)

Even when children are known to have suffered brain injury, their EEGs are often normal (Black, 1973; Freeman, 1971). These findings are due to the brain's ability to compensate for abnormalities, and the fact that EEGs reflect gross brain electrical activity but overlook complicated patterns associated with complex learning. Therefore, an abnormal EEG is of uncertain value in determining whether a brain injury is causing or is likely to cause poor learning.

Hard and Soft Neurological Signs. Besides the abnormal EEG, many investigators have examined behavioral signs that are always associated with brain injury. These are called *hard neurological signs*. They also studied relative lags in the ability to process neurological inputs (for example, understanding language — speaking; seeing a design — copying), assuming that these lags also could be due to brain malfunctioning. These are called *soft neurological signs* because they are abnormal only with respect to the child's age — they should have disappeared with maturity. Table 3-1 lists some accepted hard and soft signs of neurological damage.

Hard and soft sign studies have fared no better than medical indicators or EEGs as correlates of learning disabilities. There are groups of clearly brain-injured, learning-disordered children like the cerebral palsied, who do have more hard and soft signs than typical learners (Bortner, Hertzig & Birch, 1972; Dykman, Ackerman, Clements, & Peters, 1971). But underachievers who are not clearly brain-injured generally have no more of these signs than do typical learners (Myklebust & Boshes, 1969; Owen & colleagues, 1971). In one study, children with the most neurological signs actually had the fewest learning disorders (Ingram, Mason & Blackburn, 1970). In another study, the learning-disabled did have more hard (95 percent) and soft (90 percent) signs than did typical learners; nevertheless hard (55 percent) and soft (75 percent) signs were highly prevalent in the control group as well (Meier, 1971). Since hard and soft signs are typical among normal learners, their presence cannot prove that brain damage has caused or will cause learning problems.

The hard and soft signs of brain injury "are open to debate and may reflect 'soft' or 'equivocal' methods of detection or interpretation (Page-El & Grossman, 1973, p. 601). In fact, these signs can be related to many factors besides brain injury: inherited traits (Owen, et al., 1971; Matousek & Petersen, 1973), maturational patterns which are outgrown (Dykman et al., 1971; Routh &

Table 3-1   Signs of neurological damage

SOFT SIGNS (ABNORMAL ONLY WITH REFERENCE TO AGE; NORMAL IN EARLIER DEVELOPMENT)	HARD SIGNS (ABNORMAL AT ANY AGE)
Persistent primitive reflexes	Strabismus
Immature perceptual–motor organization	Blindness
Hyperactivity	Deafness
Impulsivity	Jerky, choreic, or athetoid
Distractibility	movements
Perseveration	Cerebral palsy
Inability to inhibit movements in one limb when moving the other limb	Seizures
	Hydrocephaly
Difficulty with rapid alternating hand movements	Microcephaly
	Persistent tilting of the head
Inadequate balance, coordination, gait	Pathological reflexes
Inability to detect where touched on body when eyes are closed	Visual or cranial nerve abnormality
Poor eye-hand coordination	Dysfunction of one side of the body
Articulation and language delays	Inability to touch finger to nose
Awkward walking of straight line and walking on tiptoe	
Poor differentiation of right from left	
Poor imitation of body movements	
Mixed laterality	
Arms drop when standing erect with eyes closed and arms outstretched	

Roberts, 1972), and environmental influences such as socioeconomic status (Bortner et al., 1972; John et al., 1977b).

Researchers are not discarding their assumptions about brain–behavior relationships because gross neurological tests haven't worked. They are trying instead to better understand the brain processes behind a child's learning strengths and weaknesses, rather than concentrating on the diagnosis of brain injury.

Neurological Patterns

Examining differences in *brain* functioning *patterns* of typical and poor learners has begun to clarify the relationship between the brain, learning, and behavior. These patterns have been revealed through modern neuropsychological assessment methods, summarized in Research Box 3-2.

Patterns of Typical Learners.   One historical theory of brain functioning claims that each brain region performs a certain function (*brain specificity*). The other major theory claims that most areas are capable of performing all functions (*brain equipotentiality*). Both theories are partially correct. Primary brain

RESEARCH BOX 3-2
Neuropsychological Research Methods

Researchers of the 1950s and 1960s clarified brain-behavior relationships by noting behavioral changes following specific brain lesions and onset of behavior when stimulating specific brain sites during surgery (Penfield & Roberts, 1959). Advances in instrumentation and computer technology in the 1970s brought rapid gains in knowledge concerning specific patterns of typical and atypical brain functioning. Each hemisphere's preference for certain types of tasks (*lateral asymmetry*) was found to be very important in typical maturation and learning. The poor learner often has atypical asymmetries. Several methods for studying brain-behavior relationships are presented below.

Split-Brain Research

Neuropsychologists have isolated the function of one brain hemisphere from another by studying individuals whose severe seizures were terminated when the *corpus callosum,* nerve fibers connecting the two cerebral hemispheres, were severed. Once this was severed, it was possible to present information to either hemisphere alone, thereby isolating the function of each cerebral hemisphere, and observing which activities necessitate interhemispheric communication.

Sperry's (1968) studies used the apparatus pictured below. Visual information is presented only to the left or right halves (visual field) of each eye. A picture presented to the left visual field is represented in the right cerebral hemisphere. Sperry's patients could not report in speech or writing what had been seen because these language functions are controlled by the left hemisphere. Some subjects even reported seeing nothing or just a flash of light. These same subjects' left

hands were able to find the objects through touch, because both the left side of the body and left visual fields are represented in the same cerebral hemisphere. Only input to the right visual field (which projects to the left hemisphere) could be described in speech or writing. Only objects placed in the right hand could be named, because all these functions are controlled by the left hemisphere. Even though they could perform the high-level task of naming, as long as the object remained in their right hands, subjects could not match it to a picture projected to the right cerebral hemisphere (through the left visual field).

Visual-half Field and Dichotic Listening Research

Simultaneous presentation of two different stimuli to the left-right visual fields or ears is a reasonably reliable and valid means of revealing the relative efficiency of each hemisphere in processing certain types of information (Bakker, Van der Vlugt, & Claushius, 1978). Each visual field is represented in the opposite hemisphere. In contrast, the left and right ears project only a majority of auditory information to the opposite hemisphere. By determining which hemisphere is more accurate on a task one can presume its greater specialization for that particular function.

These techniques have been adapted to a tactile *dichhaptic stimulation* task (Witelson, 1974). This method asks the subject to perceive meaningless shapes or name letters through touch. Again, objects in the left hand are primarily perceived by the right cerebral hemisphere and vice versa. In naming letters, the right hemisphere is as useful as the left because it can analyze the spatial information while the left hemisphere provides the name. With nonlinguistic stimuli, the left hand's perceptions prove superior because their interpretation relies on the right hemi-

RESEARCH BOX 3-2
(continued from preceding page)

sphere's spatial skills. Using these measures, researchers are discovering the typical degree of specialization of each hemisphere, as well as the inefficiencies of the poor learner.

Average Evoked Potential

Average evoked potentials, the computer summing of EEG recordings of electrical potentials, also reveal differences between good and poor learners. Recordings may be taken from as many as twenty brain sites while the subject has eyes open or closed, reads letters or words, looks at meaningful or nonmeaningful shapes and objects, looks at light flashes, or listens to sounds or words. Usually fifty to one hundred stimuli are presented at one-second intervals. The computer sums the amplitude (microvolts) of peaks and measures the milliseconds from the onset of stimulation to peaks or a return to normal. This procedure allows the brain's responses to the stimuli to stand out against its background electrical activity. In the noncomputerized EEG, this background activity, as well as unreliable judgments, may obscure significant, abnormal wave patterns (Freeman, 1967).

Computer-Assisted Tomographic Scanning (CATSCAN)

The CATSCAN is an x-ray that scans the skull and detects the absorption differences between spinal fluid, white and gray matter, and blood. Brain lesion detection is enhanced by an intravenous injection of an x-ray dense dye. An extension of the CATSCAN method, *positron-emission tomography,* involves injecting radioactive isotopes into the carotid artery, which feeds most cerebral areas. When the subject is asked to do something, blood flow concentrations change due to the more active areas needing to metabolize more glucose (80 percent of the brain's energy comes from glucose) and to take up more oxygen. These concentrations are apparent in photographs of the cortical areas being activated by these activities. Thus, we can discover the degree of activation required of which areas when performing certain tasks.

Drugs

Drugs may be used to temporarily anesthetize a hemisphere so that the functions which do and do not become impaired can be noted. For example, Osgood and Miron (1963) demonstrated how a drug could induce language impairment in an adult. Their subject had been able to name common objects displayed to him: cigarette, spring, paper clip, colors, fingers. Injection of Nembutal into the right carotid artery (which feeds the right cerebral hemisphere) had no effect on this naming behavior. But an injection into the left carotid artery produced jargon-like misnaming of the same articles. In addition, movement difficulties on the right side of the body became apparent. The effect of the Nembutal lasted four minutes, after which the subject could again identify the objects correctly. Obviously, his speech functions were located in his left hemisphere. This method has become known as *Wada's technique,* after its discoverer (Wada & Rasmussen, 1960). It often is used prior to brain surgery as a precaution against inadvertently disturbing the patient's language centers.

(Research Box continues on following page.)

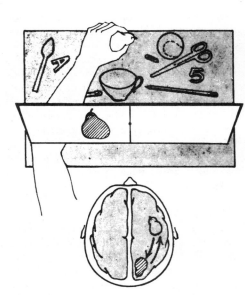

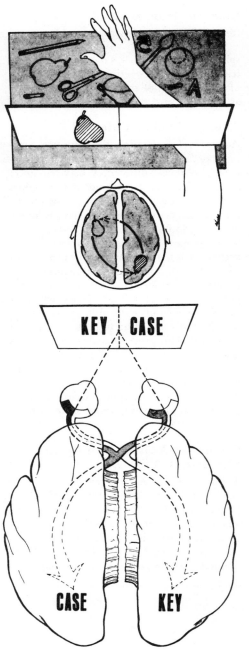

Sperry's (1968) split-brain apparatus (above). Visuo-tactile associations succeed between each half of the visual field and the corresponding hand. They fail with crossed combinations in which visual and tactual stimuli are projected into opposite hemispheres (p. 730).

Diagram of visual field projection sites (right). Things seen to the left of a central fixation point with either eye are projected to the right hemisphere and vice versa (p. 725).

SOURCE: From Sperry, R. W. "Hemisphere Deconnection and Unity in Consciousness Awareness," *American Psychologist*, 1968, *23*, pp. 723–733. Copyright 1968 by the American Psychological Association. Reprinted by permission of the publisher and the author.

regions are critical to specific functions, but many areas connecting these primary regions are capable of performing multiple functions by taking over for other damaged areas (Luria, 1966).

Structure-Function Relationships. Figure 3-1 shows the function of these areas of the human cerebral cortex. The numbers label primary and overlapping areas of specialization in the typical brain. Figure 3-2 depicts the arrangement of and relative area subsumed by brain cells responsible for body movements and sensations.

Dynamic Interrelationship of Brain Areas. Brain regions rarely work in isolation. The areas are intimately interconnected and any type of information processing generally activates several regions, each to a different degree. Because of this, an impairment in one brain region may decrease performance in seemingly unrelated areas as well (Mountcastle, 1962).

Figure 3-3a, reproduced from an actual photograph of activation of brain areas, shows that reading aloud activates seven cortical centers in each hemisphere. Even during silent reading, the areas responsible for listening and speech are stimulated slightly. This is why after reading all day for exams your mouth feels stiff and dry and you have a scratchy throat. What happens when you are resting with your eyes closed, listening to nothing and doing nothing? Your brain is still likely to be at work thinking; the brain areas involved in planning, selecting, and reflecting upon behavior are very active (Figure 3-3b).

Computerized brain wave recordings from different brain regions distinguish females from males and left- from right-handers (Dimond & Beaumont, 1974). By evaluating waves that increase and decrease with age these recordings help estimate mental maturity levels (Matousek & Petersen, 1973) and ages (Myklebust & Boshes, 1969; Satterfield, Lesser, Saul, and Cantwell, 1973).

Maturation of Brain Functions. Although we know a great deal about the adult's brain functions, we are just beginning to gain an understanding of the child's developing brain. As a child grows up, one cerebral hemisphere becomes more specialized than the other for certain functions, such as talking and art appreciation. This specialization process continues in predictable ways through adolescence (Lenneberg, 1967; Satz et al., 1975). The more specialized an area becomes, the less able it will be to take over for another area that becomes damaged. The term for the specialization differences between the two hemispheres is *brain asymmetry*. Brain asymmetry is an important area of study in learning disabilities because learning efficiency and styles are influenced by the degree to which one cerebral hemisphere has become superior to the other for given functions.

In addition to an average degree of brain asymmetry, adequate attentional processes are critical to learning efficiency. As children pay greater attention, their brain wave amplitudes increase and the time needed for the brain to

Figure 3-1 Brain structure-function relationships

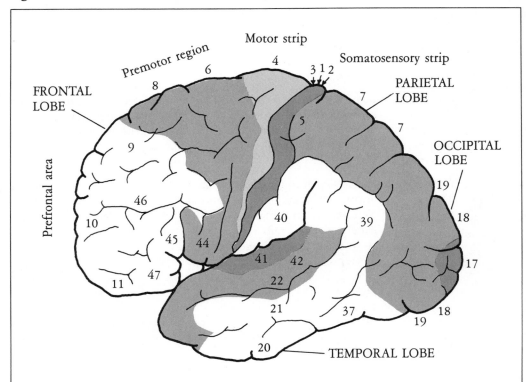

The cerebral cortex controls all conscious activity. The two halves of the cerebral cortex are almost identical in construction and metabolism, but differ in function. All brain activity is controlled by the biological structure and chemical transmissions of the nervous system.

Left Hemisphere: In most individuals, the *left hemisphere* responds to language stimuli such as inner thought, words, symbols that have verbal meaning, and memory for verbal material (Luria, 1976). It usually contains Broca's area, the region for speech. Over 95 percent of right-handed individuals (Rossi & Rosadini, 1967) and 50 percent (Geschwind, 1968) to 71 percent (Rossi & Rosadini, 1967) of left-handers have speech located in the left hemisphere. The left hemisphere receives information from the right visual field of each eye and the right side of the body. It specializes in information processing that involves analytic thinking, evaluating details, and sequencing. Due to the left hemisphere's use of words to reason, it also plays an important role in skilled math analysis and computation.

Right Hemisphere: The *right hemisphere* processes information as wholes (rather than details) and deals primarily with nonverbal stimuli such as body awareness (orientation in space), time sense, directional orientation (up–down), pictorial perception, mental imagery, spatial perception (Ketchum, 1967), memory for visual stimuli (Luria, 1976), complex forms, color, and environmental sounds, Due to its visual perceptual skills it plays an important role in appreciation of and talent in music, art, dance, sculpture, and geometric and perspective drawing (Tarnopol & Tarnopol, 1977). The right hemisphere, if not dominant for language, is still able to understand simple language and perform simple arithmetic (adding two digits). It receives information from the left visual field of each eye and the left side of the body.

Temporal Lobe: The *temporal lobe* is responsible for language reception and comprehension. Sixty percent of nerve fibers that transmit sound come from the opposite body side's ear. Forty percent come from the same

Figure 3-1 continued

side's ear. Because language is important in learning, the hemisphere that contains these skills is called *"dominant,"* even when one's writing hand is controlled by the opposite cerebral hemisphere. The temporal lobe also plays an important role in emotions and behavior because its proximity to the limbic system.

Area 41:   primary auditory reception field

Area 42:   also receives auditory input; together with area 4, it contains Heschl's gyrus which analyzes sound frequencies, lower frequencies being more centrally located

Areas 21, 22:   auditory association area capable of higher order auditory analyzes due to connections with other regions; works with area 42

Areas 21, 37:   controls auditory memory and sequencing, word meaning, searching for words.

Frontal Lobe: The *primary motor strip* (area 4) in the right hemisphere controls voluntary muscular movements of the left side of the body. The left hemisphere's motor area controls right side voluntary muscular movements. Each hemisphere contains some nerve fibers that control minor movements of the same side hand and arm.

Areas 6, 8, 44:   These are the secondary or "premotor" regions that coordinate, organize, stop, or change movement that has already begun. They formulate complex motor activities through interconnections with the sensory association regions, primary motor strip, and somatosensory strip. Area 44 is called Broca's area and is usually located in the left hemisphere. It controls speech movements and, if damaged, results in articulation difficulties.

Area 4 + premotor + sensory connections: permit visual-motor, auditory-motor, and tactile, kinaesthetic-motor associations.

Prefrontal Areas (9, 10, 11, 45, 46, 47):   control judgement, reasoning, abstract thinking, motives, planning, purposeful activity, perseveration, following plans, vigilance, and restraint of emotional impulses (Luria, 1977).

Parietal Lobe: The *somatosensory strip* (areas 1, 2, 3) in the right hemisphere receives feelings of touch, texture, pain, movement, weight, and temperature from the left side of the body. The left hemisphere's strip receives sensations from the right side. Lesions on the strip result in a loss of sensation for specific body parts. (See Figure 3–2)

Areas 5, 7:   These are the secondary association areas which, through their connections with other regions, can analyze and synthesize more complex tactile-kinesthetic information. Lesions in these areas result in partial loss of sensitivity.

Angular Gyrus: The *angular gyrus* (area 39) is located in the dominant cerebral hemisphere and works together with area 40. Visual, auditory, and kinesthetic areas of the brain are connected here. If it is damaged, the individual will have deficits in reading, writing, spelling, understanding language, and body image.

Occipital Lobe: The *occipital lobe* processes visual stimuli. The right occipital lobe processes information from the left visual field of each eye. The left occipital lobe processes information from each eye's right visual field.

Area 17:   responds to simple visual stimuli (lines and edges)

Area 18, 19:   secondary visual areas with connections to other areas that permit higher order visual functions: analyzing angles, rectangles, movements; figure-ground discrimination; recognizing and describing 1 or more objects; synthesizing parts of objects into wholes; controlling eye tracking; visual-auditory, visual-motor, and visual sensory associations

SOURCE: Tarnopol, L, and Tarnopol, M., *Brain Function and Reading Disabilities,* p. 9. Baltimore: University Park Press, 1977. Reprinted by permission of the authors. *General Sources:* Hecaen & Albert (1978); Heilman & Valenstein (1979); Luria (1966); Tarnopol & Tarnopol (1977); Walsh (1978).

Figure 3-2   The homunculus. The human body is represented in each hemisphere's motor strip (area 4 of the frontal lobe) and somatosensory strip (areas 1, 2, 3 of the parietal lobe) as an inverted fetus, a "homunculus". A relatively large brain area is devoted to the face, tongue, thumb, and fingers. These body parts, in turn, are able to move in more specialized fashions and to sense more acutely than are other body parts.

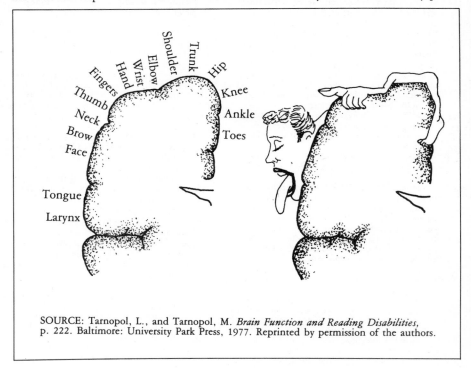

SOURCE: Tarnopol, L., and Tarnopol, M. *Brain Function and Reading Disabilities,* p. 222. Baltimore: University Park Press, 1977. Reprinted by permission of the authors.

respond decreases (Haider, 1967; Spong, Haider, & Lindsley, 1965). Interestingly, it takes more neural energy to attend to something and then not to react, than to actually respond. In fact, Soviet research has found that some brain cells' function is to inhibit response — they tell us to do nothing (Ekel, 1974). This explains teachers' comments that many learning disabled children just can't help attending to distractions, even when they are trying so hard to attend only to their work. As we learn more about the average student's brain development, we also gain a better understanding of learning disabled children whose brain patterns are atypical.

Patterns of Poor Learners. Neuropsychological measuring techniques are indicating clear patterns of differences between good and poor learners. The majority of learning disabled children have some features in common. Other patterns differentiate one LD subgroup from another.

Features Common to Poor Learners. Teachers often comment that their learning disabled students are immature in many ways, must try much harder than others to pay attention, and take a long time to finish tasks. Neuropsychological measures now explain why this is so. We find that the brain wave patterns of immature and duller children approximate those of younger, normally developing children (Buschsbaum & Wender, 1973; Matousek & Petersen, 1973). Their brain asymmetry is poorly developed (Calloway, 1975). Similarly, learning disabled children's left and right hemisphere areas of specialization are not as strongly established as they should be (Bakker, 1980).

Those brain waves that represent attention often are lower in amplitude in learning disabled than in typical achievers (Preston, Guthrie, & Childs, 1974). Therefore, learning disabled children must put far greater than normal effort into paying attention in order to process information (Shields, 1973). This effort is observable in marked increases in brain wave amplitudes. Learning disabled children's nervous systems also respond slower than typical; therefore, they require a longer time to process information and perform tasks (Satterfield et al., 1973; Shields, 1973).

When reading, good learners share a great deal of activity between the same locations in the two hemispheres. Poor readers, however, seem to overuse one hemisphere instead of adequately activating the other (Hanley & Sklar, 1976). Many LD youngsters also suffer some amount of motor incoordination because smooth, well-planned motor movements depend on the brain's ability to integrate all incoming and stored information with motor output. When they have deficiencies at any of these points, motor actions are impaired (Calanchini & Trout, 1971).

Patterns Differentiating LD Subgroups. Neuropsychological measures' sensitivity to learning patterns reflecting atypical brain asymmetries allows computerized measurements of brain wave patterns to discriminate children with higher verbal IQs from those with higher performance IQs (Black, 1973; Connors, 1970); higher from lower scoring children on visual perceptual, reading, and spelling tests (Black, 1973); arithmetic underachievers from verbal underachievers; and the most from least learning-impaired children (John et al., 1977b). Depending on the subjects studied, measurement methods, and experimental tasks, we are finding patterns of brain functioning that are unique to subgroups of poor achievers (Denckla, 1973; John et al., 1977a). Three major patterns have been identified thus far: overuse of right hemisphere, overuse of left hemisphere, and motor difficulties.

Good learners' left hemispheres generally are highly specialized for language processing. Since language is the content of reading, spelling and writing, left hemisphere language proficiency is important to achievement in these areas. When mature readers read words projected to one or the other cerebral hemisphere, their left hemispheres read far more accurately than do their right hemispheres (Kershner, 1977; Marcel, Katz, & Smith, 1974). In contrast, poor

Figure 3-3 Emission tomographic recordings of brain structure–function relationships.

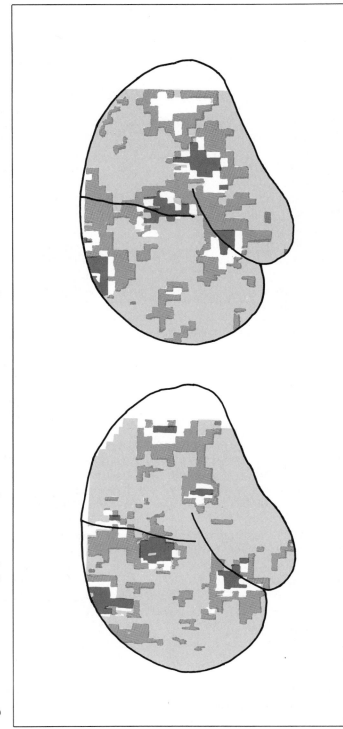

(a) Reading silently and reading aloud involve different patterns of activity in the cortex. Reading silently (left) activates four areas: the visual association area, the frontal eye field, the supplementary motor area and Broca's speech center in the lower part of the frontal lobe. Reading aloud (right) activates two more centers: the mouth area and the auditory cortex. The left hemisphere is shown in both cases, but similar results have been obtained from the right hemisphere. Adding the primary visual cortex, which is not reached by the radioactive isotope, the act of reading aloud calls for simultaneous activity in seven discrete cortical centers in each hemisphere.

Figure 3-3 continued

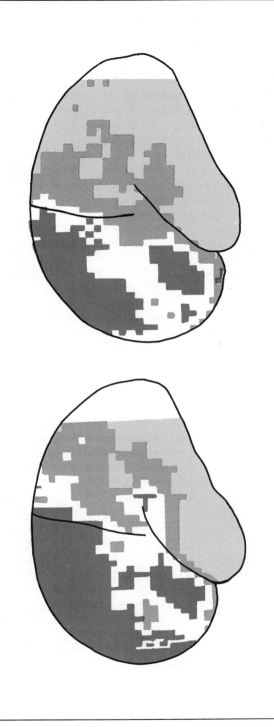

(b) Resting pattern of nerve-cell activity in the left and right hemispheres of the normal cerebral cortex was revealed by measuring regional blood flow, which is closely coupled to metabolic rate and hence to functional activity. The images were generated by a computer and the data obtained by detecting the passage of the radioactive isotope xenon 133 through the cortex. Each pixel, or picture element, represents a square centimeter of cortex. On the color scale for these figures, the mean flow is medium gray, rates up to 20 percent below the mean are light gray, and rates up to 20 percent above the mean are dark gray. Images suggest that in resting state the frontal areas are notably active.

Source: Lasson, N. A., Ingvar, D. H., and Skinhøj, E. "Brain Function and Blood Flow." *Scientific American*, 1978, *239*, 62–71. Used by permission of N. A. Lasson, M. D.

readers are often less accurate than good readers in their left hemisphere language processing (Bakker, Smink, & Reitsma, 1973; McKeever & Van Deventer, 1975; Witelson & Rabinovitch, 1972). Some poor readers' right hemispheres actually read better than their left hemispheres (Witelson & Rabinovitch, 1972; Zurif & Carson, 1970). This right hemisphere superiority is seldom found even among good readers who tend to process unusual amounts of language with their right hemispheres. The right hemisphere's style of attending to wholes (such as configuration of whole words) is incompatible with the phonetic analysis of words and the linguistic sequencing of sentences and stories that is required for reading progress. This analysis and sequencing is a left hemisphere function.

A second subgroup of poor readers overuses left hemisphere learning strategies. For example, Bakker (1980) recorded EEGs while children read words flashed to one and then the other hemisphere. He found that good readers preferred their right hemispheres at young ages, but by the end of second grade switched to their left hemispheres. While some poor readers overused their right hemispheres at all ages, others consistently overused left hemisphere information processing strategies. Unlike the former group, the left hemisphere overusers couldn't recognize whole words rapidly because they concentrated too much on analyzing word parts.

A third major pattern that poor learners show is articulation, hand movement, or gross body movement dyscoordination. This can occur even when all other learning processes appear intact (Mattis, French, & Rapin, 1975).

Continued modern neuropsychological research may help us understand how the brains of handicapped learners are electroneurologically unique and how teaching strategies might be matched to these patterns. Since researchers are just now learning which factors to investigate and how to study them, studies involve methodological errors and often yield contradictory results. A comprehensive picture of different information processing patterns is a long way off. As the prevalence of different brain functioning profiles and their relationship to learning strengths and weaknesses become clearer, some neuropsychologists feel that a new way of evaluating children, *neurometrics* (the collection of neurological norms), will emerge (John, et al., 1977a). They foresee a potential in neurometrics for instructional treatments based on the precise brain cause of a learning problem rather than on the behavioral symptoms, as is current practice.

Research that matches interventions with brain patterns is in its infancy. We have long known that stimulation facilitates brain development (Greenough, 1976). The question the neuropsychologists must now deal with is what type of stimulation is best for whom. Animal studies show better learning results when animals' stronger senses are used for instruction (Thatcher & John, 1977). Similarly, educators generally advise using children's strengths to remediate their weaknesses. Yet some neuropsychological research suggests that academic proficiency may increase even more rapidly when the weaker neuropsychological processes are exercised, as when a child reads words only through the underdeveloped hemisphere (Bakker, 1980). Frostig and Maslow (1979) concur that teaching might be more effective if it went beyond remediation of isolated learning disabilities to the remediation of their common cause:

> Any disturbed brain function that finds its expression in behavior change will probably cause other behavior changes as well. Treatment directed solely to isolated behaviors or disabilities will probably not carry over to other situations. On the other hand, sometimes seemingly unrelated behaviors have a common origin in the same brain function. For example, difficulties in verbal logical behavior, mathematical skills, and spatial orientation may be overcome if the perception of spatial relationship is improved.
>
> A teaching rule is suggested by neuropsychological research: *do not neglect to train basic psychological functions* — that is, functions that are common to and necessary for a wide variety of behaviors (p. 543).

Since nobody precisely understands all the factors involved in learning, our schools generally adopt broad-scoped programs that use children's stronger information processing channels for new learning but also try to remediate academic skill weaknesses that may interfere with progress.

Conclusions

Brain injury may occur prenatally, during the birth process, or after birth. It is frequently associated with impaired learning ability. Because of the brain's plasticity, however, the nature and extent of functional impairment caused by the injury is hard to predict. Much depends on the reason for the damage, its location, its extent, the individual's maturity at the time of injury, the time and retraining efforts since injury, and the person's maturity level at testing. Since brain injury indicators are also common among good achievers, a diagnosis of brain injury does not have much direct educational relevance. In addition, brain irregularities on these measures may be caused by factors other than brain damage, such as heredity, environmental influences, or maturational patterns. Consequently, a brain injury diagnosis is not very useful in explaining or predicting a learning disorder for any one child.

Studying the patterns of brain functioning has much potential value. Though the neuropsychological assessment field is still young, it has begun to clarify how brain-behavior patterns of good and poor learners differ. It also has confirmed that educational tasks and home environments impact significantly on brain as well as learning functions. Until brain patterns can be linked with valid educational interventions, programming will be based on psychoeducational assessments and classroom observations, using children's stronger information-processing channels for new learning while remediating academic skill weaknesses that may interfere with progress.

Hereditary Factors

Pioneers in learning disabilities like Werner, Strauss, and Orton had proposed a genetic link to learning disorders. It is unlikely that learning disabilities would be exempted from genetic causes when hereditary factors have been linked to so many other disorders affecting learning: phenylketonuria (PKU) (Hardy, 1965), Turner's syndrome (Money & Alexander, 1966), schizophrenia (Rosenthal, 1970), and depression (Gershon, Dunner, & Goodwin, 1971). It seems that different brain structures, patterns of brain maturation, biochemical irregularities, or susceptibility to diseases that impair brain functioning may be genetically transmitted.

Many early investigators documented specific cases in which reading disorders seemed to be passed down from one generation to the next or existed among several siblings (Eustis, 1947; Fisher, 1905; Hinshelwood, 1907, 1911; Marshall & Ferguson, 1939; Stephenson, 1907; Thomas, 1905). The case study on page 103 describes a youngster whose reading disorder seems related to many other handicaps among his relatives.

Large-scale research projects support the observation that learning disorders often run in families (see Table 3-2). Owen and her colleagues (1971) completed one of the best-controlled of these studies. They found that their learning disabled students' siblings shared similar learning difficulties, whereas the siblings of typical learners did not have learning problems. The LD students' parents had poorer adult reading abilities and high school English grades than did control group parents.

Table 3-2 Incidence of shared learning disorders among children and their families

INVESTIGATION	NATIONALITY	DISORDER	SHARED INCIDENCE
Hallgren (1950)	Swedish	general learning difficulty	88% shared with their family members
Critchley (1970)	European	reading	60% shared with relatives
Denckla (1973)	American	reading and spelling	88% shared with similar family histories or subtle language disorders
Ingram, Mason, & Blackburn (1970)	American	speech	more frequent in the family histories of poor readers than normal readers
Silver (1971b)	American	learning disabilities	39% shared with parents and siblings, even if the LD children's difficulties could possibly be attributed to brain trauma

CASE STUDY:
Familial Learning
Disorder

. . . a right-handed though partly ambilateral [uses both hands] boy with a severe dyslexic [reading] handicap. . . . Regarding
familial incidence, the following points are of
interest.

1. His father stated that as a boy he had had
relatively severe writing and spelling
problems which had not, however, pre-
vented him from qualifying in medicine
though he had had great difficulty in passing his examinations. His verbal learning
had always been poor and written composition slow and effortful. Indeed as a
medical student he had worked out a special technique to enable him to write
examination answers as quickly and
concisely as possible. He reported some
difficulty in visualising words [imagining

word forms] and was apt easily to lose the
place in reading, often tracking with his
forefinger. Apart from poor spelling and
relatively uncertain auditory memory, he
had managed to cope effectively with his
work as a rural general practitioner.

2. One of the boy's paternal uncles was reported to be ambilateral and a poor speller
who had had difficulties similar to those
of his brother at school, more especially
with language subjects.

3. The boy's mother had at no time difficulty with reading or spelling but in-
formed us that both her father and one of
her brothers were stammerers. This and
one other brother had also had difficulty
with reading and spelling.

4. Two of the boy's younger brothers were
likewise dyslexic although less markedly
so than himself. His youngest brother is
still too young for one to be able to assess
his reading capacity (Wyke, 1978, pp.
5–6).

One of the major objections to studies on the heritability of learning
disorders is that, even when the degree of genetic similarity among subjects is
known, concordance of learning disorders could still be due to some unique
environment that they have shared (Bijou, 1971; Gordon, 1971). How many
times have you been told that you look, act, or learn like your parents, sisters,
or brothers? Are these characteristics that you have no control over because
they've been genetically endowed to you? How many are due to influences on
each other to dress, behave, or value achievement similarly? If you have an
inherited disability, can you learn to overcome it or must you learn to live with
it?

One way to explore this heredity-environment question is to study twins,
siblings, and parents so that genetic and environmental influences can be controlled. These studies have examined two important factors in achievement,
the heritability of learning disorders and intelligence. We shall discuss these
factors, as well as the relationship between handedness and learning disorders,
because handedness is often an inherited trait.

Heritability of Learning Disabilities

Studies of the genetic versus environmental contributions to learning disorders
compare identical with fraternal twins, siblings, and parents. Identical twins
come from the same ovum and share the same genetic material. Fraternal twins

share no more genetic material than do sibling pairs, but they are more likely to share environmental influences. These studies have found a genetic link to psychological and physiological characteristics that can influence learning, such as hyperactivity (Morrison & Stewart, 1973; Willerman & Plomin, 1973), autonomic responses underlying emotionality (Jost & Sontag, 1944), and personality type (Vandenberg, 1966). They also have revealed a powerful genetic role in learning disabilities. Studies report that learning disorders are shared 33 percent of the time between fraternal twins and 100 percent of the time between identical twins (Hallgren, 1950; Hermann, 1959; Lopez, in Omenn, 1973; Norrie, 1959).

Some of the most fascinating data on the heredity-environment question comes from measuring the brainwaves of siblings and parents. One early study of identical twin pairs reported that "the [EEG] records from one twin resembled those from the other as closely as the records of the same person on successive tests" (Davis & Davis, 1936, p. 1222). Another study found identical twins' EEGs to be identical 85 percent of the time, while those of fraternal twins were alike only 5 percent of the time (Lennox, Gibbs, & Gibbs, 1945). More recently, Connors (1970) reported the same abnormal flattening of EEG waves in a father and his four children. All had reading problems. The mother had no learning problems and no EEG abnormality. Finally, the Swedish team of Matousek and Petersen (1973) found that similarities in brain wave patterns increased in the following order: triplets, siblings, fraternal twins, identical twins. The triplet data is most likely least similar because of the additional brain changes that often accompany their prematurity and birth process.

Apparently, psychological, physiological, learning, and brain functions carry genetically influenced patterns and potentials. But what has been laid down by the genes can be strongly modified by the environment. No body of literature attests to this modifiability as strongly as does the investigation of genetic versus environmental components of intelligence.

Heritability of Intelligence

Studies on the heritability of intelligence (IQ) are important because of the role of IQ in academic achievement and in LD identification. These studies find that learning potential is predetermined, but extremely modifiable through positive environmental events (Gray & Miller, 1967; Hunt, 1961).

Jensen's (1969) famous monograph estimated the heritability of IQ as ranging between 49 and 64 percent. These correlations are remarkably close to the 50 percent of genes actually shared between parents and offspring. Studies find that IQ correlations increase in direct proportion to the increase in genetic relationship. Sharing of environmental influences further increases IQ correlations. Therefore, fraternal twins' IQs are more highly correlated than are siblings' IQs, even though both share the same genetic endowment (McCall, Applebaum, & Hogarty, 1973). Similarly, identical twins who are reared together have higher IQ correlations (87 percent) than those reared apart (75 percent) (Erlenmeyer-Kimling & Jarvik, 1963).

What does the high correlation between genetic endowment and IQ actually mean? Marjorie Honzik's (1957) work found that, whether children were reared by their biological parents or by adoptive parents, their IQs correlated significantly with their biological mothers' IQs and the educational levels of their biological fathers and mothers. No IQ relationship existed between the adopted children and their foster parents. Yet, the adopted children's average IQ was 106, whereas their biological mothers' average IQ was only 86.

Another classic example of the impact of environment on intelligence is Skeels' and Skodak's (1966) follow-up of retarded orphans who had been placed in the care of adult retarded institutionalized women before they were 2½ years old. These children were returned to the orphanage six months to four years later. Their average IQ upon return was 92. The IQ of the group that had remained in the orphanage had steadily decreased to 51. Twenty-one years later, the average experimental child had graduated from high school and one-third of them had gone on to college. In contrast, half of the control group was unemployed; of the remainder, most worked as unskilled laborers. Clearly, even if genes significantly correlate with intellectual abilities, these abilities can be greatly altered through parenting and teaching.

Inherited Handedness

Handedness is often an inherited trait. Although the body side a person prefers is established at birth, hand preference doesn't become obvious until later in the preschool years (Gesell, 1939). Whereas right-handers use their right hands for most activities, left-handers do not use their left hands for all activities. Left-handedness is actually some degree of ambidexterity.

Left-handers have been deprecated throughout the centuries, with *left* being a synonym for bad or odd qualities (*sinister* in Latin, *gauche* in French). These deprecations are not deserved. Left-handedness does not cause learning difficulties or odd behavior. These difficulties occur only when a brain dysfunction has caused both the left-handedness and poor performance. Left-handers ruin every neat theory of cerebral functioning because their brains have unique distributions of functions.

Handedness and Brain Dysfunction. Early studies reported two to seven times greater prevalence of learning disorders among left- than right-handers (Harris, 1957; Wall, 1945, 1946, in Critchley, 1970). More recent studies show that left-handedness is only more frequent among learning disabled than typical learners when a left hemisphere injury or severe developmental delay has forced the student to become left-handed, as in cerebral palsy, epilepsy, and mental retardation (Kinsbourne & Caplan, 1979). These individuals most likely would have been right-handed had it not been for the condition that also caused their learning disability (Satz, 1972). Their left-handedness did not cause their learning problems (Hicks & Kinsbourne, 1978a).

Studies of individuals whose left-handedness is definitely *familial* (genetic) in origin find that they have no greater incidence of learning disorders than do right-handers (Hardyck & Petrinovich, 1977). Studies also find no differences in intelligence or perceptual skills between familial left- and right-handers (Newcombe & Ratcliffe, 1973).

Handedness and Language Dominance. In the past, the preferred hand mistakenly was thought to indicate which hemisphere was dominant (more specialized) for language. Because language abilities are highly related to efficient reading and higher level reasoning, some investigators hoped to increase language and learning efficiency by training right- or left-sided body movements (Delacato, 1966). This reasoning has proved faulty. Language dominance cannot be inferred so simply from handedness.

Neuropsychological techniques are used to reveal in which hemisphere language skills are located. Table 3-3, using this information, shows that handedness and language dominance are not always related, especially for the left-handed. Handedness reflects motor dominance, while language dominance is yet another matter. It is language dominance that more seriously concerns us in learning disabilities.

The advantages or disadvantages to the familial left-hander's having language skills located in either or both hemispheres is debated. Many familial

Table 3-3 Language dominance and handedness

HANDEDNESS	INCIDENCE	LANGUAGE DOMINANCE
Right-handers	70–90% of people are right-handed (Kershner, 1975)	95% have speech located in the left hemisphere (Kershner, 1975); their right hemispheres can still process some simple language (Searleman, 1977)
		5% have speech located in the right hemisphere
Left-handers	8–10% of people are left-handed (Hardyk & Petrinovich, 1977)	50% (Geschwind, 1968) to 75% (Rossi & Rosadini, 1967) have speech located in the left hemisphere
	more boys (10.5%) than girls (8.7%) are left-handed (Hardyk, Petrinovich, & Goldman, 1976)	12–25% have speech located in the right hemisphere (Rasmussen & Milner, 1975)
	if ambidextrous people with mild left-hand preferences are counted, then as high as 30% of people might be left-handed (Annett, 1972)	12–25% have speech located in both hemispheres (Rasmussen & Milner, 1975)

left-handers who have language represented in both hemispheres recover function following brain injury much more rapidly than do individuals who have language in only one hemisphere (Luria, 1970a). Hardyck and Petrinovich (1977), therefore, conclude that the familial left-hander's two heads might in fact be better than the right-hander's one! Others, however, claim that left-handers' unique, and at times imbalanced and crowded, cerebral organizational patterns increase the risk of learning disorders (Denckla, 1979; Witelson, 1976).

Conclusions

Intellectual, psychological, physiological and brain wave patterns have a hereditary component and relate to learning difficulties. Family history information often reflects a child's developmental patterns and suggests teaching approaches that have been successful with similarly handicapped relatives. Despite these genetic links, the environment is a powerful influence on helping us reach the limits of our potential.

Left-handedness too can be hereditary. Individuals who have become left-handed due to a left hemisphere dysfunction have a greater incidence of learning disorders than do right-handers. Most investigators no longer claim that the left-handedness is causally linked to the learning disorders. They acknowledge that both the left-handedness and learning disorder may have the same cause. Handedness continues to be studied, but not because it represents a brain malfunction that must be retrained in order to enhance learning. Instead, handedness is a particularly useful criterion for defining and studying groups that vary in cerebral organizational patterns.

Biochemical Irregularities

Several biochemical irregularities may lead to learning disorders in children who otherwise might have been conceptually competent. Some of these imbalances cause severe brain injury. Others create a hyperactive or hypoactive behavioral state that makes it difficult for the child to attend appropriately to learning tasks. Although the activity level is not in itself an important issue, the inattention that it represents is critical. An inability to focus and sustain selective attention greatly hampers information processing, and may result in learning disabilities (Ross & Ross, 1976).

There are at least seven types of hyperactivity (Connors, 1972). One is a biochemical irregularity which results in *hyperkinetic* (hyperactive) behavior by creating a short attention span, distractibility, and poor impulse control. These in turn lead to restless, inappropriate, and nongoal-directed body movements. Causes of hyperactivity other than biochemical irregularities include brain injury, maternal smoking during pregnancy, lead poisoning, anxiousness, and emotional disturbance (Denckla & Heilman, 1979).

O'Malley & Eisenberg (1973) reported that 5–10% of school-aged children may be hyperactive. Boys far outnumber girls in these statistics. Parents report that their hyperactive children can't sit still, are disobedient and moody, can't complete what they begin, and can't play well with others for prolonged periods of time. They are "unleashed tornadoes" (O'Malley & Eisenberg, 1973, p. 95) because they run all the time, seem not to tire, and injure themselves and objects around them. In class these children may disturb others, not respond to directions, become easily frustrated, and get distracted when working in a group.

Darrell's story, which appears on page 109, vividly describes how hyperactivity can interfere with school success. It also highlights how there is often more than inattention behind some learning disabled children's extreme impulsivity, social difficulties, and poor learning (Denckla & Heilman, 1979). When the teacher demands work on a structured task, Darrell cannot modulate his attention. It wanders to other things; he impulsively responds to these attention getters; and he is consequently more active and restless than his classmates. Opportunities for learning the teacher's material are lost. Darrell's mind does not go blank and stop thinking when his attention drifts. Rather, he learns many other things, most of which are irrelevant to the teacher's intentions (Kinsbourne & Caplan, 1979).

Whereas hyperactive children's attention is underfocused, hypoactive children are overfocused. They ponder too long, are overly attentive to details, and cannot arrive at decisions rapidly. They are lethargic, sluggish, and need more sleep. They are unmotivated, ask few questions, and command very little attention in the classroom because they are not disruptive. A teacher might overlook such a child but eventually will notice the slow completion of assignments and difficulty answering rapidly.

The four types of biochemical irregularities that have been linked to learning disorders and hyperactive/hypoactive behavior are abnormal neurochemical transmissions, vitamin deficiencies, glandular disorders, and hypoglycemia.

Abnormal Neurochemical Transmissions

Biochemical imbalances in the brain cannot be measured directly. Therefore, the link between abnormal neurochemical transmissions and the attention difficulty represented by hyperactive or hypoactive behavior has been surmised from knowledge of how certain drugs affect the brain, and their observed effects on attention, learning, and behavior.

Many hyperactive children focus attention better and refrain from mentally and physically responding to diversions when given stimulant medication. These stimulants seem to energize their cerebral cortex's inhibitory mechanisms so that distractions are screened out. The stimulants also sensitize specific brain systems to incoming stimuli. Although stimulants facilitate at-

CASE STUDY: Darrell

At the time of evaluation, Darrell was 8 years and 7 months of age. He started school in the fall of 1966 at the age of 6 years and 2 months. His parents saw him as a bright, likeable little boy — not perfect, of course, for he seemed on the immature side. He could not dress himself and his speech was somewhat unclear. His father worried a bit about his lack of coordination; his mother was anxious that the other children might not let him play with them.

In his second year of school, his teacher referred him to the school's Special Services Department for psychological testing "to determine why he was not achieving at the level of average intelligence indicated by a group test." After the evaluation the parents were told Darrell's intellectual functioning was above average, but that he was below average on certain tasks requiring visual perception and visual-motor integration. Testing also revealed he was hyperactive and could not concentrate well. . . .

A year later, in February, 1969, his parents had become quite concerned about him. His rate of academic progress was slower than in the previous two years. They had had many conferences at school, always hearing that Darrell was "immature, fidgety, distractible, and unable to concentrate." The teacher said he required constant personal attention and help. They had tried seating him at the back of the room, at the front, and immediately beside the teacher, but nothing seemed to help. The parents were confused and discouraged. . . .

The following is a direct quote from the father, a nice-looking, personable, 30 year old college graduate: "I'm concerned mainly about two things; his lack of coordination and his inability to concentrate on anything for over sixty seconds. He wants to compete and to excel in sports — he wants to so badly! — but he can't. He gets his feet mixed up and can't even kick a football. He is uncoordinated. . . .

The mother has a warm, ready smile. She is 29 years old and has a high school education. She expresses in a healthy way her mixed feelings about her son. There was the hint of tears as she said, "It upsets me when he comes home and says the kids don't want to play with him because he's not as good as they are." Later, her irritation came through as she fumed, "He can never find anything to occupy him for longer than a few minutes. He nags me for something else to do, somewhere to go, someone to see. My patience wears out. Sometimes I feel like knocking him down."

She told us about a visit to his classroom this year. It was depressing for her. Darrell was up and down, distracting other children from their work and constantly wiggling. He got very little work done; he couldn't copy things from the board. She felt like shaking him and wondered how the teacher could abide him (Clements, Davis, Edgington, Goolsby, & Peters, 1971, pp. 26–27).

tention processes and behavioral management of the drug responder, drugs have negative side effects and are not the answer to long-term social and academic adjustment.

In contrast to hyperactive youngsters, many hypoactive children seem to suffer from overactive inhibitory mechanisms. Sedatives quiet these mechanisms and allow more stimuli to come to their attention.

Underactive Inhibitory Mechanisms and Hyperactivity. Most writers concur that the hyperactive child's problem is one of under- rather than over-arousal. Hyperkinetic behavior was once thought to be a response to lowered excitability of the brain's reticular activating system, which modulates sensory input. The child's high activity level appeared to be an attempt to increase this input (Satterfield & Dawson, 1971). The current explanation is that the under-arousal exists within the central nervous system's inhibitory chemicals. Hyperactive children may have too little of the chemical needed to inhibit neural transmissions. The neurons containing these chemicals may have been destroyed (Wender, 1976), or their synapses (where nerve endings come together) may not be sensitive enough to the chemical inhibitors (Kinsbourne & Caplan, 1979). Consequently, children cannot inhibit attending and respond to everything.

Stimulants such as dextroamphetamine (Dexadrine), methylphenidate (Ritalin), pamoline (Cylert), and Benedryl, activate the chemicals that inhibit neurotransmissions. Therefore, when on stimulants, both normal and hyperactive children become more able to screen out distracting and irrelevant stimuli (Rapoport et al., 1978; Shetty, 1971). Sustained attention is generally enhanced and motor restlessness is reduced.

Many excellently controlled, "double-blind, cross-over" studies (see Research Box 3-3) support the underarousal theory. Soviet laboratories have shown that the cerebral process involved in inhibiting action is much more

RESEARCH BOX 3-3
Stimulant Medication Research Methods

In the past ten years drug studies have made great strides with respect to control groups. Data on drug responders is separated from data on nonresponders to more clearly parcel out how well the former group's learning is enhanced. The placebo effect is being dealt with. A *placebo* is a fake pill given to a control subject who believes he is receiving stimulants. In eight studies that used placebo controls, there was a 39 percent improvement rate in hyperactivity within the placebo groups (Barkley, 1977).

Double-blind methods try to overcome the effect of positive expectancies. Neither the experimenter nor the subjects know who is on drugs and who is on placebos. However, even double-blind studies aren't perfect because individuals may be able to guess who is on drugs from the side effects (Sprague & Sleator, 1973).

Because of variability in individual responses, each child in a drug study is used as his or her own control. This method is called a *cross-over* design because children receive the drug treatment followed by placebos, or vice versa. Since drug effects may only show up if both instruction and post-testing occur when the child is on drugs (Swanson & Kinsbourne, 1976), recent studies are sensitive to having children either on or off drugs at both pre- and post-testing times. These improvements in research design help determine exactly for whom, in which situations, and on which criteria stimulants are helpful.

complex, delicate, vulnerable, and difficult than the process involved in paying attention (Ekel, 1974). Stimulants seem to increase the activity of these inhibitory mechanisms. They also make specific excitatory brain systems more sensitive, thereby augmenting the impact of incoming stimuli on sensory and attending systems (Barkley, 1977; Kinsbourne, 1977b).

Stimulant Medication and Hyperactivity. Studies show that anywhere from 60–90 percent of children treated with stimulants improve to varying degrees (Whalen & Henker, 1976). These children are called *drug responders*. On rating scales such as those in Tables 3-4 and 3-5, parents and teachers indicate large reductions in hyperkinetic symptoms. But these scales are of uncertain reliability and validity, often indicating enhanced adult perceptions rather than child behavior. The ratings do not agree with psychological and physical measures that more objectively tap attention mechanisms (Barkley, 1977). Such objective measures of drug effects on attention span and activity level have been positive. However, the impact of drugs on academic achievement or long-term adjustment has been disappointing. Drugs are often accompanied by negative side effects and optimum dosage is difficult to determine. The ultimate test of drug efficacy will be long-term measures of whether or not children think, learn, and get along more effectively, not whether they are momentarily quieter and more attentive.

Attention Span. Many physiological and behavioral measures show that the drug responder's attention increases when on stimulant medication (see Table 3-6). Douglas (1972) summed up these children's enhanced impulse control, concentration, and planning as due to gains in ability to "stop, look, and listen." Their intelligence test scores also tend to increase because better attention enables these children to use their problem-solving capabilities and past knowledge to their best advantage (Barkley, 1977).

Activity Level. When they are on medication and in structured situations that demand attention, childrens' in-seat activity, and arm and ankle movements decrease. Their out-of-seat behavior in the classroom, however, still remains high. In free play situations their activity level is reduced as often as not, depending on the situation and measure used (Barkley, 1977). It seems that only when attention is task-relevantly engaged does their activity level decrease. This occurs most often in highly structured classroom situations.

Academic Achievement. Academic classroom gains after a period of drug intervention have been disappointing (Barkley, 1977). Some laboratory studies, however, have shown short-term enhancement of thinking and learning when children are put on stimulants. Although few in number, these studies report improved learning of word-pairs, short-term memory, and teacher- or examiner-paced learning (Whalen & Henker, 1976). Swanson and Kinsbourne's (1976) laboratory research found that learning may be "state-dependent." That

Table 3-4   Werry-Weiss-Peters activity scale: A parent rating scale

	NO	SOME	MUCH
During Meals			
Up and down at table	—	—	—
Interrupts without regard	—	—	—
Wriggling	—	—	—
Fiddles with things	—	—	—
Talks excessively	—	—	—
Television			
Gets up and down during program	—	—	—
Wriggles	—	—	—
Manipulates objects or body	—	—	—
Talks incessantly	—	—	—
Interrupts	—	—	—
Doing Homework			
Gets up and down	—	—	—
Wriggles	—	—	—
Manipulates objects or body	—	—	—
Talks incessantly	—	—	—
Requires adult supervision or attendance	—	—	—
Play			
Inability for quiet play	—	—	—
Constantly changing activity	—	—	—
Seeks parental attention	—	—	—
Talks excessively	—	—	—
Disrupts other's play	—	—	—
Sleep			
Difficulty settling down for sleep	—	—	—
Inadequate amount of sleep	—	—	—
Restless during sleep	—	—	—
Behavior Away from Home (except at school)			
Restlessness during travel	—	—	—
Restlessness during shopping (includes touching everything)	—	—	—
Restlessness during church/movies	—	—	—
Restlessness while visiting friends, relatives, etc.	—	—	—
School Behavior			
Up and down	—	—	—
Fidgets, wriggles, touches	—	—	—
Interrupts teacher or other children excessively	—	—	—
Constantly seeks teacher's attention	—	—	—
Subtotal Score	× 0	× 1	× 2
Total Score			

SOURCE: Werry, J. S. Developmental hyperactivity. *The Pediatric Clinics of North America*, 1968, 15(3), p. 588. Reprinted by permission.

Table 3-5 Connors' teacher rating scale for student hyperactivity

ITEM	NOT AT ALL 0	JUST A LITTLE 1	PRETTY MUCH 2	VERY MUCH 3
1. Sits fiddling with small objects				
2. Hums and makes other odd noises				
3. Falls apart under stress of examination				
4. Coordination poor				
5. Restless or overactive				
6. Excitable				
7. Inattentive				
8. Difficulty in concentrating				
9. Oversensitive				
10. Overly serious or sad				
11. Daydreams				
12. Sullen or sulky				
13. Selfish				
14. Disturbs other children				
15. Quarrelsome				
16. "Tattles"				
17. Acts "smart"				
18. Destructive				
19. Steals				
20. Lies				
21. Temper outbursts				
22. Isolates himself from other children				
23. Appears to be unaccepted by group				
24. Appears to be easily led				
25. No sense of fair play				
26. Appears to lack leadership				
27. Does not get along with opposite sex				
28. Does not get along with same sex				
29. Teases other children or interferes with their activities				
30. Submissive				
31. Defiant				
32. Impudent				
33. Shy				
34. Fearful				
35. Excessive demands for teacher's attention				
36. Stubborn				
37. Overly anxious to please				
38. Uncooperative				
39. Attendance problem				

SOURCE: From C. Keith Conners, A teacher rating scale for use in drug studies with children, *The American Journal of Psychiatry,* vol. 126:6, p. 886, 1969. Copyright 1969, the American Psychiatric Association. Reprinted by permission.

Table 3-6 Increase in physiological and behavioral indices of drug responders' attention when on stimulant medication

FINDINGS	INVESTIGATION
Physiological Indices	
Drug responder's alpha wave activity associated with inhibitory cortical processes increases when on drugs.	Shetty, 1971
Drug responder's average evoked responses (EEGs) are reduced by stimulant drugs, while those of poor responders are augmented.	Buchsbaum & Wender, 1973
The normal anticipatory heart rate decrease when attention is focused on a problem is facilitated when on medication	Sroufe, Sonies, West, & Wright, 1973
Behavioral Indices	
Reduced time to react to stimuli	Sroufe, et al., 1973; Zahn, Abate, Little, & Wender, 1975
Reduced errors on monotonous, continuous performance, vigilance tests (e.g., push a button when an X or red triangle appears on the screen)	Barkley, 1977
Better planning, reasoning, and control of impulsive responding on mazes	Barkley, 1977
Better matching of figures that differ in details or outline	Barkley, 1977
Reduction in number of toy or activity changes while in free play	Barkley, 1977
Improved attention to classroom tasks	Barkley, 1977
Ability to concentrate on the same stimuli for greater periods of time	Kinsbourne & Caplan, 1979

is, when a drug responder learns information (which of four zoos animals come from) while on drugs, the responder remembers or relearns this information well only if tested when again on drugs. Giving drugs on recall when none were given for the initial learning does not aid relearning at all.

Studies in which children remain on or off drugs at pretest, instruction, and posttest have not yet been attempted over a long period of time in the classroom. Therefore, at this time there is no long-term data with which to form conclusions about achievement increases with medication (Barkley & Cunningham, 1978).

Long-Term Effects. When compared with their peers, children who have been on stimulants for over two years are usually still more active, inattentive, impulsive, rebellious, failing in school, distractible, aggressive, and difficult to discipline (Barkley, 1977). They have few friends, engage in more antisocial behavior, lack ambition, have poor self-concepts, are sad, and often find themselves in trouble with the law (Whalen & Henker, 1976).

Adolescents no longer run away from their mothers in a supermarket, take everything off the shelves, or break grandma's best china. It seems their minds rather than their bodies wander (Kinsbourne, 1973a). Denckla & Heilman (1979) quote one adolescent as saying, "My mind is like a television set on which someone is always switching the channels" (p. 576).

No studies have shown emotional adjustment or academic performance to be any better for children who have been on medication several years than for children who had never been on stimulants. Yet when these children's medication is discontinued, any treatment gains are seldom maintained (Douglas, 1975). On the more positive side, no link between taking stimulants and later drug addiction has been documented (Beck, Langford, MacKay, & Sum, 1975).

Side Effects and Dosage. Not all hyperactive children are drug responders. Ten (Ross & Ross, 1976) to 30 percent (Kinsbourne & Caplan, 1979) even may get worse on medication. Careful teacher and parent observation and measurement, pretreatment versus treatment comparisons on different dosage levels, and controlled tests of new learning are essential to determine the drug's efficacy (Neisworth, Kurtz, Ross & Madle, 1976; Scranton, Hajicek, & Wolcott, 1978).

The most frequently noted side effects of stimulant medication are insomnia and decreased appetite. The next most frequent are weight loss, irritability, and abdominal pains. Also observed are: headaches, drowsiness, sadness, dizziness, nausea, proneness to crying, euphoria, nightmares, tremor, dry mouth, constipation, lethargy, depression, dazed appearance, nervous tics, hallucinations, and anxiety (Barkley, 1977). Growth also may be significantly depressed (Safer & Allen, 1973). With time and maturation, height and weight delays are overcome.

The drug dosage at which optimal thinking occurs for a drug responder is difficult to determine. Dosage is a major concern because attention, thinking, and behavior see-saw as the drug reaches its peak effect at $2-2\frac{1}{2}$ hours after ingestion, and wears off $1\frac{1}{2}-2$ hours later (Swanson, Kinsbourne, Roberts & Zucker, 1978). Longer-acting agents are being developed to help avoid this four hour up-down cognitive cycle.

Overactive Inhibitory Mechanisms and Hypoactivity. The central nervous system inhibitory mechanisms in the hypoactive child appear to be overactive, rather than underactive. The hypoactive drug responder may be helped by sedatives. These tone down the overactive inhibitory mechanisms, allowing more stimuli to come to the child's attention (Silver, 1977).

Vitamin Deficiencies

Allan Cott (1972), a psychiatrist, has been the chief promoter of another biochemical imbalance theory for learning and behavior disorders, the *orthomolecular* approach. The term *orthomolecular* was coined by Linus Pauling (1968) to refer to the normal chemical constituents required for optimum brain functioning. Pauling felt that the brain is more sensitive to changes in chemical concentrations than are body organs and tissues. Therefore, mental abnormalities may be observed long before physical symptoms appear. Brain imbalances also may occur when the blood exchange in the brain decreases or when the brain metabolizes important molecules too rapidly.

In keeping with Pauling's feeling that behind every twisted mind lies a twisted molecule, Cott gave megavitamin treatments to psychotic children and vitamin deficient learning disabled children. Megavitamin treatments are the ingestion of huge amounts of vitamins, often over 1000 times the usual daily requirement, to overcome chemical imbalances. Cott reported reduced hyperactivity and improved attention, concentration, and learning.

Although case reports indicate improvement in children on megavitamin treatments, there have been no well–controlled studies, using the methods in Research Box 3-3, on its efficacy (Kinsbourne & Caplan, 1979; Sieben, 1977). Therefore, the American Academy of Pediatrics' Committee on Nutrition (1976) declared that megavitamin therapy was unjustified as a treatment for psychoses and learning disorders, although it was appropriate in some physical diseases. In defense, supporters of the orthomolecular approach claim that in double–blind, cross–over studies of megavitamin treatments it is impossible to get control groups similar in behavior to the treated children. Further, the dosage adjustments preclude double–blind research designs (Adler, 1979). Consequently, megavitamin therapy must be approached cautiously; any claims for decreased hyperactivity and increased attention may reflect the adult and child's positive expectancies, rather than the results of the therapy.

Glandular Disorders

Hormonal imbalances may cause brain injury very early in life or physical states that interfere with efficient learning. Two of these biochemical irregularities are thyroid and calcium imbalances. Both are treatable with diet and standard medical practices.

Thyroid Imbalances. Both excess and insufficient thyroid hormone may create physical states that reduce learning efficiency. Hyperactivity is created by excess thyroid hormone. In contrast, thyroid deficiencies create a listless, placid individual who may not be motivated or activated to learn. Children who have thyroid deficiencies at birth are likely to become severely brain damaged. Intelligence, receptive and expressive communication, and body movements are impaired (Green & Perlman, 1971). The earlier treatment is begun, age 2½ being a critical year, the greater the probability the child will ultimately reach higher intelligence levels (Money & Lewis, 1964).

Calcium Imbalances. Abnormal elevation of calcium due to a calcium metabolism disorder can cause personality alterations bordering on psychosis (Karpati & Frame, 1964) and permanent intellectual deficits (Fraser, Kidd, Kooh, and Paunier, 1966). Fortunately, early diagnosis can prevent these outcomes. Abnormally low calcium levels in the body have not been associated with learning disorders.

Hypoglycemia

Many of us eat little while working or going to classes, and then overeat at dinner time. One hour later we find ourselves asleep on the living room couch. In effect, we have put our brains to sleep by consuming more sugar than our insulin levels were prepared to break down. Our pancreas reacted as though in an emergency by secreting more insulin than we needed, lowering our blood sugar levels far beyond normal. Because brain metabolism relies on adequate glucose supplies, our brains couldn't remain alert. This condition is called *hypoglycemia.*

It has been suggested that many learning disabled children are chronic sufferers from a similar condition (Green & Perlman, 1971). The children are tired, lethargic, confused, and unable to apply energy to learning. At times the inability to sustain attention leads to hyperactivity, because children move as different events catch and release their attention. Convulsions occur in severe cases.

Low blood sugar compromises brain development during the period of most rapid brain growth, the first two years of life. The earlier and more frequent the episodes of insufficient sugar supply, the more susceptible the brain is to damage (Green & Perlman, 1971).

If the condition goes untreated, the brain's nerve and glial (support) cells begin to deteriorate (Anderson, Milner, & Strich, 1967). Convulsions and permanent brain damage may set in by the second day of life (Koivisto, Blanco-Sequeiros, & Krause, 1972). The most common result is mental retardation, delayed motor development, and reduced brain size (Green & Perlman, 1971). Central nervous system abnormalities are evident among as many as 75 percent of children who had been hypoglycemic infants. Severe hypoglycemia is present in over 10 percent of newborns (Lubchenco & Bard, 1971), especially among those whose birth circumstances are associated with brain injury: twins, newborns of low birthweight, infants whose mothers had kidney dysfunction or were diabetic during pregnancy, and in those with inadequate intrauterine nutrition (Koivisto, et al., 1972). In these cases, central nervous system damage may have preceded and actually caused the hypoglycemia (Knobloch et al., 1967).

The more mild cases of infant hypoglycemia are associated with only limited central nervous system impairment (Griffiths & Laurence, 1974; Koivisto et al., 1972). If treated early, this damage can be limited (Anderson et al., 1967).

At older ages, single hypoglycemic episodes usually do not result in brain damage. They do temporarily affect the brain, however, creating abnormal EEGs. These EEGs return to normal when the blood sugar level is again normal (Green & Perlman, 1971). Careful control of children's eating patterns has successfully treated hypoglycemia and its secondary effects. Good research still needs to be done to confirm that episodic low blood sugar lies behind some older children's inability to profit from instruction (Kinsbourne & Caplan, 1979).

Conclusions

Biochemical irregularities appear to be responsible for the attention difficulties, and consequent hyperactive and hypoactive behavior, of some learning-disabled children. Judging from the effects of stimulant drugs which activate neural inhibitory mechanisms, it seems that one subgroup of hyperactive children is deficient in quantity or use of neurochemical inhibitors. These children's inhibitory systems, and attention and sensory systems, need to be aroused so that they will be able to block out irrelevant information and attend in a more focused manner. Sixty to 90 percent of hyperactive children respond to stimulants with some degree of improved attentiveness and reduced activity level in structured situations. Long-term learning and behavior gains have not yet been demonstrated. In contrast, some hypoactive, overfocussed youngsters respond well to sedatives that decrease inhibitory neural mechanisms so that attention is freer to wander.

Vitamin deficiency proponents have yet to support their claims with well-controlled research. In infancy, untreated low blood sugar, low thyroid levels, and elevated body calcium can be devastating to learning potential. If these imbalances appear after the first few years of life, learning efficiency, energy, and motivation may be adversely affected. These biochemical imbalances can be rectified through diet and standard medical practices.

Medical intervention may create a greater state of readiness to learn. But the answer to learning disorders is not in drugs or diet alone. Multiple interventions involving good schooling and supportive home environments are essential.

Summary

Research on physiological differences between good and poor learners has found that learning disabilities may be caused by brain injury, heredity, or biochemical irregularities. Any or all of these may impact to varying degrees on a child's abilities in different areas of development.

Because of the brain's plasticity, the nature and extent of impairment in learning caused by brain injury is hard to predict. Therefore, nearly as many positive indicators of brain damage are found among typical learners as among poor learners. Since these indicators are so common to good learners and do not reflect higher cognitive processes involved in academic achievement, they do not explain or predict any one child's learning problems. A more fruitful way to explore brain-behavior relationships is to identify neuropsychological patterns that differentiate individuals with varying learning strengths and weaknesses. It is hoped that knowledge about brain patterns may someday become linked to valid instructional approaches.

Since learning disabilities have an hereditary component, family history information may help us understand a child's developmental patterns and teaching approaches that have been successful with relatives. Medical interventions, too, help us understand the biochemical irregularities associated with hyperactive and hypoactive behavior. Medical intervention can prevent early brain injury and create greater states of readiness to learn.

Although physiological differences in children relate to learning disorders, the environment can have a major impact in charting a favorable developmental course. Social scientists and educators in the field of learning disabilities know that good parenting and teaching may enhance brain functioning, learning, and ultimate life adjustment.

Suggestions for Further Study

1. The literature on *commissurotomies,* severing of the connections between the two cerebral hemispheres, has yielded fascinating knowledge about which hemispheres are responsible for which functions. If you would like to learn more about the outcome of these studies, select the brain functions you are most interested in from among the following sources: an object will be remembered as having been seen before only if it appears both times in the same cerebral hemisphere (Sperry, 1968); on a drawing task, if two different visual stimuli are projected, one to the left and one to the right hemisphere, the left hand will draw the right sign but verbally report having drawn the left sign (Sperry, 1968); patients can't imitate one hand's posture with the other when the hands are out of sight (Sperry, 1968); the right hemisphere can look at objects and simple math problems and point to the categories the objects belong to or the digits' sums (Sperry, 1968); the right hemisphere can comprehend simple written and spoken words, when this comprehension is expressed nonverbally (Gazzaniga & Sperry, 1967); the right hemisphere is superior to the left in analyzing complex spatial relations (Bogen & Gazzaniga, 1965); sound reception (Milner, Taylor, & Sperry, 1968) and hand movements (Gazzaniga & Sperry, 1967) are controlled by both cerebral hemispheres, the opposite side relationship being most powerful.

2. There have been several attempts to directly retrain the brain. Claiborne (1906) advocated teaching dyslexics to be left-handed so "that the speech, symbol and sound centers on the right side of the brain may be cultivated to the exclusion of those on the left, or as supplemental to the defects on the left" (p. 1816). Claiborne's philosophy had a major influence on Delacato's work (1966). Orton (1937) devoted a very minor portion of his work to cerebral dominance training. More recently, Zaidel (1975) used contact lenses to direct information to one or another hemisphere. Van den Honert (1977) attempted to teach reading by exercising the left hemisphere. She directed instruction to the right ear (which mostly projected to the left hemisphere) while playing music through the left ear (which mostly connected to the right hemisphere). She also patched the left eye. Given what you've learned about the brain's structure and function, what basic mistake did she make in her neurological retraining effort? Some of the best evidence for the effect of teaching on brain functioning comes from naturalistic studies. For example, read Tzavaras' (1981) study of the brain asymmetry differences between literate and illiterate Greeks.

3. Are you a true left-hander? How can you tell? First of all, check out your family history. Secondly, read the following works to discover what types of questionnaires and hand measures most reliably and validly separate nonfamilial from familial, and strong from weak left-handers: Dee, 1971; Hardyck & Petrinovich, 1977; Hecaen & Sauget, 1971; McKeever, Gill, & Van Deventer, 1975; Zurif & Bryden, 1969.

4. Where would you guess your language dominance lies? Try tapping your right and then left hand's fingers in sequence. Now try singing syllables to the tune of Jingle Bells, or repeating nursery rhymes while again tapping (Morse code keys would be ideal). For which hand did speech interfere with tapping? Your language dominance might lie in the hemisphere opposite that hand. When the speech and hand mechanisms overlap, overloading and poorer performance is likely. If interference is equal for both hands, your language may be located in both hemispheres. This must seem like a crude method, but Lomes and Kimura (1976) used it successfully in their studies.

Now, note the position of your hand while writing. If inverted, your language may be located on the same side of the body as the writing hand. If not inverted, language is located in the opposite hemisphere. This theory, with only slight support, has been put forth by Levy & Reid (1976). Hemmes (1977) offers a good rebuttal.

Now, think about telling someone the proverbs that have developed from childhood fairy tales. Then try imagining visually all the landmarks you would follow to get home. In which direction did your eyes gaze during each activity? Kinsbourne (1972, 1974) and Lefevre, Starck, & Lambert (1977) have found that when thinking about verbal material eyes will gaze up and to the right in people who are left hemisphere dominant for language. When their thought processes involve spatial material, their eyes will gaze up and to the left. This occurs because each hemisphere subserves orientation (gaze, head and body turning) toward the opposite body side and it makes sense that when a hemisphere is activated, orientation would be directed by the same hemisphere.

Try all three experiments. Do the results agree?

5. The positive behavioral effects of drug therapy quickly dissipate when drugs are discontinued. Could it be that the drugs are indeed such powerful control agents? If so, should the child stay on drugs indefinitely? Or is there some other way to perpetuate positive drug effects? Whalen and Henker (1976) propose that since children attribute their behavioral improvements to drugs, they don't feel responsible for continuing their more adaptive behavior patterns when off drugs. Read this article to learn how children

can be trained to feel that they can control their own behavior. These writers cite adult studies in which such training did help individuals exert greater effort to overcome their problems.

6. Will biochemical interventions through drugs be able to make us smarter? A positive answer to this question is likely. Drugs that are known to act on specific brain functions such as interhemispheric transfer have already been shown to increase such skills as short-term verbal learning and motor abilities. Read Dimond (1976) for a fascinating review of this issue.

Chapter Four
Task- and Setting-Based Theories

Several task- and setting-based factors contribute to learning disabilities. Learning disabled children have significant lags in some skills and strengths in others. They often have unique styles of going about learning that require special teaching approaches. These children's weaknesses may be aggravated by curriculum materials and methods that make demands they are not able to meet. Appropriate matching of task characteristics to these children's uneven ability patterns and learning styles can facilitate their development. To focus on this, the maturational lag and cognitive style perspectives on learning disabilities are presented as *task-based* theories.

Several *setting-based* contributors to learning disabilities exist in our family and school climates. Like task-based factors, setting factors are influences beyond the child's control that, when interacting with the child's unique characteristics, may aggravate learning disorders. In extreme cases, such as nutritional deprivation or exposure to environmental toxins, these external factors can cause physiological differences in the child that then lead to developmental delays and learning disabilities.

In understanding the causes of and contributors to a particular child's learning difficulties, equal weight must be given to learner, task, and setting considerations. The child-, task-, and setting-based strengths suggest how best to intervene on the child's behalf.

Task-Based Theories

Task-based theories of learning disabilities emphasize the fact that school work is often mismatched with children's unique patterns of abilities and learning styles. These tasks can contribute to learning disorders if what and how the teacher teaches do not match what a student knows and how the student learns best. It is critical that school tasks be modified so as to build on a student's strengths, remediate weaker abilities, and minimize the interference of weaknesses with learning progress.

The *maturational lag perspective* stresses the importance of modifying curricular content to better meet these children's needs. The *cognitive style perspective* stresses modification of teaching approaches. Together they alter what and how children are asked to learn so that maximum achievement is possible.

Maturational Lags

Learning disabilities reflect slow maturation of visual, motor, language, and attention processes that underlie higher cognitive development. Since each learning disabled child has different sets of immaturities, each differs in rate and style of passing through the various stages of development. The maturational lag perspective assumes that these stages of child development follow a patterned, predictable, and orderly sequence.

Because the school curriculum is geared above the readiness levels of children with selective immaturities, these children risk school failure. Pam-

CASE STUDY: Pamela

A girl of seven years and six months in June, Pamela was a first grade failure. The public school first grade teacher indicated that Pamela would have only a social promotion to second grade as she has not completed the work satisfactorily.

. . . Pamela's behavior level is, at best, close to a six-and-a-half-year-old level but it is not up to seven, which is needed for success in second grade. It is unfortunate that at the beginning of first grade when her maturity, perceptual and learning problems were evident almost at once to the teacher, she wasn't placed in a reading readiness class.

At present, with her immaturity and fuzziness of behavior, her piecemeal way of thinking, her need of help in pulling things together and in thinking in an organized fashion, she is not ready for second grade work. She could manage a $6\frac{1}{2}$ year old type of learning experience but since that is not available, she will have to repeat first grade.

. . . Repeating first grade should help to synchronize her learning ability and the demands of the learning situation.

. . . A slower course in school should improve her academic performance (Ames, 1968, pp. 52–53).

ela's story, above, demonstrates the maturational lag theorist's tendency to favor retention, rather than push a child who is unready to profit from a given curriculum into faulty learning. Some children with maturational lags might remain in their grade but have tasks geared only toward objectives they are absolutely ready to handle. When programming is appropriate, minor lags may resolve themselves over time. When a child is "pushed into error by a hasty environment," these delays are aggravated, errors become habit, and serious learning disorders are more likely (Ames, 1968, p. 39).

The maturational lag perspective sees lags as delays in normal sequences of development. Maturational lag theorists advocate careful matching of curriculum and grade placement to a child's readiness level.

Lags in Normal Developmental Sequences. Uneven patterns of development are common to learning disabled children. It is said that "these children's mental maturation proceeds by fits and starts" (Kinsbourne & Caplan, 1979). Andrew, for example, is a bright third grader with superb drawing and mathematics skills. But his oral reading and ability to follow teachers' instructions are more like that of a first grader. Sally, Andrew's classmate, is an excellent reader, listener, and storyteller. But when asked to translate her thoughts into a written composition she barely manages to scribble three short sentences, the words are almost illegible, and the sentences make little sense. Andrew and Sally each have some skills developing at normal rates and others that represent developmental delays.

Delays such as Andrew's and Sally's are attributed to a *time lag* in the neurodevelopmental maturation rate of specific portions of their brains. This slow maturation may be caused by such factors as genetic predisposition, brain injury, neurochemical imbalances, or structural brain differences. Maturational lag theorists are not overly concerned with the cause of these delays because the treatment is the same, appropriate teaching.

Maturational lag theorists consider nothing about Andrew and Sally's learning patterns unknown in normal child development. Their slower developing skills are understood as being very much like those of younger typical children (Abrams, 1968). Andrew's following directions and reading skills, and Sally's writing skills, are qualitatively like those of entering first graders. They are quantitatively different from their normal peers, but not aberrant. Because they emphasize the normal sequence of child development, maturational lag theorists are often called *developmentalists*.

Maturational lag theorists acknowledge that some learning disabled children learn and behave differently from what is considered normal at any developmental stage. For example, Jonah's level of inattention and hyperactivity in the classroom may be atypical for even a one and a half year old. Even a one and a half year old will walk around chairs rather than try to walk through them. The one and a half year old will dump a pile of paper on the floor, be delighted with the fall, sit down, and joyfully crumple them piece by piece. But Jonah is unaware that he knocked the papers over, and only briefly glances at the papers while he steps on them on his way to the hamster's cage. Although such extremes are not known at any stage of growing up, maturational lag theorists claim that these too can best be understood as lying at the very ends of the continuum of normal child development (Kinsbourne & Caplan, 1979).

Maturational Lag Patterns. In learning disabled children, many selective immaturities, rather than one, commonly occur simultaneously. Each neurodevelopmental immaturity may become apparent at a different time (Kinsbourne, 1973b; Zangwill, 1960). That is, a child can be handicapped in different ways at different ages, as both the cognitive demands of tasks and the child's strengths and weaknesses change (Denckla & Heilman, 1979). For example Sally, the third grade poor writer, probably went relatively unnoticed until the curriculum demanded she write compositions. Only then did it become apparent that her clumsy printing infringed on expression of thoughts in writing. Andrew was slow to talk, but by school entrance spoke well. He was the kindergarten teacher's dream child because he excelled at eye-hand coordination exercises. But when reading was introduced in the first grade, it again taxed his ability to deal with language symbols. Finally he learned to read well, but in ninth grade he was introduced to French, another language symbol system, and again encountered difficulties.

Some initial lags in neural maturation catch up over time. Others do not. Immaturities that catch up are skills in which all children reach a high level of sophistication at relatively young ages. Denckla (1979) comments that these early maturing skills need only reach a "good-enough floor" in order to no longer interfere with academic progress (p. 560). One example is left–right letter reversals. These reversals only differentiate good from poor readers until age seven. By age nine the reversal tendency is gone in most children and no longer interferes with learning. Other skills that ceiling rather early (by age twelve or thirteen) are copying, sequencing, and remembering dictated digits. When the child's deficits are only in early critical skills, the prognosis for later, high-level learning is excellent. The student may stumble through the first few years of school, but, once the developmental interferences resolve themselves, the child can "lag and then leap" (p. 561).

Catch–up does not occur on more complex, late-emerging skills that have higher "good-enough" thresholds (Rourke, 1976). An example of one of these high-threshold skills is the child's ability to retrieve names rapidly from memory. What makes for success in naming also makes for successful high-level learning strategies. That is, most people memorize visual material by naming it and then rehearsing silently. When children can't rapidly name what they see momentarily (flashed words, multiplication facts, words in sentences), their ability to organize, store, rehearse, and retrieve this information is severely depressed. Naming is one of those slow-maturing skills in which lags are even evident at an adult level. It is akin to "blocking" on our best friends' names. Lags in late-maturing skills are associated with ongoing academic problems when school tasks are not adjusted accordingly. Kinsbourne (1973b) emphasizes that "there is no known way of hurrying the brain maturation on its way" (p. 273). But teaching resources can help a child circumvent these weaknesses.

Bone growth and weight gain relative to what would be expected for age or family background also frequently lag in children with learning disabilities (Dolan & Matheny, 1978; Gold, 1978; Oettinger, Majovski, Limbeck, & Gauch, 1974). Developmental immaturities are far more prevalent among boys than girls. Boys' development tends to be approximately six months behind girls at the time of school entry (Ilg & Ames, 1964). Boys' language and reading patterns do not reach maturity until the end of elementary school. Girls mature two years earlier (Bakker, Teunissen & Bosch, 1976, in Knights & Bakker, 1976; Byrden, 1970). Boys' social behavior also matures later than that of girls (Rubin & Balow, 1971). These observations are not new at all. Even those who wrote the Bible proclaimed a girl to be a mature woman at twelve years and one day, but a boy did not make it to manhood until age thirteen.

Matching Tasks to Readiness Levels. Maturational lag theorists stress that academic tasks should be geared to what children are ready to master, and not to their age and grade expectancies. When children are taught what they are ready to learn, it is believed that the need for very special teaching techniques is reduced (Kinsbourne & Caplan, 1979). Slowing the rate of instruction and grade retention help to achieve this match between readiness and school expectations.

Slowing the Rate of Instruction. Developmentalists caution against teaching too much too soon because transitory immaturities may then become permanent deficits. If Allison is forced to read before she is ready, she will make errors, learn bad habits, hate reading, avoid practicing, and take up much teacher time later on undoing the faulty learning. Since children who learn to read at ages four or six and a half will end up at the same reading level by the upper elementary grades, developmentalists urge delaying reading instruction until children are ready and learn faster.

Despite their readiness emphasis, developmentalists do not take a wait-and-see attitude. They urge remedial training with materials geared to the student's level of readiness. At times this demands very unique, intense, teaching methods that differ from the typical teaching approaches used with younger children.

The medical profession often has been criticized for adopting a wait-and-see perspective. Pediatricians, questioned by worried parents about their child's delayed walking and talking, restlessness, or hatred of school, too often reply "don't worry, he (or she) will outgrow it." Quite the opposite is true. Each child has a lot to grow into: "our society is a pressure cooker and doesn't allow a child to outgrow it" (Richardson, 1979).

Katrina deHirsch (1963) offers one of the best statements of the developmental perspective on instruction:

> We know from animal experiments that the nonuse of a function leads to atrophy. Thus, the emphasis on maturation should not be understood to mean that one should sit back and let development do the rest. The clinician's and educator's task is to study carefully the maturational level of the different modalities in each child who has difficulties. Thus, in the framework of a warm and supportive relationship, the teacher can help the child perform at the highest level of his potential (p. 69).

Retention. Ames (1977) blames our schools' tendency to fix a definite curriculum, and then automatically promote children from year to year, for aggravating learning disorders. She notes findings showing that children who were ready in the fall for the school's curriculum of kindergarten remained among the top students from grade to grade. Children who were questionably ready were only average learners six years later. Those who were unready were at the bottom of the class or had been dropped to a lower grade (Ames, 1968; Ilg & Ames, 1964). These findings have been replicated by other investigators (Derienzo, 1981; Book, 1980; Glazzard, 1982). Ames feels that if the unready and questionable children had not been promoted for one year, school tasks would have better matched their readiness levels. Perhaps then they would have ended up as adequate achievers.

Ames (1968) claims that over 50 percent of children entering kindergarten are unready for the curriculum. She suggests that they begin school when their behavior ages rather than chronological ages indicate that they are ready. In general, girls should have reached age six and boys six and a half by September of first grade (Ilg, Ames, & Apell, 1965). Boys who are young for their grade are at high risk for referral for psychological evaluations (DiPasquale, Moule, & Flewelling, 1980) and for school failure (Donofrio, 1977). Once school failure sets in, retention is necessary because schools don't give children time to catch up.

Kinsbourne and Caplan's (1979) diagram (Figure 4-1) traces the multiple problems that can follow aggravation of a simple lag. The failure of a child who is overplaced in school may affect whole groups of people that interact with the child. The child feels different, pressured to succeed, resented, adjusts with difficulty to social and vocational demands, and experiences daily failure.

When the child is not promoted, he or she still experiences the failure of retention. However, this is followed by frequent daily successes because the curriculum has been geared toward a lower level. Some schools deal with this issue by adopting Individually Guided Education or Continuous Progress Plans that eliminate the need for retention yet allow the student to progress at his or her own rate.

Cognitive Styles

Cognitive style theorists stress that school tasks can contribute to learning disabilities by making demands on children's problem-solving strategies that they are not prepared to meet. Every child's temperament reflects a preferred way of looking at and interacting with the world. At times this manner of perceiving, remembering, and problem-solving helps, and at other times it hinders success in specific types of tasks. This trait is called a *cognitive* or *conceptual* style (Keogh, 1977b; Kinsbourne & Caplan, 1979). Cognitive styles are relatively stable temperaments (Keogh, 1973; Witkin, Goodenough, & Karp, 1967) caused by such factors as personality disposition (Kagan & Kogan, 1970), brain injury (Kinsbourne & Caplan, 1979), and heredity (Morrison & Stewart, 1974).

Table 4-1 lists the very different behaviors to which writers have applied the terms *cognitive* or *conceptual* style. It illustrates why these terms lack precise meaning unless the writer clarifies exactly whose style is being referred to.

Recall Jonah, our hyperactive first grader. His teacher asks him to choose an educational game to play with quietly while she works with a small reading group. He flits from game to game, choosing one and then another. Each is discarded in favor of another that catches his attention. In the end, his activity level becomes a disturbance to others and he learns little from any one game. Julie, his classmate, is much more reflective. Given the same directions, she

Figure 4-1 The cycle of failure following selective unreadiness for first-grade entry

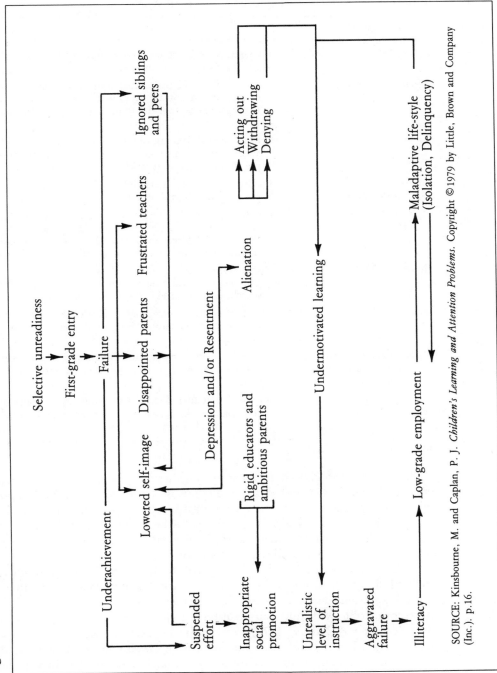

SOURCE: Kinsbourne, M. and Caplan, P. J. *Children's Learning and Attention Problems*. Copyright ©1979 by Little, Brown and Company (Inc.). p.16.

Table 4-1   Definitions of cognitive or conceptual style

SOURCE	DEFINITION
Bolles (1937)	Concrete versus abstract (continuum of preference for concrete or abstract attitudes of problem-solving)
Broverman (1960)	Conceptual versus perceptual-motor dominance (preference to concentrate on novel, difficult tasks through conceptual thinking or perceptual-motor behaviors)
	Strong versus weak automatization (strong or weak automatic response habits have been built on simple, highly practiced tasks)
Bruner, Goodnow, and Austin (1956)	Focusers versus scanners (low or high extent of sampling materials and ideas)
Gardner, Jackson, and Messick (1960)	Leveling versus sharpening (consistent individual tendency to memorize all incoming information as unconnected pieces or to sharpen memory by associating new with old information)
Guilford (1959)	Convergent versus divergent thinkers (answers are generated by allowing the information to lead or by searching in a variety of directions)
Hunt (1974)	Low versus high conceptual level (the ability to generate concepts determines how teacher-directed instruction must be)
Kagan, Rosman, Day, Albert, and Phillips (1964)	Analytic versus nonanalytic (tendency to analyze or not analyze visual arrays into their component parts)
	Impulsive versus reflective (the tendency to come to decisions quickly or slowly, not reflecting or reflecting on alternative solutions)

chooses a game and plays it over and over again while she masters all its details and double checks her performance. Time is up before she even thinks about trying another game. When the teacher asks Jonah and Julie to tell the reading group what games are available, Jonah has the answer because he's tried them all. But if the teacher asks that a game be demonstrated, only Julie is able to, because she has mastered all the details of one game.

Which child is the better learner, Jonah or Julie? In general, our society prefers Julie's style to Jonah's. Julie is more task-oriented, takes more time to arrive at solutions, and likes to analyze and memorize details. School tasks are more compatible with Julie's disposition than Jonah's (Ramirez & Castaneda, 1974; Zelniker & Jeffrey, 1976). Yet, cognitive style theorists would stress that each child learns and performs some things well and others poorly, depending on whether learning tasks are well-matched or mismatched to their

Table 4-1 continued

SOURCE	DEFINITION
Kagan, Moss, and Sigel (1963)	Analytic-descriptive (tendency to conceptualize by describing similarities in objective elements of stimuli)
	Inferential-categorical (tendency to categorize by inferring similarities based on partial objective attributes)
	Relational (categorizing on the basis of functional relationships among stimuli)
Kinsbourne and Caplan (1979)	Active versus inactive
	Sociable versus unsociable
	Placid versus emotional
	Impulsive versus compulsive (tendency to underfocus and make decisions too soon, or to overfocus, and take excessively long to make decisions)
Rotter (1966)	Internal versus external control (performance differences related to whether an individual feels that personal skill, or chance outside factors, are responsible for outcome)
Werner (1948)	Developmental levels of cognition through which one progresses
Witkin, Dyk, Faterson, Goodenough, and Karp (1962)	Field independence versus dependence (continuum of ability to apply selective attention so as to differentiate parts of complex stimulus fields versus responding to the field as a whole)

individual cognitive styles. Jonah's style does have some important virtues. For example, if the teacher asks both children to run into the classroom to find her pen, Jonah would probably find it first because his attention is all over the place at one time. Julie is more likely to systematically search one part of the room and then another until she finds the pen. Julie's style takes too long.

Cognitive style theorists presume that many learning disabled children's basic learning abilities are intact. However their styles are inappropriate to classroom demands, and interfere with efficient learning. Cognitive style theorists see the learning disabled as different from (not less able than) others in their styles of attending to information, organizing it, and rehearsing it for memory. These students, they argue, learn well when task demands suit their preferred styles, when they are taught better learning strategies, or when, through maturation, they develop more appropriate strategies (Torgesen, 1980).

Cognitive style theorists' instructional objectives stress the careful match between task and learner, and the teaching of compensatory learning strate-

CASE STUDY:
Jennifer and Sandy

Jennifer's teachers say that she is overly impulsive. When she must concentrate on a social studies paragraph, her attention is extremely underfocused. Her efforts to pay attention and the length of time that she concentrates are immature. She doesn't maintain attention long enough to get through the passage and therefore doesn't learn the material. Her attention is continually caught by other events. This distractibility makes her restless. She is very capable of learning, if only she wouldn't leave tasks before she grasps the concepts. Her answers are often wrong because she makes decisions too soon, before obtaining and reviewing enough information. Jennifer frequently stops listening to the teacher before all directions are given, answers before hearing or reading all the questions, is hard to discipline because she considers neither what the adults expect from her nor alternative behaviors, and has social difficulties because she doesn't ponder how to make friends.

Sandy is also having learning difficulties, but for quite different reasons. She is overly compulsive, concentrating so long on one bit of information that she never learns enough about the overall subject. Sandy's attention is overfocused. She is extremely slow in shifting her attention from one thing to another. Contrary to Jennifer's style on a multiple choice test, Sandy will go over and over a problem. She eventually does poorly on the test because she does not complete all the items and keeps switching answers. When disciplined, she is oversensitive to what is said and done, and she withdraws. Sandy's teachers say that she is overly reflective.

gies. They try to prevent the child's cognitive style from reducing the amount of information learned, which would create a cumulative information deficit, a potential learning disability (Keogh, 1973). The most commonly discussed styles relative to learning disabilities are impulsivity–reflectivity, directed versus nondirected instructional needs, and those falling within the broad category of learner strategies.

Impulsivity–Reflectivity. In the case study of Jennifer and Sandy, above, Jennifer has an impulsive cognitive style while Sandy is reflective. Jennifer makes others more aware of her learning problems because she creates the greater disturbance and more frequently fails. Impulsive characteristics like Jennifer's quite often differentiate the learning disabled from typical learners (Messer, 1976; Whalen & Henker, 1976).

Jennifer and Sandy's cognitive styles vary along a continuum of underfocused attention — premature decision maker — to overfocused attention — postmature decision maker (Kinsbourne & Caplan, 1979). Jerome Kagan and his colleagues (1964) led the theorizing about these impulsive and reflective styles with their use of the Matching Familiar Figures Test (MFFT). Some of the MFFT items are reproduced in Figure 4-2. On the MFFT, children had to find which one of the lower six figures matched the standard. Children who were fast and inaccurate were considered impulsive. Those who were slow and

Figure 4–2 Kagan's Matching Familiar Figures Test items

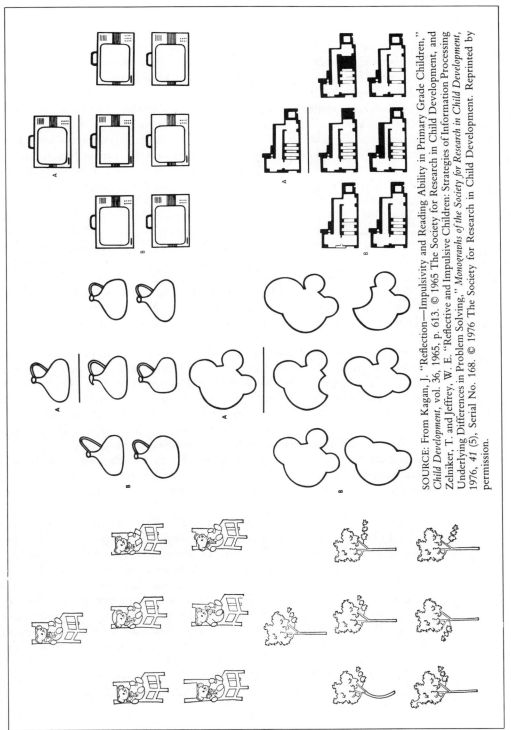

SOURCE: From Kagan, J. "Reflection—Impulsivity and Reading Ability in Primary Grade Children," *Child Development*, vol. 36, 1965, p. 613. © 1965 The Society for Research in Child Development, and Zelniker, T. and Jeffrey, W. E. "Reflective and Impulsive Children: Strategies of Information Processing Underlying Differences in Problem Solving," *Monographs of the Society for Research in Child Development*, 1976, *41* (5), Serial No. 168. © 1976 The Society for Research in Child Development. Reprinted by permission.

accurate were considered reflective. The time children took to consider alternative solutions when uncertain was called *conceptual tempo*.

Kagan hypothesized that the reflective children are anxious over getting correct answers (Kagan & Kogan, 1970). Consequently, when unsure of answers, or when dealing with intellectually demanding questions, they take longer to consider alternative solutions. The result is greater accuracy. On the other hand, the impulsive individual answers rapidly, caring less about mistakes. If the impulsive child brought the proper motivation to tasks, and scanned slower, Kagan felt that the child would be just as accurate as the reflective child.

But Block, Block, & Harrington (1974) pointed out a problem with Kagan's explanations of his children's response styles. Many children had been fast yet accurate or slow yet inaccurate. Therefore, other reasons than anxiety, motivation, and associated response speeds were needed to explain impulsive children's errors and reflective children's accuracy.

Zelniker and Jeffrey (1976) proposed that impulsive and reflective children differed in their basic information processing approaches. Reflective children preferred to scan details, taking a long time to respond. Impulsive children preferred to scan the whole, which necessitates a shorter response time. In a very important series of studies, Zelniker and Jeffrey (1976) provided evidence that the search strategies of impulsives and reflectives differ, just as they had predicted. Their studies are summarized in Research Box 4-1. They found that reflective children are superior to impulsives only when analyzing details. On items requiring more global analysis, such as dealing with outlines and themes, impulsives are equal or superior to reflectives. Further support for the differences lying in search strategies, rather than time taken to respond, comes from studies that reduced impulsive children's errors by teaching them how to search material for details. Forcing them to go slower did not help (Egeland, 1974; Heider, 1971; Meichenbaum & Goodman, 1971; Orbach, 1977; Ridberg, Parke, & Hetherington, 1971).

Impulsive and reflective children's different preferences for scanning wholes or details may be one factor accounting for their task speeds. Both styles have advantages and disadvantages, depending on which type of information the student is asked to learn. School tasks most often match the reflective child's style because they demand details, and directions urge students to take their time. Impulsive children are at a clear disadvantage. On the other hand, impulsive children are at an advantage when it comes to quickly overviewing situations, being sensitive to social cues, and solving problems that don't contain the answers (Keogh, 1973). They are more open to incidental learning (Fitzgibbons, Goldberger, & Eagle, 1965) and to an array of information (Silverman, 1967). They can also better recognize simple patterns that are rapidly exposed (Kaswan, Haralson, & Cline, 1965; Messick & Damarin, 1964).

RESEARCH BOX 4-1
Zelniker and Jeffrey's Study of Impulsive and Reflective Search Strategies

Zelniker and Jeffrey (1974) conducted four studies to test their hypothesis that impulsives and reflectives differed in the way in which they searched information.

In the first study they analyzed MFFT items by whether the correct answers required attention to global (the contour, overview) or detail features. Findings indicated that reflectives were consistently superior to impulsives on items requiring attention to detail. Although both groups performed equally well on global items, the impulsive children arrived at the solution faster.

In the second study, Zelniker and Jeffrey found that impulsive children gave more nonanalytic (looking at wholes) than analytic (looking at details) responses on the Conceptual Style Test. Reflectives showed the oppo-site pattern. This test requires the child to describe similarities between line drawings. The children are specifically told to be analytic and nonanalytic in responding. Interestingly, impulsives made more errors when told to be analytic than nonanalytic. Reflectives made more errors when told to be nonanalytic.

Children in the third study listened to sentences or looked at pictures. Impulsive children recalled themes rather than details. Reflectives recalled details rather than themes.

The fourth study used Bruner's Concept-Attainment Task which required descriptions of stimulus similarities by shape, color, and size. The impulsives named more dimensions than did the reflective children, who preferred to scan parts.

Zelniker and Jeffrey's findings suggest that impulsive and reflective children differ in information processing strategies. These strategies may influence their short and long response speeds, rather than speed itself being responsible for good or poor performance.

Directed Versus Nondirected Learners. David Hunt (1974) described a child's *conceptual level* (CL) on a continuum of ability to handle easy-to-complex information-processing under high-to-low task structure. Low CL students are categorical thinkers, dependent on rules, and less capable of generating their own concepts and considering alternatives. They have difficulty directing their own learning. High CL students, on the other hand, can generate their own concepts, provide their own rules, consider different views, and have more alternatives available for problem solving. They are more inquiring, self-assertive, and capable of independently handling complex conceptual material.

Hunt identified low and high CL students based on open-ended questions that indicated the amount of control they require from others in various circumstances. Hunt and his colleagues found that low CL students learned better by a lecture than by a discovery method (McLachlan & Hunt, 1973) and when a rule was presented before, rather than after, an example (Tomlinson & Hunt, 1971). High CL students learned equally well under all these conditions, but preferred rules after an example. They also preferred discovery methods that gave them more autonomy in learning (Hunt et al., 1974).

Maier (1980), too, found that good learners preferred to be asked questions after they had heard a folk tale because they liked to organize the information in their own way. Poor learners, however, could retell the tale only if the questions were asked before they heard the information, so that they knew what to listen for.

Schools commonly encourage children to discover relationships for themselves. Children often are asked "how do you think we could solve this problem," "what's your opinion," and "why did that happen." Less often are they directly told the key concepts or given choices to think about. There is evidence that direct teaching of the pertinent facts and concepts, and teacher guidance through rules may be just what the problem learner needs to promote greater integration and generalization of information, and an ordered approach to learning (Hunt et al., 1974; Scott & Sigel, 1965, in Coop & Sigel, 1971). Such directed instruction decreases the child's confusion and actually increases his or her conceptual flexibility. Our teaching approaches must match the child's preferred style of instruction.

Learner Strategies. Many learning disabled children are inefficient, inactive, and disorganized learners (Torgesen, 1977a, 1980). They are not aware of their own cognitive processes on a task, nor of the task demands (Flavell, 1971; Gibson, 1973, in Torgesen, 1977a). They often have little awareness that they are to put energy into learning, so their efforts are not sustained and organized (Norman, 1969). They seem unaware that memory is possible and desirable (Hagen, 1971). Left to their own styles, LD children are more dependent in intellectual activities, less hard-working, more impulsive, and less capable of understanding directions than are nonhandicapped learners (Stevenson, Friedricks, & Simpson, 1970). They do not know what kinds of strategies might help them learn.

In many cases learning disabled students do not have deficits in their actual ability to learn. It is their learning strategies that prevent them from using their basic abilities to their best advantage. They seem to have *performance deficits* rather than *ability deficits* (Brown, 1975; Gibson & Levin, 1975).

When these children are taught appropriate strategies or when teaching methods circumvent their inefficiencies, their learning either improves significantly or is no longer different from that of other children. For example, Torgesen (1977b) asked good and poor readers to push one button for each of seven pictures, with the goal of remembering them in order. Not only did the poor readers demonstrate worse recall than the good readers, but they also had little insight into a strategy to use for learning. Some didn't rehearse at all, others pushed the buttons in reverse order, and others rehearsed in random order. The good readers, on the other hand, systematically named the pictures and rehearsed in sequence from left to right. Interestingly, when Torgesen pushed the buttons in sequence for the poor readers, their recall was equal to that of good readers.

Torgesen (1977c) next required that twenty-four cards belonging in four categories be memorized. Good readers were initially superior to poor readers. They more often named the cards and grouped them into categories, spent more time moving the cards, and had less off-task behavior than did the poor readers. But when the poor readers were trained to look for categories and use mnemonic devices, their off-task behavior dropped and their memory was no longer different from that of the good readers. Poor readers also learned well when they were instructed to name the cards and actively sort them into categories (Torgesen, Murphy, & Ivey, 1979).

Since many learning disabled children may underachieve because their learning strategies are inappropriate, inactive, and inefficient, many investigators have attempted *cognitive training* methods (Abikoff, 1979; Meichenbaum, 1976, 1977). These methods teach children to stop and think before responding, to verbalize and rehearse what they have seen, to monitor their own inappropriate behaviors, to visually imagine what they must remember, to preplan task approaches, and to organize their time. The success of these approaches has led to more altering of task attributes so as to elicit more efficient learning. When tasks are matched to how a student learns best, what seemed to be basic ability deficits often disappear.

Setting-Based Theories

Many environmental factors create learning disorders in perfectly normal, healthy children, or aggravate weaknesses that already exist. One of the clearest ways society creates disabilities is through its value system's rejection of certain behaviors as deviant (Blatt, 1970; Szasz, 1967). Homosexuality, for example, used to be listed by the American Psychological Association (APA) as a disease needing treatment. Yet societal attitudes changed, and, a few years ago, the APA voted that homosexuality was no longer a psychological disorder. Society for a long time stamped marijuana users criminals. Today marijuana use is being decriminalized.

The learning disabled are our most recent educationally handicapped because they fail to meet society's standards for academic success. Many learning disabled individuals could acquire knowledge well, were it not for the fact that reading usually is the required vehicle for this learning. Often other strengths in the individual are overlooked and not developed as we endlessly pursue progress in reading. Society places such importance on reading as a tool for acquiring knowledge that this value structure forces an otherwise knowledgeable and well-adjusted individual to be considered handicapped. This is highlighted in the case study on page 138.

CASE STUDY:
The Unlettered

"Although sharp at all other things," the boy could not read. He was thirteen years old: at thirteen years a boy's reading lessons should be over and done. Yet he could not read: or, if he might read at all, it was only such words as "cat" and "rat."

Therefore he died, which seems heavy punishment for being dull at his reading. The tramway which runs on Southend Pier is an electric tramway. It is fenced about with railings. What are railings that they should keep a boy from climbing over them? But, besides the railings, there were placards warning all who should approach of the dangers of the live rail.

If the boy could have read the placards he would not have climbed the railing. But the placards told him nothing, he being able to spell out only the simplest of words. So he climbed and took his death from the current.

The world is like that, a perilous world for those who cannot learn to read. It must be so. We cannot fence every peril so that the unlettered may take no harm from it. There is free and compulsory education: at least everybody has his chance of learning his lessons in school. The world's business is ordered on the understanding that everybody can at least spell out words.

We walk in obedience to the written word. All about us are boards and placards, telling us to do this thing or to keep from doing that other thing. Keep to the Right, we are bidden, or else we are to Keep to the Left. By this stairway we are to descend to enter the train that goes Westward; by that we go to the Eastward train. Way Out and Way In; Private; Trespassers will be Prosecuted; Pit Entrance; the street's name and the name of the railway station — all of these things are cried out to us by that wonderful device of letters, a babble of voices which make no sound.

It is hard for us to understand the case of those to whom these many signs and warnings say nothing. They must move as though bewildered, as though they were blind and deaf. No warning touches them, not even that of the board which, like the board of the Southend tramway, cries Danger and Beware.

For such as he is, the days of school-time must be long days and weary days. I will not say that all the time is mis-spent: life nowadays is safer for the boy who can read the warning board, although painfully. But the case of the boy who could read only "cat" and "rat," although he was "sharp at other things," should have its lesson for those who are taken by the strong delusion that we may see a world of book-learned men and women if we will spend the money handsomely. For it is not so: there will always be those who cannot get beyond "cat" and "rat," even some who cannot get so far. (Critchley, 1970, pp. xiii–xv)

Who is devalued as handicapped varies from one culture to another. A striking example of this occurred while recently travelling through the Sinai desert. When we stopped for lunch, a little Bedouin boy galloped over to us on his camel. He could neither speak nor hear. He used hand and tongue movements to indicate that he'd like our food scraps to feed to the camels. We gave them to him, and he galloped away. By the pats he received on his head, it was clear that the elder Bedouins were pleased with the job he had done. The

Bedouins found a task at which this child could succeed. He was an important link in their life line. I wondered whether this child was considered handicapped in his society, and whether he could have become equally valued in our society. I also wondered whether he would have been able to speak and hear had he been born in Western society.

Some of the ways — in addition to our Western system — in which the environment creates learning disorders or reduces a child's ability to learn to full potential are insufficient nutrition and stimulation, sociocultural differences, emotional climate, environmental toxins, and poor teaching.

Insufficient Nutrition and Stimulation

School breakfast and hot lunch programs demonstrate educators' concern over nutrition's effect on learning. Certainly, a hungry child is not likely to be very motivated in school tasks. The same is true for children in poor physical health (for example, allergies, chronic colds; Cook, 1974).

Nutritional deficiencies negatively affect the maturation of the brain and central nervous system (Birch & Gussow, 1970; Winick, Meyer & Harris, 1975). Malnutrition affects brain weight (Chase, 1973) and has lasting effects on learning and behavior (Cravioto & DeLicardie, 1975; Pasamanick & Knobloch, 1966). It is particularly damaging during the first six months of life because this is when maximal brain cell development occurs. Cravioto (1972) demonstrated this by testing Mexican children who had been admitted to a hospital for malnutrition, prior to age two and a half, and the sibling closest in age to them. IQ and performance on learning tasks were significantly lower for the previously malnourished children than for their siblings.

Early sensory deprivation also adversely affects brain maturation and learning (Dennis, 1960; Spitz, 1945). Research Box 4-2 reviews how reduced learning opportunities affect animal brain tissue and subsequent learning. It is generally assumed that the same is true in humans.

Sociocultural Differences

Learning disabilities are more prevalent among lower socioeconomic status individuals, and racial and cultural minorities. Statistics show that 12 percent of seventeen-year-old American students are illiterate. They can handle less than 75 percent of simple reading materials encountered in everyday life (NAEP, 1976; in Lerner, 1981). Forty-four percent are semiliterate, handling less than 90 percent of easy, everyday reading material. Among black students the illiteracy rate rises to 40 percent and semiliteracy to 80 percent. Since these statistics include only those students who have not dropped out of school, illiteracy rates are likely to be even higher when the 20–25 percent of Americans who drop out are also considered.

The shockingly poor achievement of some socioculturally different individuals is due in part to insufficiencies in nutrition and medical care, both of which compromise brain development. Almost all complications of prenatal

RESEARCH BOX 4-2
The Environment's Impact on the Brain

What we learn from our environment is represented neurochemically in our brains. Mark Rosenzweig and David Krech were able to prove Sömmering's (1791) suggestion that thinking induces growth of the brain and Spurzheim's (1815) hypothesis that brain "organs increase by exercise" (in Rosenzweig, 1966). Their subjects were rats who, at twenty-five days of age, were placed in either environmentally rich or impoverished living circumstances. The enriched condition consisted of ten to twelve animals housed in a large cage, a bright room with much other research activity going on, provision of different toys each day (ladders, wheels, boxes, platforms), half-hour group (five or six rats) exploration of a three-by-three-foot field whose pattern of barriers was changed daily, and formal maze training after thirty days in this stimulating environment. The impoverished situation consisted of one rat per cage with no way of seeing or touching another rat, and a quiet and dimly lit room. The animals were from the same litters and were fed similarly. Experimenters who later analyzed the rats' brains were unaware of which brain belonged to which condition.

Data from twelve of these experiments conducted over a five-year period showed that the cortex of 80 percent of the enriched rats weighed 4 percent more than that of the restricted rats (Rosenzweig, 1966). This was due to the development of thicker gray matter in enriched rats' visual centers. Their brains also contained greater numbers of glial cells (which provide structural and nutritional support for the brain's neurons), as well as more of the chemicals used in neural transmission. Control groups indicated that these results could not be accounted for by the differences in locomotion, handling, and isolation alone. Animals reared in complex but dark environments demonstrated shrinkage of the visual centers but growth in touch and body movement areas. Those reared in isolation had decreased brain tissue growth (Krech, Rosenzweig, & Bennett, 1966).

Rosenzweig found that brain weight could be increased even in old rats. Their learning ability also increased. He jokingly commented that, "If these cerebral changes reflect learning and storage of memory, these results may be encouraging to those of us who are gray around the edges." (p. 327).

Many other investigations have supported Rosenzweig and Krech's findings (Altman & Das, 1964; Coleman & Riesen, 1968; Valverde, 1967). For example, Bell's research group (1971) found that mice reared in crowded living conditions had reduced concentrations of brain protein and nucleic acids, and decreased DNA synthesis.

Recently the influence of learning on the human brain's neural transmission has been demonstrated (Bakker, 1980; John et al., 1977; Tzavaras, 1981). This research may help us understand how teaching programs modify children's information-processing on a physiological level.

life, pregnancy, labor and delivery, and postnatal diseases and accidents which are potentially damaging to the infant's brain development are disproportionately high among low income groups (Kavale, 1980a). Furthermore, these individuals do not share the major culture's emphasis on educational achievement and fostering of appropriate learning strategies. This puts them at a disadvantage when they enter school. They also enter with a set of cognitive structures and learning experiences that are mismatched with the content and structure of the middle-class school curriculum (Kagan, 1968). Language differences constitute one of the greatest of these mismatches (Baratz & Shuy, 1969; Bernstein, 1960). The teacher's verbally based content and methods may play an important role in handicapping their learning (Hallahan & Cruickshank, 1973).

Many other correlates of low socioeconomic status are associated with poor school learning: delayed development of language specialization in the brain (Geffner & Hochberg, 1971; Kimura, 1967); greater impulsivity (Schwebel, 1966); lower intelligence on standard intelligence tests which predict success in standard curricula (Mumbauer & Miller, 1970; Skeels & Skodak, 1966); lower parental educational level (Kagan & Moss, 1959; Rees & Palmer, 1970); families with over five children (Reed & Reed, 1965); home climate (toys, books, experiences; parental example & encouragement; emotional atmosphere; child emotional adjustment) (Moore, 1968); lack of variety in sensory stimuli (Uzgairis, 1970); minimal encouragement of scholastic success within the home (Larsen, 1978); and less time on task in the classroom and in homework (Lerner, 1981).

There is substantial evidence that learning experiences actually alter the pattern of electrical activity in the brain. For example, John's research group (1977b) found EEGs to discriminate among socioeconomic groups. Myklebust and Boshes (1969) reported that EEG pattern analyses differentiated Jewish from non-Jewish brain waves. Studies that tested brain waves, taught, and then retested brain waves find changes in brain wave specialization attributable to the teaching strategies used (Bakker, 1980; Ludlam, 1981). Since prior learning is neurochemically represented in the brain, this learning is likely to impact future achievement. Prekindergarten and compensatory education programs attempt to offer socioculturally different children learning experiences that better match the school's cognitive structures, thereby promoting school success.

Adverse Emotional Climate

Learning difficulties in children are associated with atypical emotional climates such as family disorganization (Owen et al., 1971), divorce and emotional instability (Meier, 1971), maternal stress during pregnancy (Sontag, 1941; Stott, 1973; Turner, 1956), parental temperament patterns, and reinforcement of behaviors incompatible with school success (Ross & Ross, 1976). Emotional stresses may cause, intensify, or be a response to learning and behavior disorders (Lassen, Ingvar, & Skinhøj, 1978).

Emotional states can cause neurological diseases (such as tension headaches), intensify a disease process (bring on seizures), or simulate a neurological disorder (hysterical paralysis of limb) (Valenstein & Heilman, 1979). Since any type of stress, pain, or effort activates the brain through increased blood flow (Lassen, Ingvar, & Skinhøj, 1978), emotional behaviors are represented as changes in the brain, just as learning strengths and weaknesses are. If environmental stress can trigger emotional states which then become unique brain states, then these brain states can contribute to learning disabilities.

Environmental Toxins

Behavioral toxicologists warn about the adverse effects of environmental toxins on health and learning. These toxins can cause severe learning disorders before and after birth.

The fetus has neither a placental barrier against toxic substances nor the capacity to detoxify them (Moya & Smith, 1965; Spyker, 1974). Toxins such as thalidomide do not affect the pregnant mother but do affect the developing fetus (Lenz, 1962; Taussig, 1962). Other toxic prenatal effects are not immediately apparent at birth. For example, a high incidence of vaginal cancer has been found among adult daughters of mothers who took DES to prevent miscarriage. These daughters have a 69 percent greater chance of miscarriage or giving premature births than do daughters of mothers who did not take DES during pregnancy (Barnes et al., 1980). Maternal cigarette smoking is associated with hyperactivity in the offspring (Denson, Nanson, & McWatters, 1975) and excessive maternal alcohol consumption is associated with later learning disabilities (Clarren & Smith, 1978). Clearly, many prenatal toxic effects are likely to be associated with later learning disorders.

The possible deleterious effects on learning and behavior of contact with environmental toxins after birth are listed in Table 4-2. Parents bring many of these industrial toxins home on their clothing, bodies, and shoes, contaminating family members (Danziger & Possick, 1973; Wood, Weiss, & Weiss, 1973). As educators we have a responsibility to try to prevent toxins' potential for impairing students' neurological and behavioral development.

Another toxin involves individual sensitivity to certain foods. Mayron (1979) estimates that 60 to 80 percent of individuals are allergic to at least one food. Toxic reactions include hives, headaches, and stomach problems. Wunderlich (1970) and Feingold (1975) proposed that hyperactivity and poor learning also are due to certain foods' toxic effects. Many clinical studies report hyperactive behavior following ingestion of artificial food colors and flavors (Chafee & Settipane, 1967; Feingold, 1976; Green, 1974; Lockey, 1977), salicylates (aspirin-like compounds occurring in natural fruits and vegetables) and aspirin (Douglas, 1975; Samter & Beers, 1968; Settipane & Pudupakkam, 1975), and preservatives (Lockey, 1972; Michaelsson & Juhlin, 1973). Feingold attributes these responses to a toxic effect on the central nervous system rather than to allergies, as do Wunderlich and others (Havard, 1973; Rapp, 1979).

Recent research at the National Institute of Neurological and Communicative Disorders and Stroke (NINCDS) supports Feingold's contention. The NINCDS research group found that some dyes readily enter brain cells and interfere with chemical communications by inhibiting nerve cells' uptake of neurotransmitters. It is hypothesized that, because the particular enzyme that is

Table 4-2 The effects of environmental toxins on learning and behavior

TOXIN	EFFECT	INVESTIGATORS
Lead poisoning through paint and gasoline	Learning impairment due to neurological damage	Walzer & Richmond, 1973
High lead content in the blood or hair	Hyperactivity associated with aggressiveness and restlessness	David, Clark, & Voeller, 1972; Pihl & Parkes, 1977
Elevated dentine lead levels in baby teeth	Disturbance in understanding and using language, attention, classroom behavior, poor persistence on school tasks, distractibility	Needleman, Gunnoe, Leviton, Reed, Peresie, Maher, & Barrett, 1979
Small doses of carbon monoxide	Time discrimination difficulties	Beard & Wertheim, 1967
Flickering fluorescents	Seizures	Millichap, 1977
Carbon disulfide exposure	Neurological and psychological changes	Lilis, 1974
Mercury contamination	Gum disease, tremors, insomnia, irritability, memory defects, and impaired judgement	Wedig, 1974
Air pollution	Reduces the oxygen-carrying capacity of the newborn	Behrman, Fisher, & Paton, 1971
Carbon monoxide exposure of highway toll collectors	Slower motor performance	Johnson, Cohen, Struble, Setzer, Anger, Gutnick, McDonough, & Hauser, 1974
Marijuana	Deters ability to sustain attention	Moskowitz, 1974
Extremely high doses of artificial food colors	Transient deterioration in memorization ability for some individuals	Swanson & Kinsbourne, 1980

affected by the dye is controlled by a child's genetic makeup, some children respond negatively to food dyes and others do not (report in *ACLD Newsbriefs*, No. 142, Jan./Feb., 1982).

Sabo (1976) reports that Americans typically ingest five pounds of food additives per year. Research indicates that a very small subgroup of young, hyperactive children responds to these additives with an increase in hyperactivity.

When placed on Feingold's additive-free diet (see Table 4-3), one-fourth to one-third of hyperactive children participating in well-controlled studies responded with decreased hyperactivity (Mayron, 1979). In these studies children alternated two experimental diets, Feingold's diet and one disguised as

Table 4–3 Feingold's diet

The following foods should be eliminated:

I. *Foods*
Almonds
Apples
Apricots
Blackberries
Cherries
Currants
Gooseberries
Grapes or raisins
Nectarines
Oranges
Peaches
Plums or prunes
Raspberries
Strawberries
Cucumbers and pickles
Tomatoes

II. *Flavorings (Omit artificially flavored foods and drinks)*
Ice cream
Oleomargarine

Gin and all distilled beverages (except vodka)
Cake mixes
Bakery goods (except plain bread)
Jello®
Candies
Gum
Cloves
Oil of wintergreen
Toothpaste and toothpowder
Mint flavors
Lozenges
Mouthwash
Jam or jelly
Lunch meats (salami, bologna, *etc.*)
Frankfurters (Hot Dogs)

III. *Beverages*
Cider and cider vinegars
Wine and wine vinegars

Kool Aid® and similar beverages
Soda pop (all soft drinks)
Diet drinks and supplements
Gin and all distilled drinks (except vodka)
All tea
Beer

IV. *Drugs and Miscellaneous*
1. All medicines containing aspirin, such as Bufferin,® Anacin,® Excedrin,® Alka-Seltzer,® Empirin,® Darvon compound,® *etc.*
2. Perfumes
3. Toothpaste and toothpowder
(A mixture of salt and soda can be used as a substitute or Neutragena® soap unscented)

Note: Check all labels of prepared foods or drugs for artificial flavoring and coloring.
SOURCE: Feingold, B. F. *Introduction to Clinical Allergy.* Courtesy of Charles C Thomas, Publisher, Springfield, Illinois.

Feingold's diet but containing additives. Neither children, parents, teachers, nor experimenters knew when a child was on or off Feingold's diet.

Despite the high percentage of improvement on Feingold's diet, there is little consistency within each of these studies. At times teachers noted significant improvement while parents did not (Connors et al., 1976). At other times parents noted significant, positive changes, while teachers noted fewer changes, and neuropsychological tests, objective observers, and laboratory observations indicated none (Harley, Ray, Tomasi, et al., 1978). When children who responded favorably to Feingold's diet continued on the diet but ingested cookies, candy bars, or sodas containing additives, they demonstrated very little of the expected deterioration in behavior. Behavioral deterioration occurred in only one child out of nine (Harley, Matthews, & Eichman, 1978), one child of twenty-two (Weiss et al., 1980), and three children out of fifteen (Goyette, Connors, Petti, & Curtis, 1978). Those who responded to the additives with hyperactivity were generally the youngest among the studies' samples.

Because of these inconsistent findings, some experts suggest that most favorable results on Feingold's diet actually are due to other things: heightened expectations if families guess when their child is on the diet, increased attention to the child, altered family dynamics, or changes in general nutritional status (Stare, Whelan, & Sheridan, 1980). Others argue that positive results would be more frequent if children were removed from all possible contact with additives, in addition to meal time (Mayron, 1979), if behavior ratings occurred frequently enough to reflect small changes in behavior, and if quantities of additives tested were not so far below the typical amount ingested in any one day (Connors, 1980).

Certainly the deleterious effects of additives do not seem to be as widespread as Feingold and his supporters have claimed. Nevertheless, artificial flavors, colors, and preservatives may produce toxic behavioral responses in an extremely small subgroup of young, hyperactive children. In two studies, additives also adversely affected learning and performance. Swanson and Kinsbourne (1980) found that a select group of children, hyperactive stimulant drug-responders, deteriorated in their ability to learn to pair numbers with animal pictures after ingesting dye. The same deterioration did not occur with nonhyperactive children. Similarly Goyette and colleagues (1978) found that, although behavior did not deteriorate for most children, the additives temporarily deterred performance on a visual-motor tracking task that required attention. Clearly the whole matter needs to be much more carefully studied.

In the past decade public awareness of food additives has heightened. More than 100 parent groups have joined with natural food advocates to demand packaged foods labelled "no artificial ingredients." Similarly, the dramatic effects of environmental toxins on the child's development before and after birth have increased public sensitivity to drug abuse, nuclear reactor sites, solid waste disposal, industrial hazards, and environmental pollution.

Poor Teaching

Poor teaching has also been accused of contributing to learning disorders. Poor teaching involves far more than an inappropriate matching of tasks to learner characteristics. It also involves teacher bias, teacher abilities, teacher understanding of individual differences and normal child development, teaching environment, narrow curricula, nonmotivating materials and methods, school grouping practices, and radical, unvalidated changes in instructional methods. Adelman (1971) explains how these factors affect learning:

> . . . the greater the discrepancy between the child's characteristics and the program characteristics, the greater the likelihood of poor school performance.
> . . . there are children whose learning difficulties are due, primarily, to the fact that their classroom programs are not effectively personalized to accommodate individual differences. . . . the greater the teacher's ability in personalizing instruction, the fewer will be the number of children in his

classroom who exhibit learning problems; conversely, the poorer the teacher's ability in personalizing instruction, the greater will be the number of children with learning problems (Adelman, 1971, p. 529).

When instruction is not personalized, some children may be erroneously labelled LD because they have not had appropriate learning opportunities (Larsen, 1978). Since some children do learn rapidly when taught appropriately, their discrepancy between potential and achievement is a pseudodiscrepancy. For other children, poor teaching further aggravates already existing learning problems. Cohen (1971) gives the facetious label *dyspedagogia* to this "dreaded psychoeducational disease" (p. 251).

Lieberman (1980a) points out that "in some school systems 30 to 40 percent of the children are functioning below grade level. This is not an epidemiological survey of handicapping conditions but an indictment of educational practices" (p. 67). Given such staggering figures of underachievement, Bateman (1974) recommended that the term "LD" be replaced by the term "teaching disabilities," so as to focus on the inadequacies of teachers' skills and the teaching environment, not the child's inadequacies. After all, if children are going to change, it is only in interaction with changes in the tasks and settings that impact their learning. Responsibility for child development must rest with the system and not just the child (Throne, 1973). Rubin and Balow (1971) aptly reflect this in their discussion of the strikingly higher incidence of learning disorders in males than in females:

> The findings suggest that schools and teachers are oriented to a narrow band of expected pupil behaviors which are not consonant with typical behavior patterns of young boys; any pupil outside of that narrow range is treated as needing special attention. The definitions of exceptionality used here reflect problems in the interaction of pupils with teachers, curricula, and materials — the total system. Thus the interpretation of these high percentages of handicap should be made against an ecological model. . . . Clearly, the problem is not in the child alone. . . . Clearly, these data suggest a need for diagnostic and remedial procedures directed toward school systems at least equivalent to those directed toward school children (pp. 298–299).

Summary

Learning disabled children enter the classroom with unique patterns of strengths and weaknesses. Some basic abilities relevant to academic achievement are well-developed, while others are immature. They often have fairly stable styles in approaching learning tasks. Whether any of the child's unique ability patterns and learning styles become severe liabilities depends on the nature of the school tasks they are expected to accomplish, and the settings in which they study, live, and play.

Learning success is facilitated when school tasks are well-matched to a child's ability levels and learning style. Maturational lag theorists feel that learning disabled children's selective immaturities make them unready for the work of their grade. Since their delays are qualitatively like that of younger normal children, similar teaching strategies often can be employed for both groups. Teaching beyond these students' capability levels can cause distortions in the normal learning process, leading to more permanent deficits. Cognitive style theorists note that children's stable predispositions toward perceiving and interacting with information are advantageous to learning progress in some circumstances, but detrimental in others. Detail-oriented classroom goals and discovery-oriented teaching methods are mismatched with the cognitive styles and learning strategies that many children bring to school tasks. Such task-based factors may contribute to learning disorders.

Besides appropriately matching the curriculum to the child's characteristics, efficient learning is enhanced when environmental factors that may deter learning are minimized. These include inadequate nutrition and stimulation, sociocultural differences, emotional climate, environmental toxins, and poor teaching.

Much responsibility for learning success falls on modifications educators and parents make in tasks and settings. Consequently, when exploring what contributes to a student's learning problems, we must consider how specific task- and setting-based factors interact with the child's physiological and personality characteristics. When the positive attributes of each are combined, the chances for learning and behavioral progress are maximized.

Suggestions for Further Study

1. If you are interested in the cognitive development of mildly retarded as well as average intelligence children, consult Edward Zigler's (1969) article. Zigler presents the view that children with cognitive delays progress through the same stages as typical children, but at a slower pace and with different upper limits. He contrasts this developmental idea with that of others who feel that delays indicate that these children are different in kind from typical children.

2. An old area of research in adult cognitive styles, but relatively new to children, is *internal-external control* (I-E). I-E is the source to which children attribute responsibility for outcomes. Children who perceive a strong sense of personal responsibility are *internal*. They see themselves as having abilities and will put effort into learning. *External* children place responsibility on other people or systems: fate, teacher affection for them, smudged dittos, bad breakfast prepared by hassled mother, or gray day. Try to interpret the poor achievement of learning disabled children with respect to their being externally controlled. Do they relinquish responsibility for learning and therefore not put initiative and persistent effort into achievement? Excellent basic references to begin with are Phares' (1973) and Weiner's (1974) texts, and Rotter's (1966) and McGhee and Crandall's (1968) articles. Also check Whalen and Henker's (1976) review of stimulant research. They provide interesting dialogues with learning disabled children indicating that the children see the drugs rather than themselves as responsible for their good behavior. This, of course, makes it easy to blame bad behavior on "not taking the pill."

Other topics under which to search for I-E information are "locus of control" and "attribution theory."

3. One cognitive style that children adopt after many failure experiences is *learned helplessness*. They feel that it doesn't even pay to try. They think themselves incapable and even compliments won't help. If you are interested in exploring the implications of such an attitude, you might begin with the following articles: Dweck (1975), Dweck and Reppucci (1973), and Grimes (1981).

4. Reflective-impulsive temperaments are common among adults. Try an experiment on your friends. Choose ten friends whom you regard as overly reflective in their decision making, and ten others whom you regard as highly impulsive. Ask each to solve the problems in Figure 4-2. Time each person's response on each problem and record the scores. Did the slow responders solve the analytic problems (television, step-like design, Teddy Bear) faster than the rapid responders? Were the latter friends more rapid on the global problems (jug, cloud-like design, tree)? Think about your friends' conversations. Do the reflectives' conversations (slow responders) dwell on analyzing details, and the impulsives (fast responders) dwell on overall issues? Do your friends' styles seem related to which courses they excel in (chemistry, art) or their vocational choices? When the reflectives study for exams do they concentrate on details so much that at times they lose the main idea? Do the impulsives ignore the details? Do you find that your friends have stable predispositions toward interacting with learning tasks and people?

5. If you find it interesting that emotional states are represented in different brain states, read the literature that considers emotional disturbance a physiological disorder (Hertzig & Birch, 1968; Wikler, Dixon, & Parker, 1970), personality disorders as caused by temporal lobe asymmetries or epilepsy (Bear & Fedio, 1977; Greene, 1976); schizophrenia as caused by neurological deficits (Goldstein, 1978); depression (Kiev, 1975) and masculinizing of body in females (Ehrhardt & Money, 1967) as caused by hormone imbalances; and autism as a severe receptive language disorder (Denckla, 1977). Since learning disabilities also have physiological origins, could these emotional disturbances be understood as lying on the more extreme end of the learning disabilities continuum?

6. Explore how the science of behavioral toxicology began, and what its methods are. Ekel's (1974) article explains how United States interest in behavioral toxicology began in the late 1950s, after Russia set stringent standards for its industrial air quality. The Soviets use sensory thresholds, EEG orienting responses, and very sensitive conditioned reflex responses to detect toxic effects in their employees. American studies usually use biochemical and behavioral observation methods. They also use ingenious physical and chemical stresses (raise body temperature, inject sodium amytal) to test the brain's reserve powers. The latter often reveal a depleted brain reserve, although the individual doesn't appear behaviorally impaired (Lehrer, 1974). Can you think of ways of testing for the effects of environmental toxins by incorporating both the Soviet and American research designs?

7. For a thorough review of studies evaluating the effects of food additives on learning and behavior, consult Mattes & Gittleman's (1981) paper.

Chapter Five
Information–Processing Modes Underlying Learning Disorders

When a learner-, task-, or setting-based factor contributes to a learning disability, what exactly has happened? What processes important to learning could have been affected? In the short history of the LD field, studies have focused on five different processes that may be affected by learner-, task-, or setting-based contributors to learning disabilities: peripheral-visual functions (seeing), visual-perceptual skills (processing what is seen), motor skills, language skills (auditory perception and verbal expression), and attention.

Peripheral-visual defects do not seem to cause learning disabilities, although they can aggravate existing disorders. Motor difficulties make expression of knowledge difficult, thereby interfering with success. Visual-perceptual processes appear important to reading and math achievement at young ages and, in very subtle ways, are related to some later spelling, writing, and conceptual difficulties. They do not seem essential to a major portion of skills involved in higher-level academic progress. Research finds that language and attention deficits appear to play the greatest role in severe, long-lasting learning problems.

Since these information-processing abilities, combined with cognitive, social, and motivational characteristics, constitute memory, they have an important impact on learning. It should be noted that, because the majority of investigations identify their subjects by reading underachievement, more is known about the relationship of information-processing modes to reading than to performance in other academic areas.

Peripheral-Visual Functions

As Kim and Jackie's case, page 151, illustrates, poor vision and coordination of eye movements do not seem to be the root of most reading disorders.

One of the first papers published on reading problems was written by an opthalmologist named Morgan in 1896. He called his patient's reading difficulty "congenital word-blindness," although his patient's eyesight was good. Like other opthalmologists (Hinshelwood, 1917; Nettleship, 1901; Witty & Kopel, 1936), Morgan felt that the reading disorder was caused by a congenital defect in the brain's ability to register and store visual memories of words. Subsequent physicians, however, jumped to the conclusion that the difficulty was at the peripheral level — with seeing alone. These physicians observed that reading disorders often coexist with such peripheral visual abnormalities as poor eye fusion (bringing the image of each eye together at the same point in space) (Eames, 1934) and poor coordination of the eyes (Betts, 1936; Dearborn, 1933; Eames, 1932). It was even suggested that eye movements compete in people who do not consistently favor one body side over the other; as each eye tries to pull away from the center of the body, visual perception becomes confused and poor reading results.

By the 1930s, orthoptics, the retraining of peripheral-visual weaknesses, had become a popular practice among ophthalmologists who believed in a

CASE STUDY:
Kim and Jackie

Kim was born with a congenital defect of the iris. She is legally blind and must hold paper four inches from her face in order to be able to see print. Jackie was born with a muscle imbalance in her eyes. Since the muscles of one eye don't coordinate movements with the other, she can use only one eye at a time. When Jackie is reading with the teacher, the teacher often can't tell if she's even looking at the page. Her left eye has been doing the reading — all of a sudden it wanders off and the right eye is doing the looking. In spite of their visual difficulties both girls read extremely well. They are well liked by their classmates and are actively involved in all class activities and discussions. Only in art class is their work never chosen for display; nor are they chosen first for any team in gym class.

connection between the actual working of the eye and reading disorders. The practice faded when later studies found an organic cause (brain injury accompanying prematurity, Eames, 1955; seizure disorders, Elterman, et al., 1980) for the coexistence of visual and reading difficulties. When children's learning difficulties could not be traced to organic causes, there were no differences between peripheral-visual functions of good and poor readers (Benton, 1969; Letourneau, Lapierre & Lamont, 1979; Myklebust & Boshes, 1969). In fact, at times, fusion and muscle imbalance difficulties have been reported more often among good than poor readers (Witty & Kopel, 1936), and even people with poor eye movements usually read well (Gruber, 1962).

Farsightedness is the only peripheral visual function that differentiates poor from good readers (Bond & Tinker, 1967). Clearly farsightedness hinders reading because it means that one can't see well at a reading distance. But even farsightedness only aggravates rather than causes reading disorders. Reading primarily depends on the ability to process perceptual and cognitive information beyond the peripheral level of the eye (Lawson, 1968; Park & Linden, 1968). It is for this reason that reading-disordered children also are deficient in learning to read symbol systems that avoid vision, such as Morse Code and Braille (Rudel, Denckla, & Spalten, 1976).

Despite the above evidence, the relationship of eye movements to reading disorders continues to be actively explored. In addition, visual training once again has become popular.

Eye Movements During Reading

Children with reading disorders, but no eye muscle imbalances, sometimes show eye movement irregularities when following a line of print (Abercrombie, Davis, & Shackel, 1963; Mosse & Daniels, 1959; Zangwill & Blakemore, 1972). Instead of progressing smoothly from one fixation (a glance at a word) to another, they need more fixations, pause longer between fixations, and retrace part of the line toward the left. Instead of a large leftward sweep once the line is finished, the sweep resembles a staircase (multiple, small fixations) or moves diagonally in addition to horizontally. If these irregular eye movements had actually caused the reading problems, then they should also be apparent on nonreading tasks such as searching pictures. But they are not (Adler-Grinberg & Stark, 1978). Therefore, the cause of the eye movement difficulty seems to be inherent in the reading task itself.

Some researchers suggest that a comprehension difficulty may be responsible for these children's faulty eye movements (Ciuffreda, Bahill, Kenyon, & Stark, 1976). That is, the poor reader's search for specific information while reading is what causes irregular eye movements (Lefton, Lahey, & Stagg, 1978). When good readers read a foreign language or a difficult chemistry text, their eyes, too, in order to make sense out of the information, retreat to the left, needing multiple fixations.

Visual Training

Since peripheral-visual difficulties may aggravate an already existing reading disorder, optometrists have pursued visual training. They note that some ocular functions become more efficient with practice (Heath, Cook, & O'Dell, 1976), and that correction of these visual inefficiencies can reduce reading fatigue, avoidance, discomfort, loss of energy and motivation, and impediments to comprehension (Flax, 1968). Also provided are exercises to improve the brain's ability to attend to, integrate, and recall visual information. With the exception of using prisms and glasses, the optometrist's exercises closely resemble what the preschool, kindergarten, adaptive physical education, and resource or remedial reading teacher uses to encourage visual-perceptual development.

Despite the popularity of visual training, greater ocular efficiency does not significantly enhance reading acquisition (Benton, 1973). In 1972 the American Academy of Pediatrics, the American Academy of Ophthalmology and Otolaryngology, and the American Association of Ophthalmology issued a joint statement denouncing the visual training practice (reprinted in Flax, 1973). They urged medical specialists to leave remediation of reading difficulties to the educator: "Medical specialists may assist in bringing the child's potential to the best level, but the actual remedial educational procedures remain the responsibility of educators" (pp. 332–333). While correction of peripheral visual problems that create discomfort when reading is appropriate, visual trainers were cautioned that that is where the relationship between the eye and reading ends.

Visual–Perceptual Skills

With growing evidence that peripheral-visual functions aggravate rather than cause learning problems, the major thrust of visual research shifted to the brain's ability to process visual information. Although the term *visual perception* is commonly used to refer to the way in which the brain receives, orga-

CASE STUDY:
Joseph

Despite subtle visual-perceptual difficulties, Joseph has graduated from college and has earned a master's degree in political science. Now, at twenty-three, he is applying to law school.

Joseph's accomplishments have not come easily. They have required determination and hard work. He has had to drop some advanced math and business statistics courses because he cannot envision how two-dimensional circles could become three-dimensional, how planes can intersect, and how graphs are constructed. He cannot perceive where certain numbers should fall along a continuum, as in estimating the height of an average woman or the degree of temperature at which water might feel hot. Since he cannot conjure up mental images, his spelling of phonetically irregular words is poor, and his reading progress has been hampered. Although Joseph is a slow reader, he learned to read at a satisfactory level because he can analyze words into their sounds, and he comprehends language very well.

Joseph generally overanalyzes and must force himself to attend to the overall concepts being conveyed. Typically, he will memorize all the details in an assignment, understand the ideas to which they relate, yet be unable to list the main ideas in an organized fashion. For example, if Joseph is shown two circles (one red, one blue) and two squares (one black, one green), and asked how the two sets differ, he will say the red circle turned into a green square. When asked for the overall principle that distinguishes both sets, Joseph will repeat his analysis of the details. When then given a choice of the right answer — color, size, number, or shape — however, he will immediately say "shape." Typically, again, Joseph may know the answer all along, yet such generalities do not automatically occur to him.

Because he has excellent language abilities, Joseph will probably make it through law school, but he will have to work hard to overcome his preferred detail-bound style. He may need a tutor in each course to guide him to look more at overviews and many "canned briefs" to tell him exactly what is and is not important. He might also dictate his exams, to compensate for his spelling difficulties, and request extra time to fulfill required reading assignments.

nizes, stores, interprets, and transmits information received from the eye, it has no single accepted definition. Hammill's (1972) review of thirty-three definitions of visual perception found that some applied the term only to the process of taking in information, while the majority included the process of making meaning out of what is seen. Visual perception is here understood as encompassing both the processes of taking in and gaining meaning from non-symbolic (size and color) and symbolic (objects, written words) visual stimuli.

Joseph's case study, above, illustrates a few ways in which severe visual-perceptual lags may interfere with performance even into adulthood. Research indicates that visual-perceptual difficulties have the greatest relationship to academic progress in the early school years. For some individuals, however, visual-perceptual interferences with learning persist at mild to moderate levels even at older ages. Their visual processing inefficiencies may relate to visual images that linger too long as perceptual traces. This limits the time

Table 5-1 Visual-perceptual factors differentiating good from poor readers

FINDINGS	INVESTIGATORS
Visual-perceptual functions	
Discriminating visual forms	Benton, 1962; Colarusso, Martin, & Hartung, 1975
Figure-ground perception	Bender, 1938; de Hirsch, 1952; Strauss & Lehtinen, 1947
Spatial orientation	Davol & Hastings, 1967
Spatial disorientation	de Hirsch, 1952
Visual memory	de Hirsch, 1952; Lyle & Goyen, 1968; Samuels & Anderson, 1973; Vande Voort & Senf, 1973
Memory for sequence, form, and directionality	Guthrie & Goldberg, 1972
Directional sense	Benton, 1962; Samuels & Anderson, 1973
Finding embedded figures	Tjossem, Hansen, & Ripley, 1962
Spatial judgment	Brenner, Gillman, Zangwill, & Farrell, 1967; Colarusso, et al., 1975
Ability to reverse figure and ground	Snyder & Freud, 1967
Ability to perceive and integrate wholes	de Hirsch, 1963
Motor-related functions	
Clumsy gait and movements	Brenner, et al., 1967
Labored handwriting (slow, poor execution)	Clements et al., 1971
Confusion in direction of letters during writing	Orton, 1937
Drawing a human figure	Ingram, Mason & Blackburn, 1970
Visual-motor organization (planning space; construction)	de Hirsch, 1963
Poor manual skills and sloppy work	Brenner, et al., 1967
Reversals and rotations of figures when copying from short-term memory	Tjossem, Hansen, & Ripley, 1962
Poor copying of designs	Keogh, 1969; Koppitz, 1970
Primitive movement patterns	de Hirsch, 1952
Balance and reaction time	Skubic & Anderson, 1970
Fine-motor control (copying)	de Hirsch, 1963; Denckla, 1968; Lachmann, 1960
Poor movements in space	de Hirsch, 1963
Subtle fine-motor anomalies (finger movements)	Denckla, 1973
Right-left response immaturity	Belmont & Birch, 1965; Denckla, 1973
Retention of immature reflexes	Bender, 1963
Language-related functions	
Reversal of letter order in reading and writing	Orton, 1937
Reversal of letter name when the reading of letters depends on directional cues (p, q, d, b)	Orton, 1937
Auditory-visual integration	Birch & Belmont, 1964, 1965; Lovell & Gorton, 1968
Visual-auditory integration	Samuels & Anderson, 1973
Visual sequential memory for letters	Amoriell, 1979
Simultaneous visual-auditory recall	Senf & Freundl, 1971

they have to transfer this information to short–term storage. Other individuals continue to have difficulty mastering the visual–perceptual initial phases of reading. As adults they have trouble quickly recognizing words and remembering the spellings of irregular words that need to be revisualized.

Table 5-1 lists some visual–perceptual areas in which students like Joseph perform poorer than more successful learners. Since many of these abilities actually require that language and motor connections be made with the visual inputs, many apparent weaknesses in visual perception actually may be due to poor language, motor, attention, or memory skills. In many cases inefficient use of language to aid memory also impairs children's ability to use visual–perceptual competencies to their best advantage. Therefore, our research cautions against hastily blaming children's visual–perceptual systems for learning difficulties.

Visual Perception and Reading

Studies of performance on psychometric tests and the tachistoscope (an apparatus that briefly exposes visual stimuli) indicate that visual perception correlates highly with reading achievement in kindergarten and first grades. By second or third grades the correlation begins to decline. By third grade, auditory–perceptual abilities become more highly related to reading success than do visual–perceptual skills (Rudnick, Sterritt, & Flax, 1967). In part, the correlation between visual perception and reading declines with age because the test items become too easy. In the few instances where test items have been made more difficult, the measures continue to be sensitive to visual–perceptual weaknesses and to correlate with reading success, even at the sixth grade level (Kahn & Birch, 1968). Nevertheless, these correlations generally remain very low (Kavale, 1982; Keogh & Smith, 1967) because few of the skills required for performance on the perceptual tasks are the same as those involved in reading.

Because higher–level reading relies more on the comprehension of a language system than the visual analysis of the symbols themselves, visual–perceptual weaknesses are unlikely to have a major influence on the most persistent, severe reading disabilities. Nevertheless, a few very subtle visual–processing differences do distinguish some poor from good readers. These weaknesses present continuing, mild to moderate obstacles to learning progress.

Research suggests that a weak visual–perceptual strategy in beginning reading may result in poor recognition of words at a glance and poor memory for phonetically irregular spellings. Slow visual information processing time also results in difficulty remembering what is seen.

Visual to Language Shifts in Reading Acquisition. The right hemisphere of the brain specializes in functions involving perception of visual forms and the overall arrangement of these forms in their allotted space (*visuo-spatial* functions). The left hemisphere usually specializes in language skills and the analysis and sequencing of details. An easy way to remember this difference is to think of the person with right hemisphere strengths as an artist, and the individual with stronger left hemisphere abilities as an English professor. It has been suggested that reading acquisition first relies on the artist's strengths, and later switches to those of the English professor.

With its visuo-spatial strengths, the right hemisphere seems better at processing complex and nonconventional typefaces. But people recall simple and conventional typefaces better with their left hemispheres (Bryden & Allard, 1976). Using this information, Bakker (1979, 1980) proposed that young children find letters and words nonconventional and visually complex. Therefore, they need to use their right hemispheres' visuo-spatial abilities for beginning reading. With practice, these words no longer appear visually complex, making fewer demands upon the right hemisphere. In the meantime, reading has become more linguistically complex and dependent on meaning. Therefore, the left hemisphere's language analysis and sequencing abilities have had to take on a greater role.

As children's reading skills develop, they gradually shift from attending to how words look as whole shapes, to how word parts sound, how they are strung together, and what the words mean. The initial visual reliance on global shapes explains why a child can recognize his or her name at age three, long before he or she can name any of the letters. It also explains why preschoolers recognize the words "McDonald's," "Burger King," and "Coca-Cola." Their reading relies on the shapes of these names and the contexts in which they appear, rather than how their parts sound.

Neuropsychological studies supporting a shift from right to left hemisphere processing preferences in reading acquisition are reviewed in Research Box 5-1. If research continues to support this shift, it will explain why visual-perceptual tests lose their relationship to reading success as a child gets older. It should be noted that, regardless of hemispheric preference, both hemispheres continue to have a dynamic interaction during the reading process.

Right Hemisphere Weaknesses. Some children never develop a strong visual-perceptual strategy in beginning reading (Bakker, 1980; Boder, 1973; Ingram, Mason, & Blackburn, 1970; Myklebust, 1965). They approach reading in an overanalytic, linguistic manner. They have trouble looking at words and immediately sensing, from their configurations alone, what they are. Instead, they sound out words or guess at them from the sentence's grammar or meaning.

These visually weak children do learn sounds of letters and can sound out and spell words that sound as they look (for example, park). Their language skills help them manage higher-level reading, although their ability to recognize words quickly when read or flashed (as in television commercials) remains deficient. They especially continue to have trouble spelling words that cannot be sounded out and can only be remembered by mentally imagining their visual images (for example, precious, knight) (Boder, 1971).

RESEARCH BOX 5-1
Reading Acquisition:
A Shift from Right
to Left Hemisphere
Processing Preferences

Bakker's (1980) hypothesis that reading entails a gradual shift from right to left hemisphere processing preferences is supported by studies reporting:

- □ left visual field (right hemisphere) preferences for complex and nonconventional typefaces but right visual field (left hemisphere) preferences for simple and conventional typefaces (Bryden & Allard, 1976),
- □ better recall of single letters through the left visual field (right hemisphere) by normal first graders, but no longer for third, fifth, or seventh graders (Carmon, Nachshon, & Starinsky, 1976),
- □ clear right visual field superiority for word recognition emerging by grade four and persisting through college age (Miller & Turner, 1973),

- □ right visual field preferences for single letters (Bryden, 1965) or words (MacKavey, Curcio, & Rosen, 1975) in adults,
- □ inferior right visual field performance in fifth grade poor readers when compared with good readers (Kershner, 1977),
- □ grade five reading success being correlated with left ear [right hemisphere] advantage on dichotic listening tasks at kindergarten age, but right ear [left hemisphere] advantage by the end of first grade (Bakker, 1979).

Using dichotic listening tasks, Leong (in Bakker, 1979) provided evidence for Bakker's hypothesis that right hemisphere readers evaluate visual perceptual cues whereas left hemisphere readers evaluate meaning more carefully. The child who was more correct when processing auditory information with the right hemisphere made fewer word recognition errors (because sensitive to the script's perceptual features) than did the child with left hemisphere preferences. However, the latter was the more rapid reader because linguistic comprehension guided the reading (Bakker, 1979).

Visual Information-Processing Time. Some poor readers take so much time to process visual information that they have difficulty remembering what they have seen. To understand exactly what happens, imagine that you see the letter *B* quickly flashed on a television screen. This visual information persists in your mind as an image for at best only one-third of a second. During this period, you code what you have seen and transfer it to short-term storage. The short-term storage can last only one and two-thirds of a second longer. If you haven't figured out some way to remember the image by then (saying the letter's name, conjuring up its image again, thinking of a word that begins with *B*), then you won't remember what you've seen.

It seems that when some poor readers see something, this visual information persists as an image far longer than for good readers (Lovegrove, Billing, & Slaghuis, 1978; O'Neill & Stanley, 1976). This then reduces the one and two-thirds seconds of time left for the information to be coded for memory. Therefore, if more than the first one-third of a second has passed by, some poor readers cannot recognize the letters and forms they have seen as well as can good readers (Morrison, Giordani, & Nagy, 1977). In such cases, when two figures must be looked at in less than two seconds, the visual trace of the first figure will still persist when the second figure is looked at. Since the first image has not yet been transferred to short-term storage, the two figures are not perceived separately; they overlap (Stanley & Hall, 1973). When the second stimulus completely overlaps the one that has persisted too long (the letter *d* over the letter *o*), then the first stimulus (*o*) isn't seen at all.

Imagine the beginning reader who focuses on the first letter in a word, then a second letter, a third letter, and so forth. If visual processing time is slow, all letters but the last may become occluded before each can be adequately coded and stored. In the end, the word can't be read; its first few letters have not been remembered at all.

Visual Perception and Arithmetic

Learning disabled children are often delayed in arithmetic as well as reading skills. Visual-perceptual abilities relate to success in arithmetic, especially at younger ages. As children get older and the math tasks become more difficult, however, verbal abilities become more highly related to arithmetic progress.

Arithmetic achievement has not been studied as extensively as has reading, most likely because society values it less. The few studies that have been conducted indicate that arithmetic success at young ages relates to such abilities as visuo-spatial organization and visual-motor coordination (Rosner, 1973). For example, to count ten blocks, a kindergartener is aided by spacing them in an orderly fashion; if they are scattered all over a table the child is likely to count several twice (Johnson & Myklebust, 1967). The child must also organize visual-motor movements so that only one block is touched and counted at a time, and each is remembered (Kaliski, 1962).

The connection between elementary mathematics and visual perception is also thought to lie in the ability to imagine and mentally manipulate spatial relationships (Michael, Guilford, Fruchter, & Zimmerman, 1957). For example, when dealing with the number five, a third grader can mentally move around three and two dots, or four and one oranges, as though on a mental grid. The child recognizes "fiveness" in all its visual combinations and positions. The child can even easily count up four more oranges to combine with the five already visualized.

In a review of 600 studies that had correlated academic achievement with visual-perceptual factors, Larsen and Hammill (1975) found the highest relationships between arithmetic and visual discrimination (noting differences between figures), memory for visual sequences, and visual-motor coordination (copying). Yet, the correlations between these factors and arithmetic indicated that the two skills only shared about 10 percent of the same attributes. As in reading, verbal abilities are most highly related to later mathematics success. Higher-level mathematics is logical, making demands on linguistic analysis, sequencing, comprehension, and reasoning. The greater contribution of verbal over visuo-spatial factors to higher-level arithmetic abilities holds true even for such skills as dealing with money, time, and measurement (McLeod & Crump, 1978).

Visual Perception and Language

As task difficulty increases, learning problems become associated more with language than with visual-perceptual processes. Yet, historically, overwhelming numbers of LD children were thought to suffer from visual-perceptual disabilities. We have since learned that many of the significant visual-perceptual findings in early studies were actually artifacts of language disabilities. These language difficulties impacted on attention to and memory for what children saw, thereby accounting for many of these children's weaknesses on visual memory and auditory-visual integration tasks.

Visual Memory and Language. Poor readers have difficulty remembering what they have seen (Amoriell, 1979; Samuels & Anderson, 1973). Some can't remember well because of slow visual information-processing. Others can't remember well because they don't use verbal labeling to aid memory. The latter children remember what they've seen most recently, but have difficulty remembering items that they saw earlier (Spring & Capps, 1974).

Verbal labelling is essential to visual memorization of nameable information because people store visual images of letters, words (Baddeley, 1970; Kintsch & Buschke, 1969), and objects (Conrad, 1972) in memory as sounds rather than images. For example, the picture of the animal bat might be recalled a week later as a baseball bat because the sounds, not the images, were stored. Similarly, when a word is sounded out, the sound of each letter rather than its image is held in memory. That is why reading errors that appear to be due to visual misperceptions or visual memory distortions (din/bin, cob/cod, sung/snug, lion/loin) also can be due to language difficulties involving the analysis, recall, and sequencing of sounds.

Children's memory abilities are strongly tied to their use of language to label what they have seen. These labels help to organize, store, rehearse, and recall the visual information. This labeling process is called *mediation*. Studies show that children who verbally label what they see remember meaningful material better than those who don't use verbal mediation. But mediators lose their advantage over nonmediators when memorizing meaningless figures because these figures cannot be named (Groenendaal & Bakker, 1971).

Since reading is a meaningful language task, poor readers seem to have visual memory problems more often because they fail to use language to mediate what they have seen, than because they misperceive the stimuli or have other visual processing inefficiencies. For example, Vellutino's research group found that poor readers and good readers had equal difficulty remembering what, to them, were meaningless images of Hebrew words (Vellutino, Pruzek, Steger, & Meshoulam, 1973; Vellutino, Steger, DeSetto, & Phillips, 1975). Both groups showed such classic visual-perceptual errors as omitting and distorting what had been seen. On the other hand, children who had studied Hebrew could use these language skills to help them better remember which letters they had seen (Vellutino, Steger, DeSetto, & Phillips, 1975; Vellutino, Steger, Kaman, & DeSetto, 1975).

Again, language's role in visual perception is illustrated when poor readers can correctly write short words that they have just seen from memory, although they often cannot pronounce them (Allington, Gormley, & Truex, 1976; Vellutino, Smith, Steger, & Kaman, 1975; Vellutino, Steger, & Kandel, 1972). Writing only becomes a problem as increasingly longer words begin to tax short-term memory capabilities (Vellutino et al., 1972). That is, for any of us to remember more than five, six, or seven letters, these need to be recoded into more manageable chunks (Miller, 1956). Good readers use their verbal reading and spelling knowledge to do this chunking. But poor readers can't. Without verbal mediation to aid memory, poor readers have difficulty remembering longer words.

In a very complex study showing that memory deficits are usually linked to verbal mediation of information, Ceci, Ringstorm and Lea (1981) had children with auditory-memory and visual-memory weaknesses learn semantic information (belonging to nameable categories) or nonsemantic perceptual information (color, sound). Memory for semantic information in the children's weaker modalities was what differentiated them from children who had no modality weaknesses. Within their one impaired modality, memory for semantic information was significantly weaker than semantic memory in their nonimpaired modality. Only children with both auditory and visual memory problems, and therefore no stronger modality, had both semantic and nonsemantic memory difficulties. Findings like these have led many investigators to feel that the child with visual-perceptual deficits, but strong verbal mediation abilities, has a good chance of making up for perceptual handicaps.

Auditory-Visual Integration. Besides visual-memory weaknesses, investigators historically have attributed reading and writing difficulties to *cross-modal integration* difficulties. These are weaknesses in transferring visual (letter forms) to auditory (sounds) information, and vice versa. As shown in Table 5-1, there was much evidence to support their views. Yet, as with visual memory weaknesses, recent research shows that what appear to be auditory-visual integration difficulties instead may be poor use of language to aid memory.

Research on auditory-visual integration difficulties began when Birch & Belmont (1964) found that poor readers were inferior to good readers in their ability to match patterns of pencil taps on the edge of a table to the dot patterns presented in Figure 5-1. In a more recent study, poor readers were slower in learning to associate dictated words (bat, cup, dog) with abstract designs (Samuels & Anderson, 1973). Such findings made popular the idea that children become reading disabled because of an inability to connect auditory with visual information.

This idea was soon questioned because the integration difficulty could also be due to the weak attention (Samuels & Anderson, 1973) or language skills

Figure 5-1   Birch & Belmont's auditory-visual integration stimuli. Large and small spaces represent approximate time intervals of 1 sec. and 0.5 sec., respectively.

Auditory tap patterns	Visual stimuli		
Examples			
A • •	••	• •	•••
B • ••	•••	• ••	•• •
C •• •	•••	• ••	•• •
Test items			
1 •• ••	• •••	• •• •	•• ••
2 • •••	••••	• •••	••• •
3 ••• ••	•••••	•• •••	••• ••
4 • •• •	• •• •	•••••	•• ••
5 ••• •• •	••• •• •	•• ••• •	• ••• ••
6 •• •••	••• ••	•• •••	•••• •
7 •• •• ••	•• •• ••	•••• ••	••• • ••
8 ••• ••• •	•• ••• ••	••• •• ••	••• ••• •
9 •• • •••	•• •• ••	•• • •••	•• ••• •
10 • ••• ••	• •• •••	• ••• ••	•• • •••

SOURCE: From Herbert Birch and Lillian Belmont, "Auditory-Visual Discrimination in Normal and Retarded Readers." Reprinted, with permission, from the *American Journal of Orthopsychiatry;* copyright 1964 by the American Orthopsychiatric Association, Inc.

(Zigmond, 1969) that these children often had. The contribution of language to auditory-visual integration abilities has been illustrated in several studies. When visual stimuli are not nameable, good and poor readers' auditory-visual integration abilities generally are equivalent. Vellutino, Steger and Pruzek (1973), for example, had good and poor readers learn to pair meaningless, unnameable symbols with such auditory stimuli as a high hum, a cough, a hiss, and a kissing sound. All the children learned these auditory-visual pairs equally well. They were also equally proficient at learning to pair just visual or just auditory pairs. But, when the material can be named (pictures of objects and capital letters) poor readers become less proficient than good readers at pointing to what they have seen (Bakker, 1967). Good readers seem to verbally label meaningful material more often than poor readers, and therefore remember it better. Poor readers do not benefit from this mediation since they don't automatically verbally label what they see.

In reconsidering Birch and Belmont's tapping task, we see that it, too, necessitated the use of language. Children had to somehow code the order of taps in order to organize them in memory and then match the taps with dot patterns. Their inability to verbally code nonverbal stimuli so as to recall them in sequence (saying one-three-two silently as they heard the taps) seems to be at the root of what looked like an auditory-visual integration difficulty (Blank & Bridger, 1966; Blank, Weider, & Bridger, 1968).

This area of research is very complicated and is still being actively studied. Although in some children these integration problems may indeed be caused by poor visual perceptual or auditory-visual integration skills, in a great many cases they seem directly tied to language processing weaknesses.

Motor Skills

Learning disabled children very often have difficulty with gross-motor, hand, and oral movements (Bender, 1963). Sensori-motor disturbances in gaining information through touch and movement also are frequent. Joseph, the law school applicant, also has severe motor difficulties. The effect of these throughout his life is presented in the case study on page 163.

Over 75 percent of all poor readers have motor disturbances (Critchley, 1970). Since only 25 percent of these have visual perceptual disturbances, motor weaknesses are most often not the result of underlying visual-perceptual deficits. Similarly, although articulation difficulties may result from an inability to hear sounds accurately, they more often represent a problem with oral movements alone.

Despite the prevalence of motor difficulties among the learning disabled, motor difficulties don't relate highly to learning problems. Instead they make it difficult for children to show what they have learned. For example, in some cases misarticulation of what has been heard may lead educators to believe that a child has not correctly discriminated the auditory input, when in fact she or he has (Matthews & Seymour, 1981).

Studies find that copying activities are among the most consistent correlates of early math (Larsen & Hammill, 1975) and reading success (Kavale, 1982; Keogh, 1965; Keogh & Smith, 1967; Larsen, Rogers & Sowell, 1976). Yet, these correlations are of such low magnitudes that the motor difficulty cannot predict whether or not any single individual will fail academically. This is because motor incoordination is only one of many variables impacting on learning problems.

Coordination difficulties are a frequent concomitant of learning disorders because a very large area of the sensori-motor and motor cortex subserves hand, finger, body, and oral sensations and movements. When there is a

CASE STUDY: Joseph

As a youngster, Joseph always had a difficult time with recess, gym class, youth-group dances, and summer camp activities, and his coordination has not improved with time. At the age of twenty-three, Joseph cannot walk a straight line or touch his nose if his eyes are closed. With his eyes open he cannot skip or jump without difficulty.

When Joseph is unsure of what he wants to say, his speech becomes slurred. Since he has difficulty visualizing symbols in his mind, he still reverses letters and numbers when he writes. He cannot correct these errors through proofreading, because he has no mental picture against which to check his errors.

Fortunately, these motor handicaps need not deter Joseph's career as a lawyer. He can dictate his work and delegate proofreading to someone else. His coordination difficulties need not affect his socializing. Given America's enthusiasm for spectator sports, Joseph most likely will fit in nicely with the sports buffs.

dysfunction in the adjoining auditory and associative brain areas that are essential to cognitive and academic performance, there is a good deal of opportunity for things to go wrong in the sensori-motor and motor cortex as well. In addition, these areas receive messages about how to feel and move from all other brain areas. Any inability to attend to, organize, store, or retrieve visual, auditory, tactile, or kinesthetic (sensations from body movements) information necessarily comes out in motor or verbal inefficiencies. This is why a child who hasn't watched the ball bats poorly. This is also why children stutter when they're not sure of what they want to say. Some of these incoordinations are due to perceptual inefficiencies. But the majority are primarily motor problems.

Coordination difficulties result in such problems as sloppy and illegible handwriting, reluctance to complete lengthy written assignments, math computation errors due to illegibility and poor alignment of numerals, articulation difficulties, incompetence in sports, social difficulties on the playground, and clumsiness in dressing. As in Joseph's case, such problems do not help children to win friends. They're often frustrated by understanding much more than they can express orally or in writing. Their grades suffer. If a child's difficulties are only at the motor end, and he or she can bear the deprecation and poor grades on written work, then the outlook for eventual success is good.

Language Skills

A majority of children with reading disorders have weaknesses in receiving, processing, or expressing language and were delayed in language acquisition at younger ages (Vogel, 1975). Reading delays continue long after the language delays seem to be resolved (Garvey & Gordon, 1973; Griffiths, 1969). Many individuals believe that language and reading disabilities both reflect a common problem in dealing with symbolic systems (Bloom, 1978; Denckla, 1979). Therefore, even when the ability to read words becomes proficient, the language weaknesses may still interfere with reading comprehension and written expression. Due to the symbolic nature of foreign languages and poetry, these too are predictable stumbling blocks.

Reading and writing translate language's symbol system into a different vehicle for thinking and communicating about linguistic information. It follows that reading disabled children with higher verbal skills tend to improve in reading ability faster than those with weaker verbal abilities (Trites & Fiedorowicz, 1976).

Like many reading disabled children, Peter, in case study below, has a multitude of language weaknesses. Some of the language weaknesses associated with reading disorders are listed in Table 5-2. In contrast with the diminishing relationship between visual-perceptual skills and reading as children get older, language measures become increasingly capable of differentiating good from poor readers (Lyle, 1969).

Some language factors directly related to reading disorders include weak left hemisphere language-processing, auditory-processing weaknesses, and difficulty with understanding or expressing the linguistic components of language. The auditory-processing difficulty in analysis, sequencing, and recall of

CASE STUDY:
Peter

Peter is now in second grade and has had a terrible time learning to read. He is a cute fellow and well-liked by his peers. On the playground, or in gym and art classes, he's as much a member of the in group as anyone else. But in music class, reading group, and class discussions he's on the periphery. Peter has a terrible time in music class because he has no sense of rhythm and can't say the words in a song fast enough to keep up with the beat. It is not uncommon for the group to pause at the completion of a phrase of music and for all heads to suddenly turn — giggles are heard — Peter has either not sensed the pause, and is rushing on to the next phrase, or was so slow in remembering the words that he's just completing the previous phrase.

In his reading group, Peter takes so long to think of which sound goes with which letter in a word, that he's forgotten the beginning sounds by the time he gets to the end of the word. Often the word he comes up with is utter nonsense. He can't even guess at words well because he doesn't understand the grammatical structure of the sentences and word meanings well enough to guess correctly. In class discussions Peter raises his hand eagerly because he knows the answers. But when he is called on, the light fades from his eyes as he struggles to pull the right words out of his head. He finally gives up as the class echoes "call on us, we know."

Peter has severe deficits in several aspects of language: learning linguistic rules, learning meanings of words, and being able to quickly retrieve sounds and words from memory. Since all these abilities are involved in reading, he has reading difficulties.

Table 5-2   Language weaknesses associated with reading disabilities

WEAKNESS	INVESTIGATORS
Rate of early language development	Miles, 1974; Owen, Adams, Forrest, Stolz, & Fisher, 1971
Auditory memory (recalling digits & sentences), auditory closure (reconstituting fragmented words), auditory figure-ground (repeating a word when there is background noise)	Keir, 1977
Verbal-coding ability	Blank, Weider, & Bridger, 1968
Ability to differentiate statements of information from questions	Vogel, 1974
Comprehension of sentence structures	Semel & Wiig, 1975
Expressive language	Semel & Wiig, 1975
Speaking vocabulary, fluency, and linguistic patterns	Fry, Johnson, & Muel, 1970
Knowledge of grammatical rules	Vogel, 1977; Wiig, Semel, & Crouse, 1973
Ability to define words, provide verbal opposites, formulate sentences, and converse	Wiig & Semel, 1975
Sequencing of verbal and visual material	Doehring, 1968
Understanding verbal categories of space and time	de Hirsch, 1952
Learning puns, synonyms, homonyms	Maier, 1977
Frequently verbal intelligence scores are lower than performance IQs	Kinsbourne & Warrington, 1963; Myklebust & Boshes, 1969
Processing complex verbalizations and forming sentences	de Hirsch, 1952
Naming objects; cluttered and disorganized speech	de Hirsch, 1952
Sentence and digit repetition	Denckla, 1973
Minor articulation difficulties	Miles, 1974
Comprehension of rapid, lengthy, complex spoken language	Denckla, 1977; Mattis, 1978

sounds in words may be caused by a combination of factors: the child may need longer processing times to perceive certain sounds; pulling sounds out of memory may get harder the more one has to do it; and auditory retrieval of sounds and names (naming) is a struggle. This naming difficulty makes it very hard for a child to use verbal mediation as a memory aid.

Left Hemisphere Weaknesses

In the normal process of development, the left hemisphere in most individuals becomes more specialized for language processing than does the parallel area in the right hemisphere. Even as young as four and five years of age, American children perform more accurately when auditory information is presented to the right ear (sound is processed primarily by the left hemisphere) than when presented to the left ear (sound is processed primarily by the right hemisphere) (Berlin, Hughes, Lowe-Bell, & Berlin, 1973; Geffner & Hochberg, 1971).

Some learning disabled children follow this same pattern (Witelson & Rabinovitch, 1972), but many do not. Instead, they may have no language dominance differences between hemispheres (Pettit & Helms, 1979), have right hemisphere preferences (Sparrow & Satz, 1970; Zurif & Carson, 1970), or prefer to process one type of material (digits) with one hemisphere and another type (words) with the other (Sommers & Taylor, 1972). Most children's left hemisphere language regions are anatomically wider than the same regions in their right hemispheres. Yet poor readers with language weaknesses may have the reversed anatomic pattern (Hier, LeMay, Rosenberger, & Perlo, 1978).

These language specialization differences have led to very interesting speculation regarding the role of language in reading disorders. Recall the proposal that the typical reading process involves a shift from right to left hemisphere preferences. This shift occurs around second or third grade (Bakker, Teunissen, & Bosch, 1976; Kershner, 1977) and corresponds with a change to a more mature reading style. Instead of concentrating on words' visual configurations, words now are guessed from the passage's linguistic meaning. While some reading disordered children may have skipped the right hemisphere phase, the opposite also can happen (Bakker, 1980). These children seem to overuse their right hemispheres in reading and do not switch to the left hemisphere's more analytic, language processing mode. Unfortunately, the right hemisphere's structure and holistic information processing style are not well-suited to the high level, analytic language functions involved in reading and comprehension (Hier et al., 1978; LeMay, 1977).

Witelson's (1976) research suggests that, in some reading disabled boys, the right hemisphere's visuo-spatial functions have partially shifted to the left hemisphere. This overloads the language-processing capacity of the left hemisphere. Not only is their language ability reduced, but they bring a holistic style to language processing that is incompatible with high levels of reading accomplishment.

Children who have left hemisphere weaknesses and overuse right hemisphere information-processing styles seem to be the most severely reading disabled. They read by fixating on the visual configuration of words rather than their sounds and parts. Phonetic analysis is a slow, laborious process and they read syllable by syllable (Boder, 1973; Denckla, 1977; Ingram, Mason, & Blackburn, 1970; Myklebust, 1965).

Auditory-Processing Weaknesses

Integration of data from over 100 studies shows that auditory-perceptual abilities are second only to general intelligence in contributing to reading success (Kavale, 1981). The ability to analyze, sequence, and remember auditory stimuli is essential to reading progress (Lindamood & Lindamood, 1971;

Shankweiler & Liberman, 1976). Most children with learning disabilities are able to discriminate sounds of letters from one another (for example, b from f) (Keir, 1977). But when these sounds are put into words, they may no longer recognize the differences (bed, fed) (Eisenson, 1968; McReynolds, 1966). They may experience difficulty analyzing sentences into words, words into syllables, and syllables into the sequence of individual sounds.

Some experts suggest that, besides auditory-analysis weaknesses, reading disabled children are hampered by *short-term auditory memory* difficulties (Bauer, 1979; Rosenthal & Eisenson, 1970). They can't remember a sound from one moment to the next. Other professionals find that these children have *auditory-sequential memory* difficulties. They cannot remember several items in sequence, such as numbers, words, and sounds (Bakker, 1970; 1972; Eisenson, 1972). If children can't retain sounds in sequence, then they won't be able to read from the beginning to end of a word. They cannot omit the beginning, middle, or ending sound in a word and substitute a new sound for it. Analyzing, omitting, substituting, and retaining sounds in sequence are important to beginning reading where a sound must be applied to a letter, then remembered while the next sound is recalled, then the two are blended, and so on (Rosner, 1974; Weaver & Rosner, 1979). These auditory analysis, sequencing, and memory abilities also are important to higher-level reading and comprehension skills. Some of the reasons behind these difficulties include slow auditory information processing time, auditory memory scanning weaknesses, and auditory retrieval difficulties.

Auditory Information-Processing Time. Just as with visual processing, some learning disabled children seem to need a significantly longer time between auditory stimuli to process them (Tallal & Piercy, 1978). That is, when two auditory stimuli are presented too close in succession, some children can't tell which came first. Their performance improves when the interval between stimuli becomes longer or the stimuli themselves last longer.

These children have the most trouble with brief stop consonant sounds (such as b) that can't be sustained to allow more time for auditory processing to take place. Vowel sounds, on the other hand, present less of a problem because they can be sustained. Since the brief consonant sounds rather than longer duration vowels carry the meaning in our language, Tallal and Piercy suggest that children may be unable to comprehend much of what is said because the consonant sounds pass by before they can be processed. When reading, this slow auditory processing time may interfere with analysis, sequencing, and recall of word sounds as well as comprehension.

Auditory Memory Scanning. Besides needing a longer time to perceive sounds, some poor readers also require increasingly longer time to scan their auditory memories as the scanning process continues (as when retrieving letter sounds in a series of words). Good readers do not have this problem (Farnham-

Diggory & Gregg, 1975). Visual memory scanning in poor readers is usually more efficient than auditory scanning. Some studies find that these children have a hard time shifting from dealing with the easier visual to the harder auditory stimuli (Estes & Huizinga, 1974), while others find equal difficulty with auditory-to-visual or visual-to-auditory shifts (Lehmen & Brady, 1982). Farnham-Diggory & Gregg suggest that these children's reading confusions might be due to their eyes moving on to a second letter before they have had sufficient opportunity to retrieve the first letter's sound.

Auditory Retrieval. Our discussion of visual perceptual factors pointed out that visual memory is often impaired only when the stimuli are nameable. We commonly find reading disabled children to be much slower and less accurate at naming pictures of common objects than are average readers (Blank & Bridger, 1966; German, 1979; Wiig & Semel, 1975). When speaking, poor readers often have unusually long silent periods between words, choose the wrong words, or talk around a topic. This is because they can't quickly retrieve the words they are searching for. This slow auditory retrieval is called a *naming* or *word-finding* problem.

These children also have difficulty pulling out letter names, number names, or isolated sounds to attach to letters (Denckla & Rudel, 1976ab). Therefore, sounding out words is arduous and often unsuccessful. They forget the sounds of previous letters by the time they struggle to recall the sound of the next letter in a word. As poor readers belabor the decoding of each word, their capacity to remember and integrate information from previous sentences is also reduced and comprehension becomes impaired (Perfetti & Lesgold, 1977).

Several investigators have concluded that poor naming represents a structural brain deficit that hampers ready access to the linguistic information or codes that mediate recall (Swanson, 1982; Torgesen & Houck, 1980). Verbal mediation, you will remember, is the use of language to label information, organize it for storage, rehearse it, and remember it. This verbal review can occur only when the information has been "named" to begin with. Studies show that as overt (speaking aloud) or covert (speaking to oneself) speech increases, so does success on memory tasks (Sheingold & Shapiro, 1976). Children who can't name efficiently cannot use language as a memory aid. Spring and Capps (1974), for example, found that children who can't name at the rate of one object per second don't even attempt to use verbal mediation as a memory aid. Consequently, their memory is poor. Spring and Capps' children were shown eight cards, which were then laid face down in a row. Their task was to match a ninth card with one already on the table. Poor readers never even tried to name the cards so as to help them remember. Good readers did.

It is not surprising then that speed of naming is an excellent predictor of reading success (Jansky & de Hirsch, 1973; Mattis, French, & Rapin, 1975).

RESEARCH BOX 5-2
The Influence of Language Labels upon What We See and Think

The idea that language has a fundamental influence on thought itself was advanced by Benjamin Whorf (1956). For example, Eskimos have hundreds of terms to differentiate one type of snow from another. Non-Eskimos have very few names for snow-types and can't even imagine all the varieties that the Eskimos say exist. Tarnopol and Tarnopol (1977) report that Cree Indians live in conical dwellings and can recognize different orientations of verticals, horizontals, and diagonals equally well. But Canadians of European origin could not recognize the diagonals, with which they were unaccustomed, as well as they recognized the verticals and horizontals. Another example of language's influence on perceptions comes from work with the cerebral palsied. Wedell (1960) found that although children with right hemisphere damage should have been poorer in visual perception than those with leftsided damage, the opposite was true. Apparently, the left hemisphere's language functions aided performance in matching, copying, and construction tasks. With language deficits, but intact right hemispheres, perceptual skills surprisingly suffered greatly. Apparently, language has a great guiding influence on what people see and give meaning to. The educator of severely hearing-impaired children would agree that their language deficits greatly impact their conceptual abilities.

Poor naming causes trouble at every interface of spoken and written language because sounds can't be retrieved to read words, and words can't be retrieved to express ideas (Shankweiler & Liberman, 1976). The important role of language labels as mediators of what people see, think, and remember is explored in Research Box 5-2.

Linguistic Weaknesses

The child's linguistic abilities in listening comprehension and speech are significant factors in decoding, reading comprehension, writing, and even social performance. Consider what might happen if Peter, described in the case study on page 164, has not mastered past and future tense forms. What if he doesn't understand who did what to whom in a sentence like "mother was hit by her daughter"? Some learning disabled children are unable to comprehend such basic grammatical relations (Cromer, 1978). Their ability to make inferences and generalizations in reading comprehension suffers as a result (Berger, 1978; de Hirsch, 1963). The fluent reading process of guessing at words by anticipating what a sentence is going to say also becomes limited. For example, when reading a passage about a camping trip that occurred last week, a child with good language skills does not even have to look at the "ed" in "hiked." He or she will just glance at the "hik" and know that the rest must be "ed" if the passage is to make sense. Such lack of awareness of grammatical speech sequences makes it even more difficult for the beginning reader to understand how alphabet sounds are segmented and ordered (Shankweiler & Liberman, 1976). An impaired sense of rhythm may also interfere with patterning of these sound sequences (Cromer, 1978).

Some children understand linguistic concepts but have difficulty with the expressive language needed to explain them, either orally or in writing. Haight (1977), for example, found that learning disabled children knew how three of four visual patterns were alike and how they could be regrouped. Yet they failed the task because they could not verbally explain themselves. Such expressive difficulties become an increasing problem in the upper school grades as children's written language — compositions, term papers, and open-ended tests — are used to evaluate what they have learned.

Attention

Have you ever watched your five-year-old little niece or sister eat a messy chocolate ice cream cone and, when she was covered with brown drips, asked her to go into the bathroom to wash her hands and face? She walks down the hallway and two minutes later returns, still a mess. She innocently looks up and asks, "What did you tell me to do?" You smile, hug her, repeat the directions, pat her on the rear end, and send her on her way again. But what would your response be if she were eight or ten years old? Presumably quite negative. You might wonder whether your niece or sister can't hear, understand, pay attention, remember, or is just plain insolent.

When these questions arise with LD children, the answer often is insufficient focusing and sustaining of attention so that the information isn't learned in the first place. Attention seems to be the problem because, when information is attended to sufficiently to be learned, forgetting usually occurs no faster for learning disabled than typical learners (Gregory & Bunch, 1959; Schoer, 1962; Shuell & Keppel, 1970; Underwood, 1964).

A fundamental contributor to learning disorders, and perhaps the most common characteristic of LD children, is immature attending ability (Keogh, 1973; Keogh & Margolis, 1976; Tarver & Hallahan, 1974). This includes the ability to be *alert* to a stimulus about to be presented, be *ready* to respond, *focus* on the appropriate stimuli, *sustain* attention for adequate time periods, and then to *decide* on an answer or action. Whether information is attended to, and how the learner then organizes it for storage, are critical to whether the material will be remembered. The educator's goal is to help such children learn *selective attention* — focusing and sustaining attention on some things while ignoring others.

Studies show that most learning disabled children's attention is easily caught. Once caught, however, they have a problem focusing in on relevant stimuli and sustaining this attention. These difficulties are related to physiological factors, cognitive styles, and poor use of verbal mediation, all of which are incompatible with focused and sustained attention.

Catching and Focusing Attention

Though LD children's attention is readily caught by stimuli, many find it very difficult to appropriately focus their attention once caught. An easy way to conceptualize the difference between caught and focused attention is to imagine a typical interaction with your five-year-old niece or sister. Suppose that you are tired from a long day of studying and it's the little girl's bedtime. You have just read a ten-page story aloud to her. Apparently you read the correct words because she understood the content and is now asking all the usual "but why did" questions. Yet, you can't answer. You obviously had allowed your attention to be caught by the words and therefore read them correctly. But you failed to deliberately focus your attention so as to derive meaning from them. To answer the questions you'll have to reread the material, but this time pay focused attention.

One of several investigations suggesting that children's difficulties occur at the focusing rather than the caught phase of the attention process was conducted by Dykman and his colleagues (1970). They measured children's skin resistance, heart rate, and muscle action potentials before and after hearing a tone. When the children pulled a cord after the tone, a coin was released. Good and poor learners' attention was equally caught by the tone. But since poor learners could not maintain this alertness, they were unable to learn what to do.

The same question was studied by Porge's research group (1975). Children were given a "ready" signal, followed by a "go" signal to activate a toy racing car. Caught attention was measured by the expected increase in heart rate from five seconds before the children saw the ready signal to five seconds after. Focused attention was measured by the expected decrease in heart rate as the children then waited for the go signal. But instead of decreasing, heart rate increased during the focusing period just as it had when initially caught. These children's responses actually looked as though a distraction was being experienced and attention was being caught by something irrelevant. Stimulant medication successfully decreased focused heart rate to that of typical learners. Once again, it was LD children's ability to focus rather than catch attention that seemed deficient.

Sustaining Attention

Even after children with learning problems have had enough time to focus on all features of a stimulus, they often remember the content less well than the typical learner (Guthrie & Goldberg, 1972; Katz & Deutsch, 1967; Morrison, Giordani, & Nagy, 1977). The memory problem of many learning disabled children is said to be caused by their difficulty maintaining attention to the critical, distinctive features of a task (Keogh & Margolis, 1976; Samuels, 1973). Several reasons for this sustained attention weakness have been proposed: physiological difficulties, cognitive styles, and poor use of verbal mediation.

Physiological Difficulties. Table 5-3 demonstrates that poor attending processes are a physiological fact among the learning disabled, particularly those who are hyperactive. On laboratory tasks that demand attention, these children have trouble maintaining constant attention levels, take longer to react to

Table 5-3 Indices of poor attention in the learning disabled

FINDINGS	INVESTIGATORS
Poorer alpha wave reduction while attending	Fuller, 1978
Particular decrements in the narrow EEG band that reflects focused arousal during problem-solving	Sheer, 1976
Slow to notice stimuli and to respond	Dykman, Walls, Suzuki, Ackerman & Peters, 1970; Noland & Schuldt, 1971; Sroufe, Sonies, West, & Wright, 1973
If attending well, must put so much greater than normal effort into maintaining attention, that their EEG amplitudes become much higher than do those of good learners	Shields, 1973
Less able to switch attention away from information coming into the right ear, so as to be able to repeat competing information coming in through the left ear	Kinsbourne, 1980
Lower-than-normal anticipatory heart rate deceleration, lower basal skin conductance, and greater amplitude of skin resistance	Dykman, Ackerman, Clements, & Peters, 1971; Hunter, Johnson, & Keefe, 1972
Difficulty switching attention between visual & auditory modalities	Katz & Deutsch, 1963
Lower general EEG arousal levels, slower EEG response to stimuli, and weaker response reduction with continued stimulation	Grunewald-Zuberbier, Grunewald & Rasche, 1975
Evoked potentials on a vigilance task (press switch when an X is preceded by a B) stay at a peak for less time and decrease over time whereas typical learners' evoked potentials remain at a peak longer and the peak increases over time	Dainer, Klormen, Salzman, Hess, Davidson, & Michael, 1981

stimuli, and do not have typical physiological indices that are associated with attention. These inefficient attention processes may interfere with learning to such a degree that they actually cause visual and auditory processing deficits (Samuels & Anderson, 1973; Denckla, 1979).

Cognitive Styles. Unique cognitive styles can predispose a child to poor attention. Some cognitive styles do not permit attention to the important features of tasks nor use of appropriate task strategies. Keogh, for example, points out that distractable children, whose style is to look at all stimuli around them, are unable to organize perceptual inputs so as to attend only to a task's most important features (Keogh, 1973; Keogh & Donlon, 1972). For this reason pictures on a page often hinder rather than help distractible children's learning (Lamman & Bakker, in Bakker & de Wit, 1977; Samuels, 1967).

Impulsive response styles also are highly related to poor sustained attention (Douglas, 1974, 1976). The impulsive child is an underfocuser (Kinsbourne, 1977b), relinquishing concentration too quickly, thereby making premature decisions and responding too rapidly. This impulsivity is directly related to decreased performance in areas requiring sustained attention such as auditory and visual short-term memory (Messer, 1976), and oral reading accuracy (Kagan, 1965). As these children learn to focus, sustain, and organize their attention better, their tendency to respond rapidly and make many errors decreases (Ross, 1976). Their memory improves. Consequently, educators clarify important task features and teach appropriate task strategies to help these children improve attention and learning (Drew and Altman, 1970; Koppell, 1979).

Verbal Mediation. Immature verbal mediation also may underlie many children's poor attention (Meichenbaum, 1976). When a child does not use verbal labeling and rehearsal to focus attention on the relevant stimuli, the information that caught attention is not likely to be organized for storage; recall is typically hampered (Drew & Altman, 1970).

Torgesen and Goldman's (1977) study illustrated this point. They gave good and poor readers a picture containing seven drawings of common objects. The experimenter pointed to two, three, four, or five pictures. The child covered his or her eyes with goggles for fifteen seconds, then pointed to the previous sequence of objects. These pictures were presented in a different order on a new page. Good readers verbalized significantly more during the fifteen-second delay and remembered better than the poor readers. Poor readers who used verbal rehearsal applied this strategy less consistently than the good readers. Torgesen and Goldman then repeated the task, but instructed children to point to and name the pictures on presentation and also during the delay. The good and poor readers no longer differed in memory or amount of verbal rehearsal.

The above results indicate that children who do not spontaneously use verbal mediation to help them remember, may seem to have information-processing or memory deficiencies when in fact they don't (Miller & Rohr, 1980). Since speech helps people abstract, remember, and generalize information, many learning disordered children have been taught to increase their problem-solving skills and memory skills by literally talking to themselves (Meichenbaum, 1977). Verbal mediation even can make up for the interfering effects of overactivity on attention to tasks that require reflection (Weithorn & Kagen, 1978).

Summary

Peripheral-visual factors, such as acuity and eye movements, do not seem to underlie learning disabilities. Nevertheless, they make use of the eyes in reading uncomfortable, thereby aggravating an existing learning difficulty. Visual-perceptual factors influence learning at young ages and continue to do so in subtle ways at older ages. However, language and attention abilities are more frequent and powerful contributors to academic success and failure. Both are complexly interrelated and greatly influence how information is organized for storage, rehearsed, and recalled. Motor disabilities often accompany the visual-perceptual, language, and attention weaknesses of learning disabled students and make it difficult for these children to express what they know.

Learning disabilities are not simple to understand because no one unitary deficit hypothesis will explain all academic disorders (Fletcher & Satz, 1979ab; Satz, Taylor Friel, & Fletcher, 1978). All causes, contributors, and information-processing weaknesses may be operative to varying degrees in any one individual. Therefore, learning disabled youngsters are of a "mixed" variety. This makes it especially difficult to understand them and to predict the exact nature and extent of any one child's future learning progress. In the learning disabilities field, inconsistencies with theory are the rule rather than exception. For example, many of Birch and Belmont's (1964) poor auditory-visual integrators were nonetheless good readers, and some poor readers had no trouble on the integration task. Often children are good readers although they do not use verbal mediation (Groenendaal & Bakker, 1971). Likewise, many poor readers have no difficulty processing rapid auditory stimuli (Tallal, 1976).

The heterogeneity of the LD population has made it extremely difficult to describe subjects in a consistent manner from study to study. This limits the researcher's ability to replicate studies, to compare findings, and to make valid generalizations to classroom teaching.

All the possible combinations of causes of learning disabilities and information processing weaknesses make defining exactly what a learning disability is difficult. It makes most sense to describe learning disabilities by the observable interaction of the individual's information processing abilities and learned skills with specific task and setting attributes.

Suggestions for Further Study

1. To further explore how varying types of controls in studies may lead to conclusions about the relationship between eye function and reading that differ from those discussed in the text, read the following articles: Elterman, Abel, Daroff, Dell'Osso, & Bornstein (1980); Swanson (1972). Look at the subjects in both studies and the methodology in the latter. How do these affect the results? What modifications would you suggest if the studies were to be repeated?

2. To better understand Miller's important concept that our short-term memories begin to be overloaded with five to seven pieces of information, unless we chunk this information, have someone write two sets of seven numbers each on a piece of paper. Read the first set once and try to recall it. Now put a dash in between the third and fourth numbers of the second set, and read it as though this was a phone number. Did you find it easier to remember the second set because of the way you chunked the information? Many forms of chunking information for recall are applied automatically by good achievers, but infrequently among the learning disabled. How do you chunk information?

3. Language and learning strategies such as naming and chunking seem to be keys to a good memory. Try this experiment on yourself. Have someone cut out twelve magazine pictures of unrelated common objects and then successively present them to you, each for two seconds. After the twelfth one is removed, wait fifteen seconds and try to recall them in order. Did you remember anymore than the five to seven we would expect from information-processing theory? How did you remember the pictures? Did you name and verbally rehearse them? If you tried to remember the objects by conjuring up their visual images, were you successful? Did the images begin to fade? Did you then grope for another way of encoding — naming? Now try the experiment again on two of your friends, but use twenty-four pictures that can be sorted into four categories. Tell one friend what the four categories are, but say nothing to the other friend. Present the pictures in random order. Who remembered better? Did clustering by category help?

4. Given the strong relationship between language and reading disorders, have you ever wondered whether reading disabilities are specific to the English language? Read Critchley (1970) for a discussion of reading disabilities' prevalence in different countries. Some studies show that disabled readers can learn to read Chinese characters relatively faster than English, supposedly because Chinese words are a logographic system. The pictures don't demand alphabetic analysis, as English does (Rozin, Poritsky, & Sotsky, 1971). Others claim that the Japanese syllabic system is responsible for Japan's low illiteracy rate. Read Kinsbourne & Caplan (1979) for a discussion of factors other than the writing system that make this a complex issue because they too may account for cross-cultural differences in literacy rate (educational system, parent pressure for achievement, age of beginning reading instruction, teacher training, etc.).

5. If you wish to learn more about how memory develops as children's storage, retrieval, knowledge, and self-perceptions mature, consult the following resources: Brown (1975), Flavell (1970), Hagen, Jongeward & Kail (1975), Kail & Hagen (1976, 1977), Kobasigawa (1976), Kreutzer, Leonard, & Flavell (1975), Meacham (1975), and Ross (1976).

6. The problems with conducting, interpreting, and generalizing from research in learning disabilities are enormous. It is important for you to be familiar with these issues so that you can fully understand why most findings in learning disabilities research represent hypotheses to be explored further, rather than fact. Harber's (1981) review of research reported since 1978 in two LD journals highlights these issues. She finds that the majority of studies don't follow strict experimental designs, do not control for such important variables as intelligence and socioeconomic status in their experimental and control groups, use subjects who are not classified LD, and present too few operational definitions of subjects to permit replication, or too broad a range of identification criteria to permit generalization of the findings. Keogh's research group's (1980) sampling of the 1970–1978 LD literature from 143 journals and document sources is equally valuable reading. This article concludes with recommended variables to be used as reference points in describing LD research samples.

Part Three

The Learner

Chapter Six
The Preschooler

Everyone in the field of learning disabilities, whether teacher, psychologist or parent, must understand how typical infants and preschoolers develop. Learning disabled children generally follow the same sequence of skill development as these children, although at slower rates in their areas of weakness. Knowing about early childhood development helps LD professionals detect immaturities in individual children, define teaching objectives, and choose remedial strategies that will facilitate the young child's learning.

This chapter will review our current understanding of the development of visual-perceptual, visual-motor, gross motor, attention, and language abilities. Delays in these information-processing abilities may impact on both the efficiency of preschoolers' acquisition of knowledge and communication of what they know. When these weaknesses persist beyond the preschool years, the child is at high risk for school learning failure. Therefore, early identification and intervention are essential if we are to prevent learning disabilities.

Visual Perception

Visual perception is the process whereby a person detects and gains meaning from visual material. It occurs at the very moment the material is seen. Much of the 1960s emphasis in learning disabilities was on visual-perceptual theories. These theories, and how they relate to normal preschool development, are important for teachers in the field of learning disabilities to be aware of. Often they provide the basis for teachers' evaluation, screening, and remedial materials. When teachers understand the theory on which these materials are based, and relate the theory to data about normal development of complex visual perceptions, they can make appropriate programming judgments and plan a logical teaching progression for a learning disabled child.

We shall see that our theories and normal developmental data are not always in agreement. Research has shown that the newborn and young infant have a great deal of visual-perceptual ability — more ability than thought in the past (Cohen, 1979). This raises questions about early visual-perceptual theories which claimed that motor action is always necessary to the development of adequate visual perception. We now know that the infant can learn very complicated visual judgments with no actual movement involved. Only at later preschool ages does movement contribute to more complex perceptual learning. Such theories and research on the visual-perceptual development of infants and older preschoolers are useful not only in planning programs for the preschooler, but also in planning for the older student whose information-processing lags approximate the developmental levels of the typical preschooler.

This chapter was written by Eleanor Williams and Corinne Roth Smith.

Theories of Visual–Perceptual Development

Theories of visual-perceptual development primarily stress either the role of movement, stimulus-response connections, or attention and discrimination abilities. Each theory affects classroom teaching in somewhat different ways because each provides a particular viewpoint about the sequence of skill development and how a child's attention can be focused. The preschool teacher uses this information to decide where in the sequence the child's development falls, the order in which teaching material should be presented, and how material should be presented so as to engage attention. The preschool teacher decides which theoretical approach to teaching has merit for which child and on which tasks. No one approach is right for all children. When the preschool teacher keeps these theoretical models in mind and matches them to research data and the child's skills, he or she can creatively program for each learning disabled child.

Movement-Based Theories. Many pioneers (for example, Kephart) as well as recent theorists in learning disabilities have emphasized the central role of motor actions in perceptual development. They believe that children learn and develop perceptually primarily because they move.

One such recent position is Ayres' (1974) *sensorimotor integration theory*. Ayres suggests that proprioceptive (feedback received from the body's muscles and joints) and tactile information which enters at the brain stem level form the foundation for higher learning. She assumes that the developmental sequence of the human fetus, newborn, and young child follows the evolutionary development sequence of the human species. Therefore, according to Ayres' theory, the most primitive sense of touch, balance (vestibular system), and primitive reflexes must be intact before the later maturing sensory systems, such as auditory and visual perception, can develop. Cognitive function also must wait.

Ayres (1974, 1975) postulated a number of perceptual-motor dysfunctions: deficits in integration of the two cerebral hemispheres (as in coordinating both hands or crossing the midline of the body with one hand), deficits in motor planning (as in locating where one has been touched or assuming different postures such as extending arms for protection when falling), deficits in responding appropriately to touch, and problems in form and space perception. Ayres' therapies are based on stimulating the vestibular and tactile sensory systems. For example, a teacher might use tactile stimulation by rubbing the child's skin with a soft brush or terry cloth, or vestibular stimulation through swinging and rolling activities. Ayres believes that the resulting greater integration at the brain stem level would facilitate higher cognitive learning. Ayres' activities are far removed from actual skills needed in the classroom for reading and arithmetic, but may be useful to the child with gross motor problems.

Stimulus-Response–Based Theories. Other theorists hypothesize that visual perception matures as a function of *stimulus-response* connections. For example, Hebb's (1966) *response-oriented* theory and Zaporozhets' (1966) *motor-copy* theory suggest that each perception, whether visual, proprioceptive, auditory, or tactile, stimulates a certain set of neurons. Repeated stimulation tends to organize these same neurons into a network which becomes more intricate as the infant experiences additional sensory inputs (Salapatek, 1975).

Piaget's (1954) *stimulus-response* theory emphasizes the effects of the child's response on the stimulus and vice versa. For example, a stimulus within the child's environment may cause the child to act upon it. Such an action changes the nature of the stimulus for the child so that the child's future response to the stimulus will be different. Piaget felt that the motor movement is a requirement of early perceptual learning because motor movement is, at that age, the major avenue of learning.

Piaget's observations on stages of child development frequently have been used as steps in evaluating children with learning disabilities. Remediation techniques then are developed for tasks on which the child performed unsuccessfully (Adams, Lerner, & Anderson, 1979; Anderson, Richards, & Hallahan, 1980; Saxe & Shaheen, 1981). Using Piagetian theory, a teacher might decide to teach size discrimination of two objects through a motor activity, such as rolling different-sized clay balls. Piaget regarded such motor activities as essential. The other stimulus-response theorists further suggested that motor activity is necessary to activate nerve cells and form stimulus-response connections.

Attention- and Discrimination-Based Theories. Gibson's (1969) theory of *distinctive features* stresses visual attention and discrimination, rather than the response systems, in visual-perceptual development. Perceptual development, according to Gibson, is the process of noting differences in environmental properties and patterns of objects and events. With time, the child discovers constant features and relationships between these properties and patterns. The developing infant gradually learns what to pay attention to and what to filter out. According to Gibson's theory, motor movement is just one avenue whereby a child learns what to pay attention to.

Like Gibson, Cratty (1970) proposed that the infant has a great deal of visual-perceptual ability at birth. He suggested that this visual ability develops separately from other perceptual modes such as tactile or proprioceptive systems. The different modes combine in late infancy. This position contrasts with the movement and stimulus-response theories, which assume that the motor and proprioceptive systems are essential to early visual-perceptual development. Both Gibson and Cratty advocated motor activity to teach cognitive skills, but regarded this motor activity as supplementary. For example, a teacher would, through language, pointing, or motor activities, teach the distinctive features of a color, shape, or letter. A learning disabled child, according to Gibson, has not failed to perceive but has failed to rightly judge which features are important to note and which can be ignored. These judgments must be taught.

Recent evidence suggests that infants acquire visual-perceptual skills, such as the ability to discriminate forms and depth, before they can physically act on the environment. This data challenges the assumption that motor movement is essential to early visual-perceptual development. On the other hand, studies of the late preschool period show that both handling and seeing an object facilitate learning about it. At these older ages, movement appears to be valuable as a means of focusing attention, rather than as a primary learning mechanism, just as Gibson and Cratty hypothesized.

Visual Perception in the Infant

As noted, many visual-perceptual theorists stressed movement-oriented teaching methods because they believed that movement is essential to early learning. But recent studies show that movement is not essential to simple visual perception because these skills are learned at an age when movement in space and handling objects does not occur.

The infant's visual competencies also cast doubts on theories claiming that the origin of learning disabilities lies in difficulties with simple visual-perceptual processes. If these simple visual perceptions of, for example, form and space had not already developed, a child could hardly go about realizing where a step is, avoiding walking into a wall, and discriminating a cup from a plate. Since simple visual-perceptual skills develop so early in life, simple types of visual processing do not appear at fault when learning disabled preschoolers can't match colors and shapes or differentiate between letters. For example, some pioneers in learning disabilities such as Goldstein and Werner had implied that a learning disabled child actually cannot perceive the shape of a triangle against background figures. Even if a child is delayed in developing these visual attributes, he or she has many years to catch up before school begins. Current research suggests that it may be the efficiency with which simple visual-perceptual information is put to appropriate conceptual use, rather than the simple visual-perceptual processes themselves, that contribute to learning problems.

We will discuss three types of visual-perceptual ability in the infant: form discrimination, perceptual constancy, and space perception. Research in these areas assumes that infants perceive something visually if they respond to the stimulus with a longer fixation time, or a change in heart rate or sucking rate. Knowledge of the developmental progression in simple visual processing abilities is very important to parents and early infant teachers who need to stimulate the visual-perceptual development of an infant with developmental delays. This knowledge also helps to explain infants' reactions, such as crying fitfully when their ball rolls under a couch or when they do not recognize their mother when she has changed her hair color or style.

Form Discrimination. What does Benjie, a four-week-old baby, see? He can follow the environment with his eyes (Gibson, 1969). He also can detect high-contrast outside edges and angles of figures (Salapatek, 1975). However, Benjie at first does not scan the whole figure or fixate on its center. Similarly, when he sees a drawing of a human face, he scans and fixates on its outer edge, such as the hairline and chin, rather than on the internal features. Only when Benjie is about two months old is he able to scan all the features of a figure. Not until this time can he finally pick out and fixate on others' eyes. Parents look forward to this time. Any parent can testify to the boost of feeling and attachment when their infant finally gazes into their eyes.

Between two and four months of age, Benjie learns to combine the high-contrast edges and angles so as to discriminate simple shapes (Cohen, DeLoache, & Strauss; Schwartz & Day, 1979). But not until after four or five months does he respond to relationships among these forms (Bower, 1966). Therefore, by approximately five months, Benjie prefers drawings of smiling faces with regular features to scrambled faces, upright faces to inverted ones, and realistic faces to less realistic faces (Cohen, DeLoache, & Strauss, 1979).

Apparently, infants discriminate shapes and the way shapes interrelate to form patterns very early in life. This is long before they are expected to engage in motor movements, as in picking up objects of different colors and shapes, naming them, or matching them.

Perceptual Constancy. *Perceptual constancy* is the ability to realize that an object, person, or event is still the same even though the sensory information received about it has changed. For example, a cup is still the same thing when it is upside down, ten feet away, or partially hidden by a blanket. A young infant who has not established perceptual constancy may not recognize a parent's face when it is partially covered by a scarf, or may think a ball has disappeared when it rolls behind a couch. Researchers have tested two types of perceptual constancies in the infant: object or shape constancy, and size constancy.

In everyday life, anyone bringing a baby bottle to a hungry infant can tell that the infant recognizes the bottle even when the bottle is held in different positions. This is called *object* or *shape consistency*. By seven months of age, infants know that geometric shapes, three dimensional objects, or pictures of a face are the same no matter in what position the objects are held.

When an infant has developed object constancy (or "permanence"), the infant realizes that even when toys or parents are out of sight, they still exist. Piaget (1954) observed that this ability develops as follows:

1. In the first *three or four months,* a baby is not aware that objects exist out of sight.

2. Between the ages of *four to eight months,* the infant begins to anticipate the future position of an object as it moves. The best example is a baby dropping food from a high chair and looking toward the floor for it. In contrast, a younger infant may just continue looking for it on the tray. The older infant can imagine the course it has taken and will look downward.

3. At *eight to twelve months,* the infant can not only map out the course but also search for a hidden toy under a blanket. The toy's location is associated with the motion of placing it under the blanket. If the same toy is seen to be hidden in a second hiding place, the child still returns to search for it under the blanket because its location is associated with the motion of placing it under the blanket.

4. By *twelve to eighteen months,* the baby learns to search for the object where it was last hidden.

5. By *eighteen to twenty-four months* of age the child has a real sense of permanence. The child can conceive of invisible displacements. For example, Piaget placed a coin in his hand, hid the coin under a blanket and then withdrew his closed hand. His daughter first tried to find the coin in his hand and then looked under the blanket and found it. She was able to imagine where it had gone while invisible.

Size constancy is the ability to know that an object is the same in spite of appearing larger or smaller as it changes in distance from the observer. Although size constancy develops very early in life, the precise age is still disputed (Bower, 1966; Cohen, DeLoache, & Strauss, 1979; Day & McKenzie, 1977).

Space Perception. Space perception is the conglomerate ability to perceive surfaces, depth, solidity, and location of an object in space. Eleanor Gibson's (1969) famous work on this topic involved the use of the visual cliff, a table consisting of a deep and a shallow level. Both levels were covered with the same patterned material. The pattern of the deep side was slightly larger so that both patterns produced the same size images on the infant's retina, and the infant was not given a relative size cue for making a depth judgment. One piece of glass was extended from the shallow level over the deep level. An infant was placed on the center board and the mother alternately attempted to coax the infant to cross over the shallow side or the deep side. Most babies between six and eighteen months refused to move toward the mother when she called from the deep side. This and other studies concluded that even babies who had not yet learned to crawl had some knowledge of visual depth perception at an age when their experience in moving about their environment was limited (Campos, Langer, & Krowitz, 1970). The infant's eye was able to judge space without the body's experience directing it. Apparently, movement experience is not essential to this type of spatial judgment.

Visual Perception in the Preschooler

Very little is known about visual-perceptual development during the period between late infancy and the late preschool years. This is due to a number of factors. Anyone who has worked with toddlers knows the effort it takes to gain their cooperation and keep their attention long enough to finish a task. In addition, their language is still at an early state of development so that they may not be able to understand directions or describe what they see.

Complex visual-perceptual performance in the preschooler is highly influenced by language, cognitive development, attentional processes, and the child's ability to move about, experience, and manipulate. Knowledge becomes more abstract, more dependent on multiple information-processing systems, and less specifically visual, auditory, or tactile in nature (Goodnow, 1971). For example, children's ability to match shapes is influenced by their ability to label the forms, remember other similar forms, or learn from a form board puzzle.

Developmental steps in complex visual perceptions are important to appreciate because a learning disabled child of preschool or school age often performs immaturely. Since resolution of maturational lags often follows the normal continuum of development, understanding the order in which more complex visual-perceptual skills develop directs evaluations, helps form expectations for development, and guides remedial planning. For example, since a preference for matching by shape occurs earlier than color matching, the developmentally delayed preschooler should be taught to match shapes before colors. Shapes, rather than colors, then become the relevant cues on other types of matching tasks (matching round fruits rather than those that are red).

Knowledge of visual-perceptual development gives us such remedial hints as: helping the student discriminate verticals and symmetrical figures before left-right reversal figures, diagonals, or asymmetrical figures; dealing with configuration first, then internal elements, and finally the combination of both; and dealing with three-dimensional before two-dimensional perceptions. All these activities must take into consideration how a child's cognitive, attending, language, and motor systems also are involved in success on these more complex tasks. Two complex visual-perceptual abilities are visual discrimination and visual closure.

Visual Discrimination. Children use different matching styles at different ages because their visual discrimination preferences change. In a typical experiment, the investigator asks the child to match two forms out of an array of three or more. To do the task correctly the child must discriminate differences such as color, left-right orientation, or presence of an extra line.

A classic study by Brian and Goodenough (1929) found that, when children were asked to match objects or cutouts on the basis of color or shape, children below age three primarily used shape to make their decisions. Three to four year olds used color to make their decisions. Only at six years of age did shape again become the dominant characteristic to which the children attended. More recent studies found that this shape/color/shape cycle is completed two years earlier, by age four (Melkman, Koriat, & Pardo, 1976; Gaines, Suchman, & Trabasso, 1966). Although children make both kinds of discriminations well, at different ages they prefer one over the other when forced to make a choice.

In addition to the preference for color or form, children also use other matching styles at different ages. A three year old matches by using the overall configuration rather than internal elements (Hamilton & Vernon, 1976). Therefore, a three year old might remember the outline or shape of his or her name, but not the letters within the outline. A four year old matches the internal elements and tends to ignore the overall configuration. A five year old can handle both characteristics at once (Tampier, in Vernon, 1976). Matching is easier for any preschooler when the complex designs are symmetrical rather than asymmetrical (Gaines, 1969).

The child's ability to discriminate different forms develops over time. Preschool children can discriminate easily between two figures which are perpendicular to one another, for example a horizontal (——) and a vertical (|); or figures which differ in up-down orientation, such as ⊔ ⊓. However, they have difficulty discriminating diagonals, such as / or \, or left-right mirror images, such as [ ] (Corballis & Zolik, 1977; Hock & Hilton, 1979; Rudel & Teuber, 1963). Many form discriminations that differ in rotation, reversal, and perspective do not become easy until seven years of age (Gibson, Gibson, Pick, & Osser, 1962).

When first learning to print, children frequently write one or more letters backwards. They may also confuse the names of letters that are left-right mirror images of each other. These reversals normally disappear by the mid-elementary school years, although they persist longer for the learning disabled child. Gibson interprets the frequency of reversals in preschoolers as due to the five year old's lack of experience in learning that left-right transformations are a distinctive feature that must be taken into account. Until school age, when the way a letter faces actually changes its name (p–q, b–d), left-right orientation has not been an important characteristic. A toy truck is a truck, no matter what the orientation. Up-down transformations are not as troublesome, she feels, because children have more experience with them (it is important if a cup of milk is turned upside down, but not if facing left or right). Research Box 6-1 presents alternate explanations for reversals.

Visual Closure. *Visual closure* is the ability to recognize visual information in the face of incomplete material, such as being able to recognize that a complete dog exists when you see only part of it. The age at which a child acquires visual closure varies with tasks that measure different aspects of visual closure. For example, a three-dimensional visual closure task (a familiar object partially

RESEARCH BOX 6-1
Two Explanations of Children's Difficulty in Making Left-Right Discriminations

Huttenlocker (1967) believed that preschool children have difficulty with left-right reversals because discriminating mirror figures or symmetrical figures is a harder task than discriminating asymmetrical figures. She felt that the symmetry of the confused figures rather than the left-right reversal is the problem. She presented children with two pairs of figures from Rudel and Tueber's work, (a) ⊔ ⊓ and (b) [ ]. She also added (c) ⊒ and (d) ⊡. Her results showed that discrimination between the two figures in five year old children was more difficult for figure (b) and figure (d); figure (b) being symmetrical around the vertical axis and figure (d) around the horizontal axis.

Bryant (1974), on the other hand, emphasized the importance of the perceptual framework and in-line/out-of-line cues in determining features such as orientation and position of objects, shapes, or symbols on paper. He explained the child's problem with Rudel and Tueber's figures in terms of in-line/out-of-line cues. He noted that the easy forms for children to discriminate (⊓⊔, ⊑) are easy, not because they are symmetrical, but because their important missing lines are out of line with one another. The important lines in the hard figures are in line ([ ], ⊡). Oblique lines are also hard to discriminate because they are not parallel to the perceptual framework, whereas figures involving vertical and horizontal discriminations (— |) are parallel to one or another side of the perceptual frame. He cites research to support his thesis.

Most of the work done with the figures from Rudel and Tueber's experiments is difficult to interpret because the studies involve memory. Therefore, Over and Over (1967) used two pairs of figures (|— and /\) in a discrimination task but designed the experiment so that memory was not required. The children's performance improved but the mirror oblique figure still posed a problem. Regardless of the reason for these left-right reversals, they usually resolve themselves with maturation.

hidden behind a screen) can be solved at an earlier age (four to eight months) than a task involving drawings (Piaget, 1954).

Younger children seem to need more visual information to recognize incomplete pictures. For example, Gollin's (1960) study presented incomplete drawings to a group of children (four years old or more) and adults. The picture contained progressively greater degrees of fragmentation. In the most fragmented of the pictures, four-year-olds recognized only one out of twenty pictures. Adults recognized seven and a half out of twenty. Such findings relate to later reading acquisition because children initially need to spend time scrutinizing individual letter shapes. As they become familiar with these shapes, they recognize them quickly by orienting their attention to the distinctive features of each letter (the horizontal line in e versus c) and fill in the rest from memory. Eventually b's, p's, d's, and q's are discriminated by the directions in which they face, rather than each portion of their shape.

Visual–Motor Development

Many learning disabled children, especially preschoolers, have visual–motor coordination difficulties. They do not progress as expected in tasks such as working puzzles, stacking blocks, or copying. Since, besides speech, motor movement is their only way of demonstrating knowledge, motor movements play an important role in learning disabilities.

Motor movements can aid exploration of and learning about complex visual objects by directing the child's attention to salient features. They can also be a source of difficulty in demonstrating knowledge when the motor movements involved in paper-pencil tasks are not automatic, efficient, and well-developed.

An understanding of normal developmental landmarks in coordinating visual perceptions and motor movements aids detection of delays and planning sequences of remedial objectives. For example, such knowledge helps a teacher decide whether to encourage spontaneous or imitative drawing, and which forms to encourage first. Mastery of the easier elements should facilitate their application in more complex written forms. We shall discuss what we mean by "visual-motor," how motor exploration aids complex visual discrimination, and the development of drawing and copying abilities.

Visual and Motor Processing

Visual-motor processing is the ability to do a task which involves both visual input and fine or gross motor output. *Gross motor* refers to large body movements; *fine motor* traditionally refers to the use of the muscles of the hand. Although certain tasks are called fine motor, they usually involve skills that go far beyond simple visual inputs and hand-muscle movements. For example, when a child draws he or she uses the muscles of the upper arm in positioning the hand, and muscles of the trunk and legs in maintaining balance in the chair. The child also thinks, and uses language to clarify and guide drawing. Similarly, a child stacking blocks needs to pick up and release. This involves the motor system as well as tactile and proprioceptive sensations about the points at which a block touches the skin and the position of joints and limbs.

At four to six weeks of age a child can visually track an object with jerky fixations. These become continuous by two months of age. Within the next month, the infant can look at his or her own hand and hold it aloft while sweeping at an object. By three months the child can glance back and forth from hand to object (Gibson, 1969). Table 6-1 lists additional visual-motor milestones through four and a half years of age.

Motor Exploration
and Complex Visual Discrimination

Besides demonstrating knowledge, motor systems help to direct learning in the older preschooler. One way of studying this has been to compare how well children are able to match forms or objects by visual as opposed to manual

Table 6-1 Development of grasping and manipulatory skills

AGE	SKILL
8–12 weeks	The infant moves extremities in response to rattle
16 weeks	The infant now has arm activity in response to rattle
20 weeks	Definite arm approach movements sweeping at object
24 weeks	Grasps, lifts
28 weeks	Is able to reach with both hands
	Transfers an object from hand to hand
	Resecures an object after dropping
48 weeks	Reaching is well-coordinated
15 months	Can make a tower of two cubes
	Takes six cubes in and out of cup
18 months	Can make a tower of three to four cubes
	Dumps pellets out of jar
24 months	Places forms (circle, triangle, and square) in formboard puzzle
	Makes tower of six to seven cubes
	Aligns two or more cubes to make a train
36 months	Tower of nine cubes
	Imitates a cube bridge
	Places at least ten pellets into a bottle using one hand
48 months	Puts at least ten pellets in bottle within two to five seconds
	Geometric forms — points to eight forms when named
54 months	Geometric forms — points to nine of ten forms when named

SOURCES: Adapted from Gesell, A., *The First Five Years of Life*. New York. Harper & Row, 1940; Knobloch, H. & Pasamanick, B. *Gesell & Amatruda's Developmental Diagnosis*. New York: Harper & Row, 1974.

means. The latter is sometimes referred to as *haptic* discrimination and involves using the tactile, proprioceptive, and fine-motor systems. Children improve in both visual and haptic exploration patterns as they become older; they engage in more exploration and in a more systematic fashion (Piaget & Inhelder, 1956; Zaporozhets, 1965). The haptic exploration traces the outline of figures, whereas visual exploration searches within the figure and attends only minimally to the outline.

Visual matching is almost always more accurate than haptic matching (Pick, Frankel, & Hess, 1975). However, combining the visual with the hand seems at times to enhance a child's ability to discriminate forms. For example, a Russian researcher named Zinchenko asked children, aged three to seven, to examine flat wooden figures of irregular forms and then to recognize them later (Figure 6-1). The children could examine the figures by looking only, touching only, and by both looking and touching (Zaporozhets, 1965). The children performed worst when they were only able to touch the figure. Looking only improved their performance, but both looking and touching figures resulted in an even greater improvement. Performances improved as the age of the children increased.

Figure 6-1

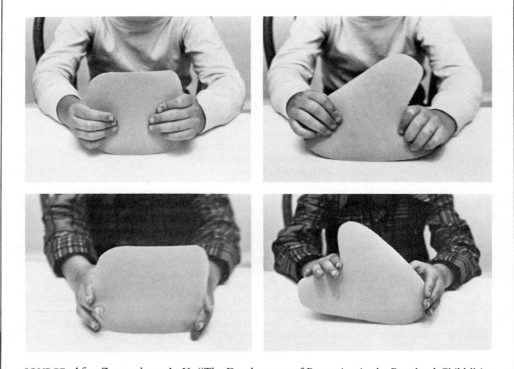

SOURCE: After Zaporozhets, A. V. "The Development of Perception in the Preschool Child," in Mussen, P. (Ed.) European research in cognitive development. *Monographs of the Society for Research in Child Development,* 1965, *30* (2), Serial No. 100.

Why does the combination of visual and haptic exploration improve a child's ability to discriminate form? Goodnow (1971) explains that combined visual and haptic exploration aids discrimination because the eye and hand scan objects in different manners. Since they each explore different features of an object, this results in better recognition and memory. In addition, touch alone seems to serve an attention-getting function. For example, Weiner & Goodnow (1970) found that, when a shape was enclosed in an eye-catching plastic globe, a child remembered just as well when looking only as when both looking and touching. They concluded that the plastic globe served the same function as touching; it helped the eye attend to a distinctive feature it might not have attended to if the children were looking at the object without the globe.

In summary, it seems that at least in the preschool years, the visual modality is superior to the haptic in matching tasks. Haptic exploration draws attention to outlines and visual search occurs within figures, so that different distinctive features are detected by each modality. Under some circumstances the combination of haptic and visual exploration is superior to either one alone because more distinctive features are sampled.

Drawing and Copying

Children's drawings include spontaneous drawings, copying of geometric forms, and drawings of a person. During the latter part of infants' first years, especially if there are brothers or sisters, children will probably manage to grab a crayon, mouth it, or pound it on a table. At around one year of age, children begin to use crayons to make marks on paper (Ilg & Ames, 1972). During the next two years children primarily scribble. This is followed by spontaneous drawing and purposeful imitation of another drawing or object.

Spontaneous Drawing. Kellogg & O'Dell (1969) analyzed the spontaneous art work of preschool children. They examined approximately one million drawings by nursery and public elementary school children, children aged four to fourteen attending art classes, and European and Asian children. They concluded that certain scribbles and forms in preschool children's drawings developed innately: dots; vertical, horizontal, diagonal, and curved lines; zigzags; loops; and circles. These were evident in children across cultures, before any instruction from adults had been given. Children universally were able to spontaneously draw simple shapes long before they were able to copy them.

Imitation Drawing. Some basic drawing landmarks are described in Table 6-2. Children are able to copy verticals first, then horizontals, and finally diagonals. Half of all children are able to successfully copy a circle at three years of age. They next learn to copy squares and then triangles. The figures' lines show that horizontals and verticals are much easier to copy than are diagonals.

Human Figure Drawing. As a child matures he begins attempting to draw pictures of the people and objects around him. How a child approaches drawing a human figure has long been of interest to parents, teachers, and developmental psychologists as an indication of visual–motor ability, emotional stability, intelligence, and social competence (Cratty, 1970). The quality of a child's drawings is assumed to reflect thoughts about him or herself and the world.

Kellogg and O'Dell (1969) traced the development of children's ability to draw human figures. The first step in the sequence is a scribble, which the child achieves at approximately two years of age. By age three the child can draw an oval, and during that year experiments with circles containing markings. Cir-

Table 6-2 Scribbling and drawing landmarks

AGE	SKILL
15 months	Imitates a horizontal scribble (〰)
18 months	Marks page with crayon and scribbles spontaneously
	Makes strokes imitatively
18–21 months	Imitates a vertical stroke (∣)
24 months	Imitates V stroke
	Imitates circular strokes
27 months	Imitates horizontal strokes
30 months	Imitates H strokes
36 months	Copies circle
	Imitates cross
48 months	Draws person with two parts
	Copies cross
54 months	Copies square
	20 percent of children print letters

SOURCES: Adapted from Gesell, A. *The First Five Years of Life*. New York. Harper & Row, 1940; Knobloch, H. & Pasamanick, B. *Gesell & Amatruda's Developmental Diagnosis*. New York: Harper & Row, 1974.

cles then begin to contain marks that represent facial features. At the same time children make drawings which Kellogg calls *suns*. Children then combine the two to form a sun containing some facial features and rays that form two arms and legs. After age three, children generally add one more feature every three months, particularly eyes, nose, mouth, body, and legs (Harris, 1963). By the time a child enters kindergarten, the human figures are fairly sophisticated, containing more detail, proportion, and two-dimensional parts (see Table 6-3).

Gross Motor Development

Gross motor function is the earliest and most obvious developmental ability evaluated at birth. Abnormalities at this time may reflect brain damage. However, academic learning would only be affected if high-level reasoning areas were also damaged. The brain's auditory, sensory, and associative areas are essential for academic and cognitive performance, and are located near the areas of the brain involved in motor function. Therefore an insult to an area involving cognitive ability could affect nearby motor areas as well (Carpenter, 1976). One of the major reasons for noting motor delays lies in the subsequent scrutiny of whether or not these delays reflect a higher-level of cognitive information-processing difficulty.

At present there is no evidence that an abnormality in the ability to perform a smooth motor act causes a cognitive disability. When the two coexist,

Table 6-3 Percentage of boys and girls showing developmental items in human figure drawings at five years of age

EXPECTED[a]	COMMON	NOT UNUSUAL	EXCEPTIONAL
Boys			
Head	Arms	Arm 2d.	Pupils
Eyes	Feet	Legs 2d.	Feet 2d.
Nose	Fingers	Arm down	5 Fingers
Mouth	Hair	Neck	Arms attached at shoulder
Body		Hands	Proportional
Legs		Ear	Nostrils
0–1 clothing item		Eyebrow	Profile
			Elbow
			Two lips
			Knee
			2–3 clothing items
Girls			
Head	Hair	Legs 2d.	Feet 2d.
Eyes	Feet	Neck	Proportional
Nose	Arms 2d.	Hands	Nostrils
Mouth	Fingers	Eyebrow	Two lips
Body	0–1 clothing item	Pupils	Elbow
Legs		Arm down	Profile
Arms		Ear	Arms attached at shoulder
		5 Fingers	Knee
		2–3 clothing items	4 clothing items

[a] *Expected* means present in 86–100% of sample of five year olds; *common* means present in 51–85%; *not unusual* means present in 16–50%; *exceptional* means present in 15% or less.
SOURCE: Adapted from Koppitz, E. *Psychological Evaluation of Children's Human Figure Drawings.* New York: Grune & Stratton, 1968, pp. 12, 16. Reprinted by permission.

they seem to be caused by common factors. Delays in gross motor function in the preschool child are predictive of future learning difficulties when brain insults have affected motor areas as well as other areas highly related to academic achievement, such as language. Since poor motor performance may reflect disorders in receiving or processing information, it is essential to analyze the source of motor delays and intervene as soon as possible.

Although poor motor coordination may not in itself cause a learning disability, it makes demonstrating knowledge difficult. It also may aggravate peer interactions.

The earliest assessment of motor function in human infants involves evaluation of the *primitive reflexes.* These are involuntary motor responses elicited by appropriate peripheral stimuli. An example is the asymmetrical tonic neck reflex. When an infant is laid on his or her back with the head turned to one side, the arm and leg will extend on the side to which the baby is facing. The arm and leg on the opposite side will flex. These reflexes form the substrate for the development of voluntary motor movement. Assessment of these primitive reflexes and other measures such as motor strength and tone, deep tendon reflexes, irritability, respiratory status, heart rate, and skin color are means for predicting future neurological development. Though some researchers (Prechtl, 1965; Roberts, 1968) had noted that neurological abnormalities at birth were prognostic of learning disabilities, most studies do not confirm this correlation (Yang, Ting, & Kennedy, 1968; Capute, et al., 1978). This is most likely because these neurological indicators do not measure the brain areas involved in high-level academic reasoning.

Beyond the immediate neonatal period, motor activity becomes more voluntary and wider in scope. Table 6-4 lists some of these activities, and the age at which approximately 50 percent of all children can perform them.

Laterality, the preference for one side of the body in hand, foot, eye, and ear use, became an issue in Orton's (1937) work in learning disabilities. Orton

Table 6-4   Gross Motor Landmarks

AGE	SKILL
Upright Posture	
16 weeks	Infant is able to raise head when lying on stomach so that head is almost perpendicular to the table surface
20 weeks	Infant makes adequate compensatory movements of the head when pulled from lying on back to a sitting posture
24 weeks	Infant can support self on extended arms in the prone position
28 weeks	In a sitting position, can hold trunk erect momentarily
36 weeks	Can hold trunk erect indefinitely
40 weeks	Can hold trunk erect and maintain balance as turns to side
44 weeks	Can go from sitting to prone to sitting positions
Standing and Walking and Running	
20 weeks	Infant is able to roll over, and momentarily support large fraction of weight
28 weeks	Crawls with abdomen in contact with floor
36 weeks	In creeping position, supports weight on toes
48 weeks	Pulls to standing and is able to walk holding on to furniture
12–18 months	Infant can walk alone with elevation of arms; feet are wide-based for support
18 months	Is able to walk sideways and backward
21 months	Walks up flight of three steps alone
2–3 years	Walking becomes automatic
3 years	Walks up stairs using alternating feet; rides tricycle
4 years	Somersaults; balances well on toes; can walk a straight line 3 meters long
5 years	Can do all previously stated activities more smoothly; hops on one foot

SOURCE: Adapted from Gesell, A., *The First Five Years of Life.* New York: Harper & Row, 1940; Knobloch, H. & Pasamanick, B. *Gesell & Amatruda's Developmental Diagnosis.* New York: Harper & Row, 1974.

proposed that failure to establish consistent usage reflects a failure of the brain to develop the necessary superiority of one hemisphere over another in language and visuo-spatial functions. This has not been shown to be true. Good learners often display this *mixed laterality*. Similarly, left- and right-handedness, a sign of hemispheric motor dominance, are unrelated to learning disabilities, except when the choice of hand has been forced by brain injury that also affected higher cognitive abilities (Hicks & Kinsbourne, 1978b, Kinsbourne & Caplan, 1979).

Handedness develops at different rates in different individuals. The earliest indication of handedness is the tonic neck reflex, in which many infants have a more frequent reflex to the right (Gesell & Ames, 1947). Another indicator of handedness in infants is length of time that one-and-a-half to four-months-old infants grasp a rattle in the left or the right hand. The hand holding the rattle longer may eventually become the writing hand (Caplan & Kinsbourne, 1976). Before handedness is fully established, the normal child does go back and forth between use of only one or both hands (Gesell & Ames, 1947). Right-handedness generally becomes predominant at around four years of age, but can be established as late as ten years. In most cases, children reach eight to ten years of age before they use the right hand for all purposes. Left-handed children exhibit varying degrees of ambidexterity throughout life. Children two-and-a-half to four-and-a-half years old who develop handedness early may have precocious mental and motor development. Yet children who are not brain-injured and do not establish hand dominance before age nine also tend to show no learning difficulties (Kaufman, Zalma, & Kaufman, 1978).

Remediation of motor delays warrants parents' and preschool teachers' attention, as well as that of the occupational and physical therapist if necessary. Although gross motor function depends largely on neurological maturity, some aspects can be influenced through teaching.

Attention

Attention disorders are major contributors to learning disabilities. Inefficient attentional processes must be observed so that modifications that enhance attention can be made in either the stimuli or the preschooler's responses. Each time a preschooler's selective attention is not engaged and maintained, an opportunity for learning is lost. Many such lost opportunities may create wide gaps in knowledge among preschoolers who might otherwise learn well. Attending mechanisms are a primary concern of the preschool teacher because without adequate attention there can be little memory for content.

Knowing the factors which influence a preschooler's attention and the developmental sequence in which they occur can aid the teacher in evaluation and teaching strategies. Aids such as color and form, handling objects, explaining a task, using three-dimensional materials, accentuating task-relevant features, and requiring recognition before recall can all be used to draw attention and increase chances for learning. Preschool development of attention and memory skills also are important for the elementary school teacher to be aware of because many attention and memory characteristics of the learning disabled school age child are similar to those of the preschooler.

There are two types of memory, short- and long-term. Flavell's (1977; Flavell & Wellman, 1976, 1977) sequence of memory development progresses from basic processes of recognition and recall, to the knowledge influencing learning, and, finally, to the use of memory strategies. Teacher direction of learning is particularly important to the preschooler because the child is too young to use intensive, planned, and goal-directed intellectual interaction with information to aid learning.

Short- and Long-Term Memory

The preschooler selects certain features of the environment to attend to and decides to ignore others. What the child selects depends on arousal. What the child ignores depends on inhibition. Investigations of *iconic* (visual) and *echoic* (auditory) memory in older preschoolers and adults indicate that there are virtually no developmental differences in the qualitative or quantitative encoding of information at the time it is received. Capacity and decay rates are similar across ages and auditory information persists slightly longer than visual information (Kail & Siegel, 1977). This process is called *short term memory*.

To store information in long term memory, a person needs to engage multiple cognitive factors, such as perception, language, thought and memory, in order to maintain selective attention and then to remember well (Pick, Frankel, & Hess, 1975; Staats, 1971). For example, in order for a preschooler to attend to and recognize a triangle, multiple cognitive skills need to guide and maintain the child's attention. These skills include the ability to abstract, review past knowledge of triangles, make comparisons to other shapes seen in the past, and group shapes by name and category. Attention matures along with accompanying changes in the psychological processes that aid selective attention.

Basic Processes

Young infants show that they are attending by exhibiting an *orienting reaction*. The orienting reaction includes looking more alert, decreasing sucking, and deceleration of heart rate. Environmental characteristics such as novelty, movement, and changes in complexity of patterns elicit orienting reactions at young ages (Pick, Frankel, & Hess, 1975).

Memory also aids attention during infancy as the baby *recognizes* previously encountered objects. It is only at the end of infancy that the ability to *recall* by retrieving a thought from memory emerges (Flavell, 1977). This is why a two year old may recognize a line by pointing correctly when asked, "show me the line," but may find it harder to name it or to recall its shape when drawing.

The basic processes of recognition memory and recall mature during the first one and one-half to two years of life. Infants can handle more complex and greater numbers of stimuli as they develop. Once an infant is able to recall, the development of these basic processes is complete.

Knowledge

Knowledge is the influence of what the child has come to know on what the child will store and retrieve. Retained knowledge undergoes continuous change over time because of changing meanings, inferences, embellishment, fit to previous knowledge, integration, rehearsal, reorganization, and recomprehending of previous experiences (Paris and Lindauer, 1977). This process results in memory representations that are simpler, easier to label, and consistent with the child's attitudes, temperament, character, developmental abilities, and conventional sociohistorical information. Clearly, memory is not an isolated mental faculty or a passive storehouse of experience. As a complex combination of an individual's perceptual, cognitive, social, and motivational characteristics, stored information is influential in guiding attention to, giving meaning to, and ultimately in storing, transforming, and retrieving new information. Therefore, the more knowledge a child has the more the child can learn.

Strategies

Preschoolers seldom use deliberate plans to remember (Paris & Lindauer, 1977). Therefore, especially with children above age three, the teacher should employ several strategies to help children focus attention during learning tasks: having the child name an item, pointing out distinctive features, instructing the child to look more and get ready to remember, and presenting items in a logical series. Planning is facilitated by knowing that children at three years of age attend better to color than to form, and by age four prefer form to color. Preschoolers attend better when allowed to handle an object, when the task is explained to them, when the object is three-dimensional, and when the relevant features are accentuated in some way (Pick, Frankel, & Hess, 1975). The preschooler also finds it easier to remember items occurring later in a sequence because that requires less long-term storage.

Efficient long-term storage requires memory strategies for which preschoolers are still too immature: continuing to repeat aloud a word they want to remember (verbal rehearsal), putting all the toys of the same color together so as to be able to recall them all (organization), noting many characteristics of a letter in order to better remember it (elaborating), and dividing a series of numbers into groups of two so as to recall the whole series (clustering). The ability to use such strategies is a developmental phenomenon too difficult for most preschool children. When they do use these strategies, they use them poorly, even after instruction. Even when taught how to use these strategies well, a child will not use them spontaneously until the early school years, and then it takes until the child is ten to fourteen years of age before they become well-developed (Hagen, Jongeward, & Kail, 1975).

Recognizing that multiple strategies can engage their students' attention and encourage learning, preschool teachers often set themes that pervade the child's day. For example, when a child does not learn to label and sequence several characters through the Gingerbread Man story, he may learn these skills by singing the Gingerbread Man song, baking gingerbread cookies, or drawing, cutting, pasting, tracing, and coloring Gingerbread Man characters.

Language Development

Language reception, processing, and expression skills can impact significantly on a child's thinking, problem-solving, social interactions, visual perceptions, regulation of motor activity, and attention and memory processes. For many learning disabled children, language disabilities persist into the elementary years and language is not used to facilitate learning; these problems slow down academic progress. Therefore, teachers and parents must carefully monitor the young child's acquisition of language and how language delays may compound or create other developmental delays. When problems become apparent, parents or teachers should intervene as soon as possible. Early intervention is critical because by the time children enter school, most have mastered the major linguistic rules used by the adults around them (Eisenson, 1972).

Although there is still no unanimity among theorists on how language actually is acquired, the typical stages of language development are well understood. These stages help us identify ways in which language-delayed children differ from their peers. Knowledge of language's impact on perception, attention, and memory also helps define objectives for preschool intervention and explain how language delays may interfere with later academic learning.

Theories of Language Acquisition

There are three major theories of how language is acquired: *environmentalist, nativist,* and *interactionist.* Each theory is supported by some empirical data, but contradicted by other data (Bloom, 1975). Most experts in the learning disabilities field have adopted the interactionist position. Its view that language and thought are intimately intertwined has provided a valuable framework within which to evaluate a preschooler's language progress, remediate language disorders, and conduct research in learning disabilities. The interactionist theory suggests several ways in which the development of LD children, who do not think or express themselves as intelligently as we would wish, can be facilitated: teaching better use of language to express meaningful thoughts, teaching specific language through which children then can better reason, and making experiences more meaningful so that words can be better understood and in turn used to convey meaning.

The Environmentalist Position. The environmentalist position is exemplified by B. F. Skinner's (1959) behavioral theory. A child's language, according to environmentalists, is shaped by others' selective reinforcements of his or her random vocalizations and speech imitations. That is, as the parent pays more attention (cuddling, fondling, excitement, imitating) to the child's approximations of speech sounds and words, the child is more apt to reproduce these again some time in the future. Sounds that are not speech-like drop out because they have attracted no unusual attention. Strings of more and more complex words are shaped through the imitation and practice that is generated by others' positive reactions.

Skinner's behavioral theory predicts that a child can't independently generate entirely new words and grammatical forms. The child first has to hear them and repeat them in the expectation of reinforcement. Once specific words and grammatical relations have been mastered, they are generalized only to other word forms and sentences that share many common features. Since children are not expected to understand sentences when the sentences' words have not been previously reinforced, the most extreme behaviorists portray humans as programmable machines in which language breeds thought. In other words, Beth would not be able to understand the concept of "mommy" until she repeatedly heard the word paired with all the wonderful things her mommy stands for.

The Nativist Position. The nativist (or biological) position gives children far more credit for being active generators of language and thought. Nativists believe that children have innate capacities to generate and deduce a grammatical theory that aids their understanding and production of infinite numbers of sentences (Chomsky, 1968). Language emerges by itself through maturation, and the environment merely triggers this unfolding process (Lenneberg, 1967). The environment does little more than provide the raw material (words) to which the child applies unique cognitive processes in order to create language. The child's maturational readiness to understand language or speak determines the level of language acquisition at any one time.

Nativists believe that thought precedes speech. For proof they point out that infants can understand complex language long before they can speak; and they express complex thoughts through very simple utterances. Nativists note that children generate their own orderly set of language rules, and don't just imitate the speech in their environment. For example, children consistently utter word combinations such as "Mommy all gone," "baby cry," "no go," "no night-night" (Braine, 1963; Brown & Bellugi, 1964; Ervin, 1964). They are certainly not hearing these word combinations from adults around them, unless of course the adults are imitating the child's speech.

Additional evidence for children's prewiring for speech comes from neuropsychological data showing the uniform emergence of cerebral specialization for language in children, and from the similarity of infant babbling and general patterns of linguistic acquisition regardless of native language. Children all over the world understand all that "mommy" connotes, but are just waiting for the right word to label their thoughts.

The Interactionist Position. Piaget's (1962) interactionist position is a compromise between environmentalist and nativist perspectives. Language is acquired as children take in (*assimilate*) the language in the environment, and then modify (*accommodate*) it with their own knowledge and thoughts. The child's reasoning processes also direct what language is assimilated. Children's language becomes more sophisticated with maturity because they understand more complex language and modify it with more complex thoughts.

Interactionists view the child as an active responder to the world. The child initiates, interacts with, and transforms his or her conceptions of reality. Consider three-year-old Beth as she pages through an animal book with her mother. Her mother points out the bear. Beth notices that the bear is feeding her cubs and transforms the character into a good mommy. Now the bear story is really a story about good mommies. Beth's language and thought develop both independently and simultaneously, each influencing the other's continued development.

Without thought as a prerequisite, children can develop no meaningful language (Flavell, 1977). But once they begin to acquire language, children use it to further shape their thoughts (Bruner, Olver, & Greenfield, 1966). MacNamara explains how thought precedes speech, yet speech modifies thought.

> . . . infants learn their language by first determining, independent of language, the meaning which a speaker intends to convey to them, and by then working out the relationship between the meaning and the language. To put it another way, the infant uses meaning as a clue to language, rather than language as a clue to meaning. . . . Obviously once he has made some progress in language, a child can use language to develop his thinking. . . . our thinking is enriched or brought into focus by language (MacNamara, 1972, p. 1).

Myklebust (1960) was a leader in applying the interactionist perspective to learning disabilities. He proposed that infants cannot develop comprehension of the spoken word (*auditory receptive language*) until their experiences have acquired such meaningfulness as to be reflected in thought (*inner language*). Only after developing auditory receptive skills do children learn to symbolize experiences through words (*auditory expressive language*). "A word without meaning is not a word" (Myklebust, 1960, p. 232); "output follows input, so the child speaks only after he comprehends" (p. 231).

Like interactionists, Myklebust proposed a reciprocal feedback between the inner, receptive, and expressive processes. Enhancement of one also enhances the other, weak receptive language also impairs expression (Myklebust, 1954), and inner language eventually involves thinking in words, using mental trial and error, grouping and classifying experiences, and talking to oneself.

This perspective has helped us conceptualize the nature of a learning disabled child's language strengths and weaknesses so as to guide remedial efforts.

Language Acquisition and Delays

As Myklebust's model suggests, inner language disturbances are the most debilitating of all language disorders. Children with inner language distur- bances do not gain meaning from experience and consequently cannot use language to represent concepts. As Myklebust proposed, studies find that receptive (understanding information) and expressive (communicating infor- mation) processes are integrally related (Denckla, 1977). Receptive disorders always result in expressive disorders, because children cannot respond mean- ingfully to someone else unless they understand what the other person has said. Children also cannot monitor their own speech well when their ability to comprehend what they are saying is impaired (Benton, 1978). Again, as Myklebust (1954) proposed, even when the major disorder appears to be ex- pressive, it is often accompanied by a receptive weakness (Wood, 1969). For a child with an expressive disorder, the lack of conversational give and take eventually impairs comprehension as well (Denckla, 1977).

Language acquisition, whether receptive or expressive, can be broken down into five components: phonology, morphology, syntax, semantics, and pragmatics. *Phonology* refers to individual sounds, *morphology* to word forma- tions, *syntax* to sentence formations, *semantics* to the understanding of words and word relationships, and *pragmatics* to the ability to engage in conversa- tional speech. Children with learning disabilities often experienced difficulties in these components of language development during their preschool years. Their phonetic and morphological weaknesses tend to resolve themselves within the elementary school years. Appropriate syntax often takes longer to acquire, and semantics and pragmatics may present difficulties throughout life. A weakness in any one of these areas also may impact on proficiency in another. For example, if Amy has difficulty in formulating the /s/ phoneme, she will be unable to express the plural morpheme, even if she is quite capable of understanding what we mean by singulars and plurals. If, at an older age, Amy is unable to understand the semantics of idioms ("go jump in the lake," "drop dead"), then her pragmatic ability to converse and get along with her peers will be seriously hampered.

Since language delays impact thought, learning, and social interactions, early intervention is critical. Most language-delayed children eventually ac- quire speech sounds (Ingram, 1969), morphemes, and syntax (Bloom, 1978; Ingram, 1976) in the same developmental order as typical children. Therefore, approaching delayed language development within a normal language acquisi- tion context benefits program planning (Menyuk, 1974; Rapin & Wilson, 1978). There are some children, however, whose language development and efficiency do not follow the typical developmental course (Menyuk, 1964; Morehead & Ingram, 1973).

Phonology. *Phonemes* are the smallest units of sound that go into forming words. They carry no meaning. For example, the words "cat" and "that" are each made up of three phonemes, /c/ or /th/, /a/, /t/, none of which have meaning by themselves. When phonemes are interchanged, however, they affect meaning (b-a-t for c-a-t). By six years of age, children usually have mastered the phonemes of the English language.

Within a month after birth newborns can discriminate speech sounds (Eimas et al., 1971; Trehub & Rabinovitch, 1972). Their left hemisphere EEGs, where speech usually becomes localized, actively respond to speech signals. Nonspeech sounds create greater activation of the right hemisphere (Molfese, 1973). Their first observable response to sound is turning in the direction from which it came (localizing the sound), and sustaining attention toward it. Next follows the ability to make nonspeech sounds (babble), to intentionally repeat sounds that have been spontaneously uttered (da-da), to distinguish and repeat individual sounds made by others, and finally to attend to the sequence of the sounds in words, so as to imitate them. Table 6-5 traces the development of infant auditory-vocal skills from birth through twelve months of age.

Frequently, a child identified as learning disabled was also delayed in infant vocalization, auditory discrimination, and articulation.

Vocalization. One of the first signs of a potential language disorder may be subtle abnormalities in a child's crying patterns (Wiig & Semel, 1980). The child also may be late in babbling and imitating adult speech sounds.

Auditory Discrimination. Learning disabled children commonly have difficulties as preschoolers in telling apart similar-sounding phonemes in words. For example, the words "bat" and "pat" may be mistaken as the same. The words "sat" and "pat" are less likely to be mistaken because their features are more distinct.

Articulation. Articulation difficulties, when unaccompanied by other delays, are not highly related to future learning disabilities. This is because articulation disorders alone represent a motor-movement or motor-planning difficulty and do not involve higher-level perceptual and cognitive abilities (Eisenson, 1972). Articulation errors, however, can disturb communication with others by distorting the child's syntax (Shriner, Holloway, & Daniloff, 1969). One of the first signs of such a motor difficulty may be sucking problems at birth (Tarnopol & Tarnopol, 1977).

When a child has difficulty discriminating between phonemes, this is reflected in articulation errors. The preschooler whose articulation disorder is caused by this type of perceptual delay, or by a conceptual inability to deal with sounds, is at higher risk for becoming learning disabled.

Other children can discriminate and articulate individual sounds well, but not when transitioning from one phoneme to another in consonant clusters, syllables, and words. Some may articulate acceptably in single word utterances but make distortions in connected speech. Poor perception of sound sequences and rhythms may result in motor patterns such as poor fluency, sound reversals (aminal for animal), jerky irregular speech, cluttered incomprehensible speech, difficulty monitoring one's own or understanding others' voice pitch and loudness, rhyming difficulty, and difficulty distinguishing and sequencing sounds.

Morphology. *Morphemes* are the smallest meaningful units in words. For example, the word "cats" is composed of two morphemes: the word "cat", and the "s" that gives the word its plural meaning. Other morphemes that lend meaning to words are prefixes (*un*dress), verb tense forms (walk*ed*), person (I walk, he walk*s*), etc. Only when the child understands the meanings of morphemes will he or she be able to eventually string several together to make meaningful sentences (Brown, 1973).

Children's understanding of language is well developed even before they can express themselves in single words. The language production stage is said to have begun when the child can say ten single words (Nelson, 1973). This usually occurs after the infant's first birthday. Among children's first words are those conveying common actions ("bye-bye") and objects that they can act upon ("bottle," "sock") (Nelson, 1973). Other early words are based on perceptual attributes that are meaningful to a baby ("up" for movement; "mmm" for taste) (Clark, 1973). Table 6-6 details the typical progression of receptive and expressive language from twelve to thirty-six months of age. By age three children can understand thousands of words and have an expressive vocabulary as high as 1000 words (Eisenson, 1972).

Table 6-7 describes the course of morphological comprehension from three and a half years on. It indicates that by the time youngsters enter kindergarten they have mastered very sophisticated word formation rules. These rules enable children to generate word forms for words they have never encountered before.

Many learning disabled children experience significant delays understanding or applying such morphological rules as third person verb forms, verb tenses, possessives, singular versus plural, irregular plurals and past tense forms, comparatives and superlatives, and prefixes (Vogel, 1974; Wiig & Semel, 1976; Wiig, Semel, & Crouse, 1973). Often these difficulties relate to limitations in auditory perception, or memory for unstressed or low information-carrying parts of phrases and sentences (such as articles and prepositions), or word endings becoming reduced in rapid conversation (Wiig & Semel, 1980). The efficiency of children's language processing also can be impaired by the speaker's style, speed, intonation, stress patterns, and the context in which the speaking is taking place. When a child has difficulty grasping the meaning of certain word forms, he or she will not use these forms to convey meaning in spoken messages. When the disability is primarily at the expressive end, the child's ability to convey meaning to others also will be compromised.

Table 6-5   The emergence of auditory-vocal skills from birth to twelve months of age

AGE RANGE	AUDITORY PROCESSING SKILLS	VOCAL-MOTOR PRODUCTION SKILLS
0–1 mo.	Responds to mother's quieting efforts. Responds to sound of bell.	Vocalizes other than crying.
1–3 mo.	Responds to sound of rattle.	Vocalizes once or twice during physical examination.
1–4 mo.	Responds to sharp sounds such as the click of a light switch.	Responds with a social smile when an examiner talks or smiles.
1–5 mo. (2.2 mo.)*	Searches with eyes for sounds of a bell or a rattle.	Vocalizes at least 4 times during physical examination.
1–5 mo. (2.3 mo.)		Vocalizes 2 different sounds.
1–6 mo. (2.7 mo.)		Vocalizes to an examiner's social smile and talk.
		Vocalizes with differentiated cries for hunger and pain.
2–4 mo.		Coos with repetitions of one syllable.
2–6 mo. (3.8 mo.)	Turns head to sound of bell.	
2–6 mo. (3.9 mo.)	Turns head to sounds of a rattle.	
3–4 mo.	Reacts to sudden noises. Heeds spoken voices.	Cries strongly. Sucks and swallows well.
		Voice quality normalizes. Responds with a meaningful smile. Vocalizes back when talked to.
4.6 mo.		Vocalizes different attitudes such as pleasure, displeasure, eagerness, satisfaction, and anger.
3–8 mo. (4.8 mo.)	Discriminates strangers.	
4–6 mo.	Turns to speaking voice. Localizes source of sounds (bell, rattle, etc.). Plays purposefully with noise-making toys. Responds appropriately to friendly or angry voices.	Laughs aloud. Tongue retracts in sucking. Eats a cookie easily. Babbles a series of syllable repetitions. Babbles several sounds on one breath. Babbles to people. Vocalizes to mirror image. Vocalizes to toys and for social contact.

Syntax. *Syntax* is the way in which words are strung together into meaningful sequences. The grammatical structure of words within a sentence is critical to meaning. For example, "You will go with your father" has a different intent than "Will you go with your father?" Each demands a different response.

Table 6-5 continued

AGE RANGE	AUDITORY PROCESSING SKILLS	VOCAL-MOTOR PRODUCTION SKILLS
4–8 mo. (5.8 mo.)	Listens with interest to sound productions of others.	
5–12 mo. (7.6 mo.)		Vocalizes 4 different syllables. Rings a bell purposefully.
5–14 mo. (7.9 mo.)	Listens selectively to familiar words such as "daddy," "dollie," "doggie."	Says "da-da" or equivalent.
7–8 mo.		Shouts for attention. Sings tones. Babbles with the inflectional patterns of adult speech. Vocalizes in recognition of familiar people.
6–14 mo. (9.1 mo.)	Responds to verbal requests such as "Give me that."	
6–13 mo. (9.4 mo.)	Places objects on command, such as placing a cube in a cup.	
8–15 mo. (9.7 mo.)	Follows directions for simple actions such as stirring with a spoon.	
7–16 mo. (10.0 mo.)	Looks at pictures.	
9–10 mo.	Responds to request to wave "bye-bye."	Waves bye-bye.
	Responds to his or her name.	Imitates a number of syllables after adults.
	Responds to request to smile and pat a mirror.	Plays peek-a-boo and patty-cake.
7–13 mo. (10.1 mo.)	Responds to inhibitory words such as "no-no."	Shakes head for no.
7–17 mo. (10.1 mo.)		Inhibits action on commands such as "no, put it down," and "don't touch."

* NOTE: Numbers in parentheses indicate average age of skill attainment.
SOURCE: Wiig, E. H., and Semel, E. M. *Language Assessment and Intervention for the Learning Disabled.* Columbus, Ohio: Charles E. Merrill, 1980, pp. 13–14. Reprinted by permission.

Although a child may be able to speak in single words beginning at around one year old, it is only at eighteen to twenty-four months of age that the child begins to understand basic grammatical relations so as to combine two words at a time ("Mommy bye-bye"). Children acquire these initial word combinations from imitation and reduction of adult speech into high-information nouns and verbs. "Do you see the milk" is imitated as "see milk" rather than as "you the." They also make deductions from other combinations that they

Table 6-6 The emergence of language skills from twelve to thirty-six months of age

AGE RANGE	LANGUAGE PROCESSING SKILLS	LANGUAGE PRODUCTION SKILLS
9–15 mo. (12.0 mo.)★		Says "mama" or "dada" or other first word.
9–18 mo. (12.5 mo.)		Imitates words such as "baby," "apple," "more," and "up."
13–14 mo.		Tries to sing simple tunes as "Jack and Jill."
10–23 mo. (14.2 mo.)		Says 2 words in a single utterance as reported by mother or examiner.
		Uses meaningful gestures such as pointing to make wants known.
15–16 mo.	Understands most simple questions. Points to own nose, eye, mouth, and other body parts on request.	Produces extensive vocalization and echoing responses.
		Has a speaking vocabulary of from 5 to 10 words.
		Uses 2-word phrases and short sentences.
		Uses expressive jargon.
		Speaks from 4 to 7 words with clear pronunciation.
13–27 mo. (17.8 mo.)		Names objects on confrontation of a ball, cup, pencil, watch, etc.
14–26 mo. (17.8 mo.)	Responds to request for play actions such as "Put the doll in the chair," "Give the doll her milk," "Wipe the doll's nose."	
14–27 mo. (18.8 mo.)		Uses words and utterances to make wants known.
17–18 mo.		Speaks 10 words with clear pronunciation.
		Asks for desired objects by naming them ("cookie," "milk," etc.)
15–26 mo. (19.1 mo.)	Points to parts of a doll such as "hand," "mouth," and "eyes" on request.	
14–27 mo. (19.3 mo.)		Names one pictured object such as a "shoe," "car," "dog," "cat," or "house."
16–28 mo. (19.9 mo.)	Points to 2 pictures of objects such as a "dog," "shoe," "cup," "clock," "house," "flag," "star," "purse," or "book" on request.	
16–20 mo. (20.6 mo.)		Produces 2-word utterances (modifier and noun; operator and lexical item) such as "Here chair," "Fix it," "Want it," "Daddy home," "Eat cookie."
16–30 mo. (21.4 mo.)		Names 2 pictured objects in a series of pictures of a "shoe," a "doll," and an "apple."

Table 6-6 continued

AGE RANGE	LANGUAGE PROCESSING SKILLS	LANGUAGE PRODUCTION SKILLS
17–30 mo. (21.6 mo.)	Points to five pictures of objects such as a "cup," "chair," "table," "house," "flag," "star," "purse," or "book" on request.	
21–22 mo.		Attempts to describe experiences after the fact. Combines 3 words to describe ideas or events such as "Daddy go bye-bye."
17–30 mo. (22.1 mo.)		Names 3 pictured objects such as "shoe," "doll," "ball," "baby," and "apple."
16–30 mo. (23.4 mo.)	Discriminates between 2 related requests such as "Give me the *cup;* Give me the *plate.*"	
17–30 mo. (24.0 mo.)		Names 3 related objects such as "socks," "shoes," "pants," "shirt."
23–24 mo.	Responds to simple requests for actions such as "Show me a dog," "Pick up the hat," "Give daddy the cup." Points to body parts such as a doll's nose, eye, and ear. Responds to questions for biographical and other information such as "What is your name?" and "What does the doggie say?"	Has discarded jargon. Shows marked decrease in sound and word repetition (echolalia). Refers to self by proper name. Produces sentences with from 2 to 4 words.
22–30 mo. (28.2 mo.)	Understands 2 prepositions such as "in" and "on."	
23–32 mo. (30.0 mo.)	Understands 3 prepositions such as "in," "on," "under."	
36 mo.	Identifies pictured objects on request when their function is indicated as in "Show me the one that you wear" or "Show me the one that you eat."	Tells his/her own sex. Indicates age by holding up fingers. Counts to 3. Repeats 5 to 7 syllable sentences, 2 to 3 nonsense syllables, 2 to 3 digits. Tells how common objects such as a fork, cup, shoe, or car are used. Produces phrases and sentences with personal pronouns, adjectives, prepositions, and/or adverbs. Uses regular noun plurals such as "dogs," "cups," "glasses."

* NOTE: Numbers in parentheses indicate average age of skill attainment.

SOURCE: Wiig, E. H., and Semel, E. M. *Language Assessment and Intervention for the Learning Disabled.* Columbus, Ohio: Charles E. Merrill, 1980, pp. 15–17. Reprinted by permission.

Table 6-7 Order of acquisition of word formation rules

WORD FORMATION RULE	APPLICATION	BY 75%		BY 90%
		AGE RANGE OF ACQUISITION		
Regular noun plurals	balls	3–6★	to	6–0 years
	coats	5–6	to	6–6 years
	chairs	6–6	to	7–0+ years
Present progressive tense	running, hitting	3–0	to	3–6 years
Present progressive tense	going	3–6	to	5–6 years
Adjective forms				
Comparative	smaller, taller	4–0	to	5–0 years
Superlative	fattest	3–0	to	3–6 years
Noun derivation				
-er	hitter	3–6	to	5–0 years
	painter	4–0	to	6–0 years
	farmer	5–0	to	6–6 years
-man	fisherman	5–6	to	6–0 years
-ist	bicyclist, pianist	7–0	to	7–0+ years
Adverb derivation				
-ly	easily, gently	7–0+	to	7–0+ years

★ 3–6 = 3 years, 6 months

SOURCE: Wiig, E. H., and Semel, E. M. *Language Assessment and Intervention for the Learning Disabled*. Columbus, Ohio: Charles E. Merrill, 1980, p. 26. Reprinted by permission.

could not have heard ("allgone," "night–night") (Brown & Bellugi, 1964). At two to two and a half years old the child's sentences begin to have subjects and predicates ("Mommy going"; "bottle fall down"). From then on sentences become more and more complex. By age three, the child has mastered subject, predicate, and object relationships and can expand each of these into phrases (Menyuk, 1969). By kindergarten age, the typical child has mastered many of the grammatical rules of adult language.

Some learning disabled children have particular difficulty understanding the concepts conveyed by sentences. These *deep structure* problems may have several causes:

1. lack of mastery of linguistic rules (Menyuk & Looney, 1972; Semel & Wiig, 1975);
2. difficulty inferring meaning ("I am playing" versus "I might play") or determining who does the acting in passive sentences ("he was chased by her") (Wiig & Semel, 1976);
3. trouble with negatives (Wiig & Semel, 1976);
4. difficulty dealing with lengthy phrases and complex or ambiguous sentences (Johnson & Myklebust, 1967);
5. trouble with "wh" questions (*what, who, when, where, why*) (Wiig & Semel, 1980);

6. trouble with sentences containing *this, that, these, those* (Wiig & Semel, 1980);
7. weak immediate recall or reauditorization (repeating in one's head) of a sentence (Wiig & Semel, 1980); and
8. trouble dealing with word sequences and meaning (Wiig & Semel, 1980).

Other LD children have *surface structure* difficulties. They comprehend the underlying meaning of individual words but do not comprehend the word order itself or the sentence meaning. These preschoolers need a lot of time to translate the words and sentence structure into meaning.

The difficulty that learning disabled children encounter in comprehending syntax is reflected in their expressive language. They omit words, add inappropriate words, use incorrect grammar, and distort the order of words and phrases (Johnson & Myklebust, 1967). They often speak in no more than two or three word sentences and have great difficulty expressing thoughts through language or having language aid their conceptual processes.

Semantics. *Semantics* provides the meaningful connection between words and sentences, and other ideas or events. Unless a child has some system of meaning, language is of no use and he or she will be incapable of understanding or learning it.

Toddlers often express semantic content through single words. For example, "cookie" may mean "I want a cookie," "look at the cookie," "there's a cookie," or "the cookie fell on the floor." Situational context obviously influences exactly what "cookie" means (Bloom, 1970). The child soon becomes able to express ideas about what is going on in the here and now. By the early elementary school years the child can choose the correct syntax to express very complex ideas about past and future events.

Children with learning disabilities often have semantic difficulties understanding and remembering words that sound alike (two, too), words that have dual meanings (block to play with versus block a punch), adjectives that are not easily described (shape and time concepts), complex verbs (evading versus running away), comparative relations (smaller than), pronouns, and strings of adjectives, adverbs, and prepositions (Wiig & Semel, 1976). Idioms, metaphors, morals, and proverbs often present life-long problems.

Difficulty naming (or word-finding) can stem from auditory-perceptual confusions between similar-sounding words, poor learning of the rules of sentence structure, and many semantic problems (Jansky & de Hirsch, 1973; Wiig & Semel, 1980):

1. concrete ways of thinking and defining words;
2. limitation in ability to mentally visualize the content of what is being said;
3. limitations in using symbols and conceptualizing;
4. narrow attribution of word meanings;
5. weaknesses in shifting from one reference point to another;

6. weak categorizing ability (gender and number);
7. poor simultaneous analysis and synthesis of critical concepts and words;
8. poor recall of word order for comparisons and interpretations; and
9. narrow or irrelevant word associations.

These children's imprecise attribution of meaning to vocabulary and vocabulary to meaning limits their expressive abilities (McGinnis, 1963). They erroneously associate their words with others in the same semantic category (tiger for lion; paper fork instead of plastic fork), opposites (aunt for uncle), those with similar phonemes (sing for sting), or they repeat the same word over and over again (Wiig & Semel, 1980).

Other children with word-finding difficulties have sufficient understanding and vocabulary to express themselves well, but lack semantic flexibility for retrieving specific words. Again, verbal fluency, flexibility, creativity, and elaboration are diminished (Wiig & Semel, 1980). Their difficulty choosing words may cause them to substitute inappropriate words, resort to synonyms, talk around and around a topic, gesture, try to define the words, stall ("you know"; "uhm"; "wait a minute"), use imprecise words ("whatchama call it"), or change the topic. It is not uncommon for parents to become impatient and tell their children to hurry up and say what they mean. After a child has finally found the right words, the parent may comment "Why didn't you just come right out and say that in the first place?"

The preschooler with naming difficulties often has later learning disabilities. This is because the abilities underlying word-finding are the same as those essential to higher-level academic learning.

Pragmatics. *Pragmatics* is competence in interpersonal communication. Pragmatics combines all the previous skills so that words can be adjusted to the particular person being spoken to, what was said right before, the topic of conversation, the goal of the discussion, and the time and setting context (Hopper & Naremore, 1973).

Pragmatic speech is becoming a major area of concern with experts because it may account in part for the learning disabled being ignored and not easily befriended by others. Learning disabled children's poor ability to interpret, infer from, compare, and respond to the speech of others may cause a good deal of their social difficulties (Bryan, 1977). Consider what happened when Lisa called Andy a jerk after he played a trick on her. Andy got angry and ran home to tell on Lisa. But Lisa only meant jerk in a playful, "You're a funny guy" manner and couldn't understand why Andy had run away from her. Imperceptions also may occur with nonverbal stimuli such as an elbowing being interpreted as "I hate you" rather than "Hi there" or "Hey, did you get a load of that?" Similarly, Andy may laugh when his nursery school teacher reprimands him because he doesn't sense the meaning behind his teacher's tone.

Pragmatics has been studied primarily in older children. Yet signs of such difficulties do appear in the preschool years, and these children need help learning to respond appropriately in social situations. They can be taught, for example, to whisper in a movie theater, to add inflection when relating a story rather than speaking in a monotone, and to read body language so as to judge whether jumping into a guest's lap is appropriate.

Language Facilitation of Memory and Behavior

The proficiency with which preschoolers use language in daily problem-solving influences what they attend to, how they connect new experiences to what they already understand, and what they store in memory, recall, and apply appropriately. The more meaningful, conceptually related, and semantically familiar new information is to what's already in a child's conceptual system, the more memorable it becomes (Flavell & Wellman, 1976). In addition, the preschooler's verbalizations, whether audible to others or just inner speech, exert a strong regulatory function on learning and behavior (Kohlberg, Yarger, & Hjertholm, 1968; Wozniak, 1972). As overt and covert (inner) speech increase, so does task success (Garrity, 1975; Jensen, 1971; Sheingold & Shapiro, 1976).

The self-regulatory function of speech gained notice from the theoretical work of Vygotsky (1962) and his student, Luria (1961). Luria proposed three stages by which verbal control is gained over behavior:

Stage 1: speech of others directing a child's behavior

Stage 2: the child's overt speech governs his behavior

Stage 3: the child's behavior becomes effectively regulated by his covert, inner speech

Uses of stages 2 and 3 increase as preschoolers get older (Flavell & Wellman, 1976). By the age of three and a half, most children already give themselves verbal self-instructions. By age five, overt self-verbalizations while trying to understand a problem typically become inaudible to others (Tarnapol & Tarnapol, 1977). At this age, self-generated instructions facilitate problem-solving just as much as instructions that adults ask children to repeat (Miller, Shelton, & Flavell, 1970).

One of the preschooler's most frequent uses of self-verbalization is self-instruction to engage in a motor act. It is not uncommon to see a three year old on a tot-cycle giggling, yelling "go-go," then tensing his arm and leg muscles, and finally moving his legs forward a few times to make the cycle go. When the cycle stops, he might self-instruct all over again.

Self-verbalization eventually can be used to refrain from doing something. Before age three and a half, self-commands often end up generating the very motor activity the child wanted to inhibit (Luria, 1977). For example, the preschooler who scoots by the hot stove and says "no touch," often goes ahead and touches. But, by age four to four and a half, the semantic content of a self-instruction overcomes the motor discharge aspect and the preschooler obeys the "no touch" self-verbalization. Inhibiting self-instructions ("I'm not going to look at . . .") may be even more helpful in maintaining attention to a task than task-facilitative self-instructions ("I'm going to look at my work") (Patterson & Mischel, 1976). This is because inhibiting behavior is much harder than actually doing something.

Most children automatically use speech to guide their behavior. Those who don't often have learning disabilities, and approach tasks in a disorganized manner. Teaching these children to use task-appropriate self-instructions can have a great impact on performance (Meichenbaum & Goodman, 1969). Learning to self-instruct aloud or silently increases the preschooler's likelihood of initiating a behavioral intention, plan, or set, and then sustaining it for a while. It helps the four year old deliberately inhibit tempting but forbidden or inappropriate behaviors, wait and suspend action, and postpone and delay gratification (Flavell, 1977).

Language plays an important role in children's ability to use their problem-solving skills to best advantage. This language usage depends on mastery of phonemic, morphologic, syntactic, semantic, and pragmatic relationships at both receptive and expressive levels, together with the intent to let language be a mediator for thought.

Summary

Learning disabilities frequently begin in the preschool years. Since learning disabled children develop in visual, visual-motor, motor, attention, and language skills at a slower than typical pace, knowledge of expected skill sequences helps to identify those areas of weakness that need to be strengthened. Knowledge of normal preschool development also helps to construct learning hierarchies and remedial techniques. For example, research indicates that infants are ready to master simple visual-perceptual, speech discrimination, and meaningful conceptual abilities, long before they can demonstrate their knowledge by manipulating objects, moving about the environment, or speaking. Remediation of developmental weaknesses is aided by knowledge that touching helps to direct the eye to distinctive features, just like verbal labeling and self-instructions help direct behavior. Besides guiding preschool interventions, knowledge of preschool development is essential because many older LD students have abilities and teaching needs similar to those of a preschooler.

Suggestions for Further Study

1. Before reading about abnormalities in child development such as learning disabilities, a student should be well-versed in normal child development. Flavell's (1977) and Mussen, Conger, & Kagan's (1979) texts thoroughly discuss the various child development theories, and data evaluating them. Gibson (1969), Salapatek (1975) and Osofsky (1979) specifically review the theories of visual-perceptual development.

2. Many investigators have contributed to the data about memory development. The reviews by Hagen & Hale (1973), Hagen, Jongeward, & Kail (1975), Brown (1975), and Kail (1979) will give the interested teacher more ideas about how to capture a preschooler's attention.

3. To learn more about various language acquisition perspectives, read the works of the following individuals: environmentalist position — Braine (1971), Jenkins & Palermo (1964), Osgood (1963), Mowrer (1960), Staats (1971); nativist position — McNeill (1966, 1970); interactionist position — Flavell (1977), Nelson, (1973), Sinclair-De-Zwart (1969), Vygotsky (1962).

4. Analysis of phonemic, morphological and syntactic structures is a complex process. Excellent resources about the common categories into which these structures can be divided are Eisenson (1972), Fromkin & Rodman (1974), Hopper & Naremore (1973), Taylor (1976), Wiig & Semel (1980), and Wood (1976). Resources detailing the order in which these structures are acquired are Bloom, Lightbrown, & Hood (1975), Brown (1973), de Villiers & de Villiers (1973). You might wish to observe in a preschool and chart the increased sophistication of the language you hear as the children get older. Do these expressive abilities parallel increased sophistication in language reception? How much earlier can these children comprehend certain language forms before they actually use these forms in their own language? Are there particular time periods during which language progress is so dramatic that it's impossible to chart?

5. Some children exhibit language differences because of dialect variations from the major culture. Jeter (1977) describes the characteristic dialectic variations between standard English and black English, Appalachian English, and southern white nonstandard English. Bartel, Grill, & Bryden (1973) describe some attributes of black English that have implications for school-related assessment devices. These children must be given fair assessment and programming, and not be presumed incapable because their language is culturally different from the major culture's language.

6. Read Denckla (1977), Geschwind (1968), and Lenneberg (1967) for a summary of literature on critical ages for language development. They find that language therapy produces rapid progress in brain-injured children as long as other brain areas haven't yet committed themselves to other specialized functions. Ages eleven to twelve appear to be a critical time. After that the brain has so specialized itself that brain damage to language areas produces lasting deficits (Geschwind, 1968; Lenneberg, 1967).

Chapter Seven

The Elementary School Student

Most research in learning disabilities has focused on first through sixth grade students and how their development differs from that of their classmates. You are already familiar with research findings on the developmental inefficiencies of LD children's information processing systems. Such weaknesses interfere with their ability to meet the school's academic objectives. To understand how to sequence learning objectives for LD students and what teaching strategies to employ, it is important for us to appreciate the way in which the average learner acquires academic and social skills. Therefore, we shall explore the typical skill acquisition process and how LD students' development differs. The discussion is geared to curriculum requirements at the primary (K–3) and intermediate (4–6) grade levels. Acquisition of reading, penmanship, spelling, and mathematics skills are discussed at the primary grade level, while the more complex aspects of comprehension, written expression, and socialization abilities are addressed within the intermediate grade context.

The Primary Grades

By first grade most children have developed sufficient information-processing skills to continue their academic learning in an orderly, predictable fashion. Many children have learned a great deal about interpreting print and spelling even before they enter school. While the typical achiever then proceeds to elaborate on this knowledge, the learning disabled student has yet to begin laying the foundation for this learning. LD students are not yet mature enough in some information-processing abilities to efficiently master the academic requirements. Their cognitive styles also interfere with the normal process and rate of acquisition of academic skills. For them, learning is a struggle to keep up. They are confused, overwhelmed, and may eventually question their own worth as individuals. Their uneven academic development is accompanied by uneven development in social areas as well. We shall begin by exploring how kindergarten lays the foundation for scholastic progress by merging a child's information-processing efficiencies with the easiest of academic requirements.

Kindergarten

Kindergarten is a year in which children's abilities to process information through visual, language, and motor channels are sharpened. The kindergarten teacher focuses on those information processing skills that match academic goals. Children in kindergarten also sharpen their ability to focus and sustain attention when faced with distractions. They learn how to organize approaches to tasks, work independently and in a group, and get along with teachers and peers. Their attitudes toward school begin to be shaped.

Much controversy in recent years has centered around whether teachers should train information-processing weaknesses in children (*process training*) or concentrate on academic instruction (*behavioral position*). Research Box 7-1

RESEARCH BOX 7-1
The Perceptual Training Controversy

Many pioneers in learning disabilities believed that foundations must be established for higher-order learning. Yet they also felt that higher-order learning should not be ignored while weaknesses were being remediated.

Kephart (1960) and Frostig (Frostig, 1961; Frostig & Horne, 1964) developed evaluation and training programs for gross-motor and eye-hand coordination abilities respectively. Their goals were to facilitate the child's interpretation of and response to the physical elements of the visual world. Kephart's procedures for the most part practiced body coordination in space, while Frostig's provided over 300 paper-pencil exercises in five areas of visual perception.

Raymond Barsch (1965), Gerald Getman (Getman & Kane, 1964; Getman, Kane, Halgren, & McKee, 1968) and Bryant Cratty (1969) developed their own programs for remediation of visual-perceptual and motor deficits. Barsch felt that perception and movement were one and the same thing; both were the cornerstone for conceptual development (Barsch, 1967, 1969). His *movigenics* curriculum, like Kephart and Frostig's exercises, found its way into the education of young typical children, the learning disabled, and those with severe physiological handicaps. Getman stressed the training of efficient eye movements. Cratty urged remediation of visual-motor deficits because efficient and accurate motor skills, such as in handwriting, are essential to demonstration of knowledge. Cratty also felt that optimum physical exercise created levels of arousal that help children sustain attention in the classroom. A game-like approach to exercise also would raise the child's motivation to learn (Cratty, 1972).

Like the visual motor theorists, Kirk felt that *psycholinguistic* training could facilitate academic learning (Kirk & Kirk, 1971). By the late 1960s several programs had been developed to train language skills thought to underlie later reading progress: auditory discrimination, memory for auditory sequences, and dealing with vocabulary, analogies and grammatical rules (Fairbanks & Robinson, 1967; Kirk, McCarthy, & Kirk, 1968; Semel, 1968).

These pioneers' objective was to enhance a child's readiness to integrate information during academic instruction. Since integration was a problem, they advocated more time in academic training while also helping information-processing on these tasks to become more efficient. Frostig, for example, urged educators not to use her paper-pencil exercises in isolation, but to integrate them with practice in: language, auditory perception, basic concepts, social skills, body image, gross and fine motor coordination, and academic tasks. She, like the others, did not expect children to make automatic gains in reading, math, and writing when exposed to perceptual-motor training. Children needed to be taught content as well. The pioneers did not advocate the remediation of weaker perceptual skills before undertaking academic instruction. Both could be done concurrently. Conceptual and perceptual development were intimately intertwined. They felt that learning in stronger areas must continue while the interfering effects of weaknesses are diminished. Weaknesses often would be trained on tasks that are the same as or share many similarities with the academic goals.

Underlying Processes and the Pioneers' Followers

Those who followed the pioneers misinterpreted their teachings. They assumed that perceptual skills must be mastered before conceptual progress can be made. They pursued the pioneers' methods and materials, not their theories. By the mid-1960s, classrooms popularly included perceptual-process training, often at the expense of academic remediation. Around the country, children were spinning, balancing, synchronizing body movements, and performing all sorts of visual discrimination and eye-hand coordination exercises that had no clear relationship to academic learning.

Two radical advocates of perceptual training, Doman and Delacato urged that no major academic interventions be given to perceptually handicapped children until underlying skills were remediated. Doman, Delacato, and their colleagues taught children to recapitulate unmastered earlier stages of normal development, such as crawling (Delacato, 1959, 1963; Doman, et al., 1960). They hoped to develop strong one-sidedness, which they thought led to stronger cerebral dominance and better learning. This practice lives on despite strong evidence that such neurological reorganization does not aid reading progress (Glass & Robbins, 1967; Robbins, 1967). Even when one-sidedness does improve after Delacato's training, neither reading nor visual-motor skills have improved (O'Donnell, 1970; O'Donnell & Eisenson, 1969).

Recently, another extremist position has become popular, Jean Ayres' (1975) sensory-integration therapy. Ayres' theory is based on a supposed link between poor learners' cognitive, language, and motor difficulties and dysfunction in the brain's cerebellar-vestibular system (Ayres, 1972a). Levinson and Frank (1973) liken the effect of cerebellar-vestibular dysfunctions to the normal reading difficulty one experiences when reading a sign from the window of a moving train. They felt that children's eye fixations and scanning of letters and words become disordered because the cerebellar-vestibular cir-

cuits do not provide harmonious, automatic, integrated motor activity of the eye muscles, head, and neck. The result is letter and word scrambling, visual perception problems, and reading and comprehension deficits. de Quirós (1976) explains further that when too much voluntary control is needed to maintain the body's posture, equilibrium, and purposeful motor acts, body-spatial information dominates neural circuits that should be used for conceptual activities. Learning remains seriously disturbed until the child is able to exclude body information from conscious awareness.

Ayres' therapy sessions aimed at enhancing vestibular (balance and coordination), proprioceptive (reflexes), and tactile functions by several means: spinning, scooter boards, swinging, rolling on tires, balancing, bilateral exercises (coordinating both body sides), and desensitization to various textures. Like Doman and Delacato, Ayres' theories have not been validated. Since studies that report more frequent reading gains among sensorially impaired learning or language-disabled children after several months of sensori-integration therapy (Ayres, 1972b, 1978; White, 1979) lack control groups, they are uninterpretable.

Efficacy of Perceptual Training
Research on the effects of training underlying visual-motor and language skills has yielded inconsistent results. In visual-motor training studies only three of seven studies showed improvement in reading readiness scores after Frostig training (Hamill, Goodman & Wiederholt, 1974). Getman's and Kephart's training program showed gains in only four out of eleven visual-motor posttests, one out of eight readiness posttests, and six out of fifteen intelligence, reading, and language posttests (Goodman & Hammill, 1973). In

(continued on following page)

Research Box 7-1
(*continued from preceding page*)

another study, reading gains after Frostig training were not maintained over time (Linn, 1968). Properly designed studies of visual-motor training efforts find no improvement in reading achievement, visual-motor skills (Hammill, et al., 1974) or math skills (Wiederholt & Hammill, 1971). Psycholinguistic training too lacked transfer of training to reading (Hammill & Larsen, 1974a; Larsen, Rogers & Sowell, 1976; Newcomer & Hammill, 1976).

These equivocal results may be due to severe methodological flaws. Subjects varied markedly from study to study, and few were like the learning disabled. Many subjects were not handicapped, remediation of visual-motor weaknesses was inappropriate, and therefore transfer of training to academic achievement was theoretically unwarranted. Subjects were most often not matched on relevant variables (social class, race, IQ, age, learning characteristics, teaching background). The design of training and teacher carry-through varied from study to study. The test used to judge a child deficient in one or another perceptual skill lacks theoretical validity (Vellutino et al., 1977; Smith & Marx, 1972). For example, the five Frostig subtests tap general perceptual organization,

IQ, or developmental age, rather than five different attributes of visual perception (Corah & Powell, 1963; Sabatino, Abbott, & Becker, 1974). At other times perceptual-motor programs have not worked because training was unwisely conducted with severely perceptually impaired (Wiederholt & Hammill, 1971) or physically handicapped (Goodman, 1973) youngsters whose extent of brain tissue damage precluded the possibility of improvement (Hartlage & Hartlage, 1977).

Due to these methodological flaws, we have not yet put perceptual training to a thorough test. There has been an understandable backlash against spending time on such training. The battle still rages as some writers point out that this type of training has aided reading progress (Lund, Foster, & McCall-Perez, 1978; McCarthy, 1976; Minskoff, 1975). Others retort that it has not (Hammill & Larsen, 1978a), and still others urge continued research (Senf, 1976). One of the goals of future research on this issue is to correct the severe methodological flaws, especially the short duration of training which does not give time for perceptual and cognitive processes to mature. Equally importantly, research has to match the training tasks to children's weaknesses, while coordinating this process with ongoing academic instruction, as the pioneers had intended.

explores the historical and research aspects of this *perceptual training* controversy. In reality, the process and behavioral positions are not that far apart once the processes that underlie higher-level learning become the same as schools' beginning academic objectives. In other words, instruction on underlying information-processing skills is legitimate when two behavioral criteria are met: the skills involved on both the underlying and academic criteria are identical or share many attributes in common, and the information-processing skills logically precede higher-level academic skills.

Keeping in mind that underlying and academic objectives should share many common attributes, learning to listen to the order of sounds in words is more justifiable than listening to the order of environmental sounds; only the former is an essential reading skill. Likewise, looking at a letter for ten seconds and finding it among a pile of letters shares many attributes with visual search and memory in reading; the same task with colors does not.

Considering that the process skills that are trained should logically precede higher level skills on the academic hierarchy, teaching the motor movements involved in gripping a pencil is justified; these are among the first items on a hierarchy of handwriting abilities. The motor movements in trampolining and crawling are not. Listening for beginning and ending sounds in words and sequencing sounds in words are skills that come before learning to sound out three-letter words. Recognizing that figures can face left and right, up and down, logically precedes learning to discriminate a "b" from "d," and "b" from "p."

To explain another way, our schools' academic tasks are analyzed into subskills. Each subskill demands more maturity to master than the previous one. Since the learning disabled process information in immature ways, they are ready to achieve at lower than typical levels on some academic hierarchies. As the teacher helps these lower-level processes mature through teaching subskills, mastery of higher-level skills benefit from these efficiencies and knowledge. The more similarities the underlying training tasks and academic goals share, the more training transfers from one to another.

Regardless of whether one believes in process training, it is important to identify, remediate and develop compensations for any information-processing inefficiencies that directly interfere with success on classroom tasks. For example, when a kindergartener has difficulty visually discriminating "b" from "d," it is unwise to ignore this, because research shows that visual perception has a low correlation with ultimate reading success. A visual training program that teaches the child to discern directions of chairs and designs is also inappropriate. The child instead needs to be taught to remember that a "b" faces one way and a "d" the other. When older children read well but are sloppy writers they must be taught to form letters accurately, dictate, or type, rather than to copy designs. When a child's spelling difficulty is due to poor memory for sequences of letter sounds, the child should be trained to memorize the auditory sound sequences or visual letter patterns in actual spelling words rather than sequences of words in sentences.

Although process theorists might call this *visual discrimination, visual-motor,* or *auditory and visual sequential memory* training, behaviorists would agree that this instruction deals with obvious, relevant academic criteria that need to be taught. This contrasts with other *underlying process* training, such as balancing and eye tracking, that may not share enough attributes with academic tasks to logically lie along the same skill hierarchy.

Since *visual-motor* and *psycholinguistic* (language) process training that meets the two criteria set forth is applicable to progress in the early school years, they remain important parts of the curriculum. They also are appropriate at older ages, when severe information processing deficits preclude adequate progress along the academic skill hierarchies (e.g., teaching a novel's grammar, word meanings, and idioms so as to facilitate comprehension of the novel) (Bush & Giles, 1977; Minskoff, Wiseman, & Minskoff, 1972). The pragmatic thing for the teacher to do is to train only those visual-motor, language, and attention abilities that have immediate, direct, transfer value to obvious skills needed for academic efficiency.

Merging of the underlying process and academic skill training hierarchies is precisely what the kindergarten curriculum tries to accomplish. Table 7-1 shows how information processing skills can be translated into educational, behavioral objectives for kindergarten children. Simple information processing abilities logically transition to more complex academic requirements. Successful mastery of kindergarten's skills also will depend on a child's cognitive abilities and ability to focus attention on relevant stimuli, sustain attention while avoiding distractions, organize information for storage, and then retrieve it.

Reading

Reading acquisition involves a progression from attending to whole visual configurations, to analyzing and sequencing the individual sounds in words, to reading for meaning with little attention to details. Some children with only mild to moderate reading difficulties follow the same developmental course as good readers, but at a slower rate. For these students, a well-chosen curriculum geared toward their readiness levels may sufficiently insure reading progress. Other students' reading patterns differ qualitatively from the typical process. They overuse either the visual, attending to wholes, or auditory, analyzing details, information processing strategies. They underuse the alternate approach. The most severely learning disabled student prefers neither process. Students with these atypical learning preferences require very specialized teaching approaches.

Reading Acquisition. The reading acquisition process involves a gradual shift from reading being a global, visual-processing task to one that analyzes, sequences, and attributes meaning to written language. How much of this process reflects our teaching methods is unknown. Kirk, Kliebhan, and Lerner (1978) described the three stages involved in this shift from visual to language processing:

Stage 1. *Reading wholes.* In this stage, children rely on clues from the visual configuration of words and their ability to remember these forms. Preschoolers are in this stage when they read Coca-Cola and Burger King signs. They tend to see these words more as patterns of shapes than as individual letters or words.

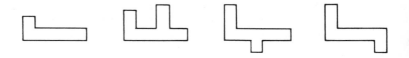

Stage 2. *Learning Details.*
    a. *Initial phase.* The child now begins to attend to the separate words that make up a phrase. To recognize the word "King" in Burger King, the child attends to the "up then down" shape:

    b. *Secondary phase.* The child begins to attend to the separate details within each word. The child is able to tell the word "king" from "wing," though still unaware of the sounds of any of the letters. Eventually the child learns the sounds associated with each of the symbols that he or she already can tell apart visually. Finally, the child is able to sequence the sounds so as to sound out unfamiliar words.
Stage 3. *Reading without awareness of details.* As facility is gained with analyzing and sequencing the sounds in words, the child becomes able to read while attending to fewer and fewer letter cues. Comprehension of thought units and ideas can occur without attending to each word's details.

    This description of the three phases of reading acquisition is supported by the neuropsychological research described in Chapter 5. This research indicates that the child begins to shift from right to left hemisphere processing preferences during Stage 2. The left hemisphere style of analyzing words' visual details is introduced, followed by application of its language analysis and sequencing abilities. By Stage 3 the left hemisphere's linguistic skills (to a greater extent) and the right hemisphere's visual processing skills (to a lesser extent) cooperate so that the meaning of a passage guides reading of words. The eye merely glances at some of the words' visual features to get a clue as to what they are. The Stage 3 process has been described with respect to anticipating grammar and meaning as well as visual and auditory processes.

Anticipating Grammar and Meaning. Goodman (1970) described the Stage 3 process as a "linguistic guessing game." That is, the reader makes hypotheses about what the words are, based on semantic (meaning), syntactic (grammar), and graphic (form) cues. A fluent reader miscalls words that fit according to the meaning and grammar of the sentence. This is all right since the meaning of the sentence is preserved. This is why, when the third grader reads "Mother told father to go to the grocery store to buy meat" as "Mom told dad to stop by the market and get meat," the teacher should not be concerned. The child is using good linguistic skills to anticipate what the passage is saying. The child is accomplishing the purpose of reading, which is gaining meaning, and not just meaninglessly pronouncing words.

Table 7-1 Underlying information processing skills translated into educational, behavioral objectives. (Sequence from beginning to end of kindergarten)

VISUAL-MOTOR	AUDITORY-VOCAL	MOTOR
☐ copies circle, cross, square, x, triangle	☐ tells full name and age	☐ walks on line or beam
☐ copies pyramid block patterns of up to 10 blocks	☐ tells birthday, address, telephone number	☐ jumps forward and backward
☐ matches abstract designs, letters, numbers	☐ names body parts: ear, finger, knee, hair	☐ stands on one foot for 8 sec.
☐ imitates clapped patterns: up-down, front-front-back, up-up-down-back	☐ counts to 5, 10	☐ runs changing directions
☐ imitates hand movements: up-down, out-cross-out-in, up-down-out-in	☐ names correct number of objects up to 10	☐ hops 7 or 8 times with both feet together, and 3 or 4 times on one foot
☐ imitates sequence of 4–5 taps on row of 5 blocks	☐ names how many eyes people have, feet they have, wheels on a tricycle	☐ gallops 15 feet
☐ finds a previously exposed visual stimulus from memory (letter, 2 shapes)	☐ responds to "which" (bigger, slower, heavier), "where" (buy gas, find a cow), "whom" (do you go to when sick), and "what" (does a fireman do, you do when sleepy or hungry, is a chair or house made of) questions	☐ catches rolled ball when sitting and rolls ball back
☐ follows directional instructions with pencil (draw a ball behind the car; draw an x in the upper left of the paper)		☐ catches bounced ball and bounces ball back
☐ matches equal sets of 1 to 10 objects		☐ catches ball
☐ screws objects into threads	☐ comprehends and describes functional relationships (what are books, stoves, umbrellas for)	☐ throws ball overhand
☐ cuts straight line and curve	☐ repeats 5–6 syllable nonsense and real words	☐ draws head, hair, eyes, nose, mouth, ears, body, arms, hands, legs, feet on a human figure
☐ draws recognizable pictures (house, people, tree)	☐ repeats 6 syllable sentences	☐ dresses self
☐ copies diamond,	☐ counts to 10	☐ uses fork and spoon appropriately
	☐ tells a story with 2–3 figures interacting	☐ brushes teeth and hair
☐ colors 95% of time within lines	☐ completes language sequences (breakfast, lunch . . .; yesterday, today . . .)	☐ cuts soft foods with knife
☐ cuts pictures out fairly close to edge	☐ completes analogies (in daytime it is light, at night it is _____; a bird flies, a fish _____)	☐ ties shoes
☐ copies upper and lower case letters and numerals well	☐ recognizes rhyming words	☐ walks balance beam backward and sideways
	☐ recites familiar nursery rhymes	☐ skips 15 feet
	☐ names first, middle, last position	☐ initiates and sustains swinging on swing
		☐ can touch thumb to each finger
		☐ hammers
		☐ dribbles ball
		☐ jumps rope once
		☐ beginning to gain balance on a bicycle
		☐ walks downstairs with alternating feet
		☐ beginning to connect bat and ball

Table 7-1 continued

VISUAL-MOTOR	AUDITORY-VOCAL	MOTOR
☐ adequately writes upper and lower case letters and numerals from memory ☐ matches capital to lower case letters ☐ prints first and last name ☐ copies simple words ☐ finds a previously exposed word or words from memory	☐ names days of week in order ☐ predicts what will happen next in stories ☐ expresses opposite relationships (how are a spoon and shoe or wood and glass different) ☐ repeats over 10 syllable sentences ☐ counts backward from 10 ☐ counts to 20 and masters writing to 100 ☐ recites alphabet song ☐ recognizes beginning and ending syllables in words ☐ recognizes beginning, ending, and middle sounds in words	

VISUAL-AUDITORY-MOTOR	VISUAL-VOCAL
☐ points to colors when named: red, blue, green, yellow ☐ points to colors when named: black, brown, orange, white ☐ points to correct number of blocks up to 10 ☐ follows directional instructions: put pencil above head and behind you, between us and then nearer to you, take 2 steps forward and 1 step backward ☐ points to penny, dime, nickel, quarter ☐ points to half and whole objects ☐ points to which one is more, less, all, longer, ☐ points to which one is in the middle, first, last, second, next to last ☐ sorts objects by category: food, clothing, animals ☐ follows simple directions (put the crayon on the book and the block in the cup) ☐ points to letters and numerals as named ☐ points to simple words when named	☐ names colors: red, green, yellow, blue ☐ names colors: black, brown, orange, white ☐ names objects by category: food, clothing, animals ☐ counts up to 10 blocks ☐ can tell a story from looking at sequence cards ☐ recalls 4 objects seen in a picture ☐ counts up to 20 objects ☐ names 10 numerals ☐ names upper- and lower-case alphabet letters ☐ names first, second, third positions ☐ adds and subtracts combinations to three ☐ sight reads ten printed words

SOURCES: Danzer, V. A., Lyons, T. M., & Gerber, M. F. *Daberon Screening Device of School Readiness*. Portland, Oregon: Daberon Research, 1972; *Meeting Street School Screening Test*. Rhode Island: Crippled Children & Adults of Rhode Island, 1969; Portage Guide to Early Education; *Pre-Kindergarten Descriptive Inventory*, Fairfield, Conn.: Fairfield Public Schools. 1974.

If our third grader used only graphic cues to read he or she would still be functioning at Stage 2. At Stage 3 the child used semantic cues to change "mother" and "father" to "mom" and "dad"; syntactic cues to know that a verb would follow the word "to" and that a preposition had to follow that verb; and graphic cues to glance at the word "meat" and guess what it was. These three types of cues are redundant so that the child could have read the word "told" by guessing from the sentence's meaning and grammar, or the word's visual configuration.

The efficient reader uses only a few cues at a time. The visual cues usually are used least. They offer the extra help needed beyond the syntax and semantics. That is, a child anticipates the grammar and meaning and then just glances at word parts in order to do a memory search for known, similar letter clusters or words (Gibson, 1965; Venezky & Calfee, 1970). Gibson explains that the child is searching for familiar spelling clusters. Even though this search process seems visual, it really depends on "what looks right" according to the sound patterns in the English language (Massaro & Klitzke, 1977).

Visual and Auditory Processes. Boder (1973) and Myklebust (1965) explain that the normal reader recognizes familiar words instantly because he or she uses efficient visual channels, which focus on wholes rather than on word parts. Unfamiliar words, however, must be read through the auditory channel, which analyzes and sequences sound patterns. There is a normal automatic interplay between these two processes. No one cerebral hemisphere can be totally responsible at any one time; fluent reading requires that many cognitive abilities come together "simultaneously and successively" (Das, Kirby, & Jarman, 1975).

The typical reading process is not really as simple as in this presentation. Experts disagree on whether or not Stage 2 is an important aspect of reading. They also have been unable to establish a valid taxonomy of reading skills that would serve as a guideline for what criteria children most easily master first, second, and so forth.

Typical Reading Patterns. Instruction in word recognition (deciphering a word rapidly), word analysis (sounding out), and comprehension typically follows a sequence such as that in Figure 7-1. By second grade the child is well into Stage 2 of reading acquisition. By third grade the typical student is transitioning to Stage 3 and the period labelled "rapid development." This progress is due to the rapid auditory and visual information processing gains (Birch & Belmont, 1965), attention, and cognitive gains (Wiig & Semel, 1980) that take place during these years. The average student reaches the refinement stage of reading and comprehension skills during the middle school years.

Most children enter school already knowing a great deal about the alphabet, sounds, and the order of sounds in familiar words (Goodman & Goodman, 1979; Read, 1975; Reid & Hresko, 1980). They generally are ready to

Figure 7-1 Sequence of reading development

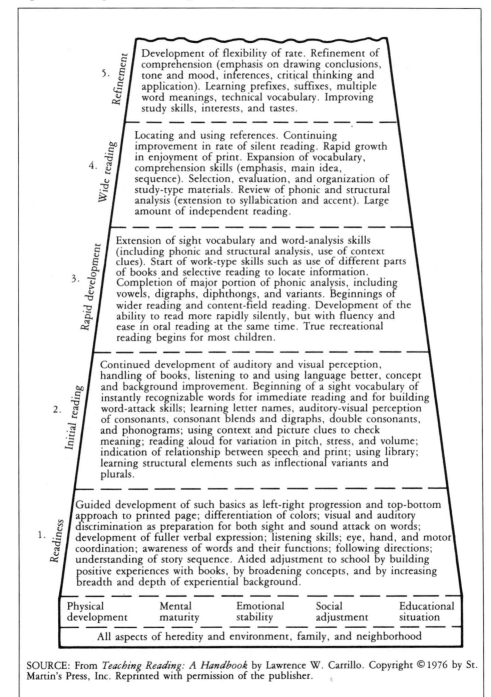

<table>
<tr><td>5.
Refinement</td><td>Development of flexibility of rate. Refinement of comprehension (emphasis on drawing conclusions, tone and mood, inferences, critical thinking and application). Learning prefixes, suffixes, multiple word meanings, technical vocabulary. Improving study skills, interests, and tastes.</td></tr>
<tr><td>4.
Wide reading</td><td>Locating and using references. Continuing improvement in rate of silent reading. Rapid growth in enjoyment of print. Expansion of vocabulary, comprehension skills (emphasis, main idea, sequence). Selection, evaluation, and organization of study-type materials. Review of phonic and structural analysis (extension to syllabication and accent). Large amount of independent reading.</td></tr>
<tr><td>3.
Rapid development</td><td>Extension of sight vocabulary and word-analysis skills (including phonic and structural analysis, use of context clues). Start of work-type skills such as use of different parts of books and selective reading to locate information. Completion of major portion of phonic analysis, including vowels, digraphs, diphthongs, and variants. Beginnings of wider reading and content-field reading. Development of the ability to read more rapidly silently, but with fluency and ease in oral reading at the same time. True recreational reading begins for most children.</td></tr>
<tr><td>2.
Initial reading</td><td>Continued development of auditory and visual perception, handling of books, listening to and using language better, concept and background improvement. Beginning of a sight vocabulary of instantly recognizable words for immediate reading and for building word-attack skills; learning letter names, auditory-visual perception of consonants, consonant blends and digraphs, double consonants, and phonograms; using context and picture clues to check meaning; reading aloud for variation in pitch, stress, and volume; indication of relationship between speech and print; using library; learning structural elements such as inflectional variants and plurals.</td></tr>
<tr><td>1.
Readiness</td><td>Guided development of such basics as left-right progression and top-bottom approach to printed page; differentiation of colors; visual and auditory discrimination as preparation for both sight and sound attack on words; development of fuller verbal expression; listening skills; eye, hand, and motor coordination; awareness of words and their functions; following directions; understanding of story sequence. Aided adjustment to school by building positive experiences with books, by broadening concepts, and by increasing breadth and depth of experiential background.</td></tr>
</table>

Physical development	Mental maturity	Emotional stability	Social adjustment	Educational situation

All aspects of heredity and environment, family, and neighborhood

SOURCE: From *Teaching Reading: A Handbook* by Lawrence W. Carrillo. Copyright © 1976 by St. Martin's Press, Inc. Reprinted with permission of the publisher.

attend to at least three stimuli and select the one most pertinent to their needs (for example, retrieving the sound of one particular letter) (Eimas, 1969). Ability to follow a line from left to right, organize visual information, and report what has been seen is usually well-established (Elkind & Weiss, 1967). Blending of isolated sounds into words, however, remains difficult until individual sounds take on more meaning (Fries, 1963).

By age six approximately 70 percent of all children are capable of segmenting words by phonemes, and 90 percent can segment by syllables (Liberman, Shankweiler, Fischer, & Carter, 1974). By age seven the child can attend to orientation of reversible letters easier (Belmont & Birch, 1963), and by age eight reversals generally disappear (Boder, 1973). Resolving mirror-images are easiest (b–d), followed by inversions (M–W), then inverted reversals (p–d) (Kinsbourne & Caplan, 1979). The average student needs two visual fixations per word in first grade, but less than one per word by the intermediate grades (Taylor, 1966). By third grade the child is adept at analyzing words based on their individual sounds or irregular patterns, configurations (length, shape), structure (roots, prefixes), clues gained from context, and clues gained from pictures.

Reading errors that children typically make include:

□ omitting letters in a word
□ omitting syllables in a word
□ omitting words in a sentence
□ inserting or omitting word endings
□ inserting extra words or sounds in words
□ substituting words that look or sound similar to the printed word
□ substituting words that have similar meanings to the printed word
□ mispronouncing initial letters, final letters, medial vowels, etc.
□ reversing whole words and the order of letters or syllables in a word (these are more often due to language sequencing or attention factors than to difficulty differentiating visual orientations)
□ transposing the order of words in a sentence
□ repeating words
□ wrong inflection
□ dialect differences

By third grade the teacher seldom listens to students read anymore. They read silently, although many subvocalize (Edfeldt, 1959). Instructional emphasis shifts to comprehension, spelling, and composition.

Reading Patterns of Learning Disabled Students. Besides being quantitatively behind their classmates in amount of reading skill acquired, reading disabled students may also show patterns that are qualitatively different from those of even younger typical learners (Reid, 1978). Some learning disabled children get stuck overusing either their visual or language information-processing abilities, and underusing the other mode, or underutilizing both processes. Therefore, they never get beyond Stage 2 reading. The normal interplay between visual and auditory processes never gets established.

Other children's reading difficulties are largely related to problems focusing and sustaining attention. Since reading is a translation of language into another symbol system, the better a child's language skills are, the more rapid reading progress is likely to be (Reid & Hresko, 1980).

Children whose reading difficulties relate to visual weaknesses have been called *visual dyslexics* (Myklebust, 1965), *visuospatial dyslexics* (Ingram, Mason, & Blackburn, 1970), and *dyseidetic dyslexics* (Boder, 1973). These children's primary deficit is in the ability to perceive and remember what letter and whole-word configurations look like.

Children whose reading delays are associated with auditory difficulties have been referred to as *auditory dyslexics* (Myklebust, 1965), *audiophonic dyslexics* (Ingram, Mason, & Blackburn, 1970), *dysphonetic dyslexics* (Boder, 1973), and *dysphonetic-sequencing disordered* (Denckla, 1977). These children have difficulty remembering letter sounds, analyzing individual sounds in words, and sequencing these into words. The most severely reading disabled students are weak in both visual and auditory abilities (Bateman, 1968; Boder, 1973). Boder calls this group *dysphonetic-dyseidetic dyslexics*, or *alexics* (without words).

One of the best descriptions of atypical reading patterns appears in Elena Boder's writings. Boder (1973) identifies the information-processing patterns of disabled readers by a simple procedure. Word lists are presented to the child to read. Those that the student recognizes within one second are listed as *sight words*. Those that the child can sound out within ten seconds also are noted. By contrasting the percentage of sight words with those that had to be analyzed, Boder can tell whether a child instantly recognizes expected numbers of words as visual wholes, has the ability to sound out unfamiliar words, or overuses either word analysis–synthesis or visual memory abilities, while underusing the other.

Boder then asks the student to spell words in his or her sight vocabulary and those that the child could not read at all. Spelling of phonetically regular (can be sounded out or follow phonetic rules) sight words measures precisely what the child has mastered about the auditory and visual aspects of sight words. On phonetically irregular sight words, the student's spelling indicates exactly which aspects of words he or she can recall visually. For example, "weight" needs to be visually stored and revisualized when spelling; only the "w" and "t" sounds can be auditorially analyzed, stored, and recalled. Although the student might have learned that "eigh" is an alternate spelling for long A, he or she must still mentally picture whether it's appropriate in this case. Finally, spelling words that could not be read at all reveals the nature of the phonetic skills that the child has mastered. The child is not expected to spell these words correctly, but is expected to at least be able to give good phonetic approximations. A good phonetic approximation of "weight," for example, might be "wate."

By using reading and spelling to determine which aspects of words children analyze and store for recall, Boder can tell whether children's preferences are for whole-word, visual gestalts (configurations), or phonetic analysis. These preferences are similar in both reading and spelling, and tend to remain continuous patterns, even as reading improves.

Tables 7-2 and 7-3 list the reading and spelling patterns of children with visual and auditory processing weaknesses respectively. Figure 7-2 illustrates these students' spelling patterns, as well as those of students who have both types of information-processing weaknesses. Some other common behaviors among children with reading difficulties are: holding the book closer than the usual fifteen to eighteen inches, thereby reflecting the energy they are putting into a hard task; fidgeting; refusing to read; reading slowly and word-by-word; unnatural voice quality; ignoring words they can't read (Jones, 1980). After such a struggle it is unlikely that the child will comprehend or store much of the passage's message.

Goodman and Burke (1972) point out that reading errors usually are not random mistakes. They are miscues and occur because information-processing preferences or past learning induces children to respond to one cue rather than

Table 7-2 Reading and spelling patterns of children with visual-processing weaknesses

- confusion with letters that differ in orientation (b–d, p–q)
- confusion with words that can be dynamically reversed (was–saw)
- very limited sight vocabulary; few words are instantly recognized from their whole configuration—they need to be sounded out laboriously, as though being seen for the first time
- losing the place because one doesn't instantly recognize what had already been read, as when switching gaze from the right side of one line to the left side of the next line
- omitting letters and words because they weren't visually noted
- masking the image of one letter, by moving the eye on too rapidly to the subsequent letter, may result in omission of the first letter
- difficulty learning irregular words that can't be sounded out (sight)
- difficulty with rapid retrieval of words due to visual retrieval weaknesses
- visual stimuli in reading prove so confusing that it is easier for the child to learn to read by first spelling the words orally and then putting them in print
- insertions, omissions, and substitutions, if the meaning of the passage is guiding reading
- strengths in left hemisphere language-processing, analytical and sequential abilities, and detail analysis; can laboriously sound out phonetically regular words even up to grade level
- difficulty recalling the shape of a letter when writing
- spells phonetically but not bizarrely (laf–laugh; bisnis–business)
- can spell difficult phonetic words but not simple irregular words

Table 7-3 Reading and spelling patterns of children with auditory-processing weaknesses

- ☐ difficulty discriminating between individual sounds in beginning reading instruction (occurs very seldom)
- ☐ difficulty processing rapid auditory inputs so that consonant sounds that cannot be sustained (p–b) are not perceived; these may then be omitted in reading
- ☐ poor ability to analyze the sequence of sounds and syllables in words; consequently they become reversed in reading words; this is akin to the problem faced orally when poor auditory analysis has taught the child such phrases as "lead a snot into temptation" and "Harold be thy name" in the Lord's Prayer, or "lmnop" being one lumped cluster in the alphabet song
- ☐ poor ability to remember individual sounds or sequences of sounds
- ☐ difficulty blending individual sounds into words
- ☐ difficulty listening to words and omitting one sound and substituting it for another (say "cat"; now take off the /c/ and put on a /f/); such abilities are essential to word analysis because that is what figuring out how to pronounce a word is all about; children usually develop this skill with initial consonants first, then final consonants, and then medial vowels or consonants
- ☐ difficulty remembering the sounds that individual letters and phonetically regular and irregular letter combinations represent
- ☐ unable to rapidly retrieve letter sounds while analyzing words so that the beginning of the word is forgotten by the time the last letter of the word is recalled (naming problem)
- ☐ difficulty analyzing unknown words due to poor knowledge of phonetic rules and analytic-sequencing problems
- ☐ word substitutions that are conceptually (person, human) or visually (horse, house), but not phonetically, related
- ☐ limited sight vocabulary because the student cannot memorize an abundance of words without the benefit of phonetic cues
- ☐ guessing at unfamiliar words rather than employing word-analysis skills
- ☐ spelling remains below reading level because it is attempted by sight rather than by ear
- ☐ correct spellings occur primarily on words that the child can revisualize
- ☐ bizarre spellings that seldom can be identified, even by the child, because they do not follow phonetic patterns
- ☐ extraneous letters and omitted syllables in spelling

a more relevant cue. Miscues have either a graphic, sound, or grammatical similarity to the written word. Goodman and Burke analyze whether the miscue represents a grammatically correct and meaningful substitution, and whether the meaning of the sentence is changed. Miscues that change the meaning of a passage (pet – pit) are more serious than those that do not interfere with comprehension (mom – mother). Since omissions and insertions seldom change the meaning of a sentence, teachers need to attend most to word-substitution errors (D'Angelo & Wilson, 1979).

Figure 7-2 Spelling patterns of students with auditory, visual, and mixed types of information-processing weaknesses

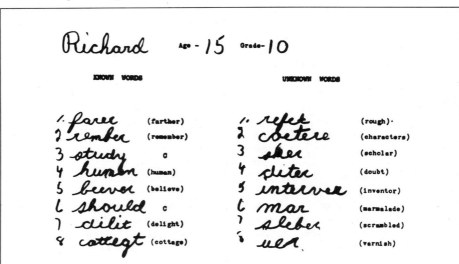

Student with auditory weaknesses has difficulty making phonetic approximations even of words in his sight vocabulary.

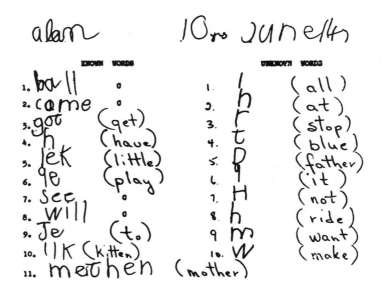

Student with a visual and auditory weakness can spell only a few words in his sight vocabulary.

Figure 7-2   continued

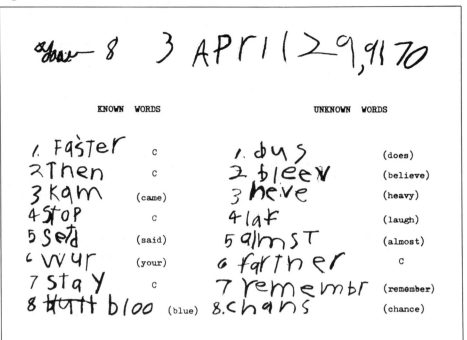

Student with visual weaknesses makes good phonetic approximations even of words he cannot read.

SOURCE: Boder, E. Developmental Dyslexia: A Diagnostic Approach Based on Three Typical Reading-Spelling Patterns. *Developmental Medicine and Child Neurology*, 1973, *15*, pp. 669–672. Reprinted by permission.

Language weaknesses more frequently and severely contribute to reading disorders than do visual deficits. Children with language strengths at least can sound out unfamiliar words, though their reading is labored because they cannot quickly recognize the words as whole gestalts (patterns). The language disabled child, on the other hand, has trouble sounding out unfamiliar words or guessing words from context, and is limited by a ceiling on most people's capacity to remember words' visual forms. Over 60 percent of Boder's LD students' profiles reveal a phonetic weakness. Less than 10 percent of the students show visual weaknesses. Approximately 20 percent show both patterns at once; some of these children show both patterns because one area of weakness impairs the capabilities of the other area. Children with either an auditory or visual weakness have a more favorable prognosis than those with both.

Very often, the visual- and auditory-processing difficulties of poor readers are complicated by poor attending abilities. At other times, inattention makes a child appear to have a visual or auditory processing disorder when the child actually doesn't. This type of child wildly guesses at words from their first letters without taking the time to sound-out and does not attend to the order of letters in words, or words in a sentence. The child does not attend to the orientation of letters that can be reversed, increases errors with effort because attention gets caught even more by irrelevant stimuli (Ross, 1976), attends to only the beginning or end of words, and does not organize what has been read for meaning and recall. Once the teacher helps this child attend systematically to words' and passages' relevant features, the teacher often finds that the child has some good abilities to deal with the words' visual and language aspects.

Apparently some learning disabled children progress slower than expected in reading but still follow the normal course of skill development. Others do not follow this course and over- or underuse auditory or visual information-processing modes or both. An awareness of how to analyze these children's error patterns helps teachers determine which abilities to capitalize on for further reading progress, and which to remediate so as to facilitate this progress.

Penmanship

A great deal of time is spent on penmanship instruction in the primary grades. Penmanship becomes increasingly important as a child progresses through school because teachers evaluate whether or not their students have mastered information by means of written tests and essays. As many as 90 percent of learning disabled students have fine-motor difficulties (Clements et al., 1971; Tarnapol & Tarnapol, 1977). Their penmanship problems often mask their underlying knowledge. The reasons underlying typical and atypical penmanship acquisition patterns are important to understand because they help direct the remediation process.

Typical Penmanship Acquisition. By the time children enter first grade, they can typically hold a pencil in a loose, comfortable three-finger grasp, print the letters of the alphabet from memory, and copy words containing three or four letters from the board or a paper. They know that printing proceeds from left to right, and can stay reasonably close to the line. Their letters may vary in size, spacing, alignment, proportion, pencil pressure (heavy, light), slant, and form (vertical, horizontal, diagonal, and circular strokes) (Freeman, 1965). Reversals of letters and order of letters are common among young elementary school students (Critchley, 1970). These usually decline by age eight to eight and one-half (Boder, 1973; Kinsbourne & Caplan, 1979).

Figure 7-3 presents handwriting samples of boys and girls whom teachers characterize as weak, average, and strong writers. By the end of third grade, children customarily have transitioned from manuscript (printing) to cursive

Figure 7-3 Handwriting samples of learning disabled, weak, average, and strong writers

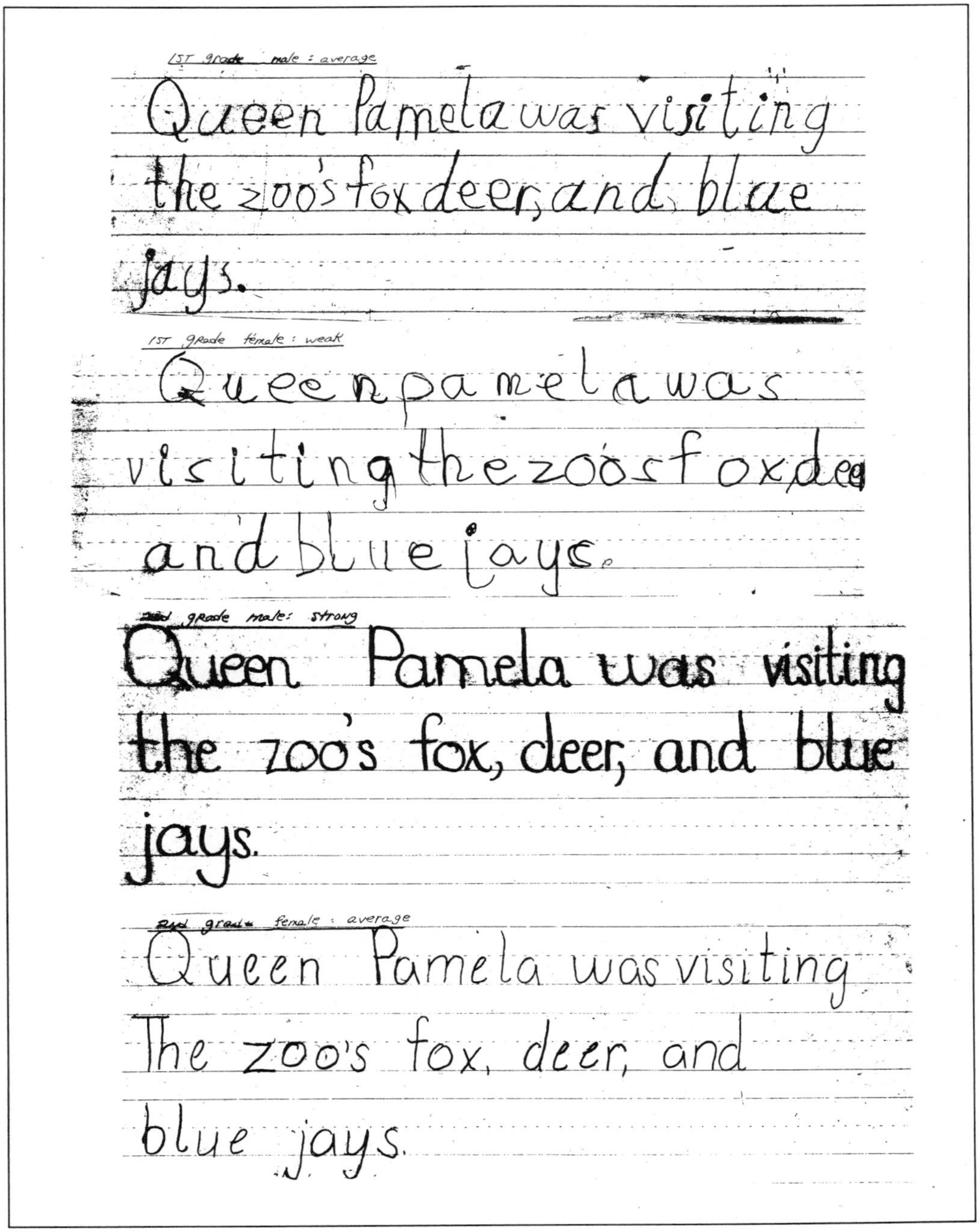

Figure 7-3 continued

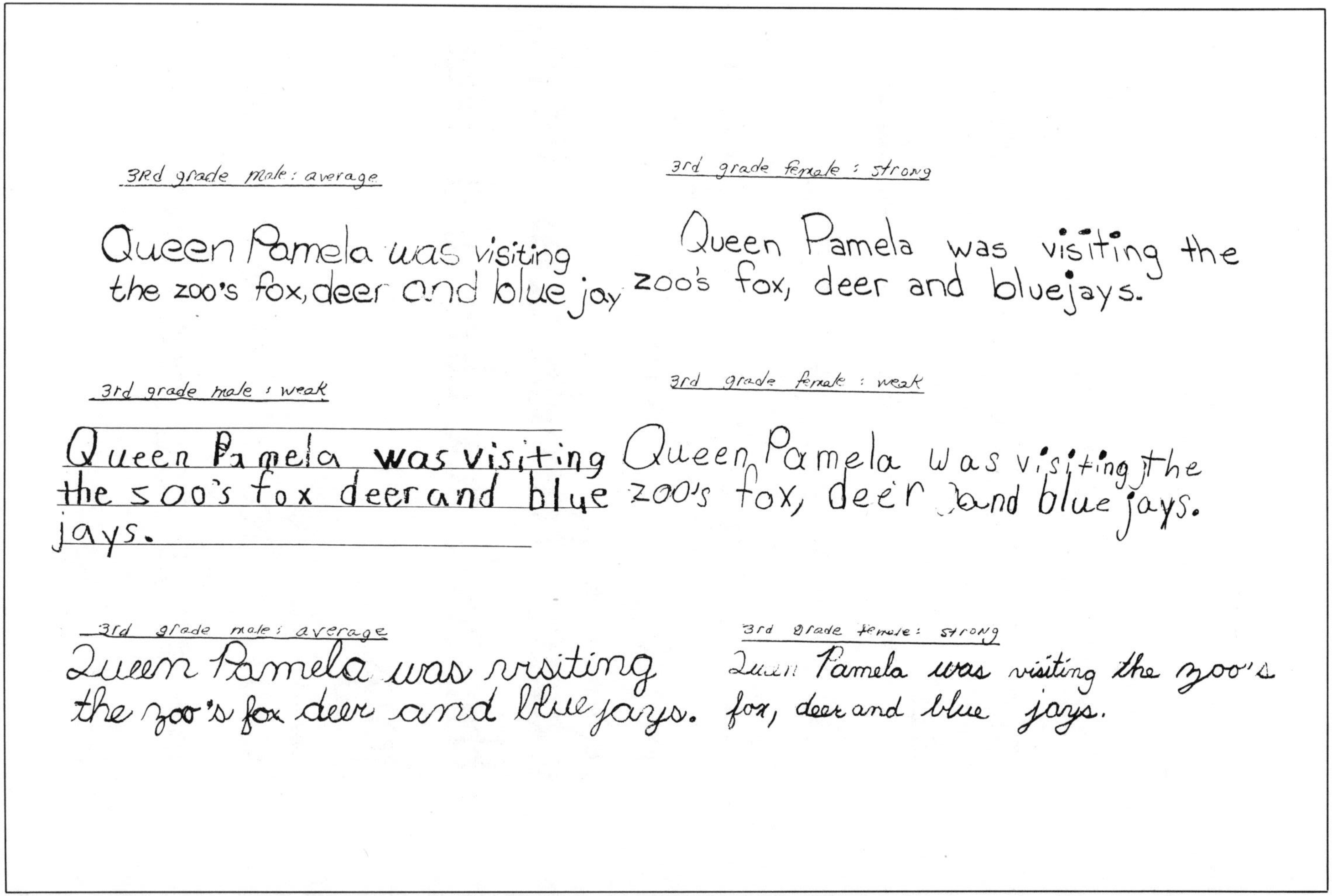

3rd grade male : average

Queen Pamela was visiting
the zoo's fox, deer and blue jay

3rd grade female : strong

Queen Pamela was visiting the
zoo's fox, deer and bluejays.

3rd grade male : weak

Queen Pamela was visiting Queen Pamela was visiting the
the zoo's fox deer and blue   zoo's fox, deer and blue jays.
jays.

3rd grade female : weak

3rd grade male : average

Queen Pamela was visiting
the zoo's fox deer and bluejays.

3rd grade female : strong

Queen Pamela was visiting the zoo's
fox, deer and blue jays.

Figure 7-3 continued

3rd grade male: weak

Queen Pamela visiting the zoo's fox deer and blue jay

4th grade male: strong

Queen Pamela was visiting the zoo's fox, deer, and blue jays.

4th grade male: average

Queen Pamela was visiting the zoo's fox, deer, and blue jays.

4th grade male: weak

Queen Pamela was visiting the zoo's fox, deer and blue jays.

3rd grade female: weak

Queen Pamela was visiting the zoo fox, deer and blue jays

4th grade female: strong

Queen Pamela was visiting the zoo's fox, deer, and blue jays.

4th grade female: average

Queen Pamela was visiting the zoo's fox, deer, and blue jays.

4th grade female: weak

Queen Pamela was visiting the zoo's fox, deer and blue jays.

Figure 7-3 continued

3rd grade male : age 9

"This is fun" said Jim, "I Am a
bit scared," said Mike, "Who cares," said
Jack, "Let's go," said Jeff.
Jeff, O.K, Fh+ said.

6th grade female: age 14

Sunday my friend came out no pass
route. She called me up to her clock
and told me that I want to past route.

— But I didn't hand to recss and
the next day I was back again next.
This didn't pleas her at all because
to my clock told not to gather the pass
fly. I never past route again

8th grade male: age 14

Summer school

I am the summer, I went to summer school.
I didn't like summer school because it
was hot and sweaty. The work was hard and
the homework was piled up way much each
day. I no two all subjects were English and
Social Studies. I couldn't take any more of it.
Finally summer school was over two weeks
before school started. I was lucky enough
to pass both courses. Thank god,
All this time to rest before school started.

Figure 7-3 continued

writing. Cursive writing skills continue to be refined in fourth and fifth grades. By sixth grade, children (especially girls) have experimented with many styles of penmanship (size, shape, slant, spacing) and usually have adopted one that will continue to distinguish their script from others'. The left-hander seldom has more trouble writing than does the right-hander. By slanting the paper in the opposite direction from that of the right-hander, the left-hander can prevent the characteristic hook (Otto, McMenemy, & Smith, 1973).

Penmanship Patterns of Learning Disabled Students. Children with penmanship difficulties generally write slowly and in a labored fashion (Clements, et al., 1971). Their writing often is sloppy and illegible, and they seldom develop an individual style of handwriting. They have difficulty taking written tests because the painstaking writing process impedes their thought processes. They have difficulty sustaining this energy long enough to put what they know down on paper. Their writing creates a real problem with teacher evaluation.

These students' pencil grips may be awkward and too tight. Their writing posture is often uncomfortable. The sizes of their letters are extremely variable and sometimes meet the line but most of the time do not. These children also have difficulty with slant, letter formations, pressure on the paper, and spacing of sentences, words, and letters (Poteet, 1980). Formation of letters containing vertical and horizontal strokes (T, L, F) present less of a problem than those containing diagonals (K) and curves (R). Confusion of capital with small letters is common.

Reversals continue longer than customary, especially for boys (Critchley, 1970), because children have not learned to attend sufficiently to the distinctive features that discriminate one from another letter or number. Reversals are not due to one side of the brain forcing its reversed image to consciousness. If this were the case, children would pick up mugs from the wrong side, try to pierce a chunk of meat by putting the fork into the other side of the plate, and so forth. Resolution of reversals comes when the children can use their visual, language, and cognitive maturities to help cue discrimination of ups from downs (p–b; u–n), lefts from rights (b–d; E-3), and rotations (b–q). Reversals of numbers tend to be resolved before that of letters, perhaps because there are fewer of them to confuse.

Penmanship problems of learning disabled students can be divided into those that are primarily due to visual-perceptual difficulties, to motor incoordination, and to attention problems.

Visual-Perceptual Difficulties. These seem to be the cause of the penmanship difficulties in only about 25 percent of LD children (Tarnapol & Tarnapol, 1977). They involve inaccurate input and recall of visual images. For example, a child occasionally may stop in the middle of writing because he or she can't revisualize (mentally picture) what a letter is supposed to look like. Similarly, the child may have trouble retaining letter sequences while copying.

Uncoordinated Motor Movements. Uncoordinated motor movements, together with difficulties in spatial judgments, are the most common cause of penmanship problems (Gerard & Junkala, 1980). These children's hands do not seem to move automatically. Their minds need to consciously direct attention to the appropriate cues (for example, spacing) or to revisualize letters for the hand to copy (Fernald, 1943). Contrary to what happens with mature writers, these children's hands seldom run away from them. They cannot daydream while writing and then look at their product and say, "Did I write that?" Their minds, instead, must actively plan, guide, and control their motor movements. When so much energy goes into the mechanics, it's no wonder that ideas become muddled, abbreviated, disorganized, or are lost altogether.

Inattention. Inattention can impact the input as well as output ends of writing tasks. Details are not observed or recalled, relationships are not evaluated, or space and motor movements are not preplanned. The inattentive child can do better when attention is focused and sustained. Since maintaining attention is difficult, the child's ideas and productivity suffer. This type of child hands in a paper that looks like it's gone through a war. When the child notices errors, he or she may just write over them in bolder print, rather than erasing. Erasing, when done, is seldom complete and the paper becomes a black smudge. When the paper is homework, by the time it gets back to school (if at all) its edges may be chewed up and the paper folded irregularly in many places.

Some educators feel that the learning disabled child should not be forced to transition to cursive writing because manuscript requires less complex movements and the printed letters are more similar to words in books (Johnson & Myklebust, 1967). They feel that it is better for the child to learn one system well, than to be confused about two. Others advocate cursive writing because spatial judgments are easier when letters connect, and the writing process is more continuous and rhythmic (Orton, 1937; Strauss & Lehtinen, 1947). Consideration of these views, and evaluation of whether the child's manuscript or cursive writing most closely approximates classmates' writing quality (Poteet, 1980), can guide the teacher's decision on this matter.

Spelling

Spelling represents what a child has been able to organize, store, and recall about the words that he or she can read. For most individuals, spelling is a much more difficult task than reading and, therefore, difficulties persist long after reading problems have been resolved. Although reading progress normally precedes spelling progress, there are some rare exceptions. Occasionally a youngster's auditory-processing abilities are so superior, and revisualization so weak, that he or she can spell words well orally but becomes confused when trying to read or perhaps write them. We shall contrast the typical process of spelling acquisition with the patterns of learning disabled youngsters.

Typical Spelling Acquisition. Spelling instruction generally does not get underway seriously until somewhere in the middle of second grade. This is because children need to have mastered many of the visual and phonic elements of reading before they can be expected to recall how words look or sound. Children recognize correct spellings of words long before they are able to spell them. As adults too, we recognize correct spellings of words such as "conscientious," but often misspell them.

English is a strange language because only approximately 50 percent of spellings follow regular phonetic rules (Hanna, Hodges, & Hanna, 1971). The only way to remember the remaining irregular words is to revisualize (mentally imagine) them. Initially children need to subvocalize when spelling (Luria, 1966; 1970b). When they are not allowed to subvocalize, their spelling errors increase. By age eight they tend to no longer need this oral aid (Tarnapol & Tarnapol, 1977).

Figure 7-4 demonstrates the spelling of a typical second grader who can analyze and sequence the phonetic elements of language but has not yet mastered irregular spellings. The ability to revisualize nonphonetic elements such as the "gh" in "sight" generally comes later than phonetic analysis skills. Primary grade children very often give good phonetic approximations for spellings. Although these are incorrect, the meaning is generally clear. By the intermediate grades children generally are able to spell over 80 percent of sight words (words that are instantly read), even if the words are phonetically irregular (Boder, 1973). Spelling instruction in the primary grades is integrated with other aspects of the language arts curriculum such as vocabulary development, grammar, and writing of increasingly complex sentences.

Spelling Patterns of Learning Disabled Students. Learning disabled children typically can spell less than half of their sight vocabularies. Their spelling errors consist of: insertion of unnecessary letters (umberella for umbrella), omission of necessary letters (famly for family), substitution of letters (mush for must), phonetic spelling (sed for said), directional confusion (was for saw), vowel changes depending on consonant order (tabel for table; doller for dollar), orientation confusion of letters (d,b; p,q; n,u; m,w), and reversed sequence (aminals for animals) (Poteet, 1980).

Learning disabled children have difficulty with phonic, visualization, or both elements of the spelling process. They typically show the same types of errors in reading as in spelling. Boder's work described how these processes work. The child with auditory processing weaknesses often has not mastered the phonetic rules. The child may be able to spell highly irregular words that need to be revisualized, but be unable to spell phonetically regular words. This child cannot spell words that have not been mastered in reading. The child

Figure 7-4 Phonetic spelling of an average second grader

Dear mom I Love you.
happy birthday.
Sinsirlys,
your dauters,
Rachael and Julie.
P.S. you should be
thank full becuse
we bought this with our own mony.
I hope you like The present
Dear Dad,
We will be back any minit.
Love, mom Julie
and ges who.
Dear
mom
We love
you We
Pland a
speshle letter
and presint
for you
I hope you
like it
if you do
Say to us
Thank you
We love
you from
Rachael Julie
and Dad

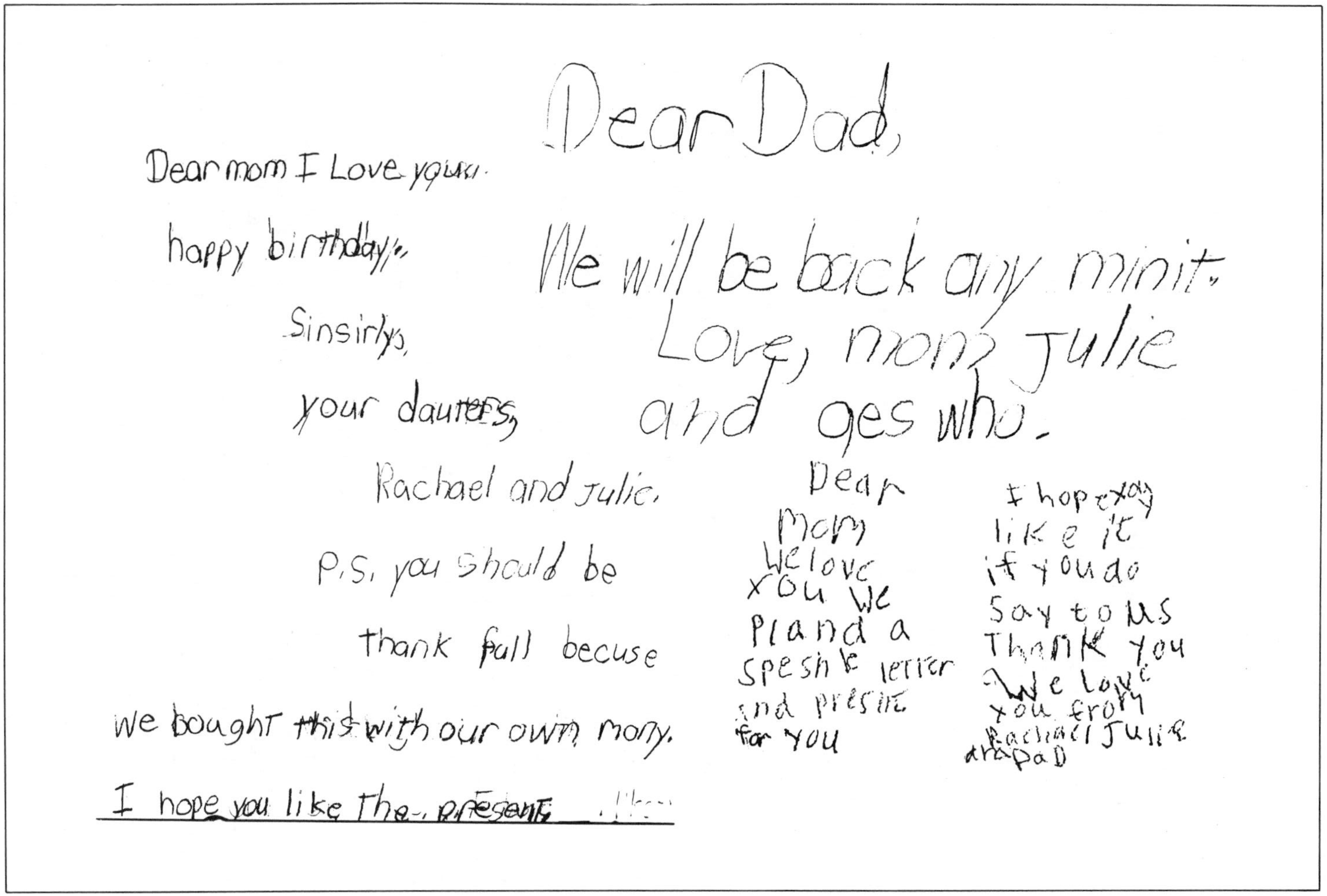

with visual processing weaknesses, on the other hand, may be able to spell phonetic words never read before, but has trouble revisualizing the irregulars.

As in reading, the child with auditory processing difficulties is the more impaired in spelling. There is a limit to how many words even a good revisualization ability could store and recall for spelling. Problems are complicated further when linguistic deficiencies deter the use of language cues to figure out spellings (for example, knowing that a past tense is being used can cue a youngster to spell "spilled" instead of "spilt").

The good reader with a spelling disorder makes far fewer phonetic spelling errors than does the child with both reading and spelling problems. The good reader's greatest problem tends to be the revisualization process, such that the wrong letters are substituted for similar-sounding letter combinations (ow for ou) (Nelson & Warrington, 1976). Finally, attentional deficits too may cause a production deficit in someone who otherwise has a good capacity to learn to spell.

Mathematics

Studies of mathematics acquisition, error patterns of learning disabled students, and teaching methods have been few in number and limited in scope. This situation is beginning to change as the computer revolution forces us to recognize that what society viewed as acceptable failure in mathematics is actually a disability.

Mathematical abilities, like reading, involve the integration of important visual, motor, language, and attentional processes. For example, higher-level visual information-processing abilities enable one to visually group and regroup objects in one's mind so as to add and subtract mentally. Motor movements help a child keep track of each object counted, write the numerals, and properly align them during calculations. Focused attention is always an important prerequisite to instruction; in word problems it aids elimination of extraneous information and use of cue words to determine the correct operation (Goodstein, 1981).

As in reading, language skills are highly related to math success because math is just another symbol system for numerical language concepts (Košč, 1981). Word problems need to be read and understood, and operations use higher-level reasoning which depends on such language flexibility as searching one's mind for a number fact while holding another fact in abeyance. The greater the linguistic complexity of a problem (vocabulary, syntax, sentence length), the more difficult mathematical solutions become for students with learning disabilities (Larsen, Parker, & Trenholme, 1978).

Before beginning formal mathematics instruction, a child must be able to:

☐ match objects by size, shape, color
☐ sort objects by size, shape, and color names
☐ compare sets of objects by amount (more, most) and size (biggest, smaller)

- arrange a series of objects by size
- match each item of one kind with a single item of another kind (for example, one napkin per person)
- recognize the amount of "one"
- match simple sets of objects by amount
- model the adding or subtracting of one or two objects from a set
- match a spoken number with correct numbers of objects
- point to correct written number when named
- name a written number accurately
- count to ten
- recall the number of objects seen accurately by naming the number or choosing the correct number of objects
- imitate and recall spatial arrangement of objects
- copy numerals accurately (Doyle, 1978)

A child is ready to progress in mathematics once he or she has mastered these skills, and once information-processing abilities are mature enough to permit reasoning about two pieces of information at once (Gelman, 1969; Piaget, 1976). That is, the child must be able to recognize that two things can be combined into a third ($2 + 3 = 5$) and that the third still contains aspects of the first two. The child must understand that one thing can be the same and different at the same time (a 2 can be more than 1 and less than 3 all at the same time) and that even though two things look different, they can still be the same ($2 + 4 = 3 + 3$).

The typical scope and sequence of the primary grade's mathematics curriculum includes one-to-one correspondence, numerals, sets, ordinal numbers (first, second, third), calculations (addition, subtraction, multiplication), word problems, geometry, measurement, money, and time. More difficult division, fractions, decimals, and word problems are introduced in the intermediate grades.

Košč (1981) describes several types of arithmetic disabilities that relate to weaknesses in different information-processing systems:

- weak finger manipulation of real objects
- disturbed ability to verbally express mathematical terms and relations (numerals, operational symbols, operations)
- disability in reading mathematical symbols
- disturbed manipulation of the mathematical symbol system in writing
- disturbance in carrying out mathematical operations
- disability in understanding mathematical ideas and relations, and thus mental calculation

Although it is commonly assumed that children with reading disabilities tend to be stronger in math, and vice versa, this is not true. In the majority of cases both disabilities coexist, although to different degrees (Reid & Hresko, 1981). This occurs because the child carries information-processing strengths and weaknesses through all academic subjects — and math, especially at higher levels, shares much in common with the language, attention and cognitive skills involved in reading (Chalfant & Scheffelin, 1969; Johnson & Myklebust, 1967; Kaliski, 1967).

The Intermediate Grades

A dramatic shift in school expectations takes place when a child enters the intermediate grades. Fourth grade begins a process of independence in studies that becomes continually more demanding for the rest of one's school career. Students' basic information-processing capabilities, reading, comprehension, and learning strategies are mature enough so that learning can take place through independent reading and research. Their penmanship, spelling, and written expression abilities are sophisticated enough so that written tests and papers can be used to assess their knowledge. Learning has become more self-directed. Assignments require long-term planning and organization. The basic skills developed in the primary grades form the foundation on which much more complex comprehension and written expression skills are now built. These skills are in turn used for learning and communicating information in content area subjects, such as social studies and science.

The learning disabled student who cannot read or comprehend well, spell, or put thoughts into writing is at a terrible disadvantage. This child does not have the basic skills with which to continue learning new content or expressing what is known. Some children do manage to get by in the primary grades, then develop large gaps in the intermediate grades when faced with the more complex comprehension, written expression, and math requirements. By this time also, the students' language weaknesses and failure experiences frequently result in lowered self-confidence, zeal to achieve, and know-how in getting along with others. The agony of poor self-perceptions and interpersonal relationships may prove even more devastating to future adjustment than the academic weaknesses themselves.

Reading Comprehension

Since the goal of reading is to gain meaning, the comprehension process is important to understand. Without decoding skills there can be no reading comprehension; but without comprehension skills even good decoding ability is useless. Typical learners become more efficient in many comprehension processes as they get older: recognizing and recalling facts and the sequence of events, recognizing and inferring main themes and relationships, making inferences, drawing conclusions, making judgments and generalizations, predicting outcomes, applying what has been learned, and following directions. Although taught in the primary grades, these abilities need to become even more sophisticated in the intermediate grades, when the student is required to be a more independent learner. While reading instruction in the intermediate grades deals with such complex aspects of written language as prefixes, suffixes, and syllabication, comprehension goals prepare the student for independent study: skimming, using reference materials, outlining, summarizing, altering reading rate and focus depending on purpose of reading, use of headings, taking notes, etc.

Some learning disabled students' reading comprehension is hampered by weak decoding skills. They expend so much time and energy struggling over words, that they cannot also attend to or remember the passage's content. When reading as the tool for gaining meaning is eliminated (e.g. using lectures, tapes), these students comprehend well and do not miss opportunities for learning.

For other LD students the problem goes far beyond decoding. These students have difficulty with comprehension because of linguistic deficits and inefficient learner strategies. These factors deter learning the content in most subject areas, whether by reading or listening.

Linguistic Deficits. The language weaknesses of preschoolers very often persist well beyond the primary grades. These children may not understand the vocabulary, morphology, syntax, and semantics that they are reading (deep structure problem). They also have difficulty comprehending the order of words in sentences and are overloaded by the sheer number of sentences themselves (surface structure problem). These problems create difficulties because the curriculum expects students to deal with such language factors as antonyms, synonyms, homonyms, idioms, metaphors, morals, proverbs, poetry, and vocabulary development. These language problems also make it difficult for these students to become Stage 3 readers, so that anticipation of meaning can guide reading. Furthermore, language expression weaknesses such as poor syntax, semantics, articulation, and naming make it hard for the student to communicate what has been comprehended. These weaknesses require extensive intervention by a language specialist, as well as by the teacher.

Inefficient Learner Strategies. Some learning disabled students approach learning tasks inefficiently, but have no other information-processing weaknesses. The inefficient learner strategies of other LD students are related to inadequate focused and sustained attention, weak visual information-processing strategies (dealing with overall ideas), weak language-processing strategies (dealing with analysis and sequencing of details, not using naming and verbal mediation to aid learning), or cognitive styles that do not match curricular expectations. Inefficient learner strategies interfere with all aspects of becoming knowledgeable, remembering, and communicating this knowledge. Therefore, high priority must be placed on matching school tasks to students' preferred learning strategies and on teaching students how to think, commit to memory, and recall more effectively. The goals of such cognitive training are guided by the way "knowing how to know" normally evolves, a research avenue that originated with the work of Piaget.

Piaget (1976) felt that self-awareness of reasoning processes enhances acquisition of information. That is, training a child to ignore distractions works best when the child understands why distracting stimuli do not help with problem-solving. Praising the child for not becoming distracted does not have the same effect. Studies on how *metacognition* (knowing about knowing) develops show that the intermediate grade student is better than the younger

RESEARCH BOX 7-2
Research on the Maturation of Metacognitive Abilities

Older children automatically store, retain, and retrieve inputs better and differently than younger children because their semantic and conceptual systems are more developed. This makes inputs more memorable because they are more familiar, meaningful, conceptually interrelated, and subject to inference and gap-filling (Flavell & Wellman, 1977). Below age five, children seldom use deliberate plans to remember. When told to memorize they perceive the information in an idle, purposeless fashion. As children mature, they recognize that intensive, persistent, planned, goal-directed intellectual interaction with the information aids retrieval. After age five, and through the teen-age years, memory strategies increase in use and efficiency (Paris & Lindauer, 1977). These strategies combine with maturing semantic and conceptual abilities, knowledge base, and awareness of how memory works to increase memory abilities with age.

Memory Strategies Used to Learn Material

Naming and Verbal rehearsal

☐ Use of spontaneous verbal rehearsal in memory tasks increases as a function of age (subjects were five, seven, and ten

years old; Flavell, Beach, & Chinsky, 1966).
☐ First grade is a transitional age for beginning to spontaneously rehearse; those who rehearse can recall picture sequences better. The nonrehearser is capable of rehearsing and can be gotten to do so with minimal instruction and demonstration, in which case memory becomes as good as that of the spontaneous rehearser. However, on another task, over half of the latter children revert to not rehearsing (Keeney, Cannizzo, & Flavell, 1967).
☐ Younger children verbalize stimulus names only while they are perceptually present; when older, they continue to verbalize these names even when the stimuli are no longer present (Flavell, Friedrichs, & Hoyt, 1970).

Clustering the organization of material

☐ When learning a list, younger children rehearse one name over and over again; older children rehearse several words together over and over again (Cuvo, 1975; Ornstein, Naus, & Liberty, 1975).
☐ Older children segregate material to be memorized by category and study same-category items together; younger children don't use clustering to aid memory.

Elaborating by using association cues

☐ Free recall of pictures is always better when each picture is accompanied by student in strategies used to learn material and awareness of how memory works. Research Box 7-2 reviews how these metacognitive skills mature.

Typical learners vary greatly in when, how, and which memory strategies they use (Butterfield, Wambold, & Belmont, 1973). The learning disabled are generally far less mature in their repertoire, awareness, and use of these strategies. They may not frequently and efficiently use spontaneous verbal rehearsal, organize information for recall, use memory cues unless prompted, use all the available cues, be aware of how memory could be facilitated, or be aware of

---

another picture that could cue memory. Cue cards work best when presented to children one at a time. When cue cards are just presented as a pile, and the same cue appears on several cards so as to cue memory for similar pictures (3 empty cage cards for 3 different animals), first graders ignore the cue or name it instead of the picture. Third graders use the cue to recall one or two pictures but do not search their memories for the remainder. They unsystematically switch from one cue category to another. Only sixth graders exhaustively search their memories for one category of cues before moving on to the next (Kobasigawa, 1974).

□ Increasing ability to recall a story from ages six to twelve is related to better ability to infer and elaborate on the story's semantic relationships (Paris & Upton, 1976).

□ Ability to use indirect, implied cues for accessing memory improves with age, thereby deepening comprehension and enhancing memory (subjects were aged seven to eleven; Paris & Lindauer, 1976).

Awareness of How Memory Works

□ Older children have a more realistic and accurate picture of their own memory abilities and limitations than do younger ones (Yussen & Levy, 1975).

□ Second and fourth graders are better than kindergarten and first graders at sensing when they've studied and learned a set of

items well enough to be able to remember them all (Flavell, Friedrichs, & Hoyt, 1970).

□ Older students are more aware of and sensitive to the need to memorize; for example, that items not recalled on tests need more study than ones that were recalled (Masur, McIntyre, & Flavell, 1973).

□ Older students have more foresight than younger ones in keeping written records of past problem-solving attempts, so as to not repeat these attempts or skip possible solution moves (Siegler & Liebert, 1975).

□ Third and fifth graders are more likely than first graders to know that a list of categorizable items is easier to remember than a list of unrelated items (Moynahan, 1973). Younger students can generate categories if asked to but don't do it spontaneously (Tenney, 1975).

□ Older students realize that opposites, or words that are meaningfully linked by a story, are easier to remember than those without these relationships. They know that information similar to that to be recalled interferes with memory. They know that it is easier to recall something in one's own words than in others' words. They can think of more ways to remember something than younger students, and these ways usually rely on internal aids ("I'll write it down") versus external aids ("I'll tell my mother to remind me") (Kreutzer, Leonard, & Flavell, 1975).

what strategies are appropriate on different types of tasks. Their most frequent response to a comprehension question is not to apply any line of reasoning at all (Kavale, 1980b).

For some children this is only a production deficiency; appropriate strategies can be induced so that learning of content becomes equivalent to that of the typical student. However, teaching such strategies will aid recall only when use of the strategies becomes automatic and effortless (Flavell, 1977; Flavell & Wellman, 1977). Teaching learning strategies to students whose information-processing weaknesses continue to hinder appropriate learning is not nearly as helpful.

Comprehension in Content Areas

Comprehension is not just a skill used during reading. It also accounts for how well children attend to, conceptualize, organize, store, and retrieve information that they hear. When language skills and learner strategies are inefficient, listening comprehension is likely to be a problem. Reading and listening comprehension difficulties interfere with achievement in all classes, including learning of content in science and social studies.

For some learning disabled students, reading comprehension, rather than listening, creates the greater difficulty because of decoding weaknesses. Others have both reading and listening comprehension difficulties. Language interferences with listening comprehension can come from weak morphology, syntax, semantics, and pragmatics. Other factors include: poor auditory perception of low-information carrying parts of sentences; inefficiencies in dealing with different speakers' styles, speeds, intonation, and stress patterns; and confusion when familiar words are used in strange contexts. Besides learning strategies, the child's cognitive preference for dealing with whole concepts or details also influences what is attended to or overlooked in reading and listening. Modifications in content area instruction are particularly important so that the learning disabled student does not become less knowledgeable with time.

Written Expression

Written language is the highest level of language accomplishment. It requires that a child translate language comprehension, reasoning, and expression skills into the visual symbol system used for reading (spelling), and then express the product through fine-motor movements (penmanship). It involves the coordination of auditory, visual, motor, and cognitive abilities (Johnson & Myklebust, 1967). This is the skill area in which many learning disabled individuals experience life-long difficulties.

Typical Written Expression Skill Acquisition. By third grade the typical school curriculum has introduced such opportunities for written expression as short stories, poems, limericks, letters, and reports. In the intermediate grades, the student continues to sharpen spelling and penmanship skills while instruction in the mechanical rules and ideational aspects of written expression is emphasized.

The mechanical rules that need to be taught include capitalization, punctuation, and grammar. The ideational aspect of written language can be divided into five categories (Poteet, 1980):

1. *Substance* concerns how well the child names the objects, people, or events written about; describes them; presents a plot; and addresses larger issues such as general themes or morality.
2. *Productivity* refers to the number of words that are written. These generally increase with age, as do the number of words per sentence. Hermreck (1979) reports that the average number of words written about a picture increases from 83 words in third grade, to 94 words in fourth grade, 141 words in fifth grade, and 200 words in sixth grade (in Poteet, 1980).
3. *Comprehensibility* represents the ease with which the reader can understand what the student has written (is it organized and logical?).
4. *Reality* refers to how realistic the author's perceptions are.
5. *Style* reflects the child's unique ways of writing. Style includes the use of different sentence forms appropriately, the tone conveyed, and the vocabulary chosen to express thoughts.

As students mature they become more able to include in their writing such aspects of comprehension as inferential thinking, critical evaluation, and abstract issues and language (e.g., metaphors). Students can better proofread their work critically and make modifications where appropriate. By the sixth grade written expression goals are similar to those in the junior high school.

Written Expression Patterns of Learning Disabled Students. Students with reading and spelling difficulties have a hard time with written expression assignments. They are significantly poorer than their peers in vocabulary chosen, maturity of themes, spelling, syntax, and format (capitalization, punctuation) (Poplin, et al., 1980). Students with visual processing difficulties and good language abilities may express themselves well in writing, but the spelling needs to be overlooked. Written expression of the child with motor production difficulties also may be good, if only the child would stick with the arduous writing process. Hermreck (1979) found that students with poor handwriting produced only about half the numbers of words written by their peers. This percentage did rise some by sixth grade (in Poteet, 1980).

The student with language disturbances is the most severely handicapped in written expression because the ideational aspect of writing is impaired. The child may lack the necessary vocabulary, grammar, spelling abilities, reasoning skills, organization, flexibility with word meanings, and ability to recall words (naming). This child cannot fluently, flexibly, and creatively translate ideas into writing and elaborate on them. At times these ideas don't even exist in such a logical, sequenced fashion that the student can relate them orally. That is, a child must be able to think about and comprehend a subject before he or she can write about it effectively. For many, this comprehension may be severely lagging. For example, a study of twelve-year-old learning disabled students found that their comprehension of ambiguous grammatical forms was equivalent to that of typical five- to six-year-old children; comprehension of multiple meanings of words equalled that of the average seven- to eight-year-old (Wiig, Semel, & Abele, 1981). This youngster has only a slim chance of mastering written expression skills unless the underlying language reception and expression disabilities are remediated.

Children whose written expression difficulties are related to attentional problems may succeed when taught very detailed rules for writing. If impulsive, these students may prefer to write about whole ideas, and not back these up with relevant details. They may cover a complex topic in several short paragraphs by dealing only with the major issues. The overly reflective student, on the other hand, may dwell so much on details that the same topic is covered in several pages, and the main issues never come clear. These students need their cognitive styles clarified for them, so that they can begin to incorporate the opposite style into their thinking and writing.

In remediating written language difficulties, teachers have been encouraged to concentrate on the ideational aspects, rather than the spelling, penmanship, or even mechanical rules (Otto, McMenemy, & Smith, 1973). Without appropriate ideas to express, the latter skills are useless. This is why teaching a formal, rule-based, grammatical method for writing tends not to improve written expression abilities (Le Fevre, 1970). Improving written expression is extremely critical because, from the intermediate grades on, this is the major means by which students' knowledge is evaluated.

Mathematics

Many learning disabled students' mathematics weaknesses persist beyond the primary grades. In the intermediate grades the math curriculum becomes conceptually more difficult. It also relies more on reading of word problems and instructions, which may in itself be difficult for the student. Mathematics concepts also become integrated to a far greater extent into the social studies and science curricula, thereby creating further problems.

To help these students, teachers must understand their strengths and weaknesses, and scrutinize the nature of past teaching. Whereas many youngsters discover important elements of reading for themselves, this is harder in math problems. Students must be systematically taught how and why they calculate as they do. Similarly, the learning of number facts, which so many LD students find very difficult, does not come automatically with time. It needs to be consciously committed to memory and drilled.

The student who cannot understand basic math relationships also often finds it particularly difficult to judge directions and time. This child has trouble finding his or her way around a city, getting to class on time, and judging when to go home for dinner. This youngster also may have a terrible time imitating rhythms in music class and on the dance floor (Wolf, 1967).

Despite these difficulties, students with severe mathematics disabilities are more fortunate than those with the same degree of reading problems. Since mathematics skills are not as highly prized in our society, a student need attain only approximately a fourth grade level competency to adjust to typical employment circumstances (Chandler, 1978). Consequently many experts suggest that children be taught to understand basic mathematical relationships and problem solving processes, but be encouraged to use calculators for computing (Capps & Hatfield, 1977; Caravella, 1977; Gawronski & Coblentz, 1976; Teitelbaum, 1978). Some feel that calculators may in fact help children improve in calculation skills (Beardslee, 1978; Creswell & Vaughn, 1979). Math educators acknowledge that computers are making it increasingly essential for students to comprehend mathematics relationships so that they can better judge manipulations of the computer keyboard, whether as a telephone operator, supermarket checkout person, or home cable TV shopper.

Social–Emotional Development

Learning disabled individuals' social adjustment is important to deal with because their success in life often has far more to do with how they feel about themselves and get along with others than with their ultimate level of academic achievement. Behavioral disturbances are more frequent among LD students than among their nondisabled peers, and among learning disabled males than females (Cullinan, Epstein, & Lloyd, 1981). Appropriate social relationships are deterred by their information-processing inefficiencies, inattentiveness, physical activity and restlessness, strong cognitive styles, maturational lags, unique temperaments, feelings engendered by others' responses to their difficulties, and past learning opportunities. Their articulation and motor problems often make interrelating through speech and group sports difficult, while such things as sloppy dress and untied shoelaces make them objects of derision. They also differ from their classmates by engaging in fewer task-oriented behaviors (Bryan & Wheeler, 1972; Bryan, 1974a), having lower self concepts (Bruininks, 1978a; Larsen, Parker, & Jorjorian, 1973), and being less socially mature (Myklebust & Boshes, 1969).

Life in the classroom is different for LD students than for their classmates. They are often ignored by teachers and peers when they initiate verbal interactions (Bryan, 1974a; Bryan & Wheeler, 1972), are judged more negatively by teachers (Garrett & Crump, 1980; Keogh, Tchir, & Windeguth-Behn, 1974), and are more often objects of negative statements, criticism, and warnings from their teachers (Bryan, 1978; Chapman, Larsen, & Parker, 1979). When their peers are asked questions such as "Whom would you like or not like to sit beside or invite to a party?", research consistently shows the LD student is less popular and accepted than others (Bryan, 1974b; Scranton & Ryckman, 1979; Serafica & Harway, 1979), or more likely to be ignored (Prillaman, 1981). As

LD students' appearance and athletic abilities improve, so does their social status among peers (Siperstein, Bopp & Bak, 1978).

Life outside the classroom is also different for LD students than for their peers. Strangers judge them more negatively after observing their nonverbal behaviors (Bryan & Perlmutter, 1979; Bryan, Sherman, & Fisher, 1980). Their parents may express less affection for them than for their siblings (Owen et al., 1971), and may expect even less of them than the learning disabled expect for themselves (Chapman & Boersma, 1979). One study found that mothers of learning disabled children viewed their children's successes less positively and their children's failures more negatively than did mothers of nondisabled children (Pearl & Bryan, 1982). They downplayed successes by attributing them to luck and compounded failures by blaming them on poor ability. Mothers of typical children, on the other hand, demonstrated precisely the opposite attribution patterns crediting success to their children's abilities and failures to bad luck.

Learning disabled students' social–emotional characteristics tend to persist over time so that, when they enter new social settings, their social isolation recurs (Bryan, 1976). Three factors appear influential in perpetuating such difficulties: language disabilities, social imperceptions, and learned helplessness. Many experts observe that LD students often have appropriate social skills but, because of these factors, fail to use them at appropriate times (Bryan & Perlmutter, 1979; Spekman, 1981).

Language Disabilities and Social Relationships. The difficulty that LD preschoolers have with pragmatic speech often persists into their elementary school years and beyond, and sharply contrasts with the excellent conversational skills of their nondisabled peers. Learning disabled students often can't adjust their language to the people they are speaking with, to what was just said, or to the topic, goal, time, or setting. Their speech is characterized by nonsequiturs. They have trouble interpreting and inferring from what others say, taking turns in responding to others, and taking others' perspectives (Wong & Wong, 1980). Problems with syntax and semantics also deter adequate communication (Bryan & Pflaum, 1978).

LD students' verbal communications more often are of a competitive than considerate nature, which in turn tends to elicit competitiveness from peers. In contrast, nondisabled students receive more consideration statements ("nice guyisms") than do their learning disabled classmates (Bryan, Donahue, Pearl, & Sturm, 1976). LD students also tend not to adjust the complexity of their language to the age level of those they are speaking with (Bryan, 1978; Bryan & Pflaum, 1978) or to provide age-appropriate descriptive information about objects and events so as to promote conversation (Noel, 1980). They take turns in conversations as cooperatively as their peers but maintain less control of the discussion because they don't use questions to engage their peers. The questions they do ask often do not require elaboration from the responder (Bryan, Donahue, & Pearl, 1981).

When their language skills are complicated by naming problems, LD students may have difficulty responding swiftly or choosing the right words, even if they are sensitive to the line and flow of conversation. All these weaknesses combined interfere with building friendships, peer acceptance, and an adequate self-image.

Social Imperceptions. Learning disabled students' social relationships are often hampered by lack of insight into the affect, attitudes, intentions, and social expectations communicated by others' verbal and nonverbal behaviors. They seem to have difficulty taking the cognitive and affective position of others (Bruininks, 1978b; Johnson & Myklebust, 1967; Wender, 1971). For example, they are less accurate than their peers at interpreting nonverbal cues of affection, gratitude, anger, and asking forgiveness (Bryan, 1977).

Taking others' perspectives, or *decentering*, makes for effective social interaction among typical learners (Chaplin & Keller, 1974; Flavell et al., 1968). With poor perspective-taking, LD students have less social insight into what is going on and how they are doing within groups. Consequently, the affective as well as cognitive quality of their interactions may differ from that of their peers (Bryan, Sherman, & Fisher, 1980). They make negative statements more often than their peers (Bryan, 1978) and laugh inappropriately (Bryan & Pflaum, 1978). These students also fail to use such social ingratiation tactics as acting interested in another speaker through eye contact and smiling (Bryan & Sherman, 1980).

LD students' problem-solving strategies do not help clarify their social perceptions. They are less likely to use questions to clarify information (Donahue, Pearl, & Bryan, 1980) and, rather than using conversations to gain task-relevant information, they tend to gather irrelevant and contradictory information (Spekman, 1981). By attending to unimportant details in social circumstances, they may fail to predict consequences within these situations (Bruno, 1981). Given their social imperceptions, it makes sense that, when in a group situation, learning disabled students are less persuasive than their peers because they tend not to disagree or hold fast to their positions. They play a submissive, deferential role, and are less likely to be leaders or to keep a group on task (Bryan, Donahue, & Pearl, 1981).

At times learning disabled students seem very much aware of their lower status among peers (Horowitz, 1981). At other times they unrealistically overestimate this status (Bruininks, 1978ab; Garrett & Crump, 1980). They often try very hard to succeed socially, and can't understand the reactions and rebuffs they get from others (Walbrown et al., 1979).

Learned Helplessness. Given their continual academic and social failure, it is no wonder that learning disabled children often give up. Although a student wishes to succeed, the repeated, inescapable failure experiences have taught the child that little relationship exists between his or her behavior and its conse-

Table 7-4 Student motivation as related to the attributional process

	TYPE OF ACHIEVEMENT RELATED TO EXPECTATIONS OF SOCIETY AND SCHOOLS	TYPE OF ADULT FEEDBACK / ATTRIBUTION MADE BY CHILD	TYPE OF AFFECT ASSOCIATED WITH INTERNAL EVALUATION OF PERFORMANCE	CHILD'S UNDERSTANDING OF HIS ROLE IN CAUSE-EFFECT RELATIONSHIPS	EXPECTATIONS AND PROBABILITY OF SUBSEQUENT BEHAVIOR
High achiever	Success is positively valued by our society. Success is defined by schools as desirable.	Positive feedback from adults. The child receives positive labels such as smart, gifted, etc. Child accepts and internalizes positive labels. / The cause of success is attributed by the child to ability and effort.	The positive affects of pride, accomplishment and competence is associated with successful performance. The child self-reinforces his performance with internal positive self-statements. The child's self-concept is enhanced.	The child perceives that his effort determines outcome. Energy is seen as a means of solving problem.	The child has expectancy of success for future performance. Increased probability of future success serves as an incentive to work harder.
Low achiever	Failure is negatively valued by our society. Failure is defined by schools as undesirable.	Negative feedback from adults. The child receives negative labels such as slow, learning problems, etc. Child accepts and internalizes negative labels. / The cause of failure by the child is attributed to lack of ability.	The negative affect of frustration, shame, indifference, and incompetence is associated with failure. Internal statements of the child are primarily negative reflecting his lack of ability. The child's self-concept is decreased.	No causal relationship is perceived between effort and outcome by the child. Therefore, the child considers effort a waste of energy. Energy is spent on avoiding the task.	The child has expectancy of failure in future. Increased probability of failure, therefore, no incentive to expend effort.

SOURCE: Grimes, L. "Learned Helplessness and Attribution Theory: Redefining Children's Learning Problems." *Learning Disability Quarterly*, 1981, 4 (1), p. 92. Reprinted by permission.

quences. Since consequences are usually negative and perceived as being out of the child's control, he or she may see no use in trying.

Table 7-4 explains why failure experiences foster the learning disabled child's attitude of "whatever I do I can't succeed, so why bother." Consequently, the term "learned helplessness" has been applied to such low-achieving children (Dweck & Repucci, 1973; Dweck, 1975; Diener & Dweck, 1978). Since these children feel that they have no control over success, they lack intrinsic motivation to prove their competence and are defeated even before they begin to learn (Adelman, 1978; Pearl, Bryan, & Donahue, 1980). Any amount of effort seems useless because the child expects failure. This helpless attitude persists, even in circumstances where the consequences could be positive. Good achievers, on the other hand, have learned to attribute success to personal effort, rather than to abilities and consequences; for them, it's always worth trying because success is likely.

When LD students constantly fail, are perceived negatively by others, are awkward in social relationships, and give up, their chances for successful life adjustment diminish. We must find ways to help these children become more socially insightful and to recognize that success is possible. Parental, teacher, and peer behavior toward LD children also must be altered so that their self-concepts are no longer on a vicious cycle downward. This is critical to paving the way for contentment with those facets of life that depend on interpersonal skills such as friendships, marriages, and relationships with children and employers.

Summary

There is a controversy over whether instruction of the young learning disabled student should focus on training underlying information-processing abilities or academic objectives. However, the two need not be considered mutually exclusive as long as the inefficiencies that are being strengthened logically lie along the academic skill hierarchy, and training occurs on the academic objectives themselves or other tasks that share many common attributes.

Reading acquisition involves a gradual shift from dealing with whole visual configurations to analysis of language details, sequencing sounds, and guessing at words from the passage's meaning. Some of this process may reflect our teaching methods. Learning disabled students may have difficulty with the visual, auditory, linguistic, or attentional portions of the reading task. These same weaknesses also impinge on spelling and the ideational aspects of written language and mathematics.

Comprehension weaknesses may affect performance in reading, listening, content area subjects, and social communication. These comprehension difficulties are often related to linguistic disabilities and inefficient learner strategies. Penmanship difficulties further complicate a learning disabled students' schooling by making it difficult for the student to communicate knowledge and for teachers to evaluate this knowledge.

In addition to academic difficulties, learning disabled students tend to be less accepted by peers and adults, to interact awkwardly with others, to be socially imperceptive, and to respond to failure by no longer trying. These social-emotional concerns need to be addressed in just as intensive a manner as the academics, to insure that these children grow up with enough personal strengths to make it through life successfully.

Suggestions for Further Study

1. To better understand how the perceptual-motor theorists intended perceptual activities to integrate with everyday learning, read Frostig (1975). In this article she illustrates how one can teach language, science, math, reading, and thinking and attention skills through perceptual training activities. Greater perceptual facility in turn facilitates the learning of skills in these other areas.

2. Parents often say that their LD children never crawled and that they still don't consistently use only one side of their body (mixed dominance). They then ask if these are related to the learning disability. Research indicates that the two are not related. Read Koupernik, MacKeith, & Francis-Williams' (1975) account of how 10 percent of all children never crawled. Instead they shuffled, hitched, scooted, or slid around while sitting (Robson, 1970). Even severely motor-impaired children can be good learners (Bibace & Hancock, 1969). Many studies have found that mixed dominance is related to learning disabilities only when a brain insult has caused both conditions (Belmont & Birch, 1965; Guyer & Friedman, 1975; Hildreth, 1945; Lyle, 1969; Myklebust & Boshes, 1969; Owen et al., 1971; Stephens, Cunningham, & Stigler, 1967; Wolfe, 1941). Mixed dominance seems to be just as common as total one-sidedness among good learners (Ekwall, 1976; Fernald, 1943; Groden, 1969; Spache, 1976).

3. Do you recall the literature on heritability of learning disorders in Chapter 4? Boder's (1973) data shows that siblings even share the same patterns of reading disorders. Run your own mini-experiment. Have a school principal identify two siblings that both have learning disabilities. Look over their work. Do their successes and failures look similar? Does the younger sibling show patterns similar to those of the older sibling at the same age? Have the same task modifications been helpful for both children? Often, evaluation of an older sibling's learning history can give clues to how to teach a younger brother or sister.

4. If you are interested in learning more about penmanship, consult the Zaner-Bloser Evaluation Scales (1968). They provide samples of varying qualities of penmanship for grades one through eight. Also inspect the scoring procedures on Myklebust's (1965) Picture Story Language Test, his 1973 volume of the same book, and the Test of Written Language (Hammill & Larsen, 1978b) to discover which features distinguish typical from atypical penmanship and written expression.

5. Visit an elementary school and browse through the teacher's guides that accompany the reading and math curricula. Each presents a detailed scope and sequence chart of the order in which certain skills should be taught. These charts are most informative about the tasks that children are expected to accomplish at different grade levels. Take particular note of the third and fourth grade objectives. Do you notice any major shifts taking place here? What kind? Why? Can you anticipate the kinds of difficulties LD students who have just managed to "get by" might face in fourth grade?

6. If you are interested in learning more about how children's attributions of success to internal or external sources affects achievement and self-concept read Grimes' (1981) excellent review article. It will help you think about techniques for modifying attributions, whether being 100 percent successful is good for children, and what the psychology of the overachiever is like.

7. Piaget has had an important influence on our understanding of a child's social, as well as academic development. If you would like to learn more about how his theories relate to research and educational practices that help LD students become more socially competent, read Pullis & Smith's (1981) excellent review article. This review melds knowledge about the LD student's social development, language competence, learner strategies, and social relationships into a framework that suggests that the LD child might best benefit from a *cooperative classroom* model (Mehan, 1979; Sharan, 1980). In this model, children work together to complete academic tasks, thereby enhancing both their interpersonal and cognitive dynamics.

Chapter Eight
The Secondary School Student

While interest, research and program development flourished during the 1960s in regard to elementary learning disabilities, there was no similar movement at the secondary level. This resulted in part from the assumption that intensive, early intervention had long-lasting, ameliorative effects. In addition, since young people at times can compensate for their weaknesses, and junior and senior high school programs typically maintain a content rather than a learner orientation, individual students' needs can easily go undetected at the secondary level.

Despite extensive elementary school programming, the learning problems of many youngsters did not go away (Mann, 1978). Nor did these remedial efforts significantly decrease the total number of children who became learning disabled adolescents (Schmid, 1979). In addition, some children, whose problems were not sufficiently acute to draw attention in the early grades, found themselves ill-equipped to cope with the more complex demands of secondary education (Goodman & Mann, 1976; Wilcox, 1970). To the practitioner, the most disheartening realization was that some of the disabilities thought to have been "cured" tended to reappear, in somewhat different forms, in the secondary years when youngsters were faced with new task, cognitive, and environmental demands.

As a result of these developments, strong interest in adolescent learning disabilities was first voiced in the mid-1970s. Secondary research and program options increased dramatically due to heightened parental and professional activism, and to Public Law 94–142, which mandated free, appropriate education for all handicapped individuals through age twenty-one.

Learning disabled adolescents, from seventh grade through graduation, often continue to have mild, or moderate to severe difficulties in any number of areas: gross and fine motor coordination, listening and speaking, reading and written expression, reasoning, and social-emotional adjustment. Many of them also have significant areas of strength. To facilitate preparation for their adult adjustment, the professional must consider their multiple needs. Remediation of basic skills is recommended when students are motivated and when such effort is warranted by their career goals and realistic potential for gains. Students can be tutored in content areas so that they continue to become knowledgeable. Their interpersonal skills can be developed, study strategies built, and vocational preparation intensified. Since in many cases weaknesses persist into adult life despite remedial gains, the primary focus in the secondary years should be on finding ways to work around and compensate for weaknesses so that students' strengths can be fully developed. Developing LD adolescents' social repertoires is equally important so that they will adjust favorably to adult work, family, and social situations and not find themselves treated differentially by employers, peers, and authorities.

This chapter was written by Debrah Shulman.

Characteristics of Learning Disabled Adolescents

Current information on the characteristics of secondary LD students is derived primarily from clinical data and classroom observations, as opposed to controlled empirical study (Cannon & Compton, 1981). Lists of characteristics, such as those presented in Table 8-1, reflect unknown degrees of variability among both the youngsters studied and observers' judgments. This makes comparing and drawing conclusions from isolated research and observational findings particularly difficult. No one has yet determined how many of which attributes apply to whom, and which characteristics, when considered together

Table 8-1   General characteristics of learning disabled adolescents

Physical	general motor awkwardness
	hyperactivity
	smaller than peers
Learning Style	excessive daydreaming
	high distractibility
	perceptual confusions
	persistent confusion
	short attention span
	impulsive decisions and judgments
	inflexibility toward ideas and activities
Cognitive/ Achievement	difficulty anticipating the behavior of others
	difficulty modifying their behavior patterns
	difficulty generalizing from experience
	difficulty interpreting and using symbols
	difficulty selecting from alternatives
	poor development of logical reasoning and abstract thinking abilities
	severe underachievement
Social/Emotional	alienation from family
	delinquency
	feelings of inadequacy
	few established principles or ideals
	frustration with self
	immaturity
	inner rage
	passive or active aggression
	quickly yields to pressure
	secondary emotional problems
	truancy

SOURCE: Schmid, R. E., in C. Mercer (ed.), *Children and Adolescents with Learning Disabilities*. Columbus, Ohio: Charles E. Merrill Publishing Co., 1979; and Wiederholt, J. L., A report on secondary school programs for the learning disabled. Final report (Project No. H12–7145B, Grant No. OEG–O–714425). Washington, D.C.: Bureau of Education for the Handicapped, 1975.

with the quality of past teaching, attitudes of parents and teachers, and the demands of the current school curriculum, identify any one individual as learning disabled. Where to draw the line between normal and learning disabled behavior is often difficult to determine.

Deshler's (1978) review of studies dealing with academic-cognitive, personality-social, and perceptual-motor factors involved in learning disabilities summarizes the general characteristics of LD adolescents:

1. LD youngsters demonstrate areas of adequacy and strength as well as weakness.
2. Many still lack skills basic to successful academic functioning.
3. By adolescence there is a high probability that the indirect effects of having a learning handicap result in poor self-perceptions, lowered self-concept and reduced motivation.
4. Maturation and compensation tend to refine and integrate many psychological, perceptual, and motor functions to the degree that problems of incoordination, hyperactivity, distractibility, and poor attention manifest themselves in more subtle or controlled ways in older students.

Because the world of the adolescent is broader than the home and classroom of the elementary school child, other age-appropriate factors also need to be considered. These include the adolescent's emerging 'sexuality, developing vocational interests, talents, future expectations, range of leisure time activities, and potential for eventual independent living. Social skills, which are at least as relevant as reading level to degree of satisfaction in later life, also need to be evaluated and intensely trained at this point.

The areas of particular interest to the LD specialist include abilities underlying academic achievement, gross and fine motor-coordination, listening and speaking, reading and written expression, mathematics, reasoning skills and social-emotional development. Research is still needed to identify the relevance and prevalence of many of these characteristics, and the ways in which they vary with chronological age and the changing demands of home and school situations. "Only when treatment variables and learner characteristics are treated concomitantly will the questions relating to each area be adequately answered" (Deshler, 1978, p. 69). To arrive at the best answers, professionals will need to follow the same individuals through both childhood and adolescence.

Abilities Underlying Academic Achievement

Many items in Table 8-1 allude to continuing problems in visual, auditory, motor and attention processes. Tests of these processes at difficulty levels suitable for teenagers show that LD adolescents often continue to differ from their typical classmates in these basic information-processing abilities (Fabian & Jacobs, 1981; Koppitz, 1981 ab). The extent to which these abilities have matured needs to be researched, as well as the relationship they have to ongoing learning (Marsh, Gearheart & Gearheart, 1978) and the longer learning histories (Estes, 1970) of secondary school students. In the absence of this research, as with the elementary student, most professionals do not advise training of these basic processes on tasks that are not the same as or similar to school tasks because transfer of training to school tasks is unlikely. Even supporters of process training for younger children hold such practices to be inappropriate and ineffective for secondary-age students, since the processes should have matured sufficiently for learning purposes by ages nine to fourteen (Wepman et al., 1975).

Most professionals agree that middle and high school teachers need to attend to underlying abilities that obviously interfere with learning, even while focusing on specific academic, career, or behavioral objectives. Perceptual irregularities in left-right discrimination may continue to be evident in industrial arts. Conversational irregularities may interfere with peer interactions. Although improved with age, these weaknesses still may be severe enough to adversely affect learning, performance, and social interactions.

Hyperactivity, for example, generally decreases with age (Bryant & McLoughlin, 1972; Menkes, Rowe & Menkes, 1967), possibly because the ability to sustain attention matures and because peers, parents, and teachers become increasingly less accepting of adolescents' annoying interruption behaviors. Nevertheless, the "frantic to-and-fro purposeless motor activity" of the five or six year old may still evidence itself in adolescent finger- or object-tapping, chair-rocking, leg-wagging, grimacing, or facial tics (Wilcox, 1970, p. 7). Longitudinal research demonstrates a frequent continuance of the related problems of inattention, poor concentration, impulsivity, excitability, and aggressiveness (Cannon & Compton, 1981).

Instead of overlooking these information-processing problems, the teacher should modify specific tasks that are troublesome so as to circumvent areas of difficulty. The industrial arts teacher, for example, might color-code the left and right portions of each piece of a project so that the student with left-right confusions can complete it correctly by matching colors. The teacher can also facilitate performance by directly teaching skills necessary for success on a task. Instead of teaching general language skills to improve social communication, the teacher might observe a student's social interactions and point out precisely what, in that situation, the student should say differently. For example, when someone says "Hi," you say "Hi" back; when your friend asks if you're going to the dance, you answer the question instead of kidding him about his girlfriend. When your friend calls you an "idiot" it means he or she appreciates you. It is not an insult and you should not slug him.

When concentration appears to be a problem, the instructor can consider shorter class sessions, less distracting home and school study environments, more varied teaching formats, and the teaching of learning strategies. The teacher can significantly influence a student's ability to attend on relevant tasks by appropriately altering the assignments or guiding the learning process. The skills being developed or compensated for can be thought of in behavioral terms; they are specific behavioral objectives on the hierarchy of subskills needed to perform academic tasks correctly. When these subskills are ignored, learning and performance continue to suffer.

Gross and Fine Motor Coordination

Although both gross and fine motor coordination generally improve with age, difficulties often persist (Wilcox, 1970; Siegel, 1974). One need only look at the gymnasium or dance floor, to see how clumsy behavior can interfere with peer relationships and impact negatively on self-esteem. Continued fine-motor coordination problems frequently evidence themselves in the illegibility and poor spacing of written school assignments. Some students find writing particularly trying because of both time pressures and the basic manipulative difficulty of the task. While typing is acknowledged to be an excellent vocational skill, and one frequently proposed as an alternative to writing, Deshler (1978) observes that the perceptual and coordination demands of typing may preclude it from being a workable solution for many learning disabled youngsters. Specific practice in writing, outlining, taking lecture notes, or shorthand may be better alternatives. While such activities should be part of secondary programs, students' performances show that, for whatever reasons (immaturity at time of initial instruction, original exposure to inappropriate teaching techniques, or insufficient opportunity for practice), many LD adolescents simply never adequately learn these skills the first time around.

Listening and Speaking

Experts have only recently begun to actively explore the possibility that language-processing deficits characterize LD adolescents as well as younger children (Wiig, Lapointe & Semel, 1977). What little evidence exists points to the fact that some secondary LD students continue to encounter difficulties in listening and speaking. Most secondary school programs are based on the premise that pupils have already mastered the primary elements and are ready to tackle tasks requiring higher-level comprehension and communication skills. This assumption is not always accurate for the learning disabled.

Listening. Man's primary mode of learning is listening; it generally is the basis for acquiring language skills. Listening also typically dominates anywhere from 30 to 65 percent of an average adult working day (Nichols & Stevens, 1957). Modern technology has provided a myriad of mechanisms to further strain listening capabilities. Telephone answering devices, dictating machines, video recorders, and talking computers have replaced business as well as leisure-time reading and writing. Each passing day increases the need to accurately receive and comprehend auditory information.

As in so many other areas of their development, LD adolescents frequently exhibit listening deficiencies. While few people can boast of fully developed listening skills, the situation is particularly critical for the learning disabled. Because they often have reading difficulties, they may need to rely on their auditory skills even more than their non-handicapped peers.

According to Wilkinson, Stratta and Dudly (1974; in Alley & Deshler, 1979), effective listening is a complicated procedure in which information is processed through many different channels. It relies on both the semantic and pragmatic aspects of language.

- The Linguistic Channel — comprehending single and multiple meanings of words and phrases; the word "party," for example, has very different connotations depending on whether it is used in conjunction with "birthday" or "political."
- The Paralinguistic Channel — understanding the tone and quality of an individual's voice, the loudness or softness of speech, of delivery, of the speed of delivery, and the use of pauses and hesitations, all of which, sometimes even more than the words themselves, convey true intent.
- The Visual Channel — gaining information from just looking at an individual (the way the speaker is groomed or attired).
- The Kinesic Channel — comprehending nonverbal modes of communication such as posture, facial expressions, eye movements, and gestures. Kinesic communication patterns may be habitual, hence meaningless, or truly informative, as when used to convey importance or emphasis. Such patterns may be culturally defined. Wilkinson et al. make the telling point that had the Americans who met the Japanese emissaries before Pearl Harbor understood that to them a smile is merely the accompaniment of any social act as opposed to a means of conveying friendship or pleasure, they might have been less likely to have been "lulled into a false sense of security" (p. 280).

Methods currently available for assessing listening abilities have been criticized with respect to validity — the degree to which they actually tap listening skills instead of other traits such as intelligence, aptitude, or hearing. Alley and Deshler (1979) stress that such evaluations tend to be confined solely to an assessment of student factors, whereas listening, like all other aspects of communication, is a two-way process. Keeping in mind that tasks and settings play a role in learning failure, teachers need to be aware of the degree to which they model appropriate listening behavior and encourage satisfactory listening on the part of students. They need to assess the kind and clarity of instructions they give, the amount of time they spend introducing new subject vocabulary, the nature of the questions they ask, the variety of activities they provide to develop listening skills, and the kind of records they keep on student growth in this area. Teachers must also consider the degree to which they effectively use nonlinguistic communication skills, organize their material, pace their presentations, use clear examples to illustrate points, and give concrete examples of abstract information. These factors are particularly important in view of the directed teaching and focusing of attention that many learning disabled students require to listen effectively.

To complete the communication cycle, a person needs to know whether or not the information presented has been correctly understood. This feedback can be either verbal or nonverbal. In a classroom setting, clues to the relative strength of both speaker and listener skills can be gleaned from the amount of teacher-student eye contact, the number of nods or expressions of disinterest, and the quantity and quality of ensuing questions and discussion.

Finally, the teacher needs to determine whether students' basic language skills are delayed to such a degree that they impinge on academic progress. Many severely reading disabled adolescents who struggle to decode first to second grade level words despite eight years of instruction, still cannot listen to a word and segment it into its individual syllables and sounds. Others experience comprehension difficulties stemming in part from the fact that idioms, innuendos, and nonverbal signals make semantics and pragmatics a puzzle.

Because of the importance of this line of inquiry, school personnel must become increasingly knowledgeable and motivated to make listening skills a greater focus of their instructional programs. Fortunately, listening skills can be effectively trained (Childers, 1970; Edgar, 1961; Erickson, 1954; Pratt, 1956). However, perhaps because it is not seen as "hard-core" curriculum, "this direct instruction is seldom given except in the context of a research project" (Cunningham, Cunningham & Arthur, 1981, p. 26).

Speaking. Such oral language abilities of LD adolescents as motor-planning, cognitive-socialization, and word-finding need to be examined (Alley & Deshler, 1979; Bartel & Bryen, 1978). It has been proposed that the language development of many LD students may simply be maturationally delayed, not different in kind from that of nonhandicapped adolescents (Fygetakis & Ingram, 1973). Other investigators, however, postulate the presence of distinct language deficits involving either higher-level cognitive-linguistic processing problems or more basic problems in the ability to name objects or recall and retrieve words from long- or short-term memory (Wiig, Lapointe, & Semel, 1977; Wiig & Semel, 1976).

Difficulties with spoken language can be dramatic, as in verbal apraxia where one experiences an inability to voluntarily make oral movements, although the power of movement remains intact. Speaking problems can also be subtle; involving a propensity toward speaking too loudly or at the wrong times. Learning disabled adolescents' behavior may vary between these extremes. Often they experience difficulty finding the right words to express their thoughts. Sometimes their speech is characterized by slower and less accurate responses to verbal questions, poorer syntax, and less developed use of logic and verbal abstractions. Because poor oral communication patterns can have a definite impact on social–emotional development, current peer acceptance, and future job adjustment, intervention deserves serious consideration.

A teacher must be aware of these language weaknesses. For bilingual or minority students, the teacher should evaluate whether the students' language conforms to their social, ethnic or regional backgrounds, and to the level of functioning expected in their environments (Wiederholt, Hammill, & Brown, 1978). Language delayed students often require special help in learning such symbol systems as foreign languages or geometry, which are introduced at the secondary level. It also is important to identify and try to improve those nonverbal aspects of communication (such as staring or standing too close) that interfere with the development of satisfactory interpersonal relationships.

Reading and Written Expression

Many LD adolescents have yet to master the higher-level skills involved in reading and written expression. Although studies in this area have methodological problems (Gillespie & Sitko, 1978; Lindsey & Kerlin, 1979), one thing appears clear: youngsters who have the least severe problems, the highest IQs, and who come from enriched, supportive homes and receive early intervention, have the most favorable prognoses (Koppitz, 1971; Muehl & Forell, 1973). Favorable outcomes depend on the interaction of learner, task, and setting characteristics.

Reading. Although reading performance in a normal junior or senior high classroom can easily range several grade levels, most students already have mastered sufficient decoding and comprehension skills to be more or less actively and independently engaged in content area studies. Many LD adolescents, however, are still acquiring essential reading skills. Problems continue in basic sight vocabulary, word attack skills, reading accuracy and rate, auditory discrimination and memory, pronunciation of vowels and consonants during oral reading, and vocalization during silent reading (Boder, 1971; Johnson & Myklebust, 1967; Myklebust, 1973). Difficulties run the gamut from incomplete memory for letters of the alphabet (Carner, 1969) to difficulty in gaining meaning from long sentences or paragraphs.

Many special remedial programs have been developed for the learning disabled. Since the learning disabled students' abilities overlap those of typical youngsters, programs developed to meet the reading needs of the younger, general school population can also be helpful in a secondary special education setting (Gillespie & Johnson, 1974).

An important way to enhance secondary reading success is to work with teachers and parents in developing strategies for teaching reading through content areas (Lindsey & Kerlin, 1979). To Cunningham, Cunningham and Arthur (1981) the success of such a program rests not only on what happens with the reading teacher or in the resource room, but also on what goes on in the regular classroom setting. They advocate a cost-efficient method by which reading is used to teach actual subject matter. Other useful interventions include overlearning specific reading skills beyond mastery and using task-analysis procedures (breaking lessons down into skill hierarchies) on the students' curricula.

Anyone working in a secondary school program needs to be aware of factors in our high schools which may actually promote reading problems for the learning disabled. These include an overemphasis on literal comprehension, poorly organized and written teaching materials, inadequate diagnostic and instructional techniques, and a lack of overall comprehensive planning for teaching reading at the secondary level (Lindsey & Kerlin, 1979). Perhaps most devastating is the assumption that if students haven't learned by now they never will. All students can learn something, particularly when provided intensive training at the proper instructional level, in an approach drastically different from the one in which failure was most recently experienced. According to Cunningham, Cunningham and Arthur (1981, p. 13): "Most dyslexia is only terminal if you believe it is!"

A critical element in the reading remediation process is student cooperation. If the learner is not highly motivated to continue working at a task, additional remedial efforts at the secondary level are no more likely to succeed than earlier ones. Equally important is the fact that whether or not these adolescents wish to continue working on basic skill development, accommodations still need to be made to insure their learning in other content areas. This may involve modifications such as tapes or readers, or curriculum materials rewritten at lower readability levels. Students must be involved in and committed to whatever approach is chosen. The programs selected must also coincide with each individual's capabilities and realistic educational-vocational career goals.

Written Expression. While facility with written expression is an important component of both academic and out of school situations, relatively little attention has been devoted to its study. Many individuals believe that societal changes and technological advances are making the ability to write well less important than it used to be. Nevertheless, writing is the way in which students are generally asked to demonstrate what they have learned. Writing is also a valuable aid in organizing thought. For individuals who lack the capacity and confidence to express themselves in writing the experience can be highly frustrating (Irmscher, 1972).

Writing problems are prevalent and difficult to remediate because proficiency in this area relies on an expanded experiential base and the development of adequate listening, speaking, and reading skills. Compared with nonhandicapped peers, LD adolescents often write at a slower pace, have poorer organization, a more limited vocabulary, and a higher frequency of mechanical errors (spelling, capitalization, and punctuation) (Myklebust, 1973). They also are less competent at monitoring their own writing errors (Deshler, 1978). Table 8-2 lists the types of written expression skills that need to be evaluated and remediated in LD students.

Efforts to improve writing skills should focus first on motivation and morale (Irmscher, 1972). Intensive remediation begins by showing students just how much they already do know and how information obtained through listening and speaking can be used in learning to write (Weiss & Weiss, 1979). The mechanics of writing follow.

Notetaking deserves special mention. It is an area in which classroom teachers need to become involved on an active, continuing basis. Students benefit from distribution of simple daily or weekly outlines which specify the topic and corresponding textbook pages, and provide explanations of new concepts or vocabulary, a few questions to be answered at the end of class discussion, and space for the student to add comments. The outline is com-

Table 8-2   Written expression skills requiring assessment and intervention in LD students

I. Attitude toward writing
  A. Emotional blocks to writing assignments
  B. Motivation to write
II. Content
  A. Reflection of the world
    1. Description
    2. Reports of happenings
    3. Procedures
    4. Retelling
    5. Summaries
  B. Conception of relationships
    1. Comparison and contrast
    2. Classification
    3. Qualitative analysis
    4. Sequential analysis
    5. Cause and effect
    6. Explanation in terms of supporting principles
  C. Projection of explanatory schemes and designs
    1. Hypothesis
    2. Conceptual schemes
    3. Design: Plan of action
  D. Expression of personal view
    1. Feelings
    2. Preferences
    3. Opinions
    4. Judgment

III. Craft
  A. Structuring paragraphs and themes
    1. Organizing ideas
    2. Sequencing ideas
  B. Vocabulary development
    1. Choosing words to express experiences
    2. Synonyms
  C. Building sentences
    Generating a variety of sentence patterns
  D. Writing questions
  E. Notetaking
    1. From class lecture
    2. From text material
  F. Summaries and paraphrases
  G. Mechanical factors
    1. Punctuation
    2. Capitalization
    3. Neatness
    4. Spelling
  H. Monitoring written expression
    1. Habits of checking for errors
    2. Ability to detect errors
    3. Ability to correct errors
  I. Written test-taking

SOURCE: Alley, G., and Deshler, D. *Teaching the Learning Disabled Adolescent: Strategies and Methods.* Denver: Love Publishing Company, 1979, p. 111. Reprinted by permission.

pleted in class, checked by the instructor, then replaced in the student's note-book. This procedure encourages careful listening during classtime and provides the learner with accurate notes, which can be used to prepare for school examinations. On tests most LD students require modifications such as extended time periods, the option of oral exams, multiple choice formats, or permission to respond in outline form.

Mathematics

The current proliferation of minicalculators notwithstanding, comprehension of basic arithmetic operations is still essential for successful daily living. First of all, not everyone is fortunate enough to always have a calculator on hand. Second, these devices are not very helpful unless the user understands which operations are to be performed and in what order. Third, the individual still needs to determine the reasonableness of the answers, and to evaluate whether or not to recalculate.

Learning disabled adolescents have all levels of mathematical abilities and skills. Cohn's (1971) studies found that improvement in arithmetical opera-tions occurred in direct relation to improvement in general neurological status, other language functions such as reading and writing, visual recall, and the ability to synthesize action posed by both simple and complex pictures. These factors, as well as limited student interest, insufficient readiness, and poor teaching techniques seem to play a role in math failure (Barney, 1972).

Relatively little research exists regarding the types of mathematical errors typically made by LD individuals. What is available highlights problems in computational operations, choice of algorithms (rules), and the handling of problem–solving situations (Cox, 1975; Lepore, 1974; in Bartel, 1978). Green-stein and Strain (1977) additionally note a preponderance of 1) spatial errors involving the incorrect alignment or placement of figures on the page, 2) subtraction problem reversals as in

$$\frac{\begin{array}{r} 25 \\ -16 \end{array}}{11}$$

3) failure to pay sufficient attention to details such as decimals and dollar signs, and 4) problems involving multiple math operations.

Several approaches exist for informally assessing a student's mathematical capabilities. These include careful examination of daily work samples as well as the results of school-made tests. An example of a more systematic approach is Cawley's Clinical Mathematics Interview (CMI) (1975; in Cawley, 1978) which entails:

1. administration of a relevant (possibly teacher-made) computational test whose items are sorted according to whether or not they were answered correctly;

2. teacher inquiry regarding the specific mathematical or cognitive strategies by which students tried to answer certain questions; and
3. subsequent representation of incorrectly answered items in a different form

(instead of being written, for example, problems may now be presented orally, by graphic symbols, or by means of materials to be manipulated). Student response formats also vary (instead of being asked to record a number, for example, they may now be required to respond orally, use graphs, number sentences, pictures or line drawings, identify the solution from a series of alternatives or actually manipulate objects).

By going beyond marking a test question as either correct or incorrect, this method identifies both the faulty learning strategies of, and the most appropriate and efficient approaches for, the individual learner. Based on the information obtained, a teacher can prepare a sequence of individualized lessons such as that presented in Figure 8-1.

Bartel (1978) suggests that mathematical instruction be geared toward the development of computational facility, mathematical understanding, and divergent, logical, and creative thinking. A positive attitude should also be encouraged and an appreciation of how math relates to everyday life. Alley and Deshler (1979) highlight other important areas for competence:

1. using numbers not involving mathematical operations — counting, measuring, reading recipes or following the Dewey decimal library system;
2. manipulating computational aids such as hand calculators and cash registers;
3. making approximations and understanding the difference, for example, between a cost estimate and an actual cost figure;
4. reading graphs, charts, and maps;
5. applying single and multidimensional geometric relations to real life situations such as determining how much paint or wallpaper to purchase; and
6. understanding the value and limitations of descriptive statistics and the importance of chance factors as they relate to daily living (poker hands, lottery tickets or supermarket games)

Reasoning Skills

What limited data exist concerning the thinking characteristics of LD adolescents suggest that they are inferior to their peers on a variety of dimensions. They tend to be more distractible and impulsive, and less able to attend selectively. They shift focus from one stimulus to another, and fail to take advantage of the organization given to class materials by either teacher or text (Alley & Deshler, 1979; Maietta, 1970). Many have trouble asking questions which would clarify their assignments and simplify their lives. Many are unaware that they can manipulate course content to more closely fit their individual styles of understanding, storing, and reproducing information. Effective decision-making, problem-solving, and time-management are definitely not the rule. Moreover, LD adolescents are often inept at organizing such multiple tasks as the everyday juggling of subjects, assignments, and social relationships.

The work of Myklebust (1973) and Brutten, Richardson and Mangel (1973) suggests that the lower cognitive test scores often obtained by LD adolescents reflect a developmental lag in logical reasoning and abstract thinking skills. Woodward (1981) proposes that these may be due to a school history that overemphasizes remediating deficits as opposed to developing areas of strength. Deshler (1978) adds that these low scores may reflect assessment procedures which, by nature of their product orientation, tend to discriminate against students who, for reasons of insufficient motivation or lack of exposure, have not adequately acquired the expected information. In addition, the perceptual preferences and attitudes that characterize an adolescent's thinking (reflective or impulsive, global or analytic, internal or external control, learned helplessness, directed or independent learning style) often do not match the requirements for success on tests or in school.

Table 8-3 lists thinking skills that need to be encouraged in LD adolescents. Such thinking is involved not only in undertaking a project, but also in self-correcting and polishing the assignment before actually handing it in. For many LD students very little thinking occurs during this timeframe as their primary goal is to get something — *anything* — down on paper, and then to hand it in as quickly as possible. This may reflect decreased capability and motivation, as well as unique cognitive styles. Deshler (1974) found LD adolescents less adept than their nonhandicapped peers at detecting errors in their

Table 8-3 Thinking skills

General Thinking Behaviors
1. Observing
2. Describing
3. Developing concepts
4. Differentiating and defining
5. Hypothesizing
6. Comparing and contrasting
7. Generalizing
8. Predicting and explaining
9. Offering alternatives
Information Organization and Management
1. Perceiving organization in material
2. Manipulating materials for organizing
3. Organizing multiple tasks
4. Using generalizations as organizers

5. Using concepts as organizers
6. Visual imagery
Problem-Solving
1. Identifying the problem
2. Analyzing the problem
3. Developing options for solving the problem
4. Decision-making
5. Executing the decision
Questioning
1. Asking questions of materials
2. Asking different kinds of questions
Self-monitoring of Performance
Time Management

SOURCE: Alley, G., and Deshler, D. *Teaching the Learning Disabled Adolescent: Strategies and Methods.* Denver: Love Publishing Company, 1979, p. 184. Reprinted by permission.

Figure 8-1 A sample remedial module consisting of algorithm, content, and mode sequences that allow error behaviors to be attacked one by one

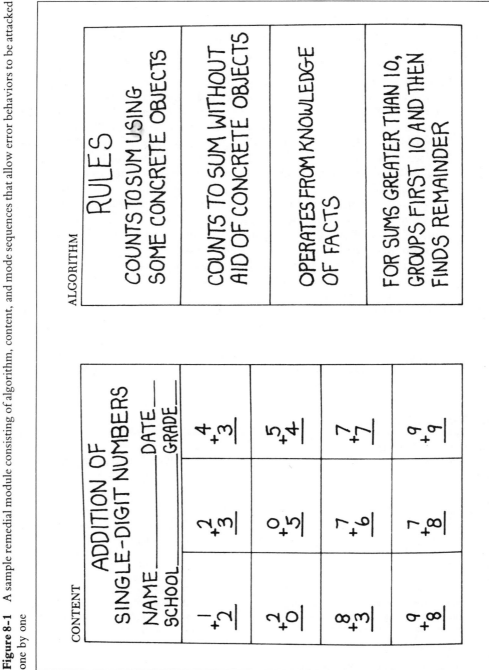

CONTENT

ADDITION OF
SINGLE-DIGIT NUMBERS

NAME_____ DATE____
SCHOOL_____ GRADE___

ALGORITHM

RULES

COUNTS TO SUM USING
SOME CONCRETE OBJECTS

COUNTS TO SUM WITHOUT
AID OF CONCRETE OBJECTS

OPERATES FROM KNOWLEDGE
OF FACTS

FOR SUMS GREATER THAN 10,
GROUPS FIRST 10 AND THEN
FINDS REMAINDER

Figure 8-1 continued

MODE

MODALITIES

INSTRUCTOR	LEARNER	INSTRUCTOR	LEARNER	INSTRUCTOR	LEARNER	INSTRUCTOR	LEARNER
CONSTRUCTS SUBSETS REPRESENTING ADDENDS	CONSTRUCTS SET REPRESENTING SUM	PRESENTS PICTURES OF TWO SUBSETS REPRESENTING ADDENDS	CONSTRUCTS SET REPRESENTING SUM	STATES TWO ADDENDS	CONSTRUCTS SET REPRESENTING SUM	GRAPHICALLY SYMBOLIZES TWO ADDENDS	CONSTRUCTS SET REPRESENTING SUM
CONSTRUCTS SUBSETS REPRESENTING ADDENDS	IDENTIFIES PICTURE OF SET REPRESENTING SUM	PRESENTS PICTURES OF TWO SUBSETS REPRESENTING ADDENDS	IDENTIFIES PICTURE OF SET REPRESENTING SUM	STATES TWO ADDENDS	IDENTIFIES PICTURE OF SET REPRESENTING SUM	GRAPHICALLY SYMBOLIZES TWO ADDENDS	IDENTIFIES PICTURE OF SET REPRESENTING SUM
CONSTRUCTS SUBSETS REPRESENTING ADDENDS	STATES SUM	PRESENTS PICTURES OF TWO SUBSETS REPRESENTING ADDENDS	STATES SUM	STATES TWO ADDENDS	STATES SUM	GRAPHICALLY SYMBOLIZES TWO ADDENDS	STATES SUM
CONSTRUCTS SUBSETS REPRESENTING ADDENDS	GRAPHICALLY SYMBOLIZES SUM	PRESENTS PICTURES OF TWO SUBSETS REPRESENTING ADDENDS	GRAPHICALLY SYMBOLIZES SUM	STATES TWO ADDENDS	GRAPHICALLY SYMBOLIZES SUM	GRAPHICALLY SYMBOLIZES TWO ADDENDS	GRAPHICALLY SYMBOLIZES SUM

SOURCE: Cawley, J. F., "An Instructional Design in Mathematics," in L. Mann, L. Goodman, & J. L. Wiederholt (eds), *Teaching the Learning Disabled Adolescent*, Boston: Houghton Mifflin Co., 1978. Used by permission.

own work. Familiarity with this skill was not totally lacking, but the strategies employed were inefficient. Because successful self-monitoring is relevant in both school and post-academic situations, it needs to be addressed directly by anyone teaching learning disabled individuals.

Formal tests exist for some higher-level thinking skills. Yet far more relevant information can be gained informally by carefully observing a student's response styles, general attitude, and pattern of risk-taking behavior and by analyzing performance on actual school tests. Answers explained or problems solved out loud can help reveal areas of ease as well as confusion. The following questions can help determine whether or not students are ready to apply independent problem-solving skills to specific reading materials:

1. Do students know how to narrow the problem to manageable proportions and to state it precisely?
2. Do they know how to set up reading targets?
3. Can they locate books and other sources of information?
4. Can students use a table of contents and an index to locate information?
5. Can they scan a passage for information?
6. Do they discriminate between what is relevant and what is irrelevant?
7. Do students evaluate what they read, selecting or rejecting after a critical appraisal?
8. Can they make notes efficiently from a number of scattered sources?
9. Can they bring the information they have collected into an orderly presentation of their own?
10. Do they keep an open mind for later evidence that may modify their solution to the problem? (Thomas and Robinson, 1977)

While Wiig, Lapointe and Semel (1977) wonder whether by this age the critical period for improvement in these skills has already passed, research on critical thinking and problem solving suggests that some students are responsive to this type of instruction. A Stanford Research Institute report, entitled *Compensatory Education in Early Adolescence* (1974; in Deshler, 1978), suggests that with certain older pupils, intensive educational efforts may be just as effective as early intervention is with others, because some students during this period experience accelerated rates of cognitive growth.

An exciting development in the area of cognitive skills training is the Learning Strategies program proposed by Alley and Deshler (1979). This approach, still awaiting external validation, assumes that it is possible to teach individuals strategies that will facilitate their acquisition, organization, storage, and retrieval of information, allowing them to more effectively cope with the social and academic demands of the secondary school curriculum.

Task modifications also can facilitate LD adolescents' problem-solving skills. They learn more efficiently when the problems appear solvable and applicable beyond the classroom. Their ability to reason is enhanced by exposure to simple, clear-cut, well-structured materials. Discrepancies between the learning strategies recommended by the teacher and the text must also be identified and clarified. Faulk and Landry (1961), for example, found only 35 percent overlap between the techniques stressed verbally by a group of teachers and those presented visually in their mathematics text. No wonder LD students are confused!

Social-Emotional Development

Adolescence is a period of great physical, social, and emotional change. It is also the time when young people engage in many important developmental tasks (Havighurst, 1972):

1. learning to accept one's physique and to effectively use one's body;
2. becoming comfortable with one's masculine or feminine role and in this role behaving in a socially responsible manner;
3. becoming less emotionally dependent on parents and other adults;
4. preparing for marriage and family life through the development of new and more mature relations with peers of both sexes;
5. selecting a career and preparing for eventual economic independence; and
6. developing an ideology, ethical code or set of values by which to live.

This is especially difficult in current cultural settings which glorify youth, promulgate legal and illegal drug use, idealize sexual permissiveness, discourage individual responsibility, and actively promote the concept that everyone should "do their own thing."

Although unique and different in many ways, adolescence does not wholly transform a person's personality from what it was as a child. "Marked changes do occur but continuity of development is the rule" (Schmid, 1979, p. 383). Learning disabled youngsters who were socially "savvy" as children tend to continue to function satisfactorily as adolescents. In fact, some of them use their superior social skills to compensate for deficits in other areas. For those who never developed these social skills, however, adolescence can be particularly trying, tackling additional important personal issues without the tools needed to either facilitate the learning or ease the transition.

At a time when peer group relations are of prime importance, the LD adolescent is often at a distinct disadvantage (Siegel, 1974). In spite of sincere intentions, the LD adolescent, by both words and mannerisms, often repels rather than attracts others. Problems in interpersonal relationships appear to stem in part from linguistic difficulties, learned helpless attitudes, and a basic lack of social perceptiveness. These youngsters often do not seem to interpret social cues the way other people do (Siegel, Siegel, & Siegel, 1978). Wiig and Harris (1974), for example, found LD adolescents less able to understand subtle communications in affective situations. They even misjudged as positive expressions viewed as negative by both investigators and nonhandicapped controls. Because social perception is such an integral part of all human interaction, deficits in this area can be the most debilitating of all learning disabilities (Minskoff, 1980a).

While comprehensive research data on the psychosocial development of these young people is sorely lacking, observational studies describe several characteristics:

1. Low motivation
2. Gullibility
3. Aloneness
4. Perseveration
5. Aversiveness
6. Low ego status (depression, low self-esteem, guilt)
7. Supersensitivity to external cues (overconcern with the way others feel about them and how they are approached and treated)
8. Paralysis of effort (extreme difficulty starting a task involving writing and spelling)
9. Ambivalence over intelligence and dependence (they think they are subnormal mentally and are sensitive about becoming dependent on others)
10. Suggestibility (prey for unscrupulous leaders)
11. Emotional lability
12. Overreaction to stimuli
13. Poor concentration
14. Demanding with other persons
15. Poor social judgment
16. Lack of awareness of social impact on others
17. Goof-offs (don't pay attention, distract others)
18. Lack of resourcefulness (inflexible, unimaginative, unable to see optional solutions) (Alley & Deshler, 1979, pp. 247–248)

Greater dependence and questioning one's own intelligence seem to be the primary social-emotional characteristics that differentiate the LD adolescent from others (Alley, Deshler & Warner, 1977; in Alley & Deshler, 1979). As with the elementary school child, the student often attributes his or her failure to basic inability rather than to lack of effort. At the same time the LD adolescent fails to credit him- or herself with successes actually achieved, attributing them instead to luck or other external, uncontrollable factors (such as easy test questions) (Tollefson, Tracy, Johnsen, Buenning, Farmer & Barké, 1982).

During adolescence the average teenager integrates childhood personality with new biological drives and wider, but often unclear, social opportunities (Erikson, 1963). The adolescent slowly, consciously, decides who he or she is and in what direction to head. Such understandings generally evolve from a sense of competence and mastery. But with their unsuccessful school histories, most LD adolescents have few positive experiences to draw on to construct such a mental image of themselves.

At this point adolescents should be beginning to view themselves as unique and separate from peer groups. The problem here, of course, is that LD adolescents often never truly develop significant peer group attachments in the first place. This diminishes their opportunity to experience new roles and explore new relationships. It also removes the one major buffer and support system society provides for easing the transition from childhood identity to a new and more separate sense of self. According to Cook (1979), youngsters who find themselves in this position often tend to make one of two debilitating decisions. They either remain excessively attached to and dependent on parental support and authority, or separate prematurely from family, without first establishing wider social horizons. For many individuals this second step could result in drifting from one adopted role to another without ever having, even temporarily, come to grips with the basic questions of "Who am I?" and "Where am I going?"

Teachers who are sensitive to these issues can facilitate the development of skills that help adolescents meet some of their emotional needs, particularly for self-esteem and esteem of others (Maslow, 1968). Berg and Wages (1982) discuss how group counseling can help in this process. The school staff can also advocate specialized social skills training where appropriate. Minskoff (1980ab), for example, has provided an extensive program for developing nonverbal communication skills in students with social perception deficits. Goldstein, Sprafkin, Gershaw and Klein (1980) have identified fifty basic social skills that can be trained by a specific, structured, small group program, based on modeling, role-playing, immediate feedback and real-life homework assignments. This procedure, with few modifications (such as telling students the steps involved in learning the skill instead of having them read them), has been used successfully with LD adolescents (Klein, 1980). Goldstein et al.'s list, in Table 8-4, is an eye-opener as to the level of social training needed.

One goal of programs such as these, as well as individual or group counselling, is to ease the transition of the LD adolescent into broader social circles. By learning active listening and appropriate behavior, the adolescents should become more socially accepted. Greater cooperativeness and verbal and non-verbal ability to instill trust in others should help the adolescent appear to be supportive and caring. This point is particularly important in view of Tubbs and Moss's (1977) contention that people who most easily acquire peer acceptance are the ones who enhance the self-esteem of those whom they are with. At the very least, social skills programs provide both a starting point and a ready-made group experience for those whose own social circles are limited. Providing such programs also helps deal with the "time panic" experienced by LD specialists who believe that adolescence is one of the most important developmental periods for social learning. Because adequate social skills are vital to personal and vocational adjustment in later life, all students who can benefit from such training deserve the opportunity.

Table 8-4   Social skills

Group I. Beginning Social Skills
1. Listening
2. Starting a conversation
3. Having a conversation
4. Asking a question
5. Saying thank you
6. Introducing yourself
7. Introducing other people
8. Giving a compliment

Group II. Advanced Social Skills
9. Asking for help
10. Joining in
11. Giving instructions
12. Following instructions
13. Apologizing
14. Convincing others

Group III. Skills for Dealing with Feelings
15. Knowing your feelings
16. Expressing your feelings
17. Understanding the feelings of others
18. Dealing with someone else's anger
19. Expressing affection
20. Dealing with fear
21. Rewarding yourself

Group IV. Skill Alternatives to Aggression
22. Asking permission
23. Sharing something

24. Helping others
25. Negotiation
26. Using self-control
27. Standing up for your rights
28. Responding to teasing
29. Avoiding trouble with others
30. Keeping out of fights

Group V. Skills for Dealing with Stress
31. Making a complaint
32. Answering a complaint
33. Sportsmanship after the game
34. Dealing with embarrassment
35. Dealing with being left out
36. Standing up for a friend
37. Responding to persuasion
38. Responding to failure
39. Dealing with contradictory messages
40. Dealing with an accusation
41. Getting ready for a difficult conversation
42. Dealing with group pressure

Group VI. Planning Skills
43. Deciding on something to do
44. Deciding what caused a problem
45. Setting a goal
46. Deciding on your abilities
47. Gathering information
48. Arranging problems by importance
49. Making a decision
50. Concentrating on a task

SOURCE: Goldstein, A., Sprafkin, R., Gershaw, N., and Klein, P. *Skill-Streaming the Adolescent: A Structured Learning Approach to Teaching Prosocial Skills.* Champaign, Ill.: Research Press, 1980, pp. 84–85. Reprinted by permission.

Programming Issues

The development of secondary LD programs has gained momentum since passage of PL 94-142. The law does not specify, however, the precise types of programs that should be provided. Basic skill instruction in reading, written expression, or mathematics is particularly relevant for individuals who have only recently been identified as LD and for whom any questions exist regarding the quantity or quality of previous training. Such instruction takes advantage of the sudden and dramatic acceleration in learning that some students experience during adolescence (Williamson, 1974–75; Stanford Research Institute Report, 1974; in Deshler, 1978). On the other hand, concentrating solely on the development of basic academic skills overlooks other needs of the secondary LD student. Some, even after benefiting from maturation and good remediation, are still plagued by severe learning problems. For these young-sters, a one-sided emphasis on basic skill attainment actually may deprive them of opportunities to acquire important knowledge in other areas. It may also prove more frustrating and less rewarding than devoting time to the develop-ment of sound compensatory skills.

Lieberman (1981) asserts that by ages fourteen to sixteen emphasis should be placed on teaching students how to live with their disabilities instead of focusing solely on trying to make them "unlearning disabled." Because dis-abilities often persist into adulthood, students must use their secondary school years to develop ways of compensating for their weaknesses, enhancing their strengths, and selecting realistic goals that capitalize on their identified areas of competence. This translates into providing direct assistance (such as tutoring) for mastery of difficult course content. It means teaching acceptable social behaviors to those who have not yet acquired them. It also includes the sys-tematic exploration of potential career opportunities, the careful selection of appropriate service delivery models, and dealing with minimum competency exams.

Career Education

Vocational goals have been part of the American educational system for over two hundred years (Cegelka, 1981). Until the 1970s, they were narrowly defined as preparing students for higher education or for direct entry into one specific job (*vocational education*). With passage of the Educational Amend-ments of 1974 (PL 93-380) came the concept of *career education,* a continuous process starting in early childhood which is intended to prepare individuals for a wide variety of social, personal, economic, avocational, and leisure-time roles. As currently offered, vocational education typically provides little for the LD adolescent. Existing courses, especially those originally developed for intellectually less capable students, are too watered down or menial in scope. Career exploration courses, on the other hand, such as may be offered to the entire student body, often present the same reading, writing, and general coping problems that make survival in other content area courses difficult.

Special care needs to be taken to include career education concerns in each pupil's individualized program and to insure the compatibility of program-ming efforts and student needs (Patton, 1981). Support for the different occu-pational skill training needs of LD and non-LD adolescents is provided by Mathews, Whang, and Fawcett (1982). They found that while both groups were equally adept at some tasks (getting a job lead from a friend, telephoning a potential employer to arrange an interview whether or not an opening exists, accepting a suggestion from an employer, and complimenting a co-worker on a job well done), LD high school students performed significantly worse on seven important job related skills: participating in a job interview, accepting criticism from an employer, providing constructive criticism to a co-worker, explaining a problem to a supervisor, writing a letter in response to a help wanted ad to request an interview, and writing a letter to follow up a job interview.

Programs developed specifically for the learning disabled have been helpful in this regard. Washburn (1975) proposes a vocational entry skills curriculum for secondary students that emphasizes:

□ *Vocational Academics* — survival reading, writing, speaking, and math relevant to daily life;

□ *Vocational Physical Education* — aimed at improving visual-motor and co-ordination problems;

□ *Vocational Resources* — learning how to obtain needed information from local community sources;

□ *Vocational Know-How*—training in skills aimed at helping a student both obtain and keep a job (interviewing, conversing, writing resumes, solving personal problems, and driving a car);

□ *Basic Vocational Entry Skills* — developing positive attitudes and building self-confidence through successful hands-on experiences in generalized work skills;

□ *Vocational Placement*—provides actual, meaningful experience in the form of volunteer work, work experience, and job placement (and replacement).

Even broader programs that include communications courses and career guidance (Williamson, 1974–5; Woodward, 1981) make sense in view of rapidly changing technology and the fact that the students of today will probably change jobs, if not career areas, at least three or four times during their lives. An approach stressing social skill development is important because the ability to get along is often weighed as heavily as technical competence by those making hiring/firing decisions.

In developing career education plans, counselors need to be aware that the learning disability label in no way precludes the possibility of higher education. Arrangements can be made for oral or untimed college entrance exams, and universities are admitting and providing special services for LD applicants who, given certain curriculum modifications, have a reasonable chance of succeeding.

Service Delivery Models

Since learning disabilities is not a unitary concept, no one school program can possibly meet the needs of all LD youngsters. Minskoff (1969; in Wiederholt, 1978) proposes a three-track program: one for students experiencing social and emotional as well as severe learning problems; a second for less disabled, noncollege-bound individuals; and a third for mildly disabled youth that modifies the regular educational program. Wiederholt (1975) suggests a six-step program ranging from noneducational (medical and welfare) services and residential schools to full-time special classes, part-time special classes, resource rooms, and consultation with regular classroom teachers. Schmid (1979) proposes an adapted general education class, in which content area specialists modify the procedures by which information is taught, but not the actual course content.

Which elements and services can or should be implemented by a specific school system can only be determined through evaluation of what best matches teaching methods, materials, styles, and school resources to student needs, and how expertise can be shared among staff (Kokoszka & Drye, 1981).

The actual services rendered should evolve from a joint parent, student, and teacher planning process (Levine, Clarke & Ferb, 1981). This involves identifying and clarifying each participant's expectations and concerns, and gathering information regarding current school performance and the results of academic, psychosocial and neuropsychological evaluations. It is also important to plan for the years remaining until the student is twenty-one, by considering the scope and sequence of school programming options and the probability, assessed in terms of time, money, personnel, and interest of realistic new program development.

In most cases, involving the adolescent in the actual planning process is critical since most teenagers intensely dislike being different or conspicuous in any way. Asking them to do anything out of the ordinary (such as altering their class schedule, meeting with the resource teacher, or using a specific notetaking procedure) can easily be viewed as threatening. Ken's story, on page 284, illustrates this point. Efforts on the part of staff not to erect unnecessary environmental barriers is extremely helpful in this regard. By working as a team, they can establish rapport, engage cooperation, and convey confidence in students' opinions and in their ability to exercise a degree of control over their own lives.

PL 94-142's mandate to educate handicapped students in as near normal an environment as is appropriate requires special support services, most often in the form of resource rooms or LD consultants to the general classroom teacher. Wiederholt (1978) highlights some of the difficulties of implementing these models at the secondary level. Problems with the resource room model stem from discrepancies between the skill-orientation of LD specialists and the content-orientation of regular classroom instructors. The latter often feel ill-prepared to modify or supplement the basic skill instruction of their students. It also is difficult for them to find the time to do so, as many already teach up to 120 pupils per day. The LD consultant's efficiency in aiding the regular classroom teacher is similarly hampered by the large numbers to be served. One possible solution rests in the use of trained peer tutors to help instruct classmates in content area courses (Haisley, Tell & Andrews, 1981).

CASE STUDY: Ken

Ken, the tall, good-looking son of a large, transient family, was not diagnosed learning disabled until fifth grade. Now fourteen years of age and in the seventh grade, he finds himself in a peculiar situation — valued by his peers because of his looks and the fact that it's "cool" to associate with older students (most of his classmates are twelve), yet academically lowest in the class. His severe (second to third grade level) reading, writing, and spelling problems necessitate his spending half of the day in the resource room. The only core subject he can successfully handle is mathematics. Even here, however, he has trouble keeping the columns of figures straight and needs to have all word problems restated in purely numerical terms.

At first glance, Ken's social skills and outside interests appear age-appropriate. He can talk a good game of sports. Yet, while his physique and erect carriage intimate athletic ability, he is a bit of a klutz. His fine-motor control is also less than satisfactory, although his writing does improve noticeably when he uses a triangular plastic pencil grip. Because he is sensitive and self-conscious, however,

he refuses to do so outside the resource room setting.

Ken never really wanted to receive extra help. He resented being singled out and was initially reluctant to participate in any appropriate remedial activities. With time and progress, his attitude has softened. He still claims not to care about school, yet his attendance is above average and he always asks to take papers home to show his family.

This year Ken has been assigned a physical education instructor with a special education background. This orientation and sensitivity have resulted in unique projects and groupings aimed at maximizing Ken's particular strengths. Most recently, for example, an impromptu boys' baseball game was converted into a football tackling session because contact sports present much less of a problem to Ken than the perceptually more demanding games of either baseball or basketball. As this type of knowledgeable concern is not common in Ken's school, it is unfortunate that, precisely when he is likely to need even more of this type of support (when his classmates come to perceive his situation more clearly and probably regard him less highly) he will in all likelihood find few other instructors similarly able to help pave the way.

Minimum Competency Tests

Minimum competency testing (MCT) programs currently exist in over three-fourths of the United States (Lerner, 1981) and are the result of public outrage over the 50-point decrease of Scholastic Aptitude Test (SAT) verbal scores and the 30-point mathematics decrease between 1963 and 1977 (Haney, 1981). In some states MCT tests are used to identify students in need of remedial instruction. Where they represent the criteria for grade-to-grade promotions and the awarding of high school diplomas, however, the situation becomes problematic.

Proponents and opponents of the MCT movement are numerous (Lerner, 1981). At the heart of the discussion is the need to upgrade society's literacy and numerical capabilities while respecting and protecting the rights of individual handicapped citizens. Advocates and critics agree that there are many unresolved issues regarding implementation of such plans. Typically these revolve around consideration of

1. the fundamental purpose of a high school education (the meaning of a diploma);
2. the possible exemption of certain handicapped children from minimum competency testing;
3. the legality of applying different criteria to handicapped and nonhandicapped individuals;
4. technical issues such as cultural and racial bias, inadequate phase-in period, test validity and reliability, value-based test items, and insufficient remedial preparation;
5. adaptions in testing procedures necessary to accommodate various types of handicapping conditions (McCarthy, 1980).

When MCTs are used to deny diplomas to LD students, they endanger the future lives of these individuals (Ewing & Smith, 1981; Ross & Weintraub, 1980). Alternative ways of meeting MCT requirements do exist, however. Some states permit tests to be read aloud and students to respond orally, to avoid the reading and writing difficulties which often interfere with performance. Others actually waive MCTs for handicapped students.

The student's Individualized Education Plan (IEP) can close the gap between state competency objectives and those of regular and special education curricula (Olsen, 1980). The IEP can specify how the MCT's requirements are to be met and how the tests should be given so as to tap only the criterion skills and not the handicapping condition itself (McCarthy, 1980). The IEP committee may select test items which best measure the student's individualized objectives, choose an instrument that best evaluates the mastery of these skills, or develop its own, comparable test for making graduation decisions (Amos, 1980). Other testing procedure modifications include flexibility in scheduling (brief sessions), testing individually or in small groups, presentation of test materials (large print), use of auditory aids (tapes or narrator), and modified methods by which answers are recorded (the proctor, a typewriter, marking answers directly in the test booklet) (Grisé, 1980).

Learning Disabilities and Juvenile Delinquency

Poor academic achievement, lack of motivation, and short attention span are terms which occur frequently in the folders of both juvenile delinquents (JD) and learning disabled adolescents. Other similarities include low frustration tolerance, negative self-concept and greater prevalence of males than females (Mauser, 1974; Miller & Windhauser, 1971). Delinquency has been empirically linked with brain damage (Berman & Siegel, 1976) and school failure (Empey, 1978; Phillips & Kelly, 1979) both of which are often descriptive of learning disabled youngsters. These observations have produced speculation about a causal relationship between LD and JD. Although learning disabilities are associated with delinquent behavior in some youngsters, they are only one of many determining factors (see Figure 8-2). "One of the few things known for sure about delinquency is that its causes are multivariate and complex" (Murray, 1976, p. 34).

The most sophisticated and comprehensive cross-sectional and longitudinal studies reported to date (see Research Box 8-1) indicate that "while only a relatively small proportion of the youth population is affected by LD, within this group learning disabilities appear to be one of the most important causes of delinquency" (Dunivant, 1981, p. 11). These findings are not attributable to sociodemographic disparities (parent education, ethnicity) or to differential tendencies of LD and non LD youngsters to disclose their socially disapproved behaviors. The data are consistent with three major hypotheses regarding the LD-JD link.

The first hypothesis, the School Failure Rationale, proposes that poor academic achievement associated with negative social acceptance erodes self-

Figure 8-2   Causes of delinquency

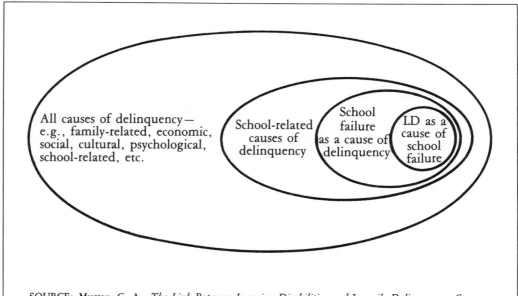

SOURCE: Murray, C. A., *The Link Between Learning Disabilities and Juvenile Delinquency: Current Theory and Knowledge.* Washington, D.C.: U.S. Government Printing Office, 1976.

RESEARCH BOX 8-1
The Link Between Learning Disabilities and Juvenile Delinquency

Dunivant (1981) summarizes the results of two major investigations of the relationship between LD and JD. In the first, a cross-sectional study involving 1,943 adolescent boys, an attempt was made to estimate the prevalence of LD among comparable groups of officially delinquent and nondelinquent youths. Classifications of learning disabilities were based on a review of school records and a battery of psychological and educational tests. A checklist was completed concerning each subject's behavior during the three and a half hour testing session, and measures of self-reported delinquent behavior, social status, ethnicity, and attitude toward school were obtained during individual interviews. All scores were submitted to computer analysis according to given diagnostic algorithms (rules) such that human error, either in the form of mathematical computations or clinical impressions, would be minimized.

The results supported the existence of a link between LD and JD. To begin with, the LD adolescents reported having committed an average of 266 delinquent acts during their lives; 81 more than the corresponding mean number for non-LD participants. Even though the mean difference in seriousness of general delinquent behavior between the groups was not significant, the LD youngsters engaged in significantly more violent acts (assault with a dangerous weapon, gang fighting), marijuana and alcohol abuse, and disruptive school behavior. LD was also strongly related to official delinquency. Weighting the sample to make it representative of the U.S. youth population, it appears that 9 out of every 100 young males with learning problems is adjudicated delinquent in comparison with only 4 of every 100 non-LD individuals. The odds of being arrested and adjudicated are approximately 220 percent greater for LD as opposed to non-LD teens. The 36 percent incidence of LD among the adjudicated population also highlights the seriousness of the problem.

The figures reported above do indeed suggest the existence of an LD/JD link. Unequivocal statements of cause and effect, however, cannot be determined from cross-sectional studies which do not follow the same individuals over time. All that can be said is that the findings are consistent with the school failure, susceptibility, and differential treatment hypotheses. A second, longitudinal follow-up study was therefore undertaken. This investigation indicated that as officially nondelinquent boys advanced through the teenage years, those handicapped by learning problems experienced significantly greater increases in delinquent behavior. This was determined by reinterviewing at one- and two-year intervals 351 boys from the official nondelinquent group contained in the cross-sectional sample, and by searching court records for evidence of subsequent juvenile court contact. Interestingly, youths who were white and from higher social class homes tended to experience relatively larger increases in delinquent behavior than the other minority and subgroups sampled. This may well reflect their own frustration and disappointment at not having been able to live up to both familial and societal expectations.

confidence to the point that, given the proper psychological and environmental incentives, the educationally disabled youngster may engage in delinquent behavior.

The second line of argument linking LD and JD focuses on increased susceptibility to delinquent behavior (Murray, 1976). It is hypothesized that because of the LD student's linguistic differences, social imperceptiveness, poor learning from experience, and impulsivity, messages often do not get through quite the way they were intended. Factors that might restrain a non-handicapped peer from committing an antisocial act simply do not have the same effect on a LD individual.

The third proposition, the differential treatment hypothesis, explains why for comparable offenses, LD adolescents are arrested and adjudicated more than their non-LD peers (Broder, Dunivant, Smith & Sutton, 1980; Keilitx, Zaremba, & Broder, 1979). It has been suggested that this increased vulnerability reflects both the learning disabled youth's weaknesses (poor expressive capabilities, ineptness at dissembling and at presenting oneself in a positive manner, and inability to grasp abstract ideas such as the protection afforded by the right of silence) and factors inherent in the judicial system itself (highly cognitive, strategy-oriented procedure, verbal mode of interaction, and frequent paternalistic attitude of judges). Dunivant (April 1982, p. 6) states that given the LD student's increased likelihood of engaging in delinquent behavior and the increased probability of his being arrested and adjudicated for the offense, "Learning disabilities are a double whammy." This "preferential treatment," however, does not seem to carry over into the final disposition of cases. Among adjudicated delinquents, LD adolescents are no more likely than their non-LD peers to receive severe disposition from the courts.

For delinquents who are reading disabled, Silberberg and Silberberg (1971) contend that it is not so much their abilities which require changing, as our society's values and institutions. They strongly recommend recognizing the adolescent's talents by using a "bookless" approach to learning. This relegates reading to an isolated skill to be taught separately, while all other avenues (such as audio-visual approaches and discussion groups) are used for the actual education of the students.

Bachara and Zaba (1978) report that LD juvenile offenders who were offered remediation in the form of special education, tutoring, or perceptual-motor training relapsed significantly less into their old delinquent patterns than did those who were not so engaged. In an extensive investigation conducted jointly by the Association for Children with Learning Disabilities and the National Center for State Courts (Crawford, 1981, Dunivant, 1981, 1982), students reacted positively to an academically oriented treatment program in which instruction was targeted to each participant's greatest deficiency, and curricular materials were compatible with the adolescent's strongest learning modalities (visual, auditory, tactile or motor). In comparison with LD delinquents not in the program, those who received the extra expressive language, math, and reading training scored higher on both intellectual and achievement posttest measures. While remediation did not significantly affect school attitudes, forty to fifty hours of instruction were found effective in preventing or controlling future delinquency. This result is credited primarily to the nature of the relationship which developed between the adolescents and the LD specialists.

Attitudinal and behavior improvements were reported in another study as a result of a one-week camping program conducted for predelinquents, normal achievers, and identified delinquents (Unkovic, Brown, & Mierswa, 1978). Emphasis during the week was on exposure to vocational opportunities, health care, recreation, fellowship, and leadership. Much of the program's success is attributed to the free interchange among individuals without the distorted perceptions frequently evoked by labels; the actual identities of the participants was not revealed until the last campfire. The recidivism rate over the next three months to one year was a low 12.9 percent. While this study did not specifically identify those delinquents who were learning disabled and how their response compared with non-LD teenagers, it highlights the variety of intervention possibilities available.

The question of a link between learning disabilities and juvenile delinquency takes LD out of the protected realm of academia and places it squarely in the public eye. It introduces a host of other professionals, such as police officers, probation workers, and juvenile court judges. The educational and social implications of an LD/JD link point to the need for further research efforts and heightened public sensitivity to this issue. While group data do point to the existence of an LD/JD link, particular caution needs to be voiced whenever individual students are discussed (Lane, 1980). Adolescents identified as LD typically have a difficult enough time functioning and being accepted. How devastating it would be for parents, teachers, and peers to begin viewing them as potential delinquents while they are still in an elementary or secondary school setting.

Summary

Interest in secondary learning disabilities has increased in recent years. This stems in part from the realization that, though improvement is the rule, particularly when the student has received extensive remediation at the elementary level, many LD adolescents still continue to lag academically and socially. While secondary students are being identified as learning disabled and programs are being developed, most remedial procedures still await external validation.

Programming efforts at the secondary level have focused primarily on the continuing development of basic reading, writing, and mathematics skills. Tutoring also has been provided in one or more content areas to insure that the learning disability does not deter the student from becoming more knowledgeable. Other areas which deserve to be addressed include developing listening, speaking, and basic thinking capabilities, as well as skill in studying, taking notes, and taking examinations. The decision to continue training in weaker abilities depends on student motivation, present level of functioning, quality of past teaching, likelihood of progress, and relevance to career goals.

Since weaknesses often persist despite gains made in remediation, secondary schools must focus on fully developing the student's strengths by working around weaknesses and developing compensatory skills. The social-emotional development of the LD adolescent also needs to be addressed by the public school system. The way adolescents feel about themselves and the way they relate to others colors not only their present performance and interactions, but also their potential for future personal and vocational success. Programs for training prosocial skills belong within a well-defined secondary LD program. Attention should also be paid to career education and the development of an adequate knowledge and skills base for students planning either to move on to higher education or directly into the world of work. To date, most such educational/vocational programs have failed to take into account the specialized needs of this segment of the student population.

The service delivery network for LD adolescents varies from self-contained special classes, to resource rooms, to teacher consultants, to the regular classroom. Because learning disabilities is neither a unitary nor simple condition, no one model can possibly satisfy all needs. The current move toward minimum competency testing is another issue which must be dealt with at the secondary level.

Current evidence supports the existence of a relationship between learning disabilities and juvenile delinquency, and several programs have been influential in curbing non-acceptable behavior in young people. The question of which program is most effective for which type of student still remains an open issue. Given the personal and societal implications of an LD/JD link, continued educational and juvenile justice efforts must be made at professional and governmental levels to design and implement proficient remedial and preventative programs.

Suggestions for Further Study

1. To determine what, if any, effects the remaining perceptual-motor problems of some LD adolescents have on their ability to drive a car, check relevant records to see whether or not these young people contribute disproportionately to the high teenage auto accident rate. If they do, what recommendations would you make regarding driver education programs, licensing, and insurance coverage?

2. Cunningham, Cunningham and Arthur's (1981) book describes two general approaches for developing listening skills in a regular classroom setting: the Directed Listening Activity and the Guided Listening Procedure. They also present a myriad of suggestions for anyone contemplating teaching reading and reading-related skills, including listening, at either the middle or secondary school level. Their book is also of value to the LD specialist who is constantly in search of new, workable techniques to offer classroom teachers in their dealings with learning disabled youth.

3. For further discussions of the use of both formal and informal means of assessing expressive language skills, read Alley and Deshler (1979) and Wiig, Lapointe and Semel (1977).

4. Specific mathematics skills can often be evaluated effectively by teacher-constructed tests. Extensive guidelines for designing such instruments are provided by Ashlock (1976), Mercer (1979), and Wiederholt, Hammill and Brown (1978). Excellent references regarding the relationship of basic psychological processes to mathematics are Chalfant and Scheffelin (1969), and McLeod and Crump (1978).

5. Formal testing exists for some, though not all, higher-level thinking skills. If you are interested in pursuing this line of inquiry, read both Alley and Deshler (1979) and a report entitled "CSE-RBS Test Evaluations: Tests of Higher Cognitive, Affective and Interpersonal Skills." The latter may be obtained from the Dissemination Office, Center for the Study of Evaluation, Graduate School of Education, University of California, 405 Hilgard Avenue, Los Angeles, California 90024.

6. Adolescents are in the midst of Erikson's (1963) Identity stage of emotional development. They also need to satisfy all of the needs proposed by Maslow (1968) — those which are physiological in nature, as well as those for safety, love, self-esteem, esteem of others and self-actualization. Think of at least ten ways in which teachers sensitive to this point can identify and facilitate the development of skills which might help teenagers meet some of the higher needs, particularly those for self-esteem and esteem of others.

7. Categorical (Sabatino, 1971) and non-categorical (Wiederholt, Hammill & Brown, 1978) resource rooms represent additional school-based programming options for LD adolescents. Other possible high school programs are discussed in both the Winter 1980 and 1981 issues of *The Forum*, the publication of the New York State Federation of Chapters of the Council for Exceptional Children: 582 Baldy Hall, SUNY/Buffalo, Amherst, New York 14260. Given the variety of settings possible, which ones do you think best meet the needs of which types of LD youngsters working on what specific kinds of tasks? Given that adolescents don't like to be different and that remedial help is difficult to accept after years of failure, is any one type of setting more likely than another to induce a youngster to choose continued remedial help?

8. Exploration of the LD/JD link has provided some of the most fascinating and confusing of all LD adolescent research findings. The proliferation of contradictory results highlights the importance of having tight research designs, appropriate statistical analyses, and controls for human error. An extensive reading list in this area is available through the National Center for State Courts, 300 Newport Avenue, Williamsburg, Virginia 23185. Particularly helpful are the observations of Noel Dunivant (1981, March 1982, April 1982).

Chapter Nine
The Adult

A special focus on the learning disabled adult is essential because, although the adolescent's weaknesses often continue into adulthood, the tasks required of the adult and the settings' expectations are different. These differences directly affect the vocational and social adjustment of individuals whose learning disabilities are more than a school-based phenomenon. Knowledge of LD adults' predictable life adjustment difficulties may lead to more appropriate preventative intervention in public schools. So important is the need to address the adjustment of LD adults that national and state advocacy organizations for the learning disabled are either taking the word "children" out of their titles, or adding the word "adults."

Little is known about learning disabled adults who are over the age of eighteen, work, live independently, are married and have children. The few case reports and research studies on these adults find that the difficulties of the learning disabled adolescent frequently do not go away with time. Despite the persistent weaknesses, many of these adults go on to postsecondary education, get good jobs, raise their children well, get along with their spouses and friends, and contribute to the betterment of their communities. Others do not. The more successful adults compensate for their learning difficulties with adequate intelligence, motivation, instruction, and emotional support. The others do not have these advantages.

When learning problems persist into adulthood, participation in postsecondary education is often limited, and vocational success may suffer. Interpersonal relations frequently remain a problem. Fortunately as society becomes sensitized to the needs of the learning disabled adult, opportunities for postsecondary education, vocational training, and transitional independent living services are increasing.

What is known about the learning disabled adult is generally in the form of investigations that are difficult to compare. These studies' subjects differ in IQ, sociocultural background, quality of educational interventions, and nature and severity of learning disorders. Consequently, conclusions can be only tentative. Given the current interest in the LD adult, there no doubt will be a larger base of knowledge on which future conclusions can be based.

Favorable Outcome Studies

Such unique individuals as Albert Einstein and Nelson Rockefeller, despite severe reading difficulties, contributed in outstanding ways to society. Critchley's (1970) report about Hans Christian Andersen and one of Sweden's kings, on page 294, demonstrates some of the types of difficulties experienced by such individuals. The outlook for other learning disabled adults appears equally favorable only when a high intelligence and socioeconomic advantages help them remediate some weaknesses, compensate for others, and find alternate routes to success.

CASE STUDY:
Hans Christian Andersen and King Karl XI

Hans Christian Andersen was also a dyslexic. He was very behind-hand in his school work, being regarded at one time as a dullard. Even as an adult he had never learned to spell correctly and his manuscripts revealed many errors of a type which are characteristic of dyslexia. Naturally enough these mistakes were usually detected and rectified by the editor. Occasionally, however, they escaped notice. Thus when Hans Christian Andersen wrote an account of his visit to Charles Dickens in London, names of English persons and places were often rendered incorrectly. These shortcomings were not always recognized by his publishers, so that they appeared in their original form in print. Among the numerous errors one may quote Schackspeare; Machbeth; Tamps or Temps (Thames); Manschester; brackfest (breakfast) (Critchley, 1970; p. 100).

Within such a category of well adjusted exdyslexics may belong the case of Karl XI (1655–97) who has been judged "one of Sweden's wisest kings." Succeeding to the throne at the age of 4 years he proved to be a most unsatisfactory scholar, mainly because of his inability to learn to read. His studies were supervised by a Professor of History at the University of Uppsala. The monarch's progress in reading was extraordinarily slow, and in adult life he always relied upon personal interviews rather than a study of reports. If handed a document he might be seen to hold the page upside-down and to pretend that he was reading the text. Throughout his life his spelling was highly unorthodox, the errors being quite unlike the usual misspellings of the uneducated. He would reverse words, omit letters, or start with letters belonging to the middle of a word. . . . Reversals and other such spelling mistakes were habitual with him up to the time of his death (pp. 114–115).

Unusually high intelligence, academic support, encouragement at home, and at times a private school education can help an individual reach high levels of reading and vocational success (Rawson, 1968; Robinson & Smith, 1962). Of Rawson's fifty-six reading disabled subjects (average IQ 131), forty-eight earned college degrees and all but two held jobs that put them in the top two socioeconomic classes. Although some spelling and reading difficulties lingered, these did not interfere with success. Robinson and Smith's subjects (median IQ 120) had been only mildly delayed in reading as children. Over half had attended private schools. Most ended up in professional, skilled, or semi-skilled occupations equivalent to those of their parents. Half even reported reading more often than did the typical person.

In a follow-up of less intelligent young adults (average IQ 100) who had severe reading disorders as children, Balow and Blomquist (1965) found that 83 percent had graduated high school, over half had gone on to college or vocational education, and all were vocationally successful. These people had not liked school, didn't read for pleasure, and had adopted negative, defeatist attitudes toward life. They did not feel as though they were masters of their own destinies. Despite their earlier reading disorders, all had achieved at least an average adult reading level.

Rogan and Hartman (1976) also followed up a group of ninety-one individuals who, as adults, tested within average ranges of intelligence. Each had received an average of three years' remedial education in a private school between ages six and thirteen. Sixty-nine percent had graduated high school, 36 percent had completed college, another 16 percent were attending college, and 8 percent completed or were pursuing graduate study. Sixty percent of the group was employed, 33 percent in clerical jobs, 23 percent in unskilled jobs, and 13 percent in professional jobs. Fifty-five percent were independent of parental supervision and 15 percent had married. There was a very low, 6 percent, incidence of adult criminal offenses. However, personality tests suggested high vulnerability to stress among the group.

What is it that helped these adults to cope relatively well with or overcome their handicaps, and adjust reasonably well to life? No doubt it has something to do with their intelligence, specific learning abilities, emotional strengths, vocational choices, home teaching, and the kind of schooling and emotional support they received. Exactly which of these learner-, task-, and setting-based factors are the most influential remains to be clarified.

Persistent Learning Difficulties

When learning disabilities are not remediated or compensated for, the adult's quality of life often suffers. The discrepancy between academic achievement and grade placement often becomes larger as learning disabled students get older, so that their weaknesses are even more pronounced in adulthood (Trites & Fiedorowicz, 1976). As adults, females generally continue to be superior to males in spelling, grammatical ability, verbal fluency, clerical speed, and accuracy. The only basic area in which males, after age twelve, excel is spatial judgment and mechanical reasoning (Heir, 1979). A relationship between persistence of learning disorders and a less satisfying quality of life has been found in a number of studies. Results from the majority of studies on what happens to LD adolescents after high school graduation are reported in the following list, but keep in mind that since the population of each study is so different and subjects and methods are not fully described, the results cannot be combined to form more than very general, tentative conclusions.

□ Twenty-year-old learning disabled adults were holding jobs with less social status and were less satisfied with their employment than non-LD adults. They were less involved in recreational activities and social organizations, were less satisfied with their contacts with relatives, used more prescription drugs, were more often convicted of crimes, were less satisfied with their school experiences and had fewer plans for future education and training. In spite of this they did not differ from other adults in number of full time jobs held, money earned, time spent unemployed, number of friends, contact with relatives, number of arrests, and time spent in jail (White, Clark, Schmaker, Warner, Alley, & Deshler, 1980).

□ 18 to 31 year old average intelligence adults retested ten years after being diagnosed as severely impaired in reading made only 1.3 years average gain in reading. Average reading grade level was 3.6, spelling level 2.9, and arithmetic level 4.6. Reversals in reading continued (on–no, saw–was) because of sound–symbol confusion, rather than visually perceiving backwards. Phonetic skills were a major problem in reading and written expression (see Figure 9-1). Amount of special reading assistance and age at which assistance began were unrelated to adult reading levels (Frauenheim, 1978).

□ Approximately 50 percent of language-impaired youngsters still exhibited communication problems 13–20 years later, but only one of eighteen articulation-impaired clients still had a disorder. Reading achievement was poorer in the language-impaired group (Hall & Tomblin, 1978).

□ Severely language- or reading-handicapped children were unable to find employment as adults that is commensurate with their intelligence (Zangwill, 1978).

□ Language-impaired adults who could read at about an 8–9 year old level but whose spoken language attainment was well below this were usually successfully employed. Although well-accepted by their workmates, they were lonely because of difficulty developing social contacts (Moor House School, 1969; in Cooper & Griffiths, 1978).

□ Reading, spelling, and visual-motor difficulties persisted into adulthood for children whose learning disabilities were due to organic factors. Although reading improved, comprehension often was still deficient (Silver & Hagin, 1964, 1966).

□ Hyperactive boys became hyperactive men. They had trouble sitting still to watch television, were nervous, restless, quick-tempered, and had difficulty concentrating. Despite normal intelligence and equal educational levels, their socio-economic job status was lower than that of their brothers and fathers (Borland & Heckman, 1976).

□ As adults, hyperactive children retained their poor educational achievements, social-emotional immaturity, poor self-esteem, and attentional difficulties (Wender, 1976).

□ A good number of hyperactive children, followed an average of twenty-four years later, still had signs of neurological abnormalities in speech and motor coordination. Many had spent time in institutions. Those who were self-supporting also had the higher intelligence levels (Menkes, Rowe, & Menkes, 1967).

□ Hyperactive individuals followed ten years after diagnosis (ages seventeen to twenty-four) did not differ from controls in height, weight, EEG's, antisocial behavior, drug abuse, serious psychiatric disturbances, work

Figure 9-1 The spelling errors of adults who were reading disabled as youngsters reflect difficulty with phonetic analysis and sequencing

Key word	Response
study	sludn, stedid, staddy, sduey, shaen, stied, sitd
kitchen	chin, kinl, kengun, ckin
city	stiy, ciedy, deit, caiy
black	billk, blane, ballk

Dictation of: "The yellow pig saw the little baby" to adults who were reading disabled as children

John	CA	19-7
Performance	IQ	111
Verbal	IQ	91

The · y pig sine the little batt.

Fred	CA	26-6
Performance	IQ	101
Verbal	IQ	83

The ellow pig sow the Bady little.

Alan	CA	20-2
Performance	IQ	100
Verbal	IQ	87

Tho — Pig sio Tno lit bobc

SOURCE: Frauenheim, J. G. "Academic Achievement Characteristics of Adult Males Who Were Diagnosed as Dyslexic in Childhood." © 1978 The Professional Press, Inc. Reprinted with permission of the publisher from *Journal of Learning Disabilities,* 11 East Adams Street, Chicago, Illinois 60603, vol. *11,* pp. 480–481.

adjustment, and living arrangements. However, their pulse rates were higher, they were more restless and less reflective, had greater scholastic difficulties, and had poorer socialization skills and feelings of well-being (Hechtman et al., 1976).

□ A ten to thirteen year follow-up of hyperactive individuals at ages 17–24 indicated poorer ratings than control subjects by teachers but equivalent ratings by employers. Self-ratings on social interaction, self-esteem and competence measures were inferior to controls, although the two groups did not differ on a psychopathology scale. The hyperactive individuals had more car accidents than controls, moved more often, and had more impulsive or immature personality traits (Weiss, Hechtman, & Perlman, 1978).

□ Language deficits persisted into adulthood although they may be very subtle (Wiig & Fleishhmann, 1978; in Wiig & Semel, 1980).

□ Young adults whose learning problems had been identified between the ages of eight and twelve persisted in mental disturbances and social maladjustment (Spreen, 1976).

□ Adult poor readers still had reversed language asymmetries (right rather than left hemisphere preferences for language processing) (Satz & Van Nostrand, 1972).

Figure 9-1 is an example of the persistent spelling difficulties of many learning disabled adults. Apparently many LD youngsters do not outgrow their problems. Their difficulties as adults are often compounded by poor vocational opportunities and social relationships.

Vocational and Emotional–Social Concerns

Vocational adjustment is a key to successful life adjustment. The type of job and level of income a person can maintain affects all facets of life: home, vacations, clothes, recreational luxuries, educational opportunities for children, and so forth. Job success is more highly related to level of schooling and personality variables than it is to intelligence.

In American society, adult income corresponds to years of schooling more than IQ (Jencks, 1972). Unskilled work is increasingly rare, accounting for only about 6 percent of all jobs (United States Department of Labor, 1976; Wattenberg, 1974). Therefore, postsecondary education is important in the competition for skilled jobs. Since schooling makes demands on reading skills, LD young adults may not continue their education, thereby compromising their vocational futures. Their success on skilled jobs, whether blue-collar or white-collar, manual or nonmanual, also depends on ability to comprehend reading material and compute figures (Lerner, 1981). Consequently, to reach high levels of vocational success in today's society, people must go through what Kinsbourne (1977c) calls a "linguistic reading bottleneck."

Many learning disabled students' reading skills do not become proficient enough to insure their success in postsecondary education or on skilled jobs.

Studies show that poor reading skills severely limit academic aspirations, slacken the pace through school, hamper postschool academic achievements, and narrow vocational options (Hermann, 1959; Preston & Yarington, 1967). A person could be successful on a job that circumvents the handicap, but the handicap can always surface again as job requirements change.

These young adults end up in lower vocational placements than would be expected from their intelligence (Zangwill, 1978). They are disappointed in themselves, they lack zeal to achieve, they feel inadequate, guilty, and embarrassed, are afraid of being discovered, and develop poor social-emotional interaction patterns. Denckla and Heilman (1979) comment that, even when an LD child outgrows a maturational lag, the emotional pressures may hinder the child from reaching his or her adult potential. These emotional pressures can create personality abnormalities and disrupt a marriage and family (Lenkowsky & Saposnek, 1978; Schwartz, Gilroy, & Lynn, 1976).

The power of emotional, relative to intellectual, factors in influencing life adjustment cannot be underestimated. The correlation between IQ and everyday life performance as an adult is no more than about .20 (McClelland, 1973). This is because IQ tests in large part measure general knowledge and problem-solving abilities (Zigler & Trickett, 1978). The tests also reflect personality attributes that are influential in ways other than academics: perseverance; ambition; optimism; zeal; willingness to try hard; eagerness to accept and attack challenges; feelings of being good, capable, and loved, and supported even through failure; knowing how to ask for and use help; and so forth. These personality attributes help individuals through life, despite less academic knowledge or problem-solving ability.

But the learning disabled are particularly handicapped in this emotional-social realm. Their learning failures may have caused, aggravated, or in part resulted from social-emotional difficulties. The learning disability may also manifest itself as social imperceptiveness. As with the learning disabled adolescent, the LD adult may be less able to interpret the emotions, attitudes, and intentions that others communicate through language, facial expressions, or body posture. Their inappropriate responses to everyday conversation, verbal subtleties, nonverbal cues, and expressions of affection or approval may end in rejection by others, feelings of insecurity, and atypical personality development. As a result, the individual is less able to call on positive emotional strengths for support in his or her drive to continue learning and become vocationally successful. Critchley (1970) writes:

> A dyslexic of sufficient ability, who is also fortunate in being endowed with unusual personality traits of application, concentration and ambition may in time overcome many of his problems even without specialized tuition [tutoring]. "Ego-strength" is what the psychiatrists call this quality, more familiar to us as "guts". . . . (p. 100)

Figure 9-2 reprints an especially poignant poem that a successful, severely reading-disabled goldsmith dictated to a friend (Devine, 1981). The right-hand

Figure 9-2   Poem written and read by a learning disabled twenty-six year old

Transcription of Reading Attempt (Note: italics indicate that the word could not be read and was supplied by a prompter.)

Teacher,	Teacher,
Teacher,	Teacher,
What do you see?	What do you see?
Can you	Can you
see	see
as far	as far
as Me?	as me?
Long school halls —	Long school halls —
closed doors!	close doors!
Where	What *Where*
could I go?	where can I go?
Where could I turn?	*Where* can I *turn*
You tried to force me	The you *tried to force me*
to look	to look
through	through
your window	to look through your window
but all I ever saw	all I all I was able ever *saw*
was	was
the sheer, blind	a solid brick *the sheer, blind*
rage	*rage*
within me.	*within me.*
Humiliation	*Humiliation*
and	*and*
anger	*anger*
forced me	my frust *forced me*
to find myself	*to find* myself
within	within
myself	myself
and not	and not
in	and not in
the printed word.	the printed word.
Struggling	*Struggling*
with a book	with a book
one day,	one day,
I said to myself,	I said
"Hey! I can	"Hey!
do it	I said a I said to myself
another way!"	"Hey! I can
And I succeeded.	do it
	another way!"
	And and and through and *and I succeeded.*

Figure 9-2   continued

(Transcription of reading attempt, continued)

Now	I known *now*
you say	I see, now I saw, *now you*'re
I was a gifted child.	*saying*
Not so.	*I was a gifted child.*
I simply	I say no, not a gifted child
never fit	just someone
on your superhighway.	which did not fit
Were all the roads	on the superhighway of a city
so wide	and I was able to stay to my own path.
you couldn't help me	path or trail.
find my trail?	
	Teacher,
Teacher.	Teacher
Teacher	I don't read,
I don't read,	I don't write.
I don't write.	When I When I look
When I look	at a book, when I look at the a *pile* of books,
at a pile of books,	I fight.
I fight!	This is a war
This war	which lasted a moment
lasted only a moment	for you
for you	a lifetime
but will last	for me.
a lifetime	
for me.	Your *tried* to
	bend to bend me
You tried to	to *fit* me
bend me	within within the jail of words
to fit	and about but
your jail of words—	[interruption from a man removing a screen]
but I am free now,	You tried to
and	bend me
stand tall	to fit me
in my	your jail of words—
own way.	but I found *I am free now*,
	and
	stand tall
	in my
	own way.

column is a transcription of his attempt to read this poem aloud to an audience at a learning disabilities convention. What the transcription cannot possibly reflect is his painful process of trying to sound out words from their first sound, but no other sounds would come out. He recognized words as wholes, or did not recognize them at all. His hesitations and even physical battle with the words (arm swinging in circles to help retrieve words, body tension, perspiring) were agonizing to witness. What takes a typical third grade reader approximately one and a half minutes to read took this adult six and a half minutes. In his own words, the author of this poem described the terrible emotional strains that accompany a learning disability:

> I have experienced first-hand the anguish, anger, despair and utter frustration of the inarticulate child who cannot tell the literate person that literacy is not the only level on which he exists; that he is a *whole person* with many ways of giving and receiving information other than by reading and writing; and that the social environment's demand for functional literacy tends to overshadow all the other potentials an individual may possess. . . . functional literacy is not the only measure of an individual and never was. My argument is with the world of education which tends sometimes to forget the relative narrowness of its focus and thereby does many of us a grave disservice. . . . it is possible to achieve a successful, fulfilling life even without the ability to read. . . . the educational system could deal with the dyslexic child by working with the strengths and talents of that individual child instead of concentrating on his or her inability to read and thus destroying the child's faith in him/herself. [I] successfully completed high school and obtained a college degree even though [I am] functionally illiterate. [I] learned with [my] heart, [my] hands, [my] mind, and [my] will, and not through literacy. . . . everyone has skills and talents, even if they are not those which our society and its educational machinery traditionally values. . . . There is a *person inside* the person the school and society is trying to teach. We must learn to respect and re-value that person. It is only because the system's view of literacy is so inflexible that dyslexia is regarded as a "learning disability" at all. What an incredibly narrow view of learning this is, and what an incredibly limiting view of the human potential! (Devine & Rose, 1981)

Sarah is a particularly good example of the impact that the social-emotional anguishes and difficulties that often accompany learning disabilities can have on life success. Sarah never read until she was eleven years old. Her one and only dream in life was to become a lawyer. But she almost never made it to law school because her self-concept was so poor that she could not admit to others that she was learning disabled.

Sarah had taken the academic route of the intellectual, hoping that her bank of facts would prove her worth and intelligence, and see her through any social encounters. She seldom dated, had few friends, and only felt comfortable among adults with whom she was assured of no ridicule or rebuffs. Sarah never asked for help in college and made it through with a low B average. Her law boards too were only average. Although she was exceptionally bright in verbal conceptual abilities, she was hampered on all tests and assignments by a reading speed equivalent to a ninth grader's and spelling and handwriting no better than a seventh grader's. Because of her overanalytic, detail-bound conceptual style, she often missed the main themes and could not organize major, relative to minor, points. She always depersonalized conversations and turned them into intellectual, political discussions. For example, when asked to write an essay about how the saying "no man is an island" applied to her life, Sarah wrote about Locke's philosophy of a state. This essay's spelling, handwriting, and thought structure appear in Figure 9-3.

At Sarah's law school interview, she was told in no uncertain terms that she was too dumb to either apply to law school or to become a lawyer. Her college grades and law boards were given as examples. When Sarah then explained her learning disability, no one believed her — it had been a secret for too long. To counter the law school's rejection, Sarah's parents begged her to ask for recommendations from all the politicians and lawyers that she had apprenticed with over the years. They had all evaluated her contributions highly, in spite of her weaknesses. Sarah was afraid to ask them for recommendations, feeling that she would lose the esteem of the only people who made her feel competent. She decided not to pursue law school any further. She would give up her dream because she could risk no more deprecation.

Sarah's parents finally prevailed on her to consider her future before her pride. She confided in those whose esteem she most needed to retain. She found that they all knew all along that something was wrong with her — she had required more tutelage in her apprenticeships than had any of her predecessors. Nevertheless, her dedication was outstanding and her work showed progress. Therefore, they wrote Sarah her recommendations and she was admitted to law school. She also began intense reading, spelling, and written language remediation.

Unlike Sarah, Marc, who had a very similar learning disability, learned early in life that others would always note his weaknesses. There was no escaping it, so he made no attempt to hide his disability. He conferenced with college professors before beginning each course; he worked out compensatory exam writing and grading systems for himself. He didn't leave anything to chance. When he wrote an exam, he sprawled in big letters at the top: "Dr. _____ please remember that I am a dyslexic. You agreed to grade me as follows. . . If you have any questions please contact me at. . ." Well Marc, like Sarah, got Bs, but was a personality-plus person. In his junior year he was elected president of the student senate. He was admitted to law school and negotiated for extended time for briefs, oral exams, and a four- instead of three-year schedule. He even made law review. Today Marc is a successful lawyer. He hires his secretaries based on their ability to spell for him. He feels like a valued individual in spite of his continuing disabilities, and never hesitates to ask for help. Sarah is just finishing law school.

Although Sarah and Marc's learning disabilities affected their learning similarly, they came to grips with the problems in different ways. Their differ-

Figure 9-3 Essay produced by learning disabled law student when asked to write an essay about how "no man is an island" applies to her life

The noted political philsopher, John Locke, writing over two hundred years ago, established the concept of the social contract. Locke held that men can be vain and selfseeking but that they also ~~have~~ have the capasity and the need to share and live collectively.

Moreove, Locke believed that man was by his very nature a social animal who, not inconsequently, ~~also~~ cried privacy on occasion. ~~but~~

In order to obtain both privacy and community, man had to give up absolute freedom in favor of a limited social contract with the other members of the community. In such a contract man submitted himself to the Judgement and the ~~law~~ law of society in exchange for protection from ~~the~~ ~~that~~ the state of nature and aid when man was invariably unable to provide for himself.

From this seemingly simple ~~compact~~ compact, the modern political state has evolved. Such a state stands as a ~~monument~~ testiment to Locke's belief that ~~no~~ man is ~~an island~~ to a ~~vary~~ varring extent a dependent being and to the extent that Locke stands ~~correct~~ correct upon this presumption, no man may ~~invariably~~ truthfully call himself an island.

Reprinted by permission of the author.

ent feelings of self-worth, not IQ or problem-solving skills, created Marc's greater chance for successful vocational and social adjustment to life as an adult.

Postsecondary Educational Options

Learning disabled adolescents who are just turning eighteen are being offered many more opportunities for educational success than in the past. Their high schools had presumably identified their learning needs and they already benefit from some individualized educational programming. In some states they may remain in public education up to age twenty-one, and sometimes even longer. This then affords them more opportunities for continued academic, work-study, career, or vocational preparation.

On high school graduation, postsecondary educational opportunities cover a wider range than in the past: training through military enlistment, technical schools (one-year business, medical, or legal secretarial training; cosmetology), two-year colleges, community colleges, night school classes offered by colleges to community residents, and modified university programs. In addition, the evaluation, counselling and training services of the Office of Vocational Rehabilitation (OVR) are now available because the government recognizes severe learning disabilities as a handicapping condition (The Rehabilitation Comprehensive Services and Developmental Disabilities Amendments of 1978; PL 95-602).

Learning disabled students can now take untimed college boards. Colleges receiving federal financial assistance cannot discriminate against the learning disabled in their recruitment, admissions, or treatment procedures (Section 504, Rehabilitation Act of 1973). Learning disabled students can apply to over 100 college programs that have made special adaptations to their needs (Martin, 1979). These programs generally offer academic advising, tutoring, and counseling as supportive services. Some colleges offer special learning centers where reading, writing, spelling, and study skill difficulties are remediated. Students are helped to explore different exam options with their professors such as untimed tests, papers, projects, and take-home or oral exams. Other colleges reduce the number of courses that a student initially takes, and carefully screen their difficulty levels (four courses instead of five: one difficult, two moderately difficult, one minimally difficult). They provide proctors when necessary for reading or writing exams. Bireley and Manley (1980) reported that the attributes most likely to lead to success in their college program are independence, motivation, acceptance of the need to expend more time and energy when studying, ability to plan study time, ability to realistically evaluate progress, and ability to match personal strengths to the requirements of course options.

Those working with learning disabled students are frequently struck by their disorganization, inability to plan time, and disabling anxiety about failure. These attributes often keep students from attempting to study in more than a cursory way. The LD college student often lives under the illusion that good students need to read material once to get it. They are so disheartened at not remembering much after the first reading, or at taking so long to read, that they give up. The compulsivity, rigor, self-discipline, and study strategies of the good student come as shocking surprises to them. Their cognitive style preferences and language disorders also contribute to continuing academic and social reasoning difficulties. Their poor self-concepts, willingness to risk failure rather than to disclose a handicap, and lack of appropriate assertiveness all deter asking their professors for program modifications that might facilitate success. The student's social-emotional adjustment certainly is highly related to his or her probability of success.

Vocational Options

Learning disabled adults have many more opportunities to enter vocations that utilize their stronger abilities today than in the past. This is due to increased post-secondary educational options, greater availability of services that support transitions to independent living, and lowering of employment barriers to the handicapped. Now that severe learning disabilities are recognized as a handicapping condition, discrimination in employment is prohibited by any program or activity receiving federal financial assistance when the individual is otherwise qualified for the job (Section 504, The Rehabilitation Act of 1973; PL 93-112).

Because of their individualized high school educations, high school graduates may be better prepared to handle complex, critical jobs than in the past. When capable of filling key roles, the learning disabled adult is assured continued employment even during economic slumps (Gold, 1976). For example, the LD adult who is the only one who can work the plastic mold machine in the shoe factory won't be laid off. The molds are essential to the stitchers' ability to do their jobs. Since there are many stitchers capable of stitching, one of these might instead lose his or her job.

Social and academic barriers to employment also are lowering. Once LD students graduate high school, many seek a trade. Young adults from middle income backgrounds find the trades for which they have talent and interest not as offensive as they might have in the past, considering high pay scales, excellent training programs and benefit packages in large corporations, and the fact that college graduates often do not have the skills to fill some high-paying trade positions. Unfortunately, vocational training programs, employment bureaus, and job applications still tend to overemphasize reading proficiency when reading is not a skill needed on the job (Silberberg & Silberberg, 1978). However, there is an increasing sensitivity to which jobs do and do not require certain levels of reading and language competency, and in the future these weaknesses may interfere less with job acquisition.

The Office of Vocational Rehabilitation and nonprofit agencies are providing increased opportunities for LD adults to make a slow transition to independent living. Supervision and counselling provided in group homes or special apartment complexes help the adult learn how to take responsibility for daily living needs (cooking, cleaning, clothing, shopping), leisure time activities (sports, clubs), and developing a social network (dates, friendships). These support services help the learning disabled adult to self-evaluate realistically, become more socially competent, and to pursue appropriate goals. The importance of these social-emotional needs cannot be underestimated. Often these attributes, more than the learning disabilities themselves, make the difference between success or failure in postsecondary education, gaining or losing jobs, and the important personal, family, and community responsibilities that come with being an independent, self-supporting adult.

Equally importantly, the LD adult's personality and behavioral styles eventually become a powerful influence on the behaviors that his or her children adopt as their own. It is important that educators be sensitive to these issues and work preventatively both before and after young adults graduate high school.

Summary

For many people learning disabilities are not just a school-based phenomenon. Since their learning problems persist into adulthood, the amount of postsecondary education that they choose to complete may be limited. Limited education, as well as the literacy requirements of skilled labor, hinders vocational options and life adjustment.

Some learning disabled adults have less severe learning difficulties, choose vocations which use their stronger abilities, have high intelligence levels that help them compensate for weaknesses, or benefit from a supportive and stimulating home and school environment. These individuals have the best chance of distinguishing themselves academically and ending up in high socioeconomic level vocations. Besides these general factors, no one can conclude exactly which learning disabled adults have the best prognosis because each study has followed very different types of individuals. Exactly which individual attributes, combined with which types of interventions and settings, most facilitate social and vocational adjustment needs to be studied further.

Success in any vocation depends a great deal on the individual's self-esteem and ability to get along comfortably with others. Therefore, it is just as important to deal with the social-emotional aspects of learning disorders as it is to deal with the learning problems themselves. Because of increasing individualized educational planning during the secondary school years, as well as a fuller range of postsecondary educational, independent living, career planning, and vocational opportunities, there is optimism that the learning disabled in the future may more successfully meet life's demands as adults.

Suggestions for Further Study

1. For further anecdotes on well-known men who may have suffered from severe learning disabilities, read Critchley (1970), Patten (1973), Thompson (1971), and Zangwill (1978). They give interesting accounts taken from the life histories and autobiographies of such individuals as Auguste Rodin, George Patton, Lee Harvey Oswald, and Woodrow Wilson.

2. If you are surprised by the low correlation between IQ and ultimate life adjustment, read the following studies: Carricker, 1957; Dinger, 1961; Krishef & Hall, 1955; Peterson & Smith, 1960; Porter & Milazzo, 1958. They report strikingly good vocational success for individuals who, during their school years, had been labelled retarded. These individuals do not distinguish themselves from others of similar socioeconomic status in such factors as getting married, raising children, successful military service, and numbers of criminal acts. The only area in which they seem to differ is emotional adjustment, which leads to frequent job changes. Emotional adjustment seems to be a key concern for the learning disabled adult as well.

3. In view of the causes, contributors, information-processing factors, and characteristics of learning disabilities, how would you go about designing a follow-up study? Which learner, task, and setting variables would you choose to identify? What would your social-emotional, vocational, and life adjustment variables be? If you have the opportunity, try a pilot follow-up project on ten adolescents seen at your university's LD clinic who are now in their twenties.

4. Gray's (1981) article deals with services to the LD adult. He describes the variability in characteristics of this group, the lack of knowledge about the validity or relevance of existing identification methods, poor fund of assessment tools, and lack of direction for providing services. Gray's references are excellent to read first hand if you are interested in designing adult instructional or support services.

5. A list of college programs for the learning disabled can be obtained from ACLD, 4156 Library Road, Pittsburgh, Pa. 15234 ($2). *A National Directory of Four Year Colleges, Two Year Colleges and Post High School Training Programs for Young People with Learning Disabilities* (1981) is available for $10.95 from Partners in Publishing, Box 50347, Tulsa, Okla. 74150. Time Out to Enjoy Inc. also publishes *A Guide to Postsecondary Educational Opportunities for the Learning Disabled* (1981) that can be obtained at 113 Garfield Street, Oak Park, IL, 60304. A relatively new group, the National Network of Learning Disabled Adults (P.O. Box 3130, Richardson, Texas, 75080) has a statewide listing of self-help and advocacy groups to support the LD adult. Recorded books are provided by: Recordings for the Blind, Inc., 215 E. 58th Street, New York City, New York 10022; National Library Service for the Blind and Physically Handicapped, The Library of Congress, Wash., D.C. 20542. Employment rights and educational opportunity information for the handicapped may be obtained from: Closer Look, Box 1492, Washington, D.C. 20013; Mainstream, Inc., 1200 15th Street, N.W., Washington, D.C. 20005. Academic Therapy Publications (20 Commercial Boulevard, Novato, Calif. 94947) provides a *Listing of Services for the Postsecondary LD Adult,* a useful compilation of college programs, community services, self-help groups, and publications. Finally, the President's Committee on Employment of the Handicapped (1979) has published a booklet which you can obtain from the government documents section of your library entitled *Learning Disability: Not Just a Problem Children Outgrow*.

6. Only since 1980 have severely learning disabled adults been granted access to vocational rehabilitation services. Read Gerber's (1981) excellent review of the factors responsible for this shift in eligibility criteria.

Part Four

The Task

Chapter Ten
Assessment

The nature and severity of any one person's learning disorders depends on the interaction of information-processing strengths and weaknesses with other personal characteristics (cognitive abilities, personality, motivation, social-emotional maturity, previous knowledge), the characteristics of required tasks (match of tasks to maturation levels and cognitive style), and the settings in which the individual lives, studies, and plays (past and present home and school attitudes and learning experiences). Therefore, appraising how the strengths of learner, task and setting components can best be matched is critical to work with learning disabled individuals. Although professionals generally agree on this multidimensional assessment framework, they disagree about appropriate evaluation strategies. There is also technical and conceptual concern about many assessment devices.

Assessment is the process of gathering data for the purpose of making decisions about or for individuals (Ysseldyke, 1979). Assessment is not the same as testing; testing is just one part of the assessment process. Assessment includes many other means of data collection such as parent, teacher, and child observations; interviews with the child and significant others in the child's life; examination of cumulative records; developmental and medical histories; checklists; evaluating curriculum requirements and options; trial teaching; task analysis; teacher attitude ratings; classroom climate measures. The primary task in assessment is to develop programs that allow the individual to grow educationally and psychologically. The prerequisites for appropriate assessment are awareness of assessment purposes, models, and methods, and securing sufficient training to evaluate and plan within multidimensional assessment domains.

Assessment Purposes

Assessment facilitates different kinds of decisions, and each decision often requires different sets of information. Ysseldyke (1979; Salvia & Ysseldyke, 1978) identified five basic purposes of assessment: screening-identification, classification-placement, psychoeducational planning, pupil evaluation, and program evaluation. Another reason for assessment is to evaluate and develop new assessment and intervention strategies, and to conduct research that might lead to a better understanding of learning disabled individuals. Our assessment purposes influence which assessment techniques are used.

Screening-Identification

One purpose of assessment is to identify children who are significantly behind their peers in one or more areas so that additional instruction or assessment can be provided. Typically, group norm-referenced tests are administered for screening purposes, so that an individual is compared with others having

This chapter was written by Harold Keller.

similar sociocultural (experiential) backgrounds and ages. For example, standardized achievement tests might identify Sharon as having learned less than expected, given her cognitive abilities, age, grade, years of schooling and quality of home and school background. Further assessment is then indicated to determine the specific factors involved. Individual vision and hearing screening are conducted routinely in schools to identify children with visual and auditory acuity problems.

Classification-Placement

To comply with state and federal laws and regulations, schools frequently assess children for administrative purposes. Such assessment supports the classification of children as learning disabled and their placement in appropriate psychoeducational environments. Haphazard and capricious placement decisions based on subjective impressions can be avoided through the appropriate integration of test data with appraisal of task and setting characteristics.

Psychoeducational Planning

Assessment data is collected to assist educational personnel in planning programs for learning disabled students that enhance their psychological adjustment and educational achievement. Within this assessment goal, emphasis is placed on determining specifically what skills children have and have not mastered, and how they approach learning tasks. The results help teachers design what and how to teach.

Pupil Evaluation

Another purpose for collecting assessment data is to help professionals, parents, and children themselves to evaluate the degree to which learning disabled students are making progress in their programs. Grades derived from teacher-constructed measures, scores on standardized tests, and behavior checklists are frequent indicators of academic and social progress.

Program Evaluation

Assessment data is also gathered to evaluate learning disability programs. Here the focus is on the program rather than the student. The school, for example, might evaluate specific reading programs or the effectiveness of specific psychological interventions such as helping a child maintain attention during math instruction. Such evaluations compare students' progress relative to stated objectives, or assess the progress of students in one program relative to progress in another program.

You are already familiar with the assessment issues involved in identifying and classifying learning disabled children. Our primary concern here is with psychoeducational planning. Assessment practices that merely lead to identification or classification-placement are not sufficient for designing instructional programs (Cromwell, Blashfield, & Strauss, 1975). Such assessment leads only indirectly to intervention. Whether the psychoeducational programming occurs in the home, the regular classroom, or other more appropriate environments, professionals and helpers in those settings must assess the child's specific learning and socio-emotional needs and how to help that child progress. The diagnostic process must be linked to intervention in ways that are continuous, and that focus on behaviors relevant to the identified problems. It must emphasize behaviors that can be changed and improved, recognize the need for a child-teacher-parent partnership, and attempt to provide specific and useful information to this partnership (Oakland, 1977b).

Once psychoeducational programs are implemented, pupil progress and program success must be evaluated systematically. Such evaluation determines whether the learning disabled child is ready to move on to a less restrictive educational setting, and whether the psychoeducational program might be used with similar students and problems in the future.

Models of Assessment

There are seven basic models of assessment (Mercer & Ysseldyke, 1977). While some focus primarily upon the learner, others focus on the learner's interactions with tasks, the learner's interactions with settings, or the learner in relation to broader sociocultural contexts.

Each model has its own set of assumptions, measures, and relationship to interventions. Each model, viewed separately, provides only a partial view of the individual and his or her strengths and weaknesses. In dealing with learning disabled students, teachers need to use an approach that views the child from multiple perspectives, including the child's interactions with tasks, settings, and broader sociocultural contexts.

Focus on Learner

When the focus is on the student, the basic assumption is that problems exist within the individual. The primary concern is with deficits. The medical model and process-deficit model both emphasize within-child problems.

Medical Model. In this model a problem is defined in terms of biological symptoms of pathology. The model assumes biological causes and views sociocultural background as irrelevant to assessment and intervention. For example, a brain injury due to oxygen deprivation during birth can be diagnosed without reference to the individual's sociocultural background. These background characteristics are pertinent to the medical model only when they cause biological symptoms, as when poor maternal nutrition causes premature birth and low birth weight.

Since many biological problems can go unrecognized, medical and behavioral assessment within the school serves an important screening function. Such screening can identify children who might be at risk for learning problems due to a medical condition (such as a visual or hearing impairment, lethargy, or hyperactivity). The child can then be referred for more thorough medical or neuropsychological assessment. Interventions involve treatment of the biological conditions or deficits, such as prescription of glasses or hearing devices, outlining a balanced diet, or drugs.

Process-Deficit Model. This model defines a problem in terms of information-processing or ability deficits related to cognitive, motor, visual perceptual, language, or attention weaknesses. As with the medical model, process deficits can also go unrecognized. A learning disabled child might be viewed as stupid or disturbed rather than as possessing disabilities that prevent learning. Therefore, again, screening is an important assessment function. Donna, for example, performs poorly in school. Assessment uncovers the fact that she does well on aurally presented and verbal tasks, but has problems with visually presented tasks and visual-motor coordination. Because most academic tasks are presented through reading, she does very poorly in school. Within this model, intervention might consist of exercises to strengthen her visual-motor coordination (remediation of deficit), while instruction is presented predominantly through an auditory mode (compensation for deficit). Her social studies lessons, for example, might be tape recorded.

Because intervention focuses on both remediation (building up deficits) and compensation (working around deficits by teaching to strengths), measures within this model identify both strengths and weaknesses. The measures assess hypothetical internal determinants of behavior.

In recent years the process model's assumptions have been questioned. Mann and Phillips (1967) question whether a child's behavior actually can be broken down into separate information-processing areas that can be independently assessed and remediated; on most tasks each process is involved to varying degrees. The reliability of measures within this general model also is often poor (Salvia & Ysseldyke, 1978; Ysseldyke, 1973, 1979; Ysseldyke & Salvia, 1974).

In addition to the measures, some authors criticize the deficit orientation in the process-deficit model (Keogh, 1972; Tarnopol, 1969). They question the assumption that hypothesized deficits exist within the child alone, and suggest that assessment focusing only on the child is too narrow. The lack of support for the basic assumption of this model is based on currently used tests and remediation procedures. As methods of identifying precisely how process deficits impair performance on components of actual educational tasks improve, support for incorporating process-deficit assumptions into remedial planning may increase.

Focus on Learner's Interactions with Tasks

The basic concern in some assessment models is with how the child relates to academic tasks as well as tasks of daily living. The Task Analysis Model is particularly concerned with child-task interactions.

Task Analysis Model. This model guides much of the instructional programming decisions described in this unit. The task analysis method helps educators discover what task attributes best match a learning disabled child's abilities and learning styles. It is basically a test-teach-test approach, geared toward the precise academic criteria on which the child experiences difficulty. Therefore, the relationship between assessment and intervention is much closer than in the process deficit model.

The task analysis model evaluates a child's general level of skill development on different aspects of a task (recognizing sight words in and out of context), or the degree of mastery of a particular skill (sounds of letters). The task is broken into its component parts while task demands and modes of presentation are altered.

Smith (1980) describes how the educator, while observing a child's performance on various assessment tasks, formulates hypotheses about possible task characteristics that get in the way of a child demonstrating knowledge. Smith suggests that the child try the task again, but with one or more task modifications suggested by the hypotheses. Instead of giving letter sounds, for example, the child could point to letters as the examiner gives their sounds. Besides analyzing tasks into their component parts to determine at what point the child is successful, Smith suggests trying task modifications that might better match the learning disabled student's learning style: directed instruction, increased time to solve the task, guided attention, self-verbalization of instructions, and motivational techniques. Success with such task modifications suggests discrepancies between the child's way-of-knowing and the way tasks are customarily presented in the classroom or on tests.

Focus on Learner's Interactions with Settings

Another way of assessing the learning disabled student is by broadening the interactional focus to include the various settings with which the child relates. Here the basic assumption is that problems relate to the child's interactions with settings. Three assessment models place primary emphasis on child-setting interactions: the social systems model, the ecological assessment model, and the behavioral assessment model.

Social Systems Model. Mercer (1979) articulated this model very clearly, with the primary focus being on social expectations for a specific role in a given setting. The learning disabled child interacts with a variety of social systems (families, classrooms, stores) and assumes a variety of social roles, such as both son and brother in a family social system. Each social role in each social system carries different expectations for behavior, so there are multiple definitions of normal and problem behaviors. The most powerful people in a given setting determine what is acceptable and what is not acceptable within various roles in the setting. For example, the school principal and teachers define standards for acceptable behavior and academic progress within a school. Within a classroom, a teacher's expectations about appropriate age-related behavior, coupled with the teacher's tolerance level, might determine whether or not a child is considered hyperactive. Thus, a person's behavior may be considered typical in one setting but judged atypical in another setting. A learning disabled child might be considered typical in math classes but atypical in reading classes.

The social systems models' basic task is to assess role behaviors and role expectations for the diversity of settings with which the child is likely to interact. Functioning well within any social system involves developing and maintaining interpersonal ties with individuals in the system, and attaining the skills necessary for functioning in particular roles in these settings. Intervention within the social systems model helps the child develop the relevant interpersonal ties (with teachers and peers) and role skills (academics) necessary for success.

Ecological Assessment Model. The ecological model is concerned primarily with the structural, affective, and organizational components of settings. One basic premise of this model is that people adapt and act selectively toward their environment to achieve a harmonious working relationship with it. Specific environments influence individual behavior and have dependable enduring effects on all individuals. To illustrate, the participants in a third grade reading group generally behave in consistent ways when in that group, even though the actual participants change throughout the morning. These consistent ways of behaving (reading silently, reading aloud when asked by teacher, answering questions about the material) are different from the ways the children act in other segments of the environment (such as the cafeteria). A lack of adaptive fit between an individual's behavior and a particular environmental setting is cause for concern. Because this model assumes that behavior and settings are mutually interdependent, an intervention (resource room) that better fits one child's needs might also cause other children to behave more appropriately in that setting.

The ecological model leads educators to examine an individual's naturally occurring behavior, the environment immediately surrounding that behavior, and the ways the individual and the immediate environment are linked. Assessment focuses on:

1. the *objective* or *structural components* of the environment (Gump, 1978): objects in the environment (number of books, learning games, bright colors), the curriculum, people in the environment (teacher, same- or multi-age peers, other support adults), presence of adult or peer praise and criticism, and others;

2. the *subjective, affective components of the environment* (Walberg, 1977): the environment from the subjective perspective of participants within the setting: "interesting," "boring," "fun," "threatening," "warm," "hostile," "organized," "chaotic."

Educators might also assess a whole organization, its interlocking systems (a school district and its buildings, support staff, interrelationships among administration and teachers), and how it influences a child's behavior within a given setting. Conoley (1980) gives as an example the effect on a boy's learning when his first grade classroom moves into a new building due to a school closing. Intervention within this model focuses on changes in the structural, affective, and organizational components of the environment.

Behavioral Assessment Model. Behavioral approaches rely heavily on direct measurement and observation to assess difficulties in their natural settings. It is used to develop psychoeducational interventions and to evaluate their effectiveness. Behavioral assessment incorporates both the social systems and ecological assessment models.

Research and interest in behavioral assessment has recently exploded (Keller, 1980a). Keller (1980c) suggested a number of conditions that appear to have brought about this increased interest: disenchantment with the use of standaridized tests; increased emphasis on adaptive behavior (daily living skills) and on multiple assessment measures; rapidly expanding and successful application of behavior modification approaches to a broad range of problems; and the major challenge to models assuming that problems exist solely within the child.

In this model each child is considered individually, and assessment takes place in many settings. Systematic observation, for example, might take place in the classroom, school halls, cafeteria, playground, home, neighborhood and in structured environments that might include role-playing or trial-teaching. Research Box 10-1 details the importance of assessing children in these settings rather than generalizing from a strange testing situation to these settings.

Assessment is not limited to behavioral actions that can be observed. It also focuses on cognitive (thoughts, images), affective (feelings, subjective meanings), physiological (increased heart rate prior to a test), and structural components (arrangement of desks) of the interaction between learner and settings. Consequently, there are a multitude of assessment strategies in the behavioral assessment model, including interviewing (Bergan & Tombari, 1975; Kanfer & Saslow, 1969), rating scales (Walls, Werner, Bacon, & Zane, 1977; Wilson, 1980), observations in natural settings (Alessi, 1980; Keller, 1980b) analogue situations (McFall, 1977; Nay, 1977), self-evaluation (Mahoney, 1977; Nelson, 1977), biofeedback monitoring (Epstein, 1976; Kallman & Feuerstein, 1977). Interventions are based on a broad social learning approach that includes diverse streams of psychological and social science research and theory (Keller, 1981; Krasner, 1971).

Focus on Learner
in Broader Sociocultural Context

This focus includes a diverse set of approaches designed to be more responsive to the cultural pluralism that exists in this country and others. It attempts to make assessments less tied to the dominant culture (in America, the middle class and Anglo-American traditions). This relatively recent focus resulted

RESEARCH BOX 10-1
The Relationship Between the Testing Situation and the Classroom Setting

Behavioral assessment is characterized by direct measurement of behaviors in settings of concern to the child and the person referring the child. Such a strategy results in fewer inferences made from the assessment setting to the intervention setting, since the settings typically are identical. In contrast, traditional assessment with standardized tests can be characterized as testing a child by a strange adult in a strange room with a strange set of questions and tasks (Bronfenbrenner, 1976). Since the child may have trouble interacting with the strange adult in an unfamiliar room (such as the psychologist's office), on irrelevant tests, inappropriate inferences may be made about the child's problems.

The need to evaluate children in the situation to which we are predicting was exemplified in a study reported by Bersoff (1973). Bersoff investigated the rate of social reinforcement in the testing situation and the classroom. He counted the number of praising comments (like "That's good" and "You're doing fine"), smiles, and positive

physical contact (pats, hugs) given to the child by the psychologist during testing. Then, for the same length of time, he observed how often the teacher praised, smiled at, and touched positively the child in the regular classroom. Bersoff demonstrated that, for a large sample of children, there was much more social reinforcement in the testing situation than in the classroom. Nonverbal social reinforcement (smiles and positive physical contact) was almost nonexistent in the classroom.

A tremendous amount of research on learning has shown that reinforcement positively influences children's learning and behavior. Apparently, traditional testing procedures make inferences about a child and the best way to help the child from a situation loaded with social reinforcement to a setting with minimal amounts of social reinforcement for the child. The social reinforcement element, along with other performance-enhancing dimensions of the testing situation, helps explain why learning disabled students' problems are often underestimated. The teacher and psychologist may respond "Well, if David can work at a third grade level during testing he certainly can in the classroom." But David can't. The situation is not the same. More direct measurement would result in a closer relationship between assessment and intervention.

from problems with test discrimination and over-representation of minorities in special education classes (Mercer, 1979; Oakland & Laosa, 1977).

Pluralistic Model. In the pluralistic model, a psychoeducational problem is defined as poor performance when sociocultural bias is controlled. The pluralistic model assumes that potential for learning is similarly distributed in all racial, ethnic and cultural groups. Individual differences in learning potential within each of these groups are acknowledged, but differences in test performance between cultural groups are assumed to be due to biases in tests and testing procedures.

Since the pluralistic model assumes that all tests assess what the child has learned about the cultural heritage represented in the tests' construction, it assumes that all tests are culturally biased. People socialized in the same cultural heritage as the test's norm sample will tend to perform better on a test than those not reared in that cultural tradition. The latter perform poorly because of differences in their socialization, not because of differences in learning potential. To illustrate, knowing who wrote *Romeo and Juliet*, a question on an intelligence test, depends on a particular cultural heritage. Assessment in the pluralistic model attempts to control for such cultural biases in testing instruments and in testing procedures.

An attempt to develop culture-free tests was made in the 1950s (Eells et al., 1951). The measures failed because they didn't predict school performance (whose goals are determined by the dominant culture) and because sociocultural differences could not be eliminated from the measures (Cronbach, 1975). The finding of sociocultural differences on so-called culture-free tests is not surprising. There are no culture-free tests, and the goal is unattainable. All tests' questions and materials must be developed within some cultural context. A test cannot be developed within a cultural vacuum.

Two alternatives to the culture-free tests are to develop culture-fair tests and many culture-specific tests. A culture fair test would balance items across cultural groups. This approach, however, would not predict performance in our predominantly middle-class, white American schools. Culture-specific tests would have the same problem — low predictability to school performance. In addition, a separate Black or Hispanic test does not recognize the considerable heterogeneity that exists within each of these groups.

Several assessment strategies have been proposed to deal with the broad focus suggested by the pluralistic model. Reschly (1979) suggests comprehensive multidimensional assessment that includes all the various domains of assessment. He emphasizes viewing nonbiased assessment as a process rather than as a set of instruments. The nonbiased assessment process must be oriented toward ensuring fairness and effectiveness of assessment and intervention decisions for all children. Complementing this strategy in pluralistic assessment are Mercer's (1979; Mercer & Lewis, 1978) System of Multicultural Pluralistic Assessment (SOMPA) and Feuerstein's (1979, 1980) Learning Potential Assessment Device (LPAD). These strategies are viewed by their respective authors not as total assessment systems but as parts of a total assessment with culturally diverse children. These two approaches are perhaps the most far-reaching attempts to deal with the issues of pluralistic assessment and nondiscriminatory testing.

System of Multicultural Pluralistic Assessment (SOMPA). Mercer's (1979) SOMPA is a norm-based measurement system specifically designed to address issues of nonbiased assessment. Mercer cautions against using the SOMPA as the only measure within a comprehensive assessment system. Three assessment models are used, each with its own set of measures: medical, social systems, and pluralistic models (see Table 10-1). Both the child and parents are sources of information. The involvement of the parent is important, especially given the mandates of PL 94-142.

Medical model measures are designed to screen for potential biological and neurological problems. Measures in the social systems model assess a child's adaptive fit to school roles, nonschool roles, and social systems. The Wechsler Intelligence Scale for Children — Revised (WISC-R), because it predicts well to schools (which reflect the dominant core culture's values, beliefs, roles, and role expectations), provides a measure of *school functioning level*. The WISC-R in SOMPA's social system model is not used as a measure of intelligence because performance on the test is clearly related to only the experiences of the dominant core society. Rather it measures the child's adaptation to the student role in the school social system.

In the pluralistic model, four sociocultural scales describe the child's sociocultural background relative to Black, Hispanic, and white norms. The degree

Table 10-1   Mercer's system of multicultural pluralistic assessment (SOMPA)

MODEL	MEASURES	DESCRIPTION	DATA SOURCE
Medical	Health history inventories	Measures past and current health conditions	Parent
	Physical dexterity tasks	Measures fine and gross motor coordination and balance	Child
	Bender Gestalt	Copying test that assesses perceptual maturity and neurological functioning	Child
	Visual acuity		Child
	Auditory acuity		Child
	Height by weight index		Child
Social systems	Adaptive Behavior Inventory for Children	Assesses child's adaptive fit to the family, community, peers, nonacademic school roles, earner consumer roles, and self-maintenance skills	Parent
	School functioning level	Based on scores on the Wechsler Intelligence Scale for Children — Revised (WISC-R), and used as a measure of adaptive fit to the student role in the school social system	Child
Pluralistic	Sociocultural scales	Assesses family's urban acculturation, socioeconomic status, structure, and size	Parent
	Estimated Learning, Potential (ELP)	Measures intellectual potential, based on WISC-R scores corrected by the family's ethnic and sociocultural characteristics	Child & Parent

of discrepancy between the child's background and the background of the dominant core culture represented in the school setting is evaluated. The major measure within the pluralistic model is the *Estimated Learning Potential* (ELP), which attempts to determine how bright the child is. The score provides an estimate of the child's WISC-R intelligence only in relation to others having similar racial, ethnic, and sociocultural characteristics. It is assumed that, by using the child's sociocultural scale scores to generate the ELP, the SOMPA compares the child's learning potential only with those having comparable life experiences, test-taking experience, familiarity with test materials, and motivation.

The SOMPA is a new assessment system, and much research is needed. One of its most serious limitations is the fact that it was standardized on California children only. How well the norms hold up across our culturally diverse country has yet to be demonstrated. Some studies suggest that we cannot readily generalize from the California sample (Oakland, 1977a; Reschly, 1978). The SOMPA has also been criticized for not providing information directly relevant to programming. But this is unwarranted, since Mercer developed the measure to ensure fair and unbiased identification, screening, and classroom placement decisions. She basically states that, as long as educators continue to ask how bright students are and place them on the basis of the answer to that question, the question should be answered in as fair and unbiased a manner as possible.

The ELP has potential use for identifying minority and socioculturally different children as learning disabled because IQs are adjusted upward. Educators are then more likely to find a potential-achievement discrepancy for these children (Reschly, 1979). Mercer (1979) argues that it is important and necessary to determine how well the child adapts to the dominant core society as well as to the child's own sociocultural settings. In this way intervention can focus on helping the child adapt to and maintain skills in the dominant society as well as in his or her own sociocultural settings.

Learning Potential Assessment Device (LPAD). Unlike the screening–classification purpose of the SOMPA, the LPAD was designed by Feuerstein (1979, 1980) to foster the development of specific psychoeducational programs for children. While Feuerstein has used the assessment system for a long time in Israel with extremely culturally diverse children, the LPAD is just now being developed formally in this country. The LPAD represents a dramatic change from norm-referenced testing, and is a significant contribution to the assessment of the learning disabled. To some extent, it appears to relate to the process-deficit model, since it purports to identify basic processes necessary for learning. The LPAD also incorporates assessment procedures somewhat analogous to those used in task-analysis procedures. Like task-analysis, it attempts to assess, not the static abilities of the child, but the child's degree of modifiability. Feuerstein believes that the primary goal in assessment is to demonstrate how program modifications allow the child to grow education-ally and psychologically.

Based upon Feuerstein's early work with Piaget, the examiner in the LPAD becomes a teacher, and the examinee a learner. These are very different roles from those assumed in the usual testing situation. The assessment strategy is to test, teach the child through a wide variety of alternative strategies that consider the child's sociocultural background and differing learning styles, and posttest to measure the amount of gain that the child makes as a result of teaching. Information is obtained on:

1. the child's ability to grasp the principles underlying the initial tasks (presented in pretest);

2. the amount and nature of effort required to teach the child the basic principles;

3. the extent to which the newly acquired principles are successfully applied to the solution of problems that become progressively more different from the initial tasks (how well can the child generalize from prior learning);

4. the child's preference for presentation and instructional modalities (figural, pictorial-concrete, verbal, numerical, spatial); and

5. the differential effects of different training strategies.

Feuerstein's (1980) companion book on his instrumental enrichment procedures describes various psychoeducational instructional strategies that might be developed directly from the assessment system.

Assessment Methods

Given the multiple purposes and models of evaluation and the need to intervene with LD students at learner, task and setting levels, the need for a multi-dimensional assessment approach is clear. Assessment can involve tests conducted with students or evaluation strategies focusing on child interactions with a variety of tasks and settings.

Tests used in assessment have been categorized by whether they are norm-referenced or criterion-referenced measures. Tests that have been standardized on a normative group, in order to compare an individual's general performance to that of his peers, are called standardized or norm-referenced tests. Criterion-referenced tests may also be normed, but they are intended to measure whether or not a person has mastered very specific skills. Norm-referenced tests indicate an individual's standing relative to others' skill development (measuring *between* individual differences). Criterion-referenced tests, on the other hand, indicate whether or not the child actually has mastered a particular skill (measuring *within*-individual skill attainment).

A test that shows Johnny has mastered math better than 15 percent of children at his grade level nationally is norm-based. A test that indicates that he can add two-digit numbers with regrouping, but cannot multiply, is criterion-referenced. The norm-referenced test judges Johnny's knowledge of letter sounds by sampling six letters and comparing his percent correct with that of the standardization sample. The criterion-referenced test may ask Johnny to give all twenty-six letter sounds.

All tests, to some extent, reflect both between-individual differences and within-individual growth. However, because of how they are developed, most tests do a better job along one dimension than the other. Norm-referenced tests are most useful for screening and classification, while criterion-referenced measures identify what to teach. How to teach is best ascertained by informal evaluation strategies particularly adapted to the questions asked about the student's interactions with tasks and settings.

Norm-Referenced Measures

Characteristics which norm-referenced tests must have in order to be useful in the decision-making process include a) reliability — stability or consistency of scores; b) validity — extent to which a test measures what it is supposed to measure; c) standardized administration; and d) norms based on standardization on a relevant comparison group.

An important function of norm-based measures is in screening children who might be at risk for subsequent psychological and educational problems. Their global screening function provides a rapid guide to further assessment questions and methods. They offer hypotheses regarding the potential problem areas and how the student might be learning or adapting to the environment. These hypotheses may be evaluated with additional assessment strategies, including criterion-referenced and non-standardized measures (Mowder, 1980; Smith, 1980). This further testing is necessitated by the fact that norm-referenced tests sample too few behaviors within a specific skill area to be of much help in intervention.

Learning disabilities teams engaging in the assessment process cannot limit themselves to the use of norm-referenced tests only, because the tests do not specify *what* and *how* to teach these children. Norm-referenced instruments gain value when, after standard administration, the examiner applies informal evaluation methods to the items on which the child erred so that the examiner can discover exactly what subcomponents of the task the student has mastered, which aspects are difficult and why, and how rapidly the student could learn the task and generalize this knowledge to new items given different instructional strategies (Smith, 1980).

Criterion-Referenced Measures

Criterion-referenced tests provide information on what to teach. While norms are not critical for these measures, knowledge of the sample of individuals with which the test was developed is important. Evaluators may not be interested in comparing a particular child with some normative sample, but information that helps them judge the appropriateness of the test's mastery criteria for a particular child is important. It is possible that individuals with certain personal characteristics or instructional backgrounds should be expected to perform differently on particular criterion tasks. Items on criterion-referenced tests are often associated directly with specific instructional objectives and thus help in the writing of individual educational plans and in evaluating pupil progress. Although criterion-referenced tests do not provide information on how to teach, application of informal evaluation strategies to the items on which the student was unsuccessful can serve this purpose.

Informal Evaluation Strategies

A variety of non-standardized assessment strategies can provide information about both what and how to teach. Task-analysis procedures, for example, break down complex instructional goals into component skills and assess mastery of these subskills (Bijou, 1970; Resnick, Wang, & Kaplan, 1973; Smith, 1980). In this way, a child can be located on a hierarchy of component skills for a given task, and the next skill to be taught is identified.

Direct systematic *observation* of the child in the classroom can also provide information about what and how to teach, whether the evaluator's goals are academic or social in nature (Alessi, 1980; Keller, 1980ab, 1981). Classroom observation has the advantage of assessing the problem in the setting where it occurs. This contrasts with traditional testing, in which a child is typically assessed in a strange room, with a strange adult, and with a strange and perhaps irrelevant set of questions and tasks (Bronfenbrenner, 1976).

Trial teaching is an assessment strategy that gets most directly at the how-to-teach question (Salvia & Ysseldyke, 1978; Smith, 1980). A variety of instructional techniques are systematically tried and evaluated, including varying materials, methods of presentation, and methods of feedback. This assessment strategy can be employed with an individual child in an office or in the classroom.

All of these nonstandardized assessment procedures relate directly to the how-to-teach question. Although time-consuming, they are necessary components in an assessment system designed to develop individual psychoeducational intervention plans. All are well-suited for assessing individual pupil progress.

Multidimensional Assessment Approaches

Public Law 94–142 mandates that multidimensional, nondiscriminatory assessment procedures be employed in evaluating learning disabled students. It also requires multiple perspectives within the assessment, decision-making, and planning processes. The primary goal of assessment with a learning disabled student is to develop effective psychoeducational programs that help the child develop educationally and personally. To do this evaluators need as much information about the child in as many domains as possible: a picture of the total child. Learning does not occur in isolation. Learning is influenced by many aspects of the child and the child's interactions with the environment. This process necessitates a team approach to assessment and to decision-making. Comprehensive assessment and intervention includes teachers, administrators, special educators, school social workers, school nurses, speech and hearing personnel, reading specialists, language specialists, school psychologists, parents, and children. The parents and, to whatever extent possible, the child are important components of the team process in assessment and planning.

Multiple Dimensions

Multidimensional assessment is conducted through an examination of many aspects or domains of the child and of the child's interaction with tasks and settings (Reschly, 1979; Tucker, 1977). Although PL 94–142's identification procedures require that "no single procedure is used as the sole criterion for determining an appropriate educational program for a child" (Federal Register, December 29, 1977, p. 65082), a thorough assessment of and plan for an LD student's daily learning program necessitates more than two measures. Possible assessment domains include language skills, sociocultural background, general and specific academic skills, intelligence, sensory–motor skills, medical, developmental and neuropsychological information, adaptive behavior, and socioemotional characteristics. Assessment should also include consideration of the curriculum and settings to which the child relates, the child's interactions with those tasks and settings, and the child's and significant others' subjective impressions concerning all these aspects. In line with these perspectives, PL 94–142 requires that the student's academic performance be observed in his or her regular classroom by a team member other than the child's regular classroom teacher. If a child is less than school age or out of school, then the observation occurs in an environment appropriate for a child of that age. Public Law 94–142 also requires that the testing materials not be racially or culturally discriminatory and that "tests and other evaluation materials are provided and administered in the child's native language or other mode of communication" (Federal Register, December 29, 1977, p. 65082).

How might this comprehensive multidimensional assessment be conducted? The format used at the Syracuse University Psychoeducational Teaching Laboratory provides one model (Smith, 1980). Initially, evaluators use structured interviews with the parents, child, and teachers during home and school visits, informal consultation, and examination of prior records. Information gained from these sources narrows the choice of measurement techniques. Next, observation systems (at school, home, and clinic) are used, along with standardized instruments that yield more accurate, but still broad-based, information. Criterion-referenced measures then narrow the range of instructional objectives. The final assessment step involves nonstandardized strategies (such as task analysis, trial teaching, and observation systems) that are less efficient but very precise. During this phase, task and setting attributes are systematically varied as measurement and consultation continue. Trial teaching spread over several weeks, as well as home and school follow-up, are important components of the final phase. The clinic staff conceptualizes its task as the assessment of the child-task-setting interactions. The goal is modification of the tasks and relevant settings to best maximize the child's strengths and continued development. The child's "way of knowing" is the key to intervention (Hunt, 1969; Silberberg, 1971).

Another format, used in some Michigan schools (Alessi, 1979), is described to some extent in Mercer (1979). When the teacher perceives a problem, he or she documents a minimum of three systematic attempts to solve the problem and the results of those attempts. When the attempts are unsuccessful, the teacher refers the child to the special support staff along with documentation of the attempts and the results. A complete multidimensional assessment is then conducted. In these districts regular classroom teachers have become much more capable of solving problems than teachers often are given credit for. Much more time is available for support staff to work on serious problems and to collaborate with the teaching staff in program development. Referrals are maintained at a more manageable level as well. This format provides a very different mind-set from the usual referral procedure. Here the teacher is more likely to perceive him or herself as part of the problem-solution process; the problem does not exist solely within the child. Initiating such a format involves tremendous change and the availability of quality support staff and collaborative consultation with teachers.

Multiple Perspectives

Public Law 94-142's regulations require participation of a multidisciplinary team including "at least one teacher or other specialist with knowledge in the area of suspected disability," as well as:

> (a) (1) the child's regular teacher; or (2) If the child does not have a regular teacher, a regular classroom teacher qualified to teach a child of his or her age; or (3) For a child of less than school age, an individual qualified by the State educational agency to teach a child of his or her age; and (b) At least one person qualified to conduct individual diagnostic examinations of children, such as a school psychologist, speech-language pathologist, or remedial reading teacher (Federal Register, December 29, 1977, pp. 65082-3).

Most often, an even wider range of professionals within the school are involved. Participation of teachers in the assessment process is important not only because they have valuable information about the child but also because this process helps to indicate the teachers' likely commitment to any subsequent interventions in their classrooms.

During an assessment, information about the child is customarily gathered from the child's parents. Hobbs (1975a) reminds educators that school professionals do not respect sufficiently those individuals (parents) who know the child most directly, for the longest duration, and over the widest range of settings. Smith (1980) too points out that when evaluators assess a child they merely arrive at hypotheses and make reasoned inferences about the problem. She suggests that the child become a partner in the assessment process. When using task-analysis procedures, evaluators might ask the child how he or she attempted to solve the problem. What was the child doing, attending to, and thinking? The student might indicate how he or she wishes that a school's curriculum or teacher characteristics would change. Such a process can prove beneficial both for the child and the evaluators.

When teacher, parents, and significant others in the environment are positively involved in the problem identification, assessment, and decision-making process, they will more likely be constructively involved in the intervention process (Keller, 1980b, 1981). They cannot merely be recipients of the assessment information and a set of recommendations. In this light, PL 94-142 assures that parents have the right to participate in the development of their LD children's individual education programs (IEP), request an impartial hearing if they disagree with the evaluation team's findings, request a free and independent assessment, petition the education commissioner if they disagree with the hearing officer's decision, engage a lawyer, have access to all public records, receive a written invitation to participate in labelling and placement decisions, receive written notices of school placement decisions, and sign their children's IEP's.

The initial stages of the assessment process (interviewing, examination of records, and observation) can help identify the specific questions of concern for a particular child. In this way, the assessment focus can be narrowed, and the process made more efficient. The degree of certainty concerning the questions determines the breadth of focus in the assessment and the makeup of the assessment team. The chair of an assessment and planning team can be rotated among the team members across referrals. With good training in leadership and group processes, rotation of the chair position helps to increase people's involvement in the process. Some schools also assign a professional (not directly involved in the assessment) for each referral, who assumes the role of child advocate. The advocacy role is rotated among professionals, and the individual is responsible for seeing that the child's needs are effectively met.

A team approach is important in terms of time and cost. More importantly, a team approach is critical to the enhancement of multiple perspectives for understanding the child. The assessment instruments, strategies, and human interactions are multidimensional and, through a team approach, attempts at understanding the problem (in terms of the learner, tasks, and settings) represent multiple perspectives. An important consequence of team involvement in the assessment process is an increased commitment to the intervention processes developed out of the assessment.

Assessment Domains

A single chapter on assessment cannot possibly do justice to all the measures available. There are complete books on assessment. In this section we shall explore the various evaluation domains and the types of assessment tools employed in each.

Those who assess children must have the necessary training and expertise to do so. A particular credential does not make a person an expert in assessment. Individuals engaged in assessment must be skilled in establishing rapport with children, familiar with appropriate strategies and tools for the specific kinds of decisions they need to make, and clear about the behaviors sampled by tests. This is particularly important when evaluating the learning disabled, who might know information in one way but not in another.

Table 10–2 and Figure 10–1 illustrate typical reading comprehension tests. The student answers questions after orally or silently reading a passage, points to the correct picture after reading silently, or adds the missing word in a sentence. Table 10–3 illustrates typical spelling assessment tests. The student writes dictated words or points to which of four spellings is correct. Clearly, each task taps different abilities in the child, only some of which are the same as those required on school work. Therefore, the evaluator needs to know not only the technical aspects of test administration, scoring, interpretation, reliability, and validity, but also the intelligent use of tests and assessment information, which includes the ability to make nonstandardized, informal use of norm-referenced, standardized instruments. Basic to such a charge is a thorough understanding of typical development of children. The evaluator must be

Table 10–2   Representative item from a reading comprehension test. The student answers oral questions after reading a passage.

Mary was going downtown to watch the parade. She skipped and ran along the street because she could hardly wait to get there. She was early and found a good place to stand.

Pretty soon she could hear the music of the bands coming down the main street. The men of the first band were dressed in scarlet, with white feathers in their hats. The men of the second band were clad in dark blue, with red feathers in their caps.

1. Why did Mary go downtown? *(to see the parade)*
2. Had the parade started before she got there? *(no)*
3. What did she hear after she found a place to stand? *(music or bands)*
4. What came first in the parade? *(band)*

SOURCE: From *Diagnostic Reading Scales* devised by George D. Spache. Reprinted by permission of the publisher, CTB/McGraw-Hill, Del Monte Research Park, Monterey, CA 93940. Copyright © 1972, 1981 by McGraw-Hill, Inc. All Rights Reserved. Printed in the U.S.A.

Figure 10-1 Representative items from reading comprehension tests. In one, the student identifies the appropriate picture. In the second item, the student fills in the blanks.

Mother sits on the bed.

"Please hurry up. We want to be sure to

_____ there on time," said Dad.

Splash! Jimmy stepped into a deep puddle.

His sneaker was all _____.

SOURCE (top): Dunn, L. M. and Markwardt, F. C. *Peabody Individual Achievement Test,* Circle Pines, Minn.: American Guidance Service, 1970. Reprinted by permission.

Table 10-3 Representative items from spelling tests. In the first, the student writes dictated words. In the second item, the student points to the correct spelling.

go	Children *go* to school.
cut	Mother will *cut* the cake.
nature	The study of *nature* is interesting.
reasonable	His request was *reasonable* and just.
appropriation	Congress made an *appropriation* for schools.

bok	boc
booke	book

faciletate	facilitate
fasilitate	facilitait

SOURCE (top): Jastak, J. F., and Jastak, S. *Wide Range Achievement Test.* Wilmington, Del.: Jastak Associates, Inc., 1978. Reprinted by Permission.
NOTE (bottom): Test item similar to Peabody Individual Achievement Test.

sensitive to the tremendous diversity among typical children as they develop, and judge the strengths and weaknesses of a particular child accordingly. Table 10-4 lists commonly used assessment measures in the various domains.

Initial Steps

The assessment process is initiated by a referral, either from the child, parents, teachers, or others in the child's environment. Necessary initial steps are examination of available records, interviews with the child and relevant others, and observations in the child's natural settings. Only then does the evaluator observe the child in analogue settings.

Appropriate use of these initial steps can make the total assessment process more efficient. At the same time, the evaluator must be careful not to narrow the focus of assessment too quickly lest he or she fail to identify some strengths or limitations of the child, tasks, or settings.

Referrals. The structure of a referral form is important because the items allow the individual to try publicly to identify the problem of concern, or the reason for requesting support services. The form's questions and format can influence an individual's view of the problem. The format might cue the person to consider the problem as within the child, or as interactional, involving the child, curriculum, settings, and teacher or parent. The form might require an individual to state the problem in descriptive terms. It might focus on a child's strengths. In addition, the form might suggest that the purpose of the assessment process is programming as opposed to identification and placement. The referral form also can be structured to communicate that the individual making the referral is important, and has significant information that will be part of the total assessment process. Because of these possibilities, care must be taken to develop a referral form that fosters perspectives that enhance children's programming opportunities.

Records. Examination of school records often provides clues as to when a problem began. Was the child absent during the presentation of key curricular material pertinent to current curriculum concepts? Are there clues about family-school relationships that might be improved or used effectively in subsequent intervention? Is the family different from the dominant school culture, so that sociocultural background needs to be assessed? What medical and developmental history data are available? Such data, in addition to yearly achievement test scores and grades, can provide useful clues as to where to begin the assessment process and what kinds of measures are needed. The accuracy of this information must be ascertained also. Are the facts verifiable, or are inferences based on tenuous information?

Interviews. The interview with teachers, parents, the referred child, and relevant others is an important component of the assessment process. The purposes of an interview are to clarify the referral reasons, specify perceptions regarding the psychoeducational problem, and determine initial assessment procedures. The interview might identify the appropriate times, places, and likely focuses of observation. It should provide clues to a variety of domains of concern, so as to make the assessment process more efficient. The primary focus of initial interviews should be on obtaining thorough descriptive information about the child and the child's interactions with task and setting conditions. It is equally important to understand people's feelings and attitudes concerning the events they describe. Like the referral format, the interview format can serve as a cue for people's behaviors and attitudes. Research Box 10-2 on page 336 reviews a study illustrating this point.

Naturalistic Observation. The use of observation early in the assessment process is important. Often observation shows that formal assessment is not needed; the perceived problem might be resolved through sensitive consultation with the teacher and others in the child's environment.

The primary reason for observation is to provide assessment information about a problem in appropriate settings. When used early and systematically in the assessment process, observational data can serve as a basis for comparing

Table 10-4   Representative assessment tools

Primary Language
  Basic Inventory of Natural Language
  Basic Language Competence Battery
  Bilingual Syntax Measure
  Pictorial Test of Bilingualism and
    Language Dominance
  Screening Test for Auditory
    Comprehension of Language
  Test of Auditory Comprehension of
    Language English/Spanish

Language
  Written Vocabulary Subtest from:
    Test of Written Language
    Myklebust Picture Story Language Test
  Expressive Vocabulary Subtests from:
    Stanford–Binet Intelligence Scale
    Wechsler Intelligence Scale for
      Children — Revised
    Test of Language Development
    McCarthy Scales of Children's Abilities
  Receptive Vocabulary:
    Peabody Picture Vocabulary Test —
      Revised
    Test of Language Development Subtest
    French Test of Pictorial Intelligence
      Subtest
  Auditory Discrimination:
    Wepman Auditory Discrimination Test
    Goldman-Fristoe-Woodcock Test of
      Auditory Discrimination
  Syntactic Ability and Articulation:
    Test of Written Language Subtest
    Northwestern Syntax Screening Test
    Goldman-Fristoe Test of Articulation
    Test of Language Development Subtest
  Language Reasoning Abilities
    Illinois Test of Psycholinguistic Abilities
    Test of Language Development Subtest
    Woodcock Johnson Psychoeducational
      Battery Language Cluster

Multiple Academic Skills (Group)
  California Achievement Test
  Metropolitan Achievement Test
  Iowa Tests of Basic Skills
  Stanford Achievement Test

Multiple Academic Skills (Individual)
  Peabody Individual Achievement Test
    (PIAT)
  Wide Range Achievement Test
    (WRAT)
  Woodcock Johnson Psychoeducational
    Battery

Diagnostic Reading Achievement
  Durrell Analysis of Reading Difficulty
  Gates–McKillop Reading Diagnostic Tests
  Gilmore Oral Reading Test
  Gray Oral Reading Test
  Spache Diagnostic Reading Scales
  Stanford Diagnostic Reading Test
  Woodcock Reading Mastery Tests

Diagnostic Mathematics Achievement
  Key Math Diagnostic Arithmetic Test
  Stanford Diagnostic Mathematics Test

Spelling and Written Expression
  Gallistel-Ellis Test of Coding Skills
  Myklebust Picture Story Language Test
  Test of Written Spelling
  Test of Written Language

Preschool Intelligence
  McCarthy Scales of Children's Abilities
  Stanford–Binet Intelligence Scale
  Wechsler Preschool and Primary Scale of
    Intelligence (WPPSI)

School-Age Intelligence
  Columbia Mental Maturity Scales
  French Test of Pictorial Intelligence
  Leiter International Performance Scale
  Raven's Progressive Matrices

observations gathered during and after psychoeducational interventions. Observational approaches can also enhance the interactions between the assessment team, school personnel, and families. Parents often perceive direct observation as an indication of genuine interest in the child. They view such data as more relevant than difficult-to-understand standardized tests. Observa-

Table 10-4   continued

Stanford–Binet Intelligence Scale
Wechsler Intelligence Scale for Children —
  Revised (WISC-R)
Wechsler Adult Intelligence Scale —
  Revised (WAIS-R)

Perceptual-Motor
Bender Visual-Motor Gestalt Test
Benton Memory for Designs Test
Frostig Developmental Test of Visual
  Perception
Physical Dexterity Tasks
Purdue Perceptual-Motor Survey
Visual Aural Digit Span Test
Illinois Test of Psycholinguistic Abilities
  Subtests

Neuropsychological Measures
Benton's Embedded Figures Test
Spreen Sentence Repetition
Finger Tapping
Right-Left Orientation Test
Aesthesiometer
Finger Localization
Auditory Reaction Time
Tactual Performance Test
Target Test
Marching Test
Gaddes Visual Retention
Speech Perception
Seashore Tonal Memory
Motor Steadiness
Dichotic Listening
Benton's Stereognosis
Lateral Dominance Examination
Handgrip (Dynamometer)
Benton's Visual Retention Test
Visual Reaction Test
Aphasia Battery

Category Test
Tactile Form Recognition Test
Progressive Figures Test
Trail-Making Test
Roughness Discrimination
Sound Recognition
Finger Proxis
Meikle Consonant Perception

Adaptive Behavior
AAMD Adaptive Behavior Scale — Public
  School Version
Adaptive Behavior Inventory for Children
Behavior Rating Profile
Children's Adaptive Behavior Scale
Devereux Elementary School Behavior
  Rating Scale
Devereux Junior-Senior High School
  Behavior Rating Scale
Public Behavior Inventory

Socioemotional
Piers-Harris Children's Self Concept Scale
Peterson-Quay Behavior Problem
  Checklist
Walker Problem Behavior Checklist
Child Behavior Checklist
Rorschach Inkblot Technique
Thematic Apperception Test
House-Tree-Person Test
School Apperception Measure

Settings
Behavior Setting Survey
Learning Environment Inventory
Classroom Environmental Scale
Classroom Activities Questionnaire
My Class Inventory
Family Environment Scale
Resource Network Assessment

tion also teaches the assessment team more about the perspectives and frustrations of individuals in the child's environment.

Extensive normative observation in schools is important because it informs the team of typical behaviors of children in the various settings and grades, about the settings themselves (very important when making placement decisions), and about expectations of personnel for the children in various

RESEARCH BOX 10-2
The Cue Function of Interview Questions

The kinds of questions asked in interviews can influence what teachers and parents say and think about a child's academic or adjustment problems. This cue function of interview questions was demonstrated in a study by Tombari and Bergan (1978). They studied the effects of specific questions (verbal cues) on teachers' statements, judgments, and expectancies concerning their students' adjustment problems. Practice teachers were systematically interviewed, one half about a problem child with questions that requested specific descriptions of child behavior and settings, and the other half with more general, open-ended questions.

The descriptive questions resulted in teacher statements and problem definitions in descriptive, behavioral terms. Teachers viewed the problems in terms of how the children interacted with their respective settings (consistent with a behavioral model). The more general, open-ended questions resulted in teacher statements and judgments of the problems that were consistent with a medical model (the problems were seen as existing within the child entirely). Teachers' expectancies with respect to their ability to solve a child's problem within the classroom were strongly influenced by the questions. Behavioral descriptive cues or questions resulted in significantly more positive teacher expectancies. Certainly a problem that involves an interaction between child and setting should be more changeable than one within the child only. With a greater expectation for change, it seems reasonable to predict a greater commitment to intervention that requires teacher participation. Therefore, questions requesting descriptive information that specifically concerns the child and settings may help develop effective interventions.

settings. This information helps the team determine whether a learning disabled student's behavior is atypical and whether the behavior might change with time in a given classroom.

Melahn and O'Donnell (1978) describe a feasible process for gathering and developing local norms based upon direct observation. Working in fifteen different Head Start centers, they spent fifteen minutes each day in normative observation of referred and randomly selected nonreferred children. An alternative strategy involves observing a referred child and randomly selected nonreferred children in the same settings before, during, and after intervention (Nelson & Bowles, 1975; Walker & Hops, 1976). Examples of behaviors that can be rated include time students spend in and out of seat, number of positive and negative comments teachers give children, behaviors that elicited these comments, number of oral reading words children need to stop and analyze, and task attentiveness in different seating arrangements. Developing such local norms is an effective strategy for identifying individual children's problems and evaluating change relative to their peers on a wide range of assessment domains.

Table 10-5 describes a variety of ways of measuring behavior during observation. In addition to observations by professional staff, volunteers such

Table 10-5 Measurement methods in observation

METHOD	DESCRIPTION	EXAMPLE
Specimen description	Detailed narrative of the stream of behaviors as they occur in relation to fully recorded structures and settings (Carlson, Scott, & Elkurd, 1980; Wright, 1960). This is used often in an early problem identification stage, although it may also be the primary observational strategy throughout.	The teacher walked toward the blackboard, John was reading at his desk, Betsy snapped John with a rubber band, John jumped out of his seat and hit Betsy, the teacher turned and reprimanded John, Betsy smiled.
Behavior setting survey	Identifying adaptive fits between behavior patterns and specific settings (Carlson et al., 1980).	Observing differences in Debbie's out-of-seat behavior in reading class, the art room, and the cafeteria.
Interval recording	A measure of the number of intervals (time blocks) within which a particular behavior occurs.	Harold was working on his math fourteen of the thirty intervals observed.
Time sampling	A measure of the number of times a behavior is observed to occur at prespecified points in time.	Whether or not Lynn is attending to her work is observed at regular five-minute intervals.
Event recording	A measure of the number of occurrences of a behavior during an observation session.	Angela spelled twenty-five words correctly in twenty minutes.
Duration recording	A measure of the exact length of time a behavior continues.	Dan studied his social studies for twenty-seven minutes.
Latency recording	A measure of the exact length of time between a specified classroom event and the onset or completion of a behavior.	The teacher asked Donna to put away her math and get out her reading book; five minutes later Donna was ready with her reading materials.
Participant or qualitative observation	Allows team to get at the subjective meaning or feeling associated with events in a person's environment (Bogdan & Taylor, 1975; Wilson, 1977).	Julian tells the observer which aspects of his classroom make him feel good and which aspects make him uncomfortable.

as aides, parents, retired citizens, and local college or high school students may be trained in systematic observational procedures (Allen et al., 1976). Observers need thorough training on techniques, on ethical issues, and on issues of confidentiality. All observers, including professional staff need frequent "booster" training.

Another way to implement observational assessment is to use observers already present in the setting. Teachers, school personnel, parents, peers, and even the referred child may conduct observations useful for assessment purposes. The use of significant people in the child's environment enhances the likelihood of implementing and maintaining a team concept in psychoeducational assessment and planning. Teachers and parents can be trained in systematic observation approaches that do not interfere with teaching or parenting. The teacher's or parent's use of such observational schemes might also indicate motivation to become involved in any subsequent intervention process.

Important adults in the child's environment can monitor their own interactions with the child. *Self-monitoring* can be conducted by children as well. For example, students can chart the number of times teachers call on them and on others. In this way children may realize they must raise their hands more often. The amount of self-monitoring might also provide an indication of the child's motivation for change and self-involvement. Self-monitoring has the added potential benefit of helping the child develop self-control and maintain intervention effects (Piersel & Kratochwill, 1979). Self-monitoring might be particularly effective when behaviors that occur infrequently and are unlikely to be observed (such as seizures or taking medication) are the objects of assessment.

Analogue Observation. Observation can take place in structured as well as naturalistic settings. Structured or analogue observations are designed to provide a controlled situation in which the behaviors of concern are highly likely to occur (Haynes, 1978; McFall, 1977; McReynolds & DeVoge, 1978; Nay, 1977). Analogue observation can increase observation efficiency, particularly with behaviors that occur infrequently.

Observation during trial teaching is an analogue assessment, as is task-analysis. The inferences derived from task-analysis and trial teaching then require testing in the actual classroom instruction and functioning of the child. Role-playing, where the child acts out various social situations, also may be used to assess various socioemotional and social skill attributes.

Campbell and his colleagues (1977) presented a structured observation approach to assess hyperactivity in preschoolers. The approach uses a teacher with a small group of children and three ten-minute time blocks of specified activities: free time at a table with many materials available, teacher-structured activity with certain materials, and instructing children to put away materials. A coding scheme for behavioral indices of hyperactivity is used.

In the Psychoeducational Teaching Laboratory at Syracuse University, evaluators frequently observe parent-child interactions through a sequence of free play by the parent(s) and child, the child playing while the parent(s) completes forms at one side of the room, the parent and child working on a cooperative task (parent turns horizontal line knob and child turns vertical line knob on magnetic board so as to create a triangle), and cleaning up materials. Similar strategies can be used to assess indices of dependence and independence, response to authority and demands for compliance, reward and discipline responses, potential liked and disliked activities that might be used in classroom interventions, and other dimensions.

Primary Language and Sociocultural Background

The evaluation team must be sensitive to language (particularly primary language competence) and sociocultural background because they affect assessment of a child in other domains. When there is considerable discrepancy between the child and the school in language and sociocultural background, the team must be very cautious in the interpretation of other assessment information, especially norm-referenced tests.

Assessment of primary language is not only a common-sense procedure, but also a requirement under PL 94-142. Assessment must be conducted in the primary language. When a child is monolingual and non-English speaking, the team should avoid norm-referenced, standardized tests of achievement and ability. While interpreters have been suggested, there are many problems with such attempts. Items do not have the same meaning, and item difficulties change with translations. Evaluation of potential-achievement discrepancies is best accomplished by comparing stronger and weaker skill areas, such as adaptive behavior with reading. If decisions must be made about intellectual ability, the team can use nonverbal tests (Gerken, 1978), though they predict less well to school functioning than verbal tests (Mercer, 1979). Monolingual, non-English speaking children must be provided an education in their native language while they learn English.

The concept of sociocultural background includes social class, race, and ethnicity. None of these are sufficient to entirely explain differences in achievement because racial or ethnic groups are extremely heterogeneous internally. The differences *within* a group are often as large or larger than differences *between* groups. Therefore, considering such additional factors as family structure, family size, and urbanization is more valid than using socioeconomic status or race alone (Mercer, 1979; Oakland, 1980; Reschly, 1978). Besides differences in language and learning experiences, the child is likely to differ from the norm group in other ways: physical problems, anxiety and emotional attributes, motivation, and socialization experiences including test-taking and interactions with test materials (Newland, 1971). When these factors are not taken into account, inappropriate identification and placement occurs (Mercer, 1973, 1979). Since the factors associated with learning disabilities are far more prevalent among lower income individuals, and greater proportions of lower than higher income children are labeled learning disabled, these are important issues to keep in mind.

Language Domain

The language domain includes assessment of listening vocabulary and productive vocabulary through speaking and writing, auditory discrimination, syntactic ability, articulation, auditory sequencing, reasoning through language, and pragmatic speech. Besides using tests that evaluate these skills, trained language therapists also evaluate spontaneously produced written and spoken language. Vocabulary, grammar, and language concepts can be analyzed from a sufficiently large written sample (50–100 sentences) and articulation can be analyzed with oral production. Spontaneous speech samples are the best way to evaluate a child's conversational abilities. Issues of reliability are just as important here as with more standardized measures.

Educational Domain

There is a wide variety of group-administered general achievement tests that serve a screening function. When using these tests as screening devices, the evaluating team must closely examine test content to determine how well it matches the school's curriculum. The less it matches, the less valid it is. When students are instructed in new math, for example, but tested in traditional math, they may perform poorly on the tests. These scores do not validly reflect their math skills. Since group-administered tests do not allow observation of individual pupil performance, evaluators lose valuable information about how a child attempts to solve problems. How learning disabled children solve problems is just as important as determining what they do and do not know.

Individually administered general achievement batteries are also commonly used for global screening purposes. Typically, the scores are inflated estimates of a student's actual ability to perform in the classroom because the tests have an easier response format and capitalize on heightened attention and motivation in the one-to-one testing situation. These tests are good general academic screening measures to guide further assessment, but *not* measures for differential diagnosis of specific academic strengths and weaknesses of the learning disabled (Reynolds, 1979).

There are a variety of individual diagnostic achievement tests for reading and mathematics. The goal of these measures is to gain information about an individual's strengths and weaknesses and how a child performs the tasks. The test user should not get caught up with grade equivalent scores on these measures because such scores are not very useful or accurate. Again, they generally yield inflated scores. General and diagnostic achievement tests often result in large discrepancies in scores on the same criterion because of differences in types of items on each test. For example, although diagnostic reading tests sample a child's oral reading of passages, on general achievement tests the examiner seldom requires a child to read more than single words.

Diagnostic reading tests vary in the skills they assess. For example, oral reading tests vary from one another in errors that are counted: how often aid is required, mispronunciations, word omissions, insertions, substitutions, repetitions, word order changes, disregarding of punctuation, and hesitations. These tests variously assess comprehension skills (literal, inferential, and listening), word-attack skills, word-recognition skills (sight vocabulary), and rate of reading.

Diagnostic math tests sample content areas such as number knowledge, fractions, algebra, and geometry, operations such as counting, computation, and arithmetic reasoning, and applications such as measurement, problem-solving, reading graphs and tables, money and budgeting, and time. With diagnostic, as with general, achievement tests the degree of match between the test content and the school curriculum is of concern.

In addition to these formal measures, classroom texts and books of varying interest and difficulty levels can be used to examine a child's reading. Task-analysis, diagnostic-prescriptive teaching, and trial teaching strategies provide extremely useful information on what and how to teach a child with learning problems. The relationship between assessment and psychoeducational intervention is very direct (Smith, 1980). Sewell (1979) has demonstrated that these strategies predict well to school learning. Learning disabled children often have skill deficits in work, study and attending skills, which decrease their achievement in spite of their adequate ability to learn. Their learning strategies need to be trained, and observational data, interview data, and checklists such as the Brown-Holtzman Survey of Study Habits and Attitudes (1965) may provide useful information on where to begin.

Intellectual Domain

First a word of caution. Intelligence is *not* a thing that exists as a trait or dimension within the individual. It is a construct based on performance on a wide variety of tasks. Intelligence tests are merely samples of behavior and are not exhaustive. Intelligence test scores change; they are not fixed for life. Intelligence tests do have excellent predictive validity after the preschool level for success in school work and verbal tasks (Cleary, Humphreys, Kendrick, & Wesman, 1975; Wesman, 1968). (Intellectual aspects tested at the preschool level are very different from those required in school.) The tests do not predict well an individual's ability to survive interpersonally or occupationally (Mercer, 1979; Oakland, 1980). Given their predictive validity to school learning, Mercer (1979) argues that intelligence measures are most appropriate as indices of adaptive fit to the student role in a school setting.

The Stanford Binet and the Wechsler Intelligence Scale for Children — Revised (WISC-R) are the most frequently used tests for school-aged children. While the Binet is often the standard against which other intelligence tests are compared, its 1972 revision has questionable merit (Salvia & Ysseldyke, 1978; Waddell, 1980). The test was standardized in only seven communities, the normative sample's characteristics are not described, and no data regarding the reliability and validity have appeared in the literature.

The WISC-R has good standardization, reliability, and validity. Kaufman (1979ab) has provided the most thorough set of guidelines for interpreting the WISC-R as a measure of learning potential. The WISC-R is composed of tests that tap verbal comprehension and perceptual organization abilities. When considered together with other evidence, subtests that rely on good focused attention (mental math manipulations, remembering dictated digits, rapidly copying a code) offer useful information about the child's Freedom from Distractibility (Kaufman, 1979a), generalized or test anxiety (Lutey, 1977), sequencing ability (Bannatyne, 1971, 1974), and symbolic skills (Meeker, 1969, 1975).

While subtest scatter — large discrepancies in subtest scores — has frequently been considered an index of neurological impairment and learning disabilities, Kaufman (1979ab) cautions that this scatter must be compared to that of typical children. He points out that the average verbal-performance discrepancy for typical children is 9.7 IQ points. Kaufman suggests that discrepancies and profile patterns may have educational significance (in that they may provide hypotheses for further assessment), but they do not have diagnostic significance unless the same fluctuations occur infrequently in the normal population.

Various WISC-R profiles are related to cognitive style (Keogh & Hall, 1974), spatial relations in learning disabled children (Rugel, 1974; Smith, Coleman, Dokecki, & Davis, 1977ab), and cognitive-processing in reading and learning disabled children (Das, 1973; Das, Kirby, & Jarman, 1975; Kirby & Das, 1977). Although these patterns are statistically significant for groups, they are not valid for making diagnostic statements about individuals.

Some schools use the SOMPA's (Mercer, 1979) ELP to identify gifted and learning disabled children from minority backgrounds (Reschly, 1979). As discussed earlier, this is a set of WISC-R scores corrected by knowledge of the child's sociocultural background. In this way the child's score is compared only with other children having comparable sociocultural and ethnic backgrounds. Considerable research is needed on this new measure to determine its use in the decision-making process.

Perceptual-Motor Domain

Measures in the perceptual-motor domain generally have inadequate norms, reliability, and validity. These measures are frequently used in the process-deficit model and involve inferences about hypothetical underlying information-processing deficits. Because motor problems are so frequent among the brain-injured, fine-motor measures screen for children whose learning problems can possibly be attributed to neurological problems. Although they cannot be used for individual diagnosis of neurological impairment (Eno & Deichman, 1980) or prediction of school achievement (Buckley, 1978), observations on these measures can guide programming efforts on related tasks, such as handwriting and vocational education.

Medical-Developmental Domain

It is important for evaluators to determine whether medical, sensory, or health factors are related to learning problems. They should examine medical records and gather medical and developmental histories. Informal medical and developmental history checklists are used to gather this information from knowledgeable sources (parents, doctors, nurses).

One limitation of these measures is the questionable accuracy of retrospective verbal reports about past events in the child's life. The SOMPA's Health History Inventories deal with this by presenting questions relating only to major health events. Standardized procedures for the parent interview allow the scores to be compared with a normative sample for screening purposes. The SOMPA uses the Health History Inventories, along with measures of visual and auditory acuity, physical dexterity, and the Bender Gestalt copying test, to screen for children needing further medical examination. More research is needed with these tasks in terms of the norms, relationships with medical model measures outside the SOMPA, and their use in psychoeducational decision-making.

A variety of medical-developmental screening tests and procedures are available (Connor et al., 1975; Meier, 1975). These include screening devices for visual impairment, hearing impairment, physical and neurological problems, as well as standard medical procedures such as metabolic measures and nutritional status. Neuropsychological assessment has a long history of use, primarily with adults. Its use with children is increasing rapidly. These procedures help direct and further focus the assessment and intervention processes by offering clues to the nature of the information-processing disorders underlying a learning disability (Gaddes, 1980). Their validity for educational program planning is still to be researched. Finally, examining the developmental and learning histories of the student's relatives, parents, and siblings offers important information about the relationship of the disability to heredity-environment factors and how these were dealt with by others.

Adaptive Behavior Domain

Adaptive behavior refers to how well a child fits the many roles he or she assumes in diverse settings. In a comprehensive, multidimensional assessment, evaluators are concerned with a child's adaptive fit not only to the student role, but also to nonacademic roles in and outside the school setting. In fact, PL 94–142 requires that assessment of adaptive behavior include nonschool settings. Adaptive behavior is defined as the degree to which the individual meets the standards of personal independence and social responsibility expected of his or her age and cultural group. Since these expectations vary across ages and cultures, so does the nature of adaptive behavior deficits (Grossman, 1973).

Norms, item distributions, reliabilities, and validities of such older adaptive behavior scales as the Vineland Social Maturity Scale and the AAMD Adaptive Behavior Scale — Public School Version (items are drawn from institutionalized population) are being revised and studied. The SOMPA's Adaptive Behavior Inventory for Children also has broadened evaluators' focus by assessing some nonschool role functioning. Peer sociometric scales (that get at a child's popularity) also are used to assess a child's adaptation to a specific peer group through such questions as "Name three children that you would most and least like to do a project with or invite to a party." Brown and Hammill's (1979) Behavior Rating Profile uses an alternate method by comparing ratings obtained from teachers, parents, peers, and the child. Much research is still needed on these measures.

Socioemotional Domain

Personality assessment has undergone tremendous changes over the past decade and a half. Mischel (1968, 1969, 1973, 1979) strongly challenged the assumptions of personality models that suggest problems exist solely within the individual. Very briefly, when an individual scores high on a particular personality trait, that same individual should score high on another measure of the same trait. Yet such consistency is rarely found. Instead, specific situations have important influences on personality test performance. Consequently, personality assessment now emphasizes assessment of settings and interactions of persons with settings, rather than individual traits. Viewed from this perspective, all adaptive behavior measures relate directly to a child's socioemotional functioning.

In addition to adaptive behavior, there are numerous other behavior checklists, and teacher and parent rating scales. When the measures have adequate behavioral and situational specificity, they can help evaluators develop appropriate social skills interventions. Using these measures requires careful attention to the samples on which the scales were developed, and to reliability and validity issues. Specifically, evaluators must determine how well these measures identify skill deficits and strengths in the area of socioemotional functioning. Self-concept measures can also help the evaluator understand how the child feels about him- or herself relative to school, home life, and peers.

Projective measures assume that children assign their own thoughts, feelings, needs, and motives to ambiguous, essentially neutral stimuli (inkblots, pictures, their own drawings, play activities). Children are assumed to project their own personalities into their responses. These tests often do not have norms, and have little or no evidence for reliability and validity. The underlying characteristics supposedly measured by these devices are unverifiable. Rating scales, checklists, and direct observation in naturalistic and analogue settings may provide more useful and verifiable information about how the child feels about him- or herself, relates to others, and deals with stressful and pleasant situations. Although drawing, play, and projective activities might help draw out a child who has been unresponsive to an interview and other measures, the relationship between projective assessment and intervention is remote at best.

Setting Domain

The importance of assessing settings should be obvious. Surprisingly, in spite of the need to examine settings alone, as well as a child's interactions with settings, few measures and strategies have been developed (McReynolds, 1979). Since many decisions with learning disabled children involve consideration of psychoeducational programming in multiple settings, evaluators must thoroughly understand those settings and how their structure and social climate can help the child.

Placement in any setting outside the regular classroom necessarily involves an assessment of other potential placements, to determine if it is the least restrictive educational environment. Conoley (1980) specifically suggests that comprehensive assessments should evaluate the kinds of curricula and instructional strategies used in various settings and the openness of teachers and peers to a child with learning problems.

Summary

There are a variety of purposes for conducting an assessment: screening-identification, classification-placement, psychoeducational planning, pupil evaluation, and program evaluation. These purposes influence the kinds of assessment strategies and measures used. Several different models of assessment help evaluators understand either the learner, the learner's interactions with tasks, the learner's interactions with settings, or the learner within broader sociocultural contexts. Each model has its own assessment instruments and is better suited to deal with one or another purpose for assessment. All models need to address such testing issues as reliability, validity, relevance of content, and appropriateness of comparison group. Testing with norm-referenced measures, criterion-referenced measures, or informal evaluation techniques constitutes only a portion of the assessment process. Referral forms, records, interviews, and observation in natural or analogue settings also are important to the assessment process. Comprehensive multidimensional assessment of children with learning problems is best implemented with a team approach. The team process can facilitate assessments that tap multiple domains and arrive at comprehensive intervention plans. By better understanding the characteristics of the child, the child's tasks, and the child's settings, the positive attributes of each can be matched to facilitate the child's academic, personal, and social growth.

Suggestions for Further Study

1. In 1974, the American Psychological Association, the American Educational Research Association, and the National Council on Measurement in Education issued a statement on the necessary characteristics of tests in a manual entitled *Standards for Educational and Psychological Tests*. If you eventually plan to use tests you should be familiar with this document. In choosing tests, you might consult O.K. Buros' *Mental Measurements Yearbooks'* thorough reviews of all major tests and how well they meet the necessary test criteria. Salvia and Ysseldyke (1978) thoroughly discuss test reliability, validity, and administration of standardized tests, all important guidelines to practice.

2. The task analysis model has been espoused by a number of investigators (Bijou, 1970; Gagné, 1970; Gold, 1972; Junkala, 1972, 1973; Resnick, Wang, & Kaplan, 1973). If you are engaged in any practicum work with learning disabled children, you will find these resources valuable for instructional planning.

3. The word "ecology" means much more than avoiding environmental pollution. The concept of ecology is applied to many disciplines, including sociology, psychology, education, and architecture. This general model is derived from the work of Barker (1968, 1978; Barker & Wright, 1955/1971), his students (Gump, 1978; Willems, 1973; Willems & Rausch, 1968), and others (Moos, 1973, 1975, 1976, 1979; Wahlberg, 1977; Wicker, 1979). If you are interested in working with learning disabled children in school settings, you will find the articles by Gump (1978), Moos (1979), and Wahlberg (1977) particularly relevant.

4. A recent explosion of research and interest in behavioral assessment is indicated by the appearance of articles, books, and two journals (*Behavioral Assessment* and *Journal of Behavioral Assessment*) devoted specifically to the topic (Ciminero, Calhoun, & Adams, 1977; Cone & Hawkins, 1977; Haynes, 1978; Haynes & Wilson, 1979; Hersen & Bellack, 1981; Keller, 1980a). If you are interested in nontest based assessment, any one of the above sources will be helpful.

5. Numerous conceptual and legal issues are related to bias in assessment. If you are interested, examine the following sources: Cleary, Humphreys, Kendrick, and Wesman (1975); Oakland (1977b), Flaugher (1978), Mercer (1979), Reschly (1979).

6. An incredible amount of information about children is gathered by and stored in schools. Care must be taken that information is accurate and verifiable, and that maintained information is still relevant to the child. Sharing of information from school records must take into account due process and rights to privacy. The Russell Sage Foundation (1970) provided a relevant document with which all school personnel should be familiar. It is entitled *Guidelines for the Collection, Maintenance and Dissemination of Pupil Records*. Prospective school employees will find this is very pertinent material.

7. Would you like to construct your own observational procedures for gaining information about a child you are working with? Keller (1980b) discussed various measurement issues with respect to the use of observation. Other sources describe procedures for developing observational skills (Boehm & Weinberg, 1977; Sackett, 1978a,b). Numerous sources have presented specific observation procedures that might be used in school and home settings (Alessi, 1980; Carlson et al., 1980; Haynes, 1978; Wahler, House, & Stambaugh, 1976; White, 1975). The Alessi (1980) article, in particular, describes specific procedures for establishing observational schedules and conducting systematic observation in the schools.

8. The area of adaptive behavior is an important one that only recently has received intensive attention. Federal and state mandates help focus this attention. How well does an LD child you are working with adapt to school and other settings? Coulter (1980; Coulter & Morrow, 1978) presents many measures of adaptive behavior and discusses numerous issues of measurement and values that may help you.

9. There are numerous formal and informal behavior checklists and teacher and parent rating scales. If you are involved in any practicum work with learning disabled children, these quickly administered measures can help you understand a child's strengths and skills. These measures have been reviewed by various investigators (Edelbrock, 1979; Haynes & Wilson, 1979; Walls et al., 1977; Wilson, 1980). Walls and colleagues (1977) is particularly helpful, describing over 200 checklists and rating scales.

Chapter Eleven
Planning Educational Interventions

Several general factors are involved in determining educational interventions: planning individualized instruction, defining and coordinating intervention roles, and deciding on categorical or noncategorical service delivery options. The goal of planning is to determine which teaching objectives, strategies, and environments are most likely to make demands on the student that he or she is prepared to meet. This is best accomplished by combining the information gained about the LD student from the multidimensional assessment with consideration of typical learning patterns, alternative teaching methods and materials, different instructional models, the school's human resources, and the attributes of available teaching settings.

Matching educational interventions to children's learning abilities and preferences is a highly individualized process due to the variability among learning disabled students. Many have severe skill and/or behavior deficits that make them hard to teach. Others have milder weaknesses that respond rapidly to appropriate structuring of learning tasks and settings. Still other LD youngsters seem to have no particular deficits but can only use their abilities to best advantage when taught in a personalized teaching environment. When the characteristics of educational tasks and settings match these children's perceptual, cognitive, and personality attributes, their learning and social adjustment are enhanced. The uniqueness of each child's learning patterns necessitates flexibility and creativity in an educational environment that encourages teachers to engage in an ongoing assessment and trial teaching process.

Planning Individualized Instruction

Individualized instruction tailors an educational program to a student's specific needs. It is an ongoing process by which the teacher's methods and materials are continually revised in order to provide the student with appropriate learning opportunities. Adelman (1971) describes the ideal individualized classroom program as one that:

a. allows for the wide range of developmental, motivational, and performance differences which exist in every 'classroom;
b. is compatible with the fostering of each youngster's desire to learn and perform; and
c. is designed to detect current and potential problem students and is able to correct, compensate for, and/or tolerate such deviant youngsters (p. 529).

Teachers, in consultation with other school personnel, parents, and the students themselves, are primarily responsible for developing these creative learning environments. The question that they must always ask themselves is: "how can I change the nature of the tasks that I expect my students to accomplish and the settings in which they must learn, to facilitate their progress?" They must keep in mind that success is contingent on increasing the congruity between a child's characteristics and his or her program (Adelman, 1971).

CASE STUDY:
The Animal School

Once upon a time, the animals decided they must do something heroic to meet the problems of "a new world." So they organized a school.

They adopted an activity curriculum consisting of running, climbing, swimming, and flying. To make it easier to administer the curriculum all the animals took all the subjects.

The duck was excellent in swimming, in fact better than his instructor; but he made only passing grades in flying and was very poor in running. Since he was slow in running, he had to stay after school and also drop swimming in order to practice running. This was kept up until his web feet were badly worn and he was only average in swimming. But average was acceptable in school so nobody worried about that except the duck.

The rabbit started at the top of the class in running, but had a nervous breakdown because of so much make-up work in swimming.

The squirrel was excellent in climbing until he developed frustration in the flying class where his teacher made him start from the ground up instead of from the tree top down. He also developed a "charlie horse" from over-exertion and then got C in climbing and D in running.

The eagle was a problem child and was disciplined severely. In the climbing class he beat all the others to the top of the tree, but insisted on using his own way to get there.

At the end of the year, an abnormal eel that could swim exceedingly well, and also run, climb, and fly a little, had the highest average and was valedictorian.

The prairie dogs stayed out of school and fought the tax levy because the administration would not add digging and burrowing to the curriculum. They apprenticed their children to a badger and later joined the groundhogs and gophers to start a successful private school.

SOURCE: Reavis, G. H. "The Animal School." *Educational Forum*, vol. 17:2, 1953, p. 141. Reprinted by permission of Kappa Delta Pi Honor Society in Education.

The "Animal School" story above humorously illustrates what can happen when child and program characteristics are mismatched. Like the animals, when a child must learn something that he or she is not ready to learn, or learn it in a way that is not natural, the child is apt to fail. This failure experience may in turn affect achievement in other academic and social areas as well. Important aspects of individualized instruction include the individualized education program, diagnostic-prescriptive teaching, instructional models, and choice of materials.

The Individualized Education Program

Following the multidisciplinary assessment process and determination that a child is learning disabled, PL 94-142 requires that the student receive an Individualized Education Program (IEP). The specific nature of the program is set down in a written IEP statement developed and reviewed annually by the child's parents or guardians, the child's special education teacher (or regular

Table 11-1 Individual Education Plan

Student _____
Date of Birth _____
Parents or Guardian _____
Address _____
Telephone _____
School _____ Grade _____
Present Placement _____
Date of Program Entry _____
Handicapping Condition _____
The committee has reviewed all pertinent data and determined that the following placement will be recommended:
Total % of Time: Regular Class _____ Special Education _____
Hours Per Week of Special Education _____

Date of Meeting _____

Participants in Meeting
Representative of School district _____
Child's teacher(s) _____
Child's parents(s) _____
Professional (skilled in assessment of the disability) _____
Other Individuals (identify) _____

NAME   ROLE
_____   _____
_____   _____
_____   _____
_____   _____

Date of Next Annual Review _____
Date of Next Reevaluation _____

Present Levels of Performance	LEARNING STRENGTHS/ STYLES	LEARNING WEAKNESSES/ STYLES
Intelligence		
Word Recognition		
Reading Comprehension		
Spelling		
Written Expression		
Math		
General Information		
Penmanship		
Coordination		
Visual-Perceptual Skills		
Language		
Social-Emotional Adaptation		
Other(s)		

Specific Special Education Assignments
Specific Regular Class Assignments

ANNUAL GOALS	SHORT TERM OBJECTIVES	SPECIFIC EDUCATIONAL SERVICES, MATERIALS, AND TEACHING STRATEGIES	EVALUATION CRITERIA AND PROCEDURES	DATES		STAFF RESPONSIBILITIES	
				BEGIN	END	NAME	POSITION

Academic and Social Objectives

class teacher if the child is not taught by a special education teacher), an administrative representative of the school who is qualified to provide for or supervise special education programming (principal, pupil personnel director), the student (when possible), and other personnel where appropriate. The IEP should include:

1. the child's present level of educational performance
2. a statement of annual goals (for example, attain a second grade reading competency)
3. a statement of short-term objectives (such as master consonant sounds, long and short vowel sounds, and blends; increase sight vocabulary)
4. the specific educational services to be provided and by whom (such as resource room for one hour per day, speech therapy twice weekly)
5. specification of materials and methods to be used and why
6. specific objective evaluation criteria and timeline for determining whether instructional objectives are being achieved
7. projected dates for initiation of services and their expected duration
8. the extent to which the child will participate in the regular educational program and extent of participation in the least restrictive environment.

Each school district may develop its own IEP format, as long as it includes this information. A representative IEP form is reprinted in Table 11-1 on the previous two pages. The report of the multidisciplinary team offers a good starting point for writing the IEP. The evaluation report in Table 11-2, beginning on page 354, illustrates how program planning is facilitated by an appropriate, multidimensional, educationally relevant evaluation.

Besides goals, methods and materials, many considerations with respect to the physical, organizational and human characteristics of settings need to be addressed during the IEP process. Chapter 15 explores these issues, stressing that before a child's IEP specifies particular placements, the educational and social advantages and disadvantages of particular settings for children with differing abilities, educational and social needs, backgrounds, goals, and so forth need to be carefully weighed. Physical aspects of settings that need to be considered include the presence of visual and auditory distractions as well as type of school and classroom design (open space, furniture arrangements, large or small school, seating arrangements, pleasantness of surroundings). Organizational considerations include a flexible continuum of educational services to provide for children's changing and diverse educational needs.

As the number, nature and severity of a child's learning disabilities increase, so does the likelihood of placement in settings that permit fewer interactions with typical peers. Placement options, from least to most segregated and specialized, include:

1. full-time regular class with the general education teacher providing an appropriately personalized environment

2. full-time regular class with the teacher receiving consultation from an LD or other specialist
3. full-time regular class with direct tutoring received several times weekly from an itinerant LD or other specialist
4. part-time regular class with one to three hours daily in a resource room or learning center
5. part-time regular class and part-time special class
6. full-time special class
7. removal from home school to a special class in another building
8. special public or private school
9. residential setting

Other organizational considerations include ascertaining whether the way in which particular teachers organize instruction matches a student's learning style (such as teacher-directed versus open-choice), and whether the organizational structure is flexible enough to ease reintegration into more typical settings.

The teacher and peer characteristics of settings are also extremely important to assess. The teacher is a far more important element in the teaching process than any single method or material. Teachers have different teaching styles just as learners have varying learning styles. When these styles match, there is an overall benefit to the student. For example, when the teacher prefers to teach in large groups, a child who works best in a smaller group setting does not benefit maximally from this teacher's approach. An impulsive teacher might bombard some students with more information than they can comfortably handle, and inadequately model reflectivity.

The teacher chosen must have a positive attitude toward special children, and his or her attitudes and behaviors must not be negatively biased by the child's sex, social class, race, or low achievement. The quality of the teacher-student relationship is critical to building student motivation, self-concept, interest in learning, and participation in honestly evaluating one's progress and planning future instructional directions and materials. The peer group must be age-appropriate, accepting, provide a good model, and be one into which the student is likely to be able to integrate successfully. Consideration of these factors enhances the likelihood that the placement choices will facilitate the learning disabled youngster's academic, social, and emotional development.

When the team decides to integrate a student into a regular classroom, the student's skills must be compatible with the existing instructional opportunities in that class. To illustrate, when the nonhandicapped students in a class are working on fractions, the IEP for an LD student present during that time period should include fractions as a short-term objective. The schedule must be carefully planned so that the LD student is in the regular class for periods when he or she can derive most benefit and enjoyment, and in the resource or special classroom during regular class activities that are inappropriate. The regular

Table 11-2 Evaluation report

Name: Marcy R.
Birthdate: February 13, 1967
Age: 14 years, 2 months
Grade: 6

Reason for Referral

Marcy was referred for evaluation because it had been three years since her previous assessment. Both her teachers and parents continued to be concerned about her spelling difficulty.

Personal Information

Marcy is the eighth of nine children. Her older brother and her younger sister, Patsy, have also experienced learning difficulties. Patsy presently attends the same learning disability resource room as Marcy.

Mr. R. reports having difficulty, even as an adult, with reading and writing. He completed a fifth grade education, quitting school to work with his family in the coal mines. Mrs. R. graduated from high school, having experienced no significant learning problems.

Mrs. R. reported no complications during her pregnancy with Marcy, and termed her birth "easy." Marcy weighed over eight pounds at birth.

Learning problems were first recognized by her parents when Marcy failed second grade in her School District. Mrs. R. also noted that she couldn't get Marcy to read at home. Despite repeating the grade, she continued to have difficulty in reading, spelling and math. Marcy's attendance record was poor, and the R.'s felt she was singled out for being in the learning disability resource room. Due to the family's growing dissatisfaction with the school system, the family moved their residence to a neighboring school district.

Though the social and general academic climate was felt to be better in the second system, Marcy continued to experience severe learning difficulties and repeated fifth grade. Her poor attendance and low achievement, however, were attributed to poor health.

Marcy's school adjustment is much improved this year. Her parents attribute this to her present learning disability teacher, with whom Marcy is said to have an excellent relationship. Marcy attends the resource room for small group instruction in reading and math. She now does her homework on her own. Her parents report that her behavior, attitude, and reading skills have greatly improved this year.

School Information

Math and spelling instruction are provided by the resource room teacher. Marcy has shown difficulty in mastery of multiplication facts, and in interpreting story problems. She is currently using Developmental Learning Material for math instruction, supplemented by practice sheets taken from the Prentice-Hall series.

The Continuous Progress series is used for Marcy's spelling instruction. In this program, clusters of words with similar sounds are introduced weekly, and Marcy is required to memorize a new unit each week. Past attempts to work on spelling have included use of word configurations for visual recognition, and use of a dictionary to check spelling. Neither of these approaches has been successful. Marcy does attempt to break words into syllables and spell phonetically, though she has not been greatly successful using this strategy.

Marcy's reading instruction, social studies, and science are provided in her 6th grade homeroom class. She is in a reading group with three other students, and they are working in a grade level reader.

Mrs. W., the homeroom teacher, reports that Marcy participates in social studies or science if no independent reading is required. Her time spent in special classes detracts from time in these subject areas. Therefore, Marcy often receives filmstrips independently and writes summaries of their content for her social studies and science lessons.

Marcy receives speech services twice a week. She has attended speech class since the second grade, primarily to clear up an "R" distortion. Working on spontaneous speech has been another goal of speech therapy, as Marcy frequently pauses during conversations, as if to organize her thoughts in mid-sentence.

Speech instruction is provided in a small group of students. Marcy works well in the group, according to the speech therapist.

Table 11-2   continued

Marcy seems to have reached a plateau in her speech progress. Although she has shown little progress in her articulation, Marcy asked to continue in the therapy program. Thus, the speech sessions are primarily supportive in nature in order to build on her prior success and maintain self-confidence.

All three of Marcy's teachers report that she is an extremely motivated student. She is able to work well independently, recognizes her difficulties, and is often able to judge her capabilities on a given task.

Marcy has a very good vocabulary, and her language skills are above average for a girl of her age. She displays maturity in both her written and oral expression. Marcy enjoys creative writing, though her spelling often impedes the readability of her written work.

The two year age difference between Marcy and her classmates, as well as her learning difficulties have served to differentiate her from the other children. While she is in the regular class, she often works with the teacher aid on a one-to-one basis, or independently on her own assignments. Thus, Marcy is separated academically and physically from the group. Mrs. R. mentioned that Marcy was chosen to participate in a Christmas play which gave her the opportunity to work with other girls in her class. She responded well to this interaction even though she did not initiate the involvement. Since that time, she has not been volunteered or appointed to participate in such activities.

Past assessment results indicated that Marcy's intelligence was within average ranges (WISC-R Verbal IQ 103, performance IQ 93, and Full Scale IQ 98). Her understanding of vocabulary on the Peabody Picture Vocabulary Test exceeded that of a sixteen year old, yet reading, spelling and arithmetic achievement ranged between second and third grade levels.

Assessment Results

Tests of reading, spelling, auditory and math abilities were given to evaluate Marcy's academic and language processing skills.

Reading

The Standard Reading Inventory (SRI) was administered to assess Marcy's word recognition, comprehension and speed of reading. In attempts to establish an independent or easy level of oral reading, Marcy was asked to read passages ranging from the primer to seventh grade levels. Her word recognition score represented errors of word substitutions, repetitions and self corrections and indicated frustration level on the early 1st grade passage.

Marcy's approach to reading words seemed to rely mainly on sight recognition and context clues. Unfamiliar words were analyzed using their first and sometimes last letters. This often resulted in real word substitutions, which she correctly or incorrectly adjusted to fit the context of the passage. Her strategy appeared to employ little systematic word attack of the letters and word parts.

Speed of reading was at instructional levels on the primer through second grade passages. Reading speed dropped to the frustration range on more difficult reading levels.

Marcy's comprehension was at an independent level for sixth grade passages. Thus, she was able to understand and remember the content of the stories, even though she had extreme difficulty in correctly reading the words.

Boder Diagnostic Word List

Graded word lists were presented to Marcy to assess sight word recognition. Marcy recognized 82 percent of the words instantly at the second grade level, and worked up to the sixth grade level, where she recognized approximately 37 percent of the words. Marcy's most common approach was to read the first sound or syllable correctly, then inserting, substituting, or omitting medial and final sounds. This pattern was exemplified in reading "pilot" for plot, "muscle" for musical, and "sheriffed" for shifted.

The Gallistel-Ellis (GE) Test of Coding Skills measured Marcy's ability to recognize the sounds for various letters, units or clusters in reading. A score of 80 percent to 100 percent in any category is considered relative mastery.

(Continued on following page)

Table 11-2   continued

Marcy scored the following: 84 percent closed syllables with single consonants, e.g.: can; 80 percent closed syllables with consonant combinations, e.g.: chest; 100 percent irregular words, e.g.: one. All other scores ranged between 72 percent and 40 percent. Therefore, Marcy has much better skill in sight word recognition than decoding.

Choral Reading

A graded passage from the *Silvaroli Informal Reading Inventory* was selected for a four step choral reading lesson: (1) The examiner read the passage aloud; (2) the examiner and Marcy read the passage together, with the examiner's voice more dominant; (3) the passage was read together again, with Marcy's voice more dominant; and (4) Marcy read the passage alone. Notes were made of the words with which Marcy had the most difficulty. Several hours later, she was asked to read these nine words out of the context of the paragraph. She did so with 100 percent accuracy. She then read the entire paragraph independently making two minor errors.

Spelling

Boder Diagnostic Spelling Procedure

Two lists of words were compiled, assessing Marcy's ability to spell words from dictation. The "known" list consisted of third, fourth and fifth grade words, the levels at which she had instantly recognized at least fifty percent of the isolated words. Her score, 40 percent, indicated poor ability to correctly spell words which are in her sight reading vocabulary.

The "unknown" word list was from grades five and six, the two levels above the "known" words. Her score was 34 percent. This indicated her poor ability to analyze words so as to write good phonetic approximations.

These scores indicate that Marcy is having difficulty using both phonetic and whole word methods as a spelling strategy.

The Gallistel-Ellis (GE) Test of Coding Skills has a spelling component which follows the word patterns used in the reading test.

Marcy was asked to spell words which she had read correctly during a previous session.

She had the most success on one syllable words with long vowels, or with vowel-r combinations. Multi-syllabic and common irregular words were more difficult. Although Marcy read 100 percent of these irregular words correctly, she spelled only 30 percent correctly.

On both the informal Boder method and the GE test, Marcy exhibited a wide variety of errors. She made errors in medial and ending places, in consonant blends and consonant-vowel-consonant combinations, and in phonetic and nonphonetic words. She was consistent, however, in beginning the word correctly. On many of the multi-syllable words, her spellings were missing a third or fourth syllable.

The Spelling subtest from the *Peabody Individual Achievement Test* was used to determine Marcy's skill in discriminating a correctly spelled word from four choices. Marcy's performance was comparable to a 3.5 grade level and was in the fourth percentile for her age. Therefore, both recognition and expression are weaknesses.

Auditory Perception

Several formal and informal measures were used to determine Marcy's skills in the area of auditory perception and processing. In the *Test of Auditory Discrimination and Auditory Vocal Repetition*, by Freer, Baldi, and Noblett, the examiner read off pairs of words and asked Marcy to tell if the words were the same or different. In a variation of this task, she was asked to repeat the word pairs. Marcy had only three errors on these eighty items, which is normal for a girl of her age.

The Auditory Closure subtest of the *Illinois Test of Psycholinguistic Abilities* tested Marcy's ability to recognize words spoken by the examiner which had consonant sounds omitted. Marcy's score was twenty-eight correct out of thirty, which again was an adequate score for her age.

Short-term auditory memory was compared to visual memory using *The Visual Aural Digit Span Test* (VADS). The VADS has four subtests: 1) the examiner read a series of digits and Marcy repeated them orally; 2) the

Table 11-2   continued

digits were presented on a card and Marcy repeated them orally; 3) the digits were spoken and Marcy wrote them; 4) the digits were presented on a card and Marcy wrote them. The same procedure was repeated with letters instead of digits. For both letters and digits Marcy was stronger on visual tasks than auditory tasks. She did best on the tasks where she had visual stimuli with a written response; here she scored in the fiftieth percentile compared to other thirteen year olds. Her score for auditory input with an oral response was the lowest, in the tenth percentile.

The Auditory-Motor Evaluation from Rosner's *Perceptual Skills Curriculum* is a hierarchy of auditory tasks working from recognizing rhythmic patterns up to substitution of speech sounds within a word. The skills tapped by this hierarchy are usually developed by age seven.

Marcy passed some items on each of the eight levels. She made several errors determining the number of syllables in compound words. For example, she broke the word motorcycle into two syllables, "motor/cycle." Analyzing the sounds in consonant blends was difficult for Marcy, as she omitted and substituted the sounds making up the blends. When saying *Boston* and *bushel* she named "bushel as the word with the "s" sound, and when given the word *snow* and asked to say *sow*, she identified "o" as the sound which had been omitted."

The ability to identify a spoken word as a series of smaller sounds was tapped using the Auditory Blending subtest from the *Woodcock-Johnson Psychoeducational Battery: Part One: Tests of Cognitive Ability*. Marcy correctly identified thirteen of the twenty-five items, showing difficulty with words that were broken into phonemes, or the basic speech sounds. Selected items were readministered informally during a later session to assess Marcy's strategy in attacking the words and to determine which word parts she could remember. On this subsequent testing, she corrected six of her previous errors, but did not master three other items. She did not remember all of the speech sounds when asked to

repeat them; for example, when the word pretend was spoken as a series of eight phonemes, Marcy recalled only, "/p/-/ĕ/-/n/-/d/."

The Lindamood Auditory Conceptualization (LAC) Test required Marcy to manipulate colored wooden blocks indicating how many sounds were heard, whether they were the same or different, and the sequential order of the sounds. In Category I, isolated sounds were presented in sequence. Category II evaluated sounds within syllable patterns.

Marcy achieved a perfect score on the 16 items in Category I. However, of the twelve items in Category II, she gave only seven correct responses. She made errors on the following tasks: substituting vowels, e.g., *ap* to *op;* deleting initial consonants, e.g., *pap* to *ap;* adding final consonants, e.g., *vop* to *vaps;* and reordering consonant sounds, e.g., *ups* to *usp.* Her total score equaled the recommended minimum score for second grade.

One week later Marcy was retested using Form B. At this time, she correctly answered ten of the twelve items. Her errors were in reordering of consonant sounds, and adding initial consonants, e.g., *asp* to *sasp.* Her total score on Form B was between third and fourth grade.

The Language Structured Auditory Retention Span Test was administered. This test assessed Marcy's ability to accurately repeat sentences of increasing length and complexity. She scored within the 15 to 18 year age range, well above expected for her age.

Mathematics

The primary tool used to assess Marcy's skill in mathematics was the *Keymath Diagnostic Arithmetic Test*. Marcy showed a wide spread in the fourteen skills tested, ranging from third grade to above ninth grade level. Her highest score was on the Missing Elements subtest, where Marcy was given an incomplete story problem and asked what information would be needed to solve the problem. Other areas of strength were the Word Problems subtest, and the Time subtest (both 5.3-grade level), where Marcy verbally

(Continued on following page)

Table 11-2   continued

answered questions dealing with time, seasons, and calendar use.

Marcy's weakest performance was on the Subtraction subtest, where she worked out written subtraction problems. Her errors were in borrowing, where she subtracted the subtrahend sum from the minuend (top from the bottom). The Addition, Multiplication, Mental Computation, Numerical Reasoning, and Measurement subtests were all at the lower fourth grade level, and the remainder of the subtests were at the fifth grade level.

An informal set of arithmetic problems and story problems supplemented the results of the Keymath test and also gave an opportunity to explore Marcy's problem-solving strategies. Marcy understood the concepts of borrowing, even on difficult problems with zeros in the sum (e.g., 101–99).

Multiplication proved to be a more difficult operation for Marcy. She has not mastered the multiplication facts, as evidenced by her response to "How much is eight times three?" Marcy attempted to count up to eight three times, by keeping a cumulative sum, and even then gave three incorrect responses.

Marcy understood the concept of carrying and applied it successfully, but had difficulties in problems with two two-digit factors. Marcy neglected to put a zero in the one's place when she began to multiply the ten's place, she forgot to multiply each numeral in the first factor, and she did not align her subproducts for summing.

Several strategies were consistently applied by Marcy in solving story problems. She was able to identify "key words" which clued her to which operations to use. She tried to subtract one answer without writing it down, but forgot to borrow. Several numerals or operations presented as words (e.g., "eight" or "divide") were misread by Marcy, changing the meaning of the problem.

Based on Marcy's errors, the examiner created a checklist of steps to follow and things to remember for multiplication. Marcy referred to this checklist and applied it to subsequent problems. Another successful strategy was for Marcy to verbalize her work.

Written Expression

Marcy was asked to write a short story which was analyzed for grammar, penmanship, and style. She selected a topic from pictures which appear on the *School Apperception Test*.

Marcy's story consisted of five sentences divided into two paragraphs, and a title to introduce the topic. Her use of compound sentences, conjunctions to join these sentences, and introductory and concluding sentences are all writing skills at or above her grade level. She did have one run-on sentence, which should have been divided by a period into two separate thoughts.

The plot of her story was fairly well developed. Marcy's character expressed regret over having misbehaved in school, and the story was titled appropriately.

Marcy's penmanship was legible, though the readability of her essay was marred by her poor spelling skills. She misspelled twenty words in her sixty-four word composition.

To compare Marcy's oral expression with her written expression, she was asked to select another picture and to tell the examiner her story. The second story was also well-developed in content and syntax.

Discussion

Marcy demonstrates a severe disability in recognizing, segmenting, and sequencing sounds beneath the word level. This is evident in reading, spelling, and auditory processing tasks. Marcy is able to make good use of meaningful language in words and sentence structures. Her memory for sentences, comprehension, and auditory closure skills are excellent. These are skills which deal with words as wholes, or gestalts. Severe obstacles are present, however, in analyzing, sequencing, and blending of sound and syllable units.

Marcy had trouble breaking words down into syllables, and breaking syllables down into separate sounds. She showed difficulty in remembering the sequence of sounds within a word or word part, and in reblending the separate sounds to form a word.

Table 11–2   continued

Storytelling, both oral and written, is a strength for Marcy. She utilizes her strong vocabulary and presents the information in a well-organized, coherent fashion.

Perceptual and auditory processing deficiencies underlie Marcy's difficulties in reading and spelling. She does not presently possess the auditory perceptual skills necessary for transfer onto the printed word in reading, spelling, and word attack skills.

Marcy did not achieve instructional level on any of the graded reading passages because of word recognition errors. Her method of trying out words in context is time-consuming, penalizing her reading accuracy and fluency. Her spelling performance is hindered as well by her inability to use the various sound and syllable patterns. Her comprehension, oral vocabulary and auditory closure skills mask the effort and frustration involved in these tasks.

Mathematics is another area where Marcy's strengths are masking underlying weaknesses. She comprehends the processes involved in addition, subtraction, and multiplication. She is able to apply these processes to story problems, and uses a consistent approach in identifying key words and operations.

However, Marcy makes computation errors in reading the operation, subtracting or multiplying numbers in the correct sequence, and aligning numbers in proper columns. She does not use methods for checking herself and detecting such errors. Rote memorization of multiplication facts also presents problems. Marcy uses a combination of addition and counting instead of automatic recall of multiplication facts. This process takes additional time and allows for more errors.

Throughout the four evaluation sessions Marcy was cooperative, determined, and hard-working. She was attentive and did her best, but she seemed to be tense and nervous, even at the last session. She responded to conversation, but did not initiate it. Her responses were short and spoken in a quiet voice.

This determination is a strength for Marcy, but beneath the determination, Marcy demonstrates anxiety about her academic performance.

Recommendations

The coordinated effort between the regular, resource, and speech teachers, already in progress, is suggested. This effort mutually facilitates Marcy's reading, spelling, listening, and social skills. Primary goals for Marcy are developing auditory analysis skills, reading and spelling through whole word approaches and continuing to make the progress in social and content areas that we know she is capable of.

Due to Marcy's difficulties with sound patterns, the resource teacher could provide reading drills using a word family approach. The Glass Analysis Approach and the *GFB Sequence of Objectives for Teaching and Testing Reading* are two examples of this approach. Rules for recognizing word structures are derived from lists for each sound pattern.

Spelling drills could parallel reading word-attack drills. The *GFB Sequence of Objectives for Teaching and Testing Spelling* provides spelling lists which are coordinated with the GFB reading component. Informal lists of spelling patterns could also be derived by the resource teacher.

To address Marcy's auditory recognition and sequencing difficulties, the speech therapist could utilize portions of the *Rosner Perceptual Skills Curriculum, Program II: Auditory Motor Skills*. Level E of this program focuses on the identification and analysis of syllable units in words.

Marcy's participation in her regular class reading group should be continued. This offers opportunities for positive social interaction as well as opportunities for Marcy to demonstrate her vocabulary, comprehension, and oral expression skills.

The Choral method used during the evaluation could be implemented in many subject areas. Social studies, science or language arts lessons could be read with Marcy, or put on tape, so that she could follow the text as she hears the material. Other students may either read the text or listen to the tape with her.

(Continued on following page)

Table 11-2   continued

Additional activities which offer academic as well as social benefits in the regular classroom include: (1) creative writing, where students collaborate on writing stories or reports; (2) vocabulary exercises for synonyms and antonyms; (3) social studies projects; and (4) science experiments. These activities could be directed by the teacher or by the teacher aide.

Remedial activities in math can be provided in the resource room with some additional drill done as homework. A variety of methods could be used for Marcy's mastery of multiplication facts: (1) practice counting by 6's, for example, filling in the blanks in a number line sequence; (2) multiplication grids can be created by Marcy for number sets she has not mastered. She could use these grids to solve multiplication or division problems. Once she has mastered a set of facts, that set could be removed; (3) The times tables facts could be put on the language master cards. This could be a self-checking method, with the answer given on the "teacher" channel of the tape strip; (4) a card game, multiplying the numbers shown on the faces of two drawn cards, would allow Marcy to drill the facts with another student.

The use of visual cues could aid Marcy in following a sequence of steps in multiplication. Model problems, with the particular digits used in each step highlighted, can serve to illustrate the sequence of steps for Marcy to follow.

a)   215
    × 83

b)   215
    × 83

c)   215
    × 83

d)   215
    × 83

e)   215
    × 83

f)   215
    × 83

g)   215
    × 83

Problem areas, such as failure to insert a zero before multiplyig by the ten's place, could be highlighted in red ink by Marcy as she solves the problem.

Another visual cue to assist Marcy in aligning her multiplication problems into proper columns is to do her problems on lined paper. She would turn the paper ninety degrees, so that the lines run vertically on the page, providing a ready-made column.

As Marcy seemed to benefit from verbalizing the processes as she solved arithmetic problems, this method is suggested as a means for Marcy to organize her work. She could work in a study carrel in the resource room, so as not to disturb other students.

Marcy could benefit from a procedure whereby she attacks problems in a systematic method and checks her work at each point in the sequence. A written check list of the steps involved in the arithmetic problem could be prepared for each type of problem (subtraction with borrowing, two-digit multiplication, etc.). Thus Marcy would have an outline of the important steps, and can mark off each step as it is completed correctly.

Anyone working with Marcy needs to be sensitive to the number and type of mistakes she makes in her written work. For example, her method of copying work needs to be observed to determine if she copies letter by letter or attempts to copy whole words. Determining the method she uses would help prevent her from making the mistake many times over.

It is essential that the many good features of Marcy's program be continued. Communication with the resource teacher at the Junior High, before the actual start of school, would greatly aid in Marcy's transition. She has already expressed some concern and anxiety about the change. Strengthening her social and academic skills now, and an orientation to the school and her future teachers may help her feel more confident about the future.

classroom and special education teachers must regularly plan, coordinate, and evaluate a student's program to aid the LD child's successful integration into the regular classroom and to assure common or complementary teaching objectives, methods, and materials.

Many professionals complain that the IEP is cumbersome to complete. Teachers report that, although they are involved in writing IEPs, they seldom consult them until the next annual IEP review (Pugach, 1982). Although the IEP can serve as a guide to instruction and an index of progress toward meeting instructional objectives, it unfortunately usually serves only a broad, administrative purpose. It can establish and monitor quantity and place of teaching, but not quality. The latter is determined by the teacher's ability, willingness, and time to engage in ongoing diagnostic-prescriptive teaching.

Diagnostic-Prescriptive Teaching

The daily classroom process by which teachers systematically try out instructional hypotheses gained from the multidisciplinary assessment is called *diagnostic-prescriptive* or *clinical* teaching. The teacher uses the assessment's conclusions and the IEP's program objectives to help with the eight steps involved in diagnostic-prescriptive teaching:

1. Objectively observe and analyze the student's classroom abilities.
2. Objectively observe and analyze the nature of the student's successes and difficulties on different types of tasks.
3. Scrutinize the characteristics of alternative tasks and settings.
4. Compare and contrast how information gained from step (3) might interact with the observations in steps (2) and (1) so as to result in more favorable achievement.
5. Consult with the student whenever possible, present the choices for modification, and decide together which ones to try.
6. Set short-term goals.
7. Make the modifications and teach.
8. Evaluate progress after a reasonable time interval; if successful, continue teaching similar but higher-level objectives; if unsuccessful retrace steps 1–7.

Clinical teaching is essentially a continuous test-teach-test process that can be used in any classroom setting. Consider the differences in outcome demonstrated by the following anecdotes when teachers do or do not use a diagnostic-prescriptive approach.

> *Ms. Harrison* — It's the third week in September and Peter still isn't paying attention. He's always daydreaming. I'm just going to make him move up closer to my desk. Then he'll have to concentrate. (The area around Ms. Harrison's desk is the busiest spot in the classroom.)
> *Ms. Dipkin* — During several periods of observation I've noticed that Lynda taps her pencil and frequently gazes at classmates while her work

remains unfinished. I asked Lynda if moving to a study carrel until her work is finished would be helpful. We decided it would be.

Ms. Dipkin's approach appropriately determines what requires modification. She observes precisely what behaviors Lynda is engaging in instead of attending to her work. She decides that a change in setting would eliminate distractions by Lynda's classmates. She then consults with Lynda, and the study carrel becomes a joint decision. Lynda's inattention is likely to be resolved.

Ms. Harrison did not objectively delineate what she meant by "daydreaming," so she did not know whether Peter's inattention was due to being distracted by his classmates, overwhelmed by too many ditto sheets, unable to follow her instructions or some other cause. She decided that the problem was in the setting, but did not analyze the distracting elements of the new setting relative to Peter's inattentiveness. She also did not enlist his cooperation in solving the problem. Peter's inattention is not likely to be resolved this time around.

Teddy's case also illustrates how important the clinical teaching process is to instructional decisions and the generalizations made from performance on one task to another. His multidisciplinary assessment concluded that seven-year-old Teddy was delayed in expressive language skills. He was unable to name letters of the alphabet other than those that appeared in his name. Learning letter names and sounds was one of the annual goals listed on Teddy's IEP.

Teddy's teacher was confused because she found that he could repeat letter sounds and match and copy letters accurately, but couldn't seem to remember them. She then task-analyzed "letter naming," and found that Teddy did remember a great deal about letter names. His problem was that he remembered in a different way from the way the teacher was asking him to remember. That is, when the teacher named letters for him and he was asked to point to them, Teddy demonstrated 100 percent accuracy. His difficulty seemed related to retrieval of isolated sounds from memory.

This task analysis of letter naming suggested that the teacher should experiment with methods that paired Teddy's weaker naming skills with his stronger motor expression and visual/auditory reception skills. The teacher pursued her diagnostic-prescriptive teaching by having Teddy draw, trace, paste, construct, and copy letters as she named them and as he repeated their names. Since Teddy could distinguish the sounds of initial consonants in each word well, the teacher tried relating the letter form to a word that began with the same letter and also had its shape. "Snake" begins with an "sss" sound, a snake can be shaped into an "s," and the letter "s" can be superimposed on it. This method seemed to work well. When seeing letters that he had been taught, Teddy seemed to rely on that visual image to discern the word's initial consonant sound and then translate this into the letter name. As his degree of mastery of letter names increased, his retrieval efficiency also increased. Teddy was not introduced to phonetic reading until he became more proficient in retrieving the sounds of letters. Instead, he was taught to compensate for his disability by learning to recognize words by sight from their visual configurations.

Could Teddy's teacher assume that he would be a poor auditory retriever on all tasks and therefore always need to go through such elaborate teaching modifications? No. We cannot generalize from one task to another. We must test our assumptions out all over again, but this time we have more clues to follow. How was Teddy at naming his numerals? Excellent. When the teacher flashed the numerals 1 through 9, he was able to name each in two seconds or less. Why the discrepancy? Perhaps numerals are more meaningful to Teddy than letter names; after all, one apple is one real thing, whereas an "s" refers to nothing real. Maybe Teddy needs all tasks to be extremely meaningful, which explains why he did best when the "s" shape was embedded in a snake. Perhaps Teddy finds nine numerals easier to master than twenty-six letters. The teacher could test out the latter hypothesis by reducing the number of letter names that she expects Teddy to master at any one time. In clinical teaching, hunches gained from one set of circumstances actually are tried out on another set, to avoid errors from unwarranted generalizations.

As another example of the need for ongoing diagnostic-prescriptive teaching, consider Teddy four years later. These are some of the strength/weaknesses patterns suggested by his three-year reevaluation, and a few of the plans outlined in his IEP.

- □ Strengths: naming numerals; math boardwork
- □ Weaknesses: recognizing words rapidly and sounding out new words; reading and math homework
- □ Remediation Objective: reading
- □ Remediation Method: teaching word families
- □ Compensation: eliminating reading from math homework assignments; ensuring suitable reading level in science and social studies assignments

Teddy had been held back a grade once and is now in a fifth-grade classroom. He is being instructed in reading at a beginning third-grade level and is progressing well in a series that teaches reading through word families (sat, bat). Math, always a strength for him, is suddenly becoming troublesome. Teddy can solve the multiplication problems that the teacher drills on the blackboard, but his homework papers contain many errors on similar types of math operations. A comparison of the boardwork and homework assignments shows that the latter depend on independent reading of directions and word problems, whereas the boardwork does not. Eliminating the need to read independently, by having Teddy's parents read the problems and directions to him, helped him achieve well in math once again. Teddy's teachers wondered whether all reading should be eliminated in science and social studies assignments as well. When they explored this question, teachers found that the social studies materials he was expected to read were indeed too difficult. The science assignments, however, were all independent experiments, and Teddy was handling this situation well. To do these projects Teddy had unknowingly enlisted the librarian's aid in directing him to books that were short and easy.

Clearly, the diagnostic-prescriptive teaching process involves a good deal of clinical intuition and guesswork, a skill that comes with adequate clinical training and many years of teaching experience. The teacher's way of analyzing student needs, matching tasks accordingly, and deciding among instructional and service delivery options may reflect several instructional models.

Instructional Models

The exact nature of teachers' instructional plans may follow several schools of thought that have characterized the learning disabilities field. The most prominent among these are the developmental, behavioral, and underlying process training viewpoints. Each differs from the other on the question of what should be taught.

The developmentalists follow a maturational lag perspective of learning disorders. They advocate teaching objectives along academic hierarchies, but only those that the student is absolutely ready to master. They maintain that children's cognitive growth proceeds in invariant stages. These stages must be passed through in an orderly fashion, each stage readying the child for the next. Mastering lower-level components of higher-level skills are the first steps toward academic progress. In contrast behaviorists believe that when tasks are appropriately structured and reinforced, even skills that the child is not entirely prepared to understand can be mastered.

The underlying process trainers stress that efficient acquisition of higher-level skills cannot occur until the deficits are remediated. They therefore advocate continued academic instruction while spending a good deal of time on shoring up the weaknesses (Bannatyne, 1971; Frostig, 1980; Hallahan & Cruickshank, 1973). At times these weaknesses are logical components of academic hierarchies (learning to listen to the order of sounds in words so as to aid decoding), and at other times they are not (locating sounds in space, trampolining, finding figures among confusing visual backgrounds). Many process-oriented individuals urge that teaching should occur primarily through the child's stronger modalities, such as visual or auditory information-processing (Johnson & Myklebust, 1967; Sabatino & Hayden, 1970; Wepman, 1967).

In the classroom, these different instructional models are often combined to varying degrees. New skills generally are taught through the student's stronger modalities while weaknesses also are built up in tasks that logically lie along academic skill hierarchies. The child's stronger ways of processing information are used to enhance learning in the weaker areas. Teachers can't justify only reconstructing deficit areas and not teaching new, higher-level material. They also can't justify teaching new material that a child's strengths enable him to learn, and ignoring the weaknesses.

The skills taught in stronger and weaker areas are those that children are ready to learn. Practice continues at one level before the child moves on to the next higher objective. Such teaching takes less time and results in less learning of errors than when the child is forced to learn things he or she is not ready to understand (Kinsbourne & Caplan, 1979). At times, however, instruction must be "forced," as when teachers initially get students to the next step on a skill hierarchy or when they teach the severely learning disabled, such as the adult who can't read beyond the second-grade level and must develop some critical reading skills: road signs, bus directions, using the telephone directory, passing the written portion of a driver's exam, filling out a job application.

Behavioral principles are commonly used for optimally structuring learning materials and methods. These principles include:

□ systematically reinforcing (repeating, attending to, praising) appropriate responses and not reinforcing errors (praising sitting in seat behavior and ignoring times out of the seat)
□ pairing neutral events (working hard) with positive reinforcers (praise) so that the neutral behavior takes on positively reinforcing value
□ highlighting cues that differentiate stimuli and pairing them with different responses (a "b" points one way, say "b"; a "d" points the other way, say "d")
□ modeling of appropriate responses (let me show you how I would talk through this algebra problem)
□ making positive outcomes (free time) contingent on less valued behaviors (one hour of library research)
□ shaping correct responses through successive approximations to the responses (ignoring the fact that the l and o of the letter "b" don't intersect properly until the individual elements can be drawn correctly; helping a student brave sitting with classmates in the lunchroom and then teaching conversational skills)
□ carefully controlling rate of presentation of new materials (introducing only three new social studies concepts or spelling words daily)
□ distributing practice over time rather than massing it (reviewing class notes daily rather than studying only the night before the exam)
□ allowing for relearning and generalization of skills (periodically insert learned material into classwork to permit relearning and application of learned concepts in new contexts)
□ continually measuring and evaluating interventions and outcomes (evaluating retention of spelling words when taught by different methods)
□ systematically presenting information with easier subskills preceding harder ones (teaching subtraction before division)

Adelman's (1971) teaching model presents a sequence of intervention approaches for LD children that incorporates the various instructional philoso-

Figure 11-1 Sequential and hierarchical teaching strategies for remedying school learning problems

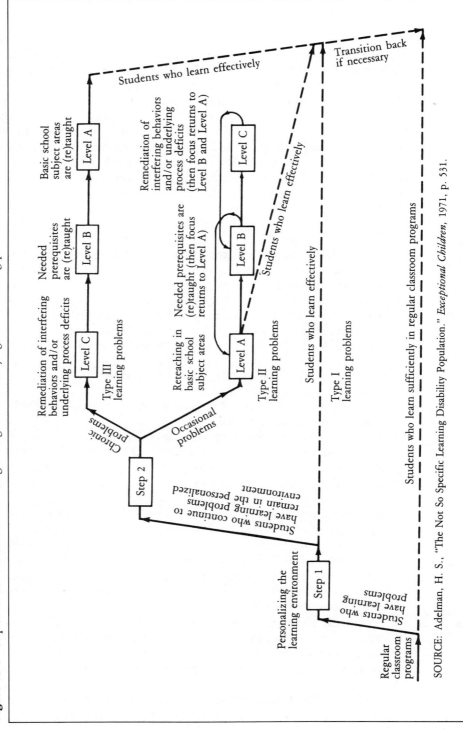

SOURCE: Adelman, H. S., "The Not So Specific Learning Disability Population." *Exceptional Children*, 1971, p. 531.

phies. This intervention model is diagrammed in Figure 11-1. Adelman describes three types of children:

- ☐ *Type I Child* — no ability disorder but learning is not rapid in a nonpersonalized instructional program.
- ☐ *Type II Child* — minor disorders can be compensated for in the appropriate learning environment.
- ☐ *Type III Child* — severe ability and perhaps behavior deficits.

Because the Type I and II students' difficulties can be ameliorated by appropriately matching the learning environment to their needs, Adelman feels that these children's difficulties are due primarily to what we have referred to as task- or setting-based causes. The source of the learning disability is a deficiency in the learning environment. The Type III student has a child-based learning disability. Learning progress for this child is also facilitated by appropriate matching of task and setting attributes. Any one child can vary between being a Type I, II, or III student in different subject areas, depending on the abilities and behavioral styles that various aspects of the curriculum tap, teacher attributes, and the nature of the different classrooms.

Adelman's hierarchy of personalized learning environments begins at Step 1, where the Type I child's program is altered, typically in the context of the regular classroom. Individual differences in development, motivation, and performance are accommodated, and a greater degree of individual variability is tolerated. By capitalizing on a child's strengths, this classroom environment becomes the prototype for prevention of learning disabilities in the regular classroom.

Type II youngsters may function effectively at Step 1 in most areas of learning, but encounter occasional problems. At this point, the teacher must decide whether to delay some instruction until a later time when learning would come more easily (developmental approach). When instruction cannot be delayed, the student requires a different level of programming in these skill areas, Step 2 (behavioral approach).

Step 2 has three levels, each of which require different types of assessment and teaching. At Level A the basic behaviors, skills, content, and concepts of the school subject are retaught, such as breaking the word "captain" into syllables to decode it. The reteaching involves qualitatively different instructional approaches: different explanations, techniques, materials, and specialized remedial approaches. When reteaching is unsuccessful, Level B is initiated. Level B involves the reteaching of prerequisites needed for success at Level A, such as learning the sound "c" for the c in "captain." When Level B is successful, the teacher returns to Level A. When Level B is unsuccessful, the teacher goes to Level C, where any interfering behavioral or underlying process deficits are assessed and remediated. The teacher, for example, assesses the child's ability to listen to sounds in sequence, to auditorially discriminate the "c" sound from other sounds or to articulate "c," and works with the child on any of these problems. Once successful at Level C, the teacher returns to Levels B and A.

The Type III student has severe, pervasive learning difficulties that necessitate resolution of interfering behaviors or information-processing deficits first (underlying process approach). The child begins at Level C (remediating weaknesses), then moves to Level B, and finally to Level A. Most Type III children still have some achievement areas that are developing normally, or that require only a Level A or B intervention.

While the Type I child may require the indirect services of an LD consultant to the regular classroom teacher, the Type II student usually requires a resource room setting for a portion of each day. The Type III child might benefit best from a special class setting. No matter which setting LD teachers are involved in, they try to gain their students' maximum motivation and cooperation. The students must understand how the special programs relate to their strengths and weaknesses, must be able to monitor and evaluate their own progress, and must play an important role in choosing and giving feedback on materials and methods.

Materials

There has been a proliferation of published special educational materials in recent years. Since research on these programs is generally conducted many years after they are published, very little data is available to substantiate any one program's approach as being better than another. How much different materials contribute to success with higher level skills is yet to be determined. Would LD children learn this information automatically as they grow older? Does one program's method work best for one or another type of student or teacher, and why? Research addressing these issues is available on only a few published programs (Hickman & Anderson, 1979).

Teachers generally must choose materials based on their teaching experience with similar LD children, on which materials have worked best for them in the past, on which materials best suit their teaching style and preferences, on which materials they are trained to use, and on which materials are readily available. In most cases the teacher needs to adapt any materials he or she chooses. These materials have been geared toward the general needs of a group of children, and not toward the needs of children with unique individual differences. No one material or method is right for all children taught by the teacher. Nor is it likely that any one program will contain exactly the right material to meet even one LD child's profile of strengths and weaknesses. The teacher, in the end, mixes parts of different programs, modifies, and improvises.

Budgetary matters are a realistic concern in choosing instructional materials. As teachers today are allocated less money for materials, deciding which published program to buy becomes very important. Without proof about which programs teach best, how can the teacher choose wisely? Teachers need to look beyond attractive packaging and marketing and evaluate the program's ability to meet their particular students' needs (Berman, 1977).

Since learning disabled students are usually instructed on the same objectives over and over again, materials should be innovative in their presentation of routine objectives (Hallenbeck, 1980). They must also expand on a child's breadth of knowledge, curiosity, and thinking skills. Even though each subject is taught as a separate entity, curriculum materials ideally integrate subject areas so that reading, writing, and math skills are reinforced through content area instruction and vice versa. The best materials are those that are designed to:

1. have a logical, hierarchical sequence of instructional objectives against which a child's current level of functioning and readiness easily can be compared;
2. have information presentation styles that are adaptable to individual learning styles (self-monitored reading, lectures, demonstrations with slides and overhead projectors);
3. have reinforcement activities adaptable to different students' learning styles (the same objectives can be accomplished by educational games, workbooks, use of audio-visual aids, term papers, community service projects);
4. rehearse the same objectives in multiple ways;
5. backtrack over easier objectives when the student has difficulty learning the present material; speed up coverage of objectives that are mastered more easily;
6. present content and directions in a consistent and simple fashion;
7. offer teachers ideas for task analysis and alternative teaching strategies;
8. pretest for where teaching should begin;
9. have a built-in evaluation mechanism for determining mastery of instructional objectives;
10. have built-in periodic rechecks on previous learning and opportunities for relearning in a different format;
11. include several evaluation formats (projects, multiple choice tests or essay exams, oral reports, homework assignments, self-checking)
12. include charts for students and teachers to easily monitor progress;
13. have built-in factors to increase student motivation;
14. be flexible so that different teaching methods may be used with the same materials;
15. allow students to proceed at their own rate and even skip objectives they have already mastered;
16. be adaptable to individualized, small-group, and large-group work
17. help students transfer skills to other contexts and practical applications.

Additional criteria for choosing instructional materials are presented in Table 11-3.

Table 11-3 Q-sheet for evaluating reading materials

Basic Q-sheet

1. *What is the stated rationale for developing the program?*

   Look for one or more statements of: (a) definition of the content area under study, e.g., reading; (b) philosophy regarding instruction in the area; or (c) dissatisfaction with specific aspects of other programs, or perhaps a previous program by the same publisher.

2. *What is the rationale for selection of program elements or content?*

   Look for comments on: (a) tradition; (b) experimental determination (always check this out in greater detail); (c) logic of the subject matter; (d) survey of other programs and their elements; or (e) the assumptions made concerning the content area, such as the linguistic base in a reading program.

3. *How can the quality of the content be checked?*

   This question is difficult. Usually some credence is given to the reputations of authors and publishers, as well as to supporting reference material. Usually "expert" opinion is needed in addition to a determination of the internal consistency of *all* program elements.

4. *What is the scope of the program?*

   Scope is the comprehensiveness or the breadth of the program. It determines how much of what it is possible to teach has been included in the program at hand. A program of limited scope may be desirable for teaching a specific skill, or as a supplement to an existing program which is weak in a particular area or variable.

5. *What is the sequencing of skills or items or units?*

   Sequence is the order the subject matter or elements are to be taught. Some materials are sequentially dependent so that mastery at each level is required before continuing to the next. Sequentially dependent curricula leave little room for flexible use or the pulling out of components. Other materials are "spiralled" so that the topic may be left and then returned to later. Paradoxically, spiralling may be helpful or detrimental. Sometimes leaving an area of

difficulty for a while has the effect of desensitization. However, it may also be possible that mastery is never actually accounted for in a spiralled curriculum except when the particular topic disappears from "mention." Sequence may also be based upon several factors other than the sequential/spiral question. Logical organization of the subject matter may be a determiner; the curriculum may proceed from immediate to remote life experiences, or it may move from concrete to abstract symbolism.

6. *How is the curriculum paced?*

   Regulation of pacing is presently one of the major ways of controlling individualization of instruction. Several bits of information provide clues to intended and actual pacing of the materials or program:

   a. Are there differing starting times for various groups or individuals, and then essentially the same pacing along the way? If so, the modification is not in "pacing" but in readiness for the program.

   b. Are "mastery" suggestions made along the way for those who need more or different experiences at various points? How is it suggested that such modifications be managed if in a group situation?

   c. Do suggested instructional time lines presented elsewhere in the program mitigate against modifications in the pacing of instruction?

7. *Is there evidence of any psychological principles of instruction which are content-free?*

   Look for reference to the systematic use of stimulus control, reinforcement, rate of introduction, set induction, etc.

8. *What are the specific techniques of instruction for each lesson?*

   The more highly structured the lessons, the less likely it is that the success of the program depends upon teacher experience and previous training. More highly structured programs also lend themselves to use by aides and volunteers under the supervision of the teacher. On the other hand, it may happen that if little teacher

Table 11-3 continued

variation is allowed or encouraged, the lesson may not be readily modifiable.

9. *What are the specific modifications suggested for individualization?*
   a. Is the individualization on a one-to-one basis, or intended for instruction within the group situation?
   b. What are the bases for the suggestions made?
   c. What is the range of suggestions or are they all pretty much alike?
   d. What range of differences is accounted for?
   e. Are the suggestions general, or are they specifically tied to potential instructional problems?

10. *Is a prerequisite skill level or information base needed to administer the program?*
    a. Is there a formalized, separate "package" of instruction available?
    b. Is the training continuous as an integral part of each unit or lesson?
    c. Are there ways to determine the instructional competency of personnel who would work with the program?

11. *Are there "readiness" behaviors specified which are prerequisites for the student?*
    a. Are assessment strategies included?
    b. How are the behaviors to be acquired or taught?

12. *How is reinforcement used in the program?*
    a. If mentioned at all, note the definition well. In the majority of nonspecial education programs there is a tendency to equate reinforcement with repetition.
    b. What kinds of reinforcement are suggested, e.g., social, tangible, edible, visual . . . ?
    c. Are there suggestions for how to determine what is reinforcing to an individual child?
    d. Are schedules of reinforcement considered?
    e. Are there specific examples, or generalized suggestions?
    f. Is there a procedure for fading from tangible to social reinforcement?
    g. Is there any discrepancy between notions of reinforcement and practices such as paper-grading or marking?

13. *What is the format of the material to be presented?*
    a. Is the material in kit, book, worksheet, chart or some other form?
    b. How are the units organized?
    c. What kind of type is used? Size? Style? Compactness?
    d. If pictures are included, what kinds are there, and what are their purposes?
    e. Are the page arrangements likely to make any difference to the learners?

14. *How independently can the material be used?*
    a. If independence of use is recommended, is there a systematic program to teach the child *how* to use the materials independently?
    b. How is progress in work habits or independence to be monitored?

15. *Has any effort been made to assess or control the complexity of the language of instruction, either receptively or expressively?*
    Does the teacher have any way of assessing whether the language level is appropriate? For example, in materials for young children, which "Wh____" questions are introduced and in what sequence? Do these correspond with the developmental sequences in language and cognition?

16. *What is the developmental interest level of the materials?*
    Materials which are obviously intended for younger children are probably inappropriate for older students. On the other hand, the teacher actually may have to develop or provide background experiences, information or interests for some students. It should be noted that statements of "mental age" do not necessarily correspond to the "interest age" or to the "social age" of the child.

17. *Are there behavioral objectives for the program or for the lessons?*
    a. Is there any attempt to justify the objectives or to determine their value?
    b. Are the objectives linked in any way to prior or to subsequent objectives?
    c. Are the statements complete in the sense of meeting behavioral criteria?

(Continued on following page)

Table 11-3   continued

d. What are the consequences of objectives assessment in terms of future instructional procedures?

e. Is the program built on predetermined objectives, or do the objectives follow from the nature of the program?

18. *What diagnostic assessments are provided?*
   a. Type
   b. Frequency?
   c. Pre/post, or continuous during instructional sequences?
   d. Feedback mechanisms to the learner and to the instructional program?
   e. What are the consequences of assessment feedback?

19. *Is this program coordinated with any other programs?*
   a. Is the program part of a series or a unified approach by the same publisher? Can it be readily separated from other components?
   b. Are there recommendations for companion programs, or for previous and subsequent programs?

20. *Have there been any attempts to determine readability or learner interest?*
   What processes have been used, and are the results available?

21. *What is the comparative cost of the program?*
   An attempt should be made to estimate the cost-effectiveness of the program. Where similar materials are available, comparisons may be made. There may also be the feasibility of using "home-made" alternatives made in a workshop or by volunteers.

22. *What is the realistic availability of the instructional components?*
   If the program is desirable because of the variety or specific inclusion of certain components, it should be determined that these are actually available from the publisher or with funds allocated. This is especially important in the case of hardware needs. The budget factor is a critical one when considering the use of consumable materials.

23. *Are testimonials, research, author claims, and publisher claims clearly differentiated?*
   a. Evidence of formative evaluation?

b. Evidence of summative evaluation?

c. Is there congruence between the program objectives and activities?

d. Are the program development processes specified?

24. *What are the target populations for whom the materials were developed?*
   If the population characteristics are stated, it is easier to assess the potential relevance of the materials to your population of interest.

25. *Is it possible to foresee — and does the author note — any potential problems which might be encountered in using these materials?*
   a. How surmountable are the problems?
   b. How readily can the materials be modified to resolve the problems?

26. *Can any of the features of this material or program be adapted or incorporated into other programs?*
   Features such as self-correctional procedures, reinforcement techniques, etc., may be noted for use in other instructional situations.

27. *Are any significant changes in the organization and management of the instructional situation required?*
   a. Are there special space and/or equipment requirements?
   b. Will the time/event schedule of the day need to be replanned?
   c. Will present child groupings be significantly affected? How?
   d. Are the descriptions of how the program is to be organized and managed stated clearly enough so that the program may be readily implemented?

28. *Is it possible to isolate sensory channels as a major instructional variable?*
   Keep in mind that for this purpose not only must the material itself be examined, but also the circumstances surrounding its actual presentation in the instructional situation.

29. *How durable are the materials?*
   Items that undergo a great deal of handling should be made of strong materials with protected surfaces. Storage or carrying of materials in kit or package form should also be considered in terms of the

Table 11-3 continued

convenience and sturdiness of the packaging materials.
30. *Is there any apparent or subtle bias toward or against a particular target group, e.g., women, blacks, Chicanos, or Indians?*
Many states or local school districts will have guidelines available for this kind of analysis.

31. *Other significant features omitted from this list but which should be noted as relevant for user purposes.*
Considerations such as potential interaction patterns, the predominance of convergent/divergent responses, or detailed linguistic analysis may be of interest to special interest users.

SOURCE: Brown, V., "Programs, Materials, and Techniques." © 1975 The Professional Press, Inc. Reprinted with permission of the publisher from *Journal of Learning Disabilities*, 11 East Adams Street, Chicago, Illinois 60603, vol. 8, pp. 412–415.

In choosing materials for a student with learning disabilities, the teacher should also check that the content is challenging despite the student's weak modes for taking in or communicating information. Subject matter, concepts, and language levels need to be equivalent to the conceptual, vocabulary, and maturity levels of the student. Aspects such as decoding, spelling, or composition requirements need to be geared toward the student's lower abilities in these areas. In this way a youngster can handle content area texts independently, while maintaining interest in progressing in basic academic skills. Thypin (1979) demonstrates how reading material can be at a high content and abstraction yet low reading level, and vice versa:

	READING LEVEL	CONTENT LEVEL
(1) The question is to be or not to be.	1st grade	High school
(2) Homo sapiens are omnivorous bipeds cohabiting among the stalagmites.	High school	4th grade

Texts that match low reading levels to higher conceptual abilities are referred to as *high interest-low vocabulary* books. They generally adapt their print size, length, and illustrations to meet the maturity level of the reader. Their goal is to help students read to learn rather than always struggling to learn to read (Weiss & Weiss, 1981).

Since no published materials are perfect, the experienced teacher usually scrounges, cuts, and pastes from all sorts of materials to create supplemental activities. The same self-made materials can be put to different creative uses. Imagine how differently magazine cut-outs of a sweater, a house, and meat could be used:

☐ pairing each picture with the corresponding reading word in the hope that visual imagery will help the student remember the printed word;

☐ using the pictures as familiar objects which, when shown to the child and placed upside down on a table, will draw sufficient attention and interest to help the child develop verbal rehearsal strategies to aid memory;

☐ teaching children categorization skills: the pictures are all the same because they are things, pictures, and are important to existence; they are different from one another in function, materials, and use.

Teacher-made materials, and innovative use of published materials, enhance the teacher's ability to individualize instruction so that appropriate learning objectives are addressed and the student's attention and interest are maximized. The teacher's decision-making will be easier once program developers field-test materials on different types of LD youngsters and with different kinds of teachers.

Defining and Coordinating Intervention Roles

The heterogeneous needs of learning disabled children require expertise in multiple areas. Yet, the large numbers of individuals whose talents can be used on behalf of learning disabled students has resulted in some difficulty with role definition. Besides school personnel, medical specialists play an important role in preventing or alleviating disease processes that can interfere with learning. The family also carries a major responsibility for the learning disabled child's growth and development. As advocate, model, and teacher, the family monitors school interventions and guides children's out-of-school hours and future lives.

School-Based Personnel

The general education teacher, LD specialist, reading and math specialist, speech pathologist, vocational educator, and the school psychologist, among others, have expertise that can serve the learning disabled. Their efforts in schools have greatly benefitted the LD child, especially through the multidisciplinary team assessment and planning process mandated by PL 94-142, and the interrelations of regular class teachers and specialists. The general education teacher has primary responsibility for most learning disabled students; this is where over three-quarters of these youngsters spend the majority of their day. The general education teacher, together with the other specialists, needs to decide precisely what academic objectives he or she is responsible for. Unfortunately, the overlapping professional roles of the specialists often confuse decisions about which one is responsible for teaching what. Recognizing these role conflicts, university training programs and state certification regulations are trying to define professional training needs so that duplication of roles is diminished and collaboration increased.

Coordination of service roles is imperative to better serve the LD child (Kline, 1975). Some individuals suggest that schools should permit those with competencies in a particular area to deal with particular problems in that area regardless of their professional labels (Abrams, 1976; Larsen, 1976; Lieberman, 1980b). Matching teaching competencies to student needs, regardless of teacher titles or training backgrounds, uses the variety of expertise in the schools to students' best advantage.

Coordination is just as important during the assessment and planning phases as the service phases. Public Law 94–142 requires that the regular class teacher (or if there is none, then a person qualified to teach a child of that age) be on the multidisciplinary LD assessment team. In many cases this teacher shares responsibility with another specialist for writing the IEP. At least one teacher or other specialist with knowledge in the area of suspected disability must also serve on the assessment team, as must a person qualified to conduct individual diagnostic examinations. Depending on the questions asked about a student and the specialists' expertise, any number of professionals may be involved on assessment teams at different times. This flexibility needs to be preplanned, negotiated, and coordinated in order for the child to benefit from the best expertise available. Exposure of specialists to one another in interdisciplinary university training and inservice programs is one means of facilitating such cooperation (Lerner, 1975; Wallace, 1976).

The General Education Teacher. The regular class teacher is responsible for referring children with learning problems for evaluation and for participating in the assessment process. The teacher's instructional responsibilities to an LD child are detailed by the IEP. The regular class teacher's role more often seems to be conferring with the special education teacher and providing information on current levels of student performance than involvement in the IEP's specification of long-term goals, short-term objectives and support services (Pugach, 1982). The regular class teacher seems more likely to participate in IEP meetings when he or she has initiated the referral, but tends to be less involved in subsequent annual IEP reviews. The regular class teacher generally assumes responsibility for educating the student in stronger areas and uses an LD consultant for more specialized instructional needs. When programming questions arise, the regular class teacher consults with the appropriate specialists.

A 1979 report indicates that 81 percent of learning disabled students are educated primarily in regular classrooms (*Progress Toward a Free Appropriate Public Education,* 1979). Although great responsibility for the handicapped is placed on regular class teachers, the general education university curriculum often has not prepared teachers to deal with extreme individual differences (Frostig, 1980). Recognizing this, the United States Office of Education has reappropriated some money from special education teacher training to regular teacher training (USOE, 1979).

Even greater sums have been allocated to inservice education of teachers working in the schools. This training has helped teachers to understand handicapped children's unique ways of learning and to creatively adapt teaching methods and materials to their needs (Tarrier, 1978). Inservice training has also built support among teachers (Yoshida, Fenton, Maxwell, & Kaufman, 1979) and high level school personnel (Biklen, 1979) for serving the special needs child in the regular classroom. These positive attitudes lead to greater teacher satisfaction with and commitment to less restrictive service options. As a consequence, the special child's integration into the regular classroom is more likely to be successful (Biklen, 1979).

The Learning Disabilities Specialist. Some states serve more LD students in special classes and facilities than in regular classes (Louisiana, Pennsylvania; *Progress Toward a Free Appropriate Public Education,* 1979). The majority, however, teach most LD students in a resource room for a portion of each day. In the resource room, LD teachers generally use special teaching techniques to remediate weaknesses and provide tutorial help in classroom subjects. They also provide formal and informal evaluation, consultation, and inservice training services to regular class teachers. They are expected to be skilled in classroom observation, interviewing, communicating and teaming with other professionals, and in the development of positive attitudes toward LD students in school personnel. Some experts have criticized these role extensions because they reduce the time and effort teachers spend directly teaching LD children who need as much intensive, specialized instruction as they can get (Wallace & McLoughlin, 1979). Others are less concerned, feeling that this consultation role will diminish as general educators become more accomplished at adapting their curricula to the learning disabled youngster's needs (Kirk, 1976).

LD teachers are considered "generalists" because they address a broad spectrum of academic and social needs. When PL 94-142 was passed, many teachers were forced to become instant LD specialists. They had only limited training in remedial reading (Horne, 1975; Jakupcak, 1973; in Jakupcak, 1975), language development and remediation (Myers & Hammill, 1976), and mathematics remediation (Fitzmaurice, 1980). Universities today are beginning to address training needs in these areas, as are state LD certification boards. When PL 94-142 passed, thirty-two states did not require a reading course for LD certification (Lewandowski, 1977), twelve states required a course in developmental reading, and only five states required a course in diagnostic and remedial reading (Sartain, 1976). States are now reexamining the competencies believed necessary for LD teacher certification.

To develop more uniform LD teacher training, certification standards, criteria for employment, and standards for monitoring professional practices, in 1978 the Council for Exceptional Children's Division for Children with Learning Disabilities published a Code of Ethics and Competencies for Teachers of Learning Disabled Children and Youth. The United States Office of

Education also is allocating funds for continuing inservice education (USOE, 1979).

Teacher training needs in learning disabilities are great. Learning disabilities is second only to mental retardation as the largest category of teacher specialization. In 1978–79 it was estimated that 60,000 new teachers specializing in learning disabilities were needed (*Progress Toward a Free Appropriate Public Education*, 1979). To meet this need, over 200 university masters and 80 doctoral-level LD degree granting programs have been established in recent years.

The Reading and Math Specialists. The reading and math teachers help organize and evaluate general education's reading and math programs, and engage in remediation. Because the remedial role overlaps the LD teacher's role, these specialists have had difficulty coming to terms with what is which person's teaching domain. At times this has resulted in professional rivalry to acquire a single budgeted job position (Sartain, 1976).

The LD specialist often has the advantage over the reading or math teacher in acquiring jobs servicing learning disabled youngsters because PL 94-142 requires that an LD student receive special services from a certified special education teacher. The LD teacher has a special education degree but the reading or math teacher most often has not. Although there is no reason why the reading and math teacher can't also teach the learning disabled student, this role is not legally required. Consequently, these teachers may end up working primarily with unlabelled children who are less severe underachievers. They are naturally puzzled by the inconsistency in a law which was designed to provide greater educational opportunities for the handicapped yet by teachers who may have less expertise in specific areas of remediation. Some university reading and math education programs are making adjustments so that their graduates can be assured of appropriate certification and employment.

The Speech Pathologist. The speech pathologist, or communicative disorders specialist, is trained to evaluate and work with children who have articulation, voice quality, stuttering, or language comprehension and expression disorders. The learning disabled child's difficulties in these areas often contribute to their learning problems. The speech pathologist is faced with the same role definition and credential conflict with the LD specialist as the reading or math specialist. The speech pathologist also is often precluded from offering therapy to many LD children daily by state caseload requirements, which can number as many as fifty to ninety children weekly. Language development instruction, therefore, often becomes the responsibility of the LD teacher, who has a more reasonable caseload, usually of twenty students.

There is one way around this problem. When the severely language impaired LD child is labelled "multiply handicapped" due to language and learning disabilities, intensive services must be made available from both the speech pathologist and the LD specialist. As with reading and math specialists, universities and state certification regulations are addressing the paucity of LD coursework required of speech pathology students (Larsen, 1976).

The School Psychologist. The school psychologist traditionally serves in an educational assessment and consultation role to the classroom teacher. Public Law 94-142 states that the school psychologist must be involved in the decision-making of the multidisciplinary group that determines the presence of a handicapping condition, but need not actually conduct the LD assessment. Since the school psychologist is well-versed in normal child development, handicapping conditions, and the physical, organizational, and human aspects of a school environment that impact learning and behavior, the LD child can benefit directly and indirectly from the psychologist's assessments, psychological services, teacher consultation, inservice training, and research on program efficacy.

The Vocational Educator. As LD youngsters reach secondary school age, they need to look toward the future. Because of their learning difficulties, many students do not choose to continue with formal education after high school. For these individuals, the skill training, career exploration, and training in how to get along on a job that are offered by a high school vocational educator are invaluable. Quite often, students graduate with skills that facilitate employment opportunities and therefore life adjustment.

Other Specialists. The school's audiologist evaluates whether hearing or auditory-processing difficulties contribute to a learning disabled youngster's problems, and intervenes appropriately. The audiologist's findings can guide a teacher in modifying instructional approaches and seating arrangements. The occupational therapist, physical therapist, and adaptive physical education teacher are invaluable resources for LD students with persistent coordination and self-help difficulties. Finally, the school's guidance and administrative personnel not only help establish the organizational framework for service delivery but also provide important personal support to students and teachers.

Medical Specialists

Public Law 94-142 mandates that any medical factors relevant to a handicapping condition must be explored and treated by appropriate medical personnel. These include the ophthalmologist and optometrist who help the child use his eyes more comfortably, the allergist who may alleviate physical conditions that take the child's mind off learning, the endocrinologist who treats glandular disorders, the geneticist who evaluates inherited learning patterns, the otologist who diagnoses and treats hearing disorders, and others. The pediatrician and neurologist are the most frequently consulted when learning disabilities are suspected.

The Pediatrician. The pediatrician is one of the first professionals to see a child after birth. It is natural for parents to turn to the pediatrician for advice regarding physical needs, as well as academic and behavioral issues. The pediatrician recognizes and deals with factors that can affect learning such as visual or auditory handicaps, malnutrition, endocrinological and metabolic disorders, and medical therapy where appropriate. The pediatrician also has a responsibility to communicate findings to educators (Garrard, 1973), encourage families to pursue special assessment and teaching programs (Richmond & Walzer, 1973), and to know the special education personnel and available community services (Bateman & Frankel, 1972).

Educators recognize that, by virtue of the status of physicians in our society, parents consult them on educational issues. Therefore, physicians should not shy away from dealing with the child's functional development (Bateman & Frankel, 1972). Recognizing this, medical schools commonly offer courses and clinical experiences relevant to assessment and treatment of learning and behavior problems. Continuing education programs for practicing physicians also often include seminars on the learning disabled.

The Neurologist. The neurologist is frequently called on when a child has a learning problem. Although not enough is known yet about brain–behavior relationships to have the neurological information suggest more than very general teaching methods, the neurologist can detect and treat ongoing neurological disease and seizure disorders, explore the family history of learning disorders, and look for signs of brain injury. The neurologist's job is complicated because the child's nervous system is still developing, and it is sometimes difficult to discriminate slow development from actual damage to the nervous system. Advances in brain and neurochemical study techniques promise a more diagnostically and instructionally relevant role for the neurologist in the future.

The Family

The child's academic and social learning is a life-long process that can be facilitated or impeded by familial circumstances (McWhirter & Cabanski, 1972). Through PL 94–142, Congress recognized that the family system bears large responsibility for positive interventions and influences on a child's life. For this reason, the law invites parental involvement in labeling, placement, and programming decisions. Government funds are provided annually to nearly 300,000 parents for training relevant to their children's handicapping conditions (*Progress Toward a Free Appropriate Public Education*, 1979).

Recognizing the key role of the family in a child's life, professionals have begun to explore learning disabilities from a more ecological perspective (Newbrough, 1978). Problems are viewed as existing in the *interaction* of individuals within the child's social system. The focus is on a malfunctioning system, and not on the individual. Changes for the child come about when the system's ways of functioning are altered. Since the family network strongly shapes a child's attitudes and habits, problem resolution becomes the responsibility of the whole family and not just the child. Chapter 14 is devoted to the critical role that the family plays as model, advocate, and teacher in a child's life.

Categorical and Noncategorical Service Delivery

Historically, educators have sought a label by which to understand a child first, then decided on educational placements based on the particular disability category, and only then dealt with specific instructional programming. Over the past decade there has been a general shift away from concentrating on the diagnosis of handicapping conditions to make placement decisions, toward assessing individuals for teaching purposes. Concomitantly, a search began for alternatives to diagnostic labelling that would focus more on instructional objectives than on children's disabling characteristics. This search was prompted in part by an awareness that academic underachievement, the primary characteristic attributed to the learning disabled, was shared by the emotionally disturbed (Kirk, 1964; Morse, Cutler, & Fink, 1964) and the educable mentally retarded (Blake, Aaron, & Westbrook, 1969; Schwarz, 1969; Schwarz & Cook, 1971).

Many individuals asked why children had to carry different labels when they actually had many characteristics in common (Blatt, 1972; Edgerton, 1967; Foster, Ysseldyke, & Reese, 1975; Gallagher, 1972; Jones, 1972; Reynolds & Balow, 1972). Given these commonalities it seemed that choice of teaching goals, methods and materials was irrelevant to particular handicapping conditions. The labelling system was criticized for the stigma it created, fixing blame for the problem within the child, programming irrelevance, lack of multiple perspectives on problems, and special class segregation that often accompanied labelling. The result of labelling and segregation was often lowered teacher expectations and poorer achievement.

In this context, the need to diagnose learning disabilities and set up learning disabilities programs, rather than just identify and deal with these students' strengths and weaknesses, also began to be questioned. The "sort," "classify," and "place" procedure of identifying "special children" was criticized for not also identifying their special needs (Gillespie, Miller, & Fielder, 1975; p. 666). It was argued that schools' broad interpretations of the federal LD definition had already diluted the label's meaning. While some individuals wished to maintain learning disabilities as a special category, others sought noncategorical service delivery options.

Categorical Service Delivery

In spite of the criticisms of diagnostic labelling practices, labelling and delivering services under the category of learning disabilities do have some advantages. Labels are essential for legislation that appropriates funds for services and research projects. Without a label with which to identify the problems and issues, advocacy work may not have succeeded in gaining the LD services we now have. Identifying children as learning disabled according to federal guidelines also helps researchers choose similar child characteristics to study, unify subject selection criteria, calculate accurate prevalence figures for planning of services, and evaluate remedial procedures and programs.

To accomplish these goals, some professionals urge learning disabilities to retain its identity by developing boundaries for the LD classification and guarding against continued expansion (Cruickshank, 1976; Larsen, 1976; Wallace & McLoughlin, 1979). Others concentrate on service delivery rather than labels by suggesting that professionals specify instructional needs while broadening the learning disabilities category to include all mildly handicapped children, whether emotionally disturbed, mildly retarded, or learning disabled (Hallahan & Kauffman, 1976). Lilly (1977) refers to this combined group as children with "special learning and behavior problems." Hallahan and Kauffman propose identifying each of these children as having a "specific learning disability in ———." For those who are developing slowly in all areas, they suggest using Dunn's (1973) term, moderate or severe "general learning disability."

Remedial instruction in a categorical system occurs in resource rooms, special classes, or special facilities specifically designated for learning disabled children. The advantages and disadvantages of these different organizational patterns are detailed in Chapter 15.

Noncategorical Service Delivery

Due to the diversity of behaviors associated with learning disabilities and its very broad definition, many experts feel that the LD label is no longer functional. They have suggested several alternative service delivery and classification systems:

Categorizing by Teaching Needs. Dunn (1968) proposed a taxonomy of eight areas that focus on analyzing learning difficulties and clinical teaching needs, while cutting across existing special education categories: environmental modifications; motor development; sensory and perceptual training; cognitive, language development, and academic instruction; speech and communication training; personality development; social interaction training; and vocational training. Lerner (1973) also believed children can be divided by instructional need rather than by historical categories of special education. In Dunn's or Lerner's systems, several children could be grouped together for similar training objectives and strategies, even though earlier they would have been classified retarded or LD and taught separately.

Some projects have successfully grouped different categories of exceptional children for instruction based on common needs (Taylor et al., 1972), and some states no longer plan services with reference to handicapping categories. This is referred to as a *noncategorical* approach.

California was the nation's leader in initiating noncategorical funding of services. Handicapped students have been referred to as "children with exceptional needs" or "learning handicapped." They are grouped on the basis of similar behavioral and educational needs, rather than on the basis of diagnostic category. Some other states classify children by the percent of time they require for individualized instruction outside of the regular classroom. The percentage time system provides school systems with a financial incentive to offer the child as much special service as would be beneficial. It also works to the advantage of the child who was previously ineligible for labelling but needed a few hours of related services (counseling, occupational therapy) weekly. Other states combine both categorical and noncategorical options by retaining the traditional categories for federal financial reimbursement purposes, and grouping students for instruction based on common needs rather than labels. One approach that has become popular in recent years is a noncategorical resource room where children with all types of exceptionalities, even the gifted, go for instruction.

These noncategorical options seem attractive because they address labelling concerns while defining teaching needs with the individual rather than diagnostic category in mind. It is up to future research to ascertain whether these noncategorical systems facilitate individualization of instruction or help teachers, peers, and others to treat exceptional children any differently than in a system based on labels (Forness, 1974).

Indexing Learning Progress. Instead of categorizing by general areas of need, Lovitt's (1976) *index of learning* system involves direct, daily measurement of what the child is learning so that individualized instruction is facilitated. Helen, who is underachieving in reading, might be called a "Lippincott C. (76/2)" (with reference to the name of the reading program): C level, seventy-six correct, two errors (p. 301). This system promotes an impression of Helen as a successful learner who will next progress to level D in the program, rather than a poor learner who is five levels behind. Such a system can apply to all exceptional children regardless of their individual handicapping conditions.

Summary

To develop appropriate individualized instructional programs for students, the multidisciplinary assessment's information is translated into an Individualized Education Program (IEP). Through the planning process involved in writing the IEP, goals are set, criteria for evaluation are established, and what types of services, by whom, and with how much participation in the regular or least restrictive environment are specified.

Daily lesson planning is the teacher's responsibility. This is not an easy task, especially considering that no one program is likely to suit the uneven development of the learning disabled student. To ascertain precisely what and how to teach, teachers engage in an ongoing, diagnostic-prescriptive teaching process. They generally follow an eclectic educational model that combines instruction in the child's weaker and stronger skill areas. They must creatively adapt published as well as self-made materials to the unique needs of each of their students.

Because of PL 94–142's "least restrictive environment" mandate, except for the most severe of learning disabilities, the regular classroom teacher tends to spend more school hours with the learning disabled student than other professionals. The LD teacher offers important assessment services, direct instruction and teacher consultation, as do reading and math teachers, the speech pathologist, the vocational educator, and the school psychologist. University training programs, state certification regulations, and professional organizations are trying to better define the roles of these specialists so that their combined skills can better serve the learning disabled student. Medical personnel also play an important role in the service delivery network, as do individuals in the learning disabled person's social system: family, close friends, relatives, and others who influence decisions. This social system primarily shapes and supports an individual's development.

To give primary attention to teaching needs and concentrate less on the diagnosis of disabilities, many states are creating noncategorical classification and service delivery systems. These systems group children together who need to work on similar instructional objectives, rather than group them because they are all labelled learning disabled. The latter categorical system neatly counts how many children require special funding and teachers, and facilitates identification of research populations. It does not, however, narrow the number and nature of teaching objectives to be met in any one class, nor does it maximize learning opportunities by creatively combining the individual needs of the child with more flexibility in tasks and settings.

Suggestions for Further Study

1. Read a learning disabled student's assessment report, and IEP. Then interview the teachers to find out what materials and strategies each is using to address teaching goals. Is the IEP outline being carried out? If not, were there other ways in which the teachers found the IEP helpful to program planning?

2. Each professional has his or her own perspective on who should teach the learning disabled youngster. The viewpoints of the LD specialist, reading teacher, and speech pathologist are contrasted in the summer 1975 volume of the *Journal of Special Education* and the October, 1976 issue of the *Journal of Learning Disabilities*. These depict how different fields of specialization view their responsibilities to the learning disabled student.

3. If both LD and reading teachers are to teach reading to the learning disabled, how do they determine who is to teach what to whom? Generally, LD experts feel that the LD teacher should remediate severe problems (List, 1975; Newcomer, 1975) or those caused by central processing difficulties (Kirk, 1975). This leaves the milder problems and those caused by environmental influences to the reading teacher. Compare these views with those presented in a reading education text. How do these perspectives impact university training practices and territorial rights conflicts among their graduates? Visit several elementary schools and interview their reading and LD teachers. How have they divided their roles? Do you find differences according to the ages of the students or individual strengths of the teachers?

4. If you are interested in exploring conceptual differences in how reading and LD specialists evaluate and teach the learning disabled, consult Lerner's (1975) article. She notes that in the real world there might even be more conceptual differences within each field than between them.

5. Cruickshank's (1966) book presents a panel of experts' recommended teaching competencies for universities to uniformly develop in their students, and the procedures for doing so. Stick (1976) notes that training programs still prepare teachers in the same way as they did twenty years before. One of the most recently prepared, national-level statements on recommended competencies for LD teachers can be found in Newcomer's (1978) article. Interview recent graduates of general education and learning disabilities programs to find out in which ways they feel they were well- or ill-prepared for their job responsibilities.

6. This country needs over 60,000 new special education teachers. Yet, we keep hearing about the oversupply of teachers. The oversupply is fact, but only among elementary and secondary teachers (about 75,000 oversupply) (*The State of Teacher Education*, 1977). Read this government document; it will help you understand how the teacher shortage of the 1950–1960s turned into a surplus by the 1970s. Factors such as these are considered: changes in university training emphases, birthrate, inflation, tenure, and turnover. Considering these factors, university reduction in elementary and secondary teacher training since 1972, together with the issues of the 1970s and 1980s (more women in the work force; later age of first pregnancy; mainstreaming; high-risk babies living), would you predict a continuation of the regular teacher oversupply or another undersupply? This issue is critical to LD children because they are for the most part educated in the regular classroom.

7. Read Kauffman and Hallahan, *Teaching Children with Learning Disabilities: Personal Perspectives* (1976), keeping in mind the question of the relevance of labelling to program planning. This book presents the retrospective, personal evaluations of many influential thinkers in the learning disabilities movement. Although these men and women's works formed the cornerstone of learning disabilities, some of them argued against establishing another category of exceptionality. Begin by reading Ray Barsch's chapter. In a touching way, he expressed the learning disabilities movement's importance as a concept clarifying the dynamics of human learning and learning failure, rather than as a category. Then read Kirk's, Frostig's, and Lovitt's contributions. Contrast these with Cruickshank's position.

Chapter Twelve
Matching Tasks to Learner Ability and Style

An essential part of the LD evaluation and planning process involves analyzing students' abilities and learning styles on the instructional tasks actually expected of them in the classroom. Only in this way can teachers ascertain precisely what and how their students need to be taught. Since learning disabilities can be aggravated or ameliorated by the nature of instructional tasks, teachers must assess the appropriateness of these tasks and how they can be modified to best meet students' learning needs. This involves analyzing the content of academic tasks and the learning processes that they require of the child. When content and process dimensions can be suitably matched to what the child is ready to learn and how he or she best learns, learning becomes a successful, forward-moving, happy adventure.

Matching tasks to children's abilities and learning styles is much easier said than done. Transferring information from the assessment process to wise decisions about teaching goals, materials, and strategies remains an ideal; it's very difficult to accomplish.

Most general education teachers have not been trained to make such analyses. Even when adequately trained, they often lack the time and energy to do so. They are overloaded with students and have little time for planning for groups of children, let alone a learning disabled child. Their limited budgets also make buying materials that benefit only one or two students unfeasible.

LD resource teachers often are appropriately trained in task analysis and diagnostic teaching procedures. Yet their ability to gear instruction to students' exact needs is limited because they must spend so much time helping students succeed in regular classroom assignments, especially at the secondary level.

Given the impossibility of matching each task to each learner, do we give up and not try? No, teachers must be realistic about what is and is not possible. The more aware teachers are of the ideal, the more likely they will be to match child and task characteristics. Besides, they cannot escape some minimal matching processes when teaching learning disabled students. Since each child is unique, a teacher must adapt most materials and teaching strategies before he or she even begins to teach.

Matching tasks to children's needs is not new. It began with such pioneers in learning disabilities as Werner, Strauss, and Fernald. Yet, it is still more an art than a science. Research Box 12-1 discusses why research on these matches, or *aptitude by treatment interactions* (ATI), is so hard to conduct. We have learned that assessment of child-task matches is an individualized, ongoing process for several reasons: not all methods work for all children (Alley & Deshler, 1979; Hagan, 1971; Wheeler & Dusek, 1973); the same method does not work on all tasks for any one child (Levin, 1976); and the same materials or methods may, after some time, no longer work for a given child. ATI research also has revealed a few methods that benefit most children, such as teaching phonics and learning strategies. Further advances in this type of research are likely to help guide future instructional decision-making.

RESEARCH BOX 12-1
Aptitude by Treatment Interaction Research

Aptitude by treatment interaction (ATI) research on how to match child and task characteristics is extremely difficult. It is nearly impossible to categorize groups of children as similar learners (for example, auditory or visual learning preferences) because precisely what each child has mastered, and how the child mastered it, varies from child to child (Bateman, 1968; Herjanic & Penick, 1972; Robinson, 1968). Therefore, one type of instruction will have nearly as many effects on the children in a study as there are children. Statistical analysis of the results of studies that teach different types of children by different methods often show no differences in gains between groups (Larrivee, 1981). Most children learn from the instruction given. Although some children probably did benefit more from one type of instruction than they would have from another, since they did not receive both types of instruction there is no way of finding this out (Haring, 1974). The group data also counterbalances the great gains of some children with the less remarkable gains of others. Aside from these factors, most studies can't be compared because of differences in design and children studied. The majority of these studies have been conducted on a short-term basis in the laboratory. In most cases researchers don't know whether the laboratory instruction transfers to classroom skills and behaviors and how long its positive effects persist.

Because of these factors, a newer trend in aptitude by treatment interaction studies is to measure an individual child's, rather than the group's, progress in the classroom (Gottman, 1973; Guralnick, 1978; Kratochwill, 1977; Kratochwill, Brody, & Piersel, 1979; Lovitt, 1975a,b; Wright, 1967). These studies teach with one method and then switch methods, so that the efficacy of different approaches with the same child can be examined. In this way researchers can discover what really works, to what degree, and for which child. The heterogeneity of a group of children does not mask individual gains. Since simulated laboratory settings are no longer required, the findings can be taken at face value and concern about generalization errors is alleviated.

The goal of this chapter is to explore the question that all teachers need to ask themselves: "In which ways must I change *what* I am expecting students to learn, and *how* I am asking them to learn it?" Which child and task attributes are the most important to consider is up to future research to determine. Three relevant types of task modifications are *task content* modified to coincide with *what* students are ready to learn, *task processes and features* modified to match *how* students prefer to go about learning, and teaching of more efficient learning strategies.

How a child's development may be affected by the daily requirements that he or she faces is demonstrated in the case study about Liza, page 388. Liza's story is an example of how adhering to rigid curriculum demands may foster success in some children but failure in others. As task demands changed, so did Liza's, her parents', and her teachers' perceptions of her as a learner. Because of

CASE STUDY:
Liza

Liza was born full term and healthy, although her mother was hospitalized with toxemia one week before delivery. At age five, Liza was placed in a small private school because her listening and expressive language skills were weak. She had not uttered single words until age two and had not combined words until age two and one-half. When she entered speech therapy at age three and one-half, she could produce almost no consonant sounds. She referred to her sister Julie as "oo-ee," bye-bye was "i - i," and bottle was "o - u." She was able to say "ma-ma" and "da-ee."

Fearing Liza might encounter academic difficulties, her parents thought that a private school's small group setting would be to her benefit. By May of her kindergarten year, Liza's teacher's support of *any* verbalizations she made ended happily. Liza had progressed from not even being brave enough to call out "Bingo" when she won a game at the beginning of the year, to constantly yelling "Hey Mrs. Thomas!" from anywhere in the room by the end of the year. All were delighted with this change.

But first grade required work and not talk. In early October the school's team told Liza's mother that she had an insolent, disobedient child who knew what to do but wouldn't do it, and destroyed the class with her disturbing chatter. Simply put — she was hyperactive and emotionally disturbed, and was potentially excludable from school. The message was clear: the mother was to go home and have a good talk with Liza. Liza should *pay attention* to the teacher, follow directions, and stop annoying others.

This type of behavior was a problem specific to the school. Although Liza chattered a lot at home, she was not a disturbance in that context. Her mother's message to the team was equally clear: "for my $2400 a year it had better be your (teachers') attitudes and task modifications that alter my daughter's school behavior." Two hours later, the team and mother agreed on what type of modifications they would make to help Liza attend better and talk less: turn her desk to the wall with her back to the others, instruct her in small groups rather than all by herself so that she would have an opportunity to learn how to listen in a group, tell her the *rules* of when talking is allowed and not allowed, compliment her on good listening, get her attention before talking to her, and ask her to repeat directions. By the next conference the mother was amused to hear from the team, "I don't know what you did but Liza has been a changed child since the very day following our conference!"

Liza's idiosyncrasies followed her wherever she went. Her chatter and inattention were predictable. Her parents decided to explore second grade in their local public school. They found that although Liza had completed all her first grade work at the private school, most of her middle-class peers in the public school had already completed second grade work. If enrolled with these children, Liza would be looked on as an underachiever among her peers. Liza's parents decided to enroll her in the public school's first grade instead. They reasoned that she had an August birthday and is somewhat immature anyhow. Liza became the brilliant class leader! She still talked a lot, didn't modulate her voice well, and couldn't judge when not to talk, but the teacher didn't notice in that large group. She still needed to hear directions twice, but the teacher repeated them automatically because of the noise in the classroom.

What is Liza? — emotionally disturbed, an underachiever relative to her peers and intelligence level (learning disabled), gifted? She is none of these, just a delightfully unique little girl who needed to find the right match between her strengths and weaknesses and school tasks to facilitate her development.

The story doesn't end all that rosily. Just as learning disabled children's resolved weaknesses reappear periodically and interfere with progress, so Liza's uniqueness creates continual challenges. Liza is now in third grade. There is some concern that she is not being challenged enough in reading and math because she is being taught the curriculum of children one year younger. Her social maturity is excellent and in some ways distances her from her peers. Yet she doesn't seem to understand their joking. She now has handwriting problems and needs to see a resource teacher twice a week. Liza is not as adept at poetry, composition, and playing with words as her classmates are. She's also too loud in the lunchroom.

Yet, she'll be okay. She's aware of her stumbling blocks but thinks of herself as a lovable, beautiful, capable child. Her biggest trauma now seems to be her strong desire to go to overnight camp at an age when most other children wouldn't consider it; but she doesn't know whether camp is worth giving up thumbsucking for, or whether the energy of hiding the thumb sucking under her blankets for four weeks is worth it!

Liza's uniqueness, neither her parents nor teachers could ever rest easy, thinking that all her problems were behind her. Similarly, teachers must continually stay on top of task content and process modifications for the learning disabled child, so that the student, teachers, and family can feel good about the positive progress being made.

Matching Task Content to Student Readiness

The comment, "my child can't learn anything" is commonly heard. Yet there is no such thing as a child who can't learn anything. Some children may not learn what they are expected to for their age and IQ, but they certainly can learn more fundamental skills that are easier for them. When task content is matched to what the child is absolutely ready to learn, then the learning process is facilitated. Achievement of higher level goals will occur more rapidly and completely when the content on which they rely is taught first (Kinsbourne & Caplan, 1979).

The maturational lag theorists warn against teaching too much, too soon and bypassing mastery of more important basic skills. Faulty habits are learned, which only need to be unlearned later on. The child who has put too much effort into learning and continually fails may lose the motivation to achieve. Consequently, teaching the appropriate material at the right time is essential.

Tables 12-1, 12-2, and 12-3 present general scope and sequence charts for instructional content in reading, math, and written expression. Teachers discover what on these tables a child is ready to learn by including several important procedures in their diagnostic-prescriptive teaching process: task analysis, evaluation of past opportunities for learning, and consultation with the child.

Table 12-1 Typical scope-and-sequence of reading skills usually taught at the elementary level

	WORD-STUDY SKILLS	COMPREHENSION SKILLS

First Grade	*Preprimer stage*
	A. Word meaning and concept building
	B. Picture clues
	C. Visual discrimination
	  1. Left-to-right progression
	  2. Word configuration
	  3. Capital and lowercase letter forms
	D. Auditory perception
	  1. Initial consonants — *b, c, d, f, g, h,*
	    l, m, p, r, s, t, w
	  2. Rhyming elements
	E. Structural analysis — ex. plural nouns:
	  adding *s*
	
	Primer stage
	Review, reteach, or teach all skills that
	child has not mastered
	Expand vocabulary
	A. Context clues
	B. Phonetic analysis
	  1. Initial consonants
	  2. Rhymes
	  3. Learning letter names — *n, l, p, d, g,*
	    r, c
	C. Structural analysis
	
	First reader
	A. All previous skills
	B. Phonetic analysis
	  1. Final analysis — *n, d, k, m, t, p*
	  2. Initial blends — *st, pl, bl, br, tr, dr,*
	    gr, fr
	C. Structural analysis
	  1. Verb forms
	    a. Adding *ed*
	    b. Adding *ing*
	  2. Compound words
		A. Associating text and pictures
		B. Following oral directions
		C. Main idea
		D. Details
		E. Sequence
		F. Drawing conclusions
		G. Seeing relationships
		
		A. All those at preprimer level
		B. Forming judgments
		C. Making inferences
		D. Classifying
		
		A. All previously taught skills
		B. Recalling story facts
		C. Predicting outcome
		D. Following printed directions

Second Grade	*Book one*
	A. Review and practice all first-grade skills
	B. Phonetic analysis
	  1. Rhyming words visually
	  2. Consonants
	    a. Initial — *j*
	    b. Final — *x, r, l*
	    c. Blends — *cr, sn, sl, pr, cl*
	    d. Digraphs — *ai, oa*
		A. All previously taught skills
		B. Making generalizations
		C. Seeing relationships
		D. Interpreting pictures

Table 12-1   continued

WORD-STUDY SKILLS	COMPREHENSION SKILLS

Second Grade

C. Structural analysis
   1. Plural of nouns — adding *s* and *es*
   2. Variant forms of verbs
      a. Adding *es, ing*
      b. Doubling consonants before adding *ing* or *ed*

Book two

WORD-STUDY SKILLS	COMPREHENSION SKILLS
A. All previously taught skills	A. Practice and use of all previously taught skills
B. Recognize words in alphabetical order	B. Making inferences
C. Phonetic analysis	C. Seeing cause-and-effect relationships

C. Phonetic analysis
   1. Consonant blends — *thr, gl, squ, apr, str*
   2. Phonograms — auditory and visual concepts of *ar, er, ir, ow, ick, ew, own, uck, ed, ex, ouse, ark, oat, ound*
   3. Vowel differences
      a. Vowels lengthened by final *e*
      b. Long and short sounds of *y*
      c. Digraphs — *ee, ea*
      d. Diphthongs — different sounds of *ow*
D. Structural analysis
   1. Contractions — *it's, I'm, I'll, that's, let's, don't, didn't, isn't*
   2. Variant forms of verbs — dropping *e* before adding *ing*
   3. Plural forms of nouns — changing *y* to *ies*

Third Grade

Book one

WORD-STUDY SKILLS	COMPREHENSION SKILLS
A. All previously learned skills	A. All skills previously learned
B. Word meaning	B. Detecting mood of situation
	C. Relating story facts to own experiences
	D. Reading pictorial maps
	E. Skimming

B. Word meaning
   1. Opposites
   2. Adding *ore, est* to change form and meaning of words
   3. Words with multiple meanings
C. Phonetic analysis
   1. Consonants
      a. Hard and soft sounds — *c, g*
      b. Recognizing consonants
      c. Digraphs
         (1) *ck*
         (2) Vowels
            (a) Silent vowels
            (b) Digraphs — *ai, ea, ou, ee, ay, ui*

(Continued on following page)

Table 12-1   continued

WORD-STUDY SKILLS	COMPREHENSION SKILLS

Third Grade

    d. Structural analysis
      (1) Contractions — *who's, we're, you're, aren't, that's, I'm, couldn't*
      (2) Possessive words
      (3) Suffixes — *en, est, ly*
      (4) Variant forms of verbs
        (a) Changing final *y* to *i* before adding *ed*
        (b) Dropping *e* before adding *ing*
    e. Alphabetizing — first letter
    f. Syllabication — up to three-syllable words

Book two

A. All previously learned skills
B. Word meaning
    1. Homonyms
      a. *dew, do*
      b. *sea, see*
      c. *whole, hole*
      d. *made, maid*
      e. *blew, blue*
      f. *ewe, you*
      g. *forth, fourth*
      h. *thrown, throne*
    2. Synonyms
      a. *throw, pitch*
      b. *quiet, still*
      c. *speak, say*
      d. *lift, raise*
      e. *tug, pull*
      f. *large, big*
      g. *swiftly, fast*
      h. *believe, think*
      i. *smart, clever*
      j. *come, arrive*
      k. *daybreak, dawn*
      l. *fastened, tied*
C. Phonetic analysis
    1. Consonants — hard and soft sounds of *g, c*
      a. *c* usually has a soft sound when it comes before *e* or *i*
      b. *g* usually has a soft sound when it comes before *e* or *i*

A. All previously learned skills
B. Problem solving

Table 12-1   continued

WORD-STUDY SKILLS	COMPREHENSION SKILLS

Third Grade

2. Vowels
   a. Diphthongs — *ou, ow, or, oy, aw, au*
   b. Sounds of vowels followed by *r*
D. Structural analysis
   1. Plurals — change *f* to *v* when adding *es*
   2. Contractions — *doesn't, you'll, they're*
   3. Suffixes
      a. Recognizing as syllables
      b. Adding *ly* and *ily*
      c. Positive comparative and superlative forms of adjectives
   4. Prefixes — *un* changes meaning of words to the opposite
E. Alphabetizing — using second letter
F. Syllabication
   1. Between double consonants
   2. Prefixes and suffixes as syllables
G. Accent — finding syllables said more heavily

Fourth Grade

Word meaning:
A. Antonyms
B. Synonyms
C. Homonyms
D. Figures of speech
E. Sensory appeals in words

Word analysis:
A. Phonetic analysis
   1. Consonants
      a. Silent
      b. Two sounds of *s*
      c. Hard and soft sounds of *c* and *g*
      d. Diacritical marks
         (1) Long sound of vowels
         (2) Short sound of vowels
         (3) *a* as in *care*
         (4) *a* as in *bars*
         (5) *u* as in *burn*
         (6) *a* as in *ask*
         (7) *e* as in *wet*
         (8) *e* as in *letter*
         (9) *oo* as in *moon*
         (10) *oo* as in *foot*

Comprehension skills (Fourth Grade):

1. All previously learned skills
2. Reading for comprehension
3. Finding the main ideas
4. Finding details
5. Organizing and summarizing
6. Recalling story facts
7. Recognizing sequence
8. Reading for information
9. Creative reading
   a. Classifying
   b. Detecting the mood of a situation
   c. Drawing conclusions
   d. Forming judgments
   e. Making inferences
   f. Predicting outcomes
   g. Seeing cause-and-effect relationships
   h. Problem solving
10. Following printed directions
11. Skimming

(Continued on following page)

Table 12-1   continued

WORD-STUDY SKILLS	COMPREHENSION SKILLS

Fourth Grade

    e. Applying vowel principles
       (1) Vowel in the middle of a word or syllable is usually *short*
       (2) Vowel coming at the end of a one-syllable word is usually *long*
       (3) When a one-syllable word ends in *e,* the medial vowel in that word is usually *long*
       (4) When two vowels come together, the first vowel is usually *long* and the second vowel is *silent*

B. Structural analysis
  1. Hyphenated words — *good-by, thirty-one, rain-maker*
  2. Finding root words in word variants
  3. Prefixes — *dis, re, un, im*
  4. Suffixes — *ly, ness, ment, ful, ish, less*
  5. Syllabication
    a. When a vowel sound is followed by one consonant, that consonant usually begins the next syllable
    b. When a vowel sound in a word is followed by two consonants, this word is usually divided between the two consonants
    c. Prefixes and suffixes are usually syllables
    d. Compound words are usually divided between the word parts
    e. In two-syllable words ending in *le* preceded by a consonant, the consonant joins the *le* and begins the final syllable
  6. Accent

Fifth Grade

WORD-STUDY SKILLS	COMPREHENSION AND STUDY SKILLS	LOCATING AND USING INFORMATION (STUDY SKILLS)
1. Antonyms — review and give practice in using context clues 2. Expand vocabulary	*Continue development in the following areas:* A. Main idea B. Sequence	

Table 12-1   continued

	WORD-STUDY SKILLS	COMPREHENSION AND STUDY SKILLS	LOCATING AND USING INFORMATION (STUDY SKILLS)

Fifth Grade	3. Review figures of speech and introduce new ones to enrich vocabulary
	4. Homonyms — review and introduce new ones
	5. Synonyms — review and introduce new ones to expand vocabulary
	6. Use of dictionary and glossary
	  a. Guide words
	  b. Accent marks
	  c. Diacritical marks
	    1. Review *â, ä, û, å, oo, oo, ëe*
	    2. Review long and short vowels
	    3. Introduce schwa, half-long *o*
	    4. Introduce italic *u, i, a, e*
	    5. Introduce ' in omitted vowel
	    6. Respellings
	7. Phonetic analysis
	  a. Review consonant sounds
	  b. Review pronunciation of diacritical marks
	  c. Review phonograms
	8. Structural analysis
	  a. Compound words
	  b. Words of similar configuration
	  c. Prefixes
	    1. Review *un-, im-, dis-, re-*
	    2. Introduce *in-, anti-, inter-, mis-*
	  d. Suffixes
	    1. Review *-en, -ment, -less, -ish, -ly, -ful, -y, -ed*
		C. Reading for details
		D. Appreciating literary style
		E. Drawing conclusions
		F. Enriching information
		G. Evaluating information
		H. Forming opinions and generalizing
		I. Interpreting ideas
		J. Using alphabetical arrangement
		K. Using dictionary or glossary skills
		L. Interpreting maps and pictures
		M. Skimming for purpose
		N. Classifying ideas
		O. Following directions
		P. Outlining
		Q. Summarizing
		R. Reading for accurate detail
		S. Skimming
		
		Introduce and teach:
		A. Discrimination between fact and fiction
		B. Perceiving related ideas
		C. Strengthening power of recall
		D. Using encyclopedias, atlas, almanac, and other references
		E. Using charts and graphs
		F. Using index and pronunciation keys
		G. Reading to answer questions and for enjoyment of literary style	

(Continued on following page)

Table 12-1   continued

	WORD-STUDY SKILLS	COMPREHENSION AND STUDY SKILLS	LOCATING AND USING INFORMATION (STUDY SKILLS)

Fifth Grade	2. Introduce -*sp*, -*or*, -*ours*, -*ness*, -*ward*, -*hood*, -*action*, -*al*;
	e. Principles of syllabication
	  1. Review rules already taught
	  2. Consonant blends and digraphs are treated as singular sounds, and usually are not divided (*ma-chine*)
	f. Application of word analysis in attacking words outside the basic vocabulary		

Sixth Grade	*Word meaning:*
	A. Antonyms — review and give practice in
	B. Homonyms — develop ability to use correctly
	C. Classify words of related meaning
	D. Enrich word meaning
	E. Review use of synonyms
	F. Use context clues in attacking new words
	G. Expand vocabulary
	H. Become aware of expressions that refer to place and time and develop skill in interpreting such expressions
	I. Use dictionary and glossary
	  1. Further ability to use alphabetical-order guide words, and pronounciation key
	  2. Review diacritical marks — introduce circumflex–breve as in *sŏft*
	  3. Review spelling
		Continue development in the following areas:
		A. Main ideas
		B. Sequence
		C. Reading for details
		D. Appreciating literary style
		E. Drawing conclusions
		  1. Predicting outcomes
		  2. Forming judgments
		  3. Seeing relationships
		F. Extending and enriching information
		G. Interpreting pictures
		H. Evaluating information
		I. Interpreting ideas
		J. Using facts to form opinions, generalizing
		
		Introduce the skills of
		A. Enriching imagery
		B. Discriminating between fact and fiction
		C. Strengthening power of recall
			Review skills in the following:
			1. Alphabetical arrangement
			2. Use of dictionary and glossary
			3. Use of encyclopedia, almanac, and other references
			4. Interpreting maps and pictures
			5. Skimming for a purpose
			6. Classifying ideas
			7. Following directions
			8. Summarizing
			9. Outlining
			10. Reading for accurate detail
			11. Using index and pronunciation keys
			12. Using charts and graphs
			13. Reading to answer questions and for enjoyment of literary style

Table 12-1 continued

	WORD-STUDY SKILLS	COMPREHENSION AND STUDY SKILLS	LOCATING AND USING INFORMATION (STUDY SKILLS)

Sixth Grade	*Word analysis:*
	A. Phonetic analysis
	  1. Review consonant sounds
	  2. Diacritical marks — interpreting pronunciation symbols
	  3. Review vowel sounds principles
	B. Structural analysis
	  1. Review compound words
	  2. Review hyphenated words
	  3. Review prefixes
	    a. Review *un-, im-, dis-, re-, in-, anti-, inter-, mis-*
	    b. Introduce *trans-, pre-, fore-, ir-, non-*
	  4. Review suffixes
	    a. Review *-en, -ment, -less, -ish, -ly, -ful, -y, -ed, -shy, -or, -er, -ous, -ness, -ward, -hood, -ation, -al*
	    b. Introduce *-able, -ance, -ence, -ate, -est, -ent, -ity, -ic, -ist, -like*
	  5. Review principles of syllabication
	  6. Review accented syllables
	  7. Apply word analysis in attacking words outside the basic vocabulary
			Introduce the following skills:
			1. Use of facts and figures
			2. Use of headings and type style — especially use of italics
			  a. To give importance to a word or expression in a sentence
			  b. To show that a sentence has a special importance to the plot of the story
			  c. To set off a special title used in a sentence or a reference
			3. Use of an index
			4. Use of library
			5. Use of table of contents
			6. Taking notes
			7. Reading of information material
			8. Reading poetry

SOURCE: Adapted from G. Kaluger and C. J. Kolson, *Reading and Learning Disabilities,* 2nd ed. Columbus, Ohio: Charles E. Merrill Publishing Co., 1978. By permission.

Table 12-2   Scope and sequence of math skills typically taught at the elementary level

		A		
GRADE LEVEL	ONE-TO-ONE	NUMERALS	SETS	ORDINALS
K	Matches one to one Matches shapes (discrimination) ○ □ △ ◇ Vocabulary of space and position Estimates distance, height, and quantity Order by height	Matches one to one Writes 0–5 Identifies 0–10 Identifies before and after 1–10 Counts orally 0–10	Matches equivalent sets 00 = 00 Recognizes sets 0–5 Recognizes sets with more or less	Understands first through fifth
1st		Identifies 0–50 Counts orally 0–100 Counts and writes by 10s to 100 and 5s to 50 Writes 0–50 Knows place value 0–50 Renames 1s & 10s through 50 Identifies odd and even numbers	Recognizes sets 6–10 Knows language of sets	Understands sixth through tenth
2nd		Counts and writes by 2s to 100; 3s to 36; 4s to 48; 5s to 100; 10s to 200 Writes 0–100 Knows place value 50–100 Renames 50–100 Knows odd and even numbers	Identifies equivalent sub-sets	Reads ordinals through twelfth
3rd		Writes in sequence 1–999 Writes from dictation 1–999 Renames 10s to 100s Knows Roman numerals I–X Knows, reads, writes 1-, 2-. and 3-place numbers	Identifies equal sets	Understands ordinals to hundredths Reads ordinals through twentieth

Table 12-2 continued

A				
GRADE LEVEL	ONE-TO-ONE	NUMERALS	SETS	ORDINALS
4th		Counts and writes by 6s to 72; 7s to 84; 8s to 96; 9s to 108 Knows place value to millions Knows Roman numerals XI–C Understands rounding of numbers to nearest 10	Identifies universal sets Identifies intersection of sets	Reads ordinals through thirtieth
5th		Reads and writes billions Knows Roman numerals C–M Understands rounding of whole numbers Identifies prime and composite numbers Understands common factors and Greatest Common Factors (GCF) Identifies multiples of numbers and Least Common Multiple (LCM)	Understands union of sets, disjoint sets, finite and infinite sets, empty sets	
6th		Understands integers, negative numbers, rational numbers, base numeration, place value to billions place	Understands solution sets, sets of ordered pairs	

B				
GRADE LEVEL	ADDITION	SUBTRACTION	STORY PROBLEMS	GEOMETRY
K			Solves oral problems using "one more" Solves oral problems using "one less"	Recognizes and reproduces ○ □ ▭ △ Recognizes and reproduces straight and curved lines

(Continued on following page)

Table 12-2   continued

			B	
GRADE LEVEL	ADDITION	SUBTRACTION	STORY PROBLEMS	GEOMETRY
1st	Knows facts 1–10 Adds facts 1–10 horizontally and vertically Adds two digits no regrouping	Knows facts 1–10 Subtracts two digits no regrouping Subtracts facts 1–10 horizontally and vertically	Solves written addition and subtraction problems 0–5	Recognizes and reproduces ◇ Recognizes line segments not closed curves
2nd	Knows facts 11–20 Adds three digits no regrouping Completes number sentences with missing digits	Knows facts 11–20 Subtracts three digits no regrouping Uses number sentences with missing digits	Solves written addition and subtraction problems through 20 One-step problems	Recognizes cone, semicircle, congruent figures, intersecting curves, labeled points
3rd	Adds two and three digits with regrouping Adds by endings	Subtracts two and three digits with regrouping Checks by addition	Solves problems using + and −, × and ÷ Two-step problems	Recognizes spheres and cylinders, rays, planes, right angles, parallel lines Understands diameter and radius
4th	Knows vocabulary Adds one-three digits and five addends with regrouping Commutative and associative properties expanded	Knows vocabulary Subtracts two-four digits with regrouping	Solves multiple-step problems + − × ÷ Writes number sentences Solves problems with averages	Recognizes prism, pyramid, cube, triangular and rectangular prisms and tetrahedron, perpendicular and intersecting lines, planes, and line segments
5th	Adds two addends with five columns Adds three addends with four columns Adds four addends with four columns	Subtracts four and five digits with regrouping Understands 0	Solves multiple-step problems using fractions, decimals, ratio, measurement graphs (bar and circle)	Measures angles Understands Pythagorean Theorem Recognizes polygons

Table 12-2 continued

		B	
GRADE LEVEL	ADDITION	SUBTRACTION	STORY PROBLEMS	GEOMETRY

GRADE LEVEL	ADDITION	SUBTRACTION	STORY PROBLEMS	GEOMETRY
	Adds equations Averages			Recognizes right, congruent, and similar triangles
				Measures triangles
6th	Adds Base 2	Subtracts Base 2	Solves problems dealing with time, work, rate, distance, and speed	Uses equations to find volume
				Finds perimeter and area
				Identifies and draws angles, isosceles and equilateral triangles

		C	

GRADE LEVEL	STANDARD MEASUREMENT	METRIC MEASUREMENT	SYMBOLS OF MATH	MULTIPLICATION
K	Understands simple comparison in length, size, and weight			
1st	Knows days of the week	Uses centimeter to find lengths	Recognizes $+$, $-$, $<>$, $=$, and $\neq$	
	Tells time on the hour, half-hour, and day			
	Knows temperature			
	Knows pint, quart, cup			
	Knows inch, foot, yard			
	Knows weight			
	Compares inch and half-inch			

(Continued on following page)

Table 12-2   continued

		C		
GRADE LEVEL	STANDARD MEASUREMENT	METRIC MEASUREMENT	SYMBOLS OF MATH	MULTIPLI-CATION
2nd	Knows months of the year Relates inches to feet Knows gallon	Uses liter and milliliter	Recognizes < >, =, and ≠	Multiplies products through 25 Relates multiplication to repeated addition
3rd	Tells time in five-minute intervals Tells time in quarter hours Converts inches, feet, yards Converts half-pint, quart Uses calendar, week, month Uses scale Measures to nearest ½ or ¼ inch Reads a digital clock Reads Celsius or Fahrenheit scale thermometer	Knows relationship of meters and centimeters, grams, and kilograms, liters and milliters	Recognizes ×, ÷, " and '	Multiplies facts through 45 Multiplies two digits by one digit, three digits by one digit, ten digits by one digit
4th	Finds perimeter of shapes Understands dry measures (weight) Understands volume, area, square inch, and square mile Converts one unit of a measure to another	Uses scale to read kilograms	Uses letter n for missing number Recognizes metric symbols: cm, m, kg, and l Recognizes ∩ intersection of sets	Knows vocabulary Multiplies facts through 81 Multiplies multiples of 100, 1,000 Multiplies with regrouping
5th	Understands zones, belts, standard time Reads graphs (bar graph, line graph, pictograph)	Shows metric comparisons Understands metric scale drawings Knows ratio of measures	Recognizes subset ⊂, super subset ⊃, union of sets ∪	Multiplies three digits by three digits Multiplies four digits by three digits Identifies prime

Table 12-2 continued

		C		
GRADE LEVEL	STANDARD MEASUREMENT	METRIC MEASUREMENT	SYMBOLS OF MATH	MULTIPLI- CATION
	Solves time prob- lems Finds area of squares and rectangles Uses solid mea- surements Reads road map Understands latitude and longitude			numbers
6th	Finds approxima- tion of area Finds area of triangle, circle Finds circumference	Understands approxi- mation of area Knows abbreviations of metric units Converts to larger and smaller units	Recognizes %, π, c	Knows modu- lar multipli- cation Knows lattice method of multiplication Knows square root Multiplies by four digits Multiplies with decimals and mixed frac- tions

		D		
GRADE LEVEL	DIVISION	FRACTIONS	DECIMALS/ PERCENT	MONEY
K		Divides shapes in $\frac{1}{2}$ Divides sets in $\frac{1}{2}$		Identifies penny, nickel, dime
1st		Divides shapes and sets in $\frac{1}{4}$		Identifies quar- ters Compares value of penny, nickel, dime

(Continued on following page)

Table 12-2   continued

		D		
GRADE LEVEL	DIVISION	FRACTIONS	DECIMALS/ PERCENT	MONEY
2nd		Divides shapes and sets in $\frac{1}{3}$		Knows symbols $ ¢ Substitutes money values: penny, nickel, dime, quarter Identifies change after purchase
3rd	Divides facts through 45 Divides problems with remainders Divides using multiples of ten	Divides shapes and sets in $\frac{1}{2}$, $\frac{1}{4}$, $\frac{1}{3}$		Compares money value 50¢ and $1.00 Adds and subtracts money problems
4th	Knows vocabulary Divides facts through 81 Divides 3⟌27 3⟌638 10⟌181 Checks answers by multiplication	Adds and subtracts fractions with like denominators Adds and subtracts fractions with unlike denominators Adds and subtracts mixed numbers		Adds purchases and counts out change

Task Analysis

Task analysis involves breaking down the exact content of each task that the child is having difficulty mastering into easier steps. The teacher notes which steps the child already has mastered. The child is then ready to be instructed on the next harder step. This process leads to valid instructional conclusions because they are gained from the actual teaching objectives (Gagné, 1970; Junkala, 1972, 1973). This *principle of maximum transfer* (Ferguson, 1956 in Vellutino et al., 1977) is an advantage that most tests don't have.

Tasks also can be analyzed along process dimensions. The teacher can divide the content into input — visual or auditory — and expression — talk-

Table 12-2   continued

		D		
GRADE LEVEL	DIVISION	FRACTIONS	DECIMALS/ PERCENT	MONEY
5th	Divides by two-digit divisor with quotient remainder Divides three-digit divisor Averages	Multiplies a whole number by a fraction, A fraction by a fraction, A mixed number by a whole number, A mixed number by mixed number	Identifies place value Solves decimal-fraction and equivalence Adds, subtracts, and reads and writes decimals to tenths and hundredths Adds and subtracts two-decimal numbers to hundredths Multiplies whole numbers by decimals	
6th	Divides by divisor with three or more digits Divides with fractions Divides with decimals	Divides fractions with like and unlike denominators Divides improper fractions Divides mixed numbers	Understands, reads, writes through billions Extends meaning through millionths Counts by tenths, hundredths, thousandths Adds and subtracts two decimals to thousandths Writes decimal equations for proper and improper fractions Multiplies decimal by decimal Divides by whole number or decimal number Computes percent of a number	

SOURCE: Mann, P. H., Suiter, P. A., and McClung, R. M. *Handbook in Diagnostic-Prescriptive Teaching,* Abridged second edition. Boston: Allyn & Bacon, 1979. pp. 251–256. Reprinted by permission.

ing or writing. Virginia Sperry (1974) lists other useful dimensions to consider when analyzing tasks from most to least difficult:

☐ *external to internal communication* — expressive skills are harder than mastering material receptively.

☐ *social to nonsocial situations* — working in a group is more difficult than working in a one-to-one situation.

☐ *abstract to concrete materials and responses* — pairing a word with a picture representing its meaning is more difficult than pairing it with an action.

Table 12-3   Scope and sequence of written expression skills typically taught at the elementary level.

GRADE 1	GRADE 2	GRADE 3
Capitalization		
The first word of a sentence	The date	Proper names: month, day, common holidays
The child's first and last names	First and important words of titles of books the children read	First word in a line of verse
The name of the teacher, school, town, street	Proper names used in children's writings	First and important words in titles of books, stories, poems
The word "I"	Titles of compositions	First word of salutation of informal note, as "Dear"
	Names of titles: Mr., Mrs., Miss	First word of closing of informal note, as "Yours"
Punctuation		
Period at the end of a sentence which tells something	Question mark at the close of a question	Period after abbreviations
Period after numbers in any kind of list	Comma after salutation of a friendly note or letter	Period after an initial
	Comma after closing of a friendly note or letter	Use of an apostrophe in a common contraction such as isn't, aren't
	Comma between the day of the month and the year	Commas in a list
	Comma between name of city and state	
Vocabulary		
New words learned during experience	Words with similar meanings; with opposite meanings	Extending discussion of words for precise meanings
Choosing words that describe accurately	Alphabetical order	Using synonyms
Choosing words that make you see, hear, feel		Distinguishing meanings and spellings of homonyms
		Using the prefix *un* and the suffix *less*
Word usage		
Generally in oral expression	*Generally in oral expression*	Use of *there is* and *there are*; *any* and *no*
Naming yourself last	Double negative	Use of *let* and *leave*; *don't* and *doesn't*; *would have*, not *would of*
Eliminating unnecessary words (my father he); use of *well* and *good*	Use of *a* and *an*; *may* and *can*; *teach* and *learn*	Verb forms in sentences:
Verb forms in sentences:	Eliminating unnecessary words (this here)	throw, threw, thrown
is, are	Verb forms in sentences:	drive, drove, driven
did, done	rode, ridden	wrote, written
was, were	took, taken	tore, torn
see, saw, seen	grow, grew, grown	

Table 12-3   continued

GRADE 1	GRADE 2	GRADE 3
Sentences Write simple sentences	Recognition of sentences; kinds: statement and question Composing correct and interesting original sentences Avoiding running sentences together with *and*	Exclamatory sentences Use of a variety of sentences Combining short, choppy sentences into longer ones Using interesting beginning and ending sentences Avoiding run-on sentences (no punctuation) Learning to proofread one's own and others' sentences
Paragraphs Not applicable	Not applicable	Keeping to one idea Keeping sentences in order; sequence of ideas Finding and deleting sentences that do not belong Indenting

GRADE 4	GRADE 5	GRADES 6, 7, AND 8
Capitalization Names of cities and states in general Names of organizations to which children belong, such as Boy Scouts, grade four, etc. Mother, Father, when used in place of the name Local geographical names	Names of streets Names of all places and persons, countries, oceans, etc. Capitalization used in outlining Titles when used with names, such as President Lincoln Commercial trade names	Names of the Deity and the Bible First word of a quoted sentence Proper adjectives, showing race, nationality, etc. Abbreviations of proper nouns and titles
Punctuation Apostrophe to show possession Hyphen separating parts of a word divided at end of a line Period following a command Exclamation point at the end of a word or group of words that make an exclamation	Colon in writing time Quotation marks around the title of a booklet, pamphlet, the chapter of a book, and the title of a poem or story Underlining the title of a book	Comma to set off nouns in direct address Hyphen in compound numbers Colon to set off a list Comma in sentences to aid in making meaning clear

(Continued on following page)

Table 12-3   continued

GRADE 4	GRADE 5	GRADES 6, 7 AND 8
Comma setting off an appositive		
Colon after the saluation of a business letter		
Quotation marks before and after a direct quotation		
Comma between explanatory words and a quotation		
Period after outline Roman numeral		

Vocabulary		
Dividing words into syllables	Using antonyms	Extending meanings; writing with care in choice of words and phrases
Using the accent mark	Prefixes and suffixes, compound words	In writing and speaking, selecting words for accuracy
Using exact words which appeal to the senses	Exactness in choice of words	Selecting words for effectiveness and appropriateness
Using exact words in explanation	Dictionary work; definitions; syllables; pronunciation; macron; breve	Selecting words for courtesy
Keeping individual lists of new words and meanings	Contractions	Editing a paragraph to improve a choice of words
	Rhyme and rhythm; words with sensory images	
	Classification of words by parts of speech	
	Roots and words related to them	
	Adjectives, nouns, verbs — contrasting general and specific vocabulary	

Word Usage		
Agreement of subject and verb	Avoiding unnecessary pronouns (the boy he . . .)	Homonyms: *its*, and *it's*; *their, there, they're*; *there's, theirs; whose, who's*
Use of *she, he, I, we,* and *they* as subjects	Linking verbs and predicate nominatives	Use of parallel structure for parallel ideas, as in outlines
Use of *bring* and *take*	Conjugation of verbs, to note changes in tense, person, number	Verb forms in sentences:
Verb forms in sentences:		beat, beat, beaten
blow, blew, blown	Transitive and intransitive verbs	learn, learned, learned
drink, drank, drunk	Verb forms in sentences:	leave, left, left
lie, lay, lain	am, was, been	lit, lit, lit
take, took, taken	say, said, said	
rise, rose, risen		

Word Usage		
ate, eaten	know, knew, known	chose, chosen
went, gone	bring, brought	climbed

Table 12-3 continued

GRADE 4	GRADE 5	GRADES 6, 7 AND 8
came, come gave, given	drew, drawn began, begun ran, run	broke, broken wore, worn spoke, spoken sang, sung rang, rung catch, caught
Grammar Not applicable	Not applicable	Nouns: recognition of singu- lar, plural, and possessive Verbs: recognition
Word Usage teach, taught, taught raise, raise, raise lay, laid, laid fly, flew, flown set, set, set swim, swam, swum freeze, froze, frozen steal, stole, stolen	fall, fell, fallen dive, dived, dived burst, burst, burst buy, bought, bought Additional verb forms: *climb, like, play, read, sail, vote, work*	forgot, forgotten swing, swung, swung spring, sprang, sprung shrink, shrank, shrunk slid, slid, slid
Grammar Nouns, common and proper; noun in complete subjects Verb in complete predicate Adjectives: recognition Adverbs: recognition (telling how, when, where) Adverbs modifying verbs, ad- jectives, other adverbs Pronouns: recognition of sin- gular and plural	Noun: possessive; objective of preposition; predicate noun Verb: tense; agreement with subject; verbs of action and state of being Adjective: comparison; predi- cate adjective; proper adjec- tive Adverb: comparison; words telling how, when, where, how much; modifying verbs, adjectives, adverbs Pronouns: possessive; objec- tive after prepositions Prepositions: recognition; prepositional phrases Conjunction: recognition Interjection: recognition	Noun: clauses; common and proper nouns; indirect ob- ject Verb: conjugating to note changes in person, number, tense; linking verbs with predicate nominatives Adjective: chart of uses; clauses; demonstrative; de- scriptive, numerals; phrases Adverb: chart of uses; clauses; comparison; descriptive; *ly* ending; modification of ad- verbs; phrases Pronoun: antecedents; declen- sion chart — person, gen- der, case; demonstrative; indefinite; interrogative; personal; relative Preposition: phrases Conjunction: in compound subjects and predicates; in subordinate and coordinate clauses

(Continued on following page)

Table 12-3   continued

GRADE 4	GRADE 5	GRADES 6, 7 AND 8
		Interjection: placement of, in quotations
		Noun: antecedent of pronouns; collective nouns; compound subject; direct object; indirect object; object of preposition
		Verb: active and passive voice; emphatic forms; transitive and intransitive; tenses, linking verbs
		Adverb: as modifiers; clauses; comparing adverbs; adverbial phrase, use of *well* and *good*
		Adjectives: as modifiers; clauses; compound adjectives
		Pronouns: agreement with antecedents; personal pronoun chart; indirect object; object of preposition; objective case, person and number; possessive form
		Preposition: in phrase
		Conjunction: coordinate; subordinate; use in compound subjects; compound predicates; complex and compound sentences
Sentences		
Command sentences	Using a variety of interesting sentences: declarative; interrogative; exclamatory; and imperative (*you* the subject)	Development of concise statements (avoiding wordiness or unnecessary repetition)
Complete and simple subject; complete and simple predicate		Indirect object and predicate nominative
Adjectives and adverbs recognized; pronouns introduced	Agreement of subject and verb; changes in pronoun forms	Complex sentences

□ *verbal to nonverbal materials and responses* — language tasks are usually harder than visual-motor tasks. For example, a child may be able to match the word "cat" with another word "cat," note that it is different when embedded among three "bat's," and copy the word "cat." However, applying language to the visual symbol for reading is more difficult. For most children, conjuring up the language and visual symbols from mem-

Table 12-3 continued

GRADE 4	GRADE 5	GRADES 6, 7 AND 8
Avoiding fragments of sentences (incomplete) and the comma fault (a comma where a period belongs) Improving sentences in a paragraph	Compound subjects and compound predicates Composing paragraphs with clearly stated ideas	Clear thinking and expression (avoiding vagueness and omissions)
Paragraphs Selecting main topic Choosing title to express main idea Making simple outline with main idea Developing an interesting paragraph	Improvement in writing a paragraph of several sentences Selecting subheads as well as main topic for outline Courtesy and appropriateness in all communications Recognizing topic sentences Keeping to the topic as expressed in title and topic sentence Use of more than one paragraph Developing a four-point outline Writing paragraphs from outline New paragraphs for new speakers in written conversation Keeping list of books (authors and titles) used for reference	Analyzing a paragraph to note method of development Developing a paragraph in different ways: e.g., with details, reasons, examples, or comparisons Checking for accurate statements Use of a fresh or original approach in expressing ideas Use of transition words to connect ideas Use of topic sentences in developing paragraphs Improvement in complete composition — introduction, development, conclusion Checking for good reasoning Use of bibliography in report based on several sources

SOURCE: Hammill, D. D. and Poplin, M. "Problems in Writing," in Hammill, D. D. and Bartel, N. R. (eds.), *Teaching Children with Learning and Behavior Problems,* 2nd ed. Boston: Allyn & Bacon, 1978, pp. 186–191.

ory and writing them down, as in writing "cat" from memory, is the most difficult task of all.

☐ *symbolic to nonsymbolic materials and responses* — dealing with the concept of "justice" is much more difficult than dealing with punishment after hitting another child; understanding language when translated into another symbol system (letters) is often harder than understanding the same content in oral speech.

☐ *sequential to static items and responses* — dealing with elements in a series is more difficult than dealing with each one in isolation.

□ *long-term recall to short-term memory to no memory* — remembering something for a long period of time is more difficult than remembering it for the moment; not having to remember is easiest of all.

A task analysis for letter-naming is presented in Table 12-4. It analyzes the task from hardest to easiest with reference to the modalities and memory skills required. Any instructional modifications resulting from such a procedure are appropriate for one particular child on that one task. The assumptions on which these modifications are based may not be appropriate for the same child on other tasks or for different children on the same task (Levin, 1976). Such task analyses help to determine both remediation methods and compensatory instructional approaches that use the child's strengths to work around the weaknesses in order to facilitate continued success.

Sally's example illustrates the task analysis of a motor and spelling difficulty. This is her profile:

□ Strengths: language skills, reading, visual recognition of spelling words
□ Weaknesses: copying, writing, written recall of spelling words
□ Remediation Objective: drawing letters and spelling

Table 12-4 Task analysis of letter-naming.

| | | MODALITY | | |
		INPUT	OUTPUT	TASK REQUIREMENTS
Harder →	*Memory* recall	auditory	motor	write the letter "C" when "C" is dictated by the teacher
	recall	visual	oral	read the letter "C" when presented on a card
	recognition	auditory	motor	teacher says "C"; student points to the "C"
	recognition	visual	oral	teacher points to a "C" and asks "is this a "C"; student responds yes or no
Easier ←	*No Memory* discrimination	visual	motor	student matches the "C" with another "C" among several distractor letters
	discrimination	auditory	vocal	teacher says "C — C," are they the same or different? "C — P" are they the same or different?; student responds
	repetition	auditory	vocal	teacher says "C"; student repeats "C"
	repetition	visual	motor	student copies a model of "C"

☐ Remediation Method: drawing letter parts, combining visual recognition and language skills with writing to aid recall of spelling words
☐ Compensations: dictating compositions

Sally, a first grader, has an excellent listening and speaking vocabulary. Yet when asked to look at simple words and copy them from the board she loses her place, skips words, changes the order of letters in words, and alters the sizes and shapes of letters in such a way that they're often not recognizable.

When the teacher begins to task analyze by having Sally copy from a sample placed on her desk, Sally does not do much better. The teacher then has her copy the letters one by one, and finds that this doesn't help either. The teacher analyzes the strokes involved in making letters: circles, verticals, horizontals, and diagonals. She finds that Sally's circles are perfect, but don't make appropriate contact with vertical lines. For example, the vertical and circle in d, p, q, and b overlap so much that one wouldn't know which of the letters she's trying to print. Sally is able to copy vertical and horizontal lines very well. But her diagonals most often are produced like verticals and horizontals. The teacher now knows what she has to teach: diagonals, and the meeting of two strokes at a specified point. She uses stencils, tracing paper, verbal explanations and practice to help Sally master these skills. Once diagonals are mastered, these are integrated into letter forms containing diagonals (k, v, x, N, M, w, z, Q, A). Within a few months Sally can reasonably copy the morning message from the blackboard together with the rest of the class.

But writing never comes easily to Sally. She continues to need to double check letter shapes on the board one by one. By the time she is in fourth grade, she has transitioned to cursive writing and is doing reasonably well. She also reads well and is able to apply her excellent language abilities to comprehension tasks. But she seems unable to pass her spelling tests in class.

Sally is referred to the psychologist for testing. The psychologist administers a spelling test and reports to the teacher that Sally actually can spell at average fourth grade levels. Now the teacher doesn't know what to do. Sally is still failing her spelling tests in the classroom and her compositions are terrible. The teacher concludes that Sally isn't trying hard enough and that everyone should crack down on her to make her work.

However, a task analysis of the psychologist's test indicates that it merely measured Sally's ability to recognize (point out) which one of four words was correctly spelled. It did not measure whether she could actually produce (write) the correct spellings. The task analysis clarified the test's interpretation. The test showed that Sally's mastery of visual recognition of correct spellings was equivalent to that of the tests' fourth grade standardization population. This visual recognition was a strength that could be incorporated creatively into a teaching program. Sally did know something about spelling the words on which she was tested, but her way of knowing was not the same as the way in which she was required to demonstrate her skills in the classroom. The teacher decided to combine Sally's good visual recognition (matching tasks) and language skills (saying the letters aloud) with writing, to help her gain proficiency in spelling.

Sally's compositions were graded without counting off for spelling. But they were still poor. The teacher hypothesized that the spelling difficulty and some residual handwriting problems were interfering with Sally's ability to express herself in writing. Therefore, Sally was permitted to dictate compositions into a tape recorder. When she transcribed her dictations, the spelling errors became the content of spelling lessons, and extra writing instruction was provided. In this manner Sally received instruction in her weaker areas, while also succeeding on compositions and perceiving herself as a capable student. Her successes helped give her the energy and ambition to get through those lessons that were more of a struggle for her.

Evaluating Previous Learning Opportunities

Evaluation of the instructional objectives to which a student previously has been exposed is essential to understanding the child's present capabilities. When considered together with the effort involved in attempting to teach skills that the child hasn't mastered, evaluating past learning opportunities offers a valuable perspective on the reasons for and degree of modifiability of the child's weaknesses.

Alan's profile demonstrates this point.

☐ Strengths: learning words from their visual configurations
☐ Weaknesses: figuring out sounds that correspond with letters
☐ Remediation Objective: teaching sound–symbol relationships
☐ Remediation Method: no special remediation, just teaching the sound symbol relationships as for any other child, but with more practice
☐ Compensation: none necessary once letter sounds were mastered

Alan transferred school systems in the middle of first grade and experienced immediate difficulty in reading because he didn't know the sounds of letters. When given the word "sand" to read he just stared at it and guessed. An analysis of Alan's previous curriculum indicated that he had been taught to look at words and recognize them from the shapes of their outlines. During such teaching, most children begin to figure out the sounds that individual letters make on their own. However, Alan was not this type of learner. When taught the sound–symbol relationships by his new teacher, he required more practice and teaching sessions than many of his peers. Once he learned this material, he retained it relatively well. What initially looked like a disability was largely a lack of opportunity to learn.

Consulting the Child

It is impossible to know for sure what is going on in a child's mind. Teachers can observe a child's task execution in fine detail, and analyze successes and errors, but their conclusions are still only hypotheses. Making the child a partner in the evaluation process, and asking how he or she goes about solving the task often proves to be a beneficial learning situation for both teacher and child.

A unique example of the value of conferring with the child occurred with five year old Rachael. Consider her profile:

- ☐ Strengths: drawing, understanding of left–right, memory
- ☐ Weaknesses: *apparent* directional confusion in printing
- ☐ Remedation Objective, Methods, and Compensation: none necessary after asking her why she was reversing letters

Rachael entered kindergarten at the age of five years, one month, printing her name in capitals from left to right, but with inconsistent reversals of all letters (except for A and H). Her drawing ability was far beyond age expectations, showing excellent attention to detail and appreciation of spatial relationships. She understood left and right on her body as well as in space. After her first two months of school, Rachael continued to reverse letters and began to sign her name from right to left on the paper (LƎAHƆAя). When the teacher corrected her she would respond "I know," in a most put-off manner. The next day she would again print her name from left to right under one picture and from right to left under another.

In time, Rachael's letter reversals became consistent: when she wrote from left to right they were always correctly oriented; when she wrote from right to left they were mirror-images. Her consistency in changes of letter orientation, together with her drawing talents, did not lend themselves to an interpretation of visual discrimination problems or poor directionality on drawing tasks.

Shortly thereafter, the teacher noted Rachael's excellent memory and backwards sequencing skills: Rachael began producing her name on the right side of the page and reversed, beginning with the " ⌐ " in the center of the page and proceeding in reverse order toward the right. The teacher approached Rachael and asked her to please clarify her confusion about the matter. Rachael responded, "Well isn't this the way I'm supposed to write my name in Hebrew?" Her excellent understanding of directionality, for all this time, actually had presented itself as a deficit in the classroom. Because she had been told so often by the teacher to write from left to right, she had decided to do it that way in Hebrew also, still reversing all letters. Although Rachael's case is unique, it does strikingly illustrate the worthiness of consulting with children whose thinking processes we're attempting to second guess.

Matching Task Processes to Student Learning Preferences

Once we have discovered *what* a student is ready to learn, we cannot assume that the child will automatically be able to absorb the material we present. Myklebust and Boshes' (1969) well-known study agrees with many others that there is "a difference in [LD children's] psychology of learning which appears critical in planning for special education" (p. 142). Each student has unique ways of going about learning that make it easier for him or her to master material when it is presented in a particular way. In order to promote acquisition of knowledge, tasks must be altered to best match *how* each student learns.

Meichenbaum (1976) suggests deciding on task modifications by means of three consecutive steps:

1. Manipulate the task —
   a. Find out under what circumstances a child can demonstrate competence (for example, using several modalities for information presentation, seeing if more salient stimulus cues generate correct answers, observing generalization of a successful strategy on one task to a similar but harder task).
   b. Find out where performance breaks down (for example, speeding response requirements or rate of stimulus presentation so that memorizing through rehearsal can't take place).
2. Alter the environment — find out if the child can do well in an ideal environment and what aspects of the environment reinstate the deficit (for example, use rooms with and without distractors, increase or decrease anxiety by varying interpersonal factors).
3. Provide supports — observe success when providing task aids (memory prompts, describe task demands part by part, give feedback on performance, require notetaking) or instructional aids (help the student self-evaluate, appraise task requirements, focus attention).

This section illustrates further task modification strategies that can meet some of the unique learning characteristics of LD students: difficulty focusing and sustaining attention, slow information-processing speeds, overloading with certain amounts and types of practice, modality strengths and weaknesses, impulsivity-reflectivity, a need for directed instruction, internally or externally controlled cognitive styles, a tendency not to generalize learning from one task or setting to another, and a need to have teachers' instructions match their learning strategies.

After deciding on several possible approaches to teaching, the teacher should offer the student a choice of methods. Allowing students to choose among equally acceptable alternatives is often associated with more rapid gains than when student preferences are not considered (Kosiewicz, Hallahan, & Lloyd, 1981).

Matching Tasks
to Students' Attending Strategies

Since learning disabled children's attention often varies from one time to another, teachers may perceive students' capabilities as greater than they really are. Ross and Ross (1976) vividly describe these misperceptions:

> A teacher who sees a child act like a disorganized tornado for the first two weeks of school and then suddenly switch to being obedient and industrious

has a hard time believing that the child's behavior is out of his control. Furthermore, his grades often fluctuate from high to low, so that the teacher usually concludes that having done it once he could do it again if he wanted to (p. 43).

Many children cannot do it again even if they wanted to. They need to have their attention facilitated by the settings they are in, and engaged by task characteristics, instructions, and explanations that draw their interest and participation more than do distractors.

Maximizing Attention–Sustaining Setting Variables. Children's attention and corresponding activity levels vary greatly across settings. Even a hyperactive child is not always hyperactive. To illustrate, Kalverboer's (1976) observations of 117 children in six different situations found only one child who was consistently among the 20 percent most active in each setting. Therefore, teachers must observe children carefully and define that environment in which each has the greatest opportunity to maximize attention. That environment is then ideally suited for instruction.

Maximizing Attention–Sustaining Task Variables. Learning disabled students' learning tends to be more influenced by instructional variables than is their peers'. They often require reduced stimulus complexity and response competition. For example, Bryant and Gettinger (1981) found that both LD children and typical learners were better at learning to associate geometric figures with nouns (a task simulating sight word reading) when only one figure (versus all) appeared on a card and when mastering one pair at a time (instead of running through all items on the list until mastery was reached). The LD students' more marked improvement under conditions of reduced visual complexity and response competition reflects their greater sensitivity to such task variables than typical learners.

Reduced Stimulus Complexity. The attentional value of tasks' perceptual features is important to evaluate because LD children often rely exclusively on the perceptual characteristics of materials instead of using their past knowledge to think through solutions (Reid, 1980). These children's attention also commonly becomes overloaded when they have to attend to more than three or four elements or ideas at a time. Bryant and Gettinger (1981) suggest that this overloading may be related to slow processing speed, failure to automatize input and output, tendency to fatigue early, or distractability causing unnecessary processing of irrelevant information. When a student is distracted or overloaded by the perceptual features of tasks, the teacher can easily give the child fewer bits of material to look at or listen to at once.

Academic tasks also can be structured in such a way as to draw a child's attention toward those features that the teacher wants the child to attend to. Vertical discriminations, for example, are much easier for young children than horizontal discriminations (Davidson, 1935; Hendrickson & Muehl, 1962). Children find the horizontal discrimination between b–d much easier when the two are lined up, one on top of the other $\frac{b}{d}$, rather than side by side (Pick & Pick, 1970). On the other hand, the vertical differences between p–b are much more noticeable if the letters are placed horizontally than vertically, $\frac{p}{b}$. Clearly, the way the teacher arranges the figures can help draw the student's attention to their distinctive features.

Another way to build attention-getters into tasks is by noting the child's preferences for color, shape, or size. These preferences can be used to aid concept attainment (Odom & Corbin, 1973; Suchman & Trabasso, 1966). When teaching the difference between the numerals 1 and 2, for example, teachers can make materials more distinctive by varying the sizes (big 1 and small 2), shapes (the 1 is pasted on a square background and the 2 on a circular background), or colors (red 1 and yellow 2). The well-known fact that less mature children's attention is best grabbed by three-dimensional rather than two-dimensional objects can also be utilized. For example, a block with the number three painted on it can be used instead of a piece of paper with a three on it.

Reduced Response Competition. Since children's attention can be drawn away to irrelevant attributes of an assignment, these must be minimized. Many learning disabled children are distracted by the pictures in their reading books. They gather comprehension clues from the pictures and then guess at the words rather than trying to analyze them. Consequently, in some cases, word recognition gains are more rapid when pictures are eliminated. Similarly, Radosh and Gittleman (1981) found that typical learners had more math calculation errors when their problems were bordered by appealing toys, animals, and objects than when bordered by abstract paintings, or nothing. But hyperactive children experienced far greater distraction and even found the abstract pictures significantly more disruptive than just a blank border.

Another manner of reducing response competition is to cluster information into categories for LD children (Cartelli, 1978; Torgesen, 1977). Suiter and Potter (1978), for example, gave learning disabled children forty pictures of objects to remember. Some children were shown the pictures in groups of four objects belonging to the same category (food, household items, animals, toys). The remaining children were also shown four pictures at a time, but no two belonged to the same category. Those who received the organized presentation recalled the information significantly better. In a similar study, learning disabled students were able to recall information such as "red – heart" easier than "yellow – log" due to their association value (Senf, 1969). Building association values into tasks is referred to as *external paradigmatic organization.*

At times the presence of similar information distracts the LD youngster from learning more than the typical student (Cermak et al., 1981). Consequently, the reduction of similar items that may prove confusing or interfere with retrieval is often necessary. For example, a teacher might elect not to teach *b* at the same time as *d*. Only when the student has learned to retrieve the sound of *b* efficiently would *d* be introduced.

Response competition may also result when students must engage in too much new learning or too many memory searches at once. The teacher needs to determine the optimum unit size for each pupil and limit material accordingly. Bryant (1980), for example, found that temporarily dropping learned items from lists of new items reduces response competition and facilitates mastery. In another study, Bryant, Drabin, and Gettinger (1981) tried to teach LD students three spelling words on each of three consecutive days. They found that 62 percent of the students achieved the experimenters' criterion for mastery. However, the percentage reaching criterion on the original nine words decreased to 30 percent when given one additional word to learn each day, and to 17 percent when given two additional words to learn each day. Bryant's research suggests that the optimal unit size for instruction may be five words for reading, but only three for spelling (Bryant, 1980).

Using Attention-Sustaining Instructions and Explanations. How children are instructed to interact with materials greatly impacts their attention. Building labelling into tasks, for example, may help the memory performance of learning disabled students become equivalent to that of typical learners (Torgesen & Goldman, 1977). In one study Torgesen (1977) found that poor readers could memorize picture cards better when they were told to label them as the experimenter sorted them into categories. They learned even more when instructed to sort the cards into the categories by themselves. Similarly, Koenigsberg (1973) found that preschoolers learned to discriminate b from d only when the experimenter verbally explained the difference, using a transparent overlay. Having the child merely say whether or not the overlay and standard were the same did not teach the discrimination. They needed the instructor to draw their attention to the distinctive features to be learned.

Besides highlighting distinctive features, labelling, and categorizing, experienced teachers have discovered many additional means of aiding attention, memory, and retrieval. Teachers, for example, instruct students to apply new ideas to practical problems in a different setting (Dechant, 1973), to use mnemonic tricks (for example, the first letters of *every good boy does fine* name the treble clef lines), to pair words for memory, to actively question during reading, to review material periodically, to immediately rehearse what has been seen or heard, and to attend to the organization of the information presented (Kaluger & Kolson, 1969).

Matching Time Limits
to Information-Processing Speed

Professionals are becoming increasingly sensitive to the differences between children in information-processing time. When children need longer periods of time to solve certain types of problems, they are penalized by timed assignments and tests. We must decide on time limits that give the youngster a reasonable opportunity to show his or her knowledge. In addition, time limits on new learning in the classroom must be sufficient to allow opportunities for labelling and verbal rehearsal and for small chunks of information to be learned at separate intervals in order to avoid overloading.

Matching Task Repetitions to Students' Practice Needs

It seems axiomatic that "Practice makes perfect." But it may not always be so for the learning disabled. The finding that poor readers may get worse with practice when scanning their memories for auditory information, but more efficient when scanning for visual information needs to be investigated further (Farnham-Diggory & Gregg, 1975; Lehman & Brody, 1982). It seems that switching from one to another modality does not aid recovery. Soviet investigators too have found that LD children may not improve motor performance with practice, as do those with normal learning abilities (Wozniak, 1972). Therefore, we must be careful that the number of repetitions of tasks assigned to students does not overwhelm and exhaust them. The teacher must also consider what amount of overlearning is needed by a pupil, at what intervals, and what types of review best speed up the overlearning process.

Matching Tasks to Students' Stronger Modalities

While the idea of matching task attributes to youngsters' stronger information-processing modalities makes intuitive sense, the research literature does not consistently support this practice. Studies generally indicate that these matches produce either greater or no greater learning rates than mismatches such as teaching an auditory learner through a visual reading approach. In other words, matching task attributes to learners' stronger modalities either helps or can't hurt (Bateman, 1968; Robinson, 1968; Hagan, 1971; Levin, 1976; Wheeler & Dusek; 1973). This occurs because the child's preferred modality may direct learning, even when the method of teaching capitalizes on the weaker modality; and because every method teaches regardless of whether it matches the stronger or weaker modality (Tarver & Dawson, 1978).

With respect to matching reading programs to modality strengths, investigators have suggested that either the modality model is invalid or, given current limitations in educational assessment and programming techniques, it is not applicable (Arter & Jenkins, 1977; Bateman, 1979). Discussion of whether educators should teach only through children's stronger modalities, remediate the weaker ones, or both, will continue until researchers can run well-designed studies and replicate their findings (see Research Box 12-1).

It must be recognized that even if modality matching has merit, some subject areas are just not flexible enough to permit altering tasks to match a child's stronger information-processing channel. At times it is impossible to find a better instructional match than the child's weakness. For example, when auditory or visual processing skills are weaknesses, the former are still essential for reading progress, and visuo-spatial skills must still be used in early math achievement.

Matching Tasks
to Students' Cognitive Styles

Research has indicated that children may not be able to break away from their preferred way of perceiving their environments. McKenney & Keen's (1976) study, for example, found that three-fourths of subjects used one problem-solving style on all types of problems. Only one-quarter switched styles to more appropriately match task requirements (in Ewing, 1977).

Since individuals have difficulty altering their conceptual styles, learning can be facilitated when teachers alter materials and methods to be congruent with student cognitive styles. Several studies have demonstrated the facilitating effect of such matches (Beller, 1967; in Coop & Sigel, 1971). Pascarella and Pflaum (1981), for example, found that learning disabled students who attributed success to their own efforts (internal locus of control) benefited more when encouraged to determine the correctness of their responses on context clue exercises. Conversely, students who attributed success to external factors (external locus of control) benefited more when the teacher pointed out and corrected their errors. In another study, Maier (1977) told a story to fourth grade language and learning disabled students. One-third of the way through she told the children, "Now you will hear the problem." Two-thirds of the way through she told them, "Now you will hear how he solved the problem." Given this focus on details, the experimental group was able to recall and infer better than the control group. Researchers have explored several means of modifying task attributes to better match the cognitive styles of impulsive-reflective and low-high conceptual level students.

Impulsive and Reflective Learners. Children with impulsive conceptual tempos do not stop to reflect on correct alternatives. This tendency is in part due to their global, rather than detail-oriented, approach to tasks. Looking at the overall picture takes them less time than studying each of the parts.

Impulsive children commonly do not double check their work, ignore details, write before thinking and planning, leave off word endings, do not organize compositions, copy sloppily from the board, and do not self-correct. On the other hand, they might be able to get the main idea of a passage, remember general concepts, overview situations, and visually discriminate contours very well.

Since educational tasks usually ask for detail analysis, the true capabilities of the impulsive student may not be tapped a good deal of the time. Consider which instruction we hear most often in school, "go slower and you'll find the information" or "hurry, skim the passage, and give me the main idea"? It is usually the former, which favors the reflective student's style.

Tasks must be modified to utilize the child's preferred style of problem-solving whenever possible, while also minimizing the style's interfering effects. For example, when teaching word attack skills, the teacher might tell the impulsive child the whole word and then ask him or her to describe why the parts combine to sound as they do, rather than the other way around; working from the parts to whole is difficult for the impulsive child. The teacher might approach the rules for regrouping in multiplication by pasting on the child's desk a number fact chart and a list of the math steps. These could be used as a reference for organizing the various problem-solving steps. Attention to details might be facilitated by having the child skim pictures and use a text's main ideas to guess the details; the child then checks the passage to see whether he or she was on target. Pictures might be covered over on a page so that the student is forced to attend to the individual words and phrases to derive meaning. The child also might correct his or her own papers, underline word endings, and outline stories to help adapt attention to the more detail-oriented, longer response time strategy that schools emphasize.

The schools' bias in favor of the reflective student does not mean that the reflective student always has an easy time of it. The reflective style means taking longer to discover main points. It is a clear disadvantage on timed tests when students spend too much time pondering the ramifications of every multiple choice. The reflective student also might be at a disadvantage on speed drills and games calling for more rapid information-processing (Coop & Sigel, 1971).

Low and High Conceptual Level Learners. Many learning disabled children are low conceptual level students. During learning they prefer structured tasks and externally imposed rules. They have difficulty generating their own concepts and considering alternative solutions. For these youngsters, teaching pertinent facts and key concepts, giving rules before instead of after examples, and lecture rather than discovery methods match their styles and promote more rapid learning. Hunt's (1974) work suggests that these methods may be just what the problem learner needs to promote greater integration of information, generalization, and order in learning. When, instead of asking children "what do you think?" teachers expand their thinking by giving them more alternatives to consider, they do not leave the acquisition of information to chance. In effect teachers increase their students' conceptual flexibility.

All too often teachers expect children to assimilate information on their own, instead of instructing them in the precise criteria to be learned. Marc is a good example. Marc is a twelve-year-old, very bright young man attending a private school with other bright youngsters. His reading, math, and comprehension skills are excellent. His spelling, however, is terrible. Marc's teachers asked his parents to have him evaluated for a learning disability. Trial teaching approaches were used during the evaluation, and no difficulty with learning to spell either phonetic or nonphonetic words could be found. Marc learned well with typical teaching methods and was even able to generalize spelling forms learned on one word to new words (such as commer*cial* to superfi*cial*). When these findings were explored with his teachers, they commented, "but we never teach spelling as a subject; these children just pick it up." Well, this student did "soak up" most information, but not spelling. Marc needed directed teaching in spelling all along. We must be careful not to expect students to learn information incidentally. Instruction that gives children direction on what to attend to and how to think about information gives them more options with which to think intelligently.

Matching Incentives to Cognitive Styles

Nothing maximizes attention like a highly motivating learning situation. This motivation can come from outside factors (*extrinsic motivation*) or from inside the child (*intrinsic motivation*). Externally controlled children hold outside factors responsible for success and failure ("I got an F because the teacher hates me"). Internally controlled children, on the other hand, feel that they personally control success and failure ("I deserved an F because I went to the movies instead of studying"). Internally controlled children are usually self-motivated, although they will also work for external rewards. Since many learning disabled students are externally controlled, they need immediate external incentives for achievement while we help them work toward increased internal motivation. Motivational techniques produce greater increments in performance for learning disabled than for typical learners because LD children's initial performance is often diminished by low motivation (Adelman & Chaney, 1982).

Extrinsic Motivators. Extrinsic incentives help children who avoid challenges to put more effort into learning. Point systems that reward children for improved attention and learning have particularly powerful effects on learning rate (Brigham, Graubard & Stans, 1972; Heiman, Fischer, & Ross, 1973). Often these points are accumulated and then traded in for a prize. In one study that used pennies as reinforcers, selective attention, spontaneous use of verbal rehearsal strategies, and recall increased. The children had the ability to use verbal rehearsal all along, but had not bothered (Hallahan, Tarver, Kauffman, & Greybeal, 1978). In another study, daily reinforcement of a whole classes' decreased reading error rate was just as effective as graphing and reinforcing each individual's daily progress, but less time–consuming and easier to implement (Thorpe, Chiang, & Darch, 1981).

Other examples of extrinsic motivators are charting successes, earning stars or candy, praise, and contracting. Contracting is particularly useful because the youngster actually makes his or her own decisions about what to achieve, and what the pay-off will be. The success of contracting is attributed to the *Premack principle:* when the child completes x, y, z activities which are less valued, he or she has earned the privilege of doing a, b, or c, higher-valued activities. These positive consequences are strong incentives to put effort into least-favored learning activities.

External reinforcement also can come from classroom materials and requirements that are highly motivating. It would be nice if the learning material were so fascinating that the student is eager to dig into it. Unfortunately, the LD child, defeated by failure, seldom generates this kind of enthusiasm. Yet, the interest level of materials can still be manipulated so as to impact student performance. Consider Bobby, a twelve-year-old student, with excellent decoding skills but inconsistent comprehension of what was read. Comprehension could vary anywhere between 40 percent and 100 percent whether on a first or sixth grade level passage. This variability greatly concerned his teachers since at times he absorbed less than half of the information they presented. They administered an interest inventory and found that he was enthusiastic about sports and outer space. When Bobby was asked to read passages on these topics he consistently demonstrates 95–100 percent comprehension, even when the passages had a sixth grade reading difficulty. Although high interest materials would be ideal for Bobby all day long, in reality he must also deal with less interesting material. Therefore, high interest reading materials were used as often as possible, and alternative extrinsic motivators were added to lessons at other times.

As Bobby's case illustrates, a child's response to extrinsic motivators is a very individual thing. Teachers must search for the incentive that best matches the child's interests, because not every method induces all children to put more energy into learning.

Intrinsic Motivation. The best form of motivation comes from within the child. Haywood's research has shown that children who gain satisfaction from engaging in tasks with responsibility, creativity, and effort can perform equivalently to those who are 20 IQ points brighter (Paris & Haywood, 1973). In other words, when intellectual or basic learning ability is limited, high motivation may partially overcome these deficiencies.

The best teacher of internal motivation is the child's family. Children model their own families' striving for academic success. After a while they no longer associate their joy in achieving with the standing ovations they got when they spoke their first baby words, or the hugs and kisses they received when they first learned the alphabet. Achievement becomes a highly valued entity in its own right. Yet when school learning comes hard to these children, they blame their failure on external factors or on being inferior human beings. In extreme cases, they find it safer to expect little, try nothing, and be helpless (Dweck, 1975). This learned helplessness can begin to be turned around by the kind of feedback teachers give children.

When teachers help children to attribute failure to something other than external sources and their own self-worth, then they may regain their interest, enthusiasm, and motivation to put energy into learning. This is why Dweck

(1975) suggests that teachers attribute children's successes and failures to the *amount of effort they put into learning*, rather than giving general praise or reproofs ("good try at sounding out" versus "you're great"). The latter are internalized as "I am capable" or "I am incapable" messages. Since these children do not believe that they are capable, general praise means little. Instead, praising of effort reduces self-criticism and shifts attention to what can be done to achieve. For example, Adelman and Chaney (1982) found large increases in performance on a coding task when LD students were complimented on the expectation that they would be the type to try hard and also help out by volunteering for the study.

As LD children's success increases, a gradual shift back to self-attributions for improvement may occur (Bandura, Jeffery, & Gajdos, 1975.) Positive self-attributions are an important goal for encouraging a style of interacting with the world that is oriented toward doing one's best.

Building Generalization into Tasks

When Marc was asked if he would remember to apply the new spelling words he had learned to his English compositions, he responded "No." We cannot expect that a child automatically will transfer information to appropriate situations. Learning sets, too, are unlikely to be generalized (Wirtenberg & Faw, 1975). Therefore, teachers are responsible for making sure that new learning is generalized (McLeskey, Rieth, & Polsgrove, 1980).

To better understand the kind of reminders that everyone uses to cue generalization of knowledge, recall an experience taking a French, or any other, final exam in a strange (chemistry) lecture hall. Did you do poorly and then blame it on the room? If so, your blaming was probably not all projection, as the Freudian analyst would say. The room was not filled with "French cues" that would facilitate recall. You might have looked around the room during the exam, hoping to reconstruct the teacher's voice while writing the conjugation of the verb être on the blackboard. But it's awfully hard to imagine this when all you see are chemistry molecules and formulas around you. With insufficient environmental cueing, you may not have been able to recover from memory what you knew you had put there. This same kind of stimulus interference occurs with the learning disabled. Therefore, it is important for the teacher to think of ways to help students generalize all academic objectives, such as transferring headings taught in English class to math assignments, or applying a math operation learned in the resource room to classroom assignments.

Stokes and Baer's (1977) research review suggests several ways in which generalization might be enhanced:

1. Students should be taught to cue teachers to reinforce their use of appropriate task strategies.
2. Teachers should use many examples to deepen application of learned skills.

3. Teachers should use consistency and structure in initial teaching but later vary formats, procedures, and examples to promote generalization.
4. The same information should be instructed by many people, in many settings and conditions.
5. Teach initially using a consistent reinforcement schedule but then change to delayed and intermittent reinforcement.
6. Students should be told to generalize using verbal mediation.
7. Students should be instructed to self-report generalization and to apply self-recording and self-reinforcement techniques.
8. Information should be taught in connection with naturally occurring stimuli (peers, physical stimuli).

In order not to waste very important time, teachers must make sure that what they teach has maximal transfer value to academic goals. Rosen (1966), for example, divided over 600 first grade children into two equivalent groups. One received half-hour daily visual-perceptual training while the other received extra classroom reading instruction. At the end of one month, the perceptually trained group was superior on the perceptual tests, and the control group was superior in reading comprehension. Each learned what it was taught, but only one made reading gains. Clearly, given limited teaching time, teachers need to put their efforts into teaching those subskills that are clear components of academic goals (Gagné, 1970).

Matching Teacher Instructions to Students' Learning Strategies

Teachers can improve students' accuracy on tasks when they carefully match their own behaviors to students' preferred learning strategies. Coop and Sigel (1971), for example, point out that the impulsive teacher may overwhelm the reflective student with a constant barrage of information. On the other hand, the reflective teacher's slow-paced, detailed approach may bore the impulsive student. For the student who profits best from directed instruction or who becomes overloaded with a barrage of materials and verbal directions, brevity, simplicity, and directness are important; excess, irrelevant, and distracting information, such as interesting tangents, need to be eliminated.

It is also important that the directions given by teachers, textbooks, and tests match, so that students have one consistent strategy to follow (Faulk & Landry, 1961). When the way in which students are asked to complete similar assignments varies from time to time, some of them may get confused and lose their previous "mental sets." The same variability, on the other hand, will excite and motivate others.

As children get older they become able to operate at higher levels of conceptual complexity, reflectivity, and independence. Teachers need to help each child move to higher conceptual levels as he or she becomes ready. Julie, for example, can organize and plan her work, but needs to be reminded continually to do so. When given ten addition and subtraction problems to work independently, Julie solved all of them correctly, but placed them every which way on the page. Julie put neither the customary heading nor her name on the piece of paper. The teacher recognized the paper and made a point next time to cue Julie to organize herself: "Julie, you do a great job paying attention to your plus and minus signs; now remember to organize your work." This simple cueing resulted in well-placed problems and a heading. The teacher was also able to help Julie attend to oral directions by simply catching Julie's attention (standing in front of her desk, looking her in the eye) and making sure that directions were repeated twice (asking someone to repeat the direction). In this manner failure due to not understanding instructions was minimized. In both instances, the teacher matched her approach to Julie's readiness to move beyond needing precise direction through every aspect of her work.

Several studies have shown that teachers' styles can have a major impact on their students' cognitive styles. Yando and Kagan (1968) found that students taught by reflective teachers showed greater increases in reflective style than did those taught by impulsive teachers. Similarly, Scott and Sigel (1965; in Coop & Sigel, 1971) taught fifteen science concepts to children in grades four, five, and six. Half were taught by an inquiry method and half by a conventional directive approach. On a cognitive style test at the end of the school term, children tended to respond in the same style as they had been instructed in science. Coop and Sigel (1971) suggest that, since a child may not be able to break away from his or her preferred mode of perceiving a situation, teachers should explain content from a perceptual framework that accommodates the child's style, while also guiding the child toward more appropriate styles.

Teaching Efficient Learning Strategies

Noting the positive impact that task modifications can have on the performance of learning disabled children, some individuals believe that many of these students are impaired in learning strategies rather than basic ability to learn (Adelman, 1971; Alley & Deshler, 1979; Torgesen, 1980). The way in which they go about learning is inefficient. To better understand the difference between ability deficits and learning strategy inefficiencies, consider the times when you haven't remembered the names of people you were introduced to. You complain about your awful memory, but you know very well that your memory is good. What really happened is that you just never consciously bothered to remember. You never repeated, organized, or rehearsed the names so as to remember them for more than a few seconds. Had the person you were introduced to been particularly good looking, famous, or of interest in some other way, you might have made more of an effort to remember his or her name.

Flavell referred to "knowing how to go about learning and desiring to do so" as *metacognition*. An important goal for teachers of the learning disabled is to help their students employ more efficient metacognitive strategies by teaching what Bryant (1980) calls "LD efficient" lessons. Others call this process *cognitive training*. Much of cognitive training is built on Flavell's (1971) notion that mental and memory abilities are one and the same:

> It has long been clear that what we know and how we think profoundly determines what and how we perceive, or speak, or imagine, or problem-solve, or predict; it is now becoming equally clear that all that knowledge and all that thinking also profoundly shape what and how we learn and remember. . . . memory itself is mostly applied cognition. . . . the human mind knows more and thinks better as it grows older, and these changes in what it knows and how it thinks have powerful effects on *what* it learns and remembers, *how* it learns and remembers, and even perhaps *when* it learns and remembers (p. 273).

Therefore, memory is "the development of intelligent structuring and storage of input, intelligent search and retrieval operations, and intelligent monitoring and knowledge of these storage and retrieval operations — a kind of 'meta-memory'" (p. 277).

Examples of metacognition include: knowing that one is forgetful and therefore writing reminder notes, recognizing one's weaknesses and strengths and planning accordingly, and knowing to think about all alternatives before choosing an answer (Flavell, 1976). These behaviors are akin to what we have historically labelled good study skills (Brown, 1978). Both become better with age because the older child is more active, flexible, planful, and efficient in learning and retrieval strategies (Hagan, Jongeward, & Kail, 1975).

Flavell's notions relate to the learning disabled because when these young-sters are taught more efficient use of their cognitive abilities, they often learn more intelligently. This approach has longer-lasting possibilities than contin-ually modifying task characteristics. Learning strategies are most effective when self-generated because they comfortably match the individual's learning style (Hagan, 1971; Levin, 1976). When the student doesn't self-generate these approaches as he or she gets older, they need to be taught. Early adolescence has been suggested as a prime time for such instruction because the students are developmentally mature enough to profit from and apply the teaching (Rohwer, 1971).

Researchers who study ways of altering learning strategies are frequently referred to as *cognitive psychologists*. Visual imagery, verbal mediation, search strategy training, and modeling are among the methods that have helped youngsters learn to attend spontaneously to the appropriate elements of their assignments, to organize them for recall, and then to retrieve them.

Visual Imagery

Teaching some youngsters to mentally imagine the material they are studying has been very helpful in aiding vocabulary and grammar acquisition (Moeser & Bregman, 1973; Moeser & Olson, 1974), word and phrase comprehension (Levin et al., 1974), prose learning (Lesgold, McCormick & Golinkoff, 1975), and learning picture pairs (Kerst & Levin, 1973). Levin's (1973) study, for example, found that poor readers' reading comprehension increased when they thought of a picture associated with each sentence of a passage. Paivio (1969) suggests that for some children imagery may be far more important to memory than verbal mediation.

Verbal Mediation

Self-verbalization's powerful effect on learning was demonstrated by Bandura, Grusec, and Menlove (1966). As children observed a scene, they either verbalized all the model's actions, just watched, or verbalized irrelevant material. The investigators found that imitation of the model's behavior occurred more often with appropriate verbalization, less with just watching, and least with inappropriate verbalization.

Donald Meichenbaum (1977) uses Bandura's principles in his "speech for self" method which teaches children to use private speech in a more mature, instrumental, and self-guided fashion during learning. His method helps youngsters to focus their attention on task-relevant stimuli and behaviors, and to organize their thinking. First, the child observes the instructor modeling such task-appropriate behaviors as sizing up the problem, focusing on relevant aspects, doing the task, self-evaluating performance, and correcting errors. The child next goes through three stages of performing the task: 1) under the instructor's verbal directions; 2) on his or her own while self-instructing aloud or in a whisper; and 3) on his or her own while self-instructing silently.

Meichenbaum's method appears most useful to youngsters who don't spontaneously analyze their experience in verbal terms, and therefore don't planfully approach problem-solving. By literally talking to themselves, impulsive children have increased their problem-solving skills dramatically (Meichenbaum & Goodman, 1969, 1971; Orbach, 1977; Weithorn & Kagan, 1979). This method has also improved learning disabled children's handwriting, attention to task, and arithmetic productivity (Hallahan et al., in Hresko & Reid, 1980).

Students can also be taught cognitive strategies for monitoring their own inappropriate behavior tendencies. The child's behavior is broken down into small units, and he or she is made aware of the sequence of situations that typically result in specific, inappropriate behavioral and cognitive reactions. The child's verbal self-instructions then help the child to interrupt a chain of events early and alter responses that he or she typically would have made. Meichenbaum (1976) also urges the use of cognitive self-training methods for overcoming the negative self-statements with which LD children often approach tasks ("I'll never be able to do that"). These task-irrelevant thoughts contribute to inadequate performance.

Search Strategy Training

Many cognitive training studies have taught children how to scan material appropriately before deciding on their answers. The approach used by Palkes, Stewart, and Kahana (1968) is presented in Figure 12-1. *Stop, Listen, Look,* and

Figure 12-1   Cognitive training technique to increase reflectivity

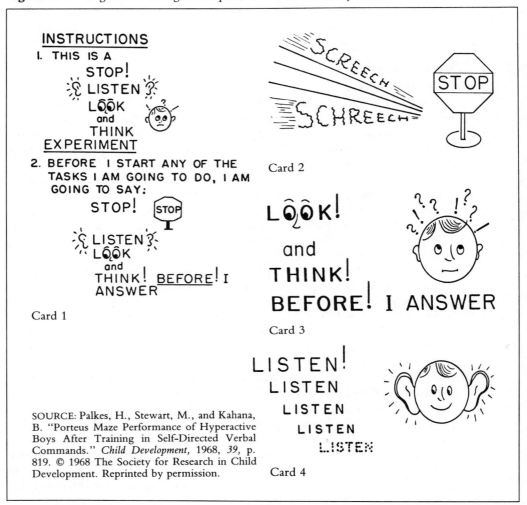

SOURCE: Palkes, H., Stewart, M., and Kahana, B. "Porteus Maze Performance of Hyperactive Boys After Training in Self-Directed Verbal Commands." *Child Development*, 1968, *39*, p. 819. © 1968 The Society for Research in Child Development. Reprinted by permission.

Think cards remained on the children's desks as constant reminders of what to do while solving mazes. Those children who read and verbalized the commands before doing the mazes had fewer errors than those who were not instructed in this self-direction method. This study was later replicated (Palkes, Stewart, & Freedman, 1971). Other investigators have shown equally good results on Kagan's visual matching task by training students to delay responding while examining alternatives, breaking the task down into parts, looking for similarities and differences, and systematically eliminating alterna-tives. The positive effects of search strategy training persist longer than train-ing the child only to delay responding (Egeland, 1974).

Children have demonstrated transfer of laboratory learned cognitive tech-niques to paper-pencil tests of impulsivity, oral reading, and comprehension. But in only two studies did classroom behavior ratings improve following cognitive training (Abikoff, 1979). This is most likely due to insufficient over-lap between the skills taught in these laboratory training studies and classroom behavioral expectations (Meichenbaum, 1977), as well as differences between the laboratory strategies and those needed by the teacher to manage classroom behaviors (Abikoff, 1979). Researchers need to further study the generalization effects of cognitive training and also the maintenance of training using periodic review sessions (Douglas, Parry, Marton, and Garson, 1976).

Modeling

Watching others perform correctly can have a strong vicarious effect on learn-ing strategies. Many studies have successfully used modeling to increase re-flectivity in impulsive, LD children (Cullinan, Epstein, & Silver, 1977; Nagle & Thwaite, 1979; Ridberg, Parke, & Hetherington, 1971). Imitating the model's actions has an even greater effect (Cullinan, Kauffman, & LaFleur, 1975).

Modeling is an important means of drawing attention to aspects of tasks that the student ordinarily would not have noticed. Similarly, problem-solv-ing in a group can be especially beneficial to the LD youngster, who profits from modeling the stragegies used by peers (Alley & Deshler, 1979).

Other Metacognitive Approaches

Other metacognitive approaches that can help students to spontaneously ana-lyze their experiences, form rules for active problem-solving, and make infor-mation more memorable are:

- □ training students to detect their own errors (LD youngsters are weak in this even at the high school level) (Deshler, 1978);
- □ clustering to aid memory (LD students often do not respond to the group-ing of material even if it is organized into categories (Parker, Freston, & Drew, 1975);
- □ using mnemonic memory tricks (remembering a shopping list by using a single word: PEAR = popcorn, eggs, apple sauce, roast beef);
- □ developing personal approaches to material that aid recall;
- □ using questioning techniques during reading to guide comprehension;
- □ reviewing material at distributed intervals;
- □ improving recall through associations by:
  - — highlighting relationships in the material;
  - — generating principles and inferences;

— drawing conclusions;
— creating new ideas;
— making judgments;
— elaborating ideas and connecting them to previously learned information to add meaning and increase the chances for recall (Paris & Haywood, 1973);

□ spontaneously forming associations to facilitate recall (LD students tend not to spontaneously do this) (Wiig & Semel, 1975);

□ distinguishing between recognition memory (multiple choice) and recall ability (fill in answers, essays) and planning appropriately (Alley & Deshler, 1979).

Although studies and applications of these metacognitive approaches are new, they hold great promise for productive educational interventions and enhancement of children's thinking processes.

Summary

Teachers must be involved in ongoing evaluations of their instructional approaches because the LD student's progress depends upon how his or her unique characteristics interact with what is taught and how it is taught. When the nature of classroom tasks are well-matched to what the child is ready to learn and how he or she prefers to go about learning, learning progress can be maximized. Task analysis, evaluation of previous learning opportunities, and consultation with the student aid the matching of task content to student readiness. When matching task processes to student learning preferences, such factors as student attending strategies, information-processing speed, and cognitive style need to be considered. It is also fruitful to teach the child more efficient ways of approaching problem-solving. The potential benefits of such task modifications give practical meaning to our scrutiny of individual differences in children.

Brainstorming about the best possible ways to match school expectations to special students' needs is not new. But the attempt to empirically validate these "aptitude by treatment" interactions received a major impetus only in the past ten years. Conducting well-designed studies on this issue is difficult, unless the researcher studies only single children's responses to different instructional methods. This is because what works with one child often does not work with others. Nor is what works with one child in one subject area necessarily appropriate for the same child in other subject areas, or in the same area months later. Evaluation of the best match between learner and task characteristics needs to be an individualized, ongoing process. Our current means of matching reflect a "state of the art," and not yet a science.

Much responsibility for change is on our tasks, since a child's behavior does not exist apart from how his or her individuality interacts with specific task requirements and expectations. Therefore, teachers must keep trying to tease out what constitutes matches and mismatches between task and child attributes, so as to better understand what task modifications best promote success.

Suggestions for Further Study

1. An effective way to discover what is entailed in modifying tasks to meet children's learning needs is to try to teach a young child a high-level skill. Borrow a neighbor's four year old and see how long it takes you to teach the child to recognize five words when you flash them. Make sure the words are all four-letter words, and that some begin and others end with the same letters. If the child didn't learn them, what kinds of task modifications and instruction in learner strategies did you have to engage in before the words were mastered? If the child was able to master the words, try teaching some harder, more confusable words. What is the teaching struggle like as the words get harder? What kinds of modifications do you find yourself making?

2. If you would like to learn more about aptitude by treatment interaction research, read Bateman (1968), Hagan (1971), Levin (1976), Robinson (1968), Tarver and Dawson (1978), and Wheeler and Dusek (1973). They clarify the problems that ATI studies faced in reading research: the tasks on which children were classified shared very little in common with subskills involved in reading; the different reading approaches highlighted different cues for learning but all ended up teaching children the same thing — how to match sounds with visual symbols; many of the children were not in need of specialized training since they learned well by all methods; different types of subjects, designs, and ways of identifying modality preferences were used; validity of tests was questionable; and training periods were too short.

3. The principle of maximum transfer is a key to good educational assessment and planning. Read Taylor's (1980) article for an example of how visual discrimination and visual memory can be evaluated on the very same instructional items that a child uses in the classroom. Such an evaluation is far more meaningful to instructional planning for a learning disabled student than inferences made from standardized tests of visual discrimination and memory.

4. What types of cognitive styles can make one more or less sensitive to praise and punishment? What type of child is more likely to evaluate him- or herself negatively? Why? How can teachers modify their reinforcement strategies to meet these children's needs? Sources that will help you with these questions are Guyer and Friedman (1975), Randolph (1971), and Ramirez and Castaneda (1974).

5. Integrating what you know about the stigma of labelling and the social difficulties of learning disabled youngsters, how do you think these students might feel about tasks specially geared toward their needs? Might you predict that such special educational techniques would make LD youngsters feel even more different? How could you use the involvement of the student in evaluation and planning to deal with this issue?

Chapter Thirteen
Instructional Strategies

You are familiar with how school tasks can be analyzed in many ways and then modified to match what a student is ready to learn and how he or she best goes about learning. These learner-task matches are extremely important to consider when choosing among available instructional materials and methods. In this chapter we shall discuss general instructional approaches from which teachers of the learning disabled can choose at the preschool, elementary, and secondary levels. No one chapter or even book could do justice to all there is to know about such instructional strategies. Therefore, this chapter's purpose is to help the reader appreciate the variety of materials and methods that are available, by offering a brief sampling at different age levels.

Preschool Programming

Parents and professionals should intervene as soon as possible when developmental weaknesses are detected in children's abilities, cognitive styles and learning strategies. Intervention not only offers children a head start in overcoming these weaknesses, but also encourages their continued growth in stronger areas. With appropriate programming, the risk of a serious learning disorder may decrease and a youngster may find it easier to reach his or her potential. Experts agree that teachers and parents can't wait and see whether preschoolers will automatically outgrow their weaknesses; they may not (Richardson, 1979).

Programming needs to focus on the preschooler's attending abilities, gaining of information through visual and auditory information-processing skills, and communicating of knowledge through language and motor production. While language and attending abilities have the most to do with severe learning disorders, inefficiencies in visual and motor processes also interfere with acquisition and communication of knowledge, although in more subtle ways. The preschool years are also an important time for shaping appropriate learning strategies, motivation to learn, and positive attitudes toward self, peers, and those in authority.

Most preschoolers' information-processing abilities develop in predictable ways when they are presented with appropriate learning opportunities. For the learning disabled preschooler, however, this maturational process is not always smooth. Some of these children are capable of learning well, but only in a personalized learning environment. They need to be encouraged to stay with a task and to have learning objectives systematically presented in a way that matches their attending and learning styles. Other preschoolers' weaknesses make learning harder. They need to be taught and retaught very basic skills along the normal continuum of preschool development. Both types of children require directed instruction because they tend not to discover relationships for themselves or to generalize learning to new situations (such as transferring the ability to count three people to counting three pennies).

435

The preschool is an ideal setting for building both stronger and weaker skills through modelling of peers, cooperating in group games, manipulating attention-drawing toys, and engaging in teacher-directed lessons. Because preschool programs generally do not segregate children by type of handicapping condition, investigations into the efficacy of preschool programs have studied a mixed variety of children. Programs with highly structured goals, reinforcements, and teacher direction seem to benefit children more in the important areas of intelligence, language, visual perception, and school readiness than more open, less academically structured programs (Karnes, Hodgins, & Teska, 1969; McDaniels, 1975). The latter, more flexible programs encourage children to take greater responsibility for success, and to be more independent and cooperative (Stallings, 1974). All of these attributes are important to later school success.

Experts in learning disabilities advocate teaching preschoolers normal developmental skills that they have not yet mastered (Kinsbourne, 1977a). They warn against wasting money and time engaging in nonsensical remediation approaches, such as crawling as an aid to language development.

The format of the preschool child's program is generally mixed between independent, teacher-child, small-group, and large-group activities. Group activities encourage such social behaviors as listening, sharing, turn-taking, and attending in a group by various means: games, songs, physical education activities, dancing, snacktime, and listening to records and stories. They also are used to expand a child's breadth of knowledge, inquisitiveness, and problem-solving abilities. Children, for example, might learn the principles of gravity by dropping objects of various sizes and weights, or discover the effect of heat and cold on solids and liquids by experimenting with water, ice, and snow, or learn about nesting and child-rearing behaviors by raising gerbils.

Individual classroom time is usually spent in visual-motor (clay, coloring, cutting, tracing), language (labelling shapes, colors, sizes, categorizing), and school readiness (counting blocks) activities that are intended to enhance knowledge and to sharpen the child's information reception, expression, and thinking skills. As their teacher explains tasks to children, they begin to develop such learning strategies as self-instructing aloud and stop-look-listen. Most activities have multiple purposes. Coloring, for example, is an eye-hand coordination activity, a language activity (naming colors), a visual perceptual activity (noting the differences among colors), a following external and internal directions activity, a sustained attention training activity, and a conceptual activity (deciding on specific colors to use by matching colors of real objects).

Children who do not make adequate gains through typical preschool activities can benefit from many language development and visual-motor training programs that can be adapted to their learning needs and styles. The language programs stimulate children's receptive, thinking, and expressive language (Dunn, Horton, & Smith, 1968), systematically teach the construction of sentences (Folkes, 1976), encourage problem-solving and generalization of information through dialogues (Blank, 1973), teach object names, and train such skills as description, classification, logical reasoning, opposites, synonyms, analogies, questioning, absurdities, describing functions, and analyzing sentence structure (Englemann & Osborn, 1975).

Excellent activities for language, visual-motor (buttoning, cutting, drawing), and gross-motor (hopping, climbing steps) development are suggested in the teaching guides written by the pioneers in learning disabilities and their followers: Barsch (1967), Frostig & Maslow (1973), Furth & Wachs (1974), Johnson & Myklebust (1967), Kephart (1971), Kirshner (1977), and Vallett 1967). When the preschooler is severely delayed in language acquisition or visual-motor skills, early assessment and intensive remedial programming by such specialists as speech pathologists, occupational therapists, and physical therapists are very much in order.

Intervention within a preschool program is only the beginning of a long educational process. Growth rate is better the longer the intervention continues (Caldwell, 1974), and cognitive gains are maintained only when individualized educational efforts continue into the elementary grades (Cicirelli, 1969; Cicirelli, Evans, & Schiller, 1970; Horowitz & Paden, 1973).

The family also has a very important influence on long-term maintenance of gains (Bronfenbrenner, 1975a). In fact, early intervention projects find that a family-centered rather than child-centered focus may. be the most effective means of enhancing long term effects (Bronfenbrenner, 1974; Caldwell, 1974). As positive linkages are built between parents and their children, and parents become aware of how to encourage motivation and learning opportunities, they can have a far greater impact on schooling success than any six-hour, ten-month school program. Several programs have experimented successfully with home-based, parent-child training (Garber & Heber, 1973; Lambie & Weikart, 1970). Paraprofessionals also have effectively modelled teaching approaches in the home (Gordon, 1975). This type of training has helped to reinforce the role of the parent as teacher, model, and advocate for continued educational gains.

Elementary School Programming

The elementary school learning disabled student's achievement in different areas has been uneven, and the child brings unique cognitive styles and information-processing strengths and weaknesses to school tasks. Consequently, the teacher must adapt the curriculum to what the child already knows, still needs to learn, and how the child learns best. At times minor program modifications are sufficient. At other times, very special approaches are needed. The area of reading instruction has the greatest availability of special materials and approaches. Although these exist in other areas as well, they are more sparse. Often the teacher has to ingeniously mix and match from several programs so that children can continue to grow in stronger and weaker skills.

A special focus at the elementary level must be placed on reading, written expression (handwriting, spelling, composition), mathematics, content area instruction, and building social–emotional skills. Often physical education, art, and music instruction must also be adapted to the LD student's individual needs.

Chapter 12's scope and sequence charts are the teaching objectives to which we apply the materials and strategies discussed here. Our intervention strategies generally use children's strengths to both remediate their weaknesses and to continue learning progress by working around these weaknesses. Although clinicians report the greater efficacy of one or another of these instructional approaches for specific types of learners, research validating such matching still needs to be conducted.

Reading

Reading difficulties are the major factor distinguishing children who fail from those who succeed in school (Strang, 1969). These difficulties then create problems in other academic areas as well.

There are several general approaches to reading instruction: visual, phonetic, linguistic, language experience, personalized, and programmed methods. These are described, in simplified form, in Table 13-1. Some of these methods emphasize the meaning of the language that is being read (visual, language experience, personalized reading), while others stress the ability to break the code (phonics, linguistic, programmed methods) (Chall, 1967). Those methods that emphasize meaning help teach learning disabled children who have visual processing strengths but whose deficits are in the areas of phonetic analysis, auditory sequencing, blending, and retrieval of sounds. They also better match the language systems of children with linguistic deficits or those who are socioculturally different.

Phonics methods are useful to LD students whose language abilities are superior to their visual information-processing skills. Since linguistic approaches cluster sounds, they are helpful to the child who is unable to analyze and sequence separate elements in a word. Since programmed approaches do not build in individualized phonetic instruction, they are useful only to children who can learn phonetics independently, and who work well with minimal teacher direction; this is seldom true of the learning disabled.

With the exception of language experience and personalized instruction approaches, reading programs generally follow the skill sequence outlined in the scope and sequence chart in Chapter 12.

For most children, phonetic approaches that teach decoding and sequencing of individual sounds in words seem to work better than other methods. Research Box 13-1 describes why researchers have had difficulty coming up with more than this general conclusion from studies. Many experts agree that a code emphasis is an appropriate first step in reading. Once the code is mastered, comprehension becomes the major focus of reading instruction (Chall, 1967; Heilman, 1968; Rosner, 1975). At this point, however, not enough is

Table 13-1   Approaches to reading instruction

GENERAL APPROACHES	CAUTIONS WITH RESPECT TO LD STUDENTS
1. Visual Approaches Visual methods are often referred to as "look-say" because words are taught by visual discrimination of letters and remembering what several letters grouped together look like. The contours of the words are highlighted in order to help children distinguish and remember them:  Many basal readers (graded series developed for the average reader) incorporate a visual approach in beginning reading (e.g., *Scott Foresman*). Eventually decoding skills are added. Comprehension is emphasized throughout.	The visual approach encourages the poor reader's implusive "look-guess" strategies. Most children will deduce phonetic rules when they have learned enough words, but poor readers won't.
2. The Phonics Approach The phonics method teaches children to associate printed letters with their corresponding sounds. Children can then use these phonic skills to analyze sound sequences, blend them together, and pronounce new words. "Pond" will be sounded out (pu – ah – nn – di) and then blended together again. A variety of reading series emphasize the phonic method (e.g., Engelmann & Bruner's (1969) *Distar* program, Open Court, Ginn, Lippincott Publishers). Supplemental programs emphasizing phonics skills are a useful adjunct to any program (e.g., Spaldings, *The Writing Road to Reading*). Other published programs combine the phonetic and visual approaches (e.g., *The Phonovisual Method*; Schoolfield & Timberlake, 1960).	The phonics method will be difficult for the child who has trouble discriminating among sounds and initial and terminal letter sounds, blending sounds into words, or remembering the sounds of letters and words (Wallace & Kauffman, 1973). Phonics will be difficult for the child who takes so long to retrieve one sound that the previous ones are forgotten.

(Continued on following page)

known about the reading process itself to determine one hierarchy that reading instruction should follow for all children (Smith, 1971).

For many LD children, wise matching of reading program approaches to their learning strengths leads to reading progress. For children with severe

Table 13–1 continued

GENERAL APPROACHES	CAUTIONS WITH RESPECT TO LD STUDENTS
3. *The Linguistic Approach* Linguistic theorists emphasize the strong relationship between printed words and the reader's oral language skills. Since meaning precedes the printed word, and individual sounds don't occur in oral language (there is no real word such as "pu - ah - nn - di"), the linguistic method tries to short cut combining letters to yield words, so that the reader can concentrate on meaning (Bloomfield & Barnhart, 1961; Fries, 1963). Once the student has learned to decode, reading for meaning can take place (Glass, 1973). In a way, the linguistic approach combines visual and phonic methods. Word stems like "at" and "ick" are taught as sight words and then individual sounds are substituted at the beginning of the stems: *p*at, *r*at, *c*at; *p*ick, *k*ick, *s*ick. Stems are taught that can be placed at the beginning (e.g. un, dis), end, or middle of words. There is a definite sequence to the presentation of words, regular spelling patterns first, followed by irregular forms. Linguistic series include the *Merrill Linguistic Readers* (Fries, 1962), *SRA Program*, *Sullivan Programmed Readers*, Traub's *Recipe for Reading*.	Some programs assume that the reader will be able to independently discover the relationship between the sound and the letter; this link may be difficult for the disabled reader. Although this system has the advantage of using visual analysis while reducing the phonetic load, students may still be overloaded by having to learn too many sounds at once (*Recipe for Reading* is an exception).
4. *Language Experience Methods* The language experience method emphasizes comprehension because the child's language is the foundation upon which reading skills are built (Allen, 1968, 1976; Lee & Allen, 1963). The child uses his vocabulary to orally relate personal experiences. The teacher writes these on wall charts. If the child can answer meaningful questions about his story, he is directed to look at the individ-	Though capitalizing on visual processing, motivation, and reading for meaning, it is unlikely that LD students will discover sound-symbol relationships for themselves. The variety of words that need to be read and remembered may be confusing. Most LD students need a systematic approach to phonics instruction.

deficits, however, the curriculum generally needs to be dramatically modified to include special alphabets or special reading strategies. At times the regular curriculum is set aside altogether if it cannot compliment the special approaches.

Table 13-1 continued

GENERAL APPROACHES	CAUTIONS WITH RESPECT TO LD STUDENTS
ual words and letters and try to remember them. Activities such as illustrating, editing, and making permanent charts or books are encouraged. This approach encourages creativity, motivation for learning to read, and aids speaking, listening, spelling, and writing skills (Allen & Allen, 1970).	
5. Personalized Reading Approach The personalized reading approach has been adopted by many alternative schools that wish children to read what is most meaningful to them. The goal is to erase the stigma of being behind everyone else that comes from being assigned to the "Blue bird" graded reading group instead of the "Hawks." It represents a much broader way of thinking about reading than other approaches (Lazar, 1957). The student chooses material which is of personal interest (books, magazines, newspapers) and reads at his or her own rate. It is highly motivating for students to participate in this type of independent approach.	Teachers must engage in systematic and continuous review because the LD reader may be "getting in over his head." Subtle difficulties could go undetected and cause the student great difficulty later on. The student may be denied opportunities for learning what is important to other schools and, if transferring schools or taking national competency tests, may fail (e.g., comprehension and composition skills, grammatical analysis).
6. Programmed Instruction Programmed instruction materials are the most extreme behaviorally oriented materials. They allow the student to be actively involved in learning and to progress at his or her own rate. The teacher is merely a guide. Programmed materials are presented in small sequential steps. The reader gets immediate feedback about whether or not the answers are correct, and then engages in additional examples of those skills in which he needs further practice.	The lack of presentation of material in small steps and constant review may compound the LD child's learning difficulties and reinforce learning of errors. LD students usually need active teacher guidance and feedback; they cannot take independent initiative for learning, self-pacing, and self-correcting. LD students usually need teacher checks on learning; they may be using the wrong cues for learning and find it easy to copy answers rather than problem solve independently.

Most often several approaches need to be combined in teaching the learning disabled. Some help a child make progress through stronger learning channels while weaknesses are remediated with other approaches. Since fluent reading necessitates the recognition of words at a glance, gaining meaning

RESEARCH BOX 13-1
Research Matching Reading Methods with Student Characteristics

Studies conducted in the classroom that test phonic against visual approaches to reading have generally found that the auditory emphasis has an advantage (Bateman, 1968; Bliesmer & Yarborough, 1965; Potts, 1968; Silberberg, Iversen, & Goins, 1973). Developing sound-blending skills is essential to reading achievement (Richardson, Di Benedetto & Bradley, 1977). Studies that add a kinesthetic element like tracing to a combined auditory-visual approach find that this method provides no additional benefits (Ringler & Smith, 1973). Bateman's study is of particular interest because it used the different approaches throughout the first grade year and analyzed the data separately for auditory and visual learners. Even the visual learners, who were theoretically mismatched with the phonetic teaching technique, profited more in reading and spelling with a phonic approach than a visual approach. Apparently, "breaking the code" is facilitated by concentrating the instructional program on these sound-symbol relationships. Even when this skill doesn't come easily to visual learners, it is essential to reading progress, and will benefit them in the long run.

Studies testing the superiority of one teaching method over another are particularly difficult to run, interpret, and compare because children improve just because the teachers know they're being studied (Hawthorne Effect), because diagnostic instruments for defining a child as one or another type of learner are of questionable reliability and validity, because it is difficult to homogeneously group very heterogeneous children, and because it is difficult to get adequate control groups. Most studies differ from one another in child characteristics and the training's time period and specific nature (Larrivee, 1981; Ysseldyke, 1973). Since all programs' skills overlap, it is also difficult to determine which are the strong and weak points of a particular program (Englemann, 1967). Bond and Dykstra's (1967) work underscores the very important point that all programs teach; the teacher, rather than the program, may be the critical variable in such studies and the most important variable in a child's learning.

from words, as well as the analysis, sequencing, and retrieval of sounds, no one process can be concentrated on to the exclusion of another. It makes sense to teach reading largely within content materials rather than just word lists since context aids word recognition and since the child's reading errors eventually become regulated by the semantic and syntactic constraints of a passage (Krieger, 1981).

Regardless of the materials and methods chosen, a primary goal must be to increase the time spent teaching reading per day. Research shows that those students who spend more time on tasks also make the greater gains (Allington, 1977; Guthrie, 1980). One study showed that LD students averaged only twenty-seven minutes of reading per day (Zigmond, Vallecorsa, & Leinhardt, 1982). In contrast, fifty-five minutes per day were spent in waiting (for the teacher, for the rest of the class, for equipment) or management tasks (getting ready, finding materials, putting things away). If students could spend only a few of these wasted minutes in additional reading each day, their reading achievement is likely to be positively affected.

We shall next discuss the special alphabets and reading strategies. Comprehension skills will be explored within issues of content area instruction.

Special Alphabets. Several major obstacles need to be overcome in learning to read English: English spelling does not correspond with individual letter sounds (the "a" in *many* is pronounced as a short "e"), several letters may represent one sound (the "o" sound in *although* is spelled "ough"), and only one-half of all words follow phonetic rules. These obstacles prove especially difficult for the learning disabled child who has trouble remembering sounds, learning when an "a" should sound like a long "a" or a short "a," "e," "i" (stomach), and "u" (infamy), or revisualizing how words should look.

When, as beginning readers, LD students have difficulty mastering these irregular relationships, special alphabets may help. Sometimes the reading series is temporarily set aside while the special alphabet becomes the primary tool for instruction. Several of these approaches follow.

Initial Teaching Alphabet (i.t.a.). The i.t.a., devised by Sir James Pitman, uses an alphabet containing forty-four characters. Each symbol represents one speech sound. For example, *sh* and *th* each have symbols, and letters that sound alike (q, k) share a symbol. A word is spelled the way it is pronounced; *six* is "siks" and *many* is "meny." Students are taught each symbol's sound, and they write using lower case letters. By the second year, i.t.a. symbols are phased out into the traditional alphabetic system. Making this transfer is a difficult process for all children, but especially for disabled readers (Hayes & Nemeth, 1965; Heilman, 1968).

Coding by Color. Two systems code the alphabet by color. *Words in Color* (Gattegno, 1962) uses forty-seven colors, each representing a single speech sound in the English language. The sound of a long "a" as in *plate* is always colored green, whether it is represented by *a, ay, eigh, ea, ei, ey,* or *ai*. The student color codes while using the traditional alphabet for reading and spelling. Teaching is done from wall charts or the blackboard, using a visual dictation process — pointing to the letters while saying the corresponding sounds. Drills begin with short vowel sounds which are then blended with consonant sounds. A practical problem with this system is that teachers find it hard to have all the colors needed, and in the correct order. They also are unable to find sustained reading materials printed in this code.

In contrast to *Words in Color*, the *Color Phonics System's* (Bannatyne, 1966) letter sounds do not all have corresponding colors. The *Color Phonics* approach allows the student to generate his or her own verbal content, whereas the content in *Words in Color* is highly organized. When the teacher feels that the student can benefit from traditional materials, these approaches are phased out.

While color may be a helpful decoding aid for some children, it may confuse others. Transitioning from color codes to black and white letters also may be difficult (Berstein, 1967).

Peabody Rebus Reading Program. Picture stories, such as are what the Rebus program is all about. The Rebus program (Woodcock & Clark, 1969) replaces traditional printed words with a rebus. A *rebus* is a symbol that is assumed to provide an easier link to the spoken word than do spelled words (see Figure 13-1). As the program progresses, many rebuses transition into sight words, so that the child can read over 100 printed words.

The Rebus program capitalizes on the good visual perceptual abilities of many disabled readers while working around the need to analyze, sequence, and blend sounds. It also provides beginning readers with an idea of what reading is like. Since children still need to learn their phonic skills to decode unfamiliar words, the Rebus idea has been adapted to letter forms (see Figure 13-2). Often associating a letter with an object that is shaped like the letter and begins with the same sound aids recall of the letter's shape and sound.

Special Reading Strategies.   Several specialized reading approaches have been used with severely disabled readers. These methods can replace the standard program, or be used to reinforce its content. All but the last of these methods follow a multisensory approach similar to that advocated by the pioneers in learning disabilities. They are based on the knowledge that when children actively involve all senses in the learning process, then attention to distinctive features and learning might be facilitated. Unlike general programs which require children to *recognize* words in print through reading, some multisensory approaches work directly on what is most difficult for LD children — organizing what they see so that it can be *recalled* in writing or oral spelling when the word is no longer in front of them. Although using all senses may be beneficial for many children, the choice of multisensory methods should be carefully evaluated because indiscriminate bombardment may overload some children's central nervous systems and literally tune them out (Johnson & Myklebust, 1967; Kirk & Kirk, 1971).

The Fernald Approach. The Fernald method, also known as the VAKT (Visual-Auditory-Kinesthetic-Tactile) method, was developed by Grace Fernald (1943). Words are taught through a multisensory approach focusing on the whole word and not its individual sounds. The following is a typical variation of Fernald's method.

Stage 1 1. The story is dictated by the child. The greater opportunity the child has to create his or her own story, the more willing the child will be to follow it through all the steps.

Figure 13-1   Example of Rebus symbols

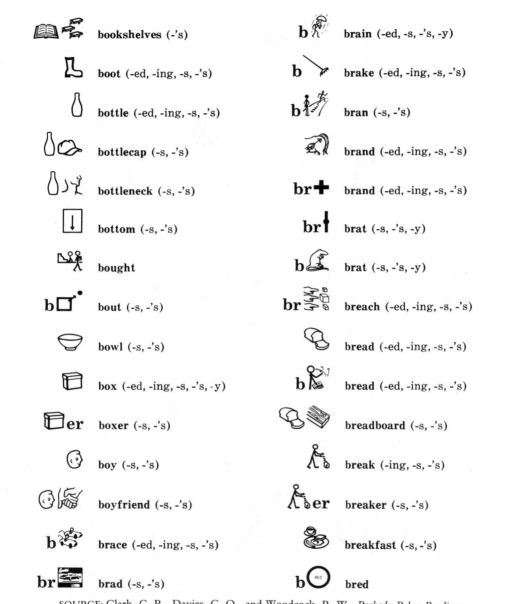

bookshelves (-'s)

boot (-ed, -ing, -s, -'s)

bottle (-ed, -ing, -s, -'s)

bottlecap (-s, -'s)

bottleneck (-s, -'s)

bottom (-s, -'s)

bought

bout (-s, -'s)

bowl (-s, -'s)

box (-ed, -ing, -s, -'s, -y)

boxer (-s, -'s)

boy (-s, -'s)

boyfriend (-s, -'s)

brace (-ed, -ing, -s, -'s)

brad (-s, -'s)

brain (-ed, -s, -'s, -y)

brake (-ed, -ing, -s, -'s)

bran (-s, -'s)

brand (-ed, -ing, -s, -'s)

brand (-ed, -ing, -s, -'s)

brat (-s, -'s, -y)

brat (-s, -'s, -y)

breach (-ed, -ing, -s, -'s)

bread (-ed, -ing, -s, -'s)

bread (-ed, -ing, -s, -'s)

breadboard (-s, -'s)

break (-ing, -s, -'s)

breaker (-s, -'s)

breakfast (-s, -'s)

bred

SOURCE: Clark, C. R., Davies, C. O., and Woodcock, R. W., *Peabody Rebus Reading Program*. Circle Pines, Minn.: American Guidance Service, 1974. Reprinted by permission.

Figure 13-2 Pairing letter sounds with object shapes

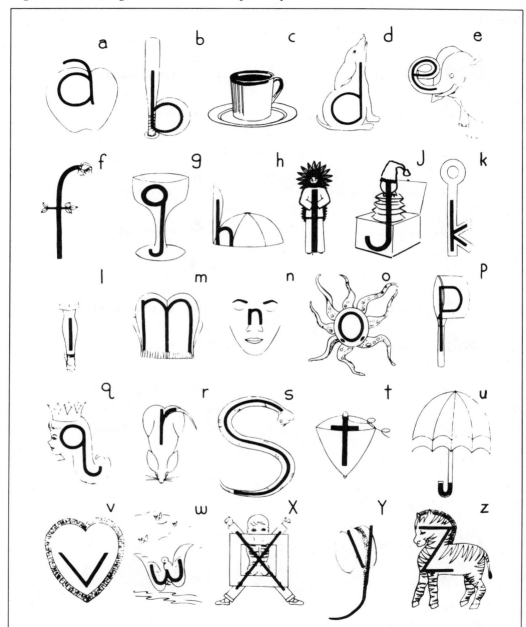

SOURCE: Isgur, J., "Establishing Letter-Sound Associations by an Object-Imaging-Projection Method." © 1975 The Professional Press, Inc. Reprinted with permission of the publisher from *Journal of Learning Disabilities,* 11 East Adams Street, Chicago, Illinois 60603, vol. *8,* p. 351.

2. The teacher writes the words of the story on strips of paper using cursive writing. There is one word on each piece of paper and the word must be large enough for the child to trace.
3. The child then traces the word with two-finger contact while slowly saying the word in syllables. The teacher insures that the child traces the word correctly every time. Tracing is repeated until the child can write the word without copying it.
4. The child writes the word on a slip of paper. If it is correct, it may be added to other correctly written words to form a story. If it is incorrect, step 3 is repeated.
5. The teacher keeps the strips of paper in a file until all the words necessary for the story are accumulated. The teacher then types the story so that the child can read it in print, and it is given to the child.

Stage 2 At this stage the child can learn words by looking at, saying, and writing them; tracing the words is no longer necessary. The other steps remain the same.

Stage 3 The student reads directly from the printed word without writing and does not require the teacher to write it first. Basal readers may be introduced, and new words are reviewed and written from memory. The teacher periodically reviews these words.

Stage 4 The child's ability to generalize becomes important at this stage. Disabled readers may need assistance in recognizing how new words resemble those already known. Mastery is required at each stage before the student is allowed to move to the next.

The Gillingham-Stillman Method. Gillingham and Stillman's (1970) multisensory approach to reading, spelling, and writing is based on Orton's (1937, 1966) theories. In contrast to Fernald's whole-word focus, this is an alphabetic system, stressing letters and their sounds. Spelling and writing are used as avenues for reading achievement. This highly structured approach requires that the child be given instruction five times a week for at least two years.

Each sound is learned one at a time using auditory, visual and kinesthetic stimuli, and some tracing. These single sounds are then blended into sound clusters and finally into short words. Word analysis is begun by the teacher speaking words and the child responding by pointing to them. The Simultaneous Oral Spelling process is introduced next. The teacher says the word, followed by the child saying the word, naming the letters and writing the letters as he or she names them.

Slingerland (1974) has produced a more recent adaptation of the Gillingham-Stillman method. Because the student is required to use this method exclusively, the teacher must make arrangements for subject area materials in science and social studies to be read to the student.

Manual Alphabet Method. A recent multisensory teaching tool for disabled readers is the signed alphabet of the deaf. Vernon, Coley and DeBois (1980) maintain that the manual alphabet can remediate reading difficulties because children benefit from a multisensory approach (Myers, 1976), physical involvement in the reading process (Offir, 1976), and heightened motivation to learn. McKnight (1979) suggests that a hand sign be used for each letter or phoneme. When a student loses his or her place or starts to reverse a word, the teacher can sign the first letter of the correct word.

Braille-Phonics. Another new multisensory method involves teaching braille as an aid to phonics acquisition (Fishbein, 1979). Braille-Phonics combines the tactile (Braille), phonic, and visual processing systems in the hope that learning through one system facilitates learning through another. The child learns the braille letters first while blindfolded. Phonics rules are taught next, and then words comprised of both braille and print are presented. In the word *shame*, for example, the "a" and "e" might be represented in braille and the "sh" and "m" in print to emphasize the silent "e" rule. Fishbein (1979) states that children with weak visual receptive or strong auditory memory abilities benefit most from using Braille-Phonics.

The Neurological Impress Method. The neurological impress method (Heckelman, 1969) uses auditory modelling by having the student and teacher read a passage aloud in unison. The child points to the words as they are read. At first the teacher's voice is louder and faster than the child's. As the child's confidence and sight recognition increase, the teacher's voice softens and lags behind the student's. Lorenz and Vockell (1979) note some secondary benefits of this approach: students and teachers formed a closer relationship; students were motivated to learn and showed more self confidence; students improved in their ability to express themselves orally; they showed increased left to right progression while reading; they increased verbal fluency; and they benefitted from being introduced to new materials.

Other Methods. Today's teacher has a myriad of special reinforcement methods available that add variety, excitement, and greater individualization to the learning process. These include tape recorders, educational games, filmstrips, film reels that children can operate and view independently, overhead projectors, records with accompanying books, and tachistoscopes that flash words at various rates. Educational TV is popularly used, as are teaching machines. These machines vary from simple "language masters" (in which a child writes and tape records a word on a computer card, and then sees and hears it as it runs through the machine), to more complex talking typewriters (developed by O. K. Moore) that speak the name of the letter a child types as a screen flashes the letter. Some complex computers automatically proceed to harder material when children punch in correct responses, and review easier material when children make errors. Such equipment is usually available to teachers through the resource room or school reading laboratory.

Written Language

Written language skills most often present the biggest stumbling block for the learning disabled. They represent the pinnacle of applying reading, spelling, listening, speaking, and thinking skills (Johnson & Myklebust, 1967). Instructional strategies in written language address the areas of handwriting, spelling, and written expression.

Handwriting. The goals of handwriting instruction include holding and directing a writing utensil, and correctly, easily, and legibly forming manuscript (printing) and cursive writing. There is some controversy concerning whether children with writing disabilities should be taught manuscript or cursive writing first. Students typically begin with printing and then transition to cursive writing in about the third grade. Manuscript is generally easier to learn and more closely resembles the print found in books. When the child has struggled but finally mastered the manuscript form reasonably well, school personnel might suggest not transitioning to cursive writing. Cursive writing, on the other hand, has the advantage of limiting reversals because all letters are formed from left to right; its connecting letters and continuous writing rhythm also help to eliminate irregular spacing. An advantage of beginning with cursive writing is that the LD child will not have to learn to transfer from one form to another (Johnson & Myklebust, 1967).

Teachers' instructional approaches will vary, depending on whether the child is having difficulty visualizing and recalling the correct letter forms or employing visual-spatial judgments and visual-motor movements to produce them (Gerard & Junkala, 1980). Table 13-2 presents a checklist of these handwriting difficulties that is helpful in planning remedial strategies. When, for example, the difficulty is at the visual input end, the student needs instruction in recognizing and recalling the size, shape, and directions of letters. Instruction eventually focuses on such production skills as the spacing, organization, and formation of letters. Proper positioning of the hand, paper (left handed tilted opposite to right handed), writing instrument, and posture all affect the child's ability to write.

Often workbook exercises requiring students to copy a model or follow dotted lines do not offer sufficient instruction in these visual and motor processes. An interesting approach that maximizes the modelling principle by gradually decreasing visual supports is the *trace and fade* method. The child traces a letter or word, then inserts a piece of tracing paper between the model and the product, shifts the paper and traces again. More and more tracing paper is inserted, until the model's image finally fades away. The child is left forming letters or words from memory.

Other methods that are useful in handwriting instruction impact primarily on learning strategies and motivation: teaching students to recognize their errors (Tagatz et al., 1969), reinforcing self-instruction and self-correction procedures (Kosiewicz, Hallahan, Lloyd, & Graves, 1982), using systematically programmed materials that have built-in rewards for correct responses

Table 13-2 Checklist indicating area of handwriting difficulty. A handwriting sample should be obtained by having the child copy at least three lines of writing either from the board or another paper. The example to be copied from should not exceed 18 letters and/or spaces per line. The child should be instructed to copy the example exactly.

IF THESE THINGS ARE OBSERVED	THE CHILD EXPERIENCES DIFFICULTY IN:			
	VISUAL-PERCEPTION-INPUT	VISUAL-SPATIAL	VISUAL-MOTOR	VISUAL RECALL
Parts of letters not connected	X			
Shape of letters distorted	X			
Reversed letters★	X			
Upside down letters★	X			
Twisted letters★	X			
Unequal spacing of letters		X		
Unequal size of letters		X		
Letters not on the line		X		
Heavy use of the pencil			X	
Light use of the pencil			X	
Tense grip while writing			X	
Pencil held in fist grip			X	
Wavering lines			X	
Deterioration of letter shape as repeated across line			X	
Letters copied out of sequence				X
Letters omitted or words omitted				X

★ These must be constant and not just an occasional learning error.

SOURCE: Gerard, J., *Correcting Handwriting Problems,* in association with the Lexington Teacher Training Program, Lexington, Mass. and Merrimack Education Center, Chelmsford, Mass., Lexington, Mass.: Lexington Public Schools, 1974, p. 18.

(Brigham, Finfrock, Breunig, & Bushell, 1972), or having a positive experience (free time) contingent on good handwriting quality (Hopkins, Schutte, & Garton, 1971). Generally, these methods initially concentrate on letter forms, then words, then short phrases, and finally sentences.

Teaching handwriting is one area in which the teacher can be creative: developing templates in the form of letters, creating dot–to–dot letter–like figures and finish–the–picture activities, covering models of letters with acetate to be used for tracing, or using paper with different–sized lines to help the children stay within boundaries. Also available are pencil grippers that help mold the correct pencil grips (and scotch tape to hold the paper in the correct position). Many special commercially prepared materials and programs provide systematic writing exercises (Brenner, 1967; Noble, 1966; Townsend; Zaner–Bloser, 1968), and can even turn the paper yellow with a gray dot when the writing instrument goes where it's supposed to (Skinner & Krakower, 1968).

Spelling. Spelling problems may be experienced for a number of reasons: trouble with phonetic sequencing, recall of auditory patterns, or recall of spelling patterns that can only be memorized visually (e.g., the spelling of "rough" must be memorized; it can't be sounded out) (Otto, McMenemy, & Smith, 1973). Handwriting difficulties may also interfere with spelling. Again, the instructional method chosen depends on the teacher's analysis of why the child is experiencing spelling difficulties. The child's reading and language arts curriculum includes spelling objectives which can be reinforced with special teaching strategies. Some of these are reviewed below.

Error Scanning Approach. Error scanning is a self–discovery approach that particularly helps the youngster who reads well but has trouble with the visual imagery needed to recall irregular words (Yukovitz, 1979). Good word recognition skills are used to scan a page and find the spelling errors. The student experiments with various spellings as the teacher reinforces correct approximations. The teacher then focuses the child's attention on the differences between the incorrect and the correct spellings, to highlight discrepancies in how the words look (Kauffman et al., 1978).

Multisensory Approach. The Fernald remedial reading strategy has also been used successfully with students who have spelling disabilities. Students use all their senses in acquiring the spellings of words they choose to learn. The Gillingham–Stillman method actually uses oral and written spelling to teach reading. The Fernald method might be appropriate for the student with stronger visual–processing skills because of its whole–word emphasis. The Gillingham–Stillman approach might best benefit the student who has good ability to analyze and sequence the sounds of letters in words.

Linguistic Approach. Linguistic approaches to spelling systematically incorporate phonological, morphological, syntactic, and semantic rules (Benthul et al., 1974). Basal spelling series generally stress phonology and morphology. The phonological aspect teaches children to transfer individual sounds into print (/c/ /a/ /t/). The morphological aspect groups the rules for meaningful speech units into a systematic instructional approach (such as adding common prefixes or word endings to stems: *un-, dis-, -s, -ed, -ing*). Arranging words by their common spelling patterns is a beneficial instructional method (Hanna, Hodges, & Hanna, 1971; Lovitt, 1975b). It enables the learning disabled child to more readily generalize these word forms to others that follow the same rule (such as, double the consonant when adding "ing" if preceded by a short vowel).

A different approach is followed by Kottmeyer and Claus' (1972) *Basic Goals in Spelling*. Here the student discovers the relationships between the sounds and symbols for him- or herself and generates the rules governing these relationships. Analysis of the phoneme is emphasized, and basic word lists and enrichment activities are presented.

The choice of methods depends on whether the child is in need of directed instruction or whether the child's cognitive style is such that he or she discovers relationships alone. In most cases, the learning disabled fall into the first category. Not until the LD student begins written expression activities will he or she learn to spell according to the syntactic (they're, their, there; its, it's) and semantic (new, knew; one, won; plain, plane) aspects of a sentence.

Written Expression. Written expression competencies are used throughout the school years for notetaking, written homework assignments, essay exams, compositions, creative writing (poetry, short stories), and letters. They involve conceptualization of the syntactic and semantic aspects of what is to be written. These include capitalization, punctuation, grammatical forms, appropriate vocabulary and word order, paragraph construction, theme development, and the basic ability to read, write and spell. The Case Study about Larry and Mike, on page 453 illustrates how written expression difficulties can be due to lack of experiences, the skills to turn these experiences into written expression, or production difficulties (handwriting and spelling).

For those who lack motivating experiences to write about, the teacher can provide enriching experiences such as field trips, discussions, and creative fantasies. The teacher can also help students to be creative in recounting their everyday activities. Other students have the experiences to relate but are reluctant to write them down. They may need instruction in such prerequisite skills as handwriting, spelling, the rules of written language, and oral grammar and vocabulary.

Emphasis in written language instruction should be placed on idea development, vocabulary usage, and the mechanical rules of writing (punctuation, capitalization, theme development, and organization of content). Very often, the written expression goals are identical to the oral goals that language development specialists emphasize: subject–verb agreement, appropriate verb tense,

CASE STUDY:
Larry and Mike

One fall a teacher gave her class an assignment to write an essay entitled "What I did during my summer vacation." She particularly noticed the papers of two students, Larry and Mike. Both boys handed in their assignments late and wrote down experiences which could be summarized as "Not much." But they did so for different reasons. Both of Larry's parents work long hours and, except for his paper route and a trip to a local fish hatchery, Larry characterized his summer as boring. When questioned by the teacher he said, "I didn't have anything interesting to write about." Mike, on the other hand, was overheard telling a group of classmates about his trip across the country. He enthusiastically related numerous experiences he had had. When the teacher asked Mike why he had not mentioned his trip before, he replied, "Because then I would've had to write it all down." Mike's grammar and vocabulary development were poor and he didn't even know how to begin a paragraph. Even had he known what to do, his spelling and handwriting were so poor that he would have gotten an F. He figured "Why bother?"

ability to use synonyms, vocabulary development, organization of thoughts, and comprehension of idioms. Teachers need to be particularly sensitive to whether their written expression goals require reinforcement in oral syntax and semantics training as well.

The greater the variety and frequency of writing activities, the greater the opportunity for improvement. Exercises can pertain to content area subject matter and practical skills such as writing letters, as well as creative writing. Students need to be encouraged to write down experiences and reactions which are important to them. Language experience activities are ideal for this purpose, as is maintaining a personal journal. The student may dictate into a tape recorder, and transcribe the tape personally or have it transcribed by someone else. The teacher then uses the finished product as the focus of instruction. Since the teacher's red marks are likely to catch up with the learning disabled in any number of written expression components, teachers need to focus on specific goals while overlooking others. Before doing written assignments, students should know whether their teacher is concerned with written format or content. They can then direct their energies selectively to grammar, spelling, and mechanical rules or to clarity in thinking, expression of ideas, and creativity.

Mathematics

A learning disabled child may have difficulty understanding basic number concepts, time, measurement, money, or computational processes. The child also may have little success with solving word problems, because these require reading in addition to mathematical reasoning and computation abilities. To choose the best remediation approach, the teacher must determine exactly what the student has and has not mastered on hierarchies of math skills such as those presented in Chapter 12. Then the teacher should explore additional factors to better understand what may be interfering with the child's mathematical progress: such as, poor past teaching, conceptual difficulty, motor problems, reading difficulty, inattentiveness to details, poor recall of number facts. This will help the teacher plan how to go about teaching.

Arithmetic remediation methods are far less developed than are reading strategies. The teacher must use ingenuity in setting up pages for students who have difficulty aligning calculations (use graph paper, turn lined paper sideways), drilling number facts (tachistocope; fact sheet pasted to desk for in-class problem-solving), helping students read word problems (transcribe them into numerals), helping students attend to all elements of a problem (set up self-checking devices), avoiding student overload with too many problems on a page (cut each ditto into four segments), and so forth. Several special approaches, such as behavioral techniques and the use of concrete materials, have been devised to aid conceptual attainment in mathematics.

Behavioral Techniques. Behavioral methods systematically program the sequence of skill acquisition and give students immediate feedback on accuracy. In the *Sullivan Basal Math Program,* for example, students progress through a series of programmed workbooks. The development of computation skills in addition, subtraction, multiplication, division, fractions, and decimals is emphasized. The student progresses at his or her own rate. The workbooks are self-correcting, providing immediate feedback concerning right or wrong responses. The teacher administers a test as each workbook is completed. Since the program does not require any reading, it is useful for students whose mathematical difficulties are complicated by their inability to read directions and word problems. However, since it doesn't teach the basic concepts underlying computations, the program needs to be supplemented with materials which highlight these concepts. As with programmed readers, the program must be appropriately matched to the conceptual style of the child.

Another programmed approach is the *Distar Arithmetic Program I, II, III* (Englemann & Carnine, 1976) in which the teacher must adhere to a prescribed set of instructions. The child is actively involved by responding orally and in writing to a rapid presentation of problems. The activity and motivation implicit in this approach helps engage students' attention. Whether it is appropriate, for those LD students who process information very slowly and have trouble responding well to aural directions, needs to be evaluated.

Concrete Materials. Many children have difficulty conceptualizing the numerals on paper as representing real things. These students benefit from seeing and manipulating the quantities about which they are reasoning. By touching actual objects, impulsive students' counting speed slows down and their accuracy increases. Concrete materials also help the child perform the type of thinking that Piaget notes underlies mathematical ability: reasoning about two pieces of information at once. Cuisenaire rods and Stern's *Structural Arithmetic* (Stern, 1965) follow this teaching strategy.

Cuisenaire rods (Davidson, 1969) have been helpful as a supplemental or math readiness program. They were invented in 1953 by George Cuisenaire, and were further developed by Caleb Gattegno. The rods are wooden and belong to any one of five color groups, each representing different quantities. Students use the rods to learn mathematics in five stages.

1. The child explores the rods.
2. The child and teacher discuss the relationships that have been discovered through directed activities, but no mathematical notation is used.
3. The child engages in teacher-directed activities. Mathematical notation is used but no number value is assigned to the rods.
4. The child engages in directed activities in which both mathematical notation and number values are assigned to the rods.
5. The child is encouraged to rely less on the rods and to perform the calculations mentally (Hammill & Bartel, 1978).

The child using Stern's approach actively manipulates rods and other concrete materials while discovering different number concepts. Sequential steps engage the child in activities ranging from simple number facts through complex problem-solving. Functional illustrations are presented in workbooks to help the students reconstruct any forgotten number facts.

Content Area Instruction

In the elementary school, content area instruction occurs primarily in social studies and science courses. These subjects are generally taught orally, but by fourth and fifth grade textbooks might be introduced. At this level, the student is required to engage in independent research projects and written assignments. It is critical that the LD student's reading, written expression, and study skill weaknesses not be allowed to interfere with acquiring content or demonstrating knowledge in these areas.

To evaluate whether the content area textbook is appropriate, the teacher must check vocabulary, sentence complexity, prior knowledge, and whether the readability level is appropriate for the student. The text should have an organizational pattern which highlights important relationships, avoids overloading with new concepts and details, and gives concrete examples for complex concepts. It might also provide visual aids, learning checks, interesting content and style, and practical applications of information. Any unmet criteria must be modified to match the student's needs. The teacher can employ one of several readability formulas discussed later in this chapter to evaluate the reading level of the material.

When the material is clearly too hard for the student to read independently, the resource teacher, reading teacher, or regular classroom teacher can read the content to the student before class. They could also rewrite the material in vocabulary that the student can manage, or help the student create an outline so only key words need to be read. The student might also tape record answers to homework assignments or tests. A teacher, peer, or parent can then transcribe these answers and use them for instruction in reading, spelling, and written language.

Even when accommodations are made for the student's reading and writing levels, comprehension still may present a problem. The reading curriculum generally works on several types of meaning: details, main ideas, sequencing events, organizing ideas, drawing inferences, and reaching conclusions. But the student may not be able to apply these skills to content area material independently, especially at higher levels of problem-solving and information evaluation. Several approaches aid comprehension under these circumstances. Generally, these methods create a purpose for reading by telling the student ahead of time what information to look for or what types of judgments the student will have to make.

A technique called SQ3R (Robinson, 1961) teaches the child to Survey the reading materials first (chapter title, introductory statement, main headings, illustrations, summary). Then the students read the Questions to discover the purpose of reading, or formulates his or her own questions from the headings. The 3 Rs follow: Read the material to find the answers to these questions, Recite the answers to the questions, and Review the material to check accuracy or gain new information and ideas. Variations of the SQ3R technique have been adapted to science (Spache, 1963) and mathematics content (Fay, 1965).

The teacher also can enhance the student's comprehension and retention of information by assigning shorter segments of passages, and immediately following each with questions. The questions should jump to higher level inferences only when the child is ready to handle such thinking. Manzo's (1969) *Request* technique has the child and teacher ask each other reciprocal questions after each has read the material silently. The questioning aids retention and evaluation of information. Such *Directed Reading-Thinking Activities* (Stauffer, 1969) have been most helpful to the learning disabled.

At least one study has found that giving word aids (explaining vocabulary) and sentence aids (explaining syntactical relationships of words in the sentence) can increase comprehension even more than setting a purpose for reading or giving prior knowledge to which the new content can relate (Pflaum, Pascarella, Auer, Augustyn & Boswick, 1982). Structuring material by building in questions, verbal rehearsal, and cognitive training strategies (modelling an instructor's performance, stop-look-listen, covert rehearsal) very often raises the learning disabled student's level of recall to that of typical learners. Recall is enhanced because students are better able to focus attention on relevant information and organize it for storage. Learner strategies also are improved by making children more aware of what they need to memorize on specific tasks, what their typical strategies are, and how they might substitute better strategies. Such training helps impulsive children attend to details, be more reflective, and delay responding. The overly reflective student can be aided by the teacher highlighting themes and concepts rather than details, and helping the student to respond faster.

Building Social-Emotional Attributes

Oliver Wendell Holmes once attended a meeting in which he was the shortest man present. "Doctor Holmes," quipped a friend, "I should think you'd feel rather small among us big fellows." "I do," retorted Holmes, "I feel like a dime among a lot of pennies" (Canfield & Wells, 1976, p. 55).

We are all perceived differently by our friends, our family, and people we meet. Certain attributes are noticed by some individuals and not by others. These men focused on how Holmes was different from them, equating the difference with inferiority. Holmes was able to change their observation to reflect self-worth. Similarly, the teacher who focuses student attention on the strengths of individuals, and their similarities, rather than differences, can help counter the many negative stereotypes applied to handicapped children. The teacher plays a significant role in developing students' positive self-images. The better children feel about themselves, the more likely they will be to use strengths to their benefit and to face up to, and try to overcome, weaknesses. The learning disabled student is in jeopardy of social failure as a result of academic failure, social imperceptions, and linguistic difficulties. Because self worth and social skills play a significant role in present and future adjustment, schools are beginning to develop approaches to programming in this very important area.

Peer Pairing. The teacher can help the LD student develop friendships by judiciously pairing children for instruction, projects, seat work, and special privileges. Peer tutoring also has been beneficial to both friendships and academic work (Chiang, Thorpe, & Darch, 1980; Gartner, Kohler & Riessman, 1971; Strain, Cooke, & Apollini, 1976). The LD child can be tutored by an older student, or can tutor younger children. The mutual give and take that develops goes a long way toward making a learning disabled youngster feel worthwhile. Peer pairing works on the social psychological principle that people become friendliest with those with whom they have the most contact. College students, for example, are often friendliest with roommates, and the strength of their attachments decline the further away their dormitory rooms are from others' rooms. The same principle can be applied to children to help them find at least one friend to whom they are important.

Formal Social Skills Building Programs. Several social skills training programs help children appreciate the worthiness of their own and others' ideas and attributes. Bessell and Palomares' (1972) *Human Development Program* offers children the opportunity to communicate in a group about their attitudes and emotions. The children sit in a "magic circle" and share their own feelings while becoming attuned to what other members of the group are feeling. The teacher acts as facilitator to get the group started and encourage participation, without overly directing the group's focus. Anyone may suggest topics for discussion. Children can pass and not contribute to the group, if they wish. Children are not permitted to comment on each other's statements, so that no value judgments occur. With such safety measures built in, children who choose to listen eventually become participants.

A very different approach is taken by Dinkmeyer's (1970) *Developing Understanding of Self and Others (DUSO)* program. The DUSO kit contains preplanned lessons using puppets, songs, and built-in role-playing. Topics are designed to enhance the emotional and social development of elementary school students by discussing similarities and differences among children, helping, sharing, independence, decision-making, personal feelings, and so forth. In the upper elementary grades this program transitions into *Toward Affective Development* (TAD), which has more sophisticated topics.

In addition to such programs, direct lessons teaching socially imperceptive children how to behave and "read" others are very much in order. LaGreca and Mesibov (1981), for example, describe how students learned greeting, joining, and conversational skills by observing leaders model appropriate and inappropriate skills, discussing how and when to use these, role-playing, critiquing videotapes, and practicing in and out of sessions followed again by discussion.

Classroom Environment. Teachers should systematically plan time devoted daily to social-emotional learning. But helping children to better appreciate themselves and others is not something that can be scheduled into only a twenty minute curriculum slot. The teacher must model respect, trust, honesty, and positive expectations throughout the school day. These are reflected in the teacher's behaviors (grading only things that children get right, eliminating red marking pencils, turning errors into opportunities for learning by using progress charts) and the types of activities the teacher encourages: sharing family trees, picking a student of the week, including a child in curriculum decisions, sharing individual successes with classmates, plays, role playing, puppetry, having each child write something good about another student and then having the class guess which statement describes whom, and so forth.

One interesting activity is to have each child award one point at the end of the day to a classmate who helped him or her. The helpful act is reported to the class, and if the child requests it, the class can vote to award up to two points. The teacher can also award one point to anyone observed being helpful to another. When individual points build up, the teacher auctions items collected from the children's and the teacher's homes. Children bid with their points, go home with the trinkets they won, and come to school the next day ready to be helpful.

Helpfulness breeds gratitude, friendship, and good feelings about oneself. When the child's self-confidence and trust in others is built, he or she is more likely to try harder to succeed in all ways. The teacher can be instrumental in raising motivation by giving the student feedback suggesting that effort can lead to success.

Besides the classroom and resource teachers, the school psychologist and guidance counselor can provide psychological services. The art, gym, and music teachers can enhance students' self-esteem by helping them achieve in areas in which they show special promise. The school custodian is often one of the most valued pals that students have, and the librarian can guide students to books in which characters have learned to cope with situations that the students also deal with. One of the most popular authors of this type in recent years is Judy Blume. Her *Tales of a Fourth Grade Nothing*, *Blubber*, and others ring familiar to many. The cartoon in Figure 13-3 shows the attitude with which children will hopefully leave school.

Figure 13-3 Self-concept: An important goal of schooling

© 1971 by United Feature Syndicate, Inc.

Secondary School Programming

Whether the student was identified as LD in the elementary grades, or was able to slip by as weaknesses matured and compensations developed, he or she is likely to develop additional difficulties on entering secondary school. The adolescent not only experiences learning-related problems but must concurrently deal with the changes in his or her body, emotions, and social environment. Like nonhandicapped students, the learning disabled adolescent does not pass smoothly through these changes (Jacks & Keller, 1978). Disruptions in his or her life patterns and adjustment are to be expected (Lidz, 1968).

If individualizing instruction was difficult at the elementary school level, it is even more so at the secondary level (McCandless, 1970; Miller, 1978). Gaps between potential and achievement are wider, and greater variability in individual characteristics and program requirements must be dealt with. Strengths must be enhanced and compensations must be developed. Providing that the adolescent is motivated to try to overcome his or her weaknesses, remedial programming is also important. Remedial instruction in reading, mathematics, written language and survival skills are the customary interventions offered to the learning disabled. Only recently have educators become aware that far more is needed relative to instruction in basic comprehension, speaking, thinking, study, social, and prevocational skills.

Reading

The goal of secondary level reading instruction is to help students cope with the secondary school's academic demands (Wepman et al., 1975). Reading skills are taught in isolation, through the content areas, or both. Some programs developed for younger learners continue to be useful with secondary students: VAKT (Thorpe, Lampe, Nash & Chiang, 1981), *Words in Color*, and the language experience approach. Most, however, are inappropriate or require retailoring for adolescents (Lerner, Evans, & Meyers, 1977).

The severely reading disabled still need to be taught basic decoding strategies. Mastery of nonphonetic patterns and rapid recognition of sight words continue to present problems. For these students, more sophisticated-looking, high interest-low reading level texts have been developed. Even when the student can decode adequately, the process may require such energy that he or she can't at the same time attend to the content. A large majority of the secondary school learning disabled require instruction in reading for meaning, vocabulary development, and reading rate. Whatever reading instructional approach is used, it must be chosen carefully and have mature content, appearance, and format. Positive attitudes toward reading also need to be rebuilt, since the attitude with which students leave the secondary school characterizes their orientation toward reading throughout adulthood (Ribovich & Erikson, 1980).

Reading Comprehension. Comprehension problems are the most frequent and debilitating reading difficulty at the secondary level due to persistent language weaknesses and inefficient learner strategies. Students are expected to recall facts; but extraction of facts often is complicated by poorly written and disorganized texts (Gagné, 1970) that vary widely in reading levels. Anthologies, for example, can have a reading range of nine grade levels, and business and vocational texts are often far above appropriate reading levels (Aukerman, 1972).

Due in part to an overemphasis on the easiest type of comprehension, literal comprehension, by content area teachers, LD students are often trained in a limited range of comprehension strategies (Lindsey & Kerlin, 1979). It is essential to broaden these skills to enable students to profitably use information they are exposed to. As with the elementary school teacher, the secondary teacher can aid the types of comprehension depicted in Table 13-3 by using questioning strategies (Taba, 1967). Mutual questioning can take place between the teacher and student, as the teacher carefully controls the level of cognitive ability required in asking or responding to questions (Hori, 1977;

Table 13-3   Question types that aid comprehension

LEVEL OF COGNITIVE ABILITY	QUESTION TYPE	STUDENT EXPECTATION
Easier	Knowledge	a) regurgitation of facts b) dealing with information through sequencing, classifications and categories, knowledge of criteria, methods or processes c) knowledge of generalizations
	Comprehension	a) ability to translate from one form to another b) interpret the basic ideas c) make inferences
	Application	application of what the student learned at the knowledge and comprehension levels
	Analysis	a) of what someone says or writes b) of the relationship between the elements c) of the overall structure
	Synthesis	a) produce some form of communication which reflects the student's own ideas and feelings b) plan a solution to given situations c) generalize based on information given
Harder	Evaluation (performed throughout all the levels)	a) analyze conclusions b) make judgments about these conclusions

SOURCE: Adapted from Bloom, B. S., Englehart, M. D., Furst, E. J., Hill, W. H., and Krathwohl, D. R. *Taxonomy of Educational Objectives, Handbook I: Cognitive Domain.* New York: David McKay, 1956.

Manzo, 1969). The student needs to learn strategies for answering questions at easier levels before he or she can succeed at the next level. Stauffer's (1969) Directed Reading-Thinking Activity (DR-TA) enables students to generate their own questions and then read to find solutions. To illustrate, a student may read a mystery story, conjecture "who done it," and read further to discover whether the guess was correct.

Questioning strategies aid comprehension by actively involving students in applying thinking skills to reading material. This type of cognitive training procedure is also helpful in improving memory for the information presented. The teacher's goal is for students to internalize these strategies and then apply them to other content material and new experiences. The LD student commonly will require reminders to generalize these strategies.

Vocabulary. You are familiar with studies showing that the words we use often guide our thinking processes, and that ability to name what we see and verbally rehearse information enhances memory: The implication is that building LD students' vocabularies is important. Providing opportunities to use new words in everyday language or to read new words through a broad range of reading materials strengthens students' abilities to communicate orally, to read, to comprehend, to recall information, and to write meaningfully.

A technique called *SSR* (sustained silent reading) encourages the student to read anything for a set period of time each day, and guarantees no interruptions. The student is neither questioned nor tested on the material. Reading is for enjoyment alone, and vocabulary and comprehension tend to increase. The student reads what he or she wishes and builds more positive attitudes toward reading (Cline & Kretke, 1980; Minton, 1980).

The language experience approach is also helpful in expanding oral and reading vocabularies. The teacher is responsible for ensuring adequate instruction of the new words and developing a classroom environment in which students feel secure enough to try new words and thinking processess without fearing negative consequences from others (Deighton, 1970).

Reading Rate. Reading rate is a significant problem for learning disabled students. They need to learn to adjust their reading rates to the difficulty of the material and the purpose for reading (Alley & Deshler, 1979; Miller, 1974). For students who are unable to vary reading rate, teachers need to clarify the difference between skimming and reading for details, and help them choose which to use for particular types of reading (Maxwell, 1973). This assistance is essential because LD students often are not very mature in recognizing how their learning strategies need to be altered to meet task demands.

Thomas and Robinson (1972) have divided skimming into three useful levels:

Level I Scanning for points that are easily recognizable
Level II Scanning for a specific answer to a question

Level III Scanning for information which goes beyond simple answers to questions (the author's style or main idea; reviewing class notes)

When you opened this textbook and flipped through it for the first time, what enticed you to stop and look at a page? Illustrations, charts, and headings may have caught your eye. You were scanning on Level I. You scanned on Level II if you wondered whether the text would address the learning disabled adult. Learning disabled students begin to have difficulties at this level. They often seem unaware of the common organization of material, not knowing where to look first (Alley & Deshler, 1979). Therefore they have trouble searching for summarized data and then deciding whether to return to the information for more intensive reading. Scanning at Level III is most difficult for LD students because it requires intensive reading and good comprehension (Alley & Deshler, 1979). These students often require assistance in judging which reading passages are most important to spend time on and reread, and which can be passed over quickly (Grayum, 1967).

Teaching Reading and Comprehension Through Content Areas. Content area teachers often are stumped about how to meet the needs of the LD adolescent in the regular classroom. Several strategies are available for increasing reading and comprehension abilities while enhancing learning of course content.

Reading. Suppose that you need to select one of five available American history textbooks to use with your students. How do you determine if the readability level will be suitable for your LD students? You would be wise to use readability formulas, an informal reading inventory, and a Cloze procedure to make your judgments, as well as considering how interesting, relevant and up-to-date the text is.

Readability formulas help you roughly estimate the reading grade level of written materials. These formulas determine difficulty levels by considering such factors as average numbers of syllables or letters per word, sentence length, and degree of unfamiliar vocabulary. Readability formulas appropriate at the secondary level include Dale & Chall's (1948) Formula, Flesch's (1951) Reading Ease Formula, the SMOG Grading Formula (McLaughlin, 1969), and Fry's (1972) formula, which appears in Figure 13-4. Each formula yields somewhat different grade level estimates (Jongsma, 1972).

The Informal Reading Inventory asks the student vocabulary, fact, sequence, and inference questions after he has read a portion of the text silently. If over 90 percent of the responses are correct, the student is capable of independently comprehending the material. Roughly 75–90 percent correct represents an appropriate instructional level. Anything below 75 percent is far too difficult. If the student can orally read less than 95 percent of the words correctly, then the text also is too difficult (Galeese, 1973). Finally, the teacher should check to see whether the student is capable of using the table of contents, glossary, and index independently.

Figure 13-4   Fry graph for estimating readability

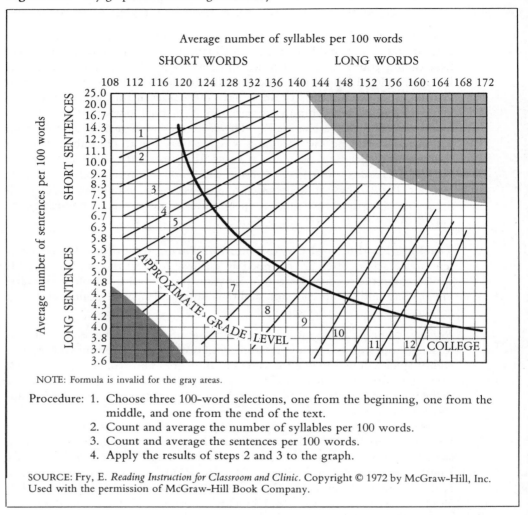

Average number of syllables per 100 words

SHORT WORDS   LONG WORDS

NOTE: Formula is invalid for the gray areas.

Procedure: 1. Choose three 100-word selections, one from the beginning, one from the middle, and one from the end of the text.
2. Count and average the number of syllables per 100 words.
3. Count and average the sentences per 100 words.
4. Apply the results of steps 2 and 3 to the graph.

SOURCE: Fry, E. *Reading Instruction for Classroom and Clinic.* Copyright © 1972 by McGraw-Hill, Inc. Used with the permission of McGraw-Hill Book Company.

In the *Cloze procedure* (Bormuth, 1968), every fifth word of a 250-word passage is *clozed* by a blank. The student fills in the blanks orally or in writing. The teacher then judges whether the student's comprehension permits him or her to anticipate a significant enough portion of the text (usually around 50 percent) for the text to be appropriate for instructional purposes.

When these techniques suggest no appropriate textbook, the resource teacher may need to rewrite the text (shorter words and sentences, less sophisticated vocabulary and phrasing) for the LD student. Once the reading material is established, it can be used for instruction of basic reading and comprehen-

CASE STUDY: Terry

Terry attends regular subject area classes as well as spending one period a day in the resource room. His English 10 class was beginning Hamlet, and Terry was overwhelmed. "The teacher says I have to read it." Using two different readability formulas, the resource teacher estimated that the grade level for this particular version of *Hamlet* was eighth grade. Terry reads independently at the fourth grade level. The teacher found another edition of Hamlet published at the fifth grade level by a high-interest/low reading-level book company. The resource teacher

approached the English teacher about the possibility of Terry reading the alternate edition. By using this edition instead, Terry would successfully be able to read *Hamlet*. The English teacher then had to decide whether her goal was to have the student read and understand *Hamlet* the classic, or the *Hamlet* published by a particular company. She decided that the theme of the classic, rather than Shakespeare's vocabulary, was the best goal for Terry and therefore opted for the lower reading-level version. The resource teacher used the latter text for comprehension exercises and slowly began to introduce vocabulary from the harder version.

sion skills as well as content. Content area assignments likewise provide an ideal opportunity for teaching spelling and written expression skills. Terry's example, above, illustrates how this can occur. At times, a particular student will profit more from having the complex text recorded on tape than from reading a watered-down version. This decision is best made from exploring reading versus listening performance using the actual classroom materials (Wiseman, Hartwell, & Hannafin, 1980).

Comprehension. Besides developing comprehension through the reading materials, the teacher can use oral classtime to increase comprehension through listening exercises. Purposes for listening are set, the student listens, literal and inferential questions are asked, and the student listens again if he or she had errors in understanding (Cunningham & Cunningham, 1976). Manzo (1975) provides a guided listening procedure for stimulating these skills.

Training listening skills in itself is valuable because greater competence increases the amount of information LD students internalize, remember, and can think about, without needing constant teacher guidance. The more intelligently a youngster can pick up information from the environment, the greater the likelihood of success in school and in everyday life.

Written Language

Written language remains one of the most unsuccessful areas for learning disabled adolescents. Spelling and penmanship remediation needs to continue when appropriate. Compensations also need to be built by learning to use a dictionary, asking someone else to proof for spelling, and learning to type.

Typing is a welcome relief for some LD students. For others, however, it presents the same fine-motor difficulty as does handwriting.

Conceptual writing must also be attended to. Try constructing your own essay following Kerrigan's (1974) approach, which is presented in Table 13-4.

Table 13-4   Method for teaching written composition skills

STEPS	DESCRIPTION
I	Write a short, simple, declarative sentence that makes one statement. This should be a sentence about an idea you have and not merely a description of how something looks or directions on how to make something.
II	Write three sentences about your subject in Step I that are clearly and directly about the entirety of that subject and not just some small aspect of it. A key to this step would be to think of the questions someone would typically ask about your subject. A) _____ B) _____ C) _____

III	Write four or five sentences about each of the three sentences in Step II.
	A) _____
	  1) _____
	  2) _____
	  3) _____
	  4) _____
	B) _____
	  1) _____
	  2) _____
	  3) _____
	  4) _____
	C) _____
	  1) _____
	  2) _____
	  3) _____
	  4) _____

IV	Make the material in the four or five sentences in Step III as concrete and specific as possible. Go into detail. Give examples. Don't ask, "What will I say next?" Say some more about what you have just said. Your goal is to say a lot about a little, not a little about a lot. Kerrigan stresses the importance of details. Avoid abstract terms.
V	In the first sentence of the second paragraph and every paragraph following, insert a clear reference to the idea in the preceding paragraph. In this step, relate each paragraph to the preceding paragraph and provide smooth transitions in the composition.
VI	Make sure every sentence in your theme is connected with, and makes clear reference to, the preceding sentence. Once again, the importance of clear references is emphasized.

SOURCE: Adapted from Kerrigan, W. S., *Writing to the Point: Six Basic Steps.* New York: Harcourt Brace Jovanovich, 1974.

In this approach, content is the focus, and spelling, punctuation and handwriting errors are disregarded until after the student's ideas are developed. This method provides a systematic opportunity for the student to express his or her own creative thoughts.

Another useful technique for encouraging writing is Allington's (1975) *USSW* — Uninterrupted *Silent* Sustained *Writing*. Students write anything that comes to mind for five to ten minutes, several times a week. They write quickly, without making corrections. Best of all, the product need not be shared with anyone! Its objective is simply to get students over the hurdle of being unwilling even to try to write.

The need to teach the LD adolescent how to write cannot be overemphasized. On high school graduation, the student will apply for jobs or higher educational opportunities. In either case, the written product plays a part in determining the individual's future options.

Mathematics

In high school, mathematics may become particularly difficult even for those learning disabled students who succeeded at the elementary level. This is because the subject matter (algebra, geometry, trigonometry) demands a new vocabulary, sophisticated reasoning through language and visual imagery, the learning of new symbols ($\sqrt{}$), and the solution of word problems. Several mathematics remediation methods have been specifically designed to meet the secondary level student's needs. As in other academic areas, teaching problem-solving strategies can be most beneficial for those who can't conceptualize the math processes or organize an approach to lengthy problems.

LeBlanc (1977) lists four problem-solving stages: 1) understanding the problem, 2) planning the solution, 3) solving the problem, and 4) reviewing the solution within the context of the initial problem. Rereading at each step enables the student to better understand and plan a solution (Earp, 1970). Learning to check answers for wrong operations, computations, algorithms, and random errors in the mathematical process also is helpful (Ashlock, 1972; Roberts, 1961). Charts for independent student activities offer another means for students to independently solve mathematics problems by teaching an organized, stepwise approach to problem-solving (Collins, 1972). For example,

Solve: $3 + 2(5 + 1) = ?$

1st Step:	2nd Step:	(Solution)
$5 + 1 = 6$	$2(6) = 2 \times 6 = 12$	$3 + 12 = 15$

Initially, the student is instructed in the use of these steps. The teacher then gradually fades out assistance to encourage independent use of these strategies. Cawley's *Project MATH* represents a combination of these approaches, using visual aids and an active verbal problem-solving approach to math acquisition (Cawley et al., 1976).

By far the greatest problem that learning disabled students face in mathematics is word problems. First of all, the problems must be read. Secondly, not all the information is usually given. Students must apply some additional knowledge to solve the problem. The necessary math vocabulary is embedded in the problem, must be translated to a math operation, and the problem's solution must be translated back into this language (Sharma, 1981).

Manheim's (1971) model is helpful to students having difficulty with word problems. It lists all the formulas, data, and other information needed to perform the operations, and eliminates reading. Manheim calls this an "imaginary" word problem. While some individuals advocate use of such nonword problems and computer devices (Shaw, 1981), others stress the importance of instructing students in word problems as a means of increasing math vocabulary as well as preparing the student for similar real life problem-solving (Sharma, 1981).

Study and Test-Taking Skills

If students are to retain what they are taught, they must develop good study skills. This includes notetaking, outlining, library, and test-taking skills. The key word to success in each of these areas is *organization*.

It is critical for students to be able to organize their time and have a disciplined study approach (Pauk, 1974). Assume that you have a term paper due in two months. Do you wait until the last two days, get it done the first week, or dabble in it over the two months? Do you grab an hour here and there, or do you set aside large chunks of time? Do you outline first, leave reminder notes to yourself, and produce a rough copy, or do you sit down and type as you write?

Whatever your style, you need an organized approach. Pauk (1974) suggests that a student note the essential activities for that particular day and a quick reminder of what needs to be done a day, two days or weeks from now on 3″ × 5″ index cards. When LD students share these time reminder cards with their teachers, realistic daily and longer-term goals can be set (Alley & Deshler, 1979). Another approach has students observe their peers' study habits and generate their own academic aids. Such a technique increases student involvement in learning and application of good study habits (Starks, 1980).

Notetaking Skills. If you open one of your textbooks you are apt to find the trails of a yellow marking pen. But for LD students who have language weaknesses, underlining books even within their readability ranges may not be beneficial; they may still have to go back and reread all the material when exam time nears, so as to understand the context of the underlined phrases (Alley & Deshler, 1979). Notetaking can be an effective alternative strategy (Dyer, Riley & Yekovich, 1979).

Courtney (1967) suggests four components to notetaking:

1. The student should use his or her own words, and not those of the author, when taking notes.
2. The student should experiment and find a format that suits his or her style and use it consistently.
3. The date and source of notes should be jotted down.
4. The notes should be complete and easily deciphered.

Teachers can help by providing structured lessons on notetaking and reinforcement for taking organized and thorough notes.

Outlining Skills. Outlining is a useful tool for identifying the main ideas of a passage or taking notes in a classroom. By design, outlines can assist the adolescent in organizing ideas about what he or she is writing, what an author has written, or what a lecturer is saying. Fisher (1967) suggests that the student ask several questions:

I. Does this reflect an important component of the topic?
   A. Does this help develop the main heading?
      1. Does this detail,
      2. as well as this detail, relate to the subdivision in sequential order?

Teachers can structure assignments and lessons to allow the student opportunities to learn outlining as a skill for organizing information. The inverse of Fisher's technique, working from details to subheadings to main ideas, is an alternate method for organizing notes. Try one of these when preparing for your next essay exam. See which one works for you.

Library Skills. Libraries can be a source of information or a source of confusion for anyone, especially the learning disabled. Students need to become comfortable with the library's organization (Dewey Decimal System, card catalogue) and reference aids (indexes to periodicals, bibliographies, dictionaries, encyclopedias, almanacs, atlases) to profitably use libraries (Burmeister & Stevens, 1974). The teacher can undertake a variety of activities to promote library use and to facilitate the student's view of the library as an ally rather than enemy. Opportunities for using libraries' multimedia materials can also motivate LD adolescents to become involved in learning in a nontraditional fashion. For many LD students these materials, rather than reading, are the primary tool for acquiring knowledge throughout life. When they don't become comfortable with a library during school years, their opportunities for learning may be diminished later on.

Test-Taking Skills. Having taken many quizzes and exams, you undoubtedly have discovered test-taking strategies which work for you. In contrast,

Table 13-5a   Procedures for preparing for tests

1. The student should ask the teacher exactly what the material will be on the test and what aspects of it will come from the notes, lectures, or textbooks. The student should also ask what the format of the test will be: true-false, essay, short answer, or multiple choice.
2. The student should obtain copies of previous exams (and their answer sheets) from other students who have taken the course or from teachers themselves. Students should be "test wise" and know what type of questions are usually on the exams and which topics are emphasized.
3. The student should be instructed in setting up and following a study schedule. This alleviates some of the necessity of cramming for tests, an ineffective method for all students — especially for LD students who have reading problems. A brief review of the material following each class helps the student remember the content.
4. The student should understand testing terms such as *compare, contrast, illustrate, briefly describe, define,* and *elaborate.* The student should also note the relative point value the teacher places on different test items. This is an indication of how much information is needed to adequately answer the questions and how much time the student should spend answering it.
5. Students should be encouraged to approach the testing situation with a positive mental attitude. Discussing feelings ahead of time can be helpful and provides the teacher with an opportunity to reinforce the student's abilities and reasons for assuming a positive outlook toward the test.

most LD adolescents need to be taught test-taking strategies to enable them to at least accurately show what they know.

Alley and Deshler (1979) proposed a five-step procedure for preparing for tests, which appears in Table 13-5a. Table 13-5b also illustrates Carman and Adams' (1972) SCORER technique, which is helpful to the student taking tests.

Survival Skills and Career Education

Adolescents need to learn practical skills with which to survive in their own as well as adult worlds. Presumably, this is what their reading (reading a menu), comprehension (figuring out how to work a voter's booth), math (budgeting), written expression (completing job applications), and study skills (studying for a driver's test) curricula have intended to do (Cassidy & Shanahan, 1979). Yet many secondary LD students are weak in these basic skills or don't generalize them from the classroom to practical life. These weaknesses, compounded by social and emotional difficulties, frequently forecast a less than adequate life adjustment, making survival skill instruction a necessity.

A major move toward independence for many high school students is obtaining a driver's license. For students who have a learning disability, the process can be complicated. Passing the written test may be difficult. The performance test may take extra effort for those with visual perceptual, coordination, and attentional difficulties. The driver's manual often is a motivating

Table 13–5b Scorer technique

S = *schedule* your time. How many questions are there, and how much time is there to complete the exam.

C = *cue* words. *All, never* and *always* rarely indicate a true answer on a true-false test but *usually* or *sometimes* often do.

O = *omitting* or setting aside the difficult questions. Answer the easiest questions first and then go back.

R = *read* the directions and examples carefully.

E = *estimate* the approximate range of possible answers for a question; e.g., the area of a shoe box will be in square inches, so answers in square feet may be disregarded. You should also "guesstimate" the answer if credit is not taken off for doing so.

R = *review* your work. Make sure all questions are answered with the correct letter or number and be very cautious about changing answers without substantiation for the new choice.

SOURCES: a. Alley, G. and Deshler, D. *Teaching the LD Adolescent: Strategies and Methods*. Denver: Love Publishing Company, 1979; and b. Carman, R. H., and Adams, W. R., Jr. *Study Skills: A Student's Guide for Survival*. New York: Wiley, 1972.

instructional tool for the teacher. Lessons can be structured using concepts to be learned such as parking requirements, meaning of signs, and also informal problem-solving such as how to get the car for a Saturday night date.

Other important survival skills include getting and keeping a job, as well as obtaining and completing job applications (Joynes, McCormick, & Heward, 1980). Figure 13-5's employment application demonstrates that even seeking a job requires reading and writing abilities. Similarly, functional reading is essential in such daily living tasks as buying food, finding shelter, obtaining medical help, and dealing with money matters involving credit cards and tax returns (Kirsch & Guthrie, 1978). Interview skills are also necessary to a job search. Role-playing various employment situations will help students prepare for job interviews.

Money management is another important area for survival training. Opening, maintaining, and balancing a bank account can be learned using actual bank checks and bankbooks, or through a variety of commercially published materials.

Given that LD students have so very much to prepare for, school goals and materials must have very practical, everyday value to them (Cassidy & Shanahan, 1979). This includes preparing them for such skills essential to independent living as cooking, cleaning, shopping, and how to spend leisure time.

Equally important is the teacher, guidance counselor, and other school personnel's assistance in exploring career options. Vocational training needs to become a higher priority in the education of the learning disabled. Unfortunately, many of the currently existing programs are geared toward the "dumbies" and "delinquents." Since many learning disabled adolescents don't want to associate with these groups, they often forego prevocational experi-

Figure 13-5 Sample job application form

Master Employment Application

Please print

Personal

Name	Last	First	Middle		Date
Date of birth	Age	Social Security Number		□ M □ F Sex	
Married □ Yes □ No No. of Dependents		Weight	Height		

Are you a citizen of the U.S.? □ Yes □ No   Phone No.

| Present Address | No. | Street | City | State | Zip Code |
| Previous Address | No. | Street | City | State | Zip Code |

Physical

Do you have any physical disabilities? _____ If yes, describe. _____

Have you had any major illness in the past 5 years? _____
If yes, describe. _____

In case of an emergency, notify, Name _____

Address _____   Phone No. _____

Education

Name of School	Attended From to	Did you graduate?
Elementary		
High School		
College or University		
Other		
Other		

Do you plan to continue your education? _____

Last grade completed _____   Grade point average _____

Extracurricular activities _____

List any special office skills that you have. _____

Employment history

List below your last three employers:

Name and Address	Salary	Position	Date From—To
1.			
2.			
3.			

Military

Have you ever served in the U.S. armed forces? □ Yes □ No
If yes, what branch? _____
Dates of Duty: From _____ To _____
Rank at Discharge _____

References

List below three names of people not related to you, whom you have known at least one year.

Name	Address	Phone No.	Years Acquainted
1.			
2.			
3.			

Do you have any relatives in this company? _____

Job performance

Type of work desired _____

Date available _____   Hours available _____

Starting expected salary _____

Why do you want this job? _____

General information

Have you committed any felonies or violations? _____

If yes, explain. _____

Are you a licensed driver? □ Yes □ No

List here any additional comments that you think are important to us in considering you for employment: _____

Signature

To the best of my knowledge the above statements are complete and are true. False statements may be cause of dismissal.

Date _____   Signature _____

SOURCE: Joynes, Y. D., McCormick, S., and Heward, W. L. "Teaching Reading Disabled Students to Read and Complete Employment Applications." *Journal of Reading*, May 1980, 23, 712–713. Reprinted with permission of the authors and the International Reading Association.

ences in favor of continued academic failure. In the absence of appropriate vocational programs, flexible, individualized scheduling can facilitate actual job sampling during the school day (Betchkel, 1980). The family's involvement in all this training is essential because, after graduation, the responsibility for guidance is largely theirs (Fafard & Haubrich, 1981).

Social-Emotional Development

Although school is generally looked on as a place for learning facts, "education is essentially a social process" (Stanford & Roark, 1974, p. viii). The quality of human interactions, more than academic knowledge or even intelligence, make for life success.

Adolescents spend a great deal of time and energy pondering the answers to such questions as, "will I be invited to the party," "do you think he (or she) really likes me," "will I be asked to join the team?" The social training aspect of secondary school is a critical stepping stone to adult emotional and social adjustment. The more positive the student's social relationships, and the higher his or her self-esteem, the more likely the student is to be successful in life.

Positive social relationships and self-esteem don't come easily to many learning disabled students. Poor social skills handicap them probably more than any other skill deficit (Cook, 1979; Gordon, 1969). LD students' failures to be accepted by nonhandicapped peers are often related to their social imperceptions, linguistic difficulties, and secondary reactions to school failure. They also may have personality difficulties related to unsatisfactory resolution of typical adolescent conflicts: separation from dependent relationships, identification with values and ideas that are different from those in childhood, formation of satisfactory peer relationships, and discovery of faith and commitment to a future process (Cook, 1979). The school's role in building social relationships, speaking skills, self-esteem, and thinking skills is important to the enhancement of these students' social-emotional adjustment.

Social Relationship Training. Teachers need to help LD students practice acceptable social behaviors. This is particularly important for students who have insufficient opportunities to interact with nonhandicapped students because of the time they spend in special education. Group discussions have helped promote positive social-emotional growth and self-understanding among adolescents. Environments conducive to sharing feelings help youngsters learn much about themselves and others' willingness to listen (Jourard, 1964).

In Glasser's *Reality Therapy* (1965) and classroom meeting approach (1969), students learn to engage in behavior that satisfies their own personal needs without interfering with the needs of others. This responsibility requires them to use decision-making skills based on careful, systematic consideration of the implications and consequences of alternative actions, a process which is difficult for many LD adolescents. Methods using chaining, modeling, shaping, cueing, movies, and role-playing to help students observe and practice new behaviors have also been successful in teaching social skills (Goldstein, et al., 1980; Krumboltz & Krumboltz, 1972).

Curricula that develop nonverbal skills in socially imperceptive adolescents are particularly important. Minskoff (1980a), for example, offers a detailed approach to learning about body language cues, use of space, sensitivity to vocal pitch, loudness, pause and rate, cosmetics, and clothing. Her teaching sequence involves discrimination of these social cues, followed by understanding their meaning, appropriate usage, and their application to actual social problems.

Speaking Skills Training. Edmund Muskie said, "Never say anything that doesn't improve upon silence." LD students' speaking skills often violate this premise. Alley & Deshler (1979) suggest several important strategies for teaching students to respond to questions or converse more appropriately.

1. *Wait time.* Students should be encouraged to organize their thoughts before speaking (Warriner, Renison, & Griffith, 1965). This is crucial in classroom and social situations. Teachers can encourage and reinforce students when they control irrelevant or inappropriate comments.

2. *Rehearsal.* Rehearsal can involve group interaction and role-playing. Students try out what they want to say to a teacher or friend and receive feedback from the class. Strategies can be discussed and generalizations drawn to assist the students in real situations. They can also rehearse for formal situations, such as giving a speech.

3. *Interpersonal sensitivity.* Recognizing how the LD adolescent's speech impacts socially on listeners is important (Warriner, et al., 1965). Teachers should help students discover what makes a person interesting to listen to. The LD student can then model that behavior. Good eye contact, enthusiasm, and genuine interest in the conversations of others, are just some behaviors that create such positive situations.

4. *Surface counseling.* Teachers are responsible for giving accurate feedback to their students by disclosing what behavior they observed, which behaviors impact the peer group, and the teachers' own reaction to the behavior.

When speaking skills improve, students' social relationships will benefit.

Building Self-Esteem. The teacher has many options for enhancing a student's self-esteem in the classroom. Techniques besides those discussed for the elementary school student include directed writing activities, self-evaluation of locus of control, Q-sorts, assertiveness training, values clarification exercises, and rap sessions.

Directed Writing Activity. If you ever have dug through attic treasures and unearthed an old diary, you probably discovered that underneath all the dust and cobwebs was an insightful incantation of feelings, thoughts, and experiences. Teachers too can encourage students to jot down reactions to their daily lives in a structured, journal format. Alley and Deshler (1979) suggest that students write daily reactions to both a positive and negative experience, and focus on their own abilities and short-comings. The journals should be read by the teacher at least once a week and discussed with the student.

Evaluating Locus of Control. Kohlberg and Turiel (1971) maintain that education's goal is to facilitate higher stages of autonomous moral reasoning and people's inner ability to govern themselves. But many LD students view their lives as controlled by others and place the responsibility for their actions on someone else: "I didn't pass the test because the teacher made it too hard." The student who accepts more responsibility for his or her own actions might say, "I didn't pass the test because I didn't study the right stuff."

Felton and Davidson (1973) suggested teaching students to identify and apply the fundamentals of locus of control to their daily lives. Role-playing and simulation activities help students discover whether their locus of control is coming from outside themselves or is internal. The value of internal control is highlighted. Problems are identified and can be dealt with in a supportive manner. Throughout the process the teacher needs to be a good listener and supportive of the overall self-esteem of the students.

Q-sort. Kroth (1973) suggests using a Q-sort, the sorting of descriptive adjectives into piles, to enable students to analyze their perceptions of their "existing" behavior and their "ideal" behavior. Students then select a behavior that they wish to change and are reinforced for progress toward this goal.

Assertiveness Training. Assertive behavior is characterized as honest and straightforward expression to others and ourselves about how we feel. It is simply open, direct, spontaneous, and appropriate interaction (Rimm & Masters, 1974). Assertive does not mean aggressive. It is a tool of social contact. With assertiveness training, students learn to feel better about themselves and less anxious about sharing their own feelings and ideas (Fensterheim & Baer, 1975; Smith, 1975). The nonassertive student often gets hurt. Assertiveness training ties into the locus of control concept because nonassertive students allow others to shape their goals. Assertive students more often make their own decisions.

Essential components of assertive behavior include (Alberti & Emmons, 1978):

1. good eye contact, appropriate body language and facial expression consistent with verbal expression (for example, not smiling when you are dissatisfied)

2. spontaneous reactions to others' actions, and judgment about the most appropriate timing of comments
3. honest content of communication illustrating that the student assumes responsibility for feelings ("I am angry with you for breaking my watch" rather than "you are so clumsy!")
4. gauging the intensity of one's response to a situation (not "blowing up" when someone bumps you in line).

Through assertiveness training, students learn to substitute positive, honest, open behaviors for nonassertive, self-destructive actions. They can also learn

Table 13-6   Procedures for improving students' thinking skills

STUDENT BEHAVIOR	TEACHER BEHAVIOR
Observing	Provide a number of experiences
Describing	Ask open-ended questions about an observation
Developing concepts	Ask questions which require students to: a) observe a situation b) describe what they observed (list items) c) group those items d) identify their common characteristics e) label the groups f) incorporate any other items they have listed under those labels g) recombine items to form new and different groups
Differentiating and defining	Identify new attributes of a definition and provide opportunities for students to differentiate between examples and nonexamples of the concept discussed. Teachers should provide concrete examples of abstract concepts
Hypothesizing	Ask students systematic questions to help them formalize their hypotheses
Comparing and contrasting	Introduce the use of an organizational chart where students can arrange the information they've received in a clear, organized schema
Generalizing	Encourage students to a) observe at least two incidents b) describe what happened c) describe in their own words why they think the incidents occurred d) identify similarities and differences e) explain in their own words these differences and similarities f) offer a generalization based upon what they have discovered
Predicting and explaining	Ask a sequence of questions which guides students through the process of applying the generalizations they have made to new situations
Offering alternatives	Encourage students to think about situations in new ways and consider options using the available information

to analyze and respond appropriately to others' nonverbal behaviors (facial expressions, body positions) (Gallaway, 1974).

Values Clarification. "School is boring. Should I quit?" "Why do I bite my nails?" "Do I really care what my friends think of me?" These and hundreds more personal and theoretical questions are asked by adolescents trying to clarify the values they adopted from their parents, friends, teachers, and their own experiences (Simon, Have, & Kirschenbaum, 1972). When a student becomes clear about what he or she prizes, what to believe and how to behave,

Table 13-7   Techniques for teaching thinking skills

TECHNIQUE	DESCRIPTION
Brainstorming	Brainstorming involves an entire group in the problem-solving process. First developed by Alex Osborn in the late 1930s, there are four basic rules (Osborn, 1963):
	1. Criticism is not allowed. No one should criticize the ideas of another. This deferred judgment is essential. 2. "The wilder the idea the better." Freedom of expression stimulates more creative ideas. 3. Generate a vast number of ideas. Come up with as many as you can and make sure someone or something (tape recorder, videotape) is recording them. 4. Expand on each other's ideas. Try combining and improving upon other's suggestions.
	Feldhusen and Treffinger (1977) add that the students should be given a typed list of all ideas generated. These listed items can then be expanded on. In this way students are exposed to a good deal of creative thinking and learn that their input is accepted and valuable.
Attribute listing	Attribute listing involves taking specific aspects of a problem and focusing on each one separately to generate new ideas. This method of analysis provides a thoughtful means of approaching everyday problem situations.
Synectics	Synectics enables the student to creatively use analogies and metaphors to analyze problems from different viewpoints (Gordon, 1961). The student engages in three types of analogies:
	☐ fantasy — students search for the ideal solution to the problem. ☐ direct — students find comparable situations in real life. ☐ personal — students place themselves in a role within the problem situation.
Problem-solving	Problem identification, analysis, evaluation of possible solutions, and action plans to implement the solution are essential steps (Patton and Griffen, 1973). The student must accept the problem as a challenge and be willing to take responsibility for his or her own decisions.

and acts accordingly, important choices and social interactions are facilitated (Raths, Harmin, & Simon, 1966).

Rap Sessions. Loughmiller (1971) suggests rap sessions to help students understand their behaviors and how these behaviors are perceived by others. In this context, a skilled professional incorporates psychological principles that help students better understand how they get along. Transactional analysis theory is one common approach to these sessions (Berne, 1964; Freed, 1971; Harris, 1969; James & Jongeward, 1971). Other approaches include nondirective and behavior therapy.

Thinking Skills Training. Adolescents continuously test their abilities to think about and react to a myriad of new situations in which they find themselves. Fraenkel (1973) outlined several procedures which can be employed to improve students' thinking skills. These are listed in Table 13-6 on page 476. DeBono (1977) also emphasizes the importance of acquiring lateral thinking methods for problem-solving and information-restructuring; there is a difference between vertical thinking (or "digging the same hole deeper") and lateral thinking (or "digging a hole somewhere else").

Students need to be shown the value of challenging assumptions in their daily lives to gain new insights and perspectives. Students must learn to look at underlying information in a different light. A stimulating way of doing this is to reverse roles: the student becomes the teacher, and the teacher the student. Other techniques to teach thinking skills include: brainstorming, attribute listing, synectics, and problem-solving strategies (Feldhusen & Treffinger, 1977). These are described in Table 13-7 on page 477. Peer relationships can reap many benefits from sharpened thinking skills.

Summary

Special interventions for the learning disabled begin in the preschool years and often continue beyond the secondary school years. Materials and approaches are chosen on the basis of what students need to learn, how they learn best, and what learning strategies need to be taught. Exactly which materials and approaches teach which students best remains to be clarified through research. Some LD children require moderate task modifications to be successful, while others require intense remediation.

The teacher is the key to good teaching and the student's family is the key to supporting a youngster's efforts. Both the teacher and family have the responsibility to attend as much to the affective as to the academic development of the youngster.

This chapter reviewed approaches for affective and academic development at the preschool, elementary and secondary school levels. These approaches foster skills in both strong and weak areas. They also help to continue academic, daily living, and vocational preparation by capitalizing on strengths and developing compensations for weaknesses.

Suggestions for Further Study

1. Suppose that you have just been hired as a learning disabilities resource room teacher in a school that has never had a resource room. It's July 15th and school begins in six weeks. You have no materials. What would you do? Several computerized information retrieval systems can help you. If you know your future students' present reading grade levels, and the content areas, general skills, and grade level ranges that you will be teaching, you can feed this information into one of these systems. In some systems you also can feed in the teaching format you desire (games, kits, programmed instruction), interest level of the material, and type of teacher direction (one on one, small group). Once you have narrowed your search, you can seek out and personally explore your options. Visit your nearest Regional Resource Center or school district. With several hypothetical children in mind, ask to collect data from their retrieval systems. The most well-known of these are the Prescriptive Materials Retrieval System (PMRS; Winch & Assoc., Torrance, Calif.), the National Instructional Materials Information System (NIMIS; National Center for Educational Media/Materials for the Handicapped, Columbus, OH) and a manually operated system called the Educational Patterns Incorporated Retrieval System (EPI; Rego Park, NY).

2. To learn more individualized educational techniques, read the following excellent resources: Lerner, Dawson, and Horvath (1980), Shrag (1977), Torres (1977), and Turnbull, Strickland, and Brantley (1978).

3. Several excellent articles on research in early intervention programs review the outcome of university sponsored projects and the government's Head Start and Follow Through programs: Cicirelli, Evans, and Schiller (1970); Karnes, Hodgins, and Teska (1969); Levitt and Cohen (1975); McDaniels (1975); Payne, Mercer, Payne and Davidson (1973); Stallings (1974); Tjossem (1976); and Weikart (1972). They distinguish between programs that follow very structured, academic curricula (Bereiter & Engelmann, 1966, and Montessori programs), the Piagetian developmental model, and the traditional nursery school.

4. Do reading disabled children have difficulty learning to read languages that don't require analyzing, sequencing, and blending sounds? There is some evidence that they do not. Read Rozin, Poritsky, and Sotsky's (1973) study, which found that reading disabled students learned to read Chinese characters as rapidly as good readers. Also read Kinsbourne and Caplan's (1979) review of reading disability rates in China and Japan. What do you think happens to children with visual processing deficiencies when they learn Chinese?

5. Excellent resources to consult for elementary school programming in reading and written expression are Anderson (1968), Frostig and Maslow (1973), Gillingham and Stillman (1970), Hammill and Bartel (1978), Johnson and Myklebust (1967), Otto, McMenemy, and Smith (1973).

6. Additional resources for arithmetic instruction can be found in Johnson (1979), May (1974), and Cawley and colleagues' Project MATH (1976). All offer excellent ideas on how to adapt mathematics programs to individual learning preferences.

7. For the most complete review of secondary education methods for the learning disabled, read Alley and Deshler (1979). You might consider purchasing this text for your own library. It has very practical value for daily instructional practices.

Part Five

The Setting

Chapter Fourteen
The Family

Setting variables, interacting with learner and task characteristics, can aggravate or help overcome learning disabilities. Children's most important setting is their family. The members of the child's family, especially his or her parents, provide the surroundings which nurture the child's intellectual and learning abilities, social attitudes and behaviors, and ultimate adult adjustment. The importance of personal-social adjustment is obvious. No matter what children's abilities, they will have a much easier time if they learn to get along with others by telling the truth, following the rules, acting in a considerate and altruistic way, trusting others, and being willing to listen to and learn from them. The parents' responsibility is to encourage the child to develop these prosocial attitudes and behaviors. Parental example and discipline teach children values, assertiveness, self-confidence and achievement orientation, all qualities important for school performance and life adjustment.

Because the family has a great influence on the development of the learning disabled child, it is important for the teacher to get to know the parents and join in a parent-teacher partnership. To do this, teachers need to be sensitive to parental needs for information and emotional support. Teachers also need to know how to go about assessing factors within the families that may relate to their children's learning progress and social adjustment. Finally, teachers need to be aware of how to intervene to help family systems better use their strengths and minimize their weaknesses, helping parents to become better teachers, advocates, and sources of support for their children. One way of encouraging this is to recognize the parent as a valuable resource in the assessment, planning, and intervention process.

Families and Learning

Parents are truly children's first teachers; home is the child's first school (Friedman, 1978). Children come into the world with certain potentials, but how they learn in their "first school" most affects their ultimate cognitive development. Throughout their children's lives, parents serve as models for behavior and stimulate their children to interact with and learn from the world. The learning disabled child's problems with cognitive development, school achievement and social development relate to the family environment in many ways. As teachers of preschoolers and older youngsters gain an understanding of these family factors, they can play an important role in family interventions aimed at increasing children's learning opportunities.

Cognitive and School Achievement

Early childhood is an important time, because parents of a learning disabled child often first note delays in development during the child's preschool years.

This chapter was written by Eleanor Williams.

483

During this period parents can also maximize their child's opportunities for cognitive development and acquisition of learned skills.

Family factors that play a role in children's developmental delays include home press for achievement, language models, encouragement to explore beyond the home, intellectual interests and activities in the home, work habits taught at home, fostering of independence, father presence, activities with adults, variety of stimulation, positive affect, emotional and verbal responsiveness of mother, avoidance of punishment, organization of time and objects in the home, appropriate play materials, and books. Many other factors are also important: style of parents when they teach; the parents' initiative, energy level, learning style, task orientation, interpersonal skills; sibling and secondary caregivers' behaviors; and traumatic events such as divorce, death of a parent, birth of a sibling, and moving (Bradley & Caldwell, 1978; Walberg & Majoribanks, 1976).

Of the above considerations, environmental stimulation has received the most research attention. Provence and Lipton's (1962) vivid descriptions of children raised in an orphanage clearly show how maternal deprivation causes developmental delay. But the home need not be as barren as the orphanage to produce children who fall behind in preschool development. Yarrow and his associates (1975) noted that intellectual competence of five- and six-month-old infants was associated with such parenting and environmental qualities as auditory stimulation, amount of kinesthetic stimulation, mother's responsiveness to stress vocalization, amount of time parent and infant spent gazing at one another, and variety and responsiveness of toys. For example, the vocalization of a very competent child's mother was a distinct response to a specific vocalization from the baby; toys did something back to the baby when she banged or moved them (a piece of newspaper crackles whenever it is hit). White (1980) noted that the more competent preschoolers spent more of their time gaining information visually, were talked to more, and were provided with more of a variety of social and play activities by their caretakers. Differences between these children and less competent children persisted even at five years of age.

Early intervention studies have attempted to influence the life history of a group of children who, because of family and environmental factors, were at high risk for retardation or school failure. These have usually been children of poor or retarded parents. The interventions have generally been of two types: placing the child at an early age in a preschool program, or putting primary emphasis on involving the parents in the educational process and nurturing their parenting abilities. Placing children in preschool settings outside the home produce greater gains than leaving the children in the home situation, but the gains are lost once the program is stopped (Bronfenbrenner, 1975b). In contrast, gains in home-based intervention programs have lasted three to four years after the intervention has ended. The earlier that either intervention occurred, the greater the gains. These studies indicate that home-based programs can be successful with children as late as the sixth grade.

When the home stimulation that a child receives in early childhood impedes development, these immaturities are likely to adversely affect the child's readiness to profit from school instruction. Direct teaching of children and parents, however, can begin to reverse this cycle. Let us explore the relationship of socio-economic factors, parent-child interactions, and physical surroundings to cognitive and social achievement.

Socio-Economic Studies. The study of the children of Kauai (Werner, 1971, 1977) and the Collaborative Perinatal Project (Broman, 1977) provide evidence about the relative influence of socio-economic status versus trauma on school failure. The Kauai study followed every child born in a certain time period on the island of Kauai, Hawaii. Assessments were conducted during pregnancy, at two, ten, and eighteen years of age. One of the most startling conclusions reached was that the effects of socio-economic status are more powerful than those of perinatal complications. Werner (1980) reported that, at twenty months of age:

1. Children growing up in [upper] middle class homes who had experienced the most severe perinatal complications had mean scores on the Cattell Infant Intelligence Scale . . . almost comparable to children with no perinatal stress who were living in lower socio-economic status homes.

2. The most developmentally retarded children (in physical, intellectual, and social maturity) were those who had both experienced the most severe perinatal complications and who were also living in the poorest homes.

3. Social status differences provided for a greater difference in mean Cattell scores (37 points) for children who had experienced severe perinatal stress than did perinatal complications for children living in favorable environments. By age 10 children with and without severe perinatal stress who had grown up in [upper] middle class homes both achieved mean PMA IQ . . . above the average. The family's socio-economic status shows significant associations with the type of behavior that is usually subsumed under MBD syndrome, that is, language problems, perceptual problems, reading problems, and overaggressive behavior (pp. 215–216).

The Collaborative Perinatal Project followed some 50,000 women who were registered for prenatal care in twelve university medical centers. The children born to these women were followed from birth to eight years (Broman, 1977). The project found that a greater proportion of children with learning disabilities came from lower socio-economic groups. Again, learning disorders were more strongly related to social class than to amount of perinatal stress. Apparently a healthy, supportive, stimulating environment goes a long way toward overcoming the effects of physical trauma at birth.

Parent-Child Interaction. The Kauai study measured parent-child interaction factors in the home that turned out to be even more powerful than perinatal complications and socio-economic status in determining a child's achievement. Children with symptoms characteristic of learning disabilities were more likely to come from a home in which the father was absent, or the family environment was unstable. An even more powerful determinant of low achievement was lack of educational stimulation and emotional support, as when less emphasis was placed on intellectual pursuits by the parent, the parents did less reading themselves; few books, magazines, and learning supplies were in the home; less time was spent reading to the child; and parents showed less interest in the child's school and homework. Homes that were positive in these features produced children with the highest academic achievement and they ameliorated the influence of severe perinatal stress. There were many examples of children who had experienced oxygen deprivation at birth and yet, at ten years of age, performed academically at their grade level with an IQ only a few points lower than children·of the same social class who had experienced no stress.

Other long term investigations, such as a twelve-year follow-up of all children entering a suburban kindergarten, have shown similar home situation influences (Bell, Abrahamson & McRae, 1977). Bell's work noted the contribution to school achievement and social performance of behaviors that children brought to school from their homes, such as competence, self-concept, stability, awareness, interest, and set toward further learning.

Clearly, parenting that does not match school goals can handicap a child's future school success. Appropriate parenting skills can make up for a poor start in life and actually contribute a great deal to good academic performance. Keogh and Becker (1973) suggest that some parents of learning disabled children may be too anxious and understanding of their children's problems. Therefore, in their interactions with their children, they do not have high enough expectations and do not push the children enough to ensure that they work to the best of their ability. This is where the feedback of teachers regarding what a child is and is not able to accomplish, and with how much effort, can be most helpful to parents.

Physical Surroundings. Books, magazines, and school supplies available to the child are related to school success. A less obvious factor in the home's physical environment which has received recent attention is television. Some professionals have postulated a connection between hyperactivity and echoic speech in the preschooler and fast-paced TV programs (Halpern, 1975). They think that fast-paced television shows further aggravate the cognitive styles of learning disabled children by reinforcing impulsiveness and lack of reflectivity. Research also has found that aggressiveness and acceptance of violence increase in children immediately after viewing a television program portraying violence and aggression (Drabman & Thomas, 1976; Feinbloom, 1976; Liebert, Neale, & Davidson, 1973). These results have not been related specifically to the learning disabled, but excessive viewing of particular television shows by a learning disabled child is worthy of investigation because it may relate to secondary behavioral problems and may further aggravate the learning problems. On the other hand, slow-paced television shows, such as *Mister Rogers' Neighborhood,* are believed to lengthen children's attention spans, increase reflectivity, and result in greater retention of information (Singer & Singer, 1979).

Social Development

In addition to academic underachievement, a learning disabled child may have problems in social interactions with parents, teachers, and peers or may behave in a hyperactive and impulsive manner. Wender (1971) summarized parents' observations of the hyperactive preschooler as being an infant "King Kong." Parents of learning disabled children often describe their children as being unable to control their impulses (Owen et al., 1971). They are less considerate and open to affection than their peers (Strag, 1972). Teachers see these children as having limited social skills, being more aggressive, less responsible, less cooperative and having less tact than their classmates (Bryan & McGrady, 1972; Keogh, Tchir, & Windeguth-Behn, 1974). Consequently, learning disabled children often have difficulty building close friendships with their peers (Bryan, 1976; Bryan et al., 1976; Bryan, 1978). Although social problems are not present in every learning disabled student, they are more prevalent than in a typical child population and are a serious problem. They do not, however, develop in a vacuum; the environment plays an important role in shaping children's behaviors and self-concepts.

This section will review how children learn to interact successfully within society, to adopt attitudes and practices which are socially acceptable, how this social learning process may possibly be disrupted in the learning disabled child, and how parents can foster or impede this development.

Normal Patterns of Prosocial Development. When children behave in socially acceptable ways their behavior is influenced by their ability to judge what is and is not appropriate behavior. They have learned to make moral judgments by developing attitudes about what is right or wrong. As with other developmental characteristics, moral development changes with age and is influenced by cognitive abilities.

Jean Piaget's (1948) classic investigations interviewed children and asked them questions about what they would do in certain situations and why. The vignettes he posed to these children (ages six through twelve) elicited information about their knowledge of social rules and how they judged lying and punishment. Piaget noted that children under the age of seven or eight very often do not understand why something is right or wrong but accept some external source, such as a parent or an older child, as the authority. This frequently results in very rigid interpretations of rules: a particular thing is wrong under all circumstances. For example, the children considered lying wrong because a parent would punish them. Factors such as the intentions of the speaker (sparing someone from some hurtful information) or the speaker's ignorance of the truth were not considered by this younger age group. A white lie was judged the same as a lie told in order to hurt someone. Another characteristic of young children is their concreteness in judging the magnitude of a lie. Their judgment is based on how far the lie departs from the truth. More than one six-year-old thought that saying one saw a cow in the street, when in truth it was a dog, was a greater lie than pretending to have good marks in school (Piaget, 1948, p. 147). There was a more obvious discrepancy from the truth in the "cow for a dog" lie.

In children over eight, Piaget noted a gradual shift toward a final stage of development, which is reached around ages eleven or twelve. During this intermediate stage, a child learns a great deal about codifying rules and works toward greater self-reliance for rules and judgments. The child relies less on the parent as the final authority in making moral judgments. The child may vacillate between taking into account or not considering the circumstances or motives surrounding an action before making a moral judgment.

By age eleven or twelve, a child notes that rules arise from a social surrounding, out of a give and take with others, and by mutual consent with others. Piaget termed this stage *equalitarian*. At this time the child realizes the social value of rules and how they make life easier. The child regards lying as wrong because it makes social intercourse impossible. How could the world operate if everyone told lies? Who could be trusted? The twelve year old is equitable in taking into account the intentions of the liar and whether the lying was purposeful.

To summarize, children in kindergarten may decide that taking another child's toy was wrong because their parents had said so, or they knew they would be punished. In grade school, they learn to take into account motives of the wrongdoer, realize that certain acts are wrong because they harm others, realize that rules help make life more orderly, and take into account remorse and willingness to reform. By the time children reach eleven or twelve years, in most cases they formulate rules based on universal principles of justice, taking into account particular circumstances and motives surrounding an act. This progression in making moral judgments is extremely important for teachers to appreciate and communicate to parents who are not aware of it.

Prosocial Development and the Learning Disabled Child. When the academic behavior of an LD student resembles that of a younger child, his or her ability to make social judgments may also be at a less mature level. A nine year old may still rely almost entirely on a parent or authority figure for cues to appropriate ways to act in social situations. This is an almost impossible way to function in school, where numerous situations arise which demand immediate decisions and action, and about which the child's authority figures have never made a ruling.

Consider what happens when a ten-year-old impulsive child must make a social judgment. The child has difficulty focusing attention on several aspects of a problem at once, and does not delay responding while considering alternatives or sequencing thoughts. The child is clearly at a disadvantage in even contemplating whether an action is socially correct or not. He or she may be unable to form a mental hierarchy as to which actions are more correct and which apply in different situations. The child, for example, might need to determine whether lying to avoid hurting someone's feelings is more correct than telling the truth. This involves looking at a situation from another's perspective, a skill with which many learning disabled children have difficulty. It also involves evaluating both verbal and nonverbal situational cues, another skill with which many LD children have difficulty. Finally, it involves choosing which words to use or not to use, a decision influenced by linguistic skills and how the child feels the listener will react. All these factors influence a child's interactions with others and the feedback he or she will get from them.

In addition to an academic assessment, the teacher needs to evaluate where students fall on the continuum of ability to make social judgments. When the teacher knows what stage students are at, he or she can then gear teaching to help them progress to a higher level. The teacher, for example, may need to explain in a very concrete manner why another child may react negatively to the too aggressive, affectionate bear hug of an LD child. An LD boy may need to learn to insult and tease other boys and still stay within the boundaries of friendship, to learn when roughhousing is appropriate, and to learn when to fight and when not to fight on the playground. All these lessons can be illustrated in the classroom through discussion groups, puppetry, or role playing. These lessons need to be paralleled in the child's most important school, the home. The teacher can be an objective information giver and consultant to the child's parents.

Parental Role in Prosocial Development. How do parents influence a child's prosocial development? Is there something unique about the family environment of a learning disabled child which could interfere with development of prosocial behaviors such as cooperativeness, sharing, honesty, following rules, and acting in a considerate way? Knowing some of the family factors that can disrupt a child's social development helps teachers assess the situation and intervene from multiple dimensions.

Children learn from their parents by identification (wanting to be like them), modeling, and through direct training (Mussen, Conway, & Kagan, 1979). The three are intertwined and influence one another. Some data indicates that learning disabled children and their parents may not be as effective as other families in these three processes. The match between parent and child temperaments can also impact prosocial development.

Identification and Modeling. Children see their parents follow a certain code of behavior. When the father always lends a helping hand in neighborhood projects, his son sees this model, wants to be like his dad, and will probably willingly join in. He may help other children in the neighborhood or, as an adult, be active in neighborhood causes. A daughter may be tempted to lie, but recall her parents' example and fear the loss of her parents' respect if she does not do the right thing. These processes of identification and modeling are fostered by warmth and love on the part of the parents (Baumrind, 1975; Becker, 1964). These processes influence such prosocial traits as kindness, honesty, generosity, resistance to cheating and lying, obedience to rules and regulations, and consideration of the rights and welfare of others.

Studies which investigate warmth of parents of learning disabled children are few. Those that do exist show atypical attitudes of some parents toward their learning disabled children. Owen and her associates' (1971) study of school-age children illustrates the disruptive patterns that may develop between learning disabled children and their parents. A mother tended to withhold affection from her learning disabled child if he or she was irresponsible or disorganized. This affection was transferred to the sibling when the sibling had higher verbal ability, persevered in school tasks, and worried the mother less. Fathers' losses of affection were also greater for the learning disabled than the sibling, even when both had poor concentration, poor impulse control, or were worried and apathetic.

Chapman and Boersma (1979) noted in questionnaires given to mothers of learning disabled children that they had more negative reactions toward their children than the control group of mothers. Similarly, Pearl and Bryan (1982) found that mothers of learning disabled children viewed their children's successes less positively, and their failures more negatively, than did mothers of nondisabled children. Success was attributed more to luck and less to ability than in typical children, and failure was attributed less to bad luck and more to inability. These studies offer at least one clue as to what makes social learning through identification with and modeling of parents more difficult for the learning disabled child — a less supportive and warm attitude on the part of the parents.

In order for parents to promote modeling of appropriate behaviors, they must not only have favorable attitudes toward their children but also arouse the child's attention, facilitate memory for the behavior, encourage practice of the behavior, and add incentive for adopting this behavior. These four steps, as discovered through Bandura's experiments (1969), are detailed in Table 14-1.

Parents use these processes in influencing their children, though most often unconsciously. Effectiveness is increased when the parent of the learning disabled child realizes what a powerful model he or she is and preplans the use of modeling techniques. The parent is a high status person in the child's life. Children literally watch their parents as a way of learning.

Some learning disabled children may have problems attending to and retaining modeled behavior. Schwartz and Bryan (1971) showed that a group

Table 14-1 Bandura's four processes of modeling

PROCESS	DESCRIPTION
Attention	For modeling to be effective, the observer's attention must be aroused. This can be facilitated by a number of factors such as the model being a high status person, the clarity or the discriminability of the modeled behavior, and the observer's ability to process the information.
Retention	The child must be able to remember or retain the modeled behavior. This involves being able to symbolically code the behavior and rehearse it. The rehearsal can be overt but more often it is covert.
Motor reproduction	Modeling behavior improves when the child has the opportunity to actually practice the behavior beforehand. The behavior must also be within the child's physical limitations.
Incentive and motivation	Seeing the model rewarded for certain behavior provides the observer incentive to try and repeat that behavior. If the observer is rewarded when he exhibits modeling behavior, this also aids retention of the new behavior.

SOURCE: Adapted from Bandura, A. *Principles of Behavior Modification*. New York: Holt, Rinehart & Winston, 1969.

of children with learning difficulties had more difficulty than a control group in picking up information from modeling cues and verbal explanations. Bryan (1977) also found that learning disabled children did not do as well as controls in interpreting what a model was doing and what emotions the model was expressing. Therefore, the LD child's parent may need to explain more, highlight important aspects, and even help the child rehearse. The parent needs to keep in mind that the child may have motor or verbal problems, making physical or oral practice harder than it is for the nondisabled child. The learning disabled child may also have less incentive to keep on trying because of past failures.

An additional difficulty for learning disabled children is that the parents themselves may be poor models. Learning disorders often show a familial pattern, with children and their parents sharing cognitive problems and inappropriate behavioral styles (Cantwell, 1975; Decker & DeFires, 1980; Morrison & Stewart, 1971; Owen et al., 1971; Pearl & Bryan, 1982). These parents have difficulty explaining what is appropriate social behavior and why, because they themselves may model many inappropriate behaviors for their child. Consequently, these parents will have to scrutinize and modify their own behavior at times.

Parents who keep in mind their own characteristics as models, where their child may have problems in the modeling process, and who then modify their actions and the modeling process to suit their child, make modeling more effective as a teaching method.

Direct Training. Direct training is another avenue whereby parents influence prosocial behavior. Discipline is a type of direct training by which parents attempt to correct behavior which is contrary to the goals, attitudes, and behavior they wish to instill in their children. Threats of punishment or power exhortations to do the right thing are less effective than explanations and reasoning about why the child should do the right thing. Research done by Becker (1964) and Baumrind (1972, 1975) on methods of discipline illustrate this point.

Baumrind investigated child rearing practices in middle class parents of preschool children. She identified three general patterns: authoritative, authoritarian, and permissive. Authoritative parents were controlling and demanding. They had high demands for obedience, academic achievement, and sharing in household tasks. At the same time these parents were warm, willing to discuss a child's reasons for not wanting to comply, and responded positively to independent behavior. Authoritarian parents were more punitive and rejecting. They also had high standards for behavior, but these were absolute, and power measures were used to set compliance. These measures were not accompanied by reasoning and communication, compliance was valued for its own sake, and there was little verbal give and take. Permissive parents, in contrast, were very accepting of all their children's impulses, and did not enforce rules and standards of conduct and achievement.

Baumrind correlated parental authoritative patterns with preschool behaviors which were socially responsible and independent, friendly to peers, cooperative, achievement-oriented, dominant, and purposeful. When authoritative parents also valued nonconformity, they produced the most dominant and purposeful children in the study. Children of authoritarian parents tended to be discontent, withdrawn, and distrustful. Children of permissive parents tended to be the least self-reliant, self-controlled, and explorative. Baumrind found that:

> the following adult practices and attitudes facilitated the development of socially responsible and independent behavior in both boys and girls:
>
> 1. Modeling by the adult of behavior which is both socially responsible and self-assertive, especially if the adult is seen as powerful by the child and as eager to use the material and interpersonal resources over which he has control on the child's behalf.
> 2. Firm enforcement policies in which the adult makes effective use of reinforcement principles in order to reward socially responsible behavior and to punish deviant behavior, but in which demands are accompanied by explanations, and sanctions are accompanied by reasons consistent

with a set of principles followed in practice as well as preached by the parent.

3. Nonrejecting but not overprotective or passive-acceptant parental attitudes in which the parent's interest in the child is abiding, and, in the preschool years, intense; but where approval is conditioned upon the child's behavior.

4. High demands of achievement, and for conformity with parental policy, accompanied by receptivity to the child's rational demands and willingness to offer the child wide latitude for independent judgment.

5. Providing the child with a complex and stimulating environment offering challenge and excitement as well as security and rest, where divergent as well as convergent thinking is encouraged (Baumrind, 1972, p. 118).

Baumrind (1975) reassessed these children and their families almost nine years later. Her conclusions were not much different than her earlier conclusions. Demanding parental practices were associated with qualities of assertiveness and independence; cognitive training was associated with children who were cooperative, purposeful, and challenged themselves cognitively; and firm discipline was associated in girls with socially confident behavior, and in boys with cooperation with adults. Warmth of parents was not significant in the preschool age, but in the second assessment warmth in fathers was associated with altruistic and cooperative behavior in girls, and warmth in mothers with purposeful behavior and creativity in boys.

If clear expectations, firm discipline, and positive reinforcement are important for the child without learning disabilities, they would seem to be even more so for the learning disabled child. Rappaport (1981) comments that this structure is essential to what she terms the "executive function" of the family:

. . . when family life is consistent it has a stabilizing influence on children's development. When parents are compromising and flexible they balance their adult needs with the needs of children. Goal-directed parents work for a physically and psychologically healthy family. They are prevention-minded in every situation. When parents recognize that in childrearing they are training successors, then they teach that parenting is the most important job to be undertaken in life (p. 22).

Considering that some parents of learning disabled children are poor models and that some learning disabled children find it hard to model, many factors which contribute to good discipline may be lacking in the home environment of some learning disabled children. Only a few studies have dealt with this question. Chapman & Boersma's (1979) study of eighty-one learning disabled children showed that mothers expected less of their LD children than these children actually expected of themselves. Owen and colleagues (1971) reported less structure and less emotional stability in the homes of children who were educationally handicapped. Pearl and Bryan's (1982) study found that mothers evaluated their own abilities as poorly as their LD children's.

At present researchers postulate that some families of learning disabled children have more attitudes and practices which interfere with social development than do matched families of nonhandicapped children. However, other groups of parents have attitudes that are well suited to a learning disabled child. Humphries and Bauman (1980), for example, found that the close control, structure, and reduced hostility which mothers practiced with their learning disabled children was an appropriate response to the children's disorganization and impulsivity.

At times the disorganization of learning disabled children and their families may represent a vicious cycle: the child's behavior causes disruption in the family, which in turn is increasingly unable to provide the structure and discipline the child needs. Studies on temperament show how this vicious cycle of interactions may occur. They illustrate how academic and social success depends a great deal on the interaction of the child's unique characteristics with those of the family.

Parent-Child Temperament Match. The child brings to the family environment characteristics, other than cognitive, which are uniquely his or her own. These can be termed the child's *temperament* — the child's cognitive or behavioral style. Temperament is the "how rather than the what (abilities and content) or the why (motivations) of behavior" (Thomas & Chess, 1977, p. 9). To illustrate, two boys may approach learning to ride their two-wheel bikes in different styles. One may eagerly, immediately try to pedal and move the bike, end up falling hard, cry hard but get up and try again. The second child may look at the bike or walk it around for a few days, may need the presence of a parent, and then cautiously try to balance, stop for a while, complain, become irritable and return later to try again. Both end up being competent bike riders but their approaches to the task are very different. One approaches immediately, loudly, and vigorously, while the other approaches more slowly and negatively.

Much research has been done to determine the origin of these styles, how parents' temperamental styles fit with those of their children, and whether children's styles can be modified. Thomas and Chess (1977), with their late colleague Birch, conducted the most thorough studies on temperament to date. Their studies vividly illustrate the benefits of a good fit between parent and child temperaments, how parental practices can modify and improve a child with hard-to-live-with temperamental characteristics, and conversely how parental practices can create even more problems.

Thomas, Chess, and Birch followed a number of children from infancy through adolescence. They classified the infants into three styles: the easy child, the difficult child, and the slow-to-warm-up child. They used nine categories to make these discriminations (see Table 14-2). The easy child was characterized by "regularity, positive approach to new stimuli, high adaptability to change and mild or moderately intense mood which is preponderantly

Table 14-2   Nine categories of temperament and their definitions

1. *Activity Level:* the motor component present in a given child's functioning and the diurnal proportion of active and inactive periods. Protocol data on motility during bathing, eating, playing, dressing and handling, as well as information concerning the sleep-wake cycle, reaching, crawling and walking, are used in scoring this category.
2. *Rhythmicity (Regularity):* the predictability and/or unpredictability in time of any function. It can be analyzed in relation to the sleep-wake cycle, hunger, feeding pattern and elimination schedule.
3. *Approach or Withdrawal:* the nature of the initial response to a new stimulus, be it a new food, new toy or new person. Approach responses are positive, whether displayed by mood expression (smiling, verbalizations, etc.) or motor activity (swallowing a new food, reaching for a new toy, active play, etc.). Withdrawal reactions are negative, whether displayed by mood expression (crying, fussing, grimacing, verbalizations, etc.) or motor activity (moving away, spitting new food out, pushing new toy away, etc.).
4. *Adaptability:* responses to new or altered situations. One is not concerned with the nature of the initial responses, but with the ease with which they are modified in desired directions.
5. *Threshold of Responsiveness:* the intensity level of stimulation that is necessary to evoke a discernible response, irrespective of the specific form that the response may take, or the sensory modality affected. The behaviors utilized are those concerning reactions to sensory stimuli, environmental objects, and social contacts.
6. *Intensity of Reaction:* the energy level of response, irrespective of its quality or direction.
7. *Quality of Mood:* the amount of pleasant, joyful and friendly behavior, as contrasted with unpleasant, crying and unfriendly behavior.
8. *Distractibility:* the effectiveness of extraneous environmental stimuli in interfering with or in altering the direction of the ongoing behavior.
9. *Attention Span and Persistence:* two categories which are related. Attention span concerns the length of time a particular activity is pursued by the child. Persistence refers to the continuation of an activity in the face of obstacles to the maintenance of the activity direction.

SOURCE: Thomas, A. and Chess, S. *Temperament and Development.* New York: Brunner/Mazel, 1977, pp. 21–22. Reprinted by permission.

positive" (p. 23). Difficult children had traits of "irregularity in biological functions, negative withdrawal to new stimuli, nonadaptability or slow adaptability to change, intense mood and expressions which are frequently negative" (p. 23). Learning disabled children may have many of the traits which characterize the difficult child. Slow-to-warm-up children were characterized "by mild intensity of reactions, whether positive or negative, and by less tendency to show irregularity of biological functions" (p. 23).

The difficult children were at greater risk for future behavior problems. However, this was not a certain outcome nor, necessarily, did temperamental traits remain static. Thomas and Chess concluded that the stability of traits and the child's outcome were the result of an interaction of temperament and environment. A good fit between the temperament of parent and child facilitated the child's development. The case study of Norman, below, who shows many behaviors of the LD student, is a good example of how temperament and environment interact, sometimes to the detriment of the child.

In Norman's case his parents expected more than he could handle. Instead of accepting his short attention span, and arranging the environment to help him, they imposed more pressure and standards that were developmentally beyond him. By the time he reached adulthood, he still had his original problems, but now they were distorted by his poor self-image and depression. Norman's temperamental characteristics and life experiences are like those frequently associated with learning disabled children. When they grow up in a warm, supportive home, which adapts to their needs and temperaments, they have a better chance of avoiding secondary behavior problems. But if the home

CASE STUDY: Norman

Norman was seen at age seventeen by one of us (S.C.), who had followed him since age four and a half because of persistent behavior disturbance. At age seventeen he had already dropped out of two colleges in one year, and was planning to go abroad for a work-study program. He was in good contact but dejected and depressed. He was extraordinarily self-derogatory, said he could not finish anything he started, was lazy, and didn't know what he wanted to do. "My father doesn't respect me, and let's face it, why should he." He talked of "hoping to find myself" in a vague, unplanned way.

Norman had always been a highly distractible child with a short attention span. Intelligent and pleasant, the youngest in his class throughout his school years due to a birth date, he started his academic career with good mastering. However, at home his parents were impatient and critical of him even in his preschool years because of his quick shifts of attention, dawdling at bedtime, and apparent "forgetfulness." By his fifth year he showed various reactive symptoms such as sleeping difficulties, nocturnal enuresis, poor eating habits and nail tearing.

Year by year his academic standing slipped. His father, a hard-driving, very persistent professional man, became increasingly hypercritical and derogatory of Norman. The father equated the boy's short attention span and distractibility with irresponsibility, lack of character and willpower. He used these terms openly to the boy and stated that he "disliked" his son. The mother grew to understand the issue, but no discussion with the father as to the normalcy of his son's temperament and the impossibility of the boy's living up to his standards of concentrated hard work succeeded in altering the father's attitude. He remained convinced that Norman had an irresponsible character and was headed for future failure — indeed a self-fulfilling prophecy. There were several times when the boy tried to comply with his father's standards and made himself sit still with his homework for long periods of time. This only resulted in generalized tension and multiple tics and Norman could not sustain this effort so dissonant with his temperament — another proof to himself and his father of his failure. Direct psychotherapy was arranged in early adolescence, but Norman entered this with a passive, defeated attitude and the effort was unsuccessful. His subsequent development was all too predictable (Thomas & Chess, 1977, pp. 167–169).

is hostile and critical, and parental expectations are beyond the child's capability, then the outcome is likely to be less favorable.

Family Adjustment

A number of parental reactions to having a handicapped child have been described (Brown, 1969; Farber & Ryckman, 1965; Olshansky, 1966; Rosen, 1955). These reactions may interfere with the evaluation of and delivery of services to the learning disabled child. They may also contribute to poor interactions between the LD child, parents, and siblings. A teacher who is aware of these reactions may be in a better position to offer the family support.

Parental Adjustment

Much of the literature on parent reactions has been based on work done with parents of mentally retarded children. The learning disability handicap is not the same and is not as severe. The learning disabled child has a good chance of leaving home and becoming self-sufficient, while the retarded child may remain partially dependent for the rest of his or her life. The learning disability diagnosis is more socially acceptable than the mental retardation diagnosis. Nevertheless, professionals working in the field of learning disabilities have noted similar parental reactions to these diagnoses (Abrams & Kaslow, 1976; Kinsbourne & Caplan, 1979).

On first learning that their child has a learning disability, parents may experience a crisis. The school or the physician often informs the parent and, as bearer of bad tidings, becomes the object of the parent's anger. A parent may also blame him or herself, or the spouse, or may review past actions and events trying to locate a cause for the child's problems. Many parents experience sorrow on learning that their child has a disability. Sometimes a parent completely denies that any problem exists at all. This last response is usually only partially successful and is often followed by a search for a more favorable opinion from other professionals.

Almost every professional in the field of learning disabilities has at some time been the fourth or fifth person to evaluate a child in the parent's search to find someone who will tell them there is no problem, what the cause is, or what the cure is. In a field which has as many unanswered questions concerning causation and remediation as the field of learning disabilities, obtaining a second opinion is, in theory, a prudent course of action. A problem exists when the search for other opinions or emotional reactions interferes with making definite plans for remediation, and with fully accepting the child regardless of his or her abilities and disabilities.

Some parents react to their own anger and disappointment by becoming overprotective and overindulgent. Overprotection deprives LD children of important learning experiences, can make the children feel fragile, weak, and unable, and withdraws them from conflict experiences, such as arguing with siblings, independent of parental interference. An overindulgent parent does not provide the guidance and limits that all children need. In finally coming to grips with the reality of having a handicapped child, many parents must "mourn" the loss of the idealized concept of their child.

Some investigators believe that, although some parents exhibit such reactions as guilt and denial, these reactions are less frequent than described in the literature (Heifetz, 1980; Olshansky, 1966; Robinson & Robinson, 1976). They imply that these responses by the parent are not bad, but are valid reactions to the many information voids in the field of learning disabilities or to the problem of finding adequate evaluations and interventions. Dembrinski and Mauser's (1977) investigation illustrates this point.

In a questionnaire sent to parents who were members of the Association for Children with Learning Disabilities, parents were asked to recall their reactions at the time when they were first told of their child's disability. When their reactions were tallied, most were accepting and relieved but frustrated. Fourteen percent recalled being shocked or feeling guilty and 7 percent were angry or disbelieving. A second question asked for recommendations parents would give to professionals based on their experience. The parents replied that:

1. Professionals in general use too much jargon;
2. Both parents should be included in the interviews;
3. Reading material should be available which helps parents;
4. Parents should receive written reports;
5. Interdisciplinary communication should be improved;
6. Parents want advice for home management;
7. Parents want information about their child's social progress from the teacher.

The replies of these parents illustrate their need for more information. Most of the parents who sought the consultation of a second professional were seeking more information.

When parents exhibit shock, anger, guilt, denial, sorrow, or mourning on learning of their child's learning disability, the professional, other members of the child's family, or even the child may become the object of these emotions. These emotions can interfere with adequate evaluation and intervention. Klein and her colleagues (1981ab), for example, point out that many parents' adverse attitudes toward authority lead them to communicate dissatisfaction with the school system to their children. Their children get the message to resist the school curriculum or authorities because these are to blame for the child's problem.

Some parents' denial of the gravity of the problem does not support school goals because the children are not held responsible for learning in an active and motivated way. Other parents place too much educational responsibility on the child, and don't involve themselves at all. While some parents' subcultures are not concerned with intellectual motivation, others push until the child rebels. In all cases, parental attitudes have exacerbated learning and attitudinal problems.

Professional attitudes sometimes make the parent feel less than adequate and guilty for the child's poor progress. Most parents seem to be saying, "Yes, we sometimes show inappropriate emotional reactions, but most of all we would like information, guidance, and good communication." The teacher, if aware of his or her own reactions and those of the parents, can be a valuable resource to the family. Just knowing that the teacher may be the object of anger, or that parents may deny that there is a problem, should give the teacher the patience to weather emotional crises and remain available for support. The teacher can then become the source of much needed information about learning disabilities.

Sibling Adjustment

Siblings are affected by their LD brothers or sisters, and they in turn influence the LD child's behavior. Most siblings are not told much about the initial diagnosis and may regard the LD child's problem as mysterious. When they get no explanation from parents, children frequently arrive at their own conclusions based on their own experiences, fantasies, and levels of development. Their conclusion may be very anxiety-provoking. They may conclude that their sibling's problem is their fault, is an infectious disease, or is a fatal disease. Honest parental explanations to siblings about the LD child's problem can avoid or alleviate these difficulties.

Siblings may resent the increased attention and time the LD child gets from parents, especially if discipline is different for the LD child. They also may be embarrassed by their brother or sister's behavior or performance at school.

The LD child in turn can suffer from comparisons to a higher achieving sibling, especially if that brother or sister is younger. The LD child has much to gain from siblings. They may be good models for social and school behavior, and they provide peer experience. Their love and acceptance may make home a happy place for the LD child, somewhere where the child can be safe and important.

Many of the problems with siblings are unavoidable, but parents can minimize them in a number of ways. Including siblings as much as possible in discussions and planning makes them feel less neglected, and allows them to become invested in helping alleviate the LD child's problems. Parents should accept the negative feelings which predictably arise. Special care must be taken so that each child in the family gets all the nurturing he or she needs.

Family Assessment

One of the most important yet most difficult tasks of a teacher is to assess the family. Such an assessment is important because the family plays a primary role in fostering a child's intellectual, emotional, and social growth. Good parenting can overcome a poor start in life, while poor parenting can fail to provide the intellectual stimulation and social skills needed for success in school. Unfortunately, teachers often do not have the time for such assessment or for planning interventions.

Ideally, family assessment should center around the emotional atmosphere, methods of discipline, and attitudes toward learning. Emotional factors include the warmth and affection between family members, the support and encouragement given to children, the fostering of independence, the presence of hostility, and the parents' attitudes toward their child's handicap. Methods of discipline involve evaluating such factors as maintenance of rules, explanation of rules, and use of corporal punishment. Assessment of attitudes toward learning includes attitudes toward education and reading, and whether or not academic achievement is valued. Assessment also should include information about prenatal and perinatal history, nutrition, general health, accidents, toxins in parental work-places, and the family history of learning problems.

Family assessment may also be done by a school social worker or psychologist using interview and home observation methods. Some tools have been developed to aid the professional. Sloman and Webster (1978) published a semistructured list of interview questions which assess parental strengths and weaknesses (see Table 14–3). Harmer and Alexander (1978), and others (Schaefer & Bell, 1958; Emmerich, 1969) also use questionnaires to determine parental attitudes. The ability of these instruments' items to predict or correlate with specific school variables such as reading achievement has yet to be demonstrated. Therefore, to assess those variables that have the most direct relevance to a specific child's circumstances, the teacher is advised to make up his or her own questionnaire or list of areas to cover in a family assessment.

A teacher can gain valuable and even more complete information through frequent and informal contact with the family. As parents get to know and trust the teacher, they may be more willing to share their family experiences and enter into a partnership with the teacher. Using the parents' information, teachers can provide for types of intellectual stimulation not present in the home. They can help parents become better models, teachers, and advocates. They can also provide needed emotional support and information.

Family Intervention

How can the teacher and school personnel intervene in the pattern of family life to help parents become more able models, teachers, and advocates? One of the major ways of doing this is by providing information. Parents are faced with a new set of educational jargon when they first learn their child has a learning disability. Many parents have never heard of such terms as *visual perception, auditory sequencing, receptive language,* or *criterion referenced tests.* The interpretive conference at which the parents are initially given the results of the schools' evaluation and recommendations can inform them while providing a frame-

Table 14-3 Interview questions

1. Are there any activities that you particularly enjoy doing with _____? (child's name)
2. What do you feel are some of _____'s greatest problems?
3. Are there any ways in which you have been able to help him with this?
4. Do you feel that this approach has helped?
5. How do you come to try this?
6. Inquire specifically about areas that have not been covered (i.e., physical, social, language, academic).
7. Do you feel that it is important for a child to learn to do things and to manage on his own? Give examples of things _____ does on his own? Give examples of things _____ does on his own at home. How often during the day do you find yourself helping _____ with something?
8. When you think about _____, do you ever feel that he grew up too fast, or not fast enough?
9. Does _____ give up easily with things he finds difficult to do? Give an example of the type of thing he might give up on.
10. Do you feel that _____ needs a lot of praise and encouragement? Give examples of situations where you would give him this.
11. Is _____ very affectionate with you?
12. In what ways does _____ express his affection? Physically? Verbally? How often?
13. Are there any ways in which _____ gives you more pleasure than your other children? Or are there any little things about _____ that you especially enjoy? Give examples.
14. Are there any ways in which _____ is more difficult to enjoy than your other children? Give examples.
15. When during the day does _____ place the most demands on you?
16. Does _____ ever become annoyed when you try to help him with something? Give an example.
17. When do you become most annoyed with _____? How frequently do you end up feeling irritated and angry with _____?
18. When is _____ the easiest to manage? When is _____ the most difficult to manage?
19. Give an example of a recent situation where _____ really wanted to do something that you didn't want him to do. What happened?
20. When during the day do you feel that you place the most demands on _____?
21. Do you have any special rules for _____ in your home? Do these apply to your other children as well?
22. Are there ever situations that are likely to end up with both you and _____ feeling angry or frustrated with each other? Give an example.
23. Can you give me a recent example of a situation where you lost your temper with _____? What did _____ do? What did you do?
24. How do you usually express your affection for _____? Verbally? Physically? Special privileges or presents?
25. Do you feel you more often show your affection when _____ has achieved something?
26. Are there ever times when you show your affection for no special reasons?
27. Are there any particular situations when you are more apt to show your affection for _____? Give examples.

SOURCE: Sloman, L. and Webster, C., "Assessing the Parents of the Learning Disabled Child: A Semistructured Interview." © 1978 The Professional Press, Inc. Reprinted with permission of the publisher from *Journal of Learning Disabilities*, 11 East Adams Street, Chicago, Illinois 60603, vol. 11, p. 27.

work for continued assessment and intervention through a give and take relationship between home and school.

Rockowitz and Davidson (1979) offer an outline for conducting such a conference (see Table 14-4). They emphasize that the conference must be preceded by adequate preparation, the information must be imparted in clear, understandable terms, and, most importantly, the conference should be conducted so as to elicit information and participation from the family. This can be done by actively seeking the parents' feedback, by keeping the group small (two or three professionals at most), and by arranging for privacy and freedom from interruption. At Syracuse University's Psychoeducational Teaching Laboratory this is frequently accomplished by explaining, interpreting, and eliciting opinions and information from parents as they observe all evaluation procedures. If appropriate, a written report is mailed to them prior to the conference. The parents then come to the conference ready to engage in dialogue, questions, or rebuttals. The conferences tend to be working sessions, clarifying basic understandings and intervention plans, rather than primarily information-giving.

Teachers and other school professionals acquainted with the causes of learning disabilities can help clarify for parents the possible reasons why their child has a learning difficulty and can deal with the question which is initially the foremost in most parents' minds: "What did I do to cause this problem?" Parents also want to know what remediation is available in the school and community. A variety of different services and therapies are available in the field of learning disabilities such as the use of medication, diet therapy, sensorimotor therapy, or various academic tutoring plans. Some are valid for a spe-

Table 14-4   Interpretive conference format outline

I. Entry pattern
   A. Introductions
   B. Review of evaluation procedures
   C. Parents' perceptions of child's functioning
   D. Restatement of parental concerns
      1. Main worry
      2. Additional concerns
II. Presentation of findings
   A. Encapsulation: brief overview
   B. Reaction by parents and child
   C. Detailed findings
      1. Strengths
         a. Reactions
      2. Deficits
         b. Reactions

III. Recommendations — only after time has been allowed for reactions
   A. Restatement of concerns with both parents
   B. Recommendations — one at a time
   C. Reactions after each recommendation
   D. Sharing with child
IV. Summary
   A. Repetition of findings, in varied wording if possible
   B. Restatement by parents or patient
   C. Planning for future contacts

SOURCE: Rockowitz, R. J. and Davidson, P. W., "Discussing Diagnostic Findings with Parents." © 1979 The Professional Press, Inc. Reprinted with permission of the publisher from *Journal of Learning Disabilities,* 11 East Adams Street, Chicago, Illinois 60603, vol. *12,* p. 13.

cific child with certain characteristics, and others have very little validity. Educators need to provide guidance in these areas.

Once a course of remediation has been decided on, both teachers and parents need feedback from one another as to how things are going. This is best done through daily or weekly notes, phone calls, or conferences.

Parents may also need help with problems at home such as increasing the child's academic motivation, improving attention, providing structure for an inattentive child, organizing the manner in which their child approaches homework, or improving methods of discipline. A teacher, for example, can help parents learn to model more academic interest at home by pointing out that if parents themselves read more, talk favorably about the academic achievement of others, show an interest in their child's school work by reviewing school papers, positively reinforce academic activity, and provide learning games and activities at home, this will encourage their child's efforts in school. Using Bandura's (1969) four processes of modeling, the parent and teacher can map a plan to model specific behavior for the child.

The inattentive, hyperactive LD child needs a consistent daily routine that has been explained clearly and repeatedly. Since impulsivity and hyperactivity can be increased by anxiety (Berman, 1979), parents must eliminate factors at home that may cause anxiety in their child. Parents also need to learn to modify their behaviors relative to their child's abilities. For example, when parents speak to a child who has a disability in auditory processing, they need to speak slowly, use short sentences, and repeat often.

Most importantly, the teacher can point out to parents how important they are in maintaining their child's self-respect and self-worth. By providing a warm supportive atmosphere at home, they can make their child feel loved and wanted, not a disappointment to them. There is usually some activity that the LD child is good at, and parents are the perfect people to provide opportunities for their child to shine.

Parents also need emotional support from the school in dealing with their own adjustment to having a handicapped child. School personnel have approached this in various ways. Many books which they can recommend to parents explain the terminology of LD, the roles of various professionals, causation, and ideas about home management (Schrag & Divoky, 1978; Smith, S., 1980; Stephens, 1977). Individual sessions with parents are useful, as well as small informational groups held after school hours or as part of a PTA program. Some schools provide useful workshops for parents (Adams, Lerner, & Anderson, 1979).

Parents themselves have organized to hold informational meetings and conferences, and to provide emotional support. The value of a parent meeting other parents of LD children cannot be underestimated. Parents learn that others have gone through similar experiences, that others have been frustrated by their child's behavior and have been sad or angry at their own situation. Parents share behavior management techniques and provide information about community services. Parent groups also can provide vocational counseling services to adults with learning disabilities. A teacher or member of the school system is a valuable source of information and support as part of such a parent group.

Parents can also be a valuable asset to teachers because they may not see many of the behaviors at home that their children, teachers, and peers agree occur in school (Glow & Glow, 1980; Levine, Clarke & Forb, 1981). They can offer tips to teachers on home environment factors that could be simulated in the classroom to produce home-like, appropriate behavior. Teachers also may encourage parents to observe in class and learn about their children's variability across settings. With sufficient education and support, parents can become excellent teachers and advocates for their children.

Parents as Teachers

The role of a parent as teacher and provider of services has, until recently, not been given much attention. It is an area in need of exploration for a number of reasons. There is a huge gap between the number of children with learning disabilities needing services and the number of professionals available. Parents could be used to fill the gap. Professionals can reach more families and multiply their own services by training groups of parents. This frees the professional from having to work with each child personally. Parents may also supplement regular school work at home by working on specific academic skills.

Both parents and teachers gain from the exchange of information which occurs in a parent-teacher team. Parents become more effective because they clearly understand the goals of the teacher. The teacher becomes more aware of the behavior of the student in situations other than school, and the strengths and weaknesses of the home situation. It can only do a child good to have a trusting relationship built between the school and home. How can a child be motivated to learn if at home the parents grumble about the school personnel not doing an adequate job? The child will carry these same attitudes of mistrust into the classroom.

What are some of the ways in which parents have become teachers? Most studies have taught parents the use of behavior modification techniques in handling behavior problems, and have then measured effectiveness of the teaching. The majority of the subjects have been parents of mentally retarded children (Doernberg, 1972; Graziano & Berkowitz, 1972). Baker and his colleagues' project (1976, 1977, 1978) developed a series of training manuals for parents of mentally retarded children. These manuals involve teaching in three areas: self-help skills, developing receptive and expressive language, and managing behavior problems. Parents were divided into four groups which differed in learning experiences (Heifetz, 1980). One group used only the manual and received no other assistance; a second used the manual and phone consultation; a third group used manuals with group training; and a fourth group used manuals with group training and home visits.

Follow-up involved a written test on behavior modification principles and measurement of gains in self-help skills (those skills taught in the manuals and those skills which were not specifically taught). The data support the concept that parents can produce beneficial results as teachers. All four training procedures produced significantly greater gains in self-help skills in the experimental group of children than occurred in the control children. The addition of phone consultation, a group experience, or a group plus home visit showed even greater benefits. Group involvement or group involvement plus home visits, for example, fostered a greater involvement of fathers. These families also expressed greater "confidence in their ability to teach new skills and manage behavior problems" (Heifetz, 1980, p. 34).

Hetrick (1979) reported the successful use of communication training with parents. Ryback and Staata (1970) and Hickey, Imber, and Ruggiero (1979), noted improved reading skills with the use of parent-administered reinforcement techniques. Shapiro and Forbes' (1981) research review indicates that the most effective intervention for learning disabled students (such as improving reading rate, comprehension, visual-motor performance) combines parent counseling with tutoring by parents or contingent parental praise for academic performance. As more of these studies are completed, they should provide examples of how to best structure programs for students and parents.

There are equally compelling reasons to discourage parents as providers of academic services to their children. The home should be the primary source of love and support for the learning disabled child. It may be asking too much of a child to fail in school before peers and teachers, and then come home and again demonstrate failure before the most important people in the child's life, the family. A child needs time to refuel and, depending on the individual situation, this may be a more appropriate function for the family.

Parents, for various reasons, also may not be suited to the role of academic teacher. Their desire for academic success may make teaching sessions torture for both parent and child, with the parent getting more and more upset with each unsuccessful attempt on the child's part. Since heredity may be one cause of learning disabilities, the parent might also have the same learning or behavioral problems as the child. Educators must balance the fact that parents are powerful teachers and models in their own right against the dangers of burdening them with a job they may have few skills for, or undermining their important nurturing function. Each family is different and, before embarking on a parent tutoring plan, the teacher must make a careful assessment of the strengths a family has at the present time and what strengths they are capable of developing in the future.

Parents as Advocates

Parents are the most important advocates any handicapped child may have. They are committed to the child for the long haul, from birth to maturity. Their advocacy should be actively encouraged by those professionals dealing with the learning disabled child.

Parents serve as advocates for their own child and as part of parent-professional organizations which advocate for all children with learning disabilities.

Table 14-5 Stages of parental involvement

STAGES	PARENTAL ACTIVITIES	PROFESSIONAL FACILITATION
Identification	Be alert to early warning signs Be aware of etiology Be aware of services Refer child to proper service Talk to other parents	Be aware of community resources Use public service media Make information available Offer parent education groups Assure adequate funding Make services available
Assessment	Maintain a developmental log Respond to interview questions and written questionnaires Cooperate with teachers and other professionals Be a team member Agree to assessment Attend committee conferences Supply relevant information from previous evaluations	Avoid jargon Be interdisciplinary Conduct conferences slowly and clearly Be realistic Be positive Supply samples of a child's work Write understandable reports Supply assessment reports
Programming	Consider appropriate placement options and program goals Choose a placement site and program goals cooperatively Identify and choose goals for own use Attend committee conferences Visit classrooms Read parents' literature Review materials	Encourage classroom observation Explain educational curriculum Demonstrate strategies and materials Design and supply parent activities Explain placement alternatives Point out goals for parents (if advisable)
Implementation	Be a classroom aide Join parent organizations (PTA, ACLD, etc.) Support efforts of professionals Model good attitude toward program Be a tutor Reinforce child's skills at home	Supply parent education groups Support parents' organizations Supply discussion groups Maintain home programs Design materials and activities for parent use Design formal parent intervention programs in school and home
Evaluation	Hold professionals accountable Be accountable Supply feedback to professionals Help evaluate educational plans Serve on parent advisory boards Support parent activism (ACLD)	Supply parent training programs Establish parent advisory boards Support parents' organizations Include parents' contributions in evaluation procedures Facilitate communication with parents

SOURCE: McLoughlin, J. A., Edge, D., and Stoenecky, B., "Perspective on Parental Involvement in the Diagnosis and Treatment of Learning Disabled Children." © 1978 The Professional Press, Inc. Reprinted with permission of the publisher from *Journal of Learning Disabilities*, 11 East Adams Street, Chicago, Illinois 60603, vol. *11*, p. 295.

The parents' first advocacy role begins with the initial assessment that a problem exists in their child's development. This leads to a search for help in evaluation and finally a search for services. This search has in the past been an impetus for the creation of services where none existed. Public Law 94–142 also mandates schools to invite parental participation in the evaluation of their learning disabled child.

But parents' roles should not stop there. Compliance by the school district to the letter of the law does not guarantee that the learning disabled child is receiving adequate and appropriate services (Baldauf, 1975). It is part of the parents' role to watch over the initial evaluation, to ensure that it is adequately done by competent personnel, and that the instructional program and setting are appropriate. Continued monitoring by the parents helps evaluate whether the program is working. School personnel are not perfect, and well-meaning people can make mistakes. Parents should ideally be partners in the problem-solving process from the onset of evaluation, including the process of monitoring progress and future planning. Table 14–5 lists the stages of parental involvement in the course of evaluation and treatment.

The second area of advocacy involves children with learning disabilities in general. Frustrations in trying to obtain professional help and services from school systems have led parents to form parent-professional organizations. The most prominent of the groups is the Association for Children and Adults with Learning Disabilities (ACLD). These groups have been powerful advocates for legislating services to the learning disabled. Parental pressure has played a major role in the beginning of programs for the learning disabled in over half the states (Baldauf, 1975).

Professionals such as teachers, principals, and psychologists can foster parental advocacy or can place many roadblocks in parents' way. McLoughlin, McLoughlin, and Steward (1979) discussed the ways in which professionals obstruct parents' efforts to become better advocates for their children: by having too many people at a conference, thus intimidating them; with poor eye contact; by rustling papers during a conference to show they want to be somewhere else; by getting angry or defensive; or by quoting regulations to show that parents must do as they say.

No one can put in as many hours, be as committed to a handicapped child, or be as potent an influence on the child as a parent. Therefore it is important that professionals do all they can to encourage a parent to be an advocate and to provide parents with information to enhance their advocacy and teaching.

Summary

Learning disabilities may be aggravated or greatly ameliorated by the setting that is most important to the child, the family. The impact of the family, especially the parents, on a child's social, intellectual, and academic development is great. Parents influence attitudes, work habits, values, and learned skills which are compatible with school success through their attitudes toward learning, the amount of intellectual stimulation provided in the home, and through their warmth and support. Higher socio-economic status homes are more advantageous when it comes to producing academically achieving children, even when these children had experienced severe trauma at birth. More important than socio-economic status, however, is the nature of parent-child interaction patterns.

Through the processes of identification, modeling, and discipline, parents can instill in their children honesty, consideration of others, respect for rules, and independence. These are all attitudes which aid the child in social relationships with adults and peers. Some families of children with learning disabilities may lack the skills and resources to be the models and to provide the discipline and support which would help their child. Unless lessons taught in school are complemented by similar teaching at home, they seem to go unlearned.

Teachers can help parents become better educated and more effective parents in a number of ways. One is by supporting parents through emotional crises which may be painful for both the parent and the professional, and helping parents overcome sorrow, anger, or denial. Teachers can also provide information about learning disabilities and methods for modeling, discipline, and making the home conducive to learning. Parents as advocates and teachers are a natural answer to the shortage of services and school personnel to teach handicapped children. This requires further research into methods of assessing families and specific programs and tasks which comfortably fit into their life styles.

Suggestions for Further Study

1. Exactly when does a child's temperament begin to be influenced by his environment? Infants are not only temperamentally different at birth, but these differences have been related to such prenatal environmental factors as the mother's heartrate (Smith & Steinschneider, 1975). Bell's (1974), Rubin's (1971), and Thomas and Chess' (1977) works offer fascinating reading on how parent, child, and sibling temperaments shape one another. The way in which each individual's unique traits interact with another's has been described by Cameron (1977, 1978) as analogous to the origins of an earthquake. The child's temperament is akin to the fault lines. Environmental events, particularly parenting styles, are akin to the strain. Just as earthquakes result from the match between faults and strains, so behavior difficulties arise from a mismatch of certain child temperaments with certain styles of parenting.

Observe an LD preschooler with behavioral difficulties in his or her home. Can you note the faults and strains? What are the differences in individual temperaments in this family versus one where the child displays no behavior difficulties? How do parental temperament traits interact with each child's traits to affect their learning and behavior differently?

2. To learn more about stages of moral development, read Kohlberg's article, published in 1963. Another good source is Turiel (1977).

3. Investigators have been able to correlate the development of moral judgment with cognitive development. Damon (1975), Karnoil (1980), and Walter (1980) have published investigations in this area. What are the implications of their findings for learning disabled children who have specific cognitive dysfunctions?

4. An area implicated in family influences on achievement is the relationship of birth order and achievement. Adams (1972) has critically reviewed the research in this area. Run a study calculating the birth order in an LD classroom. Do you confirm Adams' findings?

5. Becoming a good parent counselor and interviewer takes experience and practice. Kroth and Simpson (1977) provide information on interview format and recording procedures, and, most importantly, on interviewing skills such as active listening and reading nonverbal cues. They provide exercises for practice with friends and relatives.

6. In your parent counseling, you may want to attend to possible problems with siblings. The LD child may suffer in comparison to his sibling or siblings may react to the specialness of their brother or sister. Abrams and Kaslow (1976) and Berman (1979) both discuss the problems of adjustment that may arise.

7. One of the concerns of parents of learning disabled children is understanding professional terminology and suggestions for home management. The following references are suggested for parents and offer discussions of some of the more frequent home management problems: Brutten, Richardson, & Mangel, 1973; Dardig, and Heward, 1976; Deibert, and Harmon, 1970; Gardner, 1973; Hall, 1970; Hayes, 1975; Levy, 1973; Patterson & Gullion, 1971; Valett, 1971; Weiss & Weiss, 1976.

8. Some parent groups have taken on the task of vocational counseling. They have done so because of the lack of programs which prepare adolescent LD students for the job market or for higher educational programs. There is also a scarcity of counseling programs which inform students of the opportunities which do exist. Survey the LD programs in local high schools or contact a federal agency such as the Office of Educational Opportunity to find out what vocational services are available in your community. What additional service components would you recommend?

Chapter Fifteen
The School

One of the major premises of this text is that children exist in settings, and that each of these settings has its own interactional and organizational patterns. In this chapter we shift our focus from family settings to ways in which school settings impact upon learning disabled children's learning and behavior.

From kindergarten through twelfth grade, the average youngster spends about 14,000 hours in classroom settings (Gump, 1978). Certainly the school is a powerful influence in the child's life. It is here that the learning disabled child is singled out because the school setting reflects society's valuing of attributes that he or she has too little of.

From a social system perspective, these children are victims of the intense demands our society places on academic achievement (Forness, 1974). Society and its schools create problems by demanding that everyone acquire skills in reading, writing, and arithmetic, or be held in contempt by their peers (Dexter, 1964). This demand is clearly reflected in states' compulsory education laws and minimum competency standards for graduation. Naturally, some children cannot gain these particular skills and will be viewed as failures by others. Unfortunately, the school setting emphasizes and values some skills, while virtually ignoring others that may be strengths for these children, such as street smarts.

Although human behavior for many years has been viewed as originating primarily within the person (Marx & Hillix, 1973), it does not. Such person-centered views of human behavior cannot account for all possible varieties of behavior in all possible situations. The context or setting in which the behavior occurs is important in its own right. This point was illustrated many years ago in a famous study by Hartshorne and May (1928). Although we commonly think of honesty or dishonesty as a trait that exists within a person, these researchers found that honest and dishonest behavior in elementary school children varied greatly according to the situation they were in.

The learning and behavior of learning disabled students also are influenced by the hundreds of variables operating in any given classroom at any given time. Robby and Laura, for example, are of similar ages and family background. Because of their short attention spans, their academic achievement has suffered, and both are considered to be learning disabled. Robby's classroom is very traditional, with seats placed in rows and few out-of-seat activities. Robby's school integrates very few special children into typical settings ("mainstreaming"), so Robby spends most of his day in his classroom. Laura, on the other hand, attends an open classroom in a school that believes firmly in mainstreaming.

Robby and Laura, despite the similarities in their backgrounds and behaviors, are likely to have different school experiences. In Robby's case, the school setting has helped him to focus attention and make academic progress. However, he has not learned to behave as his typical peers do. But Laura seems to be

This chapter was written by Robert Hiltonsmith.

slipping further and further behind. She's continually distracted and can't draw conclusions or learn on her own. She needs constant teacher direction. Yet, she's a very popular girl. She has more than an average number of social contacts with different children each day as she flitters around her setting. Her classmates like her company and she has learned to dress and behave just as they do, and to have compatible interests. Gradually, the similarities between Robby and Laura fade. This is due to differences in the following classroom characteristics: the physical environment, the organizational environment, and the human environment (Moos, 1979). These dimensions interact with child characteristics and account for or aggravate some failures while alleviating others.

This chapter will help us more fully understand how school interventions can best meet LD students' needs by coming to grips with the effects of schools' physical, organizational, and teacher and peer characteristics upon children. Research Box 15-1 offers insights into the measurement of the school setting's personality. Since these areas have yet to be extensively researched with learning disabled children, this chapter's intent is to alert you to the potential impact that school setting factors have in the education of the learning disabled.

Physical Characteristics

Not until the last ten or fifteen years have educators paid attention to broader aspects of the physical environment in which education takes place. Before that, concern with the physical environment of the school had been limited to establishing minimal standards for size, acoustics, lighting, and heating; educators assumed that as long as these basic requirements were fulfilled they could then direct their attention to other psychological, instructional, and social variables (Weinstein, 1979). Recently, educators have begun to ask whether it matters where the student sits, what shape the classroom is, whether a noisy background makes a difference in learning and other environmental questions. Although they still have more questions than answers, the answers they are getting are provocative.

Two broad sets of factors have influenced this research: ambient (or nonarchitectural) factors, such as background noise; and designed (architectural) factors, such as classroom seating arrangement. Studies in these areas support our tendencies to reduce auditory and visual distractions in classrooms, place learning disabled children in smaller schools and more pleasant surroundings, and seat them with smaller groups of children that are "front and center."

The Ambient Classroom Environment

Since Strauss' and Lehtinen's (1947) time, LD professionals have recommended reducing excessive distractions in a learning disabled child's classroom. This typically involves the reduction or elimination of extraneous noise and visual stimulation in classrooms by means of three-sided cubicles. That

---

RESEARCH BOX 15-1
Social Climate:
The "Personality"
of the Environment

Several investigators in the field of person-environment study argue that environments have "personality." They mean that various settings can be assessed for their typical characteristics, much as the personality of a person can be assessed. Just as the Rorschach Inkblots and Thematic Apperception Test measure human personality, there are tests and techniques that determine the personality of a setting. Rudolf Moos and his colleagues have done a great deal of work assessing the personality or social climate of various settings. They have devised a number of *social climate* scales that assess various settings on three common dimensions:

1. *Relationship*—the amount of personal support, spontaneity, and involvement among persons in the setting,
2. *System maintenance*—the extent to which the environment is orderly, clear in its expectations, and responsive to change, and

3. *Personal growth*—the potential in the environment for personal growth and the development of self-esteem.

One of the scales that Moos devised is the *Classroom Environment Scale* which assesses the social climate of junior and senior high classrooms. Trickett (1978) used the Classroom Environment Scale to examine the social climate of five types of public schools: urban, rural, suburban, vocational, and alternative. The Classroom Environment Scale was administered to 409 classes distributed among these five types of schools. The results revealed a complex pattern of differences in the social climates of the classrooms in the five types of schools. Alternative schools and vocational schools had the greatest contrast. The alternative schools emphasized interpersonal aspects of classroom experience and were seen by the students as being "anti-authority" and "anti-competitive." On the other hand, the vocational schools emphasized the systems maintenance portion of the Classroom Environment Scale and heavily stressed rules and regulations. The social atmospheres, or social climates, of the schools were indeed different. The implications of these different social climates on interpersonal relationships, academic achievement, and other observable behaviors is just now being studied.

---

this practice is still alive today is apparent not only from recent literature (Cruickshank, 1975; Ross & Ross, 1976) but also from simple observations of many current learning disabilities classrooms.

Research on the ambient classroom environment has examined the effects of background noise and visual distractions on the learning disabled child. These studies indicate that learning disabled children tend to be no more sensitive to these factors than typical children. Their performance becomes equally depressed. Unlike their peers, however, they can least afford lost opportunities for learning.

Background Noise. Quieter classroom environments appear to benefit all children equally. Research on background noise in the classroom has investigated how intense the background noise is, whether or not the noise is meaningful, and the effect of external classroom noise. This research has in most cases found that background noise, especially meaningful noise, lowers performance, but that learning disabled children are not affected to any signficantly greater extent than typical learners.

Weinstein (1979) offered three possibilities for depressed performance in noisy environments:

1. the noise interferes with communication in the classroom, so that children are unable to attend to or even hear the teacher and consequently miss essential instruction,

2. less communication takes place in noisy environments than in quiet environments, as illustrated in Bronzaft and McCarthy's (1975) study where teachers were forced to stop instructing for thirty seconds out of every four and one half minutes while an elevated train passed by, and

3. children in perpetually noisy environments develop an auditory screening process that filters out relevant as well as irrelevant sounds.

Intensity of Background Noise. Noise levels in classrooms vary. Under *extreme* levels of classroom noise, some evidence suggests that distractible children take longer to complete educational tasks than do nondistractible children (Somervill, Jacobsen, Warnberg, & Young, 1974). These findings, however, apply only to very high levels of environmental stimulation that are unlikely to occur in even the noisiest classrooms. At typical background noise intensities, the performance of learning disabled children and typical learners seems to be equally lowered (Bremer & Stein, 1976; Sykes, Douglas, Weiss, & Minde, 1971; Whalen et al., 1979; Zentall & Zentall, 1976). In an analogue experiment, for example, Nober and Nober (1975) examined the effects of tape recorded classroom noise on an auditory discrimination task. They found that both learning disabled and nondisabled children made more errors in the noisy condition, and that the background noise did not affect the two groups of children differently.

Meaningfulness of Background Noise. Background noise in the classroom has been studied from the standpoint of whether the noise is meaningful (talking, voices, typical classroom sounds) or nonmeaningful — random and unintelligible. Meaningful noise in the classroom appears to lower the performance of children more than does unintelligible noise of similar intensity (Joiner & Kottmeyer, 1971; Nober & Nober, 1975). The performance of both average learners and children with learning problems is affected to similar extents.

Effect of External Classroom Noise. The effects of external classroom noise have been examined in a series of fascinating studies (Crook & Langdon, 1974; Kyzar, 1977). Bronzaft and McCarthy (1975), for example, studied students attending an elementary school located very close to an elevated train line.

Approximately eighty trains passed the school at irregular intervals each day, with each train taking about thirty seconds to rush by. The noise level in the classrooms nearest the train tracks was so high when a train was going by that teachers had to scream to be heard by nearby children. When the reading achievement scores of children in classrooms on the near and far sides of the building were compared, the scores of students on the noisy side were significantly lower.

Visual Distractions. The practice of isolating learning disabled children from excessive visual distractions in the classroom is still actively advocated (Cruickshank, 1971, 1975). As with excessive noise, both learning disabled and typical children are hampered to a similar extent in educational tasks by excessive visual distractions (Carter & Diaz, 1971; Somervill et al., 1974). At least one study found no significant benefits for the task performance of either distractible or nondistractible children when visual distractions in the classroom were minimized or three-sided cubicles used (Somervill, Warnberg, & Bost, 1973).

A small and controversial body of research has argued that there is a relationship between standard cool-white fluorescent lighting in the classroom and the incidence of hyperactivity in children (Mayron et al., 1976; Ott, 1976). Mayron and his colleagues (1974) investigated the incidence of hyperactive behavior in boys who attended four windowless classrooms. In two of the rooms, the standard cool-white fluorescent tubes and fixtures were replaced with full-spectrum fluorescent lights that more closely duplicate natural daylight. The cathode ends of these full-spectrum lamps were shielded with lead foil, and the entire fixture was covered with grounded aluminum screening to prevent low-frequency electromagnetic radiation from reaching the children. In the other two rooms, the standard cool-white fluorescent lights were retained. Using time-lapse films over a six-month period to analyze activity levels of children, the investigators found that, in the control rooms without the lighting modifications, six children became less active and twenty-seven became more active; in the experimental rooms with the modified lighting, twenty-seven became less active and four children became more active. Similarly, Painter (1976) found a 32 percent drop in activity level with the removal of fluorescent lights. Because of difficulties in experimental design in these studies, the decreased hyperactive behaviors cannot be absolutely linked to the experimental treatment or to other variables, such as the positive effect on the children of being in an experiment or observer bias.

The Designed Environment

Architectural (designed) aspects of the school setting that have been investigated include school and classroom size and design. The LD student could benefit from the advantages of smaller schools, teacher and student attitudes in open-space designs, small group seating arrangements requiring a teacher to move around to supervise, pleasant surroundings, and sitting front and center.

School Size. School buildings come in a tremendous variety of sizes, from the once widespread and now fast-disappearing one-room schoolhouse, to mammoth comprehensive high schools that house thousands of students under one roof. One very detailed approach to the issue of school size has been the ecological investigations of Roger Barker and his colleagues (Barker & Gump, 1964). These investigators generally found small schools to be superior to large schools on four important variables: the variety of instruction offered, the variety of extracurricular activities, the amount and nature of student participation in school affairs, and the effects of this participation on the students. In particular, they noted that small schools give the student a better chance of participating in most aspects of school life, thereby fostering a spirit of challenge, action, close cooperation among peers, and high self-esteem. These results have stood up well in subsequent studies (Baird, 1969; Wicker, 1969).

School and Classroom Design. Recent theory and research on the physical design of school buildings and classrooms focuses on the impact of innovative designs, particularly "open plan" designs. The design of school buildings and classrooms has changed greatly through the years. Getzels (1974) argues that changes in classroom design are not merely the product of architectural and engineering advances but actually mirror changing views of the learner. The rectangular classroom design of the turn of the century reflected the then-current notion of the child as an "empty" learner, one who must sit still and be "fed" information that others decide is important. These early classrooms featured long rows of chairs fastened tightly to the floor, with a raised platform in the front of the room for the teacher.

The square classrooms of the 1930s, with movable seats and the teacher's desk at the side of the room, reflected the progressive education movement and its image of the child as an active learner.

The open-plan classroom design of the late 1960s reflects still a different concept of the child, as a "vital entity, perpetually in motion, that must be given an effective opportunity to remain in motion if it is to function and continue to live" (p. 535). Getzels points to a transaction between the learner and the educational setting: "The classrooms we build for our children are not only places where the lessons intended by the teacher are taught. These classrooms teach lessons of their own; they tell the child who he is supposed to be . . . and how he is supposed to learn" (p. 538). An assortment of school and classroom design variables have been shown to influence students' attitudes, behavior, and achievement.

Open-Space Schools. The open-space design concept received intensive scrutiny over the past decade. In a comprehensive review of this research, George

(1975) reported that over 50 percent of all schools built in this country between 1967 and 1970 were open in design. The particular design of these open-space schools varies widely, but they are generally characterized by a lack of interior walls and by instructional areas ranging in size from two ordinary classrooms to over thirty (Weinstein, 1979).

There is an important distinction between open *space* and open *education*. The former is what we are discussing here, an architectural variable. The latter is an instructional variable that relates to students' self-pacing and self-initiating of educational activities, with the teacher acting as a facilitator of their learning.

Studies of student movement and behavior patterns in open school settings show that more classroom areas, particularly library areas, are used in these schools, while less time is spent at desks (Beeken & Jansen, 1978; Rothenburg & Rivlin, 1975). Interaction between peers is more frequent but at some expense, apparently, to individual contact with the teacher. Time spent reading and writing is less common in open space schools than in traditional classrooms, although no consistent differences in academic achievement or creativity between the two designs have been shown (George, 1975).

Both teachers' and students' attitudes toward school appear to be favorably influenced by open-space schools, particularly with regard to satisfaction (Meyer, 1971), ambition (Cohen, 1973), feelings of autonomy (Meyer, 1971), willingness on the part of students to take risks (George, 1975), and feelings of cooperation and caring for fellow teachers and students (Trickett, 1978). These studies may not present an accurate picture, however, because of self-selection (Weinstein, 1979). That is, many teachers in open-space schools may differ in attitude even before they enter these classes. These attitudes may have influenced their selection for these classes or they may have asked to teach in these innovative settings. The classes' enthusiasm and ambition, therefore, may reflect teacher as well as setting differences.

Studies show that learning disabled children who are hyperactive and distractible are not necessarily at a disadvantage with the increased freedom in most open-space classrooms (Flynn & Rapoport, 1976; Rothenburg & Rivlin, 1975). Nevertheless, researchers suggest design alternatives to open space rooms in the form of graduated degrees of open-structured learning areas. For learning disabled children, the increased freedom and more relaxed structure in open space schools must be carefully weighed against their needs for structure, consistency, and teacher direction. The latter are met with more difficulty in open space designs.

Furniture Arrangement. The arrangement of furniture and the use of space in the classroom also affect student behavior (Kritchevsky & Prescott, 1969; Weinstein, 1977, Zifferblatt, 1972). Zifferblatt (1972), for example, looked at the relationship between classroom furniture arrangement and student behavior in two third-grade classrooms in which the teachers' instructional styles, the curricula, and the classroom activities were similar. In one classroom the students' attention spans appeared much shorter, and they had more inappropriate movement around the classroom and loud conversation. Zifferblatt concluded that the differences in behavior observed in the two classrooms were due to differences in the way classroom space was arranged and used.

In the classroom where behavior was not a problem, the desks were situated in less accessible areas of the room, providing some degree of privacy for the students. The desks were arranged so that only two or three children could work together. The teacher's desk was located in a corner so that she was unable to direct activities from the desk and had to move around the classroom. Several bookcases, serving as barriers, helped limit classroom-wide movement and activity.

The classroom where student behavior was a problem was designed and arranged differently, with as many as twelve student desks clustered together and no clear boundaries or barriers for specific classroom activities. The teacher's desk was in the center of the room, enabling her to manage most classroom activities from her seat, thus decreasing individual, personal contact with students. Studies like these have clear implications for learning disabled children, who often respond well to close, personal contact with the teacher in helping them stay on task.

Pleasantness of Surroundings. Preliminary evidence suggests that children persist more at educational tasks when they are in pleasant surroundings. Work by Mintz (1956), and Maslow and Mintz (1956) found a relationship between an ugly environment and feelings of discontent, the desire to escape, and fatigue. Santrock (1976), building on this, had first and second graders individually perform a motor task in a school room that was decorated with happy, sad, or neutral pictures. The results indicated that these different environments had a significant impact on persistence on the motor task, with students working longest in the "happy" room setting.

Classroom Seating and Location. Where students sit has important effects on their classroom experiences. Early studies by Walberg (1969) and Adams and Biddle (1970) noted a "front and center" phenomenon: students who sit in the front center portion of the classroom seem to place significantly higher value on learning, are more attentive, engage in more on-task behavior, and interact more with the classroom teacher. These findings have generally been confirmed in later studies (Koneya, 1976; Schwebel & Cherlin, 1972), although a few studies (Delefes & Jackson, 1972) failed to find the "front and center" phenomenon. Weinstein (1979) recently concluded that "the weight of the evidence seems to indicate that a front-center phenomenon facilitates achievement, positive attitudes, and participation, at least for those somewhat predisposed to speak in class . . . [and] it seems reasonable to hypothesize that teachers attend more to students in the front and center" (p. 580).

In light of these findings, teachers should carefully analyze the common practice of isolating learning disabled children, particularly those that are highly distractible, in the far reaches of the classroom, assuming that these areas of the room have fewer distractions. This placement may result in far less supervision and encouragement from the teacher, especially in traditional class-rooms where the teacher spends most class time in the front of the room. The diminished interaction with the teacher may outweigh any advantages of re-duced distractions.

Organizational Characteristics

Organizational aspects of school and classroom settings are operating proce-dures that allocate resources, develop curriculum, assign pupils and teachers to classrooms, and generally devise the rules for the school. The school classifies children, determines a child's placement, and organizes the child's instruction. The assumption that classification and special placements can help the learning disabled child receive more appropriate educational services must be weighed against the stigma and isolation that can accompany special education services. Alternate ways of providing learning disabled youngsters with special services, without removing them from the educational mainstream, have appeared, most notably, the resource room. These approaches seem to work well in meeting the needs of many learning disabled children, while complying with the spirit of PL 94–142 and the "least restrictive environment" concept. Since the mainstreamed environment is not the least restrictive for every learning disabled child, the needs of each learner must be carefully assessed before deciding which is the most appropriate placement. One of the most important questions an educator can ask is in which settings the student is likely to be encouraged to spend the most time on task.

Classification

In most schools, special services are provided primarily to children who have been classified as handicapped. Classification is advantageous for school sys-tems because this qualifies them for funds distributed by federal and state education agencies. Some forms of classification also facilitate organizing chil-dren for special instructional and research purposes.

Against these justifications for classification, the educator must weigh a variety of potential disadvantages. These disadvantages have been extensively researched and hotly debated in educational circles over the past ten to fifteen years.

A sizable and controversial body of research and theory has found that in some, but not all, cases a teacher's expectation about a child's ability can influence both the teacher's behavior toward the child and the child's classroom behavior (Alexander & Strain, 1978; Dusek, 1975; Meyers, Sundstrom, & Yoshida, 1974; Rosenthal & Jacobson, 1968; Rosenthal & Rosnow, 1969). This so-called "self-fulfilling prophecy" is apparent only when the teacher attends to, comprehends, and retains the expectancy, and transmits it to the student, who in turn attends to, comprehends, retains, and acts on it (McGuire, 1968). This happens only when the child's actual behavior matches expectations. That is, teachers seem to allow labels to exert influence only when behavioral information is unavailable; otherwise, they form their expectations on the basis of children's actual behaviors (Reschly & Lamprecht, 1979). The expectancy gained from the label may take some time to counteract (see Research Box 15-2). A related body of research has shown that the learning disabled label by itself can exert a biasing effect on teacher judgments of child behavior (Foster, Schmidt, & Sabatino, 1976; Sutherland & Algozzine, 1979). This label may also influence children' attitudes toward their labeled peers (Foley, 1979).

There are other disadvantages to handicapping classifications besides this biasing effect on teacher and peer attitudes. Major among these are the disadvantages of assuming that group homogeneity is increased by classification or ability grouping practices (Balow, 1964; Chandler, 1966; Hallahan & Kauffman, 1977; Richey & McKinney, 1978; Wilhelms & Westby-Gibson, 1961). When children are grouped on any one criterion, such as level of reading achievement, variability on all other characteristics is not reduced. With respect to LD students, no single common cluster of symptoms is consistently associated with the term "learning disabled." In fact, a review of forty-seven studies comparing typical and learning disabled children found there to be equal variability of performance within each group. Although the LD group

RESEARCH BOX 15-2
Can the Biasing Effect of Labels Be Reversed?

If the label "learning disabled" actually influences teacher expectations, then is it possible to reverse this bias by presenting teachers with actual behavior in the labeled student that is inconsistent with the label? Ysseldyke and Foster (1978) sought to answer this question by devising a study that examined the effects of the labels "emotionally disturbed" and "learning disabled" on initial teacher bias and, more importantly, on the ability of regular classroom teachers to disregard stereotyped expectancies when confronted with behavior that was inconsistent with the expectancies.

The investigators had the teachers rate the expected behaviors of a hypothetical normal child, an emotionally disturbed child, and a learning disabled child. The teachers were then shown a twelve-minute videotape of a normal fourth grader and were divided into three groups. These three groups were told that the videotaped child was either normal, emotionally disturbed, or learning disabled. The experimenters found that teachers did respond differently to the labels when asked to rate the expected behaviors of a hypothetical child. When the normal boy in the videotape was labeled "emotionally disturbed" or "learning disabled," the teachers rated the boy more negatively — even when they were confronted with normal behavior — behavior that was inconsistent with the label. Apparently, more than a simple videotape of normal behavior is needed to counteract the expectancies communicated by a label.

on the whole scored below typical learners, 23 percent of LD children still scored above the average nondisabled group's performance (Weener, 1981). Therefore, despite their label, LD children remain just as diverse in learning styles, behavioral repertoires, and instructional needs as they were prior to classification.

A further disadvantage of classification is that it implies only an "in-child" explanation of why the LD child has had so much difficulty, whereas the real determinants for the child's lack of success might be found, for instance, in the instructional strategies in the child's classroom. Classification also implies consistent behaviors from situation to situation. A learning disabled child is, supposedly, learning disabled not only in school, but at home, on the playground, and in the community. Yet children with mild learning disabilities or even mental retardation do not always show their learning difficulties in all settings (Mercer, 1973). A child who is classified "learning disabled" in school because of difficulties with school subjects may be indistinguishable from other children in other settings. Classifying leads us to think that the classification describes the individual, rather than the interaction of the individual and attributes of particular tasks and settings. It tells us nothing about how to intervene. Noncategorical service options are trying to address these issues.

Placement

A second broad aspect of the organizational environment of school settings concerns how schools arrange classroom placements for children with special learning needs. A range of placement possibilities exists, from regular classroom placement without any supportive services all the way to special schools that are entirely devoted to childen with learning disabilities. The choice of an appropriate, effective placement for a particular learning disabled child depends on a good understanding of special class and regular class placement options, the mainstreaming and least restrictive environment concepts, and resource room models.

Special and Regular Class Placement. The appropriateness of placing children with special needs in special classes has long been debated among special educators. As in many areas of education, policy decisions often come before empirical evidence is complete. Influential articles, particularly Dunn's (1968) on the detrimental aspects of most special class placements for mildly handicapped children, paved the way for a gradual retreat from the special class concept. Has this been a wise course of action? Are the needs of special children met better in the regular or special education classroom? What needs should we consider most important — academic or social? Are special classes appropriate for some children but perhaps not for others?

Research investigating the usefulness of special versus regular class placement for learning disabled children is just beginning. A recent analysis of fifty research studies on a broad range of exceptional children shows that inferences about the usefulness of special class placements for learning disabled children do not necessarily follow from what is known about the long history of such classes for educable, mentally retarded children (Carlberg & Kavale, 1980). These investigators found that academic achievement in special class placements was significantly inferior to regular class placement for children with below-average intelligence. But it was significantly superior to regular class placement in three studies of learning disabled youngsters.

In part, special classrooms might benefit LD students because their teacher-pupil ratios are two to three times lower than those in regular classes; this ratio maximizes the probability of intensive, individualized instruction. Glass and Smith's (1979) analysis of class-size research concluded that a strong and clear relationship exists between class size and academic achievement, with students in classrooms of fifteen or fewer pupils achieving significantly higher than pupils in classes of twenty-five or more.

Bryan's (1974) study illustrates how this might happen. She found that learning disabled students in the regular class spent 14 percent of their time waiting for the teacher to get organized. In the LD classroom only 3 percent of their time was spent waiting. This was accompanied by greater on-task behavior, more positive reinforcement from the teacher, and more interaction with the teacher than in the regular classroom. Bryan & Wheeler (1976) too reported several more positive teacher-child interaction factors in LD than in regular classrooms: greater frequency of completed interactions, fewer teacher communications to the whole group, longer duration of communications (often up to one minute), greater number of adult initiations to which children responded, and more frequent continuous communications by children and teachers.

The academic progress of learning disabled children is only half the issue. What about the social or affective development of these children in special and regular classes? Several recent studies have found beneficial effects for special class placement on learning disabled students' self-concepts. Boersma, Chapman, and Battle (1979) examined changes in academic self-concept for learning disabled and mentally retarded children over a twelve-month period before and after receiving full-time remedial placement. They found that full-time placement was accompanied by significant increases in academic self-concept, particularly in the areas of reading, spelling, and general confidence. Similar results were found by Ribner (1978). In both studies, the investigators attributed the increased self-concept ratings to achievement gains made in the special classes and the fact that youngsters entering the special class could now compare their performance to that of peers who also had learning difficulties. Yauman (1980) found that LD students in segregated LD special classes maintained as good a self-concept as typical children in regular classes despite significantly lower reading achievement, which usually correlates with self-concept. LD students who remained in regular classes but had daily tutoring had significantly lower self-concept scores than typical children, even though their reading achievement scores were higher than those of the LD students in segregated classes. It appears that regular class competition can set criteria for achievement that LD students cannot meet, thereby harming their self-concept.

Contrary to earlier research with the mentally retarded, special class placement for learning disabled children may not actually be that bad. Studies thus far indicate that these youngsters make greater gains in special class in both academic and social areas.

Mainstreaming. Studies showing that special classes for the mildly retarded did not result in special outcomes, coupled with philosophical awakenings during the period of civil rights activism, brought about profound changes in long-established practices in special education: *mainstreaming,* placement in the regular classroom. This concept was further popularized through PL 94-142, which calls for handicapped children to be educated with nonhandicapped children to the maximum extent possible. Handicapped children, according to the law, should be removed from a normal environment only when the extent and severity of their handicap precludes an appropriate education in that setting, even with additional learning aids.

Mainstreaming is such a new practice that its effects — particularly its long-term effects — have not been fully evaluated. What has been shown so far is that:

1. regular classroom teachers are generally hesitant and sometimes fearful about providing for the needs of special children in their classrooms (Alexander & Strain, 1978; Johnson & Cartwright, 1979; Mandell & Strain, 1978; Moore & Fine, 1978),

2. learning disabled children who are mainstreamed into regular classrooms generally need some supportive services, such as a resource room, to maintain the academic gains they made in the special classroom (Ritter, 1978),

3. the popularity of learning disabled children in the regular classroom is in almost all cases low (Bruininks, 1978b; Bryan, 1974b; Prillaman, 1981; Richey, Miller, & Lessman, 1981; Scranton & Ryckman, 1979; Sheare, 1978), and

4. mainstreaming may not result in greater social interaction with non-handicapped children, greater social acceptance, or modeling of typical peers' behaviors (Gresham, 1982).

Research on the closely related topics of mainstreaming and special class placement might lead to the conclusion that, at least for learning disabled children, mainstreaming into regular classrooms has many disadvantages that must be considered. This conclusion, however, must be considered tentative because the studies on which they are based vary greatly in quality and the extent to which their findings can be generalized. Their results also need to be weighed against the argument that mainstreaming's rationale does not need to be verified by research studies — it is simply ethically wrong to isolate individuals from the regular classroom and peers.

When deciding on class placements, the practical thing to do is to decide what is right for each individual child. Rebecca's placement in a class for learning disabled youngsters, for example, provides her with more individualized instruction geared to her own skill levels, the chance for more successful academic experiences, and the chance to compare her performance in school against a group of peers who also are having learning difficulties, rather than against a group of regular classroom peers who are, by and large, doing very well in school. For Jamie, placement in a similar classroom creates different results. Jamie finds that she is removed for most of the day from her friends in her regular class and is made fun of for being in the dummy class down the hall. This situation obviously demoralizes her and thus further compounds her learning difficulties.

Forness (1981) suggests that, in deciding whether or not to mainstream, educators consider such factors as the child's age, degree of handicap, needed curriculum modifications, peer relationships, social skills, numbers of children in the regular class, attitude and competency of the regular class teacher, and type of family support system. Gresham (1982) suggests preparing children for mainstreaming by teaching them the requisite social skills for effective social interaction and peer acceptance. Maher (1982) adds that mainstreaming can be far more academically successful if teachers and pupils jointly set instructional goals, use rating scales for goal attainment, and meet weekly to discuss progress and write instructional plans.

The Least Restrictive Environment. The heated debate around the broad issues of mainstreaming and special class placement frequently obscures the original intent of educators in this area. Public Law 94-142 mandated that handicapped students be educated in as near normal a setting as possible — the "least restrictive environment." Based on insights from educational research, Heron and Skinner (1981) define the least restrictive environment "as that educational setting which maximizes the learning disabled student's opportunity to respond and achieve, permits the regular education teacher to interact proportionally with all the students in the classroom, and fosters acceptable social relations between nonhandicapped and learning disabled students" (p. 116).

Public Law 94-142 reflected the view that, although many children with special needs can be appropriately educated in the regular classroom setting, some have needs best met in some form of special classroom. "Mainstreaming" and "least restrictive" are not synonymous. At times, education in the mainstream might be restrictive for a learning disabled child, for a variety of reasons: such as, lack of preparation of regular classroom teachers to deal with the learning disabled child's needs, teacher unwillingness to accept a handicapped student, lack of administrative support for mainstreaming, inappropriate class structure and curriculum, and too many distractions in the regular classroom. Therefore, placement decisions must be based on both student needs and school resources.

Recently, a fruitful middle ground has been able to somewhat defuse the special versus regular class, mainstreaming, and least restrictive environment controversies. This usually involves provision of supportive services to the learning disabled student while he or she remains in the regular classroom. The most common method for providing these services has been through the resource room.

Resource Room Models. The resource room concept emerged over the last ten or fifteen years as a promising alternative to the segregated special classroom. This concept allows the child to receive instruction individually or in small groups in a special room with a specially trained teacher. The student usually leaves the regular classroom for at least one daily period in the resource room, and at the end of instruction returns to the regular classroom.

According to Hammill and Bartel (1982), three variations of the resource room model predominate:

1. The *categorical resource room,* which is open only to those students in the school who have been classified in a specific special education category, such as retarded, emotionally disturbed, or learning disabled.

2. The *noncategorical resource* room, in which referred children are not labeled by category, but purely on the basis of instructional, emotional, or behavioral needs. Thus, even gifted children can receive services here.

3. The *itinerant program,* in which mobile resource rooms and teachers travel to various schools in the system to serve the needs of either labeled or nonlabeled students.

Miller and Sabatino (1978) report a fourth variation, the *teacher consultant model.* In this variation, the resource room teacher does not serve special needs children directly, but instead works to remediate their learning needs by improving regular teachers' skills in the regular classroom. In comparing the consultant model with the categorical resource room model, Miller and Sabatino found that academic performance gains for special needs children were equivalent.

A good deal of research has been done on the effectiveness of the resource room (Glavin, Quay, Annesley, & Werry, 1971; Reger & Koppmann, 1971; Sabatino, 1971, 1972) and generally the evidence is quite favorable (Miller & Sabatino, 1978). O'Connor, Stuck and Wyne (1979), for example, identified elementary school pupils who were a year or more behind in reading or math, and who spent low percentages of time attending to their work in the regular classroom. Half of these children were randomly assigned to participate in an intensive resource room program directed at increasing on-task behaviors, while the other half acted as controls. Twenty-four weeks later, the children receiving resource room help spent significantly more time attending to their work and achieved at significantly higher levels in reading and math than did the children who had not attended the resource room. The resource program also seems not to lower LD students' peer acceptance or self-concept below that they experience when placed in the regular classroom alone (Prillaman, 1981; Sheare, 1978), and it may enhance teacher perceptions of academic progress and personal-social adjustment (Quinn & Wilson, 1977).

Pupil gains, integration with typical children, and lowered stigma (in the noncategorical resource room) suggest that resource rooms have much to recommend them. In part, their combining the positive features of both special and regular classes has resulted in the rapid growth of these programs over the past ten years. Yet, there are still questions about resource rooms that need to be answered.

First of all, it is not clear yet if the gains made by children in the resource room wash out after they no longer receive this service. Studies report that at times, gains made by LD children in the resource room are successfully maintained on their return to the regular classroom (O'Connor, Stuck, & Wyne, 1979), and at other times are not (Ito, 1980). These studies suggest that the resource room is not a magic solution and that learning disabled students are likely to need continued, long-term support.

Second, there is a question as to what exactly about resource rooms is responsible for the academic and behavioral gains shown by students. Is it the resource room concept itself, the nature of the particular program and instruction in the room, enhanced regular teacher attitudes, or the qualified special education teacher?

In conclusion, the resource room is an organizational characteristic of the school setting that seems to be a beneficial service delivery approach to the learning disabled student. Its strength is in the fact that children can receive support for their learning problems without having to leave their peers in the school mainstream.

Organization of Instruction

Classroom teachers use a myriad of approaches to deliver instructional services to students, and different classrooms have different instructional aims and organizations. With respect to resource rooms, some focus on academic skills and remove the general education teacher from this responsibility. Others support and supplement the general academic skills that are taught in the regular classroom. Still others focus on the underlying skills thought to be prerequisites for academic learning, such as eye-hand coordination and auditory discrimination. Some resource rooms focus on counseling students, or function as a place for peer tutoring. Each of these rooms, though called a resource room, actually organizes the child's instruction in very different ways.

Elizabeth Prescott Jones conducted important research on providing instruction to children in the classroom setting. She focused specifically on the "goodness of fit" between a particular child and a particular program (Jones, 1974). She conceptualized approaches to instruction in particular programs in terms of teacher-directed group activities, teacher-directed individual activities, free play situations (where children can choose among all activities available), and free choice situations (where children are free to choose their activity but only from those that have been prepared by the teacher). Jones feels that presenting and organizing instruction in closed (teacher-directed) and open (free choice) approaches are both appropriate. Which approach to use is determined by matching the needs and characteristics of the child with the benefits and drawbacks of each approach (Jones, 1974).

The teacher's manner of organizing instruction can significantly impact students' academic and personal growth. In the late 1960s and early 1970s, replacing the traditional, teacher-directed approach with one where the teacher was a facilitator of students' self-paced, self-initiated learning was in vogue. This *open-education* instructional system was expected to foster more creativity and psychological well-being (happiness, self-esteem, lowered anxiety), and yet be as effective as the traditional approach in academic achievement (Lerner, 1981). However, study after study proved just the opposite — psychological well-being was not superior in the open-education classroom, and achievement in reading, mathematics, and other subjects was inferior to that in the traditional classroom (Bell, Sipursky, & Switzer, 1976; Bennett, 1976; Ward & Barcher, 1975; Wright, 1975). Lerner (1981) and others believe that students in traditional classes fare better because they spend more time working directly on academic tasks instead of being less goal-oriented, waiting for teacher attention, and interacting socially with peers. Time on task, whether in the classroom or on homework, is one of the most powerful predictors of achievement in all areas (Wolff, 1977). More traditional organization of instruction may benefit learning disabled students who require consistent teacher direction to focus attention appropriately, remain on task, and comprehend and remember what they have been taught.

Human Characteristics

The character of an environment depends in part on the attitudes and behaviors of its members. The most important members of the typical school environment are, of course, the classroom teacher and the students in the classroom. In this section we will look at those attributes of the classroom teacher and peers that have been shown to have an important impact on the academic and social behavior of the child in the classroom. We will find that teacher-student interactions are more numerous, positive, and of higher quality in the special classroom with special education teachers and lower with regular education teachers in normal classrooms. This is paralleled by teacher attitudes. Males, lower socioeconomic status children, minorities, and low-achieving students generally experience less favorable interactions with their classroom teachers. We also find that learning disabled children have difficulty drawing positive responses from and establishing friendships with peers.

Such teacher and peer factors may be important reasons for LD students' generally poor self-concepts. Summer workshops, inservice presentations, cross-age and peer-tutoring, and cooperative class projects are possibilities for modifying the attitudes of teachers and peers toward the learning disabled student.

Teacher Characteristics

A wide range of variables affects teachers' attitudes, expectations, and behaviors with regard to special children. Most studies conclude that many regular classroom teachers are less than accepting of children with special learning needs, particularly when these children are mainstreamed into their regular classrooms.

Attitudes Toward Special Children. Much of the recent research regarding teachers' attitudes toward students with special needs is derived from the impetus for mainstreaming such children into the regular classroom. A great deal of the success of such an effort hinges on the attitudes that teachers have toward these children. Therefore, specific information on teachers' attitudes about special needs children can help educators plan for predictable problems in regular classroom placements.

The general drift of these studies suggests that regular classroom teachers are less than accepting of special children introduced into their classes (Alexander & Strain, 1978; Bryan & Pearl, 1979). Special education teachers appear to have more favorable attitudes toward exceptional children, particularly with regard to mainstreaming these children into the regular classroom (Moore & Fine, 1978; Parish et al., 1977). Regular classroom teachers are more hesitant to accept an exceptional child into the regular classroom (Alexander & Strain, 1978; Bryan & Pearl, 1979); they generally accept those children with milder handicapping conditions more easily (Panda & Bartel, 1972).

Teacher-Student Interaction. Generally, teacher-student interactions appear to be more numerous, more positive, and of higher quality when the learning disabled child is in a special classroom with a special teacher (Dembo et al., 1978). Learning disabled children do not fare nearly as well in the mainstream. Chapman, Larsen, and Parker (1979), for example, analyzed the interactions of teachers and students of 110 first grade students in two middle class surburban schools. The interactions were monitored for seven hours per week for the first thirteen weeks of the school year. The data analysis revealed that the learning disordered children, who comprised approximately 15 percent of the children studied, received more teacher criticism concerning classroom procedures and warnings about their behavior than did their nondisabled peers.

Bryan (1978) found similar results in a series of studies that closely examined the social and verbal interactions of learning disabled children in the regular classroom setting. She reports that kindergarten through sixth grade learning disabled boys are not significantly different from their peers in the amount of time they spend interacting with teachers or peers in the classroom. Although they receive the same amount of praise and encouragement from the regular class teacher, they are given twice as much criticism and punishment as nondisabled boys. Apparently, regular class teacher attitudes and teacher-student interaction patterns are less than optimal for the learning disabled child. The teacher's attitudes are reflected in his or her nonverbal behavior and are shaped by such additional factors as student sex, social class, and achievement level.

Teacher Nonverbal Behavior. Nonverbal behavior refers to those aspects of communication between people that do not involve written or spoken words. *Body language* is the everyday term for this nonverbal communication. Research conducted on the influence of teachers' nonverbal behavior in the classroom has found that teachers communicate positive and negative judgments to children through facial expressions, body movements, and posture (Brophy & Good, 1974; Richey & Richey, 1978). These in turn impact students' self-esteem (Brophy & Good, 1974), their judgments of teacher performance and preference (Chaikin et al., 1978), and most likely classmates' attitudes toward them.

Learning disabled students are relatively isolated in their classrooms. This lower social status is highly correlated with teacher preferences for these children (Garrett & Crump, 1980). Bryan (1974) demonstrated one nonverbal way in which teachers communicate these preferences to other students: they ignore the verbal initiations of LD students significantly more often than the initiations of good learners. Likewise, Lyon (1977) found that pupils whose social-personal attributes were rated low by the teacher received significantly greater amounts of negative nonverbal behaviors from the teacher, such as avoiding eye contact, frowning, and lack of physical contact or encouragement. Other students take note of these teacher behaviors and adjust their attitudes about the LD child's social desirability accordingly (Foley, 1979).

Since students who are perceived as less desirable by the classroom teacher seem to receive more negative nonverbal behavior from the teacher, and since regular classroom teachers generally have less favorable attitudes toward handicapped children, the influence of teacher nonverbal behavior on learning disabled students' attitudes about themselves and their classmates' attitudes toward them is important. We know that children who give more positive, nonverbal behaviors to teachers are more often liked by teachers and judged to be brighter (Good & Brophy, 1972). Unfortunately, many LD students are not likely to initiate positive nonverbal interactions so as to positively alter teachers' attitudes and behaviors toward them. Hopefully, additional research will further clarify these interactions, and explain what the long–term consequences of negative nonverbal behavior from the classroom teacher mean for a mainstreamed, learning disabled child.

Sex Differences. The gender of the student influences both the quality and the quantity of the interaction between student and teacher (Washington, 1979). In both elementary and secondary schools, boys are disciplined more and receive more teacher approval and criticism than girls. Teachers also are more likely to use harsh or angry tones when talking to boys than with girls regarding equivalent misbehavior in the classroom (Brophy & Good, 1974).

Good and Brophy (1978) maintain that the disruptive behavior of boys is responsible for bringing them extra teacher criticism, rather than an overt sex bias on the part of the teacher. Another explanation they offer is that teachers generally interact more (both positively and negatively) with boys because boys stand out more in the classroom and provide more intense stimuli for teachers (Brophy & Good, 1974). Regardless of the reason, this factor is likely to play a role in teachers' interactions with learning disabled children, because the majority are boys.

Social Class and Race Differences. Social class and race differences in teacher-student interactions have also been observed. These factors are relevant to learning disabilities because socioculturally different children are known to have more of the characteristics associated with learning disabilities than other groups. Teachers give more praise, rewards, approval, support, and nonverbal reinforcement to middle-class children, whereas they neglect, punish, and misunderstand lower-class children, especially boys (Brophy & Good, 1974). Crowl and MacGinitie (1974), for example, found that experienced white teachers listening to taped responses assigned significantly higher grades to the responses to school questions given by white than black boys, even though the black and white boys gave identical answers.

Achievement Differences. Most research indicates that teacher behavior toward high- and low-achieving students differs in the quality, rather than the frequency, of interaction. Higher-achieving students are more active participants in the classroom and receive more positive teacher contact and feedback. Teachers smile, nod, maintain eye contact, and lean forward toward the child more often when they are told that the child is a high achiever, and show far fewer of these behaviors when they are told the child is a lower achiever (Good

& Brophy, 1978). The latter situation, of course, is often the case for the LD child who is less mature in learning skills.

Peer Characteristics

Teachers are only part of the human aspect of the classroom setting. Peer relationships are also important in the interaction of learning disabled children and school settings.

Tanis Bryan's research in this area indicates that a significant number of learning disabled children experience difficulty in drawing positive responses from others and in establishing friendships with peers (Bryan, 1978). In one study a sociometric technique was administered in twenty fourth and fifth grade classrooms in which there were twenty-five mainstreamed, learning disabled children (Bryan, 1976). The results indicated that learning disabled girls received a greater number of social rejection votes from peers than comparison children, and very few votes in social attraction. Many other researchers confirm these findings (Parish, Ohlsen, & Parish, 1978; Scranton & Ryckman, 1979). At times LD students seem aware of their lower status (Horowitz, 1981), and at other times they do not (Bruininks, 1978b).

Why do peers react less favorably to their learning disabled classmates? Many LD children have attributes that make social communication and friendships difficult. These include comprehension and oral production difficulties, pragmatic speech weaknesses, social imperceptions, learned helplessness, immaturity, inability to put themselves in another's place, and poor social ingratiation tactics. Rejection of learning disabled children may also be a function of the labeling process. When classmates are aware that these students have been labeled by the school as academically less adequate than others, the social status of these children can be negatively affected.

Improving Teacher–Peer Interactions

Clearly the social status of the learning disabled child is intertwined with behaviors and attitudes of the teacher and other students in the classroom. Explanations of his or her behaviors are to be found not inside the child, but in the interactions of the child and, in this instance, the human characteristics of the school setting.

Steps can be taken to improve teacher and peer classroom interactions with the learning disabled child. These steps involve modifying setting attributes so that the child's interactions in the setting become more positive. The goal of these modifications is to enable the learning disabled child, the classroom teacher, and peers to better appreciate and deal with individual differences in others.

Alexander and Strain (1978) reviewed a number of studies that are optimistic about changing teacher attitudes and interactions with the special child through education and exposure. Summer workshops, inservice presentations, and modifications of teacher training programs to include courses in special education are all effective, providing the courses and workshops are appropriate and of high quality.

Changing attitudes of peers toward learning disabled and other special needs classmates has not been researched well. However, several techniques offer exciting possibilities for changing peer attitudes. These include group contingency techniques, where the cooperative work of the group, including the learning disabled student, is necessary to ensure success at a task. Other possibilities include peer and cross-age tutoring, awarding of points for helpfulness to classmates, and affective education strategies that include the learning disabled child as an integral part of the classroom group.

Summary

Learning disabled children's behavior is best comprehended by remembering that they exist in settings with definite organizational and interactional patterns. The school and classroom settings have particular importance for learning disabled children because it is in this context that they are identified as learning disabled.

Characteristics of the physical, organizational, and human environments of school and classroom settings can affect children positively and negatively. Background noise and visual distractions are the most important ambient characteristic of the physical school environment. Their detrimental effects apply to all children equally; the learning disabled child tends not to be affected to any significantly greater extent. Small schools seem to promote greater participation and feelings of responsibility among students. Open-space schools, though providing opportunities to develop students' self-direction in learning, have a decreased amount of structure and consistency, which many learning disabled children require. Studies in classroom design and seating arrangement show that children seated near the front and center of the room interact more with the teacher. More traditional instructional approaches benefit the LD child by giving more time on tasks.

The most direct effects on the LD child of organizational attributes of schools lie in classification and placement of these children in special classes. Unlike other groups of special needs students, LD students generally benefit from separate special classes. However, general concerns with classification practices and segregation have resulted in many more learning disabled students being mainstreamed or provided with supportive services in a resource room for part of the school day. This enables special students to enjoy far more interactions with their nondisabled peers and reduces their chances of being stigmatized, which often accompanies placement in a special classroom.

Human attributes of the school setting are the attitudes, beliefs, and characteristics of teachers and peers. Mainstreamed, learning disabled children are not viewed in a particularly positive manner by most teachers and classroom peers. They receive more criticism and punishment from the teacher, and are relegated by their peers to a low status in the classroom's social structure.

Attributes of the school setting may interact with a student's attributes to contribute to the behaviors defined as learning disabilities. School settings, therefore, are important factors in "making it or breaking it" for the learning disabled individual. Evaluation of physical, organizational, and human school setting attributes gives clues regarding the ways these settings can be modified to provide healthy and productive change for the learning disabled child.

Suggestions for Further Study

1. Psychologists and educators have long argued about how much of human behavior comes from within and how much is determined by the particular setting the person is in. What do you think? Is it true that we are what we are and that most of our behavior is determined by our personality characteristics? Or does much of what we do depend on particular circumstances? The issue is unfortunately not this simple. Psychologists and educators are finding out that personality attributes interact with situation or setting attributes to determine human behavior. These interactions are complex and by no means fully understood. To learn more about this, read Endler and Magnusson (1976) or Mischel (1968).

2. The field of person-environment study is new and exciting. It combines psychologists, urban planners, ecologists, environmentalists, architects, anthropologists, sociologists, educators, and other social scientists interested in learning about the relationship between persons and the environments they inhabit. It has even produced a new field of study in psychology called *environmental and ecological psychology*. There are a number of excellent texts in this area, including Bell, Fischer, and Loomis (1978) and Proshansky, Ittelson, and Rivlin (1976). There are also excellent review articles, particularly one by Stokols (1977).

3. The literature and research on open schools is vast. You might want to investigate more fully the distinction between open education and open space schools. Are open schools as popular today as they were ten or fifteen years ago? If not, why do you think their popularity has diminished? Excellent reviews by Armstrong (1975), George (1975), and Martin and Pavan (1975) might help you find answers to these questions.

4. Getzels (1974) provides a fascinating account of how the design of schools and classrooms reflect the times and, in particular, the way society in each of those times views the learner. What was the design of the school you attended as an elementary school student? High school student? When were these schools built? What does Getzels say about how educators and architects viewed the educational enterprise during the time your school was built?

5. Santrock's (1976) study noted that children persisted longer on a task when their surroundings were "happy" rather than "neutral" or "sad." Several educators feel that the aesthetic surroundings of the school make a big difference in the enthusiasm of students. Robert Sommer, in particular, has been a vocal spokesman for this view. You might want to read several of his works, especially *Tight Spaces: Hard Architecture and How to Humanize It* (1974).

6. The classification and labeling of children has broad and important effects not only on the children labeled, but on their parents, teachers, peers, and all of society. An excellent place to look for more information on the effects of the labeling and classification process is Nicolas Hobb's *Issues in the Classification of Children* (1975b).

7. Rosenthal and Jacobson's famous study on teacher expectancy effects has been criticized often since its publication in 1968. If you are interested in the design and analysis of research in education and psychology, learn why this study has been criticized so severely. A good place to start is Alexander and Strain (1978) and Dusek (1975). In light of these criticisms, do you think teacher expectancy effects exist at all? If so, why have they been so difficult to study? Rosenthal and Jacobson were looking at positive expectations (rapid learners), whereas special education labels almost always have negative connotations. Do you think this makes a difference? Why?

8. Research into the effects of teacher characteristics on student learning and behavior is vast and diversified. For more information, consult several of the interesting and readable books by the two most prominent researchers in this area, Jere E. Brophy and Thomas L. Good. An excellent place to start is Good and Brophy's *Looking in Classrooms* (1978).

9. Nonverbal aspects of communication have recently gathered a great deal of attention. To learn more about nonverbal communication, or body language, consult an introductory social or environmental psychology textbook and look up nonverbal communication or personal space, or look through the *Journal of Nonverbal Behavior*.

References

Abercrombie, M. L. J., Davis, J. R., and Shackel, B. Pilot study of version movements of eyes in cerebral palsied and other children. *Vision Research,* 1963, *3,* 135–153.

Abikoff, H. Cognitive training interventions in children: Review of a new approach. *Journal of Learning Disabilities,* 1979, *12,* 123–135.

Abrams, A. L. Delayed and irregular maturation versus minimal brain injury. Recommendations for a change in current nomenclature. *Clinical Pediatrics,* 1968, *7,* 344–349.

Abrams, J. C. More on interdisciplinary cooperation. *Journal of Learning Disabilities,* 1976, *9,* 603–604.

Abrams, J. C., and Kaslow, F. Learning disability and family dynamics. *Journal of Clinical Child Psychology,* 1976, *5,* 35–40.

Adams, N. Birth order: A critical review. *Sociometry,* 1972, *35 (3),* 411–439.

Adams, R., Lerner, L., and Anderson, J. Children with learning problems: A developmental view for parents. *Journal of Learning Disabilities,* 1979, *12,* 315–319.

Adams, R. S., and Biddle, B. J. *Realities of Teaching: Explorations With Video Tape.* New York: Holt, Rinehart and Winston, 1970.

Adelman, H. S. The not so specific learning disability population. *Exceptional Children,* 1971, *37,* 528–533.

————. The concept of intrinsic motivation: Implications for practice and research with the learning disabled. *Learning Disability Quarterly,* 1978, *1,* 43–54.

Adelman, H. S., and Chaney, L. A. Impact of motivation on task performance of children with and without psychoeducational problems. *Journal of Learning Disabilities,* 1982, *15,* 242–244.

Adey, W. R., Kado, R. T., McIlwain, J. T., and Walter, D. O. The role of neuronal elements in regional cerebral impedance changes in alerting, orienting and discriminative responses. *Experimental Neurology,* 1966, *15,* 490–510.

Adler, S. Megavitamin treatment for behaviorally disturbed and learning disabled children. *Journal of Learning Disabilities,* 1979, *12,* 678–681.

Adler-Grinberg, D., and Stark, L. Eye movements, scanpaths, and dyslexia. *American Journal of Optometry and Physiological Optics,* 1978, *55,* 557–570.

Alajouanine, T., and Lhermitte, F. Acquired aphasia in children. *Brain,* 1965, *88,* 653–662.

Alberti, R. D., and Emmons, M. L. *Your Perfect Right: A Guide to Assertive Behavior.* 3rd ed. San Luis Obispo, Calif.: Impact Publishers, 1978.

Alessi, G. J. Personal communication. 1979.

————. Behavioral observation for the school psychologist: Responsive-discrepancy model. *School Psychology Review,* 1980, *9,* 31–45.

Alexander, C., and Strain, P. S. A review of educators' attitudes toward handicapped children and the concept of mainstreaming. *Psychology in the Schools,* 1978, *15,* 390–396.

Alexander, J. E., ed. *Teaching Reading.* Boston: Little, Brown, 1980.

Allen, G. J., Chinsky, J. M., Larsen, S. W., Lochman, J. E., and Selinger, H. V. *Community Psychology and the Schools: A Behaviorally Oriented Multilevel Preventive Approach.* New York: John Wiley & Sons, 1976.

Allen, J. E. *The Right to Read — Target for the 70s.* Washington, D.C.: U.S. Department of Health, Education, and Welfare, Office of Education, 1969.

Alley, G., and Deshler, D. *Teaching the Learning Disabled Adolescent: Strategies and Methods.* Denver: London Publishing Co., 1979.

Alley, G. R., Deshler, D. D., and Warner, M. A Bayesian approach to the use of teacher judgment of learning characteristics in identification of students with learning disabilities at the secondary level. Paper presented at the Annual International Conference, Council for Exceptional Children, Atlanta, Georgia, 1977.

Allington, R. L. If they don't read much, how they ever gonna get good? *Journal of Reading,* 1977, *21,* 57–61.

Allington, R. L., Gormley, K., and Truex, S. Poor and normal readers achievement on visual tasks involving high frequency, low discriminability words. *Journal of Learning Disabilities,* 1976, *9,* 292–296.

Amante, D., Margules, P. H., Hartman, D. M., Storey, D. B., and Weber, L. J. The epidemiological distribution of CNS dysfunction. *Journal of Social Issues,* 1970, *26 (4),* 105–136.

American Academy of Pediatrics: Committee on Nutrition. Megavitamin therapy for childhood psychoses and learning disabilities. *Pediatrics,* 1976, *58,* 910–912.

American Psychological Association. *Standards for Educational and Psychological Tests.* Washington, D.C.: American Psychological Association, 1974.

Ames, L. B. Learning disabilities: The developmental point of view. In *Progress in Learning Disabilities.* Vol. 1, edited by H. R. Myklebust. New York: Grune & Stratton, 1968.

————. Learning disabilities: Time to check our roadmaps? *Journal of Learning Disabilities,* 1977, *10,* 328–330.

Amoriell, W. J. Reading achievement and the ability to manipulate visual and auditory stimuli. *Journal of Learning Disabilities,* 1979, *12,* 562–564.

Amos, K. Competency testing: Will the LD student be included? *Exceptional Children,* 1980, *47,* 194–197.

Anderson, D. W. *Teaching Handwriting.* Washington, D.C.: National Education Association, 1968.

Anderson, J. M., Milner, R. D. G., and Strich, S. J. Effects of neonatal hypoglycaemia on the nervous system: A pathological study. *Journal of Neurology, Neurosurgery, and Psychiatry,* 1967, *30,* 295–310.

Anderson, K., Richards, H., and Hallahan, D. Piagetian task performance of learning disabled children. *Journal of Learning Disabilities,* 1980, *13,* 501–505.

Annett, M. The distribution of manual asymmetry. *British Journal of Psychology,* 1972, *63,* 343–358.

——. Laterality of childhood hemiplegia and the growth of speech and intelligence. *Cortex,* 1973, *9,* 4–33.

Armstrong, D. G. Open space vs. self-contained. *Educational Leadership,* 1975, *32,* 291–295.

Arter, J. A., and Jenkins, J. R. Examining the benefits and prevalence of modality considerations in special education. *Journal of Special Education,* 1977, *11,* 281–298.

Ashlock, R. B. *Error Patterns in Computation: A Semi-programmed Approach.* Columbus, Ohio: Charles E. Merrill, 1972.

——. *Error Patterns in Computations: A Semi-programmed approach.* 2nd ed. Columbus, Ohio: Charles E. Merrill, 1976.

Aukerman, R. C. *Reading in the Secondary School Classroom.* New York: McGraw-Hill, 1972.

Ayres, A. J. *Sensory Integration and Learning Disorders.* Los Angeles: Western Psychological Services, 1972a.

——. Improving academic scores through sensory integration. *Journal of Learning Disabilities,* 1972b, *5,* 338–343.

——. *The Development of Sensory Integrative Theory and Practice: A Collection of Works of A. Jean Ayres.* Dubuque: Kendall Hunt, 1974.

——. Sensorimotor foundations of academic ability. In *Perception and Learning Disabilities in Children.* Vol. 2, edited by W. M. Cruickshank and D. P. Hallahan. Syracuse: Syracuse University Press, 1975.

——. Learning disabilities and the vestibular system. *Journal of Learning Disabilities,* 1978, *11,* 18–29.

Bachara, G. H., and Zaba, J. N. Learning disabilities and juvenile delinquency. *Journal of Learning Disabilities,* 1978, *11,* 242–246.

Baddeley, A. D. Effects of acoustic and semantic similarity on short-term paired associate learning. *British Journal of Psychology,* 1970, *61,* 335–343.

Baird, L. L. Big school, small school: A critical examination of the hypothesis. *Journal of Educational Psychology,* 1969, *60,* 253–260.

Baker, B. L., Brightman, A. J., Carroll, N. B., Heifetz, B. B., and Henshaw, S. P. *Steps to Independence: A Skills Training Series for Children with Special Needs (Speech and Language: Level 1; Speech and Language: Level 2).* Champaign, Ill.: Research Press, 1978.

Baker, B. L., Brightman, A. J., Heifetz, L. J., and Murphy, D. M. *Steps to Independence: A Skills Training Series for Children with Special Needs (Early Self-Help Skills; Intermediate Self-Help Skills; Advanced Self-Help Skills; Behavior Problems).* Champaign, Ill.: Research Press, 1976.

——. *Steps to Independence: A Skills Training Series for Children with Special Needs (Toilet Training).* Champaign, Ill.: Research Press, 1977.

Bakker, D. J. Temporal order, meaningfulness, and reading ability. *Perceptual and Motor Skills,* 1967, *24,* 1027–1030.

——. Temporal order perception and reading retardation. In *Specific Reading Disability; Advances in Theory and Method,* edited by D. J. Bakker and P. Satz. Rotterdam: Rotterdam University Press, 1970.

——. *Temporal order in disturbed reading; Developmental and neuropsychological aspects in normal and reading retarded children.* Rotterdam: Rotterdam University Press, 1972.

——. Hemispheric differences and reading strategies: two dyslexias? *Bulletin of the Orton Society,* 1979, *29,* 84–100.

——. Hemisphere specific models and the therapies of dyslexia. Colloquium presented to the Division of Special Education and Rehabilitation, Syracuse University, April 21, 1980.

Bakker, D. J., and de Wit, J. Perceptual and cortical immaturity in developmental dyslexia. In *Brain Function and Reading Disabilities,* edited by L. Tarnopol and M. Tarnopol. Baltimore: University Park Press, 1977.

Bakker, D. J., Smink, T., and Reitsma, P. Ear dominance and reading ability. *Cortex,* 1973, *9,* 301–312.

Bakker, D. J., Teunissen, J., and Bosch, J. Development of laterality-reading patterns. *The Neuropsychology of Learning Disorders: Theoretical Approaches,* edited by R. M.

Knights and D. J. Bakker. Baltimore: University Park Press, 1976.

Bakker, D. J., Van der Vlugt, H., and Claushuis, M. The reliability of dichotic ear asymmetry in normal children. *Neuropsychologia,* 1978, *16,* 753–757.

Baldauf, R. J. Parental intervention. In *Progress in Learning Disabilities.* Vol. 3, edited by H. Myklebust. New York: Grune & Stratton, 1975.

Balow, B., and Blomquist, M. Young adults ten to fifteen years after severe reading disability. *Elementary School Journal,* 1965, *66,* 44–48.

Balow, I. H. The effects of homogeneous grouping in seventh grade arithmetic. *Arithmetic Teacher,* 1964, *11,* 186–191.

Bandura, A. *Principles of Behavior Modification.* New York: Holt, Rinehart and Winston, 1969.

——. *Aggression: A Social Learning Analysis.* Englewood Cliffs, N.J.: Prentice-Hall, 1973.

Bandura, A., Grusec, J. E., and Menlove, F. L. Observational learning as a function of symbolization and incentive set. *Child Development,* 166, *37,* 499–506.

Bandura, A., Jeffery, R. W., and Gajdos, E. Generalizing change through participant modeling with self-directed mastery. *Behavior Research and Therapy,* 1975, *13,* 141–152.

Bannatyne, A. The color phonics system. In *The Disabled Reader: Education of the Dyslexic Child,* edited by J. Money. Baltimore: Johns Hopkins Press, 1966.

——. *Language, Reading and Learning Disabilities.* Springfield, Ill.: Charles C. Thomas, 1971.

——. Diagnosis: A note on recategorization of the WISC scaled scores. *Journal of Learning Disabilities,* 1974, *7,* 272–274.

Baratz, J. C., and Shuy, R. D., eds. *Teaching Black Children to Read.* Washington, D.C.: Center for Applied Linguistics, 1969.

Barker, R. G. *Ecological Psychology.* Stanford: Stanford University Press, 1968.

——. *Habitats, Environments and Human Behavior.* San Francisco: Jossey-Bass, 1978.

Barker, R. G., and Gump, P. *Big School, Small School.* Stanford: Stanford University Press, 1964.

Barker, R. G., and Wright, J. F. *Midwest and Its Children.* Hamden, Conn.: Row Peterson, 1955. Archon Books, 1971.

Barkley, R. A. A review of stimulant drug research with hyperkinetic children. *Journal of Child Psychology and Psychiatry,* 1977, *18,* 137–165.

Barkley, R. A., and Cunningham, C. E. Do stimulant drugs improve the academic performance of hyperkinetic children? *Clinical Pediatrics,* 1978, *17,* 85–92.

Barnes, A. B., Colton, T., Gundersen, J., Noller, K. L., Tilley, B. C., Strama, T., Townsend, D. E., Hatab, P., and O'Brien, P. C. Fertility and outcome of pregnancy in women exposed in utero to diethylstilbestrol. *New England Journal of Medicine,* 1980, *302,* 609–613.

Barney, L. Problems associated with the reading of arithmetic. *The Arithmetic Teacher,* 1972, *19,* 131–133.

Barsch, R. H. *A Movigenic Curriculum.* Madison: Wisconsin State Department of Public Instruction, 1965, No. 25.

——. *Achieving Perceptual Motor Efficiency.* Seattle: Special Child Publications, 1967.

——. *Enriching Perception and Cognition.* Seattle: Special Child Publications, 1969.

——. (Ray H. Barsch.) In *Teaching Children with Learning Disabilities: Personal Perspectives,* edited by J. M. Kauffman and D. P. Hallahan. Columbus, Ohio: Charles E. Merrill, 1976.

Bartel, N. R. Problems in mathematics achievement. In *Teaching Children with Learning and Behavior Problems,* edited by D. D. Hammill and N. R. Bartel. Boston: Allyn & Bacon, 1978.

Bartel, N. R., Grill, J., and Bryden, D. N. Language characteristics of black children: Implications for assessment. *Journal of School Psychology,* 1973, *11,* 351–364.

Bartel, N. R., and Bryden, D. N. Problems in language development. In *Teaching Children with Learning and Behavior Problems*, edited by D. D. Hammill and N. R. Bartel. Boston: Allyn & Bacon, 1978.

Bateman, B. D. An educator's view of a diagnostic approach to learning disorders. In *Learning Disorders*. Vol. 1, edited by J. Hellmuth. Seattle: Special Child Publications, 1965.

————. *Interpretation of the 1961 Illinois Test of Psycholinguistic Abilities*. Seattle: Special Child Publications, 1968.

Bateman, B. The efficacy of an auditory and a visual method of first grade reading instruction with auditory and visual learners. In *Perception and Reading*, edited by H. K. Smith. Newark, Del.: International Reading Association, 1968.

————. Educational implications of Minimal Brain Dysfunction. *Reading Teacher*, 1974, *27*, 662–668.

————. Teaching reading to learning disabled children. In *Theory and Practice of Early Reading*, edited by L. B. Resnick and P. A. Weaver. Hillsdale, N.J.: Lawrence Erlbaum, 1977.

Bateman, B., and Frankel, H. Special education and the pediatrician. *Journal of Learning Disabilities*, 1972, *5*, 178–186.

Bauer, R. H. Recall after a short delay and acquisition in learning disabled and nondisabled children. *Journal of Learning Disabilities*, 1979, *12*, 596–607.

Baumrind, D. Summary of parents as leaders interview by H. Yahrais. In *Families Today, a Research Sampler on Families and Children*. Vol. 1. Washington, D.C.: U.S. Department of Health, Education and Welfare, National Institute of Mental Health Science Monographs, 1980.

————. The contributions of the family to development of competence in children. *Schizophrenia Bulletin*, 1975, *14*, 12–37.

————. Socialization and instrumental competence in young children. In *The Young Child: Reviews of Research*. Vol. 2, edited by W. W. Hartup. Washington, D.C.: National Association for the Education of Young Children, 1972.

Bayley, N. Size and body build of adolescents in relation to rate of skeletal maturing. *Child Development*, 1943, *14*, 47–89.

————. Consistency and variability in the growth of intelligence from birth to eighteen years. *Journal of Genetic Psychology*, 1949, *75*, 165–196.

————. Development of mental abilities. In *Carmichael's Manual of Child Psychology*. Vol. 1, edited by P. H. Mussen. New York: John Wiley & Sons, 1970.

Bayley, N., and Jones, M. C. Physical maturing among boys as related to behavior. In *Reading in Child Development*, edited by W. E. Martin and C. B. Stendler. New York: Harcourt, Brace & Co., 1955.

Bear, M., and Fedio, P. Quantitative analysis of interictal behavior in temporal lobe epilepsy. *Archives of Neurology*, 1977, *34*, 454–467.

Beard, R. R., and Wertheim, G. A. Behavioral impairment associated with small doses of carbon monoxide. *American Journal of Public Health*, 1967, *57*, 2012–2022.

Beardslee, E. C. Teaching computational skills with a calculator. In *Developing Computational Skills: 1978 Yearbook*, edited by M. Suydam and R. Reys. Reston, Va.: National Council of Teachers of Mathematics, 1978.

Beck, L., Langford, W. S., MacKay, M., and Sum, G. Childhood chemotherapy and later drug abuse and growth curve: A follow-up study of 30 adolescents. *American Journal of Psychiatry*, 1975, *132*, 436–438.

Becker, W. C. Consequences of different kinds of parental discipline. In *Review of Child Development Research*. Vol. 1, edited by M. L. Hoffman and L. W. Hoffman. New York: Russell Sage Foundation, 1964.

Beeken, D., and Janzen, H. L. Behavioral mapping of student activity in open-area and traditional schools. *American Educational Research Journal*, 1978, *15*, 507–517.

Behrman, R. E., Fisher, D. E., and Paton, J. Air pollution in nurseries: Correlation with a decrease in oxygen-carrying capacity of hemoglobin. *Journal of Pediatrics*, 1971, *78*, 1050–1054.

Bell, A. E., Abrahamson, D. S., and McRae, K. N. Reading retardation: A 12 year prospective study. *Journal of Pediatrics*, 1977, *91*, 363–370.

Bell, A. E., Sipursky, M. A., and Switzer, F. Informal or open-area education in relation to achievement and personality. *British Journal of Educational Psychology*, 1976, *46*, 235–243.

Bell, P. A., Fischer, J. D., and Loomis, R. J. *Environmental Psychology*. Philadelphia: W. B. Saunders, 1978.

Bell, R. Q. Contributions of human infants to caregiving and social interaction. In *The Effect of the Infant on Its Caregiver*, edited by M. Lewis and L. A. Rosenblum. New York: Wiley-Interscience, 1974.

Bell, R. W., Miller, C. E., Ordy, J. M., and Rolstein, C. Effects of population density and living space upon neuroanatomy, neurochemistry, and behavior in the C57B1/10 mouse. *Journal of Comparative and Physiological Psychology*, 1971, *75*, 258–263.

Beller, E. K. Methods of language training and cognitive styles in lower-class children. Paper presented at the annual meeting of the American Educational Research Association, New York, February 1967.

Belmont, L., and Birch, H. G. Lateral dominance and right-left awareness in normal children. *Child Development*, 1963, *34*, 257–270.

————. Lateral dominance, lateral awareness, and reading disability. *Child Development*, 1965, *36*, 57–71.

Bender, L. A visual motor Gestalt test and its clinical use. *American Orthopsychiatry Association Research Monograph*, 1938, No. 3.

————. *Bulletin of the Orton Society*, 1963.

Bennett, N. *Teaching Styles and Pupil Progress*. Cambridge: Harvard University Press, 1976.

Benthul, H. F., Anderson, E. A., Utech, A. M., Biggy, M. V., and Bailey, B. L. *Spell Correctly*. Morristown, N.J.: Silver Burdette, 1974.

Benton, A. *Right-Left Discrimination and Finger Localization*. New York: Paul B. Hoeber, 1959.

————. Dyslexia in relation to form perception and directional sense. In *Reading Disability Progress and Research Needs in Dyslexia*, edited by J. Money. Baltimore: Johns Hopkins Press, 1962.

————. Minimal brain dysfunction from a neuropsychological point of view. *Annals of the New York Academy of Sciences*, 1973, *205*, 29–37.

————. The cognitive functioning of children with developmental dysphasia. In *Developmental Dysphasia*, edited by M. A. Wyke. New York: Academic Press, 1978.

Benton, C. D. Dyslexia and dominance: Some second thoughts. *Journal of Pediatric Ophthalmology*, 1969, *6*, 220–222.

————. Comment: The eye and learning disabilities. *Journal of Learning Disabilities*, 1973, *6*, 334–336.

Bentzen, F. Sex ratios in learning and behavior disorders. *American Journal of Orthopsychiatry*, 1963, *33*, 92–98.

Bereiter, C., and Engelmann, S. *Teaching Disadvantaged Children in the Preschool*. Englewood Cliffs, N.J.: Prentice-Hall, 1966.

Berg, R. C., and Wages, L. Group counseling with the adolescent learning disabled. *Journal of Learning Disabilities*, 1982, *15*, 276–277.

Bergan, J. R., and Tombari, M. L. The analysis of verbal interactions occurring during consultation. *Journal of School Psychology*, 1975, *13*, 209–226.

Berger, N. S. Why can't John read? Perhaps he's not a good listener. *Journal of Learning Disabilities*, 1978, *11*, 633–638.

Berlin, C. I., Hughes, L. F., Lowe-Bell, S. S., and Berlin, H. L. Dichotic right ear advantage in children 5 to 13. *Cortex*, 1973, *9*, 394–402.

Berman, A. LD resource materials: The great rip-off. *Journal of Learning Disabilities*, 1977, *10*, 261–263.

———. Parenting learning disabled children. *Journal of Clinical Child Psychology*, 1979, *8*, 245–249.

Berman, A., and Siegel, A. W. Adaptive and learning skills in juvenile delinquents: A neuropsychological analysis. *Journal of Learning Disabilities*, 1976, *9*, 583–590.

Bernal, E. M. A response to educational uses of tests with disadvantaged subjects. *American Psychologist*, 1975, *30*, 93–95.

Berne, E. *Games People Play*. New York: Grove Press, 1964.

Bernstein, B. Language and social class. *British Journal of Sociology*, 1960, *11*, 271–276.

Bersoff, D. N. Silk purses into sow's ears: The decline of psychological testing and a suggestion for its redemption. *American Psychologist*, 1973, *28*, 892–899.

Berstein, M. C. Reading methods and materials based on linguistic principles for basic and remedial instruction. *Academic Therapy Quarterly*, 1967, *2*, 149–154.

Bessell, H., and Palomares, U. *Human Development Program*. San Diego: Human Development Training Program, 1972.

Betchkel, J., ed. Reform high schools, says Carnegie. *The American School Board Journal*, 1980, *167*, 12.

Betts, E. A. *The Prevention and Correction of Reading Difficulties*. San Francisco: Row, 1936.

Bibace, R., and Hancock, K. Relationships between perceptual and conceptual cognitive processes. *Journal of Learning Disabilities*, 1969, *2*, 17–22.

Bijou, S. W. What psychology has to offer education — now. *Journal of Applied Behavior Analysis*, 1970, *3*, 65–71.

———. Environment and intelligence: A behavioral analysis. In *Intelligence: Genetic and Environmental Influences*, edited by R. Cancro. New York: Grune & Stratton, 1971.

Biklen, D. *The Syracuse Metropolitan Area Special Education Study*. Unpublished manuscript, Syracuse University, 1979.

Birch, H. G., and Belmont, L. Auditory-visual integration in normal and retarded readers. *American Journal of Orthopsychiatry*, 1964, *34*, 852–861.

———. Auditory-visual integration, intelligence, and reading ability in school children. *Perceptual and Motor Skills*, 1965, *20*, 295–305.

Birch, H. G., and Gussow, J. D. *Disadvantaged Children: Health, Nutrition, and School Failure*. New York: Harcourt, Brace & World, 1970.

Bireley, M., and Manley, E. The learning disabled student in a college environment: A report of Wright State University's program. *Journal of Learning Disabilities*, 1980, *13*, 7–10.

Black, F. W. Neurological dysfunction and reading disorders. *Journal of Learning Disabilities*, 1973, *6*, 313–316.

Blake, K. A., Aaron, I. E., and Westbrook, H. R. Learning of basal reading skills by mentally handicapped and nonmentally handicapped children. *Journal of Research and Development in Education*, 1969, *2* (2), 3–120.

Blank, M. *Teaching Language in the Preschool: A Dialogue Approach*. Columbus, Ohio: Charles E. Merrill, 1973.

Blank, M., and Bridger, W. H. Deficiencies in verbal labeling in retarded readers. *American Journal of Orthopsychiatry*, 1966, *36*, 840–847.

Blank, M., Weider, S., and Bridger, W. H. Verbal deficiencies in abstract thinking in early reading retardation. *American Journal of Orthopsychiatry*, 1968, *38*, 823–834.

Blatt, B. *Exodus from Pandemonium: Human Abuse and a Reformation of Public Policy*. Boston: Allyn & Bacon, 1970.

———. Public policy and the education of children with special needs. *Exceptional Children*, 1972, *38*, 537–545.

———. Bandwagons also go to funerals: Unmailed letters 1 and 2. *Journal of Learning Disabilities*, 1979, *12*, 222–224.

Bliesmer, E. P., and Yarborough, B. H.: A comparison of ten different beginning reading programs in first grade. *Phi Delta Kappan*, 1965, *46*, 500–504.

Block, J., Block, J. H., and Harrington, D. M. Some misgivings about the Matching Familiar Figures Test as a measure of reflection-impulsivity. *Developmental Psychology*, 1974, *10*, 611–632.

Bloom, L. *Language Development: Form and Function in Emerging Grammars*. Cambridge: MIT Press, 1970.

———. Language development review. In *Review of Child Development Research*. Vol. 4, edited by F. D. Horowitz. Chicago: University of Chicago Press, 1975.

———. LD Cubed. Paper presented at the meetings of the New York Association for the Learning Disabled. New York, December 1978.

Bloom, L., Lightbrown, P., and Hood, L. Structure and variation in child language. *Monographs of the Society for Research in Child Development*, 1975, *40* (2, Serial No. 60).

Boder, E. Developmental dyslexia: Prevailing diagnostic concepts and a new diagnostic approach. In *Progress in Learning Disabilities*. Vol. 2, edited by H. R. Myklebust. New York: Grune & Stratton, 1971.

———. Developmental dyslexia: A diagnostic approach based on three atypical reading-spelling patterns. *Developmental Medicine and Child Neurology*, 1973, *15*, 663–687.

Boehm, A. E., and Weinberg, R. A. *The Classroom Observer: A Guide for Developing Classroom Skills*. New York: Teachers College, 1977.

Boersma, F. J., Chapman, J. W., and Battle, J. Academic self-concept change in special education students: Some suggestions for interpreting self-concept scores. *Journal of Special Education*, 1979, *13*, 433–442.

Bogdan, R., and Taylor, S. J. *Introduction to Qualitative Research Methods*. New York: John Wiley & Sons, 1975.

Bogen, J. E., and Gazzaniga, M. S. Cerebral commissurotomy in man: Minor hemisphere dominance for certain visuo-spatial functions. *Journal of Neurosurgery*, 1965, *23*, 394–399.

Bolles, M. The basis of pertinence: A study of aments, dements, and normal children of the same mental age. *Archives of Psychology*, 1937, *30*(Serial No. 212).

Bond, L., and Dykstra, R. The cooperative research program in first grade reading instruction. *Reading Research Quarterly*, 1967, *2*.

Bond, G. L., and Tinker, M. A. *Reading Difficulties: Their Diagnosis and Correction*. 2nd ed. New York: Appleton-Century-Crofts, 1967.

Book, R. M. Identification of educationally at-risk children during the kindergarten year: A four-year follow-up study of group test performance. *Psychology in the Schools*, 1980, *17*, 153–158.

Borland, B. L., and Heckman, H. K. Hyperactive boys and their brothers. *Archives of General Psychiatry*, 1976, *33*, 669–675.

Bormuth, J. The cloze readability procedure. *Elementary English*, 1968, *45*, 429–436.

Bortner, M., Hertzig, M. D., and Birch, H. G. Neurological signs and intelligence in brain-damaged children. *Journal of Special Education*, 1972, *6*, 325–333.

Bower, E. M., ed. Early screening programs. *American Journal of Orthopsychiatry*, 1978, *48*, 1–186.

Bower, T. G. R. The visual world of infants. *Scientific American*, 1966, *215*, 80–92.

Boyd, J. E., and Bartel, N. R. Teaching children with reading problems. In *Teaching Children with Learning and Behavior Problems*, edited by D. D. Hammill and N. R. Bartel. Boston: Allyn & Bacon, 1978.

Bradley, R. H., and Caldwell, B. M. Screening the environment. *American Journal of Orthopsychiatry*, 1978, *48*, 114–130.

Bradley, R., Caldwell, B., and Elardo, R. Home environment, social status, and mental test performance. *Journal of Educational Psychology*, 1977, *69*, 697–701.

Braine, M. The ontogeny of English phrase structure: The first phase. *Language*, 1963, *39*, 1–13.

———. On two types of models of the internalization of grammars. In *The Ontogenesis of Grammar*, edited by D. Slobin. New York: Academic Press, 1971.

Brandon, S. Overactivity in children. *Journal of Psychosomatic Research*, 1971, *15*, 411–415.

Bremer, D. A., and Stein, J. A. Attention and distractibility during reading in hyperactive boys. *Journal of Abnormal Child Psychology*, 1976, *4*, 381–387.

Brenner, L. *Training Fun with Letters.* Johnston, Pa.: Mafex Association, 1967.

Brenner, M. W., Gillman, S., Zangwill, O. L., and Farrell, M. Visuo-motor disability in school children. *British Medical Journal,* 1967, *4,* 259–262.

Brian, C. R., and Goodenough, F. L. The relative potency of color and perception at various ages. *Journal of Experimental Psychology,* 1929, *12,* 197–213.

Brigham, T. A., Finfrock, S. R., Breunig, K., and Bushell, D. The use of programmed materials in the analysis of academic contingencies. *Journal of Applied Behavior Analysis,* 1972, *5,* 177–182.

Brigham, T. A., Graubard, P. S., and Stans, A. Analysis of the effects of sequential reinforcement contingencies on aspects of composition. *Journal of Applied Behavior Analysis,* 1972, *5,* 421–429.

Broder, P. K., Dunivant, N., Smith, E. C., and Sutton, L. P. *Further Observations on the Link Between Learning Disabilities and Juvenile Delinquency.* Williamsburg, Va.: National Center for State Courts, 1980.

Broman, S. 1977. In Werner, E. E. Environmental interaction in minimal brain dysfunction. In H. E. Rie and E. D. Rie (eds.), *Handbook of Minimal Brain Dysfunction.* New York: John Wiley & Sons, 1980.

Bronfenbrenner, U. The psychological costs of quality and equality in education. *Child Development,* 1967, *38,* 909–925.

Bronfenbrenner, U. Is early intervention effective? *Influences on Human Development,* edited by U. Bronfenbrenner and M. A. Mahoney. Hinsdale, Ill.: The Dryden Press, 1975a.

———. Is early intervention effective? *Exceptional Infant: Assessment and Intervention.* Vol. 3. New York: Brunner Mazel, 1975b.

———. The experimental ecology of education. *Teacher's College Record,* 1976, *78,* 157–204.

Bronzaft, A. L., and McCarthy, D. P. The effect of elevated train noise on reading ability. *Environment and Behavior,* 1975, *7,* 517–527.

Brophy, J., and Good, T. *Teacher-Student Relationships.* New York: Holt, Rinehart and Winston, 1974.

Broverman, D. M. Cognitive style and intra-individual variation in abilities. *Journal of Personality,* 1960, *28,* 240–256.

Brown, A. L. The development of memory: Knowing, knowing about knowing, and knowing how to know. In *Advances in Child Development and Behavior.* Vol. 10, edited by H. W. Reese. New York: Academic Press, 1975.

———. Knowing when, where, and how to remember: A problem of metacognition. In *Advances in Instructional Psychology,* edited by R. Glaser. Hillsdale, N.J.: Lawrence Erlbaum, 1978.

Brown, G. W. Suggestions for parents. *Journal of Learning Disabilities,* 1968, *2,* 97–106.

Brown, L. L., and Hammill, D. D. *Behavior Rating Profile: An Ecological Approach to Behavioral Assessments.* Austin, Tex.: Pro-ed, 1979.

Brown, R. *A First Language: The Early Stages.* Cambridge: Harvard University Press, 1973.

Brown, R., and Bellugi, U. Three processes in the child's acquisition of syntax. *Harvard Education Review,* 1964, *34,* 133–151.

Brown, V. Programs, materials and techniques. *Journal of Learning Disabilities,* 1975, *8,* 407–416.

Bruininks, R. H., Glaman, G. M., and Clark, C. R. Issues in determining prevalence of reading retardation. *The Reading Teacher,* 1973, *27,* 177–185.

Bruininks, V. L. Peer status and personality characteristics of learning disabled and nondisabled students. *Journal of Learning Disabilities,* 1978a, *11,* 484–489.

———. Actual and perceived peer status of learning disabled students in mainstream programs. *Journal of Special Education,* 1978b, *12,* 51–58.

Bruner, J., Goodnow, J., and Austin, G. *A Study of Thinking.* New York: John Wiley & Sons, 1956.

Bruner, J. S., Olver, R. R., and Greenfield, P. M. *Studies in Cognitive Growth.* New York: John Wiley & Sons, 1966.

Bruno, R. M. Interpretation of pictorially presented social situations by learning disabled and normal children. *Journal of Learning Disabilities,* 1981, *14,* 350–352.

Brutten, M., Richardson, S. O., and Mangel, C. *Something's Wrong with My Child: A Parent's Book about Children with Learning Disabilities.* New York: Harcourt Brace Jovanovich, 1973.

Bryan, J. H., and Perlmutter, B. Immediate impressions of LD children by female adults. *Learning Disability Quarterly,* 1979, *2,* 80–88.

Bryan, J. H., and Sherman, R. Immediate impressions of nonverbal integration attempts by learning disabled boys. *Learning Disability Quarterly,* 1980, *3,* 19–28.

Bryan, J. H., Sherman, R., and Fisher, A. Learning disabled boys' nonverbal behaviors within a dyadic interview. *Learning Disability Quarterly,* 1980, *3,* 65–72.

Bryan, T. Social relationships and verbal interactions of learning disabled children. *Journal of Learning Disabilities,* 1978, *11,* 107–115.

Bryan, T., Donahue, M., and Pearl, R. Learning disabled children's peer interactions during a small-group problem-solving task. *Learning Disability Quarterly,* 1981, *4* (1), 13–22.

Bryan, T., Donahue, M., Pearl, R., and Sturm, C. Learning: An observational study of children's communications. *Journal of Learning Disabilities,* 1976, *9,* 661–669.

Bryan, T., and McGrady, H. J. Use of a teacher rating scale. *Journal of Learning Disabilities,* 1972, *5,* 199–206.

Bryan, T., and Pearl, R. Self-concepts and locus of control of learning disabled children. *Journal of Clinical Child Psychology,* 1979, *8,* 223–226.

Bryan, T., and Pflaum, S. Social interactions of learning disabled children: A linguistic, social, and cognitive analysis. *Learning Disability Quarterly,* 1978, *1* (1), 70–79.

Bryan, T., and Wheeler, R. Perception of children with learning disabilities: The eye of the observer. *Journal of Learning Disabilities,* 1972, *5,* 199–206.

Bryan, T., Wheeler, R., Felcan, J., and Henek, T. Come on, dummy, an observational study of children's communication. *Journal of Learning Disabilities,* 1976, *9,* 53–61.

———. "Come on, dummy": Disabled children's conversational skills — The "TV talk show." *Learning Disability Quarterly,* 1981, *4,* 250–259.

Bryan, T. H. An observational analysis of classroom behaviors of children with learning disabilities. *Journal of Learning Disabilities,* 1974a, *7,* 26–34.

———. Peer popularity of learning disabled children. *Journal of Learning Disabilities,* 1974b, *7,* 621–625.

———. Peer popularity of learning disabled children: A replication. *Journal of Learning Disabilities,* 1976, *9,* 307–311.

———. Learning disabled children's comprehension of nonverbal communication. *Journal of Learning Disabilities,* 1977, *10,* 501–506.

Bryan, T. H., and Bryan, J. H. *Understanding Learning Disabilities.* 2nd ed. Sherman Oaks: Alfred Publishing Co., 1978.

Bryan, T. H., and Wheeler, R. A. Teachers' behaviors in classes for severely retarded, multiply trainable mentally retarded, learning disabled, and normal children. *Mental Retardation,* 1976, *14* (4), 41–45.

Bryant, N. D. Modifying instruction to minimize the effects of learning disabilities. *Forum,* 1980, 19–20.

Bryant, N. D., Drabin, I. R., and Gettinger, M. Effects of varying unit size on spelling achievement in learning disabled children. *Journal of Learning Disabilities,* 1981, *14,* 200–203.

Bryant, N. D., and Gettinger, M. Eliminating differences between learning disabled and non-disabled children on a paired-associate learning task. *Journal of Educational Research,* 1981, *74,* 342–346.

Bryant, N. D., and McLoughlin, J. A. Subject variables: Definition, incidence, characteristics, and correlates. In

Final Report: Leadership Training Institute in Learning Disabilities. Vol. 1, edited by N. D. Bryant and C. E. Kass. Tucson: University of Arizona, Department of Special Education, 1972.

Bryant, P. *Perception and Understanding in Young Children.* New York: Basic Books, 1974.

Bryden, M. P. Tachistoscopic recognition, handedness, and cerebral dominance. *Neuropsychologia,* 1965, *3,* 1–8.

——. Laterality effects in dichotic listening: Relations with handedness and reading ability in children. *Neuropsychologia,* 1970, *8,* 443–450.

Bryden, M. P., and Allard, F. Visual hemifield differences depend on typeface. *Brain and Language,* 1976, *3,* 191–200.

Buchsbaum, M., and Wender, P. Average evoked responses in normal and minimally brain dysfunctioned children treated with amphetamine: A preliminary report. *Archives of General Psychiatry,* 1973, *29,* 764–770.

Buckley, P. D. The Bender Gestalt Test: A review of reported research with school-age subjects, 1966–1977. *Psychology in the Schools,* 1978, *15,* 327–338.

Burmeister, L. E., and Stevens, I. J. Using library resources. In *Reading Strategies for Secondary School Teachers,* edited by L. E. Burmeister. Menlo Park, Calif.: Addison-Wesley, 1974.

Buros, O. K., ed. *Mental Measurements Yearbook.* Highland Park, N.J.: Gryphon, 1938.

Butterfield, E. C., Wambold, C., and Belmont, J. M. On the theory and practice of improving short-term memory. *American Journal of Mental Deficiency,* 1973, 77, 654–669.

Calanchini, P. R., and Trout, S. S. The neurology of learning disabilities. In *Learning Disorders in Children: Diagnosis, Medication, Education,* edited by L. Tarnopol. Boston: Little, Brown, 1971.

Caldwell, B. M. A decade of early intention programs: What have we learned? *American Journal of Orthopsychiatry,* 1974, *44,* 491–496.

Calloway, E. *Brain Electrical Potentials and Individual Psychological Differences.* New York: Grune & Stratton, 1975.

Cameron, J. R. Parental treatment, children's temperament, and the risk of childhood behavioral problems: 1. Relationships between parental characteristics and changes in children's temperament over time. *American Journal of Orthopsychiatry,* 1977, *47,* 568–576.

Cameron, J. R. Parental treatment, children's temperament, and the risk of childhood behavioral problems. 2. Initial temperament, parental attitudes, and the incidence and form of behavioral problems. *American Journal of Orthopsychiatry,* 1978, *48,* 140–147.

Campbell, S. B., Schleiter, M., Weiss, G., and Perlman, T. A two-year following of hyperactive preschoolers. *American Journal of Orthopsychiatry,* 1977, *47,* 149–162.

Campos, J. J., Langer, A., and Krowitz, A. Cardiac response on the visual cliff in prelocomotor infants. *Science,* 1970, *170,* 196–197.

Canfield, J., and Wells, H. C. *100 Ways to Enhance Self-Concept in the Classroom: A Handbook for Teachers and Parents.* Englewood Cliffs: Prentice-Hall, 1976.

Cannon, I., and Compton, C. School dysfunction in the adolescent. In *Neurological Impairments — A Proposal for Service,* edited by C. Larson and P. Larson. New York: NYALD Developmental Disabilities Act Grant Contract No. 171365, 1981.

Cantwell, D. P. Familial genetic research with hyperactive children. In *The Hyperactive Child: Diagnosis, Management, Current Research,* edited by D. P. Cantwell, New York: Spectrum Publications, 1975.

Caplan, P. J. Sex, age, behavior, and school subjects as determinants of report of learning problems. *Journal of Learning Disabilities,* 1977, *10,* 314–316.

Caplan, P. J., and Kinsbourne, M. Sex differences in response to school failure. *Journal of Learning Disabilities,* 1974, *7,* 232–235.

——. Baby drops the rattle: Assymmetry of duration of grasp by infants. *Child Development,* 1976, *47,* 532–534.

Capps, L. R., and Hatfield, M. M. Mathematical concepts and skills: Diagnosis, prescription, and correction of deficiencies. *Focus on Exceptional Children,* 1977, *8,* 1–8.

Capute, A. J., Accardo, P., Vening, E., Rubenstein, J., and Harryman, S. *Primitive Reflex Profile. Monographs in Developmental Pediatrics.* Baltimore: University Park Press, 1978.

Carlberg, C., and Kavale, K. The efficacy of special versus regular class placement for exceptional children: A meta-analysis. *Journal of Special Education,* 1980, *14,* 295–309.

Carlson, C. I., Scott, M., and Eklund, S. J. Ecological theory and method for behavioral assessment. *School Psychology Review,* 1980, *9,* 75–82.

Carman, R. A. and Adams, W. R., Jr. *Study Skills: A Student's Guide for Survival.* New York: John Wiley & Sons, 1972.

Carmon, A., Nachshon, I., and Starinsky, R. Developmental aspects of visual hemifield differences in perception of verbal material. *Brain and Language,* 1976, *3,* 463–469.

Carner, R. L. The adult dyslexic-dilemma and challenge. In *Reading Disability and Perception,* edited by G. Spache. Newark, Del.: International Reading Association, 1969.

Carpenter, M. *Human Neuroanatomy.* Baltimore: Williams & Wilkins, 1976.

Carricker, W. R. A comparison of postschool adjustments of regular and special class retarded individuals served in Lincoln and Omaha, Nebraska Public Schools. *Dissertation Abstracts,* 1957, *17,* 2206–2207.

Carrillo, L. *Teaching Reading: A Handbook.* New York: St. Martin's Press, 1976.

Cartelli, L. M. Paradigmatic language training for learning disabled children. *Journal of Learning Disabilities,* 1978, *11,* 313–318.

Carter, J. L., and Diaz, A. Effects of visual and auditory background on reading test performance. *Exceptional Children,* 1971, *38,* 43–50.

Carvella, J. R. *Minicalculators in the Classroom.* Washington, D.C.: National Education Association, 1977.

Cassidy, J., and Shanahan, T. Survival skills: Some considerations. *Journal of Reading,* 1979, *23,* 136–140.

Cawley, J. F. *Math curricula for the secondary learning disabled student.* Paper presented at a symposium on learning disabilities in the secondary schools, Norristown, Pa., March 1975.

——. An instructional design in mathematics. In *Teaching the Learning Disabled Adolescent,* edited by L. Mann, L. Goodman, and J. L. Wiederholt. Boston: Houghton Mifflin, 1978.

Cawley, J. F., Fitzmaurice, A. M., Goodstein, N. A., Lepore, A. V., Sedlak, R., and Althaus, V. *Project MATH, Level 1.* Tulsa: Educational Progress, a division of Educational Development Corp., 1976.

Ceci, S. J., Ringstorm, M., and Lea, S. E. G. Do language-learning disabled children (L/LDS) have impaired memories? In search of underlying processes. *Journal of Learning Disabilities,* 1981, *14,* 159–162, 173.

Cegelka, P. Career Education. In *An Introduction to Special Education,* edited by A. Blackhurst and W. Berdine. Boston: Little, Brown, 1981.

Cermak, L. S., Goldberg-Warter, J., Deluce, D., Cermak, S., and Drake, C. The role of interference in the verbal retention ability of learning disabled children. *Journal of Learning Disabilities,* 1981, *14,* 291–295.

Chafee, C. H., and Settipane, G. A. Asthma caused by FD & C approved dyes. *Journal of Allergy,* 1967, *40,* 65–72.

Chaikin, A. L., Gillen, B., Derlega, V. S., Heinen, J. R. K. and Wilson, M. Students' reactions to teachers' physical attractiveness and non-verbal behavior: Two exploratory studies. *Psychology in the Schools,* 1978, *15,* 588–595.

Chaing, B., Thorpe, H. W., and Darch, C. B. Effects of cross-age tutoring on word-recognition performance of learning disabled students. *Learning Disability Quarterly,* 1980, *3* (4), 11–19.

Chalfant, J. C., and King, F. S. An approach to operationalizing the definition of learning disabilities. *Journal of Learning Disabilities,* 1976, *9,* 228–243.

Chalfant, J. C., and Scheffelin, M. A. *Central Processing Dysfunctions in Children: A Review of Research* (National Institute of Neurological Diseases and Stroke Monograph No. 9). Bethesda: U.S. Department of Health, Education and Welfare, 1969.

Chall, J. *Learning to Read: The Great Debate.* New York: McGraw-Hill, 1967.

Chandler, H. N. Confusion confounded: A teacher tries to use research results to teach math. *Journal of Learning Disabilities,* 1978, *11,* 361–369.

Chandler, T. A. The fallacy of homogeneity. *Journal of School Psychology,* 1966, *5,* 64–67.

Chaplin, M. V., and Keller, H. R. Decentering and social interaction. *Journal of Genetic Psychology,* 1974, *124,* 269–275.

Chapman, J. W., and Boersma, F. J. Learning disabilities, locus of control, and mother attitudes. *Journal of Educational Psychology,* 1979, *71,* 250–258.

Chapman, R. B., Larsen, S. C., and Parker, R. M. Interactions of first-grade teachers with learning disordered children. *Journal of Learning Disabilities,* 1979, *12,* 225–230.

Chase, H. P. The effects of intrauterine and postnatal undernutrition on normal brain development. *Annals of the New York Academy of Sciences,* 1973, *205,* 231–244.

Childers, P. R. Listening is a modifiable skill. *The Journal of Experimental Education,* 1970, *38*(4), 1–3.

Chomsky, N. A. *Language and Mind.* New York: Harcourt Brace Jovanovich, 1968.

Church, R. L., and Sedlak, M. W. *Education in the United States.* New York: Free Press, 1976.

Cicirelli, V. G. *The Impact of Head Start: An Evaluation of the Effects of Head Start on Children's Cognitive and Affective Development.* Vol. 1. Springfield, Va.: Clearinghouse, 1969.

Cicirelli, V. G., Evans, J. W., and Schiller, J. S. The impact of Head Start: A reply. *Harvard Educational Review,* 1970, *40*(1), 105–129.

Ciminero, A. R., Calhoun, K. S., and Adams, H. E., eds. *Handbook of Behavioral Assessment.* New York: John Wiley & Sons, 1977.

Ciuffreda, K. J., Bahill, A. T., Kenyon, R. V. and Stark, L. Eye movements during reading: Case reports. *American Journal of Optometry and Physiological Optics,* 1976, *53,* 389–395.

Claiborne, J. H. Types of congenital symbol amblyopia. *Journal of the American Medical Association,* 1906, *47,* 1813–1816.

Clark, E. What's in a word? On the child's acquisition of semantics in his first language. In *Cognitive Development and the Acquisition of Language,* edited by T. E. Moore. New York: Academic Press, 1973.

Clarren, S. K., and Smith, D. W. The fetal alcohol syndrome. *New England Journal of Medicine,* 1978, *298,* 1063.

Cleary, T. A., Humphreys, L. G., Kendrick, S. A., and Wesman, A. G. Educational uses of tests with disadvantaged students. *American Psychologist,* 1975, *30,* 15–41.

Clements, S. D. *Minimal Brain Dysfunction in Children: Terminology and Identification. Phase One of a Three-Phase Project* (NINDS Monograph No. 3, U.S. Public Health Service Publication No. 1415). Washington, D.C.: U.S. Government Printing Office, 1966.

Clements, S. D., Davis, J. S., Edgington, R., Goolsby, C. M., and Peters, J. E. Two cases of learning disabilities. In *Learning Disorders in Children: Diagnosis, Medication, Education,* edited by L. Tarnopol. Boston: Little, Brown, 1971.

Cline, R. K. J., and Kretke, G. L. An evaluation of long term SSR in the junior high school. *Journal of Reading,* 1980, *23,* 503–506.

Cohen, E. G. Open-space schools: The opportunity to become ambitious. *Sociology of Education,* 1973, *46,* 1–8.

Cohen, L. Commentary on visual shape perception in infancy. *Monographs of the Society for Research in Child Development.* 1979, *44,* 58–63.

Cohen, L., DeLoache, J., and Strauss, M. Infant visual perception. In *Handbook of Infant Development,* edited by J. Osofsky. New York: John Wiley & Sons, 1979.

Cohen, M., and Martin, G. Applying precision teaching to academic assessment. *Teaching Exceptional Children,* 1971, *3,* 120–128.

Cohen, S. A. Dyspedagogia as a cause of reading retardation: Definition and treatment. In *Learning Disorders.* Vol. 4, edited by B. Bateman. Seattle: Special Child Publications, 1971.

Cohn, R. The neurological study of children with learning disabilities. *Exceptional Children,* 1964, *31,* 179–185.

————. Arithmetic and learning disabilities. In *Progress in Learning Disabilities.* Vol. 2, edited by H. Myklebust. New York: Grune & Stratton, 1971.

Colarusso, R. P., Martin, H., and Hartung, J. Specific visual perceptual skills as long-term predictors of academic success. *Journal of Learning Disabilities,* 1975, *8,* 651–655.

Coleman, J. C., and Sandhu, M. A descriptive relational study of 364 children referred to a university clinic for learning disorders. *Psychological Reports,* 1967, *20,* 1091–1105.

Coleman, P. D., and Riesen, A. H. Environmental effects on cortical dendritic fields. I. Reading in the dark. *Journal of Anatomy,* 1968, *102,* 363–374.

Colletti, L. F. Relationship between pregnancy and birth complications and the later development of learning disabilities. *Journal of Learning Disabilities,* 1979, *12,* 659–663.

Colligan, R. Concurrent validity of the Myklebust Pupil Rating Scale in a kindergarten population. *Journal of Learning Disabilities,* 1977a, *10,* 317–320.

————. The Minnesota Child Development Inventory as an aid in the assessment of developmental disability. *Journal of Clinical Psychology,* 1977b, *33,* 162–163.

————. Prediction of reading difficulty from parental preschool report: A 3-year follow-up. *Learning Disability Quarterly,* 1981, *4,* 31–37.

Colligan, R. C., and O'Connell, E. J. Should psychometric screening be made an adjunct to the pediatric preschool examination? *Clinical Pediatrics,* 1974, *13,* 29–34.

Collins, E. A. Teaching styles (secondary school). In *The Slow Learner in Mathematics,* edited by W. C. Lowry. Thirty-fifth yearbook of the National Council of Teachers of Mathematics. Washington, D.C.: National Council of Teachers of Mathematics, 1972.

Compensatory Education in Early Adolescence. Menlo Park, Calif.: Stanford Research Institute, 1974.

The Condition of Education. 1980 ed. Washington, D.C.: U.S. Department of Education, National Center for Education Statistics, 1980.

Cone, J. D., and Hawkins, R. P., eds. *Behavioral Assessment: New Directions in Clinical Psychology.* New York: Brunner/Mazel, 1977.

Cone, T. E., and Wilson, L. R. Quantifying a severe discrepancy: A critical analysis. *Learning Disability Quarterly,* 1981, *4*(4), 359–371.

Connor, F., Hoover, R., Horton, K., Sands, H., Sternfold, L., and Wolinsky, G. Physical and sensory handicaps. In *Issues in the Classification of Children.* Vol. 1, edited by N. Hobbs. San Francisco: Jossey-Bass, 1975.

Connors, C. K. A teacher rating scale for use in drug studies with children. *American Journal of Psychiatry,* 1969, *126,* 884–888.

————. Symptom patterns in hyperkinetic, neurotic, and normal children. *Child Development,* 1970, *41,* 667–682.

————. Symposium: Behavior modification by drugs. II. Psychological effects of stimulant drugs in children with minimal brain dysfunction. *Pediatrics,* 1972, *49,* 702–708.

————. *Food Additives and Hyperactive Children.* New York: Plenum, 1980.

Connors, C. K., Goyette, C. H., Southwick, D. A., Lee, J. M., and Andrulonis, P. A. Food additives and hyperkinesis: A controlled double-blind experiment. *Pediatrics*, 1976, *58*, 154–166.

Conoley, J. C. Organizational assessment. *School Psychology Review*, 1980, *9*, 83–89.

Conrad, R. Speech and reading. In *Language by Ear and by Eye: The Relationships Between Speech and Reading*, edited by J. F. Kavanagh and I. G. Mattingly. Cambridge: MIT Press, 1972.

Cook, L. D. The adolescent with a learning disability: A developmental perspective. *Adolescence*, 1979, *14*, 697–707.

Cook, W. Letters to the editor: Allergy, nutrition and hyperactivity. *Journal of Learning Disabilities*, 1974, *7*, 68.

Coop, R. H., and Sigel, I. E. Cognitive style: Implications for learning and instruction. *Psychology in the Schools*, 1971, *8*, 152–161.

Cooper, J. M., and Griffiths, P. Treatment and prognosis. In *Developmental Dysphasia*, edited by M. A. Wyke. New York: Academic Press, 1978.

Corah, N. L., and Powell, B. J. A factor analytic study of the Frostig Developmental Test of Visual Perception. *Perceptual Motor Skills*, 1963, *16*, 59–63.

Corballis, M. C., and Zalik, M. C. Why do children confuse mirror image obliques? *Journal of Experimental Child Psychology*, 1977, *24*, 516–523.

Cott, A. Megavitamins: The orthomolecular approach to behavioral disorders and learning disabilities. *Academic Therapy*, 1972, *7*, 245–258.

Coulter, W. A. Adaptive behavior and professional disfavor: Controversies and trends for school psychologists. *School Psychology Review*, 1980, *9*, 67–74.

Coulter, W. A. and Morrow, H. W. eds. *Adaptive Behavior: Concepts and Measurements*. New York: Grune & Stratton, 1978.

Coulter, W. A., Morrow, H. W., and Tucker, J. A. What you always wanted to know about adaptive behavior but were too hostile and angry to ask. Paper presented at the meeting of the National Association of School Psychologists. New York, 1978.

Courtney, B. L. Organization produced. In *Developing Study Skills in Secondary Schools*, New York: Macmillan, 1967.

Cowgill, M. L., Fiedland, S., and Schapiro, R. Predicting learning disabilities from kindergarten reports. *Journal of Learning Disabilities*, 1973, *6*, 577–582.

Cox, L. S. Diagnosing and remediating systematic errors in addition and subtraction computations. The *Arithmetic Teacher*, 1975, *22*, 151–157.

Cragg, B. G. The development of synapses in cat visual cortex. *Investigative Ophthalmology*, 1972, *11*, 377–385.

Cratty, B. *Perceptual-Motor Behavior and Educational Processes*. Springfield, Ill.: Charles C Thomas, 1969.

———. *Perceptual and Motor Development in Infants and Children*. New York: Macmillan, 1970.

———. *Physical Expressions of Intelligence*. Englewood Cliffs, N.J.: Prentice-Hall, 1972.

Cravioto, J. Nutrition and learning in children. In *Nutrition and Mental Retardation*, edited by N. S. Springer. Ann Arbor: Institute for the Study of Mental Retardation and Related Disabilities, 1972.

Cravioto, J., and DeLicardie, E. R. Environmental and nutritional deprivation in children with learning disabilities. In *Perceptual and Learning Disabilities in Children*. Vol. 2, *Research and Theory*, edited by W. M. Cruickshank and D. P. Hallahan. Syracuse: Syracuse University Press, 1975.

Crawford, D. A summary of the results and recommendations from the Association for Children with Learning Disabilities Research and Development Project (National Institute for Juvenile Justice and Delinquency Prevention, Office of Juvenile Justice and Delinquency Prevention, Law Enforcement Assistance Administration, U.S. Department of Justice Grant Nos. 76-JN-99-0021 and 78-JN-AX-0022). Presented to the Federal Coordinating Council, Washington, D.C., 16 December 1981.

Creswell, J. L., and Vaughn, L. R. Hand-held calculator curriculum and mathematical achievement and retention. *Journal for Research in Mathematics Education*, 1979, *10*, 364–367.

Critchley, M. *The Dyslexic Child*. Springfield, Ill.: Charles C. Thomas, 1970.

Cromer, R. F. The basis of childhood dysphasia: A linguistic approach. In *Developmental Dysphasia*, edited by M. A. Wyke. New York: Academic Press, 1978.

Cromwell, R. L., Blashfield, R. K., and Strauss, J. S. Criteria for classification systems. In *Issues in the Classification of Children*. Vol. 1, edited by N. Hobbs. San Francisco: Jossey-Bass, 1975.

Cronbach, L. J. Five decades of public controversy over mental testing. *American Psychologist*, 1975, *30*, 1–14.

Cronbach, L. J., and Furby, L. How we should measure "change" — or should we? *Psychological Bulletin*, 1970, *74*, 68–80.

Crook, M. A., and Langdon, F. J. The effects of aircraft noise in schools around London Airport. *Journal of Sound and Vibration*, 1974, *34*, 221–232.

Crowl, T. K., and MacGinitie, W. H. The influence of students' speech characteristics on teachers' evaluation of oral answers. *Journal of Educational Psychology*, 1974, *66*, 304–308.

Cruickshank, W. M., ed. *The Teacher of Brain-Injured Children: A Discussion of the Bases for Competency*. Syracuse: Syracuse University Press, 1966.

———. The development of education for exceptional children. In *Education of Exceptional Children and Youth*. 2nd ed., edited by W. M. Cruickshank and G. O. Johnson. Englewood Cliffs, N. J.: Prentice-Hall, 1967.

———, ed. *Psychology of Exceptional Children and Youth*. 3rd ed. Englewood Cliffs, N.J.: Prentice-Hall, 1971.

———. Some issues facing the field of learning disability. *Journal of Learning Disabilities*, 1972, *5*, 380–388.

———. The education of children with special learning disabilities. In *Education of Exceptional Children and Youth*. 3rd ed., edited by W. M. Cruickshank and G. O. Johnson. Englewood Cliffs, N.J.: Prentice-Hall, 1975.

Cruickshank, W. M., William M. Cruickshank. In *Teaching Children with Learning Disabilities: Personal Perspectives*, edited by J. M. Kauffman and D. P. Hallahan. Columbus, Ohio: Charles E. Merrill, 1976.

Cruickshank, W. M., Bentzen, F. A., Ratzeburgh, F. H., and Tannhauser, M. T. *A Teaching Method for Brain-Injured and Hyperactive Children*. Syracuse: Syracuse University Press, 1961.

Cruickshank, W. M., Bice, H. V., and Wallen, N. E. *Perception and Cerebral Palsy*, Syracuse: Syracuse University Press, 1957.

Cruickshank, W. M., Bice, H. V. Wallen, N. E., and Lynch, K. S. *Perception and Cerebral Palsy*. 2nd ed. Syracuse: Syracuse University Press, 1965.

Cullinan, D., Epstein, M. H., and Lloyd, J. School behavior problems of learning disabled and normal girls and boys. *Learning Disability Quarterly*. 1981, *4*, 163–169.

Cullinan, D., Epstein, M. H., and Silver, L. Modification of impulsive tempo in learning disabled pupils. *Journal of Abnormal Child Psychology*, 1977, *5*, 437–444.

Cullinan, D. Kauffman, J. M., and La Fleur, N. K. Modeling: Research with implications for special education. *Journal of Special Education*, 1975, *9*, 209–221.

Cunningham, J. W., Cunningham, P. M. and Arthur, S. V. *Middle and Secondary School Reading*. New York: Longman, 1981.

Cunningham, P. M., and Cunningham, J. W. Improving listening in content area subjects. *NASSP Bulletin*, Dec. 1976, 26–31.

Cuvo, A. J. Developmental differences in rehearsal and free recall. *Journal of Experimental Psychology*, 1975, *19*, 265–278.

Dainer, K. B., Klorman, R., Salzman, L. F., Hess, D. W., Davidson, P. W., and Michael, R. L. Learning-disordered children's evoked potentials during sustained attention. *Journal of Abnormal Child Psychology*, 1981, *9*, 79–94.

Dale, E., and Chall, J. S. A formula for predicting readability. *Educational Research Bulletin*, 1948, *27*, 11–20; *28*, 37–54.

Damon, W. Early concepts of positive justice as related to the development of logical operations. *Child Development*, 1975, *46*, 301–312.

D'Angelo, K., and Wilson, R. M. How helpful is insertion and omission miscue analysis? *The Reading Teacher*, 1979, *32*, 519–520.

Danielson, L. C., and Bauer, J. N. A formula-based classification of learning disabled children: An examination of the issues. *Journal of Learning Disabilities*, 1978, *11*, 163–176.

Danzer, V. A., Lyons, T. M., and Gerber, M. F. *Daberon Screening Device of School Readiness*. Portland, Ore.: Daberon Research, 1972.

Danziger, S. J., and Possick, P. A. Metallic mercury exposure in scientific glassware manufacturing plants. *Journal of Occupational Medicine*, 1973, *15*, 15.

Dardig, J. and Heward, W. *Sign Here: A Contracting Book for Children and Their Parents*. Kalamazoo: Behaviordilia, 1976.

Das, J. P. Structure of cognitive abilities: Evidence for simultaneous and successive processing. *Journal of Educational Psychology*, 1973, *35*, 103–108.

Das, J. P., Kirby, J., and Jarman, R. F. Simultaneous and successive syntheses: An alternative model for cognitive abilities. *Psychological Bulletin*, 1975, *82*, 87–103.

David, O., Clark, J., and Voeller, K. Lead and hyperactivity. *Lancet*, 1972, *2*, 900–903.

Davidoff, J. B., Cone, B. P., and Scully, J. P. Developmental changes in hemispheric processing for cognitive skills and the relationship to reading ability. In *Cognitive Psychology and Instruction*, edited by A. M. Lesgold, J. W. Pellegrino, S. Fokkema, and R. Glaser. New York: Plenum, 1978.

Davidson, H. P. A study of the confusing letters b, d, p, and q. *Journal of Genetic Psychology*, 1935, *47*, 458–468.

Davidson, J. *Using the Cuisenaire Rods*. New Rochelle: Cuisenaire, 1969.

Davis, H., and Davis, P. A. Action potentials of the brain in normal persons and in normal states of cerebral activity. *Archives of Neurology and Psychiatry*, 1936, *36*, 1214–1224.

Davol, S. H., and Hastings, M. L. Effects of sex, age, reading ability, socioeconomic level, and display position on a measure of spatial relations in children. *Perceptual and Motor Skills*, 1967, *24*, 375–387.

Day, R. H., and McKenzie, B. E. Constancies in the perceptual world of the infant. In *Stability and Constancy in Visual Perception. Mechanisms and Processes*, edited by W. Epstein. New York: John Wiley & Sons, 1977.

Dearborn, W. F. Structural factors which condition special disability in reading. *Proceedings of the American Association for Mental Deficiency*, 1933, *38*, 266–283.

Debono, E. Information processing and new ideas — lateral and vertical thinking. In *Guide to Creative Action*, edited by S. J. Pames, R. B. Noller, and A. M. Biondi. New York: Charles Scribner's Sons, 1977.

Denchant, E. *Reading Improvement in the Secondary School*. Englewood Cliffs, N.J.: Prentice-Hall, 1973.

Decker, S. N., and DeFires, J. C. Cognitive abilities in families with reading disabled children. *Journal of Learning Disabilities*, 1980, *13*, 517–522.

Dee, H. L. Auditory asymmetry and strength of manual preference. *Cortex*, 1971, *7*, 236–245.

de Hirsch, K. Specific dyslexia or strephosymbolia. *Folia Phoniatrica*, 1952, *4*, 231–248.

——. *Bulletin of the Orton Society*, 1963.

de Hirsch, K., Jansky, J. J., and Langford, W. S. *Predicting Reading Failure*. New York: Harper & Row, 1966.

Deibert, A. A., and Harmon, A. J. *New Tools for Changing Behavior*. Champaign, Ill.: Research Press, 1970.

Deighton, L. C. Developing Vocabulary: Another look at a problem. In *Teaching Reading Skills in Secondary Schools: Readings*, edited by A. V. Olson and W. S. Ames. Scranton, Pa: Intext Educational Publishers, 1970.

Delacato, C. H. *The Treatment and Prevention of Reading Difficulty*. New York: Harcourt, Brace & World, 1959.

——. *The Diagnosis and Treatment of Speech and Reading Problems*. Springfield, Ill.: Charles C Thomas, 1963.

——. *Neurological Organization and Reading*. Springfield, Ill.: Charles C. Thomas, 1966.

Delefes, P., and Jackson, B. Teacher-pupil interaction as a function of location in the classroom. *Psychology in the Schools*, 1972, *9*, 119–123.

Dembo, M. H., Yoshida, R. K., Reilly, T. and Reilly, V. Teacher-student interaction in special education classrooms. *Exceptional Children*, 1978, *45*, 212–213.

Dembrinski, R. and Mauser, A. What parents of the learning disabled really want from professionals. *Journal of Learning Disabilities*, 1977, *10*, 578–584.

Denckla, M. B. Research needs in learning disabilities: A neurologist's point of view. *Journal of Learning Disabilities*, 1973, *6*, 441–450.

——. Keynote address to Association for Children with Learning Disabilities, New York, 1975.

——. Minimal brain dysfunction and dyslexia: Beyond diagnosis by exclusion. In *Child Neurology*. edited by M. E. Blaw, I. Rapin, and M. Kinsbourne. New York: Spectrum Publications, 1977.

——. Childhood learning disabilities. In *Clinical Neuropsychology*, edited by K. M. Heilman and E. Valenstein. New York: Oxford University Press, 1979.

Denckla, M. B., and Heilman, K. M. The syndrome of hyperactivity. In *Clinical Neuropsychology*, edited by K. M. Heilman and E. Valenstein, New York: Oxford University Press, 1979.

Denckla, M. B., and Rudel, R. G. Naming of object-drawings by dyslexic and other learning disabled children. *Brain and Language*, 1976a, *3*, 1–15.

——. Rapid "automatized" naming (R.A.N.): Dyslexia differentiated from other learning disabilities. *Neuropsychologia*, 1976b, *14*, 471–479.

Dennis, W. Causes of retardation among institutional children: Iran. *Journal of Genetic Psychology*, 1960, *96*, 47–59.

Denson, R., Nanson, J. L., and McWatters, M. A. Hyperkinesis and maternal smoking. *Canadian Psychiatric Association Journal*, 1975, *20*, 183–187.

de Quirós, J. B. Diagnosis of vestibular disorders in the learning disabled. *Journal of Learning Disabilities*, 1976, *9*, 39–47.

Derienzo, P. J. A predictive validity study of the Gesell School Readiness Test. Unpublished master's thesis, Syracuse University, 1981.

Deshler, D. D. Learning disability in the high school student as demonstrated in monitoring of self-generated and externally generated errors. Unpublished doctoral dissertation, University of Arizona, 1974.

——. Psychoeducational aspects of learning disabled adolescents. In *Teaching the Learning Disabled Adolescent*, edited by L. Mann, L. Goodman, and J. L. Wiederholt. Boston: Houghton Mifflin, 1978.

Deutsch, M. Minority group and class status as related to social and personality factors in scholastic achievement. *Monograph of the Society for Applied Anthropology*, 1960 (No. 2), 1–32.

deVilliers, P., and deVilliers, J. A cross-sectional study of the acquisition of grammatical morphemes in child speech. *Journal of Psycholinguistic Research*, 1973, *2*, 267–278.

Devine, R., and Rose, D. Proposal to produce a one-hour, broadcast-quality videotape on dyslexia: "To learn to learn, or to learn to read." Rochester, N.Y., 1981.

Dexter, L. A. *The Tyranny of Schooling: An Inquiry into the Problem of "Stupidity."* New York: Basic Books, 1964.

Diamond, J., Cooper, E., Turner, C., and MacIntyre, L. Trophic regulation of nerve sprouting. *Science*, 1976, *193*, 371–377.

Diener, C., and Dweck, C. An analysis of learned helplessness: Continuous changes in performance, strategy, and achievement cognitions following failure. *Journal of Personality and Social Psychology*, 1978, *35*, 451–462.

Dimond, S. J. Drugs to improve learning in man: Implications and neuropsychological analysis. In *The Neuropsychology of Learning Disorders: Theoretical Approaches*, edited by R. M. Knights and D. J. Bakker. Baltimore: University Park Press, 1976.

Dimond, S. J., and Beaumont, J. G., eds. *Hemisphere Function in the Human Brain*. London: Elek., 1974.

Dinger, J. C. Post-school adjustment of former educable retarded pupils. *Exceptional Children*, 1961, *27*, 353–360.

Dinkmeyer, D. *Developing Understanding of Self and Others (DUSO)*. Circle Pines, Minn.: American Guidance Service, 1970.

DiPasquale, G. W., Moule, A. D., and Flewelling, R. W. The birthdate effect. *Journal of Learning Disabilities*, 1980, *13*, 234–238.

Divoky, D. Education's latest victim: The "LD" kid. *Learning*, 1974, *3*(2), 20–25.

Doehring, D. G. *Patterns of Impairment in Specific Reading Disability*. Bloomington: Indiana University Press, 1968.

Doernberg, N. L. Parents as teachers of their own retarded children. In *Mental Retardation*. Vol. 4, edited by W. J. Wortis. New York: Grune & Stratton, 1972.

Dolan, A. B., and Matheny, A. P. A distinctive growth cure for a group of children with academic learning problems. *Journal of Learning Disabilities*, 1978, *11*, 490–494.

Doman, G. Children with severe brain injuries: Neurological organization in terms of mobility. *Journal of the American Medical Association*, 1960, *174*, 257–262.

Donan, R. J., Spitz, E. B., Zuchman, E., Delacato, C. H., and Soman, G. Children with severe brain injuries. Neurological organization in terms of mobility. *Journal of the American Medical Association*, 1960, *174*, 257–262.

Donahue, M., Pearl, R., and Bryan, T. Learning disabled children's conversational competence: Responses to inadequate messages. *Applied Psycholinguistics*, 1980. *1*, 387–403.

Donofrio, A. F. Grade repetition: Therapy of choice. *Journal of Learning Disabilities*, 1977, *10*, 349–351.

Douglas, V. I. Stop, look and listen: The problem of sustained attention and impulsive control in hyperactive and normal children. *Canadian Journal of Behavioural Science*, 1972, *4*, 259–282.

———. Differences between normal and hyperkinetic children. In *Clinical Use of Stimulant Drugs in Children*, edited by C. K. Conners. Princeton: Excerpta Medica, 1974.

———. Are drugs enough? — To treat or to train the hyperactive child. *International Journal of Mental Health*, 1975, *4*, 199–212.

———. Perceptual and cognitive factors as determinants of learning disabilities: A review chapter with special emphasis on attentional factors. In *The Neuropsychology of Learning Disorders: Theoretical Approaches*, edited by R. M. Knights and D. J. Bakker. Baltimore: University Park Press, 1976.

Douglas, V. I., Parry, P., Marton, P., and Garson, C. Assessment of a cognitive training program for hyper-active children. *Journal of Abnormal Child Psychology*, 1976, *4*, 389–410.

Doyle, B. A. Math readiness skills. Paper presented at National Association of School Psychologists, New York, 1978.

Drabman, R. and Thomas, M. H. Does watching violence on television cause apathy? *Pediatrics*, 1976, *57*, 329–331.

Drew, C. J., and Altman, R. Effects of input organization and material difficulty on free recall. *Psychological Reports*, 1970, *27*, 335–337.

Dunivant, N. The relationship between learning disabilities and juvenile delinquency: Executive summary (National Institute for Juvenile Justice and Delinquency Prevention, Office of Juvenile Justice and Delinquency Prevention, U.S. Department of Justice Grant No. 78-JN-AX-0028). Williamsburg, Va.: National Center for State Courts, December 1981.

———. The relationship between learning disabilities and juvenile delinquency: Brief summary of research findings. (National Institute for Juvenile Justice and Delinquency Prevention, Office of Juvenile Justice and Delinquency Prevention, U.S. Department of Justice Grant No. 78-JN-AX-0028). Williamsburg, Va.: National Center for State Courts, March 1982.

———. A note on differences between learning-disabled and non-learning-disabled teenagers in delinquent behavior: Addendum to *Some Observations* and *Further Observations* Reports (National Institute for Juvenile Justice and Delinquency Prevention, Office of Juvenile Justice and Delinquency Prevention, U.S. Department of Justice Grant No. 78-JN-AX-0028). Williamsburg, Va.: National Center for State Courts, April 1982.

Dunn, L. M. Special education for the mildly retarded: Is much of it justifiable? *Exceptional Children*, 1968, *35*, 5–22.

———. Children with moderate and severe general learning disabilities. In *Exceptional Children in the Schools: Special Education in Transition*. 2nd ed., edited by L. M. Dunn. New York: Holt, Rinehart and Winston, 1973.

Dunn, L., Horton, R., and Smith, J. *Peabody Language Development Kit: Level P*. Circle Pines, Minn.: American Guidance Service, 1968.

Durkin, D. *Teaching Them to Read*. 3rd ed. Boston: Allyn & Bacon, 1978.

Dusek, J. B. Do teachers bias children's learning? *Review of Educational Research*, 1975, *45*, 661–684.

Dweck, C. S. The role of expectations and attributions in the alleviation of learned helplessness. *Journal of Personality and Social Psychology*, 1975, *31*, 674–685.

Dweck, C. S., and Reppucci, N. D. Learned helplessness and reinforcement responsibility in children. *Journal of Personality and Social Psychology*, 1973, *25*, 109–116.

Dyer, J. W., Riley, J., and Yekovich, F. R. An analysis of three study skills: notetaking, summarizing, and rereading. *Journal of Educational Research*, 1979, *73*, 3–7.

Dykman, R. A., Ackerman, P. T., Clements, S. D., and Peters, J. E. Specific learning disabilities: An attentional deficit syndrome. In *Progress in Learning Disabilities*. Vol. 2., edited by H. R. Myklebust. New York: Grune & Stratton, 1971.

Dykman, R. A., Walls, R. C., Suzuki, T., Ackerman, P. T., and Peters, J. E. Children with learning disabilities: Conditioning, differentiation, and the effect of distraction. *American Journal of Orthopsychiatry*, 1970, *40*, 776–782.

Eames, T. H. A comparison of the ocular characteristics of unselected and reading disability groups. *Journal of Educational Research*, 1932, *25*, 211–215.

———. Low fusion convergence as a factor in reading disability. *American Journal of Ophthalmology*, 1934, *17*, 709–710.

———. The relationship of birth weight, the speeds of object and word perception, and visual acuity. *Journal of Pediatrics*, 1955, *47*, 603–606.

Earp, N. W. Procedures for teaching reading in mathematics. *The Arithmetic Teacher*, 1970, *17*, 575–579.

Edelbrock, C. Empirical classification of children's behavior disorders: Progress based on parent and teacher ratings. *School Psychology Digest*, 1979, *8*, 355–369.

Edfeldt, A. W. *Silent Speech and Silent Reading*. Stockholm: Almquist & Wiksell, 1959.

Edgar, K. F. The validation of four methods of improving listening ability. Doctoral dissertation, University of Pittsburgh, 1961.

Edgerton, R. B. *The Cloak of Competence: Stigma in the Lives of the Retarded.* Berkeley: University of California Press, 1967.

Education Daily, July 13, 1981.

Eells, K., Davis, A., Havighurst, R., Herrick, V., and Tyler, R. *Intelligence and Cultural Differences.* Chicago: University of Chicago Press, 1951.

Egeland, B. Training impulsive children in the use of more efficient scanning techniques. *Child Development,* 1974, *45,* 165–171.

Eggert, G. H. *Wernicke's Works on Aphasia: A Sourcebook and Review.* The Hague: Mouton, 1977.

Ehrhardt, A. A., and Money, J. Progestin-induced hermaphroditism: IQ and psychosexual identity in a study of ten girls. *Journal of Sex Research,* 1967, *3,* 83–100.

Eimas, P. D. Multiple-cue discrimination learning in children. *Psychological Record,* 1969, *19,* 417–424.

Eimas, S., Siqueland, E., Jusczyk, P., and Vigorito, J. Speech perception in infants. *Science,* 1971, *171,* 303–306.

Eisenson, J. *Examining for Aphasia.* New York: The Psychological Corporation, 1954.

———. Developmental aphasia: A speculative view with therapeutic implications. *Journal of Speech and Hearing Disorders,* 1968, *33,* 3–13.

———. *Aphasia in Children.* New York: Harper & Row, 1972.

Ekel, G. J. Use of conditioned reflex methods in Soviet behavioral toxicology research. In *Behavioral Toxicology,* edited by C. Xintras, B. L. Johnson, and I. de Groot. Washington, D.C.: U.S. Department of Health, Education and Welfare, 1974.

Ekwall, E. E. *Diagnosis and Remediation of the Disabled Reader.* Boston: Allyn & Bacon, 1976.

Elkind, D., and Weiss, J. Studies in perceptual development. III: Perceptual explorations. *Child Development,* 1967, *38,* 553–563.

Elterman, R. D., Abel, L. A., Daroff, R. B., Dell'Osso, L. F., and Bornstein, J. L. Eye movement patterns in dyslexic children. *Journal of Learning Disabilities,* 1980, *13,* 11–16.

Emmerich, W. The parental role: A functional cognitive approach. *Monographs of the Society for Research in Child Development.* Vol. 34. Chicago: Child Development Publications, 1969.

Empey, L. T. *American delinquency: Its meaning and construction.* Homewood, Ill.: Dorsey Press, 1978.

Endler, N. S., and Magnusson, D. *Interactional Psychology and Personality.* Washington, D.C.: Hemisphere Publishing Company, 1976.

Englemann, S. Teaching reading to children with low mental age. *Education and Training of the Mentally Retarded,* 1967, *2,* 193–201.

Engleman, S., and Carnine, D. *DISTAR: An Instructional System Arithmetic I, II, III.* Chicago: Science Research Associates, 1976.

Engleman, S., and Osborn, J. *DISTAR.* Chicago: Science Research Associates, 1975.

Eno, L., and Deichmann, J. A review of the Bender Gestalt Test as a screening instrument for brain damage with school-aged children of normal intelligence since 1970. *Journal of Special Education,* 1980, *14,* 37–45.

Epstein, L. M. Psychophysiological measurement in assessment. In *Behavioral Assessment: A Practical Handbook,* edited by M. Hersen and A. S. Bellack. New York: Pergamon, 1976.

Erickson, A. G. Can listening efficiency be improved? *Journal of Communication,* 1954, *4,* 128–132.

Erickson, M. T. The z-score discrepancy method for identifying reading-disabled children. *Journal of Learning Disabilities,* 1975, *8,* 308–312.

Erikson, E. H. *Childhood and Society.* New York: W. W. Norton, 1963.

Erlenmeyer-Kimling, L., and Jarvik, L. F. Genetics and intelligence: A review. *Science,* 1963, *142,* 1477–1479.

Ervin, S. Imitation and structural change in children's language. In *New Directions in the Study of Language,* edited by E. Lenneberg. Cambridge: MIT Press, 1964.

Estes, R. E., and Huizinga, R. J. A comparison of visual and auditory presentations of a paired associate learning task with learning disabled children. *Journal of Learning Disabilities,* 1974, *7,* 35–42.

Estes, W. K. *Learning Theory and Mental Development.* New York: Academic Press, 1970.

Eustis, R. S. Specific reading disability. A familial syndrome associated with ambidexterity and speech defects and a frequent cause of problem behavior. *The New England Journal of Medicine,* 1947, *237,* 243–249.

Ewing, D. W. Discovering your problem-solving style. *Psychology Today,* 1977, *11(7),* 69–73, 138.

Ewing, N., and Smith, J. Minimum competency testing and the handicapped. *Exceptional Children,* 1981, *47,* 523–524.

Fabian, J., and Jacobs, U. Discrimination of neurological impairment in the learning disabled adolescent. *Journal of Learning Disabilities,* 1981, *10,* 594–596.

Fafard, M., and Haubrich, P. A. Vocational and social adjustment of learning disabled young adults: A follow-up study. *Learning Disability Quarterly,* 1981, *4(2),* 122–130.

Fairbanks, J., and Robinson, J. *Fairbanks-Robinson Program, Levels 1 and 2.* Boston: Teaching Resources, 1967.

Farber, B. and Ryckman, D. B. Effects of severely retarded children on family relationships. *Mental Retardation Abstracts,* 1965, *2,* 1–17.

Farnham-Diggory, S. *Learning Disabilities: A Psychological Perspective.* Cambridge: Harvard University Press, 1978.

Farnham-Diggory, S., and Gregg, L. W. Short term memory functioning in young readers. *Journal of Experimental Child Psychology,* 1975, *19,* 279–298.

Faulk, C. J., and Landry, T. R. An approach to problem-solving. *The Arithmetic Teacher,* April 1961, pp. 157–160.

Fay, L. Reading study skills: Math and science. *Reading and Inquiry,* edited by J. A. Figurel. Newark, Del.: International Reading Association, 1965.

Federal Register. Washington, D.C., Monday, 29 November 1976, 52404–52407.

Federal Register. Washington, D.C., Thursday, 29 December 1977, 65082–65085.

Feinbloom, R. I. Children and television. *Pediatrics,* 1976, *57,* 301–303.

Feingold, B. F. *Introduction to Clinical Allergy.* Springfield, Ill. Charles C. Thomas, 1973.

———. *Why Your Child Is Hyperactive.* New York: Random House, 1975.

———. Hyperkinesis and learning disabilities linked to the ingestion of artificial food colors and flavors. *Journal of Learning Disabilities,* 1976, *9,* 551–559.

Feldhusen, J. F., and Treffinger, D. J. *Teaching Creative Thinking and Problem Solving.* Dubuque: Kendal/Hunt, 1977.

Felton, G. S., and Davidson, H. R. Group counseling can work in the classroom. *Academic Therapy,* 1973, *8,* 461–468.

Fensterheim, H., and Baer, J. *Don't Say Yes When You Want to Say No.* New York: Dell, 1975.

Ferguson, G. A. On transfer and the abilities of man. *Canadian Journal of Psychology,* 1956, *10,* 121–131.

Ferinden, W. E., Jr., and Jacobson, S. Early identification of learning disabilities. *Journal of Learning Disabilities,* 1970, *3,* 589–593.

Fernald, G. M. *Remedial Techniques in Basic school Subjects.* New York: McGraw-Hill, 1943.

Feshback, S., Adelman, H., and Fuller, W. W. Early identification of children with high risk of reading failure. *Journal of Learning Disabilities,* 1974, *7,* 639–644.

Feuerstein, R. *The Dynamic Assessment of Retarded Performers: The Learning Potential Assessment Device, Theory, Instruments, and Techniques.* Baltimore: University Park Press, 1979.

———. *Instrumental Enrichment: An Intervention Program for*

Cognitive Modifiability. Baltimore: University Park Press, 1980.

Fishbein, H. D. Braille phonics: A new technique for aiding the reading disabled. *Journal of Learning Disabilities*, 1979, *12*, 60–64.

Fisher, J. A. *Learning and Study Skills: A guide to Independent Learning*. Des Moines: Drake University Reading and Study Skills Clinic, 1967.

Fisher, J. H. Case of congenital word-blindness (inability to learn to read). *Ophthalmic Review*, 1905, *24*, 315–318.

Fitzgibbons, D., Goldberger, L., and Eagle, M. Field dependence and memory for incidental material. *Perceptual and Motor Skills*, 1965, *21*, 743–749.

Fitzmaurice, A. M. LD teachers; self-ratings on mathematics education competencies. *Learning Disability Quarterly*, 1980, *3* (2), 90–94.

Flaugher, R. L. The many definitions of test bias. *American Psychologist*, 1978, *33*, 671–679.

Flavell, J. H. Developmental studies of mediated memory. In *Advances in Child Development and Behavior*. Vol. 5, edited by H. W. Reese and L. P. Lipsitt. New York: Academic Press, 1970.

———. What is memory development the development of? *Human Development*, 1971, *14*, 272–278.

———. Metacognitive aspects of problem solving. In *The Nature of Intelligence*, edited by L. B. Resnick. Hillsdale, N.J.: Lawrence Erlbaum, 1976.

———. *Cognitive Development*. Englewood Cliffs, N.J.: Prentice-Hall, 1977.

Flavell, J. H., Beach, D. H., and Chinsky, J. M. Spontaneous verbal rehearsal in a memory task as a function of age. *Child Development*, 1966, *37*, 283–299.

Flavell, J. H., Botkin, P. T., Fry, C. L., Wright, J. W., and Jarvis, P. E. *The Development of Role-Taking and Communication Skills in Childhood*. New York: John Wiley & Sons, 1968.

Flavell, J. H., Friedrichs, A. G., and Hoyt, J. D. Developmental changes in memorization processes. *Cognitive Psychology*, 1970, *1*, 324–340.

Flavell, J. H., and Wellman, H. M. Metamemory. In *Memory in Cognitive Development*, edited by R. V. Kail and J. W. Hagen. Hillsdale, N.J.: Lawrence Erlbaum, 1976.

Flavell, J. H., and Wellman, H. Metamemory. In *Perspectives on the Development of Memory and Cognition*, edited by R. V. Kail and J. W. Hagen. Hillsdale, N.J.: Lawrence Erlbaum, 1977.

Flax, N. Visual function in learning disabilities. *Journal of Learning Disabilities*, 1968, *1*, 551–556.

———. The eye and learning disabilities. *Journal of Learning Disabilities*, 1973, *6*, 328–333.

Flesch, R. *How to Test Readability*. New York: Harper & Row, 1951.

Fletcher, J. M., and Satz, P. Unitary deficit hypotheses of reading disabilities: Has Vellutino led us astray? *Journal of Learning Disabilities*, 1979a, *12*, 155–159.

Fletcher, J. M., and Satz, P. Has Vellutino led us astray? A rejoinder to a reply. *Journal of Learning Disabilities*, 1979b, *12*, 168–171.

Flynn, N. M. and Rapoport, J. L. Hyperactivity in open and traditional classroom environments. *Journal of Special Education*, 1976, *10*, 285–290.

Foley, J. M. Effect of labeling and teacher behavior in children's attitudes. *American Journal of Mental Deficiency*, 1979, *83*, 380–384.

Folkes, J. *Folkes Sentence Builder*. New York: Teaching Resources Corp., 1976.

Forness, S. R. Implications of recent trends in educational labelling. *Journal of Learning Disabilities*, 1974, *7*, 445–449.

———. Concepts of learning and behavior disorders: Implications for research and practice. *Exceptional Children*, 1981, *48*(1), 56–64.

Forness, S. R., and Esveldt, K. C. Prediction of high-risk kindergarten children through classroom observation. *Journal of Special Education*, 1975, *9*, 375–388.

The Forum. Amherst, New York: New York State Federation of Chapters of the Council for Exceptional Children, Winter 1980.

Foster, G. G., Schmidt, C. R., and Sabatino, D. Teacher expectancies and the label "Learning Disabilities." *Journal of Learning Disabilities*, 1976, *9*, 111–114.

Foster, G. G., Ysseldyke, J. E., and Reese, J. H. I wouldn't have seen it if I hadn't believed it. *Exceptional Children*, 1975, *41*, 469–473.

Fraenkel, J. R. *Helping Students Think and Value: Strategies for Teaching the Social Studies*. Englewood Cliffs, N.J.: Prentice-Hall, 1973.

Franks, D. J. Ethnic and social status characteristics of children in EMR and LD classes. *Exceptional Children*, 1971, *37*, 537–538.

Fraser, D., Kidd, B. S. L., Kooh, S. W., and Paunier, L. A new look at infantile hypercalcemia. *Pediatric Clinics of North America*, 1966, *13*(2), 503–525.

Frauenheim, J. G. Academic achievement characteristics of adult males who were diagnosed as dyslexic in childhood. *Journal of Learning Disabilities*, 1978, *11*, 476–483.

Freed, A. M. *Transactional Analysis for Kids (and Grown-Ups Too)*. Sacramento, Calif.: Aluyn M. Freed, 1971.

Freeman, F. W. *Reference Manual for Teachers. Grades One Through Four*. Columbus, Ohio: Zaner-Bloser, 1965.

Freeman, R. D. Special education and the electroencephalogram: Marriage of convenience. *Journal of Special Education*, 1967, *2*, 61–73.

———. Special education and the electroencephalogram: Marriage of convenience. In *Educational Perspectives in Learning Disabilities*, edited by D. Hammill and N. Bartel. New York: John Wiley & Sons, 1971.

Friedman, R. Using the family school in treatment of learning disorders. *Journal of Learning Disabilities*, 1978, *11*, 378–382.

Fries, C. D. *Linguistics and Reading*. New York: Holt, Rinehart and Winston, 1963.

Fromkin, V., and Rodman, R. *An Introduction to Language*. New York: Holt, Rinehart and Winston, 1974.

Frostig, M. *The Marianne Frostig Developmental Test of Visual Perception*. Palo Alto: Consulting Psychologists Press, 1961.

———. Testing as a basis for educational therapy. *Journal of Special Education*, 1967, *2*, 15–34.

———. In *Teaching Children with Learning Disabilities: Personal Perspectives*, edited by J. M. Kauffman and D. P. Hallahan. Columbus, Ohio: Charles E. Merrill, 1976.

———. Meeting individual needs of all children in the classroom setting. *Journal of Learning Disabilities*, 1980, *13*, 158–161.

Frostig, M., and Horne, D. *The Frostig Program for the Development of Visual Perception: Teacher's Guide*. Chicago: Follett, 1964.

Frostig, M., Lefever, D. W., and Whittlesey, J. R. B. A developmental test of visual perception for evaluating normal and neurologically handicapped children. *Perceptual and Motor Skills*, 1961, *12*, 383–394.

———. *The Marianne Frostig Developmental Test of Visual Perception*. Palo Alto: Consulting Psychologists Press, 1964.

Frostig, M., and Maslow, P. *Learning Problems in the Classroom*. New York: Grune & Stratton, 1973.

———. Neuropsychological contributions to education. *Journal of Learning Disabilities*, 1979, *12*, 538–552.

Fry, E. A readability formula that saves time. *Journal of Reading*, 1968, *11*, 513–516.

Fry, M. A., Johnson, C. S., and Muel, S. Oral language production in relation to reading achievement among select second graders. In *Specific Reading Disability*, edited by D. J. Bakker and P. Satz. Rotterdam: Rotterdam University Press, 1970.

Fuller, P. W. Attention and the EEG alpha rhythm in learning disabled children. *Journal of Learning Disabilities*, 1978, *11*, 303–312.

Furth, H. G., and Wachs, H. *Thinking Goes to School*. New York: Oxford University Press, 1974.

Fygetakis, L. J., and Ingram, D. Language rehabilitation and programmed conditioning: A case study. *Journal of Learning Disabilities,* 1973, *6,* 60–64.

Gaddes, W. *Learning Disabilities and Brain Function: A Neuro-Psychological Perspective.* New York: Springer-Verlag, 1980.

Gagné, R. M. *The Conditions of Learning.* 2nd ed. New York: Holt, Rinehart and Winston, 1970.

Gaines, R. The discriminability of form among young children. *Journal of Experimental Child Psychology,* 1969, *8,* 418–431.

Gaines-Suchman, R., and Trabasso, T. Color and form preference in young children. *Journal of Experimental Child Psychology,* 1966, *3,* 177–187.

Galeese, B. *Informal Reading Inventory Program.* University of Michigan, Office of Instructional Services, School of Education, 1973.

Gallagher, J. J. Children with developmental imbalances: A psychoeducational definition. In *The Teacher of Brain-Injured Children: A Discussion of the Bases for Competency,* edited by W. M. Cruickshank. Syracuse: Syracuse University Press, 1966.

———. The special education contract for mildly handicapped children. *Exceptional Children,* 1972, *38,* 527–535.

Gallaway, C. M. Nonverbal teacher behaviors: A critique. *American Educational Research Journal,* 1974, *11,* 305–306.

Garber, H., and Heber, R. *The Milwaukee Project: Early Intervention as a Technique to Prevent Mental Retardation.* Storrs: University of Connecticut Technical Paper, 1973.

Gardner, R. A. *MBD: The Family Book About Minimal Brain Dysfunction.* New York: Jason Aronson, 1973.

Gardner, R. W., Jackson, D. N., and Messick, S. J. Personality organization in cognitive control and intellectual abilities. *Psychological Issues,* 1960, *2*(8), 1–149.

Garey. L. J., Fisken, R. A., and Powell, T. P. S. Observations on the growth of cells in the lateral geniculate nucleus of the cat. *Brain Research,* 1973, *52,* 359–362.

Garey, L. J., and Pettigrew, J. D., Ultrastructural changes in kitten visual cortex after environmental modification. *Brain Research,* 1974, *66,* 165–172.

Garrard, S. D. Role of the pediatrician in the management of learning disorders. *The Pediatric Clinics of North America,* 1973, *20*(3), 737–754.

Garrett, M. K., and Crump, W. D. Peer acceptance, teacher preference, and self-appraisal of social status among learning disabled students. *Learning Disability Quarterly,* 1980, *3*(3), 42–48.

Garrity, L. An electromyographical study of subvocal speech and recall in preschool children. *Developmental Psychology,* 1975, *11,* 274–281.

Gartner, A., Kohler, M. C., and Riessman, F. *Children Teach Children: Learning by Teaching.* New York: Harper & Row, 1971.

Garvey, M., and Gordon, N. A follow-up study of children with disorders of speech development. *British Journal of Disorders of Communication,* 1973, *8,* 17–28.

Gattegno, C. *Words in Color.* Chicago Learning Materials, 1962.

Gawronski, J. D., and Coblentz, D. Calculators and the mathematics curriculum. *Arithmetic Teacher,* 1976, *23,* 510–512.

Gazzaniga, M. S., and Sperry, R. W. Language after section of the cerebral commissures. *Brain,* 1967, *90,* 131–148.

Geffner, D. S., and Hochberg, I. Ear laterality performance of children from low and middle socioeconomic levels on a verbal dichotic listening task. *Cortex,* 1971, *7,* 193–203.

Gelman, R. Conservation acquisition, a problem of learning to attend to relevant attributes. *Journal of Experimental Child Psychology,* 1969, *7,* 167–187.

George, P. S. *Ten Years of Open Space Schools: A Review of the Research.* Gainesville: Florida Educational Research and Development Council, University of Florida, 1975.

Gerard, J. A., and Junkala, J. Task analysis, handwriting, and process based instruction. *Journal of Learning Disabilities,* 1980, *13,* 49–58.

Gerber, P. J. Learning disabilities and eligibility for vocational rehabilitation services: A chronology of events. *Learning Disability Quarterly,* 1981, *4*(4), 422–425.

Gerken, K. Performance of Mexican-American children on intelligence tests. *Exceptional Children,* 1978, *44,* 438–443.

German, D. J. Word-finding skills in children with learning disabilities. *Journal of Learning Disabilities,* 1979, *12,* 176–181.

Gershon, E. S., Dunner, D. L., and Goodwin, F. K. Toward a biology of affective disorders. *Archives of General Psychiatry,* 1971, *25,* 1–15.

Geschwind, N. Neurological foundations of language. In *Progress in Learning Disabilities.* Vol. 1, edited by H. R. Myklebust. New York: Grune & Stratton, 1968.

Gesell, A. L. *Biographies of Child Development.* New York: Harper & Row, 1939.

———. *The First Five Years of Life.* New York: Harper & Row, 1940.

Gesell, A. L. and Amatruda. C. S. *Developmental Diagnosis.* New York: Paul B. Hoeber, 1941.

Gesell, A., and Ames, L. B. The development of handedness. *Journal of Genetic Psychology,* 1947, *70,* 155–175.

Getman, G. N., and Kane, E. R. *The Physiology of Readiness: An Action Program for the Development of Perception for Children.* Minneapolis: Programs to Accelerate School Success, 1964.

Getman, G. N., Kane, E. R., Halgren, M. R., and McKee, G. W. *Developing Learning Readiness.* Manchester, Mo.: Webster Division, McGraw-Hill, 1968.

Getzels, J. W. Images of the classroom and visions of the learner. *School Review,* 1974, *82,* 527–540.

Gibson, E. J. Learning to read. *Science,* 1965, *148,* 1066–1072.

———. *Principles of Perceptual Learning and Development.* New York: Appleton–Century-Crofts, 1969.

———. Trends in perceptual development: Implications for the reading process. Paper presented at the Minnesota Symposia on Child Development, Minneapolis, October 1973.

Gibson, E. J., Gibson, J. J., Pick, A. D., and Osser, H. A. Developmental study of the discrimination of letter-like forms. *Journal of Comparative and Physiological Psychology,* 1962, *55,* 897–906.

Gibson, E. J., and Levin, H. *The Psychology of Reading.* Cambridge: MIT Press, 1975.

Gillespie, P. H., and Johnson, L. *Teaching Reading to the Mildly Retarded Child.* Columbus, Ohio: Charles E. Merrill, 1974.

Gillespie, P. H., Miller, T. L., and Fielder, V. D. Legislative definitions of learning disabilities: Roadblocks to effective service. *Journal of Learning Disabilities,* 1975, *8,* 660–666.

Gillespie, P. H., and Sitko, M. C. Reading problems. In *Teaching the Learning Disabled Adolescent,* edited by L. Mann, L. Goodman, and J. L. Wiederholt. Boston: Houghton Mifflin, 1978.

Gillingham, A., and Stillman, B. *Remedial Training for Children with Specific Disability in Reading, Spelling, and Penmanship.* Cambridge, Mass.: Educator's Publishing Service, 1970.

Glass, G. V., and Robbins, M. P. A critique of experiments on the role of neurological organization in reading performance. *Reading Research Quarterly,* 1967, *3,* 5–51.

Glass, G. V., and Smith, M. L. Meta-analysis of research on class size and achievement. *Educational Evaluation and Policy Analysis,* 1979, *1,* 2–16.

Glasser, W. *Reality Therapy.* New York: Harper & Row, 1965.

———. *Schools Without Failure.* New York: Harper & Row, 1969.

Glavin, J. P., Quay, H. C., Annesley, F. R., and Werry, J. S. An experimental resource room for behavior problem children. *Exceptional Children,* 1971, *38,* 131–137.

Glazzard, M. The effectiveness of three kindergarten predictors for first grade achievement. *Journal of Learning Disabilities,* 1977, *10,* 95–99.

Glazzard, P. H. Teacher rating and reading readiness as predictors of vocabulary and comprehension achievement in first, second, third and fourth grade. *Learning Disability Quarterly,* 1981, *3,* 35–45.

———. Long-range kindergergarten prediction of reading achievement in first through sixth grade. *Learning Disability Quarterly,* 1982, *5*(1), 85–88.

Glow, R. A., and Glow, P. H. Peer and self rating: Children's perception of behavior relevant to hyperkinetic impulse disorder. *Journal of Abnormal Child Psychology,* 1980, *8,* 4.

Gold, M. W. Stimulus factors in skill training of the retarded on a complex assembly task: Acquisition, transfer, and retention. *American Journal of Mental Deficiency,* 1972, *76,* 517–526.

Gold, M. Try another way. Conference on content and process task analyses. Syracuse University, October, 1976.

Gold, R. F. Constitutional growth delay and learning problems. *Journal of Learning Disabilities,* 1978, *11,* 427–429.

Goldman, P. S., Crawford, H. T., Stokes, L, P., Galkin, T. W., and Rosvold, H. E. Sex-dependent behavioral effects of cerebral cortical lesions in the developing rhesus monkey. *Science,* 1974, *186,* 540–542.

Goldman, R. D., and Hartig, L. K. The WISC may not be a valid predictor of school performance for primary-grade minority children. *American Journal of Mental Deficiency,* 1975, *80,* 583–587.

Goldstein, A. P., Sprafkin, R. P., Gershaw, N. J., and Klein, P. *Skill-streaming the Adolescent: A Structured Approach to Teaching Prosocial Skills.* Champaign, Ill.: Research Press, 1980.

Goldstein, G. Cognitive and perceptual differences between schizophrenics and organics. *Schizophrenia Bulletin,* 1978, *4,* 160–185.

Goldstein, K. The modifications of behavior consequent to cerebral lesions. *Psychiatric Quarterly,* 1936, *10,* 586–610.

———. *The Organism.* New York: American Book Co, 1939.

———. *Aftereffects of Brain Injuries in War.* New York: Grune & Stratton, 1942.

Gollin, E. S. Developmental studies of visual recognition of incomplete objects. *Perceptual Motor Skills,* 1960, *11,* 289–298.

Good, T. and Brophy, J. Behavioral expression of teacher attitudes. Journal of Educational Psychology, 1972, *63,* 617–624.

Good, T., and Brophy, J. *Looking in Classrooms.* New York: Harper & Row, 1978.

Goodman, D. C., and Horel, J. A. Sprouting of optic tract projections in the brain stem of the rat. *Journal of Comparative Neurology,* 1966, *127,* 77–88.

Goodman, K. S., and Goodman, Y. Learning to read is natural. In *Theory and Practice of Early Reading.* Vol. 1, edited by L. B. Resnick and P. A. Weaver. Hillsdale, N.J.: Lawrence Erlbaum, 1979.

Goodman, L. The efficacy of visual-motor training for orthopedically handicapped children. *Rehabilitation Literature,* 1973, *34,* 299–304.

Goodman, L., and Hammill, D. The effectiveness of Kephart Getman activities in developing perceptual-motor and cognitive skills. *Focus on Exceptional Children,* 1973, *4*(9), 1–9.

Goodman, L., and Mann, L. *Learning Disabilities in the Secondary School: Issues and Practices.* New York: Grune & Stratton, 1976.

Goodman, Y. M. Using children's miscues for teaching reading strategies. *The Reading Teacher,* 1970, *23,* 455–459.

———. Reading diagnosis qualitative or quantitative. *The Reading Teacher,* 1972, *26,* 32–37.

Goodman, Y., and Burke, C. L. *Reading Miscue Inventory Manual: Procedure for Diagnosis and Evaluation.* New York: Macmillan, 1972.

Goodnow, J. J. The role of modalities in perceptual and cognitive development. *Minnesota Symposium on Child Psychology,* 1971, *5,* 3–25.

Goodstein, H. A. Are the errors we see the true errors? Error analysis in verbal problem solving. *Topics in Learning and Learning Disabilities,* 1981, *1*(3), 31–45.

Gordon, E. W. Methodological problems and pseudoissues in the nature-nurture controversy. In *Intelligence: Genetic and Environmental Influences,* edited by R. Cancro. New York: Grune & Stratton, 1971.

Gordon, I. J. *The Florida Parent Education Early Intervention Projects: A Longitudinal Look.* Urbana: ERIC Clearinghouse on Early Childhood Education, 1975.

Gordon, S. Psychological problems of adolescents with minimal brain dysfunction. In *Learning Disabilities: Its Implications to a Responsible Society,* edited by D. Kronick. Chicago: Developmental Learning Materials, 1969.

Gordon, W. J. *Synectics.* New York: Harper & Row, 1971.

Gottesman, R. L., Croen, L., and Rotkin, L. Urban second grade children: A profile of good and poor readers. *Journal of Learning Disabilities,* 1982, *15,* 268–272.

Gottman, J. M. N-of-one and N-of-two research in psychotherapy. *Psychological Bulletin,* 1973, *80,* 93–105.

Goyette, C. H., Connors, C. K., Petti, T. A., and Curtis, L. E. Effects of artificial colors on hyperkinetic children: A double-blind challenge study. *Psychopharmacology Bulletin,* 1978, *14*(2), 39–40.

Gray, R. A. Services for the LD adult: A working paper. *Learning Disability Quarterly,* 1981, *4*(4), 426–434.

Gray, S. W., and Miller, J. O. Early experience in relation to cognitive development. *Review of Educational Research,* 1967, *37,* 475–493.

Grayum, H. S. Skimming in Reading: A fine art for modern needs. In *Teaching Reading Skills in Secondary Schools,* edited by A. V. Olson and W. S. Ames. New York: Macmillan, 1967.

Graziano, A. and Berkowitz, B. Training parents as behavior therapists, a review. *Behavior Research & Therapy,* 1972, *10,* 297–317.

Green, M. Sublingual provocative testing for foods and FD & C dyes. *Annals of Allergy,* 1974, *33,* 274–281.

Green, O. C., and Perlman, S. M. Endocrinology and disorders of learning. In *Progress in Learning Disabilities.* Vol. 2, edited by H. R. Myklebust. New York: Grune & Stratton, 1971.

Greene, V. T. Temporal lobe epilepsy and the clinical psychiatrist. *Journal of the Irish Medical Association,* 1976, *69,* 90–96.

Greenough, W. T. Enduring brain effects of differential experience and training. In *Neural Mechanisms of Learning and Memory,* edited by M. R. Rosenzweig and E. L. Bennett. Cambridge: MIT Press, 1976.

Greenstein, J. and Strain, P. S. The utility of the Key Math Diagnostic Arithmetic Test for adolescent learning disabled students. *Psychology in the Schools,* 1977, *14*(3), 275–282.

Gregory, S. C., and Bunch, M. E. The relative retentive abilities of fast and slow learners. *Journal of General Psychology,* 1959, *60,* 173–181.

Gresham, F. M. Misguided mainstreaming: The case for social skills training with handicapped children. *Exceptional Children,* 1982, *48,* 422–433.

Griffith, H., and Davidson, M. Long-term changes in intellect and behavior after hemispherectomy. *Journal of Neurology, Neurosurgery, and Psychiatry,* 1966, *29,* 571–576.

Griffiths, A. D., and Laurence, K. M. The effect of hypoxia and hypoglycaemia on the brain of the newborn human infant. *Developmental Medicine and Child Neurology,* 1974, *16,* 308–319.

Griffiths, C. P. S. A follow-up study of children with disorders of speech. *British Journal of Disorders of Communication,* 1969, *4,* 46–56.

Grimes, L. Learned helplessness and attribution theory: Redefining children's learning problems. *Learning Disability Quarterly*, 1981, *4*(1), 91–100.

Grisé, P. Florida's minimum competency testing program for handicapped students. *Exceptional Children*, 1980, *47*, 186–191.

Groden, G. Lateral preferences in normal children. *Perceptual and Motor Skills*, 1969, *28*, 213–214.

Groenendaal, H. A., and Bakker, D. J. The part played by mediation processes in the retention of temporal sequences by two reading groups. *Human Development*, 1971, *14*, 62–70

Grossman, H., ed. *Manual on Terminology and Classification in Mental Retardation* (Special Publication Series No. 2). Washington, D.C.: American Association on Mental Deficiency, 1973.

———. *Manual on Terminology and Classification in Mental Retardation*. 2nd ed. Washington, D.C.: American Association on Mental Deficiency, 1977.

Gruber, E. Reading ability, binocular coordination and the ophthalmograph. *Archives of Ophthalmology*, 1962, *67*, 280–288.

Grunewald-Zuberbier, E., Grunewald, G., and Rasche, A. Hyperactive behavior and EEG arousal reactions in children. *Electroencephalography and Clinical Neurophysiology*, 1975, *38*, 149–159.

Guilford, J. P. Three faces of intellect. *American Psychologist*, 1959, *14*, 469–479.

Gump, P. V. School environments. In *Children and the Environment*, edited by I. Altman and J. F. Wohlwill. New York: Plenum, 1978.

Guralnick, M. J. The application of single-subject research designs to the field of learning disabilities. *Journal of Learning Disabilities*, 1978, *11*, 415–421.

Guthrie, J. Time in reading programs. *The Reading Teacher*, 1980, *33*, 500–502.

Guthrie, J. T. and Goldberg, H, K. Visual sequential memory in reading disability. *Journal of Learning Disabilities*, 1972, *5*, 41–46.

Guyer, B. L., and Friedman, M. P. Hemispheric processing and cognitive styles in learning-disabled and normal children. *Child Development*, 1975, *46*, 658–668.

Hagen, J. W. Some thoughts on how children learn to remember. *Human Development*, 1971, *14*, 262–271.

Hagen, J. W., and Hale, G. H. The development of attention in children. *Minnesota Symposium on Child Psychology*, 1973, *7*, 117–140.

Hagen, J. W., Jongeward, R. H., and Kail, R. V. Cognitive perspectives on the development of memory. In *Advances in Child Development and Behavior*. Vol. 10, edited by H. W. Reese. New York: Academic Press, 1975.

Haider, M. Vigilance, attention, expectation, and cortical evoked potentials. *Acta Psychologica*, 1967, *27*, 246–252.

Haight, S. Concept usage and concept formation in learning disabled and normal children. Paper presented at the Association for Children with Learning Disabilities, 14th International Conference, Washington, D.C., 9–12 March 1977.

Haisley, F., Tell, C., and Andrews, J. Peers as tutors in the mainstream: Trained "teachers" of handicapped adolescents. *Journal of Learning Disabilities*, 1981, *14*, 224–226, 238.

Hall, P. K., and Tomblin, J. B. A follow-up study of children with articulation and language disorders. *Journal of Speech and Hearing Disorders*, 1978, *43*, pp. 227–241.

Hall, R. V. *Managing Behavior: Parts 1, 2, 3.* Lawrence, Kan.: H. & H. Enterprises, 1970.

Hallahan, D. P. and Cruickshank, W. M. *Psycho-educational Foundations of Learning Disabilities.* Englewood Cliffs, N.J.: Prentice-Hall, 1973.

Hallahan, D. P., Gajar, A. H., Cohen, S. B., and Tarver, S. G. Selective attention and locus-of-control in learning disabled and normal children. *Journal of Learning Disabilities*, 1978, *11*, 231–236.

Hallahan, D. P., and Kauffman, J. M. *Introduction to Learning Disabilities: A Psycho-Behavioral Approach.* Englewood Cliffs, N.J.: Prentice-Hall, 1976.

Hallahan, D. P., and Kauffman, J. M. Labels, categories, behaviors: ED, LD, and EMR reconsidered. Journal of Special Education, 1977, *11*, 139–149.

Hallahan, D. P., Tower, S. G., Kauffman, J. M., and Graybeel, N. L. A comparison of the effect of reinforcement and response cost on the selective attention of learning disabled children. *Journal of Learning Disabilities*, 1978, *11*, 430–438.

Hallenbeck, M. Tips for selecting textbooks. *The American School Board Journal*, 1980, *167*, 21–22.

Hallgren, B. Specific dyslexia ("congenital word blindness"): A clinical and genetic study. *Acta Psychiatrica et Neurologica, Scandinavica*, 1950, Suppl. *65*, 1–287.

Halpern, W., Turned on toddlers. *Journal of Communication*, 1975, *25*, 66–70.

Hamilton, V., and Vernon, M., eds. *The Development of Cognitive Processes.* London: Academic Press, 1976.

Hammill, D. Training visual perceptual processes. *Journal of Learning Disabilities*, 1972, *5*, 552–559.

———. Defining "LD" for programmatic purposes. *Academic Therapy*, 1976, *12*, 29–37.

Hammill, D. D., and Bartel, N. R. *Teaching Children with Learning and Behavior Problems.* 2nd ed. Boston: Allyn & Bacon, 1978.

———. *Teaching Children with Learning and Behavior Problems.* 3rd ed. Boston: Allyn & Bacon, 1982.

Hammill, D., Goodman, L., and Wiederholt, J. L. Visual-motor processes: Can we train them? *Reading Teacher*, 1974, *27*, 469–478.

Hammill, D. D., and Larsen, S. C. The effectiveness of psycholinguistic training. *Exceptional Children*, 1974a, *41*, 5–14.

———. The relationship of selected auditory perceptual skills and reading ability. *Journal of Learning Disabilities*, 1974b, *7*, 429–436.

———. The effectiveness of psycholinguistic training: A reaffirmation of position. *Exceptional Children*, 1978a, *44*, 402–414.

———. *Test of Written Language.* Austin, Tex.: Pro-Ed, 1978b.

Hammill, D. D., Leigh, J. E., McNutt, G., and Larsen, S. C. A new definition of learning disabilities. *Learning Disability Quarterly*, 1981, *4*(4), 336–342.

Hammill, D. D., and Poplin, M. Problems in writing. In *Teaching Children with Learning and Behavior Problems.* 2nd ed. Boston: Allyn & Bacon, 1978.

Haney, W. Validity, vaudeville and values: A short history of social concerns over standardized testing. *American Psychologist*, 1981, *36*, 1021–1034.

Hanley, J. and Sklar, B., Electroencephalographic correlates of developmental reading dyslexias: Computer analysis of recordings from normal and dyslexic children. In *Basic Visual Processes and Learning Disability*, edited by G. Leisman. Columbus, Ohio: Charles C Thomas, 1976.

Hanna, P. R., Hodges, R. E., and Hanna, J. S. *Spelling: Structure and Strategies.* Boston: Houghton Mifflin, 1971.

Harber, J. R. Learning disability research: How far have we progressed? *Learning Disability Quarterly*, 1981, *4*(4), 372–381.

Hardy, J. B. Perinatal factors and intelligence. In *The Biosocial Basis of Mental Retardation*, edited by S. F. Osler and R. E. Cooke. Baltimore: Johns Hopkins Press, 1965.

Hardyck, C., and Petrinovich, L. F. Left-handedness. *Psychological Bulletin*, 1977, *84*, 385–404.

Hardyck, C., Petrinovich, L. F., and Goldman, R. D. Left-handedness and cognitive deficit. *Cortex*, 1976, *12*, 266–279.

Haring, N. G. Norris G. Haring. In *Teaching Children with Behavior Disorders*, edited by J. M. Kauffman and C. D. Lewis. Columbus, Ohio: Charles E. Merrill, 1974.

Haring, N. G., and Ridgway, R. W. Early identification of

children with learning disabilities. *Exceptional Children*, 1967, *33*, 387–395.

Harley, J. P., Matthews, C. G., and Eichman, P. Synthetic food colors and hyperactivity in children: A double-blind challenge experiment. *Pediatrics*, 1978, *62*, 975–983.

Harley, J. P., Ray, R. S., Tomasi, L., Eichman, P. L., Matthews, C. G., Chun, R., Cleeland, C. S. and Traisman, E. Hyperkinesis and food additives: Testing the Feingold hypothesis. *Pediatrics*, 1978, *61*, 818–828.

Harmer W., and Alexander, J. Examination of parental attitudes within the diagnostic intervention process. *Journal of Learning Disabilities*, 1978, *11*, 590–593.

Harris, A. J. Lateral dominance, directional confusion and reading disability. *Journal of Psychology*, 1957, *44*, 283–294.

———. *Effective Teaching of Reading*. New York: David McKay, 1962.

Harris, A. J., and Sipay, E. R. *How to Teach Reading: A Competency-Based Program*. New York: Longman, 1979.

Harris, D. *Children's Drawings as Measures of Intellectual Maturity*. New York: Harcourt, Brace & World, 1963.

Harris, T. A. *I'm OK — You're OK: A Practical Guide to Transactional Analysis*. New York: Harper & Row, 1969.

Hartlage, L. C., and Green, J. B. EEG differences in children's reading, spelling, and arithmetic abilities. *Perceptual and Motor Skills*, 1971, *32*, 133–134.

Hartlage, L. C., and Green, J. B. The EEG abnormalities and WISC subtest differences. *Journal of Clinical Psychology*, 1972, *28*, 170–171.

Hartlage, L. C., and Hartlage, P. L. Application of neuropsychological principles in the diagnosis of learning disabilities. In *Brain Function and Reading Disabilities*, edited by L. Tarnopol and M. Tarnopol. Baltimore: University Park Press, 1977.

Hartshorne, H. and May, M. A. *Studies in Deceit*. New York: Macmillan, 1928.

Harvard, J. School problems and allergies. *Journal of Learning Disabilities*, 1973, *6*, 492–494.

Havighurst, R. J. *Developmental Tasks and Education*. New York: David McKay, 1972.

Hawthorne, L., and Larsen, S. The predictive validity and reliability of the Basic School Skills Inventory. *Journal of Learning Disabilities*, 1977, *10*, 44–50.

Hayes, M. L. *Oh, Dear Somebody Said 'Learning Disabilities': A Book for Teachers and Parents*. San Rafael, Calif.: Academic Therapy Publications, 1975.

Haynes, S. N. *Principles of Behavioral Assessment*. New York: Gardner, 1978.

Haynes, S. N., and Wilson, C. C. *Behavioral Assessment: Recent Advances in Methods, Concepts, and Applications*. San Francisco: Jossey-Bass, 1979.

Head, H. Hughlings Jackson on aphasic and kindred affections of speech. *Brain*, 1915, *38*, 1–190.

———. Aphasia: An historical review. *Brain*, 1920a, *43*, 390–411.

———. Aphasia and kindred disorders. *Brain*, 1920b, *43*, 87–165.

———. Speech and cerebral localization. *Brain*, 1923, *46*, 355–528.

———. *Aphasia and Kindred Disorders of Speech*. London: Cambridge University Press, 1926.

Heath, E. J., Cook, P., and O'Dell, N. Eye exercises and reading efficiency. *Academic Therapy*, 1976, *11*, 435–445.

Hebb, D. O. A *Textbook of Psychology*. Philadelphia: W. B. Saunders, 1966.

Hécaen, H., and Albert, M. L. *Human Neuropsychology*. New York: John Wiley & Sons, 1978.

Hécaen, H., and Sauget, J. Cerebral dominance in left-handed subjects. *Cortex*, 1971, *7*, 19–48.

Hechtman, L., Weiss, G., Finklestein, J., Werner, A., and Benn, R. Hyperactives as young adults: Preliminary report. *Canadian Medical Association Journal*, 1976, *115*, 625–627, 630.

Heckelman R. C. A neurological inpress method of remedial reading. *Academic Therapy*, 1969, *4*, 277–282.

Heider, E. R. Information processing and the modification of an "impulsive conceptual tempo." *Child Development*, 1971, *42*, 1276–1281.

Heifetz, L. From consumer to middleman: Emerging roles for parents in the network of services for retarded children. In *Parent Education Handbook*, edited by R. R. Abendin. Springfield, Ill.: Charles C. Thomas, 1980.

Heilman, A. W. *Phonics in Proper Perspective*. Columbus, Ohio: Charles E. Merrill, 1968.

Heilman, K. M., and Valenstein, E. *Clinical Neuropsychology*. Oxford: Oxford University Press, 1979.

Heiman, J. R., Fischer, M. J., and Ross, A. O. A supplementary behavioral program to improve deficient reading performance. *Journal of Abnormal Child Psychology*, 1973, I, 390–399.

Hemmes, N. S. Writing posture and paper orientation. *Science*, 1977, *195*, 441.

Hendrickson, L. N., and Muehl, S. The effects of attention and motor response pretraining on learning to discriminate *b* and *d* in kindergarten children. *Journal of Educational Psychology*, 1962, *53*, 236–241.

Herjanic, B. M., and Penick, E. C. Adult outcome of disabled child readers. *Journal of Special Education*, 1972, *6*, 397–410.

Hermann, K. *Reading Disability: A Medical Study of Word-Blindness and Related Handicaps*. Springfield, Ill.: Charles C. Thomas, 1959.

Hermreck, L. A. A comparison of the written language of LD and non-LD elementary children using the Inventory of Written Expression and Spelling. Unpublished master's thesis, University of Kansas, 1979.

Heron, T. E., and Skinner, M. E. Criteria for defining the regular classroom as the least restrictive environment for LD students. *Exceptional Children*, 1981, *4*(2), 115–121.

Hersen, M., and Bellack, A. S., eds. *Behavioral Assessment: A Practical Handbook*. 2nd ed. New York: Pergamon, 1981.

Hertzig, M. E., and Birch, H. G. Neurologic organization in psychiatrically disturbed adolescents: A comparative consideration of sex differences. *Archives of General Psychiatry*, 1968, *19*, 528–537.

Hess, R. D., and Shipman, V. C. Maternal influences upon early learning: The cognitive environments of urban preschool children. In *Early Education*, edited by R. D. Hess and R. M. Bear. Chicago: Aldine, 1968.

Hetrick, E. Training parents of learning disabled children in facilitative communication skills. *Journal of Learning Disabilities*, 1979, *12*, 275–277.

Hickey, K., Imber, S. C. and Ruggiero, E. A. Modifying reading behavior of elementary special needs children: A cooperative resource parent program. *Journal of Learning Disabilities*, 1979, *12*, 444–448.

Hickman, M. R., and Anderson, C. P. Evaluating instructional materials for LD children. *Journal of Learning Disabilities*, 1979, *12*, 355–359.

Hicks, R. E., and Kinsbourne, M. Differences: Lefthandedness. In *The Asymmetrical Function of the Brain*, edited by M. Kinsbourne. New York: Cambridge University Press, 1978a.

———. Human handedness. In *Asymmetrical Function of the Brain*, Cambridge: Cambridge University Press, 1978b.

Hier, D. B. Sex differences in hemisphere specialization: Hypothesis for the excess of dyslexia in boys. *Bulletin of the Orton Society*, 1979, *29*, 74–83.

Hier, D. B., LeMay, M., Rosenberger, P. B., and Perlo, V. P. Developmental dyslexia: Evidence for a sub-group with a reversal of cerebral asymmetry. *Archives of Neurology*, 1978, *35*, 90–92.

Hildreth, G. A school survey of eye-hand dominance. *Journal of Applied Psychology*, 1945, *29*, 83–88.

Hinshelwood, J. A case of dyslexia: A peculiar form of word-blindness. *Lancet*, 1896, *2*, 1451–1454.

———. A case of "word" without "letter" blindness. *Lancet*, 1898, *1*, 422–425.

———. "Letter" without "word" blindness. *Lancet*, 1899, *1*, 83–86.

———. Four cases of congenital word-blindness occurring in the same family. *British Medical Journal*, 1907, *2*, 1229–1232.

———. Two cases of hereditary congenital word-blindness. *British Medical Journal*, 1911, *1*, 608–609.

———. *Congenital Word Blindness*. London: H. K. Lewis & Co., 1917.

Hobbs, N. *The Futures of Children*. San Francisco: Jossey-Bass, 1975a.

———. *Issues in the Classification of Children*. 2 vols. San Francisco: Jossey-Bass, 1975b.

Hock, H., and Hilton, T. Spatial coding and oblique discrimination by children. *Journal of Experimental Child Psychology*, 1979, *27*, 96–104.

Hoffman, J. V. The disabled reader: Forgive us our regressions and lead us not into expectations. *Journal of Learning Disabilities*, 1980, *13*, 7–11.

Honzik, M. P. Developmental studies of parent-child resemblance in intelligence. *Child Development*, 1957, *28*, 215–228.

Honzik, M. P., Macfarlane, J. W., and Allen, L. The stability of mental test performance between two and eighteen years. *Journal of Experimental Education*, 1948, *17*, 309–324.

Hopkins, B. L., Schutte, R. C., and Garton, K. L. The effects of access to a playroom on the rate and quality of printing and writing of first and second grade students. *Journal of Applied Behavior Analysis*, 1971, *4*, 77–87.

Hopper, R., and Naremore, R. C. *Children's Speech: A Practical Introduction to Communication Development*. New York: Harper & Row, 1973.

Hori, A. K. O. An investigation of the efficacy of a questioning training procedure on increasing the reading comprehension performance of junior high school learning disabled students. Unpublished master's thesis, University of Kansas, 1977. In *Teaching the Learning Disabled Adolescent: Strategies and Methods*, edited by G. Alley and D. Deshler. Denver: Love Publishing Company, 1979.

Horn, A. *The Uneven Distribution of the Effects of Specific Factors* (Southern California Educational Monographs, No. 12). Los Angeles: University of Southern California Press, 1941.

Horne, M. D. Do learning disabilities specialists know their phonics? *Journal of Special Education*, 1975, *9*, 580–582.

Horowitz, E. C. Popularity, decentering ability, and role-taking skills in learning disabled and normal children. *Learning Disability Quarterly*, 1981, *4*(1), 23–30.

Horowitz, F. D., and Paden, L. Y. The effectiveness of environmental intervention programs. In *Review of Child Development Research*. Vol. 3, edited by B. M. Caldwell and H. N. Ricciuti. Chicago: University of Chicago Press, 1973.

Hresko, W. P., and Reid, D. K. Five faces of cognition: Theoretical influences on approaches to learning disabilities. *The Forum*, Summer, 1980, 14–15, 22–23.

Humphries, T. W. and Bauman, E. Maternal child rearing attitudes associated with learning disabilities. *Journal of Learning Disabilities*, 1980, *13*, 54–57.

Hunt, D. E. Learning styles and teaching strategies. *High School Behavioral Science*, 1974, *2*, 22–34.

Hunt, D. E., Joyce, B. R., Greenwood, J., Noy, J. E., Reid, R., and Weil, M. Student conceptual level and models of teaching: Theoretical and empirical coordination of two models. *Interchange*, 1974, *5*, 19–30.

Hunt, J. McV. *Intelligence and Experience*. New York: Ronald, 1961.

———. The early detection of potential learning disorders. *Academic Therapy*, 1969, *4*, 12–15.

Hunter, E. J., Johnson, L. C., and Keefe, F. B. Electrodermal and cardiovascular responses in nonreaders. *Journal of Learning Disabilities*, 1972, *5*, 187–197.

Hurley, R. *Poverty and Mental Retardation: A Causal Relationship*. New York: Vintage, 1969.

Huttenlocker, J. Discrimination of figure orientation: Effects of relative position. *Journal of Comparative and Physiological Psychology*, 1967, *63*, 359–361.

Hyden, H., Nerve cells and their glia: Relationships and differences. In *Macromolecules and Behaviour*, edited by G. B. Ansell and P. B. Bradley. Baltimore: University Park Press, 1973.

Ilg, F., and Ames, L. *School Readiness*. New York: Harper & Row, 1964.

Ilg, F. L., Ames, L. B., and Apell, R. School readiness as evaluated by Gesell developmental, visual, and projective tests. *Genetic Psychology Monographs*, 1965, *71*, 61–91.

Ingram, T. T. S. Developmental disorders of speech. In *Handbook of Clinical Neurology*. Vol. 4, *Disorders of Speech, Perception, and Symbolic Behavior*, edited by P. J. Vinken and G. W. Bruyn. Amsterdam: North Holland, 1969.

———. Speech disorders in childhood. In *Foundations of Language Development*. Vol. 2, edited by E. H. Lenneberg and E. Lenneberg. New York: Academic Press, 1976.

Ingram, T. T. S., Mason, A. W., and Blackburn, I. A retrospective study of 82 children with reading disability. *Developmental Medicine and Child Neurology*, 1970, *12*, 271–279.

Irmscher, W. F. *The Holt Guide to English*. New York: Holt, Rinehart and Winston, 1972.

Ito, H. R. Long-term effects of resource room programs on learning disabled children's reading. *Journal of Learning Disabilities*, 1980, *13*, 322–326.

Jacks, K. B., and Keller, M. E. A humanistic approach to the adolescent with learning disabilities: An educational psychological and vocational model. *Adolescence*, 1978, *13*, 59–68.

Jackson, G. D. Another psychological view from the association of black psychologists. *American Psychologist*, 1975, *22*, 88–93.

Jackson, H. *Selected Writings of John Hughlings Jackson*. 2 vols. London: Hodder & Stoughton, 1931.

Jakupcak, M. Job functions, roles and views of training of learning disability and remedial reading personnel. Unpublished doctoral dissertation, University of Illinois, Urbana, 1973.

———. Areas of congruence in remedial reading and learning disabilities. *Journal of Special Education*, 1975, *9*, 155–157.

James M., and Jongeward, D. *Born to Win: Transactional Analysis with Gestalt Experiments*. Reading, Mass.: Addison-Wesley, 1971.

Jansky, J., and de Hirsch, K. *Preventing Reading Failure: Prediction, Diagnosis, and Intervention*. New York: Harper & Row, 1972.

———. *Preventing Reading Failure: Prediction, Diagnosis, Intervention*. New York: Harper & Row, 1973.

Jencks, C. *Inequality*. New York: Harper & Row, 1972.

Jenkins, J. J., and Palermo, D. S. Mediation processes and the acquisition of linguistic structure. In *The acquisition of language*. Monographs of the Society for Research in Child Development, edited by U. Bellugi and R. Brown, 1964, *29*(1, Whole No. 92).

Jensen, A. Learning ability in retarded, average, and gifted children. *Merrill-Palmer Quarterly*, 1963, *9*, 123–140.

———. How much can we boost IQ and scholastic achievement? *Harvard Educational Review*, 1969, *39*, 1–123.

———. The role of verbal mediation in mental development. *Journal of Genetic Psychology*, 1971, *118*, 39–70.

Jeter, I. K., ed *Social Dialects: Differences vs. Disorders*. Rockville, Md.: American Speech and Hearing Association, 1977.

John, E. R., Karmel, B. Z., Corning, W. C., Easton, P., Brown, D., Ahn, H., John, M., Harmony, T., Prichep, L., Toro, A., Gerson, I., Bartlett, F., Thatcher, R., Kaye, H., Valdes, P., and Schwartz, E. Neurometrics. *Science*. 1977a, *196*, 1393–1410.

John, E. R., Thatcher, R., Smith, Carmel, and Kaye, H. Neurometrics. Symposium presented at the Association for Children with Learning Disabilities, 14th International Conference, Washington, D.C., 9–12 March 1977b.

Johnson, B., and Cartwright, C. A. The roles of information and experience in improving teachers' knowledge and attitudes about mainstreaming. *Journal of Special Education*, 1979, *13*, 453–462.

Johnson, B. L., Cohen, H. H., Struble, R., Setzer, J. V., Anger, W. K., Gutnik, B. D., McDonough, T., and Hauser, P. Field evaluation of carbon monoxide exposed toll collectors. In *Behavioral Toxicology*, edited by C. Xintras, B. L. Johnson, and I. de Groot. Washington, D.C.: U.S. Department of Health, Education and Welfare, 1974.

Johnson, D. J. Educational principles for children with learning disabilities. *Rehabilitation Literature*, 1967, *28*, 317–322.

Johnson, D., and Myklebust, H. *Learning Disabilities: Educational Principles and Practices*. New York: Grune & Stratton, 1967.

Johnson, G. O. Special education for the mentally handicapped — a paradox. *Exceptional Children*, 1962, *29*, 62–69.

Johnson, S. W. *Arithmetic and Learning Disabilities. Guidelines for Identification and Remediation*. Boston: Allyn & Bacon, 1979.

Joiner, L. M., and Kottmeyer, W. A. Effect of classroom noise on number identification by retarded children. *California Journal of Educational Research*, 1971, *22*, 164–169.

Jones, D. R. The dictionary: A look at "Look it up." *Journal of Reading*, 1980, *23*, 309–312.

Jones, E. P. Approaches to quality in early childhood programs. *Childhood Education*, 1974, *50*(3), 125–131.

Jones, R. L. Labels and stigma in special education. *Exceptional Children*, 1972, *38*, 553–564.

Jost, H., and Sontag, L. W. The genetic factor in autonomic nervous system function. *Psychosomatic Medicine*, 1944, *6*, 308–310.

Jourard, S. *The Transparent Self*. Princeton: Van Nostrand, 1964.

Joynes, Y. D., McCormick, S., and Heward, W. L. Teaching reading disabled students to read and complete employment applications. *Journal of Reading*, 1980, *23*, 709–714.

Junkala, J. Task analysis and instructional alternatives. *Academic Therapy*, 1972, *8*, 33–40.

———. Task analysis: The processing dimension. *Academic Therapy*, 1973, *8*, 401–409.

Kagan, J. Reflection-impulsivity and reading ability in primary grade children. *Child Development*, 1965, *36*, 609–628.

———. On cultural deprivation. In *Environmental Influences*, edited by New York: Rockefeller University Press and Russell Sage Foundation, 1968.

Kagan, J., and Kogan, N. Individual variation in cognitive processes. In *Carmichael's Manual of Child Psychology*. Vol. 1, edited by P. H. Mussen. New York: John Wiley & Sons, 1970.

Kagan, J., Moss, H. A., and Sigel, I. E. Psychological significance of styles of conceptualization. *Monographs of the Society for Research in Child Development*, 1963, *28*, 73–124.

Kagan, J., Rosman, B. L., Day, D., Albert J., and Phillips, W. Information processing in the child: Significance of analytic and reflective attitudes. *Psychological Monographs*, 1964, *78*(1, Whole No. 578).

Kahn, D., and Birch, H. G. Development of auditory-visual integration and reading achievement. *Perceptual and Motor Skills*, 1968, *27*, 459–468.

Kail, R. *The Development of Memory in Children*. San Francisco: W. H. Freeman, 1979.

Kail, R. V., and Hagen, J. W., eds. *Memory in Cognitive Development*. Hillsdale, N.J.: Lawrence Erlbaum, 1976.

———. *Perspectives on the Development of Memory and Cognition*. Hillsdale, N.J.: Lawrence Erlbaum, 1977.

Kail, R. V., and Siegel, A. W. The development of mnemonic encoding in children: From perception to abstraction. In *Perspectives on the Development of Memory and Cognition*, edited by R. V. Kail and J. W. Hagen. New York: John Wiley & Sons, 1977.

Kaliski, L. Arithmetic and the brain-injured child. *Arithmetic Teacher*, 1962, *9*, 245–251.

———. Arithmetic and the brain-injured child. In *Educating Children with Learning Disabilities*, edited by E. Frierson and W. Barbe. New York: Appleton-Century-Crofts, 1967.

Kallman, W. M., and Feuerstein, M. Psychophysiological procedures. In *Handbook of Behavioral Assessment*, edited by A. R. Ciminero, K. S. Calhoun, and H. E. Adams. New York: John Wiley and Sons, 1977.

Kaluger, G., and Kolson, C. J. *Reading and Learning Disabilities*. Columbus, Ohio: Charles E. Merrill, 1969.

Kalverboer, A. F. Neurobehavioral relationships in young children: Some remarks on concepts and methods. In *The Neuropsychology of Learning Disorders: Theoretical Approaches*, edited by R. M. Knights and D. J. Bakker. Baltimore: University Park Press, 1976.

Kanfer, F. H., and Saslow, G. Behavioral diagnosis. In *Behavior Therapy: Appraisal and Status*, edited by C. M. Franks. New York: McGraw-Hill, 1969.

Karnes, M., Hodgins, A., and Teska, J. The effects of preschool interventions: Evaluations over two years. In *Investigations of Classroom and At-home Interventions: Research and Development Program on Preschool Disadvantaged*. Final report, Vol. 1, edited by M. B. Karnes et al. Washington, D.C.: Office of Education, Bureau of Research, 1969.

Karnoil, R. A conceptual analysis of imminent justice: Responses in children. *Child Development*, 1980, *51*, 118–130.

Karpati, G., and Frame, B. Neuropsychiatric disorders in primary hyperparathyroidism. *Archives of Neurology*, 1964, *10*, 387–397.

Kass, C. E. Learning disability: An educational definition. *Journal of Learning Disabilities*, 1969a, *2*, 377–379.

———. Introduction to learning disabilities. *Seminars in Psychiatry*, 1969b, *1*, 240–244.

Kass, C. E., and Myklebust, H. R. Learning disability: An educational definition. *Journal of Learning Disabilities*, 1969, *2*, 377–379.

Kaswan, J., Haralson, S., and Cline, R. Variables in perceptual and cognitive organization and differentiation. *Journal of Personality*, 1965, *33*, 164–177.

Katz, P. A., and Deutsch, M. Relation of auditory-visual shifting to reading achievement. *Perceptual Motor Skills*, 1963, *17*, 327–332.

Katz, P. A. and Deutsch, M. Auditory and visual functioning and reading achievement. In *The Disadvantaged Child*, edited by M. Deutsch. New York: Basic Books, 1967.

Kaufman, A. A new approach to interpretation of test scatter on the WISC-R. *Journal of Learning Disabilities*, 1976, *9*, 160–168.

Kaufman, A. S. *Intelligent Testing with the WISC-R*. New York: John Wiley & Sons, 1979a.

———. WISC-R research: Implications for interpretation. *School Psychology Digest*, 1979b, *8*, 5–27.

Kaufman, A., Zalma, R., and Kaufman, N. The relationship of hand dominance to the motor coordination, mental ability and R-L awareness of young normal children. *Child Development*, 1978, *49*, 885–888.

Kauffman, J. M., and Hallahan, D. P. *Teaching Children With Learning Disabilities: Personal Perspectives*. Columbus, Ohio: Charles E. Merrill, 1976.

Kauffman, J. M., Hallahan D. P., Haas, K., Brame, T., and Born, R. Imitating children's errors to improve their spelling performance. *Journal of Learning Disabilities*, 1978, *11*, 217–222.

Kavale, K. A. Learning disability and cultural-economic

disadvantage: The case for a relationship. *Learning Disability Quarterly*, 1980a, *3*, 97–112.

———. The reasoning abilities of normal and learning disabled readers on measures of reading comprehension. *Learning Disability Quarterly*, 1980b, *3*(4), 34–45.

———. The relationship between auditory perceptual skills and reading ability: A meta-analysis. *Journal of Learning Disabilities*, 1981, *14*, 539–546.

———. Meta-analysis of the relationship between visual perceptual skills and reading achievement. *Journal of Learning Disabilities*, 1982, *15*, 42–51.

Kavale, K., and Nye, C. Identification criteria for learning disabilities: A survey of the research literature. *Learning Disability Quarterly*, 1981, *4*(4), 383–388.

Keeney, J. J., Cannizzo, S. R., and Flavell, J. H. Spontaneous and induced verbal rehearsal in a recall task. *Child Development*, 1967, *38*, 953–966.

Keeves, J. *Educational Environment and Student Achievement.* Stockholm: Malmquist & Wicksell, 1972.

Keilitz, I., Zaremba, B., and Broder, P. The link between learning disabilities and juvenile delinquency: Some issues and answers. *Learning Disability Quarterly*, 1979, *2*, 2–11.

Keir, E. H. Auditory information processing and learning disabilities. In *Brain Function and Reading Disabilities*, edited by L. Tarnopol and M. Tarnopol. Baltimore: University Park Press, 1977.

Keller, H. R., ed. Behavioral assessment. *School Psychology Review*, 1980a, *9*, 3, 89, 93–98.

———. Issues in the use of observational assessment. *School Psychology Review*, 1980b, *9*, 21–30.

———. Preface to behavioral assessment. *School Psychology Review*, 1980c, *9*, 3–4.

———. Behavioral consultation, In *Consultation in Schools: Theory, Research, Technology*, edited by J. C. Conoley. New York: Academic Press, 1981.

Kellogg, R., and O'Dell, S. *Analyzing Children's Art.* Palo Alto: National Press Books, 1969.

Keogh, B. K. The Bender-Gestalt as a predictive and diagnostic test of reading performance. *Journal of Consulting Psychology*, 1965, *29*, 83–84.

———. The Bender-Gestalt with young children: Research implications. *Journal of Special Education*, 1969, *3*, 15–21.

———. Psychological evaluation of exceptional children: Old hangups and new directions. *Journal of School Psychology*, 1972, *10*, 141–145.

———. Perceptual and cognitive styles: Implications for special education. In *The First Review of Special Education*, edited by L. Mann and D. A. Sabatino. Philadelphia: JSE Press, 1973.

———. Working together: A new direction. *Journal of Learning Disabilities*, 1977a, *10*, 478–482.

———. Research on cognitive styles. In *Changing Perspectives in Special Education*, edited by R. D. Kneedler and S. G. Tarver. Columbus, Ohio: Charles E. Merrill, 1977b.

Keogh, B. K. and Becker, L. D. Early detection of learning problems: Questions, cautions, and guidelines. *Exceptional Children*, 1973, *40*, 5–11.

Keogh, B. K., and Donlon, G. McG. Field dependence, impulsivity, and learning disabilities. *Journal of Learning Disabilities*, 1972, *5*, 331–336.

Keogh, B. K., and Hall, R. J. WISC subtest patterns of educationally handicapped and educable mentally retarded pupils. *Psychology in the School*, 1974, *11*, 296–300.

Keogh, B. K., Major, S. M., Omori, H. Gandara, P., and Reid, H. P. Proposed markers in learning disabilities research. *Journal of Abnormal Child Psychology*, 1980, *8*, 21–31.

Keogh, B. K., and Margolis, J. Learn to labor and to wait: Attentional problems of children with learning disorders. *Journal of Learning Disabilities*, 1976, *9*, 276–286.

Keogh, B. K. and Smith C. E. Visuo-motor ability for school prediction: A seven-year study. *Perceptual and Motor Skills*, 1967, *25*, 101–110.

———. Early identification of educationally high potential and high risk children. *Journal of School Psychology*, 1970, *8*, 285–290.

Keogh, B. K., Tchir, C. and Windeguth-Behn, A. Teachers' perceptions of educationally high risk children. *Journal of Learning Disabilities*, 1974, *7*, 367–374.

Kephart, N. C. *The Slow Learner in the Classroom.* Columbus, Ohio: Charles E. Merrill, 1960.

Kephart, N. C. Forward. In *Itard, Seguin, and Kephart: Sensory Education. A Learning Interpretation*, edited by T. S. Ball. Columbus, Ohio: Charles E. Merrill, 1971.

Kephart, N. C., and Strauss, A. A. A clinical factor influencing variations in IQ. *American Journal of Orthopsychiatry*, 1940, *10* 345–350.

Kerrigan, W. S. *Writing to the Point: Six Basic Steps.* New York: Harcourt Brace Jovanovich, 1974.

Kershner, J. R. Reading and laterality revisited. *Journal of Special Education*, 1975, *9*, 269–279.

———. Cerebral dominance in disabled readers, good readers, and gifted children: Search for a valid model. *Child Development*, 1977, *48*, 61–67.

Kerst, S., and Levin, J. R. A comparison of experimenter-provided and subject-generated strategies in children's paired associate learning. *Journal of Educational Psychology*, 1973, *65*, 300–303.

Ketchum, E. G. Neurological and/or emotional factors in reading disabilities. In *Vistas in Reading*, edited by J. Figural. Newark, Del.: International Reading Association, 1967.

Kiev, A. Depression as a treatable illness. *Drug Therapy*, March 1975, 67–76.

Kimura, D. Functional asymmetry of the brain in dichotic listening. *Cortex*, 1967, *3*, 163–178.

Kinsbourne, M. Eye and head turning indicates cerebral lateralization. *Science*, 1972, *176*, 539–541.

———. School problems. *Pediatrics*, 1973a, *52*, 697–710.

———. Minimal brain dysfunction as a neurodevelopmental lag. *Annals of the New York Academy of Sciences*, 1973b, *205*, 268–273.

———. Direction of gaze and distribution of cerebral thought processes. *Neuropsychologia*, 1974, *12*, 279–281.

———. Keynote address, National Association for Children with Learning Disabilities, 14th International Conference. Washington, D.C.: 9–12 March 1977a.

———. An overview of MBD — Past and present concepts. Address to SUNY Upstate Medical Center and CIBA conference, *Understanding Minimal Brain Dysfunction*, Syracuse, New York: 17 November 1977b.

———. The practical approach to MBD: Guidelines to therapy. Address to SUNY Upstate Medical Center and CIBA Conference, *Understanding Minimal Brain Dysfunction*, Syracuse, 18 November 1977.

Kinsbourne, M., and Caplan, P. *Children's Learning and Attention Problems.* Boston: Little, Brown, 1979.

Kinsbourne, M., and Warrington, E. K. Developmental factors in reading and writing backwardness. *British Journal of Psychology*, 1963, *54*, 145–156.

Kintsch, W., and Buschke, H. Homophones and synonyms in short-term memory. *Journal of Experimental Psychology*, 1969, *80*, 403–407.

Kirby, J. R., and Das, J. P. Reading achievement, IQ, and simultaneous successive processing. *Journal of Educational Psychology*, 1977, *69*, 564–570.

Kirk, S. A. *Early Education of the Mentally Retarded: An Experimental Study.* Urbana: University of Illinois Press, 1958.

———. *Educating Exceptional Children.* Boston: Houghton Mifflin, 1962.

———. Research in education. In *Mental Retardation: A Review of Research*, edited by H. A. Stevens and R. Heber. Chicago: University of Chicago Press, 1964.

———. Samuel A. Kirk. In *Teaching Children with Learning Disabilities: Personal Perspectives*, edited by J. M. Kauffman and D. P. Hallahan. Columbus, Ohio: Charles E. Merrill, 1976.

Kirk, S. A., and Elkins, J. Characteristics of children enrolled in the child service demonstration centers. *Journal of Learning Disabilities*, 1975a, *8*, 630–637.

――――. Identifying developmental discrepancies at the preschool level. *Journal of Learning Disabilities*, 1975b, *8*, 417–419.

Kirk, S. A., and Kirk, W. D. *Psycholinguistic Learning Disabilities: Diagnosis and Remediation.* Chicago: University of Illinois Press, 1971.

Kirk, S. A., Kliebhan, Sister J. M., and Lerner, J. W. *Teaching Reading to Slow and Disabled Learners.* Boston: Houghton Mifflin, 1978.

Kirk, S. A., and Lord, F., eds. *Exceptional Children: Educational Resources and Perspectives.* Boston: Houghton Mifflin, 1974.

Kirk, S. A., McCarthy, J. J., and Kirk, W. D. *Illinois Test of Psycholinguistic Abilities.* Experimental ed. Urbana: University of Illinois Press, 1961.

――――. *Illinois Test of Psycholinguistic Abilities.* Rev. Ed. Urbana: University of Illinois Press, 1968.

Kirk, W. D. A tentative screening procedure for selection of bright and slow children in kindergarten. *Exceptional Children*, 1966, 235–241.

――――. The relationship of reading disabilities to learning disabilities. *Journal of Special Education*, 1975, *9*, 133–137.

Kirsch, I., and Guthrie, J. T. The concept and measurement of functional literacy. *Reading Research Quarterly*, 1978, *13*, 485–507.

Kirshef, C. H., and Hall, M. A. Employment of the mentally retarded in Hannepin County, Minnesota. *American Journal of Mental Deficiency*, 1955, *60*, 182–189.

Klaus, R., and Gray, S. The early training project for disadvantaged children: A report after five years. *Monographs of the Society for Research in Child Development*, 1968, *33*(4, Serial No. 120).

Klausmeier, H. J., Feldhusen, J., and Check, J. *An Analysis of Learning Efficiency in Arithmetic of Mentally Retarded Children in Comparison With Children of Average and High Intelligence.* Madison: University of Wisconsin Press, 1959.

Klein, P. Personal communication. December 8, 1980.

Klein, R. S., Altman, S. D., Dreizen, K., Friedman, R., and Powers, L. Restructuring dysfunctional parental attitudes toward children's learning and behavior in school: Family-oriented psychotherapy, Part 1. *Journal of Learning Disabilities*, 1981a, *14*, 15–19.

――――. Restructuring dysfunctional parental attitudes toward children's learning and behavior in school: Family-oriented psychotherapy, Part 2. *Journal of Learning Disabilities*, 1981b, *14*, 99–101.

Kline, C. L., Ashbrenner, M., Barrington, B., and Reimer, L. *Dyslexia Quotient: An Index of Reading Ability.* Pomfret, Conn. The Orton Society, reprint No. 22.

Kline, L. W. Follow the yellow brick road — or — lost in the forest of professional educational argument. *Journal of Special Education*, 1975, *9*, 167–177.

Knights, R. M., and Bakker, D. J., eds. *The Neuropsychology of Learning Disorders: Theoretical Approaches.* Baltimore: University Park Press, 1976.

Knobloch, H., Sotos, J. F., Sherard, E. S., Hodson, W. A., and Wehe, R. A. Prognostic and etiologic factors in hypoglycemia. *Journal of Pediatrics*, 1967, *70*, 876–884.

Knobloch, H., and Pasamanick, B. *Gesell and Amatruda's Developmental Diagnosis.* New York: Harper & Row, 1974.

Kobasigawa, A. Utilization of retrieval cues by children in recall. *Child Development*, 1974, *45*, 127–134.

Kobasigawa, A. Retrieval strategies in the development of memory. In *Memory in Cognitive Development*, edited by R. V. Kail and J. W. Hagen. Hillsdale, N.J.: Lawrence Erlbaum, 1976.

Koenigsberg, R. S. An evaluation of visual versus sensorimotor methods for improving orientation discrimination for letter reversals by preschool children. *Child Development*, 1973, *44*, 764–769.

Kohlberg, L. The development of children's orientations toward a moral order. 1. Sequence in the development of moral thought. *Vita Humana*, 1963, *6*, 11–33.

――――. Montessori with the culturally disadvantaged. A cognitive-developmental interpretation and some research findings. In *Early Education*, edited by R. D. Hess and R. M. Bear. Chicago: Aldine, 1968.

Kohlberg, L., Yarger, J., and Hjertholm, E. Private Speech: Four studies and a review of theories. *Child Development*, 1968, *39*, 691–736.

Koivisto, M., Blanco-Sequeiros, M., and Krause, U. Neonatal symptomatic and asymptomatic hypoglycemia: A follow-up study of 15 children. *Developmental Medicine and Child Neurology*, 1972, *14*, 603–614.

Kokoszka, M., and Drye, J. Toward the least restrictive environment: High school L.D. students. *Journal of Learning Disabilities*, 1981, *14*, 22–23, 26.

Koneya, M. Location and interaction in row-and-column seating arrangements. *Environment and Behavior*, 1976, *8*, 265–282.

Koppell, S. Testing the attentional deficit notion. *Journal of Learning Disabilities*, 1979, *12*, 43–48.

Koppitz, E. *Psychological Evaluation of Children's Human Figure Drawings.* New York: Grune & Stratton, 1968.

――――. Brain damage, reading disability and the Bender-Gestalt Test. *Journal of Learning Disabilities*, 1970, *3*, 429–433.

――――. *Children with Learning Disabilities: A Five-Year Follow-up Study.* New York: Grune & Stratton, 1971.

――――. The Bender Gestalt and VADS test performance of learning disabled middle school pupils. *Journal of Learning Disabilities*, 1981a, *2*, 96–98, 110.

――――. The Visual Aural Digit Span Test for seventh graders: A normative study. *Journal of Learning Disabilities*, 1981b, *2*, 93–95.

Košč, L. Neuropsychological implications of diagnosis and treatment of mathematical learning disabilities. *Topics in Learning and Learning Disabilities*, 1981, *1* (3), 19–30.

Kosiewicz, M. M., Hallahan, D. P., and Lloyd, J. The effects of an LD student's treatment choice on handwriting performance. *Learning Disability Quarterly*, 1981, *4* (3), 281–286.

Kosiewicz, M. M., Hallahan, D. P., Lloyd, J., and Graves, A. W. Effects of self-instruction and self-correction procedures on handwriting performance. *Learning Disability Quarterly*, 1982, *5* (1), 71–78.

Kottmeyer, W., and Claus, A. *Basic Goals in Spelling.* New York: McGraw-Hill, 1972.

Koupernik, C., MacKeith, R., and Francis-Williams, J. Neurological correlates of motor and perceptual development. In *Perceptual and Learning Disabilities in Children.* Vol. 2, edited by W. M. Cruickshank and D. P. Hallahan. Syracuse: Syracuse University Press, 1975.

Krasner, L. Behavior therapy. *Annual Review of Psychology*, 1971, *22*, 488–532.

Kratochwill, T. R. N=1: An alternative research strategy for school psychologists. *Journal of School Psychology*, 1977, *15*, 239–249.

Kratochwill, T. R., Brody, G. H., and Piersal, W. C. Time-series research: Some comments on design methodology for research in learning disabilities. *Journal of Learning Disabilities*, 1979, *12*, 257–263.

Krech, D., Rosenzweig, M. R., and Bennett, E. L. Environmental impoverishment, social isolation, and changes in brain chemistry and anatomy. *Physiology and Behavior*, 1966, *1*, 99–104.

Kreutzer, M. A., Leonard, C., and Flavell, J. H. An interview study of children's knowledge about memory. *Monographs of the Society for Research in Child Development*, 1975, *40* (1, Serial No. 159).

Krieger, V. K. A hierarchy of "confusable" high frequency words in isolation and context. *Learning Disability Quarterly*, 1982, *4* (2) 131–138.

Kritchevsky, S. and Prescott, E. *Planning Environments for Young Children: Physical Space.* Washington, D.C.: National Association for the Education of Young Children, 1969.

Kroth, R. The behavioral Q-sort as a diagnostic tool. *Academic Therapy*, 1973, *8*, 317–330.

Kroth, R. L. and Simpson, R. L. *Parent Conferences as a Teaching Strategy*. Denver: Love Publishing Company, 1977.

Krumboltz, J. D., and Krumboltz, H. B. *Changing Children's Behavior*. Englewood Cliffs, N.J.: Prentice-Hall, 1972.

Kyzar, B. L. Noise pollution and schools: How much is too much? *CEFP Journal*, 1977, *4*, 10–11.

Lachmann, F. M. Perceptual-motor development in children retarded in reading ability. *Journal of Consulting Psychology*, 1960, *24*, 427–431.

LaGreca, A. M., and Mesibov, G. B. Facilitating interpersonal functioning with peers in learning disabled children. *Journal of Learning Disabilities*, 1981, *14*, 197–199.

Lambert, N., and Sandoval, J. The prevalence of learning disabilities in a sample of children considered hyperactive. *Journal of Abnormal Child Psychology*, 1980, *8*, 33–50.

Lambie, D. Z., and Weikart, D. P. Ypsilanti-Carnegie infant education project. In *Disadvantaged Child*, Vol. 3, edited by J. Hellmuth. New York: Brunner/Mazel, 1970.

Lane, B. A. The relationship of learning disabilities to juvenile delinquency: Current status. *Journal of Learning Disabilities*, 1980, *13* (8), 425–434.

Lapp, E. R. A study of the social adjustment of slow-learning children who were assigned part-time to regular classes. *American Journal of Mental Deficiency*, 1957, *62*, 254–262.

Larrivee, B. Modality preference as a model for differentiating beginning reading instruction: A review of the issues. *Learning Disability Quarterly*, 1981, *4*(2), 180–188.

Larsen, S. C. The learning disabilities specialist: Role and responsibilities. *Journal of Learning Disabilities*, 1976, *9*, 498–508.

———. Learning disabilities and the professional educator. *Learning Disability Quarterly*, 1978, *1*, 5–12.

Larsen, S. C., and Hammill, D. D. The relationship of selected visual-perceptual abilities to school learning. *Journal of Special Education*, 1975, *9*, 281–291.

Larsen, S. C., Parker, R., and Jorjorian, S. Differences in self-concept of normal and learning disabled children. *Perceptual and Motor Skills*, 1973, *37*, 510.

Larsen, S. C., Parker, R., and Trenholme, B. The effects of syntactic complexity upon arithmetic performance. *Learning Disability Quarterly*, 1978, *1*(4), 80–85.

Larsen, S. C., Rogers, D., and Sowell, V. The use of selected perceptual tests in differentiating between normal and learning disabled children. *Journal of Learning Disabilities*, 1976, *9*, 85–90.

Lassen, N. A., Ingvar, D. H., and Skinhøj, E. Brain function and blood flow. *Scientific American*, 1978, *239*, 62–71.

Lawson, L. J. Ophthalmological factors in learning disabilities. In *Progress in Learning Disabilities*. Vol. 1, edited by H. R. Myklebust. New York: Grune & Stratton, 1968.

LeBlanc, J. F. You can teach problem solving. *The Arithmetic Teacher*, 1977, *25*, 16–20.

Le Fevre, C. *Linguistics, English and the Language Arts*. Boston: Allyn & Bacon, 1970.

Lefevre, E., Starck, R., Lambert, W. E., and Genesee, F. Lateral eye movements during verbal and nonverbal dichotic listening. *Perceptual and Motor Skills*, 1977, *44*, 1115–1122.

Lefton, L. A., Lahey, B. B., and Stagg, D. I. Eye movements in reading disabled and normal children: A study of system and strategies. *Journal of Learning Disabilities*, 1978, *11*, 549–558.

Lehman, E. B., and Brady, K. McC. Presentation modality and taxonomic category as encoding dimensions for good and poor readers. *Journal of Learning Disabilities*, 1982, *15*, 103–105.

Lehrer, G. M. Measurement of Minimal Brain Dysfunction. In *Behavioral Toxicology*, edited by C. Xintras, B. L. Johnson, and I. de Groot. Washington, D.C.: U.S. Department of Health, Education, and Welfare, 1974.

Lehtinen, L. Appendix. In *Psychopathology and Education of the Brain-injured Child*. Vol. 2, *Progress in Theory and Clinic*, edited by A. A. Strauss and N. C. Kephart. New York: Grune & Stratton, 1955.

LeMay, M. Asymmetries of the skull and handedness: Phrenology revisited. *Journal of the Neurological Sciences*, 1977, *32*, 243–253.

Lenkowsky, L. K., and Saposnek, D. T. Family consequences of parental dyslexia. *Journal of Learning Disabilities*, 1978, *11*, 47–53.

Lenneberg, E. H. *Biological Foundations of Language*. New York: John Wiley & Sons, 1967.

Lennox, W. G., Gibbs, E. L. and Gibbs, F. A. The brain-wave pattern, an hereditary trait: Evidence from 74 "normal" pairs of twins. *Journal of Heredity*, 1945, *36*, 233–243.

Lenz, W. Thalidomide and congenital abnormalities. *Lancet*, 1962, *1*, 45.

Lepore, A. A comparison of computational errors between educable mentally handicapped and learning disability children. Unpublished manuscript. University of Connecticut, Storrs, 1974.

Lerner, B. The minimum competence testing movement: Social scientific, and legal implications. *American Psychologist*, 1981, *36*, 1057–1066.

Lerner, J. W. Systems analysis and special education. *Journal of Special Education*, 1973, *7*, 15–26.

———. Remedial reading and learning disabilities: Are they the same or different? *Journal of Special Education*, 1975, *9*, 119–131.

Lerner, J., Dawson, D., and Horvath L. *Cases in Learning and Behavior Problems: A Guide to Individualized Education Programs*. Boston: Houghton Mifflin, 1980.

Lerner, J. W., Evans, M. A., and Meyers, G. LD programs at the secondary level: A survey. *Academic Therapy*, 1977, *13*, 7–19.

Lesgold, A. M., McCormick, C., and Golinkoff, R. M. Imagery training and children's prose learning. *Journal of Educational Psychology*, 1975, *67*, 663–667.

Lessler, K., and Bridges, J. S. The prediction of learning problems in a rural setting: Can we improve on readiness tests? *Journal of Learning Disabilities*, 1973, *6*, 90–94.

Letourneau, J., Lapierre, N., and Lamont, A. The relationship between convergence insufficiency and school achievement. *American Journal of Optometry and Physiological Optics*, 1979, *56*, 18–22.

Levin, J. R. Inducing comprehension in poor readers: A test of a recent model. *Journal of Educational Psychology*, 1973, *65*, 19–24.

———. What have we learned about maximizing what children learn? *Cognitive Learning in Children: Theories and Strategies*, edited by J. R. Levin and V. L. Allan. New York: Academic Press, 1976.

Levin, J. R., Divine-Hawkins, P., Kerst, S. M., and Guttmann, J. Individual differences in learning from pictures and words: The development and application of an instrument. *Journal of Educational Psychology*, 1974, *66*, 296–303.

Levine, M. D., Clarke, S., and Forb, T. The child as a diagnostic participant: Helping students describe their learning disorders. *Journal of Learning Disabilities*, 1981, *14*, 527–530.

Levitt, E., and Cohen, S. An analysis of selected parent-intervention programs for handicapped and disadvantaged children. *Journal of Special Education*, 1975, 9, 345–365.

Levy, H. *Square Pegs, Round Holes: The Learning Disabled Child in the Classroom and at Home*. Boston: Little, Brown, 1973.

Levy, J., and Reid, M. Variations in writing posture and cerebral organization. *Science*, 1976, *194*, 337–338.

Lewandowski, G. Learning disabilities certification: A needed revision. *The Reading Teacher*, 1977, *31*, 132–133.

Liberman, I. Y., Shankweiler, D., Fischer, F. W., and Carter, B. Reading and the awareness of linguistic segments. *Journal of Experimental Child Psychology*, 1974, *18*, 201–212.

Lidz, T. *The Person: His Development Throughout the Life Cycle.* New York: Basic Books, 1968.

Lieberman, L. M. The implications of noncategorical special education. *Journal of Learning Disabilities*, 1980a, *13*, 65–68.

———. Territoriality: Who does what to whom? *Journal of Learning Disabilities*, 1980b, *13*, 124–128.

———. The LD adolescent . . . When do you stop? *Journal of Learning Disabilities*, 1981, *14*, 425–426.

Liebert, R. M., Neal, J. M., and Davidson, E. S. *The Early Window: Effects of Television on Children and Youth.* New York: Pergamon, 1973.

Lilis, R. Behavioral effects of occupational carbon disulfide exposure. In *Behavioral Toxicology*, edited by C. Xintras, B. L. Johnson, and I. de Groot. Washington, D.C.: U.S. Department of Health, Education, and Welfare, 1974.

Lilly, M. S. A merger of categories: Are we finally ready? *Journal of Learning Disabilities*, 1977, *10*, 115–121.

Lindamood, C. N., and Lindamood, P.C. *Lindamood Auditory Conceptualization Test.* Boston: Teaching Resources, 1971.

Lindsey, J. D., and Kerlin, M. A. Learning disabilities and reading disorders: A brief review of the secondary level literature. *Journal of Learning Disabilities*, 1979, *12*, 408–415.

Linn, S. H. A follow-up: Achievement report of first grade students after visual-perception training in kindergarten. *Academic Therapy Quarterly*, 1968, *3*, 179–180.

List, L. Much ado about something: Lerner's logic. *Journal of Special Education*, 1975, *9*, 139–143.

Lloyd, J., Sabatino, D., Miller, T., and Miller, S. Proposed federal guidelines: Some open questions. *Journal of Learning Disabilities*, 1977, *10*, 69–71.

Lockey, S. D., Sr. Sensitizing properties of food additives and other commercial products. *Annals of Allergy*, 1972, *30*, 638–641.

———. Hypersensitivity to Tartrazine (FD & C Yellow No. 5) and other dyes and additives present in foods and pharmaceutical products. *Annals of Allergy*, 1977, *38*, 206–210.

Lomes, J., and Kimura, D. Intrahemispheric interaction between speaking and sequential manual activity. *Neuropsychologia*, 1976, *14*, 23–33.

Lopez, R. E. Hyperactivity in twins. *Canadian Psychiatric Association Journal*, 1965, *10*, 421.

Lorenz L., and Vockell E. Using the neurological impress method of learning disabled readers. *Journal of Learning Disabilities*, 1979, *12*, 420–422.

Loughmiller, G. Keep the session alive. *Instructor*, November 1971, 73.

Lovegrove, W., Billing, G., and Slaghuis, W. Processing of visual contour orientation information in normal and reading disabled children. *Cortex*, 1978, *14*, 268–278.

Lovell, K., and Gorton, A. A study of some differences between backward and normal readers of average intelligence. *British Journal of Educational Psychology*, 1968, *38*, 240–248.

Lovitt, T. C. Applied behavior analysis and learning disabilities. Part 1, Characteristics of ABA, general recommendations, and methodological limitations. *Journal of Learning Disabilities*, 1975a, *8*, 432–443.

———. Applied behavior analysis and learning disabilities. Part 2, Specific research recommendations and suggestions for practitioners. *Journal of Learning Disabilities*, 1975b, *8*, 504–518.

———. Thomas C. Lovitt. In *Teaching Children with Learning Disabilities: Personal Perspectives*, edited by J. M. Kauffman and D. P. Hallahan. Columbus, Ohio: Charles E. Merrill, 1976.

———. The learning disabled. In *Behavior of Exceptional Children*. 2nd ed., edited by N. G. Haring. Columbus, Ohio: Charles E. Merrill, 1978.

Lowell, R. Reading readiness factors as predictors of success in first grade reading. *Journal of Learning Disabilities*, 1971, *4*, 563–567.

Lubchenco, L. O., and Bard, H. Incidence of hypoglycemia in newborn infants classified by birth weight and gestational age. *Pediatrics*, 1971, *47*, 831–838.

Ludlam, W. M. Visual electrophysiology and reading/learing difficulties. *Journal of Learning Disabilities*, 1981, *14*, 587–590.

Luick, A. H., and Senf, G. M. Where have all the children gone? *Journal of Learning Disabilities*, 1979, *12*, 285–287.

Lund, K. A., Foster, G. E., and McCall-Perez, F. C. The effectiveness of psycholingusitic training: A reevaluation. *Exceptional Children*, 1978, *44*, 310–319.

Luria, A. *The Role of Speech in the Regulation of Normal and Abnormal Behavior.* New York: Liveright Publishing Corp., 1961.

———. *Higher Cortical Functions in Man.* New York: Basic Books, 1966.

———. *Traumatic Aphasia.* The Hague: Mouton, 1970a.

———. The functional organization of the brain. *Scientific American*, 1970b, *222*, 66–78.

———. *The Neuropsychology of Memory.* New York: John Wiley & Sons, 1976.

———. Cerebral organization of conscious acts: A frontal lobe function. In *Brain Function and Reading Disabilities*, edited by L. Tarnopol and M. Tarnopol. Baltimore: University Park Press, 1977.

Lutey, C. *Individual Intelligence Testing: A Manual and Sourcebook.* 2nd enl. ed. Greenley, Colo.: Carol L. Lutey, 1977.

Lyle, J. G. Reading retardation and reversal tendency: A factorial study. *Child Development*, 1969, *40*, 833–843.

Lyle, J. G., and Goyen, J. Visual recognition, developmental lag, and strephosymbolia in reading retardation. *Journal of Abnormal Psychology*, 1968, *73*, 25–29.

Lyon, S. Teacher nonverbal behavior related to perceived pupil social-personal attributes. *Journal of Learning Disabilities*, 1977, *10*, 173–177.

MacKavey, W., Curcio, F., and Rosen, J. Tachistoscopic word recognition performance under conditions of simultaneous bilateral presentation. *Neuropsychologia*, 1975, *13*, 27–33.

Mackie, R. P. *Special Education in the United States: Statistics 1948–1966.* New York: Teachers College Press, 1969.

Mackie, R. P., and Dunn, L. M. College and university programs for the preparation of teachers of exceptional children. U.S. Office of Education Bulletin No. 13. Washington, D.C.: U.S. Government Printing Office, 1954.

MacMillan, D. L. Special education for the mildly retarded: Servant or savant? *Focus on Exceptional Children*, 1971, *2* (9), 1–11.

MacNamara, J. Cognitive basis of language learning in infants. *Psychological Review*, 1972, *79*, 1–13.

Macy, D. J., Baker, J. A., and Kosinski, S. C. An empirical study of the Myklebust Learning Quotient. *Journal of Learning Disabilities*, 1979, *12*, 93–96.

Magliocca, L. A., Rinaldi, R. T., Crew, J. L., and Kunzelmann, H. P. Early identification of handicapped children through a frequency sampling technique. *Exceptional Children*, 1977, *43*, 414–420.

Maher, C. A. Learning disabled adolescents in the regular classroom: Evaluation of a mainstreaming procedure. *Learning Disability Quarterly*, 1982, *5* (1), 82–84.

Mahoney, M. J. Some applied issues in self-monitoring. In *Behavioral Assessment: New Directions in Clinical Psychology*, edited by J. D. Cone and R. P. Hawkins. Brunner/Mazel, 1977.

Maier, A. S. The effect of focusing on the cognitive processes of learning disabled children. Paper presented at the Association for Children with Learning Disabilities, 14th International Conference, Washington, D.C., 9–12 March 1977.

——. The effect of focusing on the cognitive processes of learning disabled children. *Journal of Learning Disabilities,* 1980, *13,* 143–147.

Maietta, D. F. The role of cognitive regulators in learning-disabled teenagers. *Academic Therapy,* 1970, *5,* 177–186.

Majoribanks, K. Environment, social class, and mental abilities. *Journal of Educational Psychology,* 1972, *43,* 103–109.

Mandel, C. J., and Strain, P. S. An analysis of factors related to the attitudes of regular classroom teachers toward mainstreaming mildly handicapped children. *Contemporary Educational Psychology, 3,* 154–162.

Manheim, J. Word problems or problems with words. In *Mathematics Is a Verb,* edited by C. W. Schminke and W. R. Arnold. Hinsdale, Ill.: The Dryden Press, 1971.

Mann, L. Perceptual training revisited: The training of nothing at all. *Rehabilitation Literature,* 1971, *32,* 322–335.

——. Introduction. In *Teaching the Learning-Disabled Adolescent,* edited by L. Mann, L. Goodman, and J. L. Wiederholt. Boston: Houghton Mifflin, 1978.

Mann, L., and Phillips, W. A. Fractional practices in special education: A critique. *Exceptional Children,* 1967, *33,* 311–319.

Mann, P. H., Suiter, P. A., and McClung, R. M. *Handbook in Diagnostic-Prescriptive Teaching.* Boston: Allyn & Bacon, 1979.

Manzo, A. V. The request procedure. *Journal of Reading, 1969, 13,* 123–126.

——. Guided reading procedure. *Journal of Reading,* 1975, 7, 287–291.

Marcel, T., Katz, L., and Smith, M. Laterality and reading proficiency. *Neuropsychologia,* 1974, *12,* 131–139.

Marsh, G. E., Gearheart, C. K., and Gearheart, B. R. *The Learning Disabled Adolescent: Program Alternatives in the Secondary School.* Saint Louis: C. V. Mosby, 1978.

Marshall, W., and Ferguson, J. H. Hereditary word-blindness as a defect of selective association. *Journal of Nervous and Mental Diseases,* 1939, *89,* 164–173.

Martin, E. W. Education of the handicapped. Statement of Edwin W. Martin, Deputy Commissioner of Education, Wednesday, March 14, 1979, Senate appropriations Hearing, 96th Congress, p. 316.

Martin, J. Measuring reading outcomes and determining needs. In *Readings on Reading Instruction,* edited by A. J. Harris. New York: David McKay, 1963.

Martin, L. S., and Pavan, B. N. Current research on open space, nongrading, vertical grouping, and team teaching. *Phi Delta Kappan,* 1976, *57,* 310–315.

Marx, M. H. and Hillix, W. A. *Systems and Theories in Psychology.* 2nd ed. New York: McGraw-Hill, 1973.

Maslow, A. *Toward a Psychology of Being.* New York: Van Nostrand Reinhold, 1968.

Maslow, A. H., and Mintz, N. L. The effects of esthetic surroundings: I. *Journal of Psychology,* 1956, *41,* 247–254.

Massaro, D. W., and Klitzke, D. Letters are functional in word identification. *Memory and Cognition,* 1977, *5,* 292–298.

Masur, E. F., McIntyre, C. W., and Flavell, J. H. Developmental changes in apportionment of study time among items in a multitrial free recall test. *Journal of Experimental Child Psychology,* 1973, *15,* 237–246.

Mathews, R. M., Whang, P. L., and Fawcett, S. B. Behavioral assessment of occupational skills of learning disabled adolescents. *Journal of Learning Disabilities,* 1982, *15,* 38–41.

Matousek, M., and Petersen, I. Frequency analysis of the EEG in normal children (1–15 years) and in normal adolescents (16–21 years). In *Automation of Clinical Electroencephalography,* edited by P. Kellaway and I. Petersen. New York: Raven Press, 1973.

Mattes, J. A., and Gittelman, R. Effects of artificial food colorings in children with hyperactive symptoms. *Archives of General Psychiatry,* 1981, *38,* 714–718.

Matthews, B. A. J., and Seymour, C. M. The performance of learning disabled children on tests of auditory discrimination. *Journal of Learning Disabilities,* 1981, *14,* 9–12.

Mattis, S. Dyslexia syndromes: A working hypothesis that works. In *Dyslexia: An Appraisal of Current Knowledge,* edited by A. L. Benton. New York: Oxford University Press, 1978.

Mattis, S., French, J. H., and Rapin, I. Dyslexia in children and young adults: Three independent neuropsychological syndromes. *Developmental Medicine and Child Neurology,* 1975, *17,* 150–163.

Mauser, A. J. Learning disabilities and delinquent youth. *Academic Therapy,* 1974, *4,* 389–402.

Maxwell, M. J. Skimming and scanning improvement: The needs, assumption and knowledge base. *Journal of Reading Behavior,* 1973, *5,* 47–59.

May, L. J. *Teaching Mathematics in the Elementary School.* 2nd ed. New York: Free Press, 1974.

Mayron, L. W. Allergy, learning, and behavior problems. *Journal of Learning Disabilities,* 1979, *12,* 32–42.

Mayron, L. W., Mayron, E. L., Ott, J. W. and Nations, R. Light, radiation, and academic achievement: Second year data. *Academic Therapy,* 1976, *11,* 397–407.

Mayron, L. W., Ott, J., Nations, R., Mayron, E. L. Light, radiation and academic behavior: Initial studies on the effects of full-spectrum lighting and radiation shielding on behavior and academic performance of school children. *Academic Therapy,* 10, 33–47.

McCall, R. B., Appelbaum, M. I. and Hogarty, P. S. Developmental changes in mental performance. *Monographs of the Society for Research in Child Development,* 1973, *38,* (3, Serial No. 150).

McCall, R. B., Hogarty, P. S., and Hurlburt, N. Transitions in infant sensorimotor development and the prediction of childhood IQ. *American Psychologist,* 1972, *27,* 728–748.

McCandless, B. R. *Adolescents — Behavior and Development.* Hinsdale, Ill.: The Dryden Press, 1970.

McCarthy, J. J. Rebuttal. The validity of perceptual tests: The debate continues. *Journal of Learning Disabilities,* 1976, *9,* 332–337

McCarthy, M. Minimum competency testing and handicapped students. *Exceptional Children,* 1980, *47,* 166–173.

McClelland, D. C. Testing for competence rather than for "intelligence." *American Psychologist,* 1973, *28,* 1–14.

McDaniels, G. L. The evaluations of follow through. *Educational Research,* 1975, *4* (11), 7–11.

McFall, R. M. Analogue methods in behavioral assessment: Issues and prospects. In *Behavioral Assessment: New Directions in Clinical Psychology,* edited by J. D. Cone and R. P. Hawkins. New York: Brunner/Mazel, 1977.

McGhee, P. E., and Crandall, V. C. Beliefs in internal-external control of reinforcements and academic performance. *Child Development,* 1968, *39,* 91–102.

McGinnis, M. *Aphasic Children: Identification and Education by the Association Method.* Washington, D.C.: Volta, 1963.

McGuire, W. Personality and susceptibility to social influence. In *Handbook of Personality Theory and Research,* edited by E. Borgatta and W. V. Lamber. Chicago: Rand McNally, 1968.

McIntosh, D. K., and Dunn, L. M. Children with major specific learning disabilities. In *Exceptional Children in the Schools: Special Education in Transition.* 2nd ed, edited by L. M. Dunn. New York: Holt, Rinehart and Winston, 1973.

McKeever, W. F., Gill, K. M., and VanDeventer, A. D. Letter versus dot stimuli as tools for "splitting the normal brain with reaction time." *Quarterly Journal of Experimental Psychology,* 1975, *27,* 363–373.

McKeever, W. F., and Van Deventer, A. D. Dyslexic adolescents: Evidence of impaired visual and auditory language processing associated with normal lateralization and visual responsivity. *Cortex,* 1975, *11,* 361–378.

McKenney, J. L., and Keen, P. G. W. How managers' minds work. *Harvard Business Review*, 1976, *52*, 14–21.

McKnight, J. C. Using the manual alphabet in teaching reading to learning disabled children. *Journal of Learning Disabilities*, 1979, *12*, 581–584.

McLachlan, J. F. C., and Hunt, D. E. Differential effects of discovery learning as a function of conceptual level. *Canadian Journal of Behavioral Science*, 1973, *5*, 152–160.

McLaughlin, H. G. SMOG grading: A new readability formula. *Journal of Reading*, 1969, *12*, 639–646.

McLeod, J. Educational underachievement: Toward a defensible psychometric definition. *Journal of Learning Disabilities*, 1979, *12*, 322–330.

McLeod, T. M., and Crump, W. D. The relationship of visuo-spatial skills and verbal ability to learning disabilities in mathematics. *Journal of Learning Disabilities*, 1978, *11*, 237–241.

McLeskey, J., Rieth, H. J., and Polsgrove, L. The implications of response generalization for improving the effectiveness of programs for learning disabled children. *Journal of Learning Disabilities*, 1980, *13*, 287–290.

McLoughlin, J., Edge, D., and Strenecky, B. Perspective on parental involvement in diagnosis and treatment of learning disabled children. *Journal of Learning Disabilities*, 1978, *11*, 291–296.

McLoughlin, J., McLoughlin, R. and Steward, W. Advocacy for parents of the handicapped. A professional responsibility. *Learning Disability Quarterly*, 1979, *2*, 51–57.

McNeill, D. The development of language. In *Carmichael's Manual of Child Psychology*. Vol. 1, edited by P. H. Mussen. New York: John Wiley & Sons, 1970.

McReynolds, L. V. Operant conditioning for investigating speech sound discrimination in aphasic children. *Journal of Speech and Hearing Research*, 1966, *9*, 519–528.

McReynolds, P. The case for interactional assessment. *Behavioral Assessment*, 1979, *1*, 237–247.

McReynolds, P., and DeVoge, S. Use of improvisational techniques in assessment. In *Advances in Psychological Assessment*. Vol. 4, edited by P. McReynolds. San Francisco: Jossey-Bass, 1978.

McWhirter, J. J., and Cabanski, C. Influencing the child: A program for parents. *Elementary School Guidance and Counseling*, 1972, *7*, 26–31.

Meacham, J. A. The development of memory abilities in the individual. *Human Development*, 1975, *15*, 205–228.

Meeker, M. N. *The Structure of Intellect*. Columbus, Ohio: Charles E. Merrill, 1969.

———. WISC-R template for SOI analysis. Available from SOI Institute, 214 Main Street, El Segundo, Calif., 1975.

Mehan, H. *Learning Lessons: Social Organization in the Classroom*. Cambridge: Harvard University Press, 1979.

Meichenbaum, D. Cognitive factors as determinants of learning disabilities: A cognitive-functional approach. In *The Neuropsychology of Learning Disorders: Theoretical Approaches*, edited by R. M. Knights and D. J. Bakker. Baltimore: University Park Press, 1976.

———. *Cognitive-Behavior Modification: An Integrative Approach*. New York: Plenum, 1977.

Meichenbaum, D., and Goodman, J. Reflection-impulsivity and verbal control of motor behavior. *Child Development*, 1969, *40*, 785–797.

———. Training impulsive children to talk to themselves: A means of developing self-control. *Journal of Abnormal Psychology*, 1971, *77*, 115–126.

Meier, J. H. Prevalence and characteristics of learning disabilities found in second grade children. *Journal of Learning Disabilities*, 1971, *4*, 1–16.

———. Assessment and intervention for young children at developmental risk. In *Issues in the Classification of Children*. Vol. 2, edited by N. Hobbs. San Francisco: Jossey-Bass, 1975.

Melahn, C. L., and O'Donnell, C. R. Norm-based behavioral consulting. *Behavior Modification*, 1978, *2*, 309–338.

Melkman, R., Koriat, A., and Pardo, K. Preference for color and form in preschoolers as related to color and form difference. *Child Development*, 1976, *47*, 1045–1050.

Menkes, M. M., Rowe, J. S., and Menkes, J. H. A 25-year-old follow-up study on the hyperkinetic child with minimal brain dysfunction. *Pediatrics*, 1967, *39*, 393–399.

Menyuk, P. Comparison of grammar of children with functionally deviant and normal speech. *Journal of Speech and Hearing Research*, 1964, *7*, 109–121.

———. *Sentences Children Use*. Cambridge: MIT Press, 1969.

———. The bases of language acquisition: Some questions. *Journal of Autism and Childhood Schizophrenia*, 1974, *4*, 325–345.

Menyuk, P., and Looney, P. Relationships between components of the grammar in language disorders. *Journal of Speech and Hearing Research*, 1972, *15*, 395–406.

Mercer, C. D. *Children and Adolescents with Learning Disabilities*. Columbus, Ohio: Charles E. Merrill, 1979.

Mercer, C. D., Forgnone, C., and Wolking, W. D. Definitions of learning disabilities used in the United States. *Journal of Learning Disabilities*, 1976, *9*, 376–386.

Mercer, J. R. The ecology of mental retardation. In *The Proceedings of the First Annual Spring Conference of the Institute for the Study of Mental Retardation*, Ann Arbor, 1970, pp. 55–74.

———. *Labeling the Mentally Retarded: Clinical and Social System Perspectives on Mental Retardation*. Berkeley: University of California Press, 1973.

———. *Technical Manual: System of Multicultural Pluralistic Assessment*. New York: Psychological Corporation, 1979.

Mercer, J. R., and Lewis, J. F. *The System of Multicultural Pluralistic Assessment*. New York: Psychological Corporation, 1978.

Mercer, J. R., and Ysseldyke, J. Designing diagnostic-intervention programs. In *Psychological and Educational Assessment of Minority Children*, edited by T. Oakland. New York: Brunner/Mazel, 1977.

Messer, S. B. Reflection-impulsivity: A review. *Psychological Bulletin*, 1976, *83*, 1026–1052.

Messick, S., and Damarin, F. Cognitive styles and memory for faces. *Journal of Abnormal and Social Psychology*, 1964, *69*, 313–318.

Meyer, J. The impact of the open space school upon teacher influence and autonomy: The effects of an organizational innovation. Stanford: Stanford University Press, 1971. (ERIC Document Reproduction Service No. ED 062 291)

Meyers, C. E., Sundstrom, P. E., and Yoshida, R. K. The school psychologist and assessment in special education. *School Psychology Monographs*, 1974, *2*, 3–57.

Michael, W. B., Guilford, J. P., Fruchter, B. and Zimmerman, W. S. The description of spatial-visualization abilities. *Educational and Psychological Measurement*, 1957, *17*, 185–199.

Michaelsson, G., and Juhlin, L. Urticaria induced by preservatives and dye additives in food and drugs. *British Journal of Dermatology*, 1973, *88*, 525–532.

Miles, T. R. *The Dyslexic Child*. London: Priory Press, 1974.

Miller, A. D., Margolin, J. B., and Yolles, S. F. Epidemiology of reading disabilities: Some methodologic considerations and early findings. *American Journal of Public Health*, 1957, *47*, 1250–1256.

Miller, G. A. The magical number seven, plus or minus two: Some limits on our capacity for processing information. *The Psychological Review*, 1956, *63*, 81–97.

Miller, J. P. Piaget, Kohlberg, and Erikson: Developmental implications for secondary education. *Adolescence*, 1978, *13*, 237–250.

Miller, L. K., and Turner, S. Development of hemifield differences in word recognition. *Journal of Educational Psychology*, 1973, *65*, 172–176.

Miller, M., and Rohr, M. E. Verbal mediation for perceptual deficits in learning disabilities: A review and suggestions. *Journal of Learning Disabilities*, 1980, *13*, 319–321.

Miller, S. A., Shelton, J., and Favell, J. H. A test of Luria's hypotheses concerning the development of verbal self-regulation. *Child Development*, 1970, *41*, 651–665.

Miller, T. and Sabatino, D. A. An evaluation of the teacher consultant model as an approach to mainstreaming. *Exceptional Children*, 1978, *45*, 86–91.

Miller, W. H. Reading diagnosis kit. New York: The Center for Applied Research in Education, 1974.

Miller, W. H., and Windhauser, E. Reading disability: Tendency toward delinquency? *Clearinghouse*, 1971, *46*, 183–186.

Millichap, J. G. A neurologist's viewpoint: Physical examination and laboratory findings. Address to SUNY Upstate Medical Center and CIBA conference, Understanding Minimal Brain Dysfunction, Syracuse, 17 November 1977.

Mills v. Board of Education of D.C., 348 F. Supp. 866, 880 (D.D.C. 1972).

Milner, B. Taylor, L., and Sperry, R. W. Lateralized suppression of dichotically presented digits after commissural section in man. *Science*, 1968, *161*, 184–186.

Minskoff, E. H. Research on psycholinguistic training: Critique and guidelines. *Exceptional Children*, 1975, *42*, 136–144.

Minskoff, E. Teaching approach for developing nonverbal communication skills in students with social perception deficits. Part I. The basic approach and body language cues. *Journal of Learning Disabilities*, 1980a, *13*, 118–124.

———. Teaching approach for developing nonverbal communication skills in students with social perception deficits. Part 2, Proxemic, vocalic, and artifactual cues. *Journal of Learning Disabilities*, 1980b, *13*, 203–208.

Minskoff, E. H., Wiseman, D. E., and Minskoff, J. G. *The MWM Program for Developing Language Abilities*. Ridgefield, N.J.: Educational Performance Associates, 1972.

Minskoff, J. G. Modifying and restructuring academics for secondary school special education. *Adams School Bulletin*, 1969, *3*, 1.

Minton, M. J. The effect of sustained silent reading upon comprehension and attitudes among 9th graders. *Journal of Reading*, 1980, *23*, 498–502.

Mintz, N. L. Effects of esthetic surroundings: II. Prolonged and repeated experience in a "beautiful" and "ugly" room. *Journal of Psychology*, 1956, *41*, 459–466.

Mischel, W. Father absence and delay of gratification: cross cultural comparison. *Journal of Abnormal and Social Psychology*, 1961, *63*, 116–124.

Mischel, W. *Personality and Assessment*. New York: John Wiley & Sons, 1968.

———. Continuity and change in personality. *American Psychologist*, 1969, *24*, 1012–1018.

———. Toward a cognitive social learning reconceptualization of personality. *Psychological Review*, 1973, *80*, 252–283.

———. On the interface of cognition and personality: Beyond the person-situation debate. *American Psychologist*, 1979, *34*, 740–754.

Moeser, S. D., and Bregman, A. S. Imagery and language acquisition. *Journal of Verbal Learning and Verbal Behavior*, 1973, *12*, 91–98.

Moeser, S. D., and Olson, A. J. The role of reference in children's acquisition of a miniature artificial language. *Journal of Experimental Child Psychology*, 1974, *17*, 204–218.

Molfese, D. Cerebral asymmetry in infants, children and adults: Auditory evoked responses to speech and musical stimuli. *Journal of the Acoustical Society of America*, 1973, *53*, 363(A).

Money, J., and Alexander, D. Turner's syndrome: Further demonstration of the presence of specific cognitional deficiencies. *Journal of Medical Genetics*, 1966, *3*, 47–48.

Money, J., and Lewis, V. Longitudinal study of intelligence quotient in treated congenital hypothyroidism. In *Brain-Thyroid Relationships*, edited by M. P. Cameron and

M. O'Connor. CIBA Foundation Study Group No. 18. Boston: Little, Brown, 1964.

Monroe, M. *Children Who Cannot Read*. Chicago: University of Chicago Press, 1932.

Moor House School. Follow-up report. Oxted, Surrey, England, 1969.

Moore, J., and Fine, M. J. Regular and special class teachers' perceptions of normal and exceptional children and their attitudes toward mainstreaming. *Psychology in Schools*, 1978, *15*, 253–259.

Moos, R. H. Conceptualizations of human environments. *American Psychologist*, 1973, *28*, 652–665.

———. Assessment and impact of social climate. In *Advances in Psychological Assessment*, Vol. 3, edited by P. McReynolds. San Francisco: Jossey-Bass, 1975.

———. *The Human Context*. New York: John Wiley & Sons, 1976.

———. *Evaluating Educational Environments*. New York: John Wiley & Sons, 1979.

Morehead, D., and Ingram, D. The development of base syntax in normal and linguistically deviant children. *Journal of Speech and Hearing Research*, 1973, *16*, 330–353.

Morgan, W. P. A case of congenital word blindness. *British Medical Journal*, 1896, *2*, 1378.

Morrison, F. J., Giordani, B., and Nagy, J. Reading disability: An information-processing analysis. *Science*, 1977, *196*, 77–79.

Morrison, J. P. and Stewart, M. A. A family study of the hyperactive child syndrome. *Biological Psychiatry*, 1971, *3*, 189–195.

———. The psychiatric status of the legal families of adopted hyperactive children.

———. Bilateral inheritance as evidence for polygenicity in the hyperactive child syndrome. *Journal of Nervous and Mental Disease*, 1974, *158*, 226–228.

Morse, W. C., Cutler, R. L., and Fink, A. H. *Public School Classes for the Emotionally Handicapped: A Research Analysis*. Washington, D.C.: Council for Exceptional Children, National Education Association, 1964.

Moskowitz, H. Drug effects in relation to industrial safety. In *Behavioral Toxicology*, edited by C. Xintras, B. L. Johnson, and I. de Groot. Washington, D.C.: U.S. Department of Health, Education and Welfare, 1974.

Mosse, H. L., and Daniels, C. R. Linear dyslexia: A new form of reading disorder. *American Journal of Psychotherapy*, 1959, *13*, 826–841.

Mountcastle, V. B., ed. *Interhemispheric Relationships and Cerebral Dominance*. Baltimore: Johns Hopkins Press, 1962.

Mowder, B. A. A strategy for the assessment of bilingual handicapped children. *Psychology in the Schools*, 1980, *17*, 7–11.

Mowrer, O. H. *Learning Theory and the Symbolic Process*. New York: John Wiley & Sons, 1960.

Moya, F., and Smith, B. E. Uptake, distribution and placental transport of drugs and anesthetics. *Anesthesiology*, 1965, *26*, 465–476.

Moynahan, E. D. The development of knowledge concerning the effect of categorization upon free recall. *Child Development*, 1973, *44*, 238–246.

Muehl, S., and Forell, E. R. A followup study of disabled readers: Variables related to high school reading performance. *Reading Research Quarterly*, 1973, *9*, 110–123.

Mumbauer, C. C., and Miller, J. O. Socioeconomic background and cognitive functioning in preschool children. *Child Development*, 1970, *41*, 471–480.

Murray, C. A. *The Link Between Learning Disabilities and Juvenile Delinquency: Current Theory and Knowledge*. Washington, D.C.: U.S. Government Printing Office, 1976.

Mussen, H., Conger, J. J., and Kagan, J. *Child Development and Personality*. New York: Harper & Row, 1979.

Myers, C. A. Reviewing the literature on Fernald's techniques of remedial reading. *Reading Teacher*, 1970, *31*, 614.

Myers, P. I., and Hammill, D. D. *Methods for Learning Disorders*. 2nd ed. New York: John Wiley & Sons, 1976.

Myklebust, H. R. Aphasia in children. *Exceptional Children*, 1952, *19*, 9–14.

———. *Auditory Disorders in Children*. New York: Grune & Stratton, 1954.

———. *The Psychology of Deafness: Sensory Deprivation, Learning, and Adjustment*. New York: Grune & Stratton, 1960.

———. *The Psychology of Deafness: Sensory Deprivation, Learning and Adjustment*. New York: Grune & Stratton, 1964.

———. *Development and Disorders of Written Language*. Vol. 1, *Picture Story Language Test*. New York: Grune & Stratton, 1965.

———. Learning disabilities: Definition and overview. In *Progress in Learning Disabilities*. Vol. 1, edited by H. R. Myklebust. New York; Grune & Stratton, 1968.

———. *Development and Disorders of Written Language*. Vol. 2, *Studies of Normal and Exceptional Children*. New York: Grune & Stratton, 1973.

Myklebust, H. R., and Boshes, B. *Minimal Brain Damage in Children*. Washington, D.C.: Neurological and Sensory Disease Control Program, Department of Health, Education and Welfare, 1969.

Nagle, R. J. and Thwaite, B. C. Modelling effects on impulsivity with learning disabled children. *Journal of Learning Disabilities*, 1979, *12*, 331–336.

National Advisory Committee on Handicapped Children. *Better Education for Handicapped Children: Second Annual Report*, Washington, D.C.: U.S. Department of Health, Education and Welfare, 1970.

National Assessment of Educational Progress. *Functional Literacy: Basic Reading Performance*. Denver: National Assessment of Education Progress, 1976.

Nay, W. R. Analogue measures. In *Handbook of Behavioral Assessment*, edited by A. R. Ciminero, K. S. Calhoun, and H. E. Adams. New York: John Wiley & Sons, 1977.

Needleman, H. L., Gunnoe, C., Leviton, A., Read, R., Peresie, H., Maher, C., and Barrett, P. Deficits in psychologic and classroom performance of children with elevated dentine lead levels. *The New England Journal of Medicine*, 1979, *300*, 689–695.

Neisworth, J. T., Kurtz, P. D., Ross, A., and Madle, R. A. Naturalistic assessment of neurological diagnoses and pharmacological intervention. *Journal of Learning Disabilities*, 1976, *9*, 149–152.

Nelson, H. E., and Warrington, E. K. Developmental spelling retardation. In *The Neuropsychology of Learning Disorders: Theoretical Approaches*, edited by R. M. Knights and D. J. Bakker. Baltimore: University Park Press, 1976.

Nelson, K. Structure and strategy in learning to talk. *Monographs of the Society for Research in Child Development*, 1973, *38*(102, Serial No. 149).

Nelson, K. E. Memory development in children: Evidence from nonverbal tasks. *Psychonomic Science*, 1975, *25*, 346–348.

Nelson, R. O. Methodological issues in assessment via self-monitoring. In *Behavioral Assessment: New Directions in Clinical Psychology*, edited by J. D. Cone and R. P. Hawkins. New York: Brunner/Mazel, 1977.

Nelson, R. O, and Bowles, E. P. The best of two worlds: Observations with norms. *Journal of School Psychology*, 1975, *13*, 309.

Nettleship, E. Cases of congenital word-blindness (inability to learn to read). *Ophthalmic Review*, 1901, *20*, 61–67.

Newbrough, J. R. Workshop on ecological assessment. Presented to the National Meeting of the Association of School Psychologists, New York, 1978.

Newcombe, F., and Ratcliff, G. Handedness, speech lateralization and ability. *Neuropsychologia*, 1973, *11*, 399–407.

Newcomer, P. Learning disabilities: An educator's perspective. *Journal of Special Education*, 1975, *9*, 146–149.

Newcomer, P. L. Competencies for professionals in learning disabilities. *Learning Disability Quarterly*, 1978, *1*, 73–76.

Newcomer, P., and Hammill, D. D., eds. *Psycholinguistics in the Classroom*. Columbus, Ohio: Charles E. Merrill, 1976.

Newland, T. E. Psychological assessment of exceptional children and youth. In *Psychology of Exceptional Children and Youth*, edited by W. Cruickshank. Englewood Cliffs, N.J.: Prentice-Hall, 1971.

Nichols, R. G., and Stevens, L. A. *Are You Listening?* New York: McGraw-Hill, 1957.

Nober, L. W., and Nober, E. H. Auditory discrimination of learning disabled children in quiet and classroom noise. *Journal of Learning Disabilities*, 1975, *8*, 656–659.

Noble, J. K. *Better Handwriting for You*. New York: Noble and Noble, 1966.

Noel, M. M. Referential communication abilities of learning disabled children. *Learning Disability Quarterly*, 1980, *3*(3), 70–75.

Noland, E. G., and Schuldt, W. J. Sustained attention and reading retardation. *Journal of Experimental Education*, 1971, *40*, 73–76.

Norman, D. A. *Memory and Attention*. New York: John Wiley & Sons, 1969.

Norrie, E. Research data reported in *Reading Disability*, by L. J. Thompson. Springfield, Ill.: Charles C. Thomas, 1959.

Novack, H. S., Bonaventura, E., and Merenda, P. F. A scale for early detection of children with learning problems. *Exceptional Children*, 1973, *40*, 98–105.

Oakland, T. Pluralistic norms and estimated learning potential. Paper presented at the meeting of the American Psychological Association, August 1977a.

———. An evaluation of the ABIC, pluralistic norms, and estimated learning potential. *Journal of School Psychology*, 1980, *18*, 3–11.

Oakland, T., ed. *Psychological and Educational Assessment of Minority Children*. New York: Brunner/Mazel, 1977b.

Oakland, T., and Laosa, L. M. Professional, legislative, and judicial influences on psychoeducational assessment practices in schools. In *Psychological and Educational Assessment of Minority Children*, edited by T. Oakland. New York: Brunner/Mazel, 1977.

O'Connor, P. D., Stuck, G. B., and Wyne, M. D. Effects of a short-term interaction resource room program on task orientation and achievement. *Journal of Special Education*, 1979, *13*, 375–385.

Odom, R. D., and Corbin, D. W. Perceptual salience and children's multidimensional problem solving. *Child Development*, 1973, *44*, 425–532.

O'Donnell, P. A. A re-evaluation of research on lateral expression. *Journal of Learning Disabilities*, 1970, *3*, 344–350.

O'Donnell, P. A., and Eisenson, J. Delacato training for reading achievement and visual–motor integration. *Journal of Learning Disabilities*, 1969, *2*, 441–447.

Oettinger, L., Majovski, L. V., Limbeck, G. A., and Gauch, R. Bone age in children with minimal brain dysfunction. *Perceptual and Motor Skills*, 1974, *39*, 1127–1131.

Offir, C. W. Their fingers do the talking. *Psychology Today*, 1976, *10*, 73–78.

Olsen, K. Minimum competency testing and the IEP process. *Exceptional Children*, 1980, *47*, 176–183.

Olshansky, S. Parent responses to a mentally defective child. *Mental Retardation*, 1966, *4*, 21–23.

Olson, J. L, and Mealor, D. J. Learning disabilities identification: Do researchers have the answer? *Learning Disability Quarterly*, 1981, *4*(4), 389–392.

O'Malley, J. E., and Eisenberg, L. The hyperkinetic syndrome. *Seminars in Psychiatry*, 1973, *5*, 95–103.

Omenn, G. S. Genetic approaches to the syndrome of minimal brain dysfunction. *Annals of the New York Academy of Sciences*, 1973, *205*, 212–222.

O'Neill, G., and Stanley, G. Visual processing of straight lines in dyslexic and normal children. *British Journal of Educational Psychology*, 1976, *46*, 323–327.

Orbach, I. Impulsive cognitive style: Three modification techniques. *Psychology in the Schools*, 1977, *14*, 353–359.

Ornstein, P. A., Naus, M. J., and Liberty, C. Rehearsal and organizational processes in children's memory. *Child Development*, 1975, *46*, 818–830.

Orton, S. T. "Word-blindness" in school children. *Archives of Neurology and Psychiatry*, 1925, *14*, 582–615.

————. Specific reading disability: Strephosymbolia. *The Journal of the American Medical Association*, 1928, *90*, 1095–1099.

————. *Reading, Writing and Speech Problems in Children.* New York: W. W. Norton, 1937.

————. The Orton Gillingham Approach. In *Disabled Reader*, edited by J. Money and G. Shiffman. Baltimore: Johns Hopkins Press, 1966.

Osborn, A. *Applied Imagination.* New York: Charles Scribner's Sons, 1963.

Osgood, C. E. A behavioristic analysis of perception and language as cognitive phenomena. In *Contemporary Approaches to Cognition*, edited by J. S. Bruner. Cambridge: Harvard University Press, 1957a.

————. Motivational dynamics of language behavior. *Nebraska Symposium on Motivation*, 1957b, *5*, 348–424.

————. Psycholinguistics. In *Psychology: A Study of a Science.* Vol. 6, edited by S. Koch. New York: McGraw-Hill, 1963.

Osgood, C. E., and Miron, M. S. *Approaches to the Study of Aphasia.* Urbana: University of Illinois Press, 1963.

Ott, J. N. Influence of fluorescent lights on hyperactivity and learning disabilities. *Journal of Learning Disabilities*, 1976, *9*, 417–422.

Otto, W., McMenemy, R. A., and Smith, R. *Corrective and Remedial Teaching: Principles and Practices.* Boston: Houghton Mifflin, 1973.

Over, R., and Over, J. Detection and recognition of mirror image obliques by young children. *Journal of Comparative and Physiological Psychology*, 1967, *64*, 467–470.

Owen, F. W., Adams, P. A., Forrest, T., Stolz, L. M., and Fisher, S. Learning disorders in children: Sibling studies. *Monographs of the Society for Research in Child Development*, 1971, *36*(4, Serial No. 144).

Padula, W. V. A point of discrimination: Public Law 94-142. *Journal of Learning Disabilities*, 1979, *12*, 682–683.

Page-El, E., and Grossman, H. Neurologic appraisal in learning disorders. *Pediatric Clinics of North America*, 1973, *20*(3), 599–605.

Painter, M. Fluorescent lights and hyperactivity in children: An experiment. *Academic Therapy*, 1976, *12*, 181–184.

Paivio, A. Mental imagery in associative learning and memory. *Psychological Review*, 1969, *76*, 241–263.

Palkes, H., Stewart, M., and Freedman, J. Improvement in maze performance of hyperactive boys as a function of verbal-training procedures. *Journal of Special Education*, 1971, *5*, 337–342.

Palkes, H., Stewart, M., and Kihana, B. Porteus maze performance of hyperactive boys after training in self-directed verbal commands. *Child Development*, 1968, *39*, 817–826.

Panda, K. C. and Bartel, N. R. Teacher perception of exceptional children. *Journal of Special Education*, 1972, *6*, 261–266.

Paris, S. G., and Haywood, H. C. Mental retardation as a learning disorder. *Pediatric Clinics of North America*, 1973, *20*(3), 641–651.

Paris, S. G., and Lindauer, B. K. The role of inference in children's comprehension and memory for sentences. *Cognitive Psychology*, 1976, *8*, 217–227.

————. Constructive aspects of children's comprehension and memory. In *Perspectives on the Development of Memory and Cognition*, edited by R. V. Kail and J. W. Hagen. Hillsdale, N.J.: Lawrence Erlbaum, 1977.

Paris, S. G., and Upton, L. R. Children's memory for inferential relationships in prose. *Child Development*, 1976, *47*, 660–668.

Parish, T. S., Eads, G. M., Reece, N. H., and Piscitello, M. A. Assessment and attempted modification of future teachers' attitudes toward handicapped children. *Perceptual and Motor Skills*, 1977, *44*, 540–542.

Parish, R. S., Ohlsen, R. L., and Parish, J. G. A look at mainstreaming in light of children's attitudes toward the handicapped. *Perceptual and Motor Skills*, 1978, *46*, 1019–1021.

Park, G. E., and Linde, J. D. The etiology of reading disabilities: An historical perspective. *Journal of Learning Disabilities*, 1968, *1*, 318–330.

Parker, T. B., Freston, C. W., and Drew, C. J. Comparison of verbal performance of normal and learning disabled children as a function of input organization. *Journal of Learning Disabilities*, 1975, *8*, 386–393.

Pasamanick, B., and Knobloch, H. The contribution of some organic factors to school retardation in Negro children. *Journal of Negro Education*, 1958, *27*, 4–9.

————. Brain damage and reproductive causality. *American Journal of Orthopsychiatry*, 1960, *30*, 298–305.

————. Epidemiological studies on the complications of pregnancy and the birth process. In *Prevention of Mental Disorder in Children*, edited by J. Caplan. New York: Basic Books, 1961.

————. The epidemiology of reproductive causality. In *Children With Learning Problems: Reading in a Developmental-Interaction Approach*, edited by S. G. Sapir and A. C. Nitzburg. New York: Brunner/Mazel, 1973.

Pasamanick, B., Knobloch, H., and Lilienfeld, A. M. Socioeconomic status and some precursors of neuropsychiatric disorder. *American Journal of Orthopsychiatry*, 1956, *26*, 594–601.

Pascarella, E. T., and Pflaum, S. W. The interaction of children's attribution and level of control over error correction in reading instruction. *Journal of Educational Psychology*, 1981, *73*, 533–540.

Patten, B. M. Visually mediated thinking: A report of the case of Albert Einstein. *Journal of Learning Disabilities*, 1973, *6*, 415–420.

Patterson, C., and Mischel, W. Effects of temptation-inhibiting and task facilitating plans on self-control. *Journal of Personality and Social Psychology*, 1976, *33*, 209–217.

Patterson, G. R., and Gullion, M. E. *Living with Children.* Champaign, Ill.: Research Press, 1971.

Patton, B. R., and Griffin, K. *Problem-Solving Group Interaction.* New York: Harper & Row, 1973.

Patton, P. A model for developing vocational objectives in the IEP. *Exceptional Children*, 1981, *47*, 618–622.

Pauk, W. *How to Study in College.* Boston: Houghton Mifflin, 1974.

Pauling, L. Orthomolecular psychiatry. *Science*, 1968, *160*, 265–271.

Payne, J. S., Mercer, C. D., Payne, R. A., and Davidson, R. G. *Head Start: A Tragicomedy with Epilogue.* New York: Behavioral Publications, 1973.

Pearl, R., and Bryan, T. Mothers' attributions for their learning disabled child's successes and failures. *Learning Disability Quarterly*, 1982, *5*(1), 53–57.

Pearl, R., Bryan, T., and Donahue, M. Learning disabled children's attributions for success and failure. *Learning Disability Quarterly*, 1980, *3*, 3–9.

Penfield, W., and Roberts, L. *Speech and Brain Mechanisms.* Princeton: Princeton University Press, 1959.

Pennsylvania Association for Retarded Children v. Pennsylvania, 334 F. Supp. 1257 (E.D. Pa. 1971).

Perfetti, C. A., and Lesgold, A. M. Coding and comprehension in skilled reading and implications for reading instruction. In *Theory and Practice in Early Reading*, edited by L. B. Resnick and P. Weaver. Hillsdale, N.J.: Lawrence Erlbaum, 1977.

Peterson, L., and Smith, L. L. A comparison of the post-school adjustment of educable mentally retarded adults with that of adults of normal intelligence. *Exceptional Children*, 1960, *26*, 404–408.

Pettigrew, T. F. *A Profile of the Negro American*. Princeton: Van Nostrand, 1964.

Pettit, J. M., and Helms, S. B. Hemispheric language dominance of language-disordered, articulation-disordered, and normal children. *Journal of Learning Disabilities*, 1979, *12*, 71–76.

Pflaum, S. W., Pascarella, E. T., Auer, C., Augustyn, L., and Boswick, M. Differential effects of four comprehension-facilitating conditions on LD and normal elementary-school readers. *Learning Disability Quarterly*, 1982, *5*, 106–116.

Phares, E. J. *Locus of Control: A Personality Determinant of Behavior*. Morristown, N.J.: General Learning Press, 1973.

Phillips, J. C., and Kelly, D. H. School failure and delinquency: Which causes which? *Criminology*, 1979, *17*, 194–207.

Piaget, J. *The Moral Judgment of the Child*. Glencoe, Ill.: Free Press, 1948.

———. *The Construction of Reality in the Child*. New York: Basic Books, 1954.

———. *The Language and Thought of the Child*. New York: World Publishing, 1962.

———. Piaget's theory. In *Piaget and His School: A Reader in Developmental Psychology*. edited by B. Inhelder, H. H. Chipman, and C. Zwingmann. New York: Springer-Verlag, 1976.

Piaget, J., and Inhelder, B. *The Child's Conception of Space*. London: Routledge & Kegan Paul, 1956.

Pick, A. D., Frankel, D. G., and Hess, V. L. Children's attention: The development of selectivity. *Review of Child Development Research* 1975, *5*, 325–383.

Pick, H. L., and Pick, A. D. Sensory and perceptual development. In *Carmichael's Manual of Child Psychology*. 3rd ed., edited by P. H. Mussen. New York: John Wiley & Sons, 1970.

Piersel, W. C., and Kratochwill, T. R. Self-observation and behavior change: Applications to academic and adjustment problems through behavioral consultation. *Journal of School Psychology*, 1979, *17*, 151–161.

Pihl, R. O., and Parkes, M. Hair element content in learning disabled children. *Science*, 1977, *198*, 204–206.

Poplin, M. S. The severely learning disabled: Neglected or forgotten? *Learning Disability Quarterly*, 1981, *4*(4), 330–335.

Poplin, M. S., Gray, R., Larsen, S., Banikowski, A., and Mehring, T. A comparison of components of written expression abilities in learning disabled and non-learning disabled students at three-grade levels. *Learning Disability Quarterly*, 1980, *3*(4), 46–53.

Porges, S. W., Walter, G. F., Korb, R. J., and Sprague, R. L. The influences of methylphenidate on heart rate and behavioral measures of attention in hyperactive children. *Child Development*, 1975, *46*, 727–733.

Porter, R. B., and Milazzo, T. C. A comparison of mentally retarded adults who attended a special class with those who attended a regular school class. *Exceptional Children*, 1958, *24*, 410–412, 420.

Poteet, J. A. Informal assessment of written expression. *Learning Disability Quarterly*, 1980, *3*(4), 88–98.

Potts, M. The relative achievement of first graders under three different reading programs. *The Journal of Educational Research*, 1968, 61, 447–450.

Pratt, E. Experimental evaluation of a program for the improvement of listening. *Elementary School Journal*, 1956, *56*, 315–320.

Prechtl, H. F. R. Prognostic value of neurological signs in the newborn infant. *Proceedings of the Royal Society of Medicine*, 1965, *58*, 3–4.

Preston, M. S., Guthrie, J. T., and Childs, B. Visual evoked responses (VERs) in normal and disabled readers. *Psychophysiology*, 1974, *11*, 452–457.

Preston, R. C., and Yarington, D. J. Status of fifty retarded readers eight years after reading clinic diagnosis. *Journal of Reading*, 1967, *11*, 122–129.

Prillaman, D. Acceptance of learning disabled students in the mainstream environment: A failure to replicate. *Journal of Learning Disabilities*, 1981, *14*, 344–346, 368.

Progress Toward a Free Appropriate Public Education. A Report to Congress on the Implementation of Public Law 94-142: The Education for All Handicapped Children Act. Washington, D.C.: U.S. Department of Health, Education, and Welfare, Office of Education, January 1979.

Proshansky, H. M., Ittelson, W. H., and Rivlin, L. G. *Environmental Psychology*. 2nd ed. New York: Holt, Rinehart and Winston, 1976.

Provence, S., and Lipton, R. C. *Infants in Institutions*. New York: International Universities Press, 1962.

Pugach, M. C. Regular classroom teacher involvement in the development and utilization of IEP's. *Exceptional Children*, 1982, *48*, 371–374.

Pullis, M., and Smith, D. C. Social-cognitive development of learning disabled children. In Piaget, Learning, and Learning Disabilities, edited by D. K. Reid. *Topics in Learning and Learning Disabilities*, 1981, *1*, 43–55.

Quay, H. C. Special education: Assumptions, techniques, and evaluative criteria. *Exceptional Children*, 1973, *40*, 165–170.

Quinn, J. A., and Wilson, B. J. Programming effects on learning disabled children: Performance and affect. *Psychology in the Schools*, 1977, *14*, 196–199.

Radosh, A., and Gittleman, R. The effect of appealing distractors on the performance of hyperactive children. *Journal of Abnormal Child Psychology*, 1981, *9*, 179–189.

Raisman, G., and Field, P. M. A quantitative investigation of the development of collateral reinnervation after partial deaffrentiation of the septal nuclei. *Brain Research*, 1973, *50*, 241–264.

Ramirez, M., and Castaneda, A. *Cultural Democracy, Bicognitive Development, and Education*. New York: Academic Press, 1974.

Randolph, L. C. A study of the effects of praise, criticism, and failure on the problem solving performance of field-dependent and field-independent individuals. Unpublished doctoral dissertation, New York University, 1971.

Rapin, I., and Wilson, B. C. Children with developmental language disability: Neurological aspects and assessment. In *Developmental Dysphasia*, edited by M. A. Wyke. New York: Academic Press, 1978.

Rapoport, J. L., Buchsbaum, M. S., Zahn, T. P., Weingartner, H., Ludlow, C., and Mikkelsen, E. J. Dextroamphetamine: Cognitive and behavioral effects in normal prepubertal boys. *Science*, 1978, *199*, 560–563.

Rapp, D. J. Food allergy treatment for hyperkinesis. *Journal of Learning Disabilities*, 1979, *12*, 608–616.

Rappaport, M. Prevention of problems in children: The executive function of the family. *The Forum*, 1981, *7*(2), 11, 22.

Rasmussen, T., and Milner, B. Clinical and surgical studies of the cerebral speech areas in man. In *Otfred Foerster Symposium on Cerebral Localization*, edited by K. J. Zulch, O. Creutzfeldt, and G. C. Galbraith. Heidelberg: Springer-Verlag, 1975.

Raths, L., Harmin, M., and Simon, S. *Values and Teaching*. Columbus, Ohio: Charles E. Merrill, 1966.

Rawson, M. B. *Developmental Language Disability: Adult Accomplishments of Dyslexic Boys*. Baltimore: Johns Hopkins Press, 1968.

Read, C. Lessons to be learned from the preschool orthographer. In *Foundations of Language Development: A Multidisciplinary Apporach*, edited by E. H. Lenneberg and E. Lenneberg. New York: Academic Press, 1975.

Reese, H. W., and Lipsitt, L. P. *Experimental Child Psychology*. New York: Academic Press, 1970.

Reeve, J. E. NCE's for Identifying Severe Discrepancies. Paper presented at the meeting of the National Association of School Psychologists, San Diego, March 1979.

Reid, D. K. Genevan theory and the education of exceptional children. In *Knowledge and Development*. Vol. 2, *Piaget and Education*, edited by J. M. Gallagher and J. A. Easley, New York: Plenum, 1978.

———. Learning from a Piagetian perspective: The exceptional child. In *Piagetian Theory and Research: New Directives and Applications*, edited by I. E. Sigel, R. M. Golinkoff, and D. Brodzinsky. Hillsdale, N.J.: Lawrence Erlbaum, 1980.

Reid, D. K., and Hresko, W. P. A developmental study of the language and early reading in learning disabled and normally achieving children. *Learning Disabilities Quarterly*, 1980, *3*(4), 54–61.

———. Mathematics (editorial comment). *Topics in Learning and Learning Disabilities*, 1981, *1*(3), vii–ix.

Reitan, R. M. Methodological problems in clinical neuropsychology. In *Clinical Neuropsychology: Current Status and Applications*, edited by R. M. Reitan and L. A. Davison, Washington, D.C.: Winston, 1974.

Reger, R. and Koppmann, M. The child oriented resource room program. *Exceptional Children*, 1971, *37*, 460–462.

Reschly, D. Comparisons of bias in assessment with conventional and pluralistic measures. Paper presented at meeting of the Council for Exceptional Children, 1978.

Reschly, D. Nonbiased assessment. In *School Psychology: Perspectives and Issues*, edited by G. D. Phye and D. J. Reschly. New York: Academic Press, 1979.

Reschly, D., and Lamprecht, M. J. Expectancy effects of labels: Fact or artifact? *Exceptional Children*, 1979, *46*(1), 55–58.

Resnick, L. B., Wang, M. C., and Kaplan, J. Task analysis in curriculum design: A hierarchically sequenced introductory mathematics curriculum. *Journal of Applied Behavior Analysis*, 1973, *6*, 679–710.

Reynolds, C. R., Factor structure of the Peabody Individual Achievement Test at five grade levels between grades one and twelve. *Journal of School Psychology*, 1979, *17*, 270–274.

Reynolds, M. C., and Balow, B. Categories and variables in special education. *Exceptional Children*, 1972, *38*, 357–366.

Ribner, S. The effects of special class placement on the self-concept of exceptional children. *Journal of Learning Disabilities*, 1978, *11*, 319–323.

Ribovich, J. K., and Erikson, L. A study of lifelong reading with implications for instructional programs. *Journal of Reading*, 1980, *24*, 20–26.

Richardson, E., Di Benedetto, B., and Bradley, C. M. The relationship of sound blending to reading achievement. *Review of Educational Research*, 1977, *47*, 319–334.

Richardson, S. Address to Grand Rounds, Upstate Medical Center, Syracuse, 11 October 1979.

Richey, D. D., and McKinney, J. D. Classroom behavioral styles of learning disabled boys. *Journal of Learning Disabilities*, 1978, *11*, 297–302.

Richey, D. D., Miller, M., and Lessman, J. Resource and regular classroom behavior of learning disabled students. *Journal of Learning Disabilities*, 1981, *14*, 163–166.

Richey, H. W., and Richey, M. N. Nonverbal behavior in the classroom. *Psychology in the Schools*, 1978, *15*, 571–576.

Richmond, J. B., and Walzer, S. The central task of childhood learning: The pediatrician's role. In *Minimal Brain Dysfunction*, edited by F. De La Cruz, B. H. Fox, and R. H. Roberts. *Annals of the New York Academy of Science*, 1973, *205*, 390–394.

Ridberg, E. H., Parke, R. D., and Hetherington, E. M. Modification of impulsive and reflective cognitive styles through observation of film-mediated models. *Developmental Psychology*, 1971, *5*, 369–377.

Rimm, D. C., and Masters, J. C. *Behavior Therapy: Techniques and Empirical Findings*. New York: Academic Press, 1974.

Ringler, L. H., and Smith, I. L. Learning modality and word recognition of first-grade children. *Journal of Learning Disabilities*, 1973, *6*, 307–312.

Ritter, D. R. Surviving in the regular classroom: A follow-up of mainstreamed children with learning disabilities. *Journal of School Psychology*, 1978, *16*, 253–256.

Roach, E. F., and Kephart, N. C. *The Purdue Perceptional-Motor Survey*. Columbus, Ohio: Charles E. Merrill, 1966.

Robbins, M. P. Test of the Doman-Delacato rationale with retarded readers. *Journal of the American Medical Association*, 1967, *202*, 389–393.

Roberts, C. J. The distribution of neurological signs in early infancy: A population study. In studies in Infancy, edited by R. MacKeith and M. Bax. *Clinics in Developmental Medicine*, 1968, *27*, 55–64.

Roberts, G. H. The failure strategies of third grade arithmetic pupils. *The Arithmetic Teacher*, May 1961, 226–233.

Robinson, F. P. Study skills for superior students in the secondary schools. *The Reading Teacher*, 1961, 29–33.

Robinson, H. M. Visual and auditory modalities related to two methods for beginning reading. *AERA Paper Abstracts*, 1968, 74–75.

Robinson, H. M. and Smith, H. K. Reading clinic clients — ten years after. *Elementary School Journal*, 1962, *63*, 22–27.

Robinson, N. M., and Robinson, H. B. *The Mentally Retarded Child*. New York: McGraw-Hill, 1976.

Robson, P. Shuffling, hitching, scooting or sliding: Some observations in 30 otherwise normal children. *Developmental Medicine and Child Neurology*, 1970, *12*, 608–617.

Rockowitz, R. J., and Davidson, P. W. Discussing diagnostic findings with parents. *Journal of Learning Disabilities*, 1979, *12*, 11–16.

Rogan, L. L., and Hartman, L. D. A follow-up study of learning disabled children as adults. Final report. Bureau of Education for the Handicapped, December 1976.

Rohwer, W. D., Jr. Prime time for education: Early childhood or adolescence? *Harvard Educational Review*, 1971, *41*, 316–341.

Rosen, C. L. An experimental study of visual perceptual training and reading achievement in first grade. *Perceptual and Motor Skills*, 1966, *22*, 979–986.

Rosen, L. Selected aspects in the development of the mother's understanding of her mentally retarded child. *American Journal of Mental Deficiency*, 1955, *59*, 522.

Rosenberg, J. B., and Weller, G. M. Minor physical anomalies and academic performance in young school children. *Developmental Medicine and Child Neurology*, 1973, *15*, 131–135.

Rosenthal, D. *Genetic Theory and Abnormal Behavior*. New York: McGraw-Hill, 1970.

Rosenthal, R., and Jacobson, L. *Pygmalion in the Classroom: Teacher Expectations and Pupils' Intelligence Development*. New York: Holt, Rinehart and Winston, 1968.

Rosenthal, R., and Rosnow, R. *Artifact in Behavioral Research*. New York: Academic Press, 1969.

Rosenzweig, M. R. Environmental complexity, cerebral change, and behavior. *American Psychologist*, 1966, *21*, 321–332.

Rosenzweig, M. R., and Bennett, E. L. Enriched environments: Facts, factors, and fantasies. In *Knowing, Thinking, and Believing*, edited by L. F. Petrinovich and J. L. McGaugh. New York: Plenum, 1976.

Rosner, J. Language arts and arithmetic achievement, and specifically related perceptual skills. *American Educational Research Journal*, 1973, *10*, 59–68.

———. Auditory analysis in training with prereaders. *The Reading Teacher*, 1974, *27*, 379–384.

———. *Helping Children Overcome Learning Difficulties*. New York: Walker, 1975.

Ross, A. O. *Psychological Aspects of Learning Disabilities and Reading Disorders*. New York: McGraw-Hill, 1976.

Ross, D. M., and Ross, S. A. *Hyperactivity: Research, Theory, and Action*. New York: John Wiley & Sons, 1976.

Ross, J., and Weintraub, F. Policy approaches regarding the impact of graduation requirements on handicapped students. *Exceptional Children*, 1980, *47*, 200–203.

Ross, O. A. Conceptual issues in the evaluation of brain damage. In *Brain Damage and Mental Retardation*, edited by J. L. Khanna. Springfield, Ill. Charles C. Thomas, 1968.

Ross, S. L. DeYoung, H. G., and Cohen, J. S. Confrontation: Special education placement and the law. *Exceptional Children*, 1971, *38*, 5–12.

Rossi, G. F., and Rosadini, G. Experimental analysis of cerebral dominance in man. In *Brain Mechanisms Underlying Speech and Language*, chaired by C. H. Millikan and edited by F. L. Darley. New York: Grune & Stratton, 1967.

Rothenburg, M., and Rivlin, L. An ecological approach to the study of open classrooms. Paper read at a conference on ecological factors in human development, University of Surrey, England, 1975.

Rotter, J. B. Generalized expectancies for internal versus external control of reinforcement. *Psychological Monographs*, 1966, *80* (1, Whole No. 609).

Rourke, B. P. Reading retardation in children: Developmental lag or deficit. In *The Neuropsychology of Learning Disorders: Theoretical Approaches*, edited by R. M. Knights and D. J. Bakker. Baltimore: University Park Press, 1976.

Routh, D. K., and Roberts, R. D. Minimal brain dysfunction in children: Failure to find evidence for a behavioral syndrome. *Psychological Reports*, 1972, *31*, 307–314.

Rozin, P., Poritsky, S., and Sotsky, P. American children with reading problems can easily learn to read English represented by Chinese characters. *Science*, 1971, *171*, 1264–1267.

———. In *Psycholinguistics and Reading*, edited by F. Smith. New York: Holt, Rinehart and Winston, 1973.

Rubin, E. Z. Cognitive dysfunction and emotional disorders. In *Progress in Learning Disabilities. Vol. 2*, edited by H. R. Myklebust. New York: Grune & Stratton, 1971.

Rubin, R., and Balow, B. Learning and behavior disorders: A longitudinal study. *Exceptional Children*, 1971, *38*, 293–299.

Rubin, R. A., Krus, P., and Balow, B. Factors in special class placement. *Exceptional Children*, 1973, *39*, 525–532.

Rudel, R. G., Denckla, M. B., and Spalten, E. Paired associate learning of Morse Code and Braille letter names by dyslexic and normal children. *Cortex*, 1976, *12*, 61–70.

Rudel, R. G., and Teuber, H. L. Discrimination of the direction of line by young children. *Journal of Comparative and Physiological Psychology*, 1963, *56*, 892–898.

Rudnick, M., Sterritt, G. M., and Flax, M. Auditory and visual rhythm perception and reading ability. *Child Development*, 1967, *38*, 581–587.

Rugel, R. P. WISC subtest scores of disabled readers: A review with respect to Bannatyne's recategorization. *Journal of Learning Disabilities*, 1974, *7*, 48–55.

Russell Sage Foundation. *Guidelines for the Collection, Maintenance and Dissemination of Pupil Records*. New York: Russell Sage Foundation, 1970.

Ryback, D., and Staats, A. Parents as behavior therapy technicians in treating reading deficits. *Journal of Behavioral Therapy*, 1970, *1*, 101–119.

Sabatino, D. A. An evaluation of resource rooms for children with learning disabilities. *Journal of Learning Disabilities*, 1971, *4*, 84–93.

Sabatino, D. Resource rooms: The renaissance in special education. *Journal of Special Education*, 1972, *6*, 335–347.

Sabatino, D. A., Abbott, J. C., and Becker, J. T. What does the Frostig DTVP measure? *Exceptional Children*, 1974, *40*, 453–454.

Sabatino, D. H., and Hayden, D. L. Prescriptive teaching in a summer learning disabilities program. *Journal of Learning Disabilities*, 1970, *3*, 220–227.

Sabo, R. The Feingold Diet. Address to the annual meeting of the School Psychologists of Upstate New York, Syracuse, October 1976.

Sackett, G. P., *Observing Behavior. Vol. 1, Theory and Applications in Mental Retardation*. Baltimore: University Park Press, 1978a.

———. *Observing Behavior. Vol. 2, Data Collection and Analysis Methods*. Baltimore: University Park Press, 1978b.

Safer, D. J., and Allen, R. P. Factors influencing the suppressant effects of two stimulant drugs on the growth of hyperactive children. *Pediatrics*, 1973, *51*, 660–667.

Salapatek, P. Pattern perception in early infancy. In *Infant Perception from Sensation to Cognition: Basic Visual Processes*. Vol. 1, edited by L. B. Cohen and P. Salapatek. New York: Academic Press, 1975.

Salvia, J., and Clark, J. Use of deficits to identify the learning disabled. *Exceptional Children*, 1973, *39*, 305–308.

Salvia, J., and Ysseldyke, J. E. Assessment in Special and Remedial Education. Boston: Houghton Mifflin, 1978.

Samter, M., and Beers, R. F., Jr. Intolerance to aspirin: clinical studies and consideration of its pathogensis. *Annals of Internal Medicine*, 1968, *68*, 975–983.

Samuels, S. J. Attentional process in reading: The effect of pictures on the acquisition of reading responses. *Journal of Educational Psychology*, 1967, *58*, 337–342.

———. Effect of distinctive feature training on paired-associate learning. *Journal of Educational Psychology*, 1973, *64*, 165–170.

Samuels, S. J., and Anderson, R. H. Visual recognition memory, paired-associate learning and reading achievement. *Journal of Educational Psychology*, 1973, *65*, 160–167.

Santrock, J. W. Affect and facilitative self-control: Influence of ecological setting, cognition, and social agent. *Journal of Educational Psychology*, 1976, *68*, 529–535.

Sarason S. B. *Psychological Problems in Mental Deficiency*. New York: Harper, 1949.

Sartain, H. W. Instruction of disabled learners: A reading perspective. *Journal of Learning Disabilities*, 1976, *9*, 489–497.

Satterfield, J. H., and Dawson, M. E. Electrodermal correlates of hyperactivity in children. *Psychophysiology*, 1971, *8*, 191–197.

Satterfield, J. H., Lesser, L. I., Saul R. E., and Cantwell, D. P. EEG aspects in the diagnosis and treatment of minimal brain dysfunction. In *Minimal Brain Dysfunction. Annals of the New York Academy of Sciences*, 1973, *205*, 274–282.

Satz, P. Pathological left-handedness: An explanatory model. *Cortex*, 1972, *8*, 121–135.

Satz, P., Bakker, D. J., Teunissen, J., Goebel, R., and Van der Vlugt, H. Developmental parameters of the ear asymmetry: A multi-variate approach. *Brain and Language*, 1975, *2*, 171–185.

Satz, P., Taylor, H. G., Friel, J., and Fletcher, J. Some developmental and predictive precursors of reading disabilities: A six-year follow-up. In *Dyslexia: An Appraisal of Current Knowledge*, edited by A. L. Benton and D. E. Pearl. New York: Oxford University Press, 1978.

Satz, P., and Van Nostrand, K. Developmental dyslexia: An evaluation of a theory. In *The Disabled Learner: Early Detection and Intervention*, edited by P. Satz and J. J. Ross. Rotterdam: Rotterdam University Press, 1972.

Saxe, G., and Shaheen, S. Piagetian theory and the atypical case: An analysis of the developmental Gertsman Syndrome. *Journal of Learning Disabilities*, 1981, *14*, 131–136.

Schaefer, E. an·d Bell, R. Development of parental attitude research instrument. *Child Development*, 1958, *29*, 339–361.

Scheibel, M. E., and Scheibel, A. B. Some thoughts on the ontogeny of memory and learning. In *Neural Mechanisms of Learning and Memory*, edited by M. R. Rosenzweig and E. L. Bennett. Cambridge: MIT Press, 1976.

Schmid, R. E. The learning disabled adolescent. In *Children and Adolescents with Learning Disabilities,* edited by C. Mercer. Columbus, Ohio: Charles E. Merrill, 1979.

Schoer, L. Effect of list length and interpolated learning on the learning and recall of fast and slow learners. *Journal of Educational Psychology,* 1962, *53,* 193–197.

Schrag, P., and Divoky, D. *The Myth of the Hyperactive Child.* New York: Dell, 1978.

Schwartz, M., and Day, R. H. Visual shape perception in early infancy. *Monographs of the Society for Research in Child Development,* 1979, *44,* 1–57.

Schwartz, M. L., Gilroy, J., and Lynn, G. Neuropsychological and psychosocial implications of spelling deficit in adulthood: A case report. *Journal of Learning Disabilities,* 1976, *9,* 144–148.

Schwartz, T. H., and Byran, J. H. Imitation and judgements of children with language deficits. *Exceptional Children,* 1971, *38,* 157–158.

Schwarz, R. H. Mental age as it relates to school achievement among educable mentally retarded adolescents. *Education and Training of the Mentally Retarded,* 1969, *4,* 53–56.

Schwarz, R. H., and Cook, J. J. Mental age as a predictor of academic achievement. *Education and Training of the Mentally Retarded,* 1971, *6,* 12–15.

Schwebel, A. I., and Cherlin, D. L. Physical and social distancing in teacher-pupil relationships. *Journal of Educational Psychology,* 1972, *63,* 543–550.

Schwebel, A. S. Effects of impulsivity on performance of verbal tasks in middle and lower class children. *American Journal of Orthopsychiatry,* 1966, *36,* 13–21.

Scott, D., Jr., and Lui, C. N. Factors promoting regeneration of spinal neurons: positive influence of nerve growth factor. In *Mechanisms of Neural Regeneration, Progress in Brain Research.* Vol. 13, edited by M. Singer and J. P. Schade. Amsterdam: Elsevier, 1964.

Scott, N., and Sigel, I. E. Effects of inquiry training in physical science on creativity and cognitive styles of elementary school children. Research report for U.S. Office of Education, 1965.

Scranton, T. R., Hajicek, J. O., and Wolcott, G. J. The physician and teacher as tram: Assessing the effects of medication. *Journal of Learning Disabilities,* 1978, *11,* 205–209.

Scranton, T. R., and Ryckman, D. B. Sociometric status of learning disabled children in an integrative program. *Journal of Learning Disabilities,* 1979, *12,* 402–407.

Searleman, A. A review of right hemisphere linguistic capabilities. *Psychological Bulletin,* 1977, *84,* 503–528.

Semel, E. *Sound Order Sense.* Boston: Teaching Resources, 1968.

Semel, E. M., and Wiig, E. H. Comprehension of syntactic structures and critical verbal elements by children with learning disabilities. *Journal of Learning Disabilities,* 1975, *8,* 46–51.

Senf, G. M. Development of immediate memory for bisensory stimuli in normal children and children with learning disorders. *Developmental Psychology Monograph,* 1969, *1* (6, Pt. 2), 1–28.

———. Future research needs in learning disabilities. In *Learning Disabilities/Minimal Brain Dysfunction Syndrome: Research Perspectives and Application,* edited by R. P. Anderson and G. Halcomb, pp. 249–267. Springfield, Ill.: Charles C. Thomas, 1976.

———. Implications of the final procedures for evaluating specific learning disabilities. *Journal of Learning Disabilities,* 1978, *11,* 124–126.

Senf, G. M., and Freundl, P. C. Memory and attention factors in specific learning disabilities. *Journal of Learning Disabilities,* 1971, *4,* 94–106.

Serafica, F. C., and Harway, N. I. Social relations and self-esteem of children with learning disabilities. *Journal of Clinical Child Psychology,* 1979, *8,* 227–233.

Settipane, G. A., and Pudupakkam, R. K. Aspirin intolerance. 3: Subtypes, familiar occurrence, and cross-reactivity with tartrazine. *Journal of Allergy and Clinical Immunology,* 1975, *56,* 215–221.

Severance, L., and Gastorm, L. Effects of the label "mentally retarded" on causal explanations for success and failure outcomes. *American Journal of Mental Deficiency,* 1977, *81,* 547–555.

Sewell, T. E. Intelligence and learning tasks as predictors of scholastic achievement in black and white first-grade children. *Journal of School Psychology,* 1979, *17,* 325–332.

Sewell, T. E., and Severson, R. A. Intelligence and achievement in first-grade black children. *Journal of Consulting and Clinical Psychology,* 1975, *43,* 112.

Shankweiler, D., and Liberman, I. Y. Exploring the relations between reading and speech. In *The Neuropsychology of Learning Disorders: Theoretical Approaches,* edited by R. M. Knights and D. J. Bakker. Baltimore: University Park Press, 1976.

Shapiro, S., and Forbes, R. A review of involvement programs for parents of learning disabled children. *Journal of Learning Disabilities,* 1981, *14,* 499–504.

Sharma, M. C. Using word problems to aid language and reading comprehension. *Topics in Learning and Learning Disabilities,* 1971, *1* (3), 61–71.

Sharon, S. Cooperative learning in small groups: Recent methods and effects on achievement, attitudes, and ethnic relations. *Review of Educational Research,* 1980, *50,* 241–271.

Shaw, R. A. Designing and using non-word problems as aids to thinking and comprehension. *Topics in Learning and Learning Disabilities,* 1981, *1* (3), 73–80.

Sheare, J. B. The impact of resource programs upon the self-concept and peer acceptance of learning disabled children. *Psychology in the Schools,* 1978, *15,* 406–412.

Sheer, D. E. Focused arousal and 40-Hz EEG. In *The Neuropsychology of Learning Disorders: Theoretical Approaches,* edited by R. M. Knights and D. J. Bakker. Baltimore: University Park Press, 1976.

Sheingold, K., and Shapiro, J. Children's verbal rehearsal in a free-recall task. *Developmental Psychology,* 1976, *12,* 169–170.

Shetty, T. Alpha rhythms in the hyperkinetic child. *Nature,* 1971, *234,* 476.

Shields, D. T. Brain responses to stimuli in disorders of information processing. *Journal of Learning Disabilities,* 1973, *6,* 501–505.

Shrag, J. A. *Individualized Educational Programming (IEP): A Child Study Team Process.* Austin, Tex.: Learning Concepts, 1977.

Shriner, T. H., Holloway, M. S., and Daniloff, R. G. The relationship between articulatory deficits and syntax in speech defective children. *Journal of Speech and Hearing Research,* 1969, *12,* 319–325.

Shuell, T. J., and Keppel, G. Learning ability and retention. *Journal of Educational Psychology,* 1970, *61,* 59–65.

Sieben, R. L. Controversial medical treatments of learning disabilities. *Academic Therapy,* 1977, *13,* 133–147.

Siegel, E. *The Exceptional Child Grows Up.* New York: Dutton, 1974.

Siegel, E., Siegel, R., and Siegel, P. *Help for the Lonely Child.* New York: Dutton, 1978.

Siegler, R. S., and Liebert, R. M. Acquisition of formal scientific reasoning by 10- and 13-year olds: Designing a factorial experiment. *Developmental Psychology,* 1975, *11,* 401–402.

Silberberg, N. E. Is there such a thing as a learning disabled child? *Journal of Learning Disabilities,* 1971, *4,* 273–276.

Silberberg, N. E., Iversen, I. A., Goins, J. T. Which remedial reading method works best? *Journal of Learning Disabilities,* 1973, *6,* 547–556.

Silberberg, N. E., and Silberberg, M. C. School achievement and delinquency. *Review of Educational Research,* 1971, *41,* 17–33.

———. And the adult who reads poorly? *Journal of Learning Disabilities,* 1978, *11,* 3–4.

Silberman, A. If they say your child can't learn. *McCall's*, January 1976, *103*, 76–81.

Silver, A. A., and Hagin, R. A. Specific reading disability: Follow-up studies. *American Journal of Orthopsychiatry*, 1964, *34*, 95–102.

———. Maturation of perceptual functions in children with specific reading disability. *The Reading Teacher*, 1966, *19*, 253–259.

Silver, L. A proposed view on the etiology of the neurological learning disability syndrome. *Journal of Learning Disabilities*, 1971a, *4*, 123–132.

———. Familial patterns in children with neurologically-based learning disabilities. *Journal of Learning Disabilities*, 1971b, *4*, 349–358.

———. The faces of MBD: Psychiatric aspects. Address to SUNY Upstate Medical Center and CIBA conference, Understanding Minimal Brain Dysfunction, Syracuse, 17 November 1977.

Silverman, J. Personality trait and "perceptual style" studies of the psychotherapists of schizophrenic patients. *Journal of Nervous and Mental Disease*, 1967, *145*, 5–17.

Simmons, G. A., and Shapiro, B. J. Reading expectancy formulas: A warning note. *Journal of Reading*, 1968, *11*, 625–629.

Simon, S. B., Have, L. W., and Kirschenbaum, H. *Values Clarification: A Handbook of Practical Strategies for Teachers and Students*. New York: Hart Publishing Company, 1972.

Sinclair-De-Swart, H. Developmental psycholoinguistics. In *Studies in Cognitive Development: Essays in Honor of Jean Piaget*, edited by D. Elkind and J. H. Flavell. New York: Oxford University Press, 1969.

Singer, J. L., and Singer, D. Come back, Mister Rogers, come back. *Psychology Today*, 1979, *12*, 59–60.

Siperstein, G. N., Bopp, M. J., and Bak, J. J. Social status of learning disabled children. *Journal of Learning Disabilities*, 1978, *11*, 98–102.

Skeels, H. M., and Skodak, M. Adult status of individuals who experienced early intervention. Paper presented at the 90th annual meeting of the American Association on Mental Deficiency, Chicago, 10–14 May 1966. In *Psychoeducational Foundations of Learning Disabilities*, edited by D. P. Hallahan and W. M. Cruickshank. Englewood Cliffs, N.J.: Prentice-Hall, 1973.

Skinner, B. F. *Verbal Behavior*. New York: Appleton-Century-Crofts, 1959.

Skinner, B. F., and Krakower, S. *Handwriting with Writing and Seeing*. Chicago: Lyons & Carnahan, 1968.

Skubic, V., and Anderson, M. The interrelationship of perceptual-motor achievement, academic achievement, and intelligence of fourth grade children. *Journal of Learning Disabilities*, 1970, *3*, 413–420.

Slingerland, B. H. *A Multi-Sensory Approach to Language Arts for Specific Language Disability Children*. Cambridge, Mass.: Educator's Publishing Service, 1974.

Sloman, L., and Webster, C. Assessing the parents. *Journal of Learning Disabilities*, 1978, *11*, 73–79.

Smead, V. S. Ability training and task analysis in diagnostic/prescriptive teaching. *Journal of Special Education*, 1977, *11*, 113–125.

Smith, C. R. Assessment alternatives: Non-standardized procedures. *School Psychology Review*, 1980, *9*, 46–57.

Smith, C. R., and Steinschneider, A. Differential effects of prenatal rhythmic stimulation on neonatal arousal states. *Child Development*, 1975. *46*, 574–578.

Smith, F. *Understanding Reading*. New York: Holt, Rinehart and Winston, 1971.

Smith, M. D., Coleman, J. M., Dokecki, P. R., and Davis, E. E. Intellectual characteristics of school labeled learning disabled children. *Exceptional Children*, 1977a, *43*, 352–357.

———. Recategorized WISC-R scores of learning disabled children. *Journal of Learning Disabilities*, 1977b, *10*, 444–449.

Smith, M. J. *When I Say No I Feel Guilty*. New York: Bantam Books, 1975.

Smith, P. A., and Marx, R. W. Some cautions on the use of the Frostig Test: A factor analytic study. *Journal of Learning Disabilities*, 1972, *5*, 357–362.

Smith, S. *Learning Disabilities: No Easy Answers*. Boston: Winthrop, 1980.

Smith, S., and Solanto, J. An approach to preschool evaluation. *Psychology in the Schools*, 1971, *8*, 142.

Snyder, R. T., and Freud, S. L. Reading readiness and its relation to maturational unreadiness as measured by the spiral aftereffect and other visual-perceptual techniques. *Perceptual and Motor Skills*, 1967, *25*, 841–854.

Somervill, J. W., Jacobsen, L., Warnberg, L., and Young, W. Varied environmental condition and task performance by mentally retarded subjects perceived as distractible and nondistractible. *American Journal of Mental Deficiency*, 1974, *79*, 204–209.

Somervill, J. W., Warnberg, L., and Bost, D. E. Effects of cubicles vs. increased stimulation of task performance by 1st-grade males perceived as distractible and nondistractible. *Journal of Special Education*, 1973, *7*, 169–185.

Sommer, R. *Tight Spaces: Hard Architecture and How to Humanize It*. Englewood Cliffs, N.J.: Prentice-Hall, 1974.

Sömmering, S. T. *Von Baue des Menschlichen Koerpers*. Vol. 5, Pt. 1. Frankfurt am Main: Barrentropp and Wenner, 1971.

Sommers, R. K., and Taylor, L. M. Cerebral speech dominance in language-disordered and normal children. *Cortex*, 1972, *8*, 224–232.

Sontag, L. W. The significance of fetal environmental difference. *American Journal of Obstetrics and Gynecology*, 1941, *42*, 996–1003.

Spache Diagnostic Reading Scales. New York: CTB/McGraw-Hill, 1963.

Spache, G. D. *Toward Better Reading*. Champaign, Ill.: Garrard Press, 1963.

———. *Investigating the Issues of Reading Disabilities*. Boston: Allyn & Bacon, 1976.

Sparrow, S., and Satz, P. Dyslexia, laterality and neuropsychological development. In *Specific Reading Disability: Advances in Theory and Method*, edited by D. J. Bakker and P. Satz. Rotterdam: Rotterdam University Press, 1970.

Spekman, N. J. Dyadic verbal communication abilities of learning disabled and normally achieving fourth- and fifth-grade boys. *Learning Disability Quarterly*, 1981, *4* (2), 139–151.

Sperry, R. W. Hemisphere deconnection and unity in conscious awareness. *American Psychologist*, 1968, *23*, 723–733.

Sperry, V. B. *A Language Approach to Learning Disabilities*. Palo Alto: Consulting Psychologists Press, 1974.

Spicker, H. H., and Bartel, N. R. The mentally retarded. In *Exceptional Children Research Review*, edited by G. O. Johnson and H. D. Blank, pp. 38–109. Washington, D.C.: Council for Exceptional Children, 1968.

Spitz, R. A. Hospitalism: An inquiry into the genesis of psychiatric conditions in early childhood. *Psychoanalytic Study of the Child*, 1945, *1*, 53–74.

Spong, P., Haider, M., and Lindsley, D. B. Selective attentiveness and cortical evoked responses to visual and auditory stimuli. *Science*, 1965, *148*, 395–397.

Sprague, R. L., and Sleator, E. K. Effects of psychopharmacologic agents on learning disorders. *Pediatric Clinics of North America*, 1973, *20*, 719–735.

Spreen, O. Neuropsychology of learning disorders: Post conference review. In *The Neuropsychology of Learning Disorders: Theoretical Approaches*, edited by R. M. Knights and D. J. Bakker. Baltimore: University Park Press, 1976.

Spring, C., and Capps, C. Encoding speed, rehearsal, and probed recall of dyslexic boys. *Journal of Educational Psychology*, 1974, *66*, 780–786.

Spurzheim, J. G. *The Physiognomical System of Drs. Gall and Spurzheim.* London: Baldwin, Cradock, and Joy, 1815.

Spyker, J. M. Occupational hazards and the pregnant worker. In *Behavioral Toxicology*, edited by C. Xintras, B. L. Johnson, and I. de Groot. Washington, D.C.: U.S. Department of Health, Education and Welfare, 1974.

Sroufe, L. A., Sonies, B. C., West, W. D., and Wright, F. S. Anticipatory heart rate deceleration and reaction time in children with and without referral for learning disability. *Child Development*, 1973, *44*, 267–273.

Stanley, G., and Hall, R. Short-term visual information processing in dyslexics. *Child Development*, 1973, *44*, 841–844.

Staats, A. Linguistic-mentalistic theory versus an explanatory S-R learning theory of language development. In *The Ontogenesis of Grammar*, edited by D. I. Slobin. New York: Academic Press, 1971.

Stallings, J. A. *Follow Through Classroom Observation Evaluation, 1972–1973.* Menlo Park, Calif.: Stanford Research Institute, 1974.

Stanford, G., and Roark, A. E. *Human Interaction in Education.* Boston: Allyn & Bacon, 1974.

Stare, F. J., Whelan, E. M., and Sheridan, M. Diet and hyperactivity: Is there a relationship? *Pediatrics*, 1980, *66*, 521–525.

Stauffer, R. *Directing Reading Maturity as a Cognitive Process.* New York: Harper & Row, 1969.

Steg, J. P., and Rapoport, J. L. Minor physical anomalies in normal, neurotic, learning disabled, and severely disordered children. *Journal of Autism and Childhood Schizophrenia*, 1975, *5*, 299–307.

Stephens, T. M. *Teaching Skills to Children with Learning and Behavior Disorders.* Columbus, Ohio: Charles E. Merrill, 1977.

Stephens, W. E., Cunningham, E. S., and Stigler, B. J. Reading readiness and eye-hand preference patterns in first grade children. *Exceptional Children*, 1967, *33*, 481–488.

Stephenson, S. Six cases of congenital word-blindness affecting three generations of one family. *Ophthalmoscope*, 1907, *5*, 482–484.

Stern, C. *Structural Arithmetic.* Boston: Houghton Mifflin, 1965.

Stevens, G. D., and Birch, J. W. A proposal for clarification of the terminology used to describe brain-injured children. *Exceptional Children*, 1957, *23*, 346–349.

Stevenson, H. W., Friedricks, A. C., and Simpson, W. E. Interrelations and correlates over time in children's learning. *Child Development*, 1970, *41*, 625–637.

Stevenson, H. W., Parker, T., and Wilkenson, A. Predictive value of teachers' ratings of young children. *Journal of Educational Psychology*, 1976, *68*, 507–517.

Stick, S. The speech pathologist and handicapped learners. *Journal of Learning Disabilities*, 1976, *9*, 509–519.

Stokes, T. F., and Baer, D. M. An implicit technology of generalization. *Journal of Applied Behavior Analysis*, 1977, *10*, 349–367.

Stokols, D., ed. *Perspectives on Environment and Behavior.* New York: Plenum, 1977.

Stott, D. H. Follow-up study from birth of the effects of prenatal stresses. *Developmental Medicine and Child Neurology*, 1973, *15*, 770–787.

Strag, G. A. Comparative behavioral ratings of parents with severe mentally retarded, special learning disability and normal children. *Journal of Learning Disabilities*, 1972, *5*, 631–635.

Strain, P. S., Cooke, T. P., and Apolloni, T. The role of peers in modifying classmates' social behavior: A review. *The Journal of Special Education*, 1976, *10*, 351–356.

Strang, R. *Diagnostic Teaching of Reading.* 2nd ed. New York: McGraw-Hill, 1969.

Strauss, A. A. Diagnosis and education of the cripple-brained, deficient child. *Exceptional Children*, 1943, *9*, 163–168, 183.

Strauss, A. A., and Kephart, N. C. Behavior differences in mentally retarded children as measured by a new behavior rating scale. *American Journal of Psychiatry*, 1940, *96*, 1117–1123.

———. *Psychopathology and Education of the Brain-injured Child.* Vol. 2, Progress in Theory and Clinic. New York: Grune & Stratton, 1955.

Strauss, A. A., and Lehtinen, L. E. *Psychopathology and Education of the Brain-Injured Child.* New York: Grune & Stratton, 1947.

Strauss, A. A., and Werner, H. Disorders of conceptual thinking in the brain-injured child. *Journal of Nervous and Mental Disease*, 1942, *96*, 153–172.

Suchman, P. G., and Trabasso, T. Stimulus preference and cue function in young children's concept attainment. *Journal of Experimental Child Psychology*, 1966, *3*, 188–198.

Suiter, M. L., and Potter, R. E. The effects of paradigmatic organization on verbal recall. *Journal of Learning Disabilities*, 1978, *11*, 247–250.

Sulzbacher, S., and Kenowitz, L. A. At last, a definition of learning disabilities we can live with? *Journal of Learning Disabilities*, 1977, *10*, 67–69.

Sutherland, J., and Algozzine, B. The learning disabled label as a biasing factor in the visual motor performance of normal children. *Journal of Learning Disabilities*, 1979, *12*, 8–14.

Swanson, J. M., and Kinsbourne, M. Stimulant-related state-dependent learning in hyperactive children. *Science*, 1976, *192*, 1354–1357.

Swanson, J. M., and Kinsbourne, M. Food dyes impair performance of hyperactive children on a laboratory learning test. *Science*, 1980, *207*, 1485–1487.

Swanson, J., Kinsbourne, M., Roberts, W., and Zucker, K. Time-response analysis of the effect of stimulant medication on the learning ability of children referred for hyperactivity. *Pediatrics*, 1978, *61*, 21–29.

Swanson, L. Verbal short-term memory encoding of learning disabled, deaf, and normal readers. *Learning Disability Quarterly*, 1982, *5*(1), 21–28.

Swanson, W. L. Optometric vision therapy: How successful is it in the treatment of learning disorders? *Journal of Learning Disabilities*, 1972, *5*, 285–290.

Sykes, D. H., Douglas, V. I., Weiss, G., and Minde, K. K. Attention in hyperactive children and the effect of methylphenidate (Ritalin). *Journal of Child Psychology and Psychiatry*, 1971, *12*, 129–139.

Szasz, T. S. The myth of mental illness. In *Theories of Psychopathology*, edited by T. Millon. Philadelphia: W. B. Saunders, 1967.

Taba, H. *Teacher's Handbook for Elementary Social Studies.* Reading, Mass.: Addison-Wesley, 1967.

Tagatz, G. E., Otto, W., Klausmeier, H. J., Goodwin, W. L., and Cook, D. M. Effect of three methods of instruction upon the handwriting performance of third and fourth graders. In *Remedial Teaching: Research and Comment*, edited by W. Otto and K. Koenke. Boston: Houghton Mifflin, 1969.

Tallal, P. Auditory perceptual factors in language and learning disabilities. In *The Neuropsychology of Learning Disorders: Theoretical Approaches*, edited by R. M. Knights and D. J. Bakker. Baltimore: University Park Press, 1976.

Tallal, P., and Piercy, M. Defects of auditory perception in children with developmental dysphasia. In *Developmental Dysphasia*, edited by M. A. Wyke. New York: Academic Press, 1978.

Tampieri, G. How does the weight of the parts change in visual perception of preschool children. Unpublished report in *The Development of Cognitive Processes*, edited by V. Hamilton and M. Vernon. London: Academic Press, 1976.

Tarnopol, L. Testing children with learning disabilities. In *Learning Disabilities: Introduction to Educational and Medical Management*, edited by L. Tarnopol. Springfield, Ill.: Charles C. Thomas, 1969.

Tarnopol, L., and Tarnopol, M. Introduction to Neuropsychology. In *Brain Function and Reading Disabilities*, edited by L. Tarnopol and M. Tarnopol. Baltimore: University Park Press, 1977.

Tarrier, R. Mainstreaming handicapped students in occupational education: Exemplary administrative practices. ERIC Reports, 1978.

Tarver, S. G., and Dawson, M. M. Modality preference and the teaching of reading: A review. *Journal of Learning Disabilities*, 1978, *11*, 5–17.

Tarver, S G., and Hallahan, D. P. Attention deficits in children with learning disabilities: A review. *Journal of Learning Disabilities*, 1974, *7*, 560–569.

Taussig, H. B. A study of the German outbreak of phocomelia: The thalidomide syndrome. *Journal of the American Medical Association*, 1962, *180*, 1106–1114.

Taylor, E. *The Fundamental Reading Skill as Related to Eye-Movement Photography and Visual Anomalies*. Springfield, Ill.: Charles C. Thomas, 1966.

Taylor, F. D., Artuso, A. A., Soloway, M. M., Hewett, F. M., Quay, H. C., and Stillwell, R. J. A learning center plan for special education. *Focus on Exceptional Children*, 1972, *4*(3), 1–7.

Taylor, I. *Introduction to Psycholinguistics*. New York: Holt, Rinehart and Winston, 1976.

Taylor, N. E. Measuring perceptual skills that are related to the learning task. *Journal of Learning Disabilities*, 1980, *13*, 17–19.

Teitelbaum, E. Calculators for classroom use? *Arithmetic Teacher*, 1978, *26*, 18–20.

Tenney, Y. J. The child's conception of organization and recall. *Journal of Experimental Child Psychology*, 1975, *19*, 100–114.

Thatcher, R. W., and John, E. R. *Functional Neuroscience: Foundations of Cognitive Processes*. Vol. 1. New York: Halsted Press, 1977.

Thomas, A., and Chess, S. *Temperament and Development*. New York: Brunner/Mazel, 1977.

Thomas, C. J. Congenital "word-blindness" and its treatment. *Ophthalmoscope*, 1905, *3*, 380–385.

Thomas, E. L., and Robinson, H. A. *Improving Reading in Every Class*. Boston: Allyn & Bacon, 1972.

———. *Improving Reading in Every Class: A Sourcebook for Teachers*. Boston: Allyn & Bacon, 1977.

Thompson, L. J. Language disabilities in men of eminence. *Journal of Learning Disabilities*, 1971, *4*, 34–45.

Thorndike, R. L. *The Concepts of Over- and Underachievement*. New York: Teachers College Press, 1963.

Thorpe, H. W., Chiang, B., and Darch, C. B. Individual and group feedback systems for improving oral reading accuracy in learning disabled and regular class children. *Journal of Learning Disabilities*, 1981, *14*, 332–334.

Thorpe, H. W., Lampe, S., Nash, R. T., and Chiang, B. The effects of the kinesthetic-tactile component of the VAKT procedure on secondary LD students' reading performance. *Psychology in the Schools*, 1981, *18*, 334–340.

Throne, J. M. Learning disabilities: A radical behaviorist point of view. *Journal of Learning Disabilities*, 1973, *6*, 543–546.

Thypin, M. Selection of books of high interest and low reading level. *Journal of Learning Disabilities*, 1979, *12*, 428–430.

Tjossem, T. D. Early intervention: Issues and approaches. In *Intervention Strategies for High Risk Infants and Young Children*, edited by T. D. Tjossem. Baltimore: University Park Press, 1976.

Tjossem, T. D., Hansen, T. J., and Ripley, H. S. An investigation of reading difficulty in young children. *American Journal of Psychiatry*, 1962, *118*, 1104–1113.

Tobias, J. Social and ethnic factors related to utilization of rehabilitative services by the mentally retarded. *Rehabilitation Literature*, 1969, *30*, 226–230.

Tollefson, N., Tracy, D. B., Johnsen, E. P., Buenning, M., Farmer, A., and Barke, C. R. Attribution patterns of learning disabled adolescents. *Learning Disability Quarterly*, 1982, *5*, 1, 14–20.

Tombari, M. L., and Bergan, J. K. Consultant cues and teacher verbalizations, judgments, and expectancies concerning children's adjustment problems. *Journal of School Psychology*, 1978, *16*, 212–219.

Tomlinson, P. D., and Hunt, D. E. Differential effects of rule-example order as a function of conceptual level. *Canadian Journal of Behavioral Science*, 1971, *3*, 237–245.

Torgesen, J. Cognitive Processes. Paper presented at the 14th International Conference of the Association for Children with Learning Disabilities. Washington, D.C., 1977.

Torgesen, J., and Goldman, T. Verbal rehearsal and short-term memory in reading disabled children. *Child Development*, 1977, *48*, 56–60.

Torgesen, J. K. The role of nonspecific factors in the task performance of learning-disabled children: A theoretical assessment. *Journal of Learning Disabilities*, 1977a, *10*, 27–34.

———. Paper presented at the meeting of the National Association of School Psychologists, New York, March 1977b.

———. Memorization processes in reading-disabled children. *Journal of Educational Psychology*, 1977c, *69*, 571–578.

———. Conceptual and educational implications of the use of efficient task strategies by learning disabled children. *Journal of Learning Disabilities*, 1980, *13*, 364–371.

Torgesen, J. K., and Houck, D. G. Processing deficiencies of learning-disabled children who perform poorly on the digit span test. *Journal of Educational Psychology*, 1980, *72*, 141–160.

Torgesen, J. K., Murphy, H. A., and Ivey, C. The influence of an orienting task on the memory performance of children with reading problems. *Journal of Learning Disabilities*, 1979, *12*, 396–401.

Torres, S., ed. *A Primer on Individualized Education Programs for Handicapped Children*. Reston, Va.: The Foundation for Exceptional Children, 1977.

Townes, B. D., Trupin, E. W., Martin, D. C., and Goldstein, D. Neuropsychological correlates of academic success among elementary school children. *Journal of Consulting and Clinical Psychology*, 1980, *48*, 675–684.

Townsend, R. *Imaginary Line Handwriting*. Austin, Tex.: Steck-Vaughan Co., 1978.

Trehub, S., and Rabinovitch, M. Auditory linguistic sensitivity in early infancy. *Developmental Psychology*, 1972, *6*, 74–77.

Trickett, E. J. Toward a social ecological conception of adolescent socialization: Normative data on contrasting types of public school classrooms. *Child Development*, 1978, *49*, 408–414.

Trippe, M. J. Conceptual problems in research in educational provisions for disturbed children. *Exceptional Children*, 1963, *29*(8), 400–406.

Trites, R. L., and Fiedorowicz, C. Follow-up study of children with specific (or primary) reading disability. In *The Neuropsychology of Learning Disorders: Theoretical Approaches*, edited by R. M. Knights and D. J. Bakker. Baltimore: University Park Press, 1976.

Tubbs, S. L., and Moss, S. *Human Communication: An Interpersonal Perspective*. New York: Random House, 1977.

Tucker, J. A. Operationalizing the diagnostic-intervention process. In *Psychological and Educational Assessment of Minority Children*, edited by T. Oakland. New York: Brunner/Mazel, 1977.

———. Ethnic proportions in classes for the learning disabled: Issues in nonbiased assessment. *Journal of Special Education*, 1980, *14*, 93–105.

Turiel, E. Distinct and developmental domains: Social convention and moral. In *Nebraska Symposium on Motivation.*, edited by H. E. Howe. Lincoln: University of Nebraska Press, 1977.

Turnbull, A. P., Strickland, B. B., and Brantley, J. C. *Developing and Implementing Individualized Education Programs*. Columbus, Ohio: Charles E. Merrill, 1978.

Turner, E. K. The syndrome in the infant resulting from maternal emotional tension during pregnancy. *Medical Journal of Australia*, 1956, *1*, 221–222.

Tzavaras, A., Kaprinis, G., and Gatzoyas, A. Literacy and hemispheric specialization for language: Digit dichotic listening in illiterates. *Neuropsychologia*, 1981, *19*, 565–570.

Underwood, B. J. Degree of learning and the measurement of forgetting. *Journal of Verbal Learning and Verbal Behavior*, 1964, *3*, 112–129.

Unkovic, C. M., Brown, W. R., and Mierswa, C. G. Counterattack on juvenile delinquency: A configurational approach. *Adolescence*, 1978, *13*, 401–410.

U.S. Department of Health, Education and Welfare. *Departments of Labor and Health, Education and Welfare Appropriations for 1980, Part 5: Hearings Before a Subcommittee of the Committee on Appropriations, House of Representatives*. Washington, D.C.: U.S. Government Printing Office, 22–23 March 1979.

————. National Institutes of Health. *Learning Disabilities due to Minimal Brain Dysfunction: Hope Through Research*. Washington, D.C.: U.S. Government Printing Office, 1977.

U.S. Department of Labor. The changing nature of work. In *Employment and Training Report to the President*. Washington, D.C.: U.S. Department of Labor, 1976.

U.S. Office of Education. *First Annual Report, National Advisory Committee on Handicapped Children*. Washington, D.C.: U.S. Department of Health, Education and Welfare, 1968.

U.S. Office of Education. *Third Annual Report of the National Advisory Committee on Handicapped Children*. Washington, D.C.: U.S. Department of Health, Education and Welfare, 30 June 1970a.

————. *Better Education for Handicapped Children: Annual Report Fiscal Year 1969*. Washington, D.C.: U.S. Department of Health, Education and Welfare, 1970b.

————. *Estimated Number of Handicapped Children in the United States, 1971–1972*. Washington, D.C.: U.S. Office of Education.

————. Education of handicapped children: Assistance to states: Proposed rule-making. *Federal Register*, 1976, *41*, 52404–52407.

————. *Education of the Handicapped*. Statement by Deputy Commissioner Edwin W. Martin before the Senate Appropriations Committee, 96th Congress. Washington, D.C.: 14 March 1979.

Uzgairis, I. C. Sociocultural factors in cognitive development. In *Social-Cultural Aspects of Mental Retardation*, edited by H. C. Haywood. New York: Appleton-Century-Crofts, 1970.

Valenstein, E., and Heilman, K. M. Emotional disorders resulting from lesions of the central nervous system. In *Clinical Neuropsychology*, edited by K. M. Heilman and E. Valenstein. Oxford: Oxford University Press, 1979.

Vallett, R. E. *Modifying Children's Behavior: A Guide for Parents and Professionals*. Palo Alto: Fearon Publishers, 1971.

————. *The Remediation of Learning Disabilities: A Handbook of Psychoeducational Resource Programs*. Belmont, Calif.: Fearon Publishers, 1967.

Valverde, F. Apical dendrite spines of the visual cortex and light deprivation in the mouse. *Experimental Brain Research*, 1967, *3*, 337–352.

Vande Voort, L., and Senf, G. M. Audiovisual integration in retarded readers. *Journal of Learning Disabilities*, 1973, *6*, 170–179.

Vandenberg, S. G. Contributions of twin research to psychology. *Psychological Bulletin*, 1966, *56*, 326–352.

van den Honert, D. A neuropsychological technique for training dyslexics. *Journal of Learning Disabilities*, 1977, *10*, 21–27.

Vellutino, F. R., Pruzek, R. M., Steger, J. A., and Meshoulam, U. Immediate visual recall in poor and normal readers as a function of orthographic-linguistic familiarity. *Cortex*, 1973, *9*, 370–386.

Vellutino, F. R., Smith, H., Steger, J. A., and Kiman, M. Reading disability: Age differences and the perceptual deficit hypothesis. *Child Development*, 1975, *46*, 487–493.

Vellutino, F. R., Steger, B. M., Moyer, J. C., Harding, C. J., and Niles, J. A. Has the perceptual deficit hypothesis led us astray? *Journal of Learning Disabilities*, 1977, *10*, 375–385.

Vellutino, F. R., Steger, J. A., DeSetto, L., and Phillips, F. Immediate and delayed recognition of visual stimuli in poor and normal readers. *Journal of Experimental Child Psychology*, 1975, *19*, 223–232.

Vellutino, F. R., Steger, J. A., Kaman, M., and DeSetto, L. Visual form perception in deficient and normal readers as a function of age and orthographic-linguistic familiarity. *Cortex*, 1975, *11*, 22–30.

Vellutino, F. R., Steger, J. A., and Kandel, G. Reading disability: An investigation of the perceptual deficit hypothesis. *Cortex*, 1972, *8*, 106–118.

Vellutino, F. R., Steger, J. A., and Pruzek, R. M. Inter- vs. intrasensory deficit in paired associate learning in poor and normal readers. *Canadian Journal of Behavioral Science*, 1973, *5*, 111–123.

Venezky, R. L., and Calfee, R. C. The reading competency model. In *Theoretical Model and Processes of Reading*, edited by H. Singer and R. B. Ruddell. Newark, Del.: International Reading Association, 1970, 273–291.

Vernon, M. D. *Backwardness in Reading: A Study of Its Nature and Origin*. Cambridge: Cambridge University Press, 1957.

Vernon, M., Coley, J., and DeBois, J. Using sign language to remediate severe reading problems. *Journal of Learning Disabilities*, 1980, *13*, 215–218.

Vogel, S. A. Syntactic abilities in normal and dyslexic children. *Journal of Learning Disabilities*, 1974, *7*, 103–109.

————. *Syntactic Abilities in Normal and Dyslexic Children*. Baltimore: University Park Press, 1975.

————. Morphological ability in normal and dyslexic children. *Journal of Learning Disabilities*, 1977, *10*, 35–43.

von Hilsheimer, G., and Kurko, V. Minor physical anomalies in exceptional children. *Journal of Learning Disabilities*, 1979, *12*, 462–469.

Vygotsky, L. S. *Thought and Language*. Cambridge: MIT Press, 1962.

Wada, J. A., and Rasmussen, T. Intracarotic injection of sodium amytal for the lateralization of cerebral speech dominance: Experimental and clinical observations. *Journal of Neurosurgery*, 1960, *17*, 266–282.

Waddell, D. D. The Stanford-Binet: An evaluation of the technical data available since the 1972 restandardization. *Journal of School Psychology*, 1980, *18*, 203–209.

Wahler, R. G., House, A. E., and Stambaugh, E. E. *Ecological Assessment of Child Problem Behavior: A Clinical Package for Home, School and Institutional Settings*. New York: Pergamon, 1976.

Wakefield, R. A. An investigation of the family backgrounds of educable mentally retarded children in special classes. *Exceptional Children*, 1965, *31*, 143–146.

Walberg, H. J. Physical and psychological distance in the classroom. *School Review*, 1969, *77*, 64–70.

————. Psychology of learning environments: Behavioral, structural, or perceptual? In *Review of Research in Education*. Vol. 4, edited by L. S. Shulman. Itasca, Ill.: F. E. Peacock, 1977.

Walberg, H., and Marjoribanks, K. Family environment and cognitive development: Twelve analytic models. *Review of Educational Research*, 1976, *46*, 527–552.

Walbrown, F. H., Fremont, T. S., Nelson, E., Wilson, J., and Fischer, J. Emotional disturbance or social misperception? An important classroom management question. *Journal of Learning Disabilities*, 1979, *12*, 645–648.

Waldrop, M., and Halverson, C. E. Minor physical anomalies and hyperactive behavior in young children. In *Exceptional Infant*. Vol. 2, edited by J. Hellmuth. New York: Brunner/Mazel, 1971.

Walker, H. M., and Hops, H. Use of normative peer data as a standard for evaluating classroom treatment effects. *Journal of Applied Behavior Analysis*, 1976, *9*, 159–168.

Wall, W. D. Reading backwardness among men in the army, pt. 1. *British Journal of Educational Psychology*, 1945, *15*, 28–40.

———. Reading backwardness among men in the army, pt. 2. *British Journal of Educational Psychology*, 1946, *16*, 133–148.

Wallace, G. Interdisciplinary efforts in learning disabilities: Issues and recommendations. *Journal of Learning Disabilities*, 1976, *9*, 520–526.

Wallace, G., and McLoughlin, J. A. *Learning Disabilities, Concepts and Characteristics*. 2nd ed. Columbus, Ohio: Charles E. Merrill, 1979.

Walls, R. T., Werner, T. J., Bacon, A., and Zane, T. Behavior checklists. In *Behavioral Assessment: New Directions in Clinical Psychology*, edited by J. D. Cone and R. P. Hawkins. New York: Brunner/Mazel, 1977.

Walsh, K. W. *Neuropsychology: A Clinical Approach*. Churchill-Livingstone, 1978.

Walter, L. J. Cognitive and perspective taking prerequisites for moral development. *Child Development*, 1980, *51*, 131–139.

Walzer, S., and Richmond, J. B. The epidemiology of learning disorders. *The Pediatric Clinics of North America*, 1973, *20*, 719–736.

Ward, W. D., and Barcher, P. R. Reading achievement and creativity as related to open classroom experience. *Journal of Educational Psychology*, 1975, *67*, 683–691.

Warren, J. Early and periodic screening, diagnosis and treatment. *Educational Research*, 1977, *6*, 14–20.

Warren, S. A. Adult expectations and learning disorders. *Pediatric Clinics of North America*, 1973, *20*, 705–717.

Warriner, J. E., Renison, W., and Griffith, F. *English Grammar and Composition*. Rev. ed. New York: Harcourt, Brace & World, 1965.

Washburn, W. Y. Where to go in voc-ed for secondary LD students. *Academic Therapy*, 1975, *11*, 31–35.

Washington, V. Noncognitive effects of instruction: A look at teacher behavior and effectiveness. *Educational Horizons*, 1979, *57*, 209–213.

Wattenberg, B. J. *The Real America*. Garden City, N.Y.: Doubleday, 1974.

Weaver, P. A., and Rosner, J. Relationships between visual and auditory perceptual skills and comprehension in students with learning disabilities. *Journal of Learning Disabilities*, 1979, *12*, 617–621.

Wedell, K. The visual perception of cerebral palsied children. *Child Psychology and Psychiatry*, 1960, *1*, 215–227.

Wedig, J. Early detection of mercurialism. In *Behavioral Toxicology*, edited by C. Xintras, B. L. Johnson, and I. de Groot. Washington, D.C.: U.S. Department of Health, Education and Welfare, 1974.

Weener, P. On comparing learning disabled and regular classroom children. *Journal of Learning Disabilities*, 1981, *14*, 227–232.

Weikart, D. P. Relationship of curriculum, teaching, and learning in preschool education. In *Preschool Programs for the Disadvantaged: Five Experimental Approaches to Early Childhood Education*, edited by J. C. Stanley. Baltimore: Johns Hopkins Press, 1972.

Weiner, B. *Achievement Motivation and Attribution Theory*. Morristown, N.J.: General Learning Press, 1974.

Weiner, B., and Goodnow, J. J. Motor activity effects on memory. *Developmental Psychology*, 1970, *2*, 448.

Weinstein, C. S. Modifying student behavior in an open classroom through changes in the physical design. *American Educational Research Journal*, 1977, *14*, 249–262.

———. The physical environment of the school: A review of the research. *Review of Educational Research*, 1979, *49*, 577–610.

Weintraub, F. J. Recent influences of law regarding the identification and educational placement of children. *Focus on Exceptional Children*, 1972, *4*(2), 1–11.

Weintraub, F. J., and Abeson, A. New education policies for the handicapped: The quiet revolution. *Phi Delta Kappan*, 1974, *55*, 526–529, 569.

Weiss, B., Williams, J. H., Margen, S., et al. Behavioral responses to artificial food colors. *Science*, 1980, *207*, 1487–1489.

Weiss, G., Hechtman, L., and Perlman, T. Hyperactives as young adults: School, employer, and self-rating scales obtained during ten-year follow-up evaluation. *American Journal of Orthopsychiatry*, 1978, *48*, 438–445.

Weiss, H. G., and Weiss, M. S. *Home Is a Learning Place: A Parent's Guide to Learning Disabilities*. Boston: Little, Born, 1976.

Weiss, H. G., and Weiss, M. Survival techniques for the adolescent with a learning disability. *The Observer*, June 1981.

Weiss, M. S., and Weiss, H. G. *The Basic Language Kit: A Teaching-Tutoring Aid for Adolescents and Young Adults*. Great Barrington, Mass.: Treehouse Associates, 1979.

Weithorn, C. J., and Kagen, E. Interaction of language development and activity level on performance of first-graders. *American Journal of Orthopsychiatry*, 1978, *48*, 148–159.

Wender, P. *Minimal Brain Dysfunction in Children*. New York: Wiley-Interscience, 1971.

Wender, P. H. Hypothesis for possible biochemical basis of minimal brain dysfunction. In *The Neuropsychology of Learning Disorders: Theoretical Approaches*, edited by R. M. Knights and D. J. Bakker. Baltimore: University Park Press, 1976.

Wepman, J. The perceptual basis for learning. In *Educating Children with Learning Disabilities*, edited by E. C. Frierson and W. B. Barbe. New York: Appleton-Century-Crofts, 1967.

Wepman, J. M., Cruickshank, W. M., Deutsch, C. P., Morency, A., and Strother, C. R. Learning disabilities. In *Issues in the Classification of Children*. vol. 1 edited by N. Hobbs. San Francisco: Jossey-Bass, 1975.

Wepman, J. M., and Jones, L. V. *The Language Modalities Test for Aphasia*. Chicago: University of Chicago Education Industry Service, 1961.

Wepman, J. M., Jones, L. V., Bock, R. D., and Van Pelt, D. Studies in aphasia: Background and theoretical formulations. *Journal of Speech and Hearing Disorders*, 1960, *25*, 323–332.

Werner, E. E. Environmental interaction in minimal brain dysfunction. In *Handbook of Minimal Brain Dysfunction*, edited by H. E. Rie and E. D. Rie. New York: John Wiley & Sons, 1980.

Werner, E. E., Bierman, J., and French, F. E. *The Children of Kauai*. Honolulu: University of Hawaii Press, 1971.

Werner, E. E., and Smith, R. *Kauai's Children Come of Age*. Honolulu: University of Hawaii Press, 1977.

Werner, H. Process and achievement: A basic problem of education and developmental psychology. *Harvard Educational Review*, 1937, *7*, 353–368.

———. Development of visuo-motor performance on the Marble-Board Test in mentally retarded children. *Journal of Genetic Psychology*, 1944, *64*, 269–279.

———. *Comparative Psychology of Mental Development*. New York: Science Editions, 1948.

Werner, H., and Bowers, M. Auditory-motor organization in two clinical types of mentally deficient children. *Journal of Genetic Psychology*, 1941, *59*, 85–99.

Werner, H., and Strauss, A. A. Problems and methods of functional analysis in mentally deficient children. *Journal of Abnormal and Social Psychology*, 1939, *34*, 37–62.

———. Causal factors in low performance. *American Journal of Mental Deficiency*, 1940, *45*, 213–218.

————. Pathology of figure-background relation in the child. *Journal of Abnormal and Social Psychology*, 1941, *36*, 236–248.

Wernicke, C. Der Aphasische Symptomencomplex: Eine psychologische studie auf anatomischer Basis. Breslau: Cohn & Weigert, 1874. Translated in *Wernicke's Works on Aphasia: A Sourcebook and Review*, edited by G. H. Eggert. The Hague: Mouton, 1977.

————. Der Aphasische Symptomencomplex. In *Deutsche Klinik am Eingange des 20. Jahrhunderts*, edited by V. Leyden and U. Klemperer. pp. 487–556, Berlin, 1906. Translated in *Wernicke's Works on Aphasia: A Sourcebook and Review*, edited by G. H. Eggert. The Hague: Mouton, 1977.

Werry, J. S. Developmental hyperactivity. *The Pediatric Clinics of North America*, 1968, *15*(3), 581–599.

Wesman, G. A. Intelligent testing. *American Psychologist*, 1968, *23*, 267–274.

Whalen, C. K., and Henker, B. Psychostimulants and children: A review and analysis. *Psychological Bulletin*, 1976, *83*, 1113–1130.

Whalen, C. K., Henker, B., Collins, B. E., Finck, D., and Dotemoto, S. A social ecology of hyperactive boys: Medication effects in structured classroom environments. *Journal of Applied Behavior Analysis*, 1979, *12*, 65–81.

Whalen, R. J. The relevance of behavior modification procedures for teachers of emotionally disturbed children. In *Intervention Approaches in Educating Emotionally Disturbed Children*, edited by P. Knobloch. Syracuse: Syracuse University Press, 1966.

Wheeler, R. J., and Dusek, J. B. The effects of attentional and cognitive factors on children's incidental learning. *Child Development*, 1973, *44*, 253–258.

White, B. L. Developing a sense of competence in young children. In *Families Today: A Research Sampler on Families and Children*. Vol 1, by H. Yahrais. Washington, D.C.: U.S. Department of Health, Education and Welfare, National Institute of Mental Health Science Monograph, 1980.

White, M. A first grade intervention program for children at risk for reading failure. *Journal of Learning Disabilities*, 1979, *12*, 231–237.

White, M. S. Natural rates of teacher approval and disapproval in the classroom. *Journal of Applied Behavior Analysis*, 1975, *8*, 367–372.

White, W. J., Clark, F. L., Schmaker, J. B., Warner, M. M., Alley, G. R., and Deshler, D. D. The impact of learning disabilities on post-school adjustment. *Forum*, 1980, *6* (4), 14–15, 21.

Whiteman, M., Brown, B., and Deutsch, M. Some effects of social class and race on children's language and intellectual abilities. In *The Disadvantaged Child*, edited by M. Deutsch and Associates. New York: Basic Books, 1967.

Whorf, B. L. *Language, Thought, and Reality*. New York: John Wiley & Son, 1956.

Wicker, A. Cognitive complexity, school size, and participation in school behavior settings: A test of the frequency of interaction hypothesis. *Journal of Educational Psychology*, 1969, *60*, 200–203.

Wicker, A. W. *An Introduction to Ecological Psychology*. Monterey, Calif.: Brooks/Cole, 1979.

Wide Range Achievement Test. New York: Jastak Assessment Systems.

Wiederholt, J. L. Historical perspectives on the education of the learning disabled. In *The Second Review of Special Education*, edited by L. Mann and D. Sabatino.

————. A report on secondary school programs for the learning disabled. Final Report (Project No. H12-7145 B, Grant No. OEG-0-714425). Washington, D.C.: Bureau of Education for the Handicapped, 1975.

————. Adolescents with learning disabilities: The problem in perspective. In *Teaching the Learning Disabled Adolescent*, edited by L. Mann, L. Goodman, and J. L. Wiederholt. Boston: Houghton Mifflin, 1978.

Wiederholt, J. L., and Hammill, D. D. Use of the Frostig-Horne visual perception program in the urban school. *Psychology in the Schools*, 1971, *8*, 268–274.

Wiederholt, J. L., Hammill, D. D., and Brown, V. *The Resource Teacher: A Guide to Effective Practices*. Boston: Allyn & Bacon, 1978.

Wiig, E. H., and Fleischmann, N. Knowledge of pronominalization, relfexivization, and relativization by learning disabled college students. Paper presented at the 54th Annual American Speech and Hearing Association Convention, San Francisco, 1978.

Wiig, E. H., and Harris, S. P. Perception and interpretation of nonverbally expressed emotions by adolescents with learning disabilities. *Perceptual and Motor Skills*, 1974, *38*, 239–245.

Wiig, E. H., Lapointe, C., and Semel, E. M. Relationships among language processing and production abilities of learning disabled adolescents. *Journal of Learning Disabilities*, 1977, *10*(5), 292–299.

Wiig, E. H., and Semel, E. M. Productive language abilities in learning disabled adolescents. *Journal of Learning Disabilities*, 1975, *8*, 578–586.

————. *Language Disabilities in Children and Adolescents*. Columbus, Ohio: Charles E. Merrill, 1976.

————. *Language Assessment and Intervention for the Learning Disabled*. Columbus, Ohio: Charles E. Merrill, 1980.

Wiig, E. H., Semel, E. M., and Abele, E. Perception and interpretation of ambiguous sentences by learning disabled twelve-year olds. *Learning Disability Quarterly*, 1981, *4*, 3–12.

Wiig, E. H., Semel, E. M., and Crouse, M. A. B. The use of English morphology by high-risk and learning disabled children. *Journal of Learning Disabilities*, 1973, *6*, 457–465.

Wikler, A., Dixon, J. F., and Parker, J. B. Brain function in problem children and controls: Psychometric, neurological, and electroencephalographic comparisons. *American Journal of Psychiatry*, 1970, *127*, 634–645.

Wilcox, E. Identifying characteristics of the NH adolescent. In *Helping the Adolescent with the Hidden Handicap*, edited by L. E. Anderson. Los Angeles: Academic Therapy Publications, 1970.

Wilhelms, F. T., and Westby-Gibson, D. Grouping: Research offers leads. *Educational Leadership*, 1961, *18*, 410–413, 476.

Wilkinson, A., Stratta, L., and Dudley, P. *The Quality of Listening*. London: Macmillan Education, 1974.

Willems, E. P. Behavioral ecology and experimental analysis: Courtship is not enough. In *Life Span Developmental Psychology: Methodological Issues*, edited by J. R. Nesselroade and H. W. Reese. New York: Academic Press, 1973.

Willems, E. P., and Rausch, H. L., eds. *Naturalistic Viewpoints in Psychological Research*. New York: Holt, Rinehart and Winston, 1968.

Willerman, L., and Plomin, R. Activity level in children and their parents. *Child Development*, 1973, *44*, 854–858.

Williamson, A. P. Career education: Implications for secondary LD students. *Academic Therapy*, Winter 1974–1975, *10*, 193–200.

Wilson, C. C. Behavioral assessment: Questionnaires. *School Psychology Review*, 1980, *9*, 58–66.

Wilson S. The use of ethnographic techniques in educational research. *Review of Educational Research*, 1977, *47*, 245–265.

Winick, M., Meyer, K. K., and Harris, R. C. Malnutrition and environmental enrichment by early adoption. *Science*, 1975, *190*, 1173–1175.

Wirtenberg, J., and Faw, T. T. The development of learning sets in adequate and retarded readers. *Journal of Learning Disabilities*, 1975, *8*, 304–307.

Wiseman, D. E., Hartwell, L. K., and Hannafin, M. J. Exploring the reading and listening skills of secondary mildly handicapped students. *Learning Disability Quarterly*, 1980, *3*(3), 56–61.

Witelson, S. Developmental dyslexia: Two right hemispheres and none left. *Science*, 1977, *195*, 309–311.

Witelson, S. F. Hemispheric specialization for linguistic and nonlinguistic tactual perception using a dichotomous stimulation technique. *Cortex*, 1974, *10*, 3–17.

———. Sex and the single hemisphere: Specialization of the right hemisphere for spatial processing. *Science*, 1976, *193*, 425–427.

Witelson, S. F., and Rabinovitch, M. S. Hemispheric speech lateralization in children with auditory-linguistic deficits. *Cortex*, 1972, *8*, 412–426.

Witkin, H. A., Dyk, R. B., Faterson, H. F., Goodenough, D. R., and Kirp, S. A. *Psychological Differentiation: Studies of Development*. New York: John Wiley & Sons, 1962.

Witkin, H. A., Goodenough, D. R., and Karp, S. A. Stability of cognitive style from childhood to young adulthood. *Journal of Personality and Social Psychology*, 1967, *7*, 291–300.

Witty, P. A., and Kopel, D. Studies of eye muscle imbalance and poor fusion in reading disability: An evaluation. *Journal of Educational Psychology*, 1936, *27*, 663–671.

Wolf, C. W. An experimental investigation of specific language disability (dyslexia). *Bulletin of the Orton Society*, 1967, *17*, 32.

Wolfe, L. S. Differential factors in specific reading disability: I. Laterality of function. *Journal of Genetic Psychology*, 1941, *58*, 45–56.

Wolff, R. M. *Achievement in America: National Report of the United States for the International Educational Achievement Project*. New York: Teachers College Press, 1977.

Wong, B. Y. L., and Wong, R. Role-taking skills in normal achieving and learning disabled children. *Learning Disability Quarterly*, 1980, *3*(2), 11–18.

Wood, B. C. *Children and Communication: Verbal and Nonverbal Language Development*. Englewood Cliffs, N.J.: Prentice-Hall, 1976.

Wood, N. *Verbal Learning*. Belmont, Calif.: Fearon Publishers, 1969.

Wood, R. W., Weiss, A. B., and Weiss, B. Hand tremor induced by industrial exposure to inorganic mercury. *Archives of Environmental Health*, 1973, *26*, 249–252.

Woodcock, R. W., and Clark, C. R. *Peabody Rebus Reading Program*. Circle Pines, Minn.: American Guidance Service, 1969.

Woodward, D. M. *Mainstreaming the Learning Disabled Adolescent: A Manual of Strategies and Materials*. Rockville, Md.: Aspen Systems Corporation, 1981.

Wortis, J. A note on the concept of the "brain-injured" child. *American Journal of Mental Deficiency*, 1956, *61*, 204–206.

Wozniak, R. H. Verbal regulation of motor behavior: Soviet research and non-Soviet replications. *Human Development*, 1972, *15*, 13–57.

Wright, H. F. *Recording and Analyzing Child Behavior*. New York: Harper & Row, 1967.

Wright, R. J. The affective and cognitive consequences of an open-education elementary school. *American Educational Research Journal*, 1975, *12*, 449–465.

Wunderlich, R. *Kids, Brains, and Learning*. St. Petersburg, Fla.: Johnny Reads, Inc., 1970.

Wyke, M.A., ed. *Developmental Dysphasia*. New York: Academic Press, 1978.

Yando, R. M., and Kagan, J. The effect of teacher tempo on the child. *Child Development*, 1968, *39*, 27–34.

Yang, D. C., Ting, R. Y., and Kennedy, C. The predictive value of the neurological examination in infancy and for mental status at four years of age. In Studies in Infancy, edited by R. MacKeith and M. Bax. *Clinics in Developmental Medicine*, 1968, *27*, 94–99.

Yarrow, L. J., Rubenstein, J. L. and Pederson, F. A. *Infant and Environment: Early Cognitive and Motivational Development*. Washington, D.C.: Hemisphere Publishing Company, 1975.

Yauman, B. E. Special education placement and the self-concepts of elementary-school-age children. *Learning Disability Quarterly*, 1980, *3*(3), 30–35.

Yoshida, R. K., Fenton, K. S., Maxwell, J. P., and Kaufman, M. J. Group decision making in the planning team process: Myth or reality? *Journal of School Psychology*, 1978, *16*, 237–244.

Ysseldyke, J. E. Diagnostic-prescriptive teaching: The search for aptitude treatment interactions. In L. Mann *The First Review of Special Education*, edited by L. Mann and D. A. Sabatino. Philadelphia: Journal of Special Education Press, 1973.

———. Issues in psychoeducational assessment. In *School Psychology: Perspectives and Issues*, edited by G. D. Phye and D. J. Reschly. New York: Academic Press, 1979.

Ysseldyke, J. E., and Foster, G. G. Bias in teachers' observations of emotionally disturbed children and learning disabled children. *Exceptional Children*, 1978, *44*, 613–615.

Ysseldyke, J. E., and Salvia, J. Diagnostic-prescriptive teaching: Two models. *Exceptional Children*, 1974, *41*, 181–185.

Yussen, S. R., and Levy, V. M. Developmental changes in predicting one's own span of short-term memory. *Journal of Experimental Child Psychology*, 1975, *19*, 502–508.

Zahn, T. P., Abate, F. A., Little, B. C., and Wender, P. H. Minimal brain dysfunction, stimulant drugs, and autonomic nervous system activity. *Archives of General Psychiatry*, 1975, *32*, 381–387.

Zaidel, E. A technique for presenting lateralized visual input with prolonged exposure. *Vision Research*. 1975, *15*, 283–289.

Zaner-Bloser Co. *Legible Print Writing*. Columbus, Ohio, 1968.

Zaner-Bloser Evaluation Scale. Columbus, Ohio: Zaner-Bloser, 1968.

Zangwill, O. L. *Cerebral Dominance and Its Relation to Psychological Function*. Edinburgh: Oliver & Boyd, 1960.

———. The concept of developmental dysphasia. In *Developmental Dysphasia*, edited by M. A. Wyke. New York: Academic Press, 1978.

Zangwill, O. L., and Blakemore, C. Dyslexia: Reversal of eye movements during reading. *Neuropsychologia*, 1972, *10*, 371–373.

Zaporozhets, A. V. The development of perception in the pre-school child. In European research in cognitive development, edited by P. Mussen. *Monographs of the Society for Research in Child Development*, 1965, *30*(2, Serial No. 100).

Zelnicker, T., and Jeffrey, W. E. Relfective and impulsive children: Strategies of information processing underlying differences in problem solving. *Monographs of the Society for Research in Child Development*, 1976, *41*(5, Serial No. 168).

Zentall, S. S., and Zentall, T. R. Activity and task performance of hyperactive children as a function of environmental stimulation. *Journal of Consulting and Clinical Psychology*, 1976, *44*, 693–697.

Zifferblatt, S. M. Architecture and human behavior: Toward increased understanding of a functional relationship. *Educational Technology*, 1972, *12*, 54–57.

Zigler, E. Developmental versus difference theories of mental retardation and the problem of motivation. *American Journal of Mental Deficiency*, 1969, *73*, 536–556.

Zigler, E., and Trickett, P. K. IQ, social competence, and evaluation of early childhood intervention programs. *American Psychologist*, 1978, *33*, 789–798.

Zigmond, N. K. Auditory processes in children. In *Learning Disabilities: Introduction to Educational and Medical Management*, edited by L. Tarnopol. Springfield, Ill.: Charles C. Thomas, 1969.

Zigmond, N., Vallecorsa, A., and Leinhardt, G. Reading instruction for students with learning disabilities. In *Lan-*

guage Disorders and Learning Disabilities, edited by K. B. Butler and G. P. Wallach. Rockville, Md.: Aspen Publishers, 1982.

Zucker, J. S., and Stricker, G. Impulsivity-reflectivity in Preschool Headstart and middle class children. *Journal of Learning Disabilities,* 1968, *1,* 578–583.

Zurif, E. B., and Bryden, M. P. Familial handedness and left-right differences in auditory and visual perception. *Neuropsychologia,* 1969, *7,* 179–187.

Zurif, E. B., and Carson, G. Dyslexia in relation to cerebral dominance and temporal analysis. *Neuropsychologia,* 1970, *8,* 351–361.

Name Index

Subject Index

Authoritative parents, 492
Average evoked potentials, 91

Behavior
  adaptive, 343–344
  language facilitation of, 213–214
  teacher nonverbal, 529–530
Behavioral assessment model, 319
Behavioral principles, 365
Behaviorism, 36–37
Behavior modification, 36–37
Behavior Rating Profile, 343
Behavior setting survey, 337
Bender Gestalt copying test, 343
Benedryl, 110
Biochemical irregularities, 107–118
  abnormal neurochemical transmissions, 108–115
  glandular disorders, 116–117
  hypoglycemia, 117–118
  vitamin deficiencies, 116
Birth, brain injury during, 84–85
Boder Diagnostic Spelling Procedure, 356
Boder Diagnostic Word List, 355
Body language, 529
Braille-Phonics, 448
Brain
  areas of, 93
  functions in, 93, 96
  hemispheres of, 32–33, 90, 99–100, 155–156, 157, 165–166
  plasticity of, 85, 86
  research methods for, 90–92
  structure-function relationships in, 93, 94–95, 96–99
Brain asymmetry, 90, 93
Brain dysfunction
  environment, learning, and, 56
  handedness and, 105–106
  minimal, 45–49
Brain equipotentiality, 89
Brain injury, 83–101
  causes of, 83–85
  definition of, 42–45
  effects of, 85–87
  neurological patterns and, 89, 93, 96, 99–101
  neurological signs of, 88
  research in, 14, 18
  testing for, 87–89
Brain specificity, 89
Brain waves, differences in, 141
Broca's area, 22, 23
Bureau for the Education of the Handicapped, 73

Calcium imbalances, 117
Career education, 281–282, 306–307, 470–473
Categorical resource room, 525
Central aphasia, 26–27
Cerebral dominance training, 32–34, 36
Child-rearing practices, 492–494
Children with Specific Learning Disabilities Act (1969), 10
Classification, 314
  disadvantages of, 519–521
Classroom
  classification in, 519–521
  design of, 516–519
  environment of, 358–359, 512–515

open-plan, 516
  testing situation and, 320
Classroom Environment Scale, 513
Clinical teaching, 35, 361–364
Cloze procedure, 464
Clustering, 199, 248
Code of Ethics and Competencies for Teachers of Learning Disabled Children and Youth, 376
Cognitive development, and family, 483–487
Cognitive psychologists, 428
Cognitive styles, 128–137
  attention and, 173
  definitions of, 130–131
  directed vs. nondirected learners, 135–136
  impulsivity–reflectivity, 132–135
  incentives and, 423–425
  learner strategies and, 136–137
  tasks and, 421–423
Cognitive training, 137, 428
Collaborative Perinatal Project, 485
Color Phonics, 443
Comprehensibility, 251
Computer-assisted tomographic scanning (CATSCAN), 91
Concept-Attainment Task, 135
Conceptual level (CL), 135–136, 422–423
Conceptual style. See Cognitive styles
Conceptual Style Test, 135
Conceptual tempo, 134
Conduction aphasia, 23
Conference on Exploration into Problems of the Perceptually Handicapped Child, 50
Congenital word blindness, 30
Connors' hyperactivity rating scale, 113
Coordination, 162–163
  See also Visual-motor development
Copying. See Drawing
Corpus callosum, 90
Council for Exceptional Children (CEC), 12, 376
Council for Learning Disabilities (CLD), 12–13
Criterion-referenced tests, 324, 325–326
Cross-modal integration, 160
Cross-over design, 110
Cuisenaire rods, 455
Cultural bias
  IQ tests and, 70
  pluralistic assessment model and, 320–324
  teachers and, 530
Cultural differences, 138, 139–141, 530
Culture-fair tests, 321
Culture-free tests, 321
Culture-specific tests, 321
Cylert, 110

Decentering, 255
Decoding, 25
Deep structure problems, 210–211, 247
Developing Understanding of Self and Others (DUSO) program, 458
Developmental aphasia, 25
Developmental imbalances, 44–45
Developmentalists, 125
Developmental Test of Visual Perception (DTVP), 19
Dexadrine, 110
Dextroamphetamine, 110
Diagnostic-prescriptive teaching, 361–364
Dichhaptic stimulation, 90